HIDDEN®
Utah

HIDDEN®

Utah

Including Salt Lake City, Park City, Moab, Arches, Zion, and Bryce Canyon

Kurt Repanshek

SECOND EDITION

Ulysses Press®

BERKELEY, CALIFORNIA

Published by:
ULYSSES PRESS
P.O. Box 3440
Berkeley, CA 94703
www.ulyssespress.com

ISSN 1527-7135
ISBN 1-56975-347-4

Printed in Canada by Transcontinental Printing

10 9 8 7 6 5 4 3 2

MANAGING EDITOR: Claire Chun
EDITOR: Lily Chou
EDITORIAL ASSOCIATES: Kate Allen, Laura Brancella,
    Caroline Cummins, Sarisa Nelson
TYPESETTER: Lisa Kester
CARTOGRAPHY: Pease Press
COVER DESIGN: Sarah Levin, Leslie Henriques
INDEXER: Sayre Van Young
COVER PHOTOGRAPHY: Larry Ulrich (Dirty Devil Arm, Lake Powell
    near Hite Marina, Glen Canyon National Recreation Area)
ILLUSTRATOR: Doug McCarthy

Distributed in the United States by Publishers Group West and
in Canada by Raincoast Books

For my parents,
who long ago instilled in me a love for the outdoors,
a passion for adventure, and a curiosity to see what lies
over the next mountain and around the next river bend.

Acknowledgments

Writing a guidebook is much like going on a road trip: you're never quite sure what exists beyond the next mountain until you get there. I received some wonderful help in negotiating the roads that led to the completion of *Hidden Utah*. It would not have been possible without assistance from Ken Kraus at the Utah Travel Council, who provided unflagging input on Utah's out-of-the-way nooks and crannies and constantly kept me apprised of new lodgings and restaurants. Chamber bureaus throughout the state were an invaluable resource. In particular, thanks go to Jason Mathis at the Salt Lake Convention and Visitors Bureau, Barbara McConvill at the Ogden/Weber Convention and Visitors Bureau, and Maridene Alexander Hancock at the Logan Convention and Visitors Bureau. Of course, a writer's work is only as solid as his or her editor, and Lily Chou deftly massaged my writing into a nicely flowing narrative. Finally, I'd like to thank my wife, Marcelle, for her patience and support throughout this project, although I'm not sure she ever really came to view my traipsing about Utah's fabulous countryside, eating in its best restaurants, and staying in some of its finer lodgings as work.

*

Ulysses Press would like to thank the following readers who took the time to write in with suggestions that were incorporated into this new edition of *Hidden Utah*: Joanne Schopflin of Walnut Creek, CA; Dave Sheingold of Hawthorne, NY; Derek Martinez via e-mail.

What's Hidden?

At different points throughout this book, you'll find special listings marked with a hidden symbol:

◀ *HIDDEN*

This means that you have come upon a place off the beaten tourist track, a spot that will carry you a step closer to the local people and natural environment of Utah.

The goal of this guide is to lead you beyond the realm of everyday tourist facilities. While we include traditional sightseeing listings and popular attractions, we also offer alternative sights and adventure activities. Instead of filling this guide with reviews of standard hotels and chain restaurants, we concentrate on one-of-a-kind places and locally owned establishments.

Our authors seek out locales that are popular with residents but usually overlooked by visitors. Some are more hidden than others (and are marked accordingly), but all the listings in this book are intended to help you discover the true nature of Utah and put you on the path of adventure.

Write to us!

If in your travels you discover a spot that captures the spirit of Utah, or if you live in the region and have a favorite place to share, or if you just feel like expressing your views, write to us and we'll pass your note along to the author.

We can't guarantee that the author will add your personal find to the next edition, but if the writer does use the suggestion, we'll acknowledge you in the credits and send you a free copy of the new edition.

ULYSSES PRESS
3286 Adeline Street, Suite 1
Berkeley, CA 94703
E-mail: ulysses@ulyssespress.com

Contents

Maps

OUTDOOR ADVENTURE SYMBOLS

The following symbols accompany national, state and regional park listings, as well as beach descriptions throughout the text.

Symbol	Activity	Symbol	Activity
	Camping		Water Skiing
	Hiking		Windsurfing
	Biking		Canoeing or Kayaking
	Horseback Riding		Boating
	Downhill Skiing		Boat Ramps
	Cross-country Skiing		Fishing
	Swimming		

ONE

Utah Wandering

Wedged into a notch high on the cliff, blending in so completely with the buff-colored sandstone that it's unnoticeable except from certain angles and under certain light conditions, the cliff dwelling is a testament to a people long gone from southern Utah's canyon-riddled landscape. Although centuries old, baskets, pottery and sometimes even woven sandals can be found occasionally in these dwellings, as if their owners had left for only a few hours with plans to return. Hours to the north, in the heavily treed and snowy mountains of the Wasatch Range, skiers and snowboarders revel in the "Greatest Snow on Earth"—snow so light, powdery and deep and terrain so challenging that the 2002 Olympic Winter Games were staged here. In the West Desert, rock hounds sift through soil for gemstones and geodes, while in the state's northeastern corner a Jurassic bone yard exists in the form of Dinosaur National Monument.

Utah is a landscape rich in geologic diversity, a state where the gritty Old West co-exists alongside the 21st-century's high-tech brain trust, where visitors exult in both world-class alpine resorts and breathtaking red-rock panoramas that have been works-in-progress for hundreds of millions of years. No single adjective succinctly captures the essence of the state's snow-capped mountains, serpentine canyonlands and rugged and desolate high desert. Utah is a state that demands to be experienced up close and in person; it can't be savored from a distance.

Those unfamiliar with the state often think first of Mormons—members of the Church of Jesus Christ of Latter-day Saints—when talk turns to Utah. And while the 84,916-square-mile state is indeed the headquarters for the LDS Church, the church is not the only religion practiced in the state nor does it define Utah. True, Temple Square in the heart of Salt Lake City is Utah's number-one tourist draw, and its magnificent temple and renowned tabernacle justify that designation. Still, there are those who would argue, and justifiably so, that southern Utah's labyrinthine canyon country, or the state's frothy whitewater, or its snow heavy mountains, or its five national parks, could easily claim that honor.

Utah is a tourist's dilemma. Should you come in summer to enjoy hiking or boating through the southern canyons, or arrive in winter to savor the alpine resorts? There's so much to be seen and sampled in this state that the average vacationer only has enough time to scratch the surface. Often those who fly into Salt Lake City to see Temple Square and research their roots in the Family History Center, or enjoy the skiing and snowboarding in the Wasatch Range, find it hard to add a five-hour drive to the south to tour one or more of the state's national parks. Conversely, those who fly into Las Vegas and drive north to Zion or Bryce Canyon national parks are put off by the three-hour drive to Capitol Reef, Canyonlands or Arches national parks, not to mention the longer treks to Salt Lake City or Dinosaur National Monument. Raise the prospect of venturing into the West Desert to explore long-forgotten Pony Express stations or dig for gemstones, to the southeast to take part in a day or more of whitewater rafting through canyons explored in 1869 by Major John Wesley Powell, or to the north to see where the transcontinental railroad was tied together and you'll produce looks of exasperation . . . and possibly disbelief that one state could offer so much.

Sandwiched between these established destinations are quaint, off-the-beaten-path waystations such as Boulder, which sits on the shoulder of one of the West's most scenic backcountry roads as well as the lip of the ruggedly beautiful Grand Staircase–Escalante National Monument, and Kamas, a sleepy, bucolic community that serves as the front door to the recreational playground known as the Uinta Mountains. Cedar City is known not only for its award-winning Utah Shakespearean Festival but also for being the gateway to Cedar Breaks National Monument, while Price offers a wonderful museum on Utah's paleontological history and a short ride to one of the state's most remote stretches of spectacular backcountry, the San Rafael Swell.

Hidden Utah, quite simply, is a guidebook. It's not an encyclopedia on Utah, nor is it intended to be. Rather, it's designed as a starting point, a genesis from which to craft your visit to the Beehive State. In the following six chapters you'll learn about the state's highlights, the places you should definitely consider visiting. Sprinkled liberally throughout the chapters are "hidden" spots— sites, accommodations and eateries not heavily publicized nor usually included on group tours. They're the kind of places you usually discover after spending a number of days in one area and learning where the locals like to go. Along with pointing out these places, the text touches on the history of the various corners of Utah. You'll learn about the Mormons' flight from religious persecution that brought them to the state, the rough-and-tumble miners who played a key role in settling the state, and a bit about the ancient Fremont and Anasazi Indians who called the state home from about A.D. 200 to about A.D. 1300 before mysteriously vanishing from the scene. Whether you're on vacation, looking for adventure, or simply out to explore America, *Hidden Utah* can make your trip to the state more enjoyable and productive.

Geographically, as noted above, Utah offers a seemingly endless array of landscapes. From the deeply eroded and colorful canyon country in the south and the desolate high-desert landscape running along the western border to the heavily forested

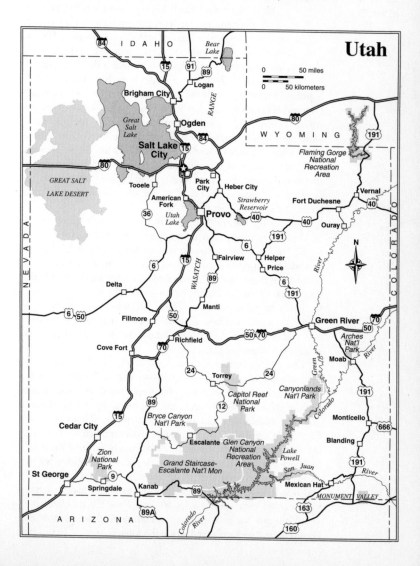

mountains of north-central and northern Utah, the state is an explorer's dream.

After dispatching helpful introductory information such as the state's geology, history and wildlife, sections that paint a portrait of Utah, this book delves into six geographic regions, starting with Salt Lake City and its surroundings (covered in Chapter Two). From there the book meanders, as any good traveler should, moving on to Northern Utah (Chapter Three), where Utah's ties to the taming of the West can be seen at Promontory Summit, where the "golden spike" was driven in 1869 to knit the transcontinental railroad together, and where the state's connection with America's space industry is rooted.

The Great Salt Lake is so salty that early mountain men mistook it for the Pacific Ocean.

Northeastern Utah (Chapter Four) is perhaps the most geologically diverse region of the state, running from the seismically sculpted Wasatch Range that is the heart of the state's ski industry to Dinosaur National Monument (truly a Jurassic park) along the Utah–Colorado border. Just as you'll recognize world-class skiing and snowboarding at Park City's three alpine resorts, you'll appreciate first-rate dinosaur digs north of Vernal in the national monument. For those interested in bucking whitewater, the Green and Yampa rivers that flow through the monument offer some of the state's best rapids.

Outwardly, Central Utah (Chapter Five) might seem several notches below the other regions in terms of attractions and things to do, but look closer. Rich in pioneer history, the area claims a national monument in the caves of Mount Timpanogos National Monument northeast of Provo, while the Cleveland-Lloyd Dinosaur Quarry south of Price is renowned for the fossils it continues to supply to paleontologists. The West Desert, with its herds of wild horses and rockhounding fields, can entertain one for days and weeks on end if you have a taste for solitude, desert and searching for gemstones.

Chapter Six probes Southwestern Utah, which boasts an iridescent red-rock landscape that's a work in progress thanks to the ever-present forces of wind and rain, freeze and thaw. Snapshots of Mother Nature's handiwork are captured by Cedar Breaks National Monument and two national parks, Zion and Bryce Canyon. While Zion is largely angular, as exemplified by the towering Watchman sandstone monolith that rises high above the park's southern entrance near Springdale, Bryce is best known for expansive stone amphitheaters crowded with whimsical goblins and hoodoos—erosion's most intricate works of arts that have been carved into southern Utah's soft Pink Cliffs. Here, too, you'll glimpse the geologic and paleontological wonders of the Grand Staircase–Escalante National Monument.

Chapter Seven explores Southeastern Utah, home of Moab—the mountain-biking capital of the free world—and Canyonlands National Park, a rugged wilderness you enter on its terms, not yours. Within this chapter you'll find Arches National Park, with the world's greatest collection of rock arches, and the Green and Colorado rivers, which run wild through Canyonlands before being funneled through Glen Canyon National Recreation Area and then spewed into the Grand Canyon.

The best of Utah—places widely known as well as some largely unknown—is packaged into this book. Whether you embark on a long, circular sweep of the state with hopes of glimpsing the highlights, or focus on one region at a time in trips spread out over several years, is up to you. It's a state that provides windows, both figurative and literal, into prehistory as well as into the future.

The Story of Utah

GEOLOGY

Utah, perhaps more than any other state, is a portal into the past. Sandstone and coal beds from Vernal to Price and south to Moab and St. George are vaults for Jurassic and Cretaceous fossils, preserving the remains and footprints of some of the most voracious dinosaurs that trod the earth. Cliff faces throughout the state were *pleine aire* easels to American Indians, beginning with the ancient Anasazi and continuing on through the Ute Nation, whose medicine men detailed their tribes' annals on the rocky walls of places such as Nine Mile Canyon. More recently, miners literally burrowed into Utah, first to extract coal, silver and gold, and then in search of oil and gas, uranium and copper.

Squeezed, tugged and buckled by North America's tectonic plates, Utah is an amalgamation of geologic provinces. The southlands are a sprawling earthen palette of high desert studded with sagebrush, juniper and cacti. They're a colorful land of crumbling red-rock vistas marked by canyons chewed deeply into the arid expanse. Farther north, jagged, steeply pitched mountains still enjoying their youth tower over much of the landscape. Impossible to overlook, of course, is the Great Salt Lake, a massive inland sea.

The Great Basin province (also known as the Basin and Range) lies west of a line drawn north to south from Idaho to Nevada through Ogden, Salt Lake City, Provo, Nephi, Cedar City and St. George. This oft-parched high-desert landscape was once inundated by prehistoric Lake Bonneville, which in its prime left parts of Utah, Idaho and Nevada awash under a freshwater inland ocean nearly 350 miles long and 145 miles wide. East of a diagonal line drawn from Vernal southwest through Price, Torrey and Kanab sprawls the Colorado Plateau, a tabletop of sedimentary rocks that erosion has sculpted into a magnificent matrix of canyons, buttes, draws and mesas.

Sandwiched between the Basin and Range and Colorado Plateau lies the high country of the Wasatch and High plateaus and the east–west running Uinta Mountain Range. Here rise the thickest of Utah's forests, as stands of conifer, aspen, oak, maple and juniper shroud much of the mountains. Bejeweled alpine lakes and tumbling mountain streams add a lushness to the landscape that's largely missing in southern Utah.

Although it's mostly unseen, the state's most significant geologic landmark, due to its active status beneath the heavily populated Wasatch Front, is the Wasatch Fault. This geologic worm is responsible for having ratcheted up its namesake mountains over the millennia. The fault, however, has long been quiescent, not having unleashed its signature magnitude 7 quake in more than six centuries.

Hoisted ever upward by the periodic shudders of this deep-seated geologic fault, the north-to-south-running Wasatch Range is a monument to the fault's energy. And unlike the East Coast's Appalachians, whose ancient age is reflected by gently rounded summits and deep forests, the Wasatch carries all the angular blemishes, mannerisms and rumblings of geologic puberty. Erosion has yet to soften the gray, granitic spires that scrape the sky; rocky escarpments left by the fault's previous subterranean grindings gash the mountains' flanks; tiny swarms of earthquakes, usually unnoticed, reverberate through the range each year.

More dramatic is southern Utah's geology. Time, wind, rain, ice and snow have conspired to chisel arches, bridges and windows into the colorful sandstone landscape that was cemented together, layer by gritty layer, by ancient oceans' sediments. Working together, the Green and Colorado rivers and their numerous tributaries have carved deep canyons.

Varying amounts of iron oxides have artfully painted the expanse with hues of reddish-brown Entrada, pinkish Navajo and

SLIPPING AND SLIDING

How does the Wasatch Fault, which has been pushing up its namesake mountains for 15 million years, work? Unlike California's more famous San Andreas fault (a "slip-strike" fault in which blocks of rock slip sideways during quakes), the Wasatch is one of the world's longest and most active "normal" faults (a "dip-slip" fault in which the blocks slip mostly vertically as the earth's crust pulls apart). To picture how this works, imagine holding three bricks in front of you by squeezing them together. If you relax this pressure, the center brick slides down. In the case of the Wasatch Fault, the Salt Lake Valley is the center brick that sinks while the adjoining mountains rise.

brilliant brick-red Wingates and Kayentas sandstones that seem to change color as the sun wheels across the sky. Locked for the moment between these ribbons and a hard layer of whitish Kaibab limestone is a brittle bed of milky Chinle sandstone. As erosion, ever the skilled craftsman, works its never-ending magic, minarets, fins and turrets are whittled into place as softer sandstones flake away.

Nothing is constant in geology, particularly when it involves this rumpled landscape. Deep under this land are massive salt and gypsum domes, which can be traced to the lost seas, that drift as the rocks above ground weigh down on them. When pressure forces the domes to slip sideways, the ground above drops, creating valleys referred to as "grabens." Above-ground formations often topple as these valleys form. Sometimes they don't, though, managing somehow to drop straight down as if on an elevator and leave behind flanks of stone pillars.

Although they've been there for more than 150 million years, only in recent years have the fossilized remains of incredible dinosaurs been unearthed in southern Utah's Grand Staircase–Escalante National Monument. As years progress and more paleontologists head to this vast land, more riddles from the time of dinosaurs are expected to be answered.

Combined, these individual geologic regions create a sprawling jigsaw puzzle that never bores the traveler.

NATIVE PEOPLE Utah is an open book, its geologic and cultural history readily available to anyone who takes the time to read the landscape. For more than 10,000 years people have roamed across Utah. They learned how to live in the state's mountains, deserts and canyonlands, finding nourishment in the streams, fields and forests.

Storytelling was an integral part of these cultures and the tribal shaman often bore the responsibility of recounting these tales through images. Painstakingly etched into rock panels throughout Utah's backcountry are symbols, characters, animals and warriors—images that ask many questions of their creators but offer few direct answers. Scattered across the state in places like Nine Mile Canyon, the San Rafael Swell, Parowan Gap and Newspaper Rock, these petroglyphs and pictographs paint a picture of both Utah's prehistoric past, a time when ancient hunters and gatherers known as the Fremont and Anasazi roamed the state, and the more recent past of Indian tribes such as the Utes, Paiutes and Shoshones, who added their own scenes to some of the rock panels first touched by the Fremont and Anasazi. At times overlapping the cultures, these exquisite patches of art often tell stories that are not always easily comprehended. While it's easy to interpret a warrior astride a horse with bow drawn, not so un-

HISTORY

derstandable are the asexual, anthropomorphic entities that seem to be clutching balloons or tossing lightning bolts.

Utah's first prehistoric groups to be given names by today's historians were the Fremont and Anasazi. While the Anasazi, also known as "ancestral Puebloans," arose around A.D. 200 in southern Utah near the Four Corners region, surviving by growing crops like corn, beans and squash, the Fremont arrived just to the north in the Great Basin and Uinta Basin by at least A.D. 500. The two cultures seemingly coexisted in Utah until around A.D. 1300. While the Fremont, who supplemented their hunting and gathering with farming of corn, beans and squash, lived in pit houses, the Anasazi lived in cliff dwellings in addition to pit houses, many of which remain today and can be seen by sharp-eyed tourists or those on guided tours.

For reasons still unclear today, these two cultures seemed to vanish from the landscape around 1300, possibly because of a long-lasting drought, perhaps due to assimilation by other peoples.

Historically, Utah was then populated by the Goisute, Navajo, Shoshone, Southern Paiute and Ute peoples, who, like the Fremont and Anasazi before them, engaged in hunting, gathering and fishing. These tribes, endemic to the Great Basin and Rocky Mountain regions, roamed the state, which is named after the Ute tribe. While the Utes lived in structures familiar to most today as tepees, the Southern Paiute, who ranged across southern Utah as well as parts of Nevada and Arizona, fashioned ice-cream-cone-shaped "wickiups" from poles and brush.

The tribes can still be found in Utah. While the Ute have a reservation that covers nearly four and a half million acres in northeastern Utah (tribal headquarters are in Fort Duchesne), the Goisute, whose ancestors roamed the West Desert and Nevada, live on the Skull Valley Reservation southwest of Tooele. The Navajo, also known as Dine', have a reservation based in northern Arizona that spills over into southern Utah near Medicine Hat; the Northwestern band of the Shoshone has small holdings in northern Utah, with an office in Brigham City. The Southern band of the Paiute has its tribal headquarters in southwestern Utah in Cedar City.

EXPLORERS AND MOUNTAIN MEN Spanish explorers are believed to have found their way into Utah in the 1700s, although somewhat more romantic tales date to the mid-1600s, a time when Spaniards supposedly roamed the Uinta Mountains and enslaved Utes during their search for gold ore and caches of gold they thought had been hidden there by the Aztecs.

Spaniard Juan Maria Rivera reached the state in 1765, entering Utah in the southeastern corner near today's Hovenweep National Monument and working his way as far north as Moab. More famous was the 1776 journey of Atanasio Dominguez and

Silvestre Velez de Escalante, two Franciscan priests searching for a route from Sante Fe, New Mexico, to Monterey, California. They sallied into the Uinta Basin near present-day Jensen and drifted as far west as Utah Lake before turning back to the southeast and Santa Fe. Their journals provided extensive notes on Utah's native peoples, vegetation and landscape.

Jim Bridger, Jedediah Smith, Miles Goodyear and scores of other mountain men hunted and trapped their way through northern Utah between 1807 and 1840. It was Bridger, then a stalwart 20-year-old, who worked his way down Logan Canyon from 1825–26 and reached the Great Salt Lake, thinking it was the Pacific Ocean because of its saltiness.

These trappers rambled wherever beaver led them. Bear Lake in extreme northern Utah was a popular gathering spot for their annual "rendezvous," as was Blacksmith Canyon south of Logan. Goodyear found the present-day site of Ogden to be a comfortable, logical place to build a trading post and erected Fort Buenaventura along the banks of the Ogden River in 1844 with hopes of growing rich from passing wagon trains en route to California.

Just as the era of the mountain man was ending in the 1840s, Congress' determination to gain a better understanding of this country brought explorer John C. Fremont into Utah on his way across the West. Fremont visited the Great Salt Lake and Antelope Island, which he named for the game he and his men shot, and explored the Great Basin.

MORMON SETTLEMENT   The influx of Mormons in 1847 ushered in the widespread settlement of Utah by whites. Under Brigham Young the church latched onto an ambitious colonization effort that established isolated communities in the state's far-flung corners and rugged interior. By 1850, just three years after the Mormons had arrived in Salt Lake City, outposts known as Bountiful, Farmington, Manti, Ogden, Provo and Tooele sprang up; hundreds more around the state would soon follow.

The name of Franciscan priest Silvestre Velez de Escalante remained in the state in the form of a town, river and national monument.

In addition to spreading the word of their gospel, the Mormons tamed the landscape. Elaborate irrigation systems nourished parched and dusty fields, orchards flourished and communities grew.

While the Mormons decided in 1849 to create their own state, a place called "Deseret," Congress withheld statehood and instead named the area the Utah Territory. Tensions between the Mormons and Congress grew heated in the 1850s, when Washington politicians condemned the Mormon practice of polygamy. Though President Buchanan sent the U.S. Cavalry to Utah in 1857 in a show of force, no battles broke out. The federal presence, however, continued during the Civil War, as President Lincoln, fearful that Utahns might side with the South, maintained a garrison of soldiers on Salt Lake City's eastern bench in the form of Fort Douglas.

The soldiers not only kept an eye on the Mormons but took to the mountains to search for valuable ores that might spur a mining boom and draw non-Mormons into the state. The move succeeded grandly: silver, gold, copper, lead and other deposits were found in Wasatch Range and mountains southwest of Provo and generated a fevered rush to the ore fields.

Among the towns that flourished under this mining boom was one nestled in a small valley on the eastern slopes of the Wasatch Range, a place called Park City. While Park City was not Utah's first ski town—Alta lays claim to that distinction, having entered the snow business in 1938—it perfected the concept and helped place Utah's ski industry on the globe.

MODERN TIMES   Utah joined the rocket age in 1957 when Thiokol Chemical Corporation came to Brigham City with plans to build a solid fuel rocket propellant plant, which it did to the west of town. The center remains today, with NASA being one of its main customers, while nearby Utah State University in Logan has developed a nationally recognized rocket curriculum through its Space Dynamics Lab.

To the south, while skiing was making the Wasatch Range fashionable, another revolution was taking placing in the Salt Lake Valley that put that part of the state on the technological map. In Provo software geniuses in the 1980s launched WordPerfect Corp. and Novell, two companies that established Utah as a serious player in the software industry. At the same time, a bit to the north in Salt Lake City, medical advances such as artificial hearts were being pioneered, and the state capital also became a financial center for the Intermountain West.

These technological and financial advances spurred a significant influx of people to the state throughout the 1980s and 1990s, though Utahns' high birth rate has remained the primary factor behind the state's booming population.

FLORA   Considering the kaleidoscopic landscape, from snow-capped peaks to arid deserts, is it any surprise that Utah's vegetative province is equally diverse? Elevations ranging from 2350 feet in the southwestern corner of the state near St. George to 13,528 feet atop King's Peak in the Uinta Range—not to mention varied moisture conditions—result in an incredible array of vegetation, from ancient bristlecone pines and unusual Joshua trees to hanging gardens and old-growth pine forests.

Utah is easily divided into three vegetative regions: the Wasatch and Uinta mountain ranges, the Basin and Range province, and the Colorado Plateau.

A quick glance across the Basin and Range and the Colorado Plateau generates the impression that these parts of the state are arid, desolate and generally inhospitable for both plants and animals. But a closer look reveals a vivid collection of plants that dab color and texture to the landscape.

Colorful pods of claret cup cacti, patches of prickly pear cacti, waves of desert globemallow and scattered stands of desert plumes are among the hardy plants that paint the southern deserts in the spring. While claret cups add rich, scarlet brush strokes to the desert when in bloom, prickly pear flowers add dashes of pink and yellow. Fields of orange-blooming desert globemallow are set off by the canyon country's vivid red rock, which also enhances the dainty stalks of yellow flowers displayed like feather dusters by desert plumes.

Black bears mainly prowl the Uinta Range, although they and cougars can be found in the Book Cliffs area.

While Zion National Park initially seems hostile to all but the most stalwart of flora, deep within Zion's canyons hang gardens nourished by runoff that erupt with dazzling displays of golden and western columbine, monkey flowers and delicate maidenhair ferns.

Odd-looking Joshua trees, a tree-like variety of yucca, as well as more common yucca plants abound in the state's southwestern corner near St. George, where the hot, arid climate provides ideal conditions for these desert lovers. Plants that overlap in the Basin and Range and Colorado Plateau areas include shrubs such as rabbitbrush, blackbrush and greasewood. Single-leaf ash trees also seem to enjoy the canyon country, often finding niches where runoff collects.

A prevalent but non-native plant that clogs many river corridors of southern and central Utah is tamarisk, also known as salt cedar. Although it displays showy plumes of purplish flowers in spring, this tenacious plant is steadily crowding out willows and other native vegetation.

While juniper and piñon can be found in some areas of southern Utah, they steadily begin to dominate the landscape as it slowly transforms from desert to mountains. Bristlecone pines, which have lifetimes measured in thousands, not hundreds, of years, anchor themselves in the rocky soils surrounding Cedar Breaks National Monument and near the southern tip of Bryce Canyon National Park.

Pine, fir, spruce, aspen, maple, scrub oak and willow are among the trees found throughout the Wasatch and Uinta ranges. Though there are open meadows that burst in spring with wildflowers such as asters, penstemons and sego lilies, patches of south-facing slopes within the mountains might also harbor sweet-scented sagebrush.

FAUNA   Though grizzly bears no longer wander Utah's mountains, long ago having been hunted out, black bears and other remnants of the "wild West" can still be found in the state. Wild mustangs continue to gallop across the prairie in areas such as the West Desert and Book Cliffs, while deer, elk and moose all graze in substantial numbers in the northern forests. On occasion, moose have stumbled out of the Wasatch Mountains and into Salt Lake City's neighborhoods, only to be rounded up by state wildlife personnel and returned to the mountains.

There are few areas of the West where bison, popularly known as buffalo, still roam wild. One is in Utah, where these shaggy animals congregate in the Henry Mountains (the last major mountain range in the country to be explored), located in the south-central region of the state. The bison there are not native, but rather descended from those in Yellowstone National Park. In 1941 three bulls and 15 cows from the Yellowstone herds were released into the San Rafael Desert with hopes that they would make the area home. Five more Yellowstone bulls were released a year later, after the first three left the area, and the animals steadily increased their numbers.

While the bison for many years drifted through the Burr Desert, in 1963 they headed into the Henry Mountains. Today the size of the herd, which averages about 400 animals, is maintained through an annual hunt. Antelope Island in the Great Salt Lake also boasts a bison herd, one that numbers in the hundreds and is actively managed by the state.

Bighorn sheep, with their magnificently curved horns, can be found in several areas of Utah, ranging from the northeastern corner of the state near Flaming Gorge National Recreation Area to Antelope Island and the Wasatch Range. Not as numerous nor quite as visible are mountain goats. Some of these shaggy, bearded creatures live around Mount Timpanogos and near the mouth of Little Cottonwood Canyon, while another herd clatters around the Tushar Mountains east of Beaver.

FLOCKING TOGETHER

Three national wildlife refuges—Fish Springs southwest of Tooele, Bear River west of Brigham City, and Ouray south of Vernal—along with the shores of the Great Salt Lake are tremendous lures for migratory birds such as avocets, stilts, white pelicans, herons, cranes, egrets, ducks, Canada geese and many more waterfowl and shorebird species. During the winter months Fish Springs is a good area to spot and photograph bald eagles, as is Willard Bay along the eastern shore of the Great Salt Lake between Ogden and Brigham City.

Nearly 3000 wild horses still cluster in parts of the state, notably the West Desert, the Uinta Basin south of Vernal and north of Green River, and the San Rafael Swell. While most of these horses are thought to have descended from mares and stallions that escaped ranches in the late 1800s, some think that many can be traced back to horses brought to the region by Spanish explorers more than a century earlier.

Elk, plentiful throughout much of northern Utah, can be spotted at the state-run Hardware Ranch near the head of Blacksmith Fork below Logan. Though once native to Utah, wolves were long ago forced out of the state as settlers and ranchers arrived. In 2003, wolves descended from those released in Yellowstone National Park in the 1990s made their way into Utah's wilds.

Southern Utah's desertscape is not devoid of wildlife. Most viewers can easily view deer and pronghorn antelope, while those with more patience will often see coyotes, kit foxes, desert tortoise and, on occasion, ringtail cats. Mountain lions also slink through the state, ranging from the northern mountains south into the area around Zion National Park.

Utah's skies harbor many bird species, from buzzing hummingbirds to raucous magpies to graceful raptors such as red-tail hawks and golden and bald eagles. A reliable spotting area for bald eagles is the Weber River near Henefer along Route 84 northeast of Park City. The eagles roost in the trees along the river throughout the winter, pulling fishy meals from the stream. When summer arrives the eagles head north while great blue herons come to use the area for a rookery. Wild turkeys frequent some areas of the state, too, and condors released near the Grand Canyon in the 1990s have been known to soar over the Grand Staircase and Bryce Canyon.

Where to Go

A vacation to Utah, unless you have three or four weeks available for wandering, does not easily afford itself to trips that will take in both the mountains and canyon country. The state is just too big and too spectacular to truly, and fairly, encompass both in a one-or two-week swing. With five national parks and seven national monuments, not to mention the cultural attractions in the Salt Lake Valley and northern end of the state, one can't possibly take in all the highlights outlined in this book in one trip. If you try to see it all, you may find yourself so focused on covering large distances that you sacrifice quiet moments to appreciate the natural beauty you came for.

Deciding what to see and where to go is a tough choice—you'll just have to keep coming back and exploring at different times of the year to get to know Utah intimately.

If you're flying to Utah, most likely you'll arrive in the **Salt Lake Valley** at Salt Lake City International Airport. On the jet's approach to the airport, you receive a panoramic view of the valley that Brigham Young and his fellow Mormons reached in July 1847 in their bid to escape religious persecution. The rugged and angular Wasatch Range defines the eastern border of the valley, while the Oquirrh Mountains do the same for the western edge. Just north of the airport is the Great Salt Lake, the largest inland lake west of the Mississippi. Salt Lake City is the spiritual center for the LDS Church. Ever since Brigham Young established the church's headquarters here, the city has served as the base of the church's world-wide operations, which today emanate from the beautiful and well-kept grounds and buildings of the Temple Square complex. But Salt Lake City is more than just a religious center—it also offers a lively cultural scene thanks to its theaters, playhouses, art galleries and restaurants, as well as the University of Utah, and is a growing business center for the Intermountain West.

Northern Utah is a veritable wilderness compared to the Salt Lake Valley. Steep and thickly forested mountains rim Ogden and Brigham City to the east, while the Great Salt Lake shimmers just to the west of these cities. At Promontory Summit west of Brigham City and atop the northern tip of the lake lies the Golden Spike National Historic Site, the spot where the transcontinental railroad was bound together. Closer to Brigham City is the Bear River Migratory Bird Refuge, a sanctuary for millions of waterfowl and shorebirds who rest here on their migrations north and south. Although Ogden is farther away from Promontory Summit than Brigham City, it is Utah's true railroad town, and the Union Station that anchors the city's historic district is a landmark rich in railroad history.

Logan, the region's only other major city, lies in the lush Cache Valley that's cupped by mountains to the east, south and west. Bear Lake, 40 miles east of Logan, is a popular and refreshing summer retreat, drawing boaters, anglers and even scuba divers to its waters, while fruit lovers arrive for the late-summer raspberry festival.

Both ski resorts and dinosaur bones are scattered throughout **Northeastern Utah**, a sprawling slice of the state that stretches from Park City's alpine slopes to Dinosaur National Monument, which straddles the Utah–Colorado border. The backside of the Wasatch Range cradles the Deer Valley, Park City and Canyons ski resorts as well as the tony resort town of Park City, which is home to the U.S. Ski and Snowboard Association, the Utah Olympic Park and dozens of top-notch restaurants. The east-to-west-running Uinta Mountains provide a more rugged recreational experience for backcountry skiers, hikers and anglers who don't mind trekking miles to access high-country lakes and tumbling streams teeming with trout. Although off the beaten path, Dinosaur National Monument is a rich treasure of this country's Jurassic past, and the Green and Yampa rivers that flow through the monument and its surrounding landscape sate the souls of many recreationalists.

Central Utah is a transition zone between the state's northern mountains and its southern canyons. Steep mountains east and south of Provo are popular with skiers, hikers and others who love the outdoors. Price, on the northern edge of the Colorado Plateau and its wondrous landscape, is home to the College of Eastern Utah and its fine dinosaur museum, while the bottom of this region is marked by the geologic wonder that is Capitol Reef National Park. Between Price and Capitol Reef lies the San Rafael Swell, a modern-day no-man's land of canyon-riddled backcountry rife with history and adventures. Just as the region is a medley of landscapes, it offers a mix of activity, too, from the buzzing high-tech districts in the Provo–Orem corridor to the sleepy towns of Panguitch and Torrey.

In Capitol Reef, the least known of Utah's national parks, one that falls in south central Utah, the remains of an old pioneer community provide a hub for a network of dirt roads and trails through side canyons and among strange rock formations.

Unless you're a diehard skier or snowboarder who has long lusted after Utah's dry powder snow, your first trip to the state should take you to the southern reaches with their national parks. Few people actually live in the wild landscape of hoodoos and slickrock canyons that comprise southwestern and southeastern Utah, but millions of visitors come each year to visit the remarkable string of five national parks, each within a few hours' drive of the next.

Southwestern Utah is home to both Zion and Bryce Canyon national parks, parcels that base their fame and drawing power on rock formations. While Zion National Park's calling cards are towering cliffs and deep slot canyons, Bryce Canyon's popularity revolves around its unusual "hoodoos and goblins" that have been carved into the colorful landscape by erosion. St. George, in the extreme southwestern corner of Utah, is a growing retirement community thanks to its mild climate and challenging golf courses.

Far across the state to the east, **Southeastern Utah** has two national parks to call its own as well. While Arches National Park is renowned for having the world's greatest concentration of red-rock arches, Canyonlands National Park is a rugged wilderness that can't be truly appreciated during a "drive-through" vacation; instead you need to get on the ground—either by hiking, via four-wheel-drive vehicle, or even a raft trip down the Colorado River. Situated between these two parks is Moab, the heart and soul of mountain biking in the Southwest with its many miles of slickrock trail.

Each of Utah's parks is strikingly different from the others. Arches, Bryce Canyon and Zion all present distinctly shaped stone landscapes—erosion as an art form. Canyonlands, the most challenging to explore thoroughly due to its ruggedness and few interior roads, is reached by any of three dead-end roads into the park that start a hundred miles apart and do not connect. Canyonlands and the Moab area are favored by backpackers, mountain bikers and river rafters. Besides the national parks, another major destination in southern Utah is Lake Powell, the largest reservoir on the Colorado River, most of its shoreline is far from any road and only accessible by boat. You can rent anything from a speedboat to a houseboat at one of the marinas and cruise for days, exploring side canyons and isolated desert shorelines.

When to Go

SEASONS

Utah's diverse landscape produces a contradiction in climates. While summers in the northern mountains are downright enjoyable (high temperatures are typically in the mid-80s and overnight lows in the 50s) with little precipitation aside from the random afternoon thunderstorm, the canyonlands of southern Utah turn into ovens under the broiling sun that reach 100 degrees and beyond. Even the Salt Lake Valley can surpass the century mark repeatedly during summer. Conversely, when winter brings heavy snows and cold, below-freezing weather to the northern half of the state, the southern half often sports highs in the 50s, 60s and occasionally the 70s, making it the perfect place to escape winter's bite.

To assure a thick snow-pack for your ski vacation, it's best to plan a Utah visit between January and early April.

The worst time to visit northern Utah is between mid-April and early June, a time derisively, and descriptively, known as the "mud season" thanks to melting snows and spring rains. This is the most unpredictable time of year, weather-wise, in the region, as sunny, mild weather one week can be replaced by snowstorms and body-numbing temperatures the next. In Park City and other ski areas, many restaurants and resort facilities shut down for several weeks when the snows are gone but the slopes are not yet dried out to handle mountain-bike and hiking traffic.

Spring brings cool, moist weather to the southern reaches of the state, making it possible to see snow showers on the high plateaus around Moab and Bryce Canyon National Park, while heavy rains soak Zion and Capitol Reef national parks. This can be a magical time in canyon country, though, as the rains spur blankets of colorful wild flowers and cascading waterfalls in an otherwise dusty landscape.

Utah's summer tourist season typically runs from Memorial Day through Labor Day (a bit earlier and later in the southern reaches of the state), and the weather generally cooperates in grand design. Meadows swell with wildflowers well into July, scant rainfall makes for optimum conditions to enjoy the outdoors, and the lack of humidity makes both the warm mountain temperatures and occasionally hot canyon and high-desert temperatures generally bearable. Thunderstorms do arise, but not as often as in neighboring Wyoming. The greatest danger these storms pose is in southern Utah, where a cloudburst ten miles away can generate deadly flash floods through slot canyons.

Statewide, July is Utah's hottest month, followed closely by August. Of course, to many the 82° that is Park City's average high in July is quite pleasant, unlike St. George's 101° average July high.

Unless you're a skier, autumn—which usually arrives by mid-September—offers Utah's best weather, in all parts of the state. The changing season paints the mountains with yellow, orange and red aspen, maple and scrub oak in the north and funnels in cooler, occasionally crisp air that's perfect for biking and hiking. It also marks harvest time in places such as Brigham City, Bear Lake, Provo and tiny Fruita. Across the south, national-park crowds diminish as families head home from vacation so children can return to school, and the oppressively hot weather that makes it uncomfortable (and sometimes dangerous) to hike through Utah's canyon country lets up.

The weather largely remains dry in the fall, even in the high country, which is a perfect retreat for the year's last backpacking trek, camping outing or fishing foray. It's not entirely out of the question, though, for the high country to witness a snowstorm in October. Generally, heavy snows don't arrive before Thanksgiving, which is the traditional kickoff to ski season in the Wasatch Range; heavy, reliable snows, in fact, often do not arrive before year's end, forcing resorts to rely on their snowmaking systems.

Winters can bring short bursts of exceptionally cold weather in the state's mountainous areas, but as a rule Utah's winters are on the mild side when compared with those in Wyoming and Montana. Sub-zero readings in the state's ski country are few and far between; instead, most winter days see high temperatures climb into the 30s in Park City as well as Little and Big Cottonwood canyons. Down south, while St. George enjoys average high temperatures in the 50s in both December and January, Moab receives readings in the 40s.

CALENDAR OF EVENTS

Festivals serve dual purposes in Utah—they lure tourists to the state and give the locals an excuse to get together. Glancing over the list of events, it's clear that Utahns have extensive tastes: music and art festivals, re-enactments of mountain-man rendezvous and settler celebrations, harvest jubilees and, in a state where the snow is widely accepted as the greatest on Earth, even a winter carnival or two. Utah's Western heritage isn't overlooked, either, as there are pow-wows, rodeos and chili cookoffs. Below is a sampling of some of the leading annual events. Check with local chambers of commerce (listed in the regional chapters of this book) to see what will be going on when you are in the area.

JANUARY   **Salt Lake Valley, Northern Utah and Northeastern Utah**   The Utah Winter Games, a cornucopia of winter-sports competitions, lures thousands of Utahns to the slopes, cross-country courses and ice rinks in a bid to see who are the best athletes. Chocoholics and snow sliders converge at Solitude Ski Resort each January to mix and match their passions during the **Chocolate Lovers Tour**, which allows you to both ski the slopes and take breaks to melt chocolate in your mouth at various booths.

Northeastern Utah   Late in the month Robert Redford presents **The Sundance Film Festival**, a marketing orgy of independent film projects that draws Hollywood actors, actresses, producers and moguls to Park City in the one mid-winter event that can over-shadow Utah's snow season.

Southwestern Utah   Brian Head Ski Resort is the stage for the **Snowmobile Drag Race**, an uphill competition featuring souped up snowmobiles.

FEBRUARY   **Southwestern Utah**   From snowshoe races to winter archery, the **Bryce Canyon Winter Festival** held just north of Bryce Canyon National Park attracts crowds of participants and spectators alike.

MARCH   **Salt Lake Valley**   Spring can't be far off once the **Home and Garden Show** kicks off in Salt Lake City with its gardening and home-improvement exhibits. Snowbird is the backdrop for the NFL **Celebrity Classic**, a charitable ski race that draws notable grid-iron warriors to the slopes. Irish eyes are smiling in Salt Lake City for the **St. Patrick's Day Parade**, which runs down 200 East Street.

Northern Utah   The railroads largely created Ogden, which honors its past with the **Railroad Festival** that features model-train layouts in Union Station.

Central Utah   As winter starts to ease its grip on this part of Utah, thousands of Lesser Snow Geese arrive in the Delta area for a stopover on their northern migration. The **Snow Goose Festival**, held the first weekend in March, welcomes these birds, which rest in fields and bodies of water between the Clear Lake Wildlife Management Area and Delta. Scots celebrate their her-itage during the **Spring Scottish Festival** in Payson with an evening of music and dining.

Southwestern Utah   "Western" music aficionados head to Cedar City for the **Canyon Country Western Arts Festival**, an extravaganza of Western music and art. In the mountains, the Brian Head Resort hosts its annual **Spring Carnival**.

Southeastern Utah Muscle-propelled locomotion is the focus in Moab when runners trot into town for the **Canyonlands Half Marathon**. Hardier souls head to Monticello to test their stamina in the **Blue Mountain to Canyonlands Triathlon**.

Salt Lake Valley Snowbird Ski and Summer Resort welcomes the season with its **Easter Sunrise Service and Easter Egg Hunt**. The **Salt Lake Stingers** open their Triple-A baseball season at Franklin Quest Field.

Northern Utah Ogden, which traces its origin to a mountain man who decided to open a trading post, celebrates its history with the **Mountain Man Rendezvous**, where black-powder musketry is demonstrated along with Dutch-oven cooking and a trader's row.

Northeastern Utah The Canyons ski resort stages its rite of spring—the **Pond Skimming Contest**.

Central Utah Some of Utah's best artworks—pastels, water-colors, oils and more—go on display in Springville when the **Annual Spring Salon** is exhibited at the Springville Museum of Art.

Southwestern Utah Spring is welcomed at Brian Head Ski Resort, which stages its **Spring Carnival**, complete with on-snow activities such as pond-skimming on skis and snowboards. The **St. George Art Festival** fills Main Street and the art center with juried art exhibits and continuous musical performances.

Southeastern Utah Off-road-vehicle fanatics turn up in Moab for the **Easter Jeep Festival**, which features displays of gleaming mean machines as well as off-road rides into the surrounding red-rock landscape. Not as big as Sundance but just as interesting is Moab's **Canyonlands Film Festival**.

Salt Lake Valley The **Great Salt Lake Festival** appreciates the briny lake as well as the shorebirds and waterfowl that flock to its shores on their migratory flights with birding outings and naturalist talks.

Northern Utah America's railroad heritage is celebrated at Golden Spike National Historic Site during the **Wedding of the Rails Anniversary and Commemoration**, when the driving of the golden spike that symbolically tied the transcontinental rail line together is re-enacted. In Logan, they remember another time with a **Mountain Man Rendezvous**.

Central Utah Ephraim's Scandinavian roots show during the **Scandinavian Festival**, which includes the "Little Denmark Supper" featuring traditional dishes, a 5K road race, a parade and a rodeo.

Southwestern Utah Cowboy country springs into action at Ruby's Inn with the **Bryce Canyon Country Rodeo**, an exhibitory event rather than competitive, that begins its summer run in May.

Southeastern Utah Artworks, craftworks and music come together in downtown Moab during its annual **Arts Festival**.

JUNE

Salt Lake Valley The Pony Express is recalled at **Simpson Springs** during a re-enactment of the horse-powered mail system, while the **Utah Arts Festival** arrives in downtown Salt Lake City. Runners head for the **Salt Lake City Classic**, which features both 5K and 10K road races.

Northeastern Utah The **Northern Utah Indian Pow Wow** is held at Fort Duchesne on the Uintah and Ouray Indian Reservation. Sponsored by the Northern Ute Tribe, the pow-wow includes traditional dance and drum contests. Runners head to Park City for the annual **Park City Marathon**.

Central Utah A theatrical re-enactment of the Mormons' flight to Utah is presented as the **Mormon Miracle Pageant** in Manti.

Southwestern Utah Shakespeare fans make way for the opening of Cedar City's **Utah Shakespearean Festival**, which continues through the fall. In addition to daily performances of Shakespeare's works on an outdoor stage, there are related seminars and entertainment events. **Tuacahn**, an outdoor amphitheater set amid the glowing red rock of St. George, opens its summer season of plays.

JULY

Statewide Bigger than the Fourth of July celebration in Utah is July 24th's **"Days of '47"** celebration, also known as **Utah Pioneer Day**, which commemorates the arrival of Brigham Young and his followers in the Salt Lake Valley on July 24, 1847.

Salt Lake Valley Jazz aficionados head into the mountains to attend the **Jazz and Blues Festival** at Snowbird Ski and Summer Resort. In conjunction with the Days of '47 Celebration is the **Deseret News Marathon and 10K** races, which cut through the heart of Salt Lake City. Antelope Island is taken over by cyclists during the **Moonlight Bike Ride** across the causeway that ties the island to the state.

Northern Utah The **Cache Valley Cruise-In** lures some of the hottest cars, hot rods, motorcycles and trucks in the West to Logan for a long weekend of activities such as the Broom Sweep, in which drivers hang a broom out their windows to sweep balls along the road. The **Utah Festival Opera Company** opens shop with three classic operas that are performed at Logan's Ellen Eccles Theater. Staged several times a week, the shows continue on a revolving basis into August.

Northeastern Utah The **Oakley Rodeo**, the best little rodeo in Utah, brings members of the Professional Rodeo Cowboy Association to this sleepy Summit County community in the days leading up to the Fourth of July. The **Utah Symphony** fills the mountains with music when it begins its summer run of performances in the open-air, slope-side band shell at Deer Valley Resort.

Central Utah   Folk dances from around the world are presented in Springville during the town's **World Folkfest**, which is performed on alfresco stages. **Summer Theater**, which usually features a nationally known musical, begins its run at Sundance Resort in an outdoor setting. Campy international B movies are honored during the **Bicknell International Film Festival** held late in the month.

Southwestern Utah   Chili is the main attraction at Duck Creek's **Chili Cook-Off**. Kanab comes alive musically with the **Southern Utah Bluegrass Festival**.

Statewide   County fairs abound during this summer month.

AUGUST

Salt Lake Valley   Belly dancing, not skiing or snowboarding, is the focus at Snowbird Ski and Summer Resort when the **Utah Belly Dance Festival** opens its doors.

Northern Utah   Raspberries are served up in shakes, jams and pancakes during **Bear Lake Raspberry Days** at Garden City on the shores of Bear Lake. The **Festival of the American West** near Wellsville recalls and re-enacts the Old West, featuring the **World Championship Dutch Oven Cookoff**. The **Annual Railroaders Festival**, offering steam-locomotive demonstrations, is held at the Golden Spike National Historic Site on the second Saturday in August. Hot air is on display during the **Eden Balloon Festival**.

Northeastern Utah   The ski town turns into an arts colony when Park City hosts the **Park City Arts Festival**, luring artists, craftsmen and thousands of shoppers looking for bargains. The **Park City International Jazz Festival** runs several days at Deer Valley Resort this month, featuring musicians of national and international acclaim. Midway's heritage is revealed during the annual **Swiss Days** celebration.

Central Utah   Tall tales, scary stories and funny contrivances are the backbone of Orem's **Timpanogos Storytelling Festival**. The **Tintic Silver Festival Celebration** in Eureka recounts the glory days of this once-upon-a-time boomtown. A golf tournament, steak fry and dance highlight the festival. The Springville Art Museum stages its annual **quilt show** inside its galleries.

Southwestern Utah   At the **Party and Children's Fishing Derby** at Fremont Indian State Park visitors celebrate the park's creation and watch as children angle for the day's best catch. At Bryce Canyon National Park hardy runners enter the **Bryce Canyon Rim Run**, a five-mile jaunt along rolling hills and paved roads. Zion National Park is the backdrop for the **Zion Jazz and Art Festival**.

Salt Lake Valley   The **Utah State Fair** sets up shop at Salt Lake City's state fairgrounds for ten days of pie contests, flower contests, rides and other fair-related activities. The city's **Greek Festival**

SEPTEMBER

offers ethnic foods, dancing and crafts. The Bonneville Salt Flats turn into the world's fastest race course when the **World of Speed** is staged. Mid-month brings the **Brewer's Festival** to downtown Salt Lake City. Oom-pah bands, brauts and beer are in abundance at Snowbird Ski and Summer Resort during **Oktoberfest**, held weekends through the month and into October.

Northern Utah   Harvest time means it's time for Brigham City's **Peach Days Festival**, Utah's oldest continuing harvest festival, with a parade, an antique car show, a Dutch-oven cookoff and a carnival.

Northeastern Utah   The hamlet of Midway in the Heber Valley recalls its heritage with the **Swiss Days** festival, which features authentic Scandinavian foods, music and dancing.

Central Utah   Utah's first capital, Fillmore, comes to life when the **Old Capitol Arts Festival** arrives mid-month with arts-and-crafts booths, pioneer demonstrations that touch on blacksmithing, weaving and candle-making, juried art exhibits, and daily "Quick Draw" competitions among artists. Onions are the glorified vegetable during Payson's **Onion Days** celebration.

Southwestern Utah   Brauts and bikes share center stage in Brian Head during the **Oktoberfest and Mountain Bike** weekend.

Southeastern Utah   The **Moab Music Festival** offers some of the hottest tickets in the state during its two-week run that brings concerts to various locations in the area. The most popular (and the toughest to land tickets for) are the concerts held in a grotto along the Colorado River. The Four Corners' Navajo heritage is remembered during the **Navajo Fair and Rodeo** in Bluff. Over in Green River, watermelons, honey dew and cantaloupes are harvested during **Melon Days**.

OCTOBER   **Salt Lake Valley**   Cowboys head to Antelope Island for the **Bison Roundup**. At historic Gardner Village in West Jordan you'll find the **Scarecrow Festival**, which offers pumpkin sales and decoration exhibits. The **Scottish Festival**, featuring traditional music, food and dancing, comes to Salt Lake City.

Northern Utah   To celebrate the coming of fall, Logan stages its **Pumpkin Walk**. Just south of Logan the American West Heritage Center offers a **corn maze**.

Northeastern Utah   The **Great Pumpkin Festival** is held in Jensen's town park in time for Halloween.

Southwestern Utah   One of the country's fastest and most scenic marathon courses lures thousands to the **St. George Marathon**.

Southeastern Utah   Mountain bikers converge on Moab for the **Canyonlands Fat Tire Mountain Bike Festival** and the **24 Hours of Moab Bike Race**.

Statewide   If the snow gods are willing, the state's **ski resorts**   **NOVEMBER**
start to open.

Salt Lake Valley   The Christmas holidays can't be far off once
the **Temple Square Holiday Lights** are lit during Thanksgiving
weekend.

Northeastern Utah   Wine lovers head to Deer Valley Resort for
the **Beaujolais Festival**, when the season's favorite is paired with
some of the tastiest foods found in ski country. Deer Valley is also
the setting for the **Navajo Rug Show**, a charitable event that raises
money for the Adopt-a-Native Elder program on the Navajo Indian
Reservation. Christmas lights that have been strung throughout
the **Dinosaur Gardens** at Vernal's Utah Field House are turned
on late in the month. Barring unseasonably warm weather, the
Park City Mountain Resort hosts the **America's Opening World
Cup** ski races.

Southeastern Utah   A **Parade of Christmas Lights**, which gives
boat owners a reason to festoon their watercraft with lights, is
held in late November around Thanksgiving on Lake Powell at the
Bullfrog Resort and Marina. Moab hosts the **Turkey Trot 5K Race.**

Salt Lake Valley   Salt Lake City stages its **First Night** New   **DECEMBER**
Year's Eve celebration in the heart of downtown with entertain-
ment and fireworks. The **Winterfest** celebration at Snowbird Ski
and Summer Resort features the country's best wines, beers and
foods over a weekend of cooking seminars. The **Nutcracker** is a
seasonal mainstay of the Ballet West troupe, which performs the
Christmas classic in the Capitol Theater. The festive **Mormon
Tabernacle Choir Christmas Concert** is always popular.

Northern Utah   Over at Golden Spike National Historic Site
west of Brigham City the **Railroad Film Festival and Winter Steam
Train Demonstrations** are staged between Christmas and New
Year's Day. **Elk Feeding** begins at the Hardware Ranch located
near the head of Blacksmith Fork Canyon south of Logan. Once
the snow covers the ground, sleigh rides are conducted through
the refuge.

Northeastern Utah   In Helper the **Electric Light Parade** revolves
around an evening parade through downtown to celebrate the
season with lighted floats.

Central Utah   At Brigham Young University's Marriott Center,
the **Christmas Around the World** festival features folk dancing
and ethnic holiday celebrations.

Southwestern Utah   Zion National Park is the setting for the
park's **Christmas Bird Count.**

Southeastern Utah   The **Canyonlands Christmas Festival** in
Moab features an electric light parade through downtown, a tree-
lighting ceremony, caroling and a holiday craft fair.

▼▼▼▼▼▼▼▼▼▼
Before You Go

**VISITORS
CENTERS**

Free visitor information packages, which include guides to accommodations throughout the state, a state highway map and details to special events, can be obtained by contacting the **Utah Travel Council**. ~ Council Hall, Salt Lake City, UT 84114; 801-538-1030, 800-200-1160, fax 801-538-1399. Much of the information is also available at the council's website: www.utah.com.

The state is divided into nine travel regions, with local tourism offices within each region that are very helpful. You can obtain detailed information from their respective websites and offices.

The **Golden Spike Empire** covers a portion of northern Utah, including the cities of Ogden and Brigham City. ~ 2501 Wall Avenue, Ogden, UT 84401; 801-627-8288, 800-255-8825; www.ogdencvb.org, e-mail info@ogdencvb.org.

The **Cache Valley Travel Region** comprises the rest of northern Utah, including Logan and Bear Lake. ~ 160 North Main Street, Logan, UT 84321; 435-752-2161, 800-882-4433; www.tourcachevalley.com, e-mail tourism@tourcachevalley.com.

Great Salt Lake Country encompasses Salt Lake City and the Bonneville Salt Flats. ~ 90 South West Temple Street, Salt Lake City, UT 84101; 801-521-2822, 800-541-4955; www.visitsaltlake.com, e-mail slvcb@saltlake.org.

Mountainland covers Park City, Provo and Heber City. ~ 586 East 800 North, Orem, UT 84097; 801-229-3800.

Dinosaurland entails northeastern Utah, including Vernal, Flaming Gorge National Recreation Area and Dinosaur National Monument. ~ 55 East Main Street, Vernal, UT 84078; 435-789-6932, 800-477-5558; www.dinoland.com, e-mail dinoland@easilink.com.

Panoramaland covers a wide swathe of central Utah, including Capitol Reef National Park, Spring City, Ephraim, Manti and Fillmore. ~ 4 South Main Street, Nephi, UT 84648; 435-623-5203, 800-748-4361.

Castle Country encompasses east-central Utah, including Price, the San Rafael Swell and the Manti-La Sal National Forest. ~ 90 North 100 East, Price, UT 84501; 435-637-3009, 800-842-0789; www.castlecountry.com, e-mail cctr@priceutah.net.

Color Country is in southwestern Utah and contains Zion and Bryce Canyon national parks, St. George, Cedar City and Brian Head. There are a number of travel offices in this region so you really can focus your research. ~ *Beaver Country Travel Council*, P.O. Box 272, Beaver, UT 84713; 435-468-5438. *Brian Head Chamber of Commerce*, 259 South Route 143, Brian Head, UT 84719; 888-677-2810; www.brianheadutah.com. *Escalante/Boulder Chamber of Commerce*, P.O. Box 175, Escalante, UT 84276; 435-826-4810; www.escalante-cc.com. *Gar-*

field County Travel Council, P.O. Box 200, Panguitch, UT 84759; 435-676-1160, 800-444-6689; www.brycecanyoncountry.com. *Iron County Travel Council*, P.O. Box 1007, Cedar City, UT 84721; 435-586-5124, 800-354-4849; www.scenicsouthernutah. com. *Kane County Travel Council*, 78 South 100 East, Kanab, UT 84741; 435-644-5033, 800-733-5263; www.kaneutah. com. *St. George Area Chamber of Commerce*, 97 East St. George Boulevard, St. George, UT 84770; 435-628-1658. *Washington County Travel Bureau*, 1835 Convention Center Drive, St. George, UT 84790; 435-634-5747, 800-869-6635; www.utahsdixie.com. *Zion Canyon Chamber of Commerce*, P.O. Box 331, Springdale, UT 84767; 888-518-7070; www.zionpark.com. *Panguitch Chamber of Commerce*, P.O. Box 400, Panguitch, UT 84759; 435-676-8585; www.panguitch.org.

> Cool temperatures often lull newcomers into forgetting that thin, high-altitude air filters out far less of the sun's ultraviolet rays; above timberline, exposed, unprotected skin will sunburn faster than it would on a Hawaiian beach.

Canyonlands covers extreme southeastern Utah and Moab, Arches and Canyonlands national parks, Lake Powell and the La Sal and Abajo mountain ranges. There are two travel offices in this region. ~ *Moab Area Travel Council*, P.O. Box 550, Moab, UT 84532; 435-259-1370, 800-635-6622; www.discovermoab. com. *San Juan County Visitor Services*, P.O. Box 490, 117 South Main Street, Monticello, UT 84535; 435-587-3235, 800-574-4386; www.southeasternutah.com, e-mail info@southeastern utah.com.

Packing for a trip to Utah can be simplified by confining your visit to either the mountains or the high desert. Of course, that's not a very realistic plan, unless you're on a ski vacation or a white-water rafting trip. The fact of the matter is, it's not unusual to have a snowstorm in the mountains in June and warm golfing weather in St. George on the same day.

PACKING

In general, though, Utahns are an informal lot, as typified by "Park City formal." What's that? Jeans go very well with your tuxedo jacket, thank you very much. For the most part, Utahns are either dressed to play, to go to church, or somewhere in between. There's no need for a coat and tie in the state, and Lycra wears very well in the mountain-bike capital of Moab.

Due to the mountains' elevation and the high desert's propensity for cooling off at night, even in summer you should pack a fleece jacket or long-sleeved flannel shirt and jeans for evenings. During the days, though, shorts and T-shirts suffice admirably. In spring, fall and winter, layers of clothing are your best bet, since the weather can change dramatically from day to day and region to region. Winters only get bone-numbing cold in the state's upper-

Text continued on page 28.

The Mormon Faith

Although Utah is universally accepted as the headquarters for the Church of Jesus Christ of Latter-day Saints, the religion's birthplace is far to the east, in New York state. And while the church flourished under the leadership of Brigham Young, the faith was originally given life in the early 1800s by Joseph Smith, who as a young man was uncertain which religion to follow.

In 1820 Smith, troubled by this dilemma, headed into a forest and prayed for God to tell him which church to join. Instead of hearing an answer, though, Smith claimed to have been visited by God and his son, Jesus Christ, and told that none of the existing religions was worthy. Three years later God was said to have dispatched the angel Moroni to lead Smith to a book of golden plates that contained the religious gospel of an alleged, long-forgotten American culture. This gospel, Smith was told, was the one true religion that he should follow. Using these writings, Smith in 1827 wrote the Book of Mormon. Three years later he organized the LDS Church.

But just as the pilgrims fled England in the 1600s because of religious persecution, Smith and his followers continually found themselves moving in search of a place where they could peacefully practice their faith. From New York the Mormons went to Ohio and then Missouri before moving on in 1839 to Nauvoo, Illinois. It was while defending his religion in 1844 that Smith and his brother, Hyrum, were killed by a mob in Carthage, Illinois, that opposed his church.

Upon Smith's death Brigham Young, who had joined the church in 1832, rose to become church president and convinced his congregation to flee to the West. On July 24, 1847, after a nearly 1300-mile-long pilgrimage, Young and a group of 148 followers found themselves near the mouth of today's Emigration Canyon on the eastern rim of the Salt Lake Valley. Although feverish and bed-ridden, Young managed to gaze down on the valley and proclaim that it was the place they would settle.

In the valley the Mormons quickly displayed a knack for taming the harsh land, building extensive irrigation systems that ferried water from the mountains to their fields. After laying out the grid that would become Salt Lake City, Young focused on spreading the church's word by dispatching missionaries to settle Utah and convert whomever they could. Young's dream of strengthening his church has been carried on by successive church presidents who continue to dispatch missionaries, not just throughout Utah but throughout the world.

Today, by sending most young male church members out on two-year missions after high school, the LDS Church has built a worldwide following of more than ten million members.

Just as Brigham Young relied on divine revelations from God to help him lead his congregation, so, too, do today's church leaders. And just as Smith and Young were viewed by their followers as prophets, so, too, is the current church president.

Roughly three-quarters of Utah's nearly two million residents members are of the LDS Church, so its substantial influence on the state should come as no surprise. Despite the generally accepted constitutional division between church and state, in Utah it's not unusual for legislative leaders to discuss proposed legislation with church leaders. The church's conservative, strait-laced nature is also reflected throughout the state and its residents.

The world-wide headquarters for the LDS Church can be found at Temple Square in the heart of downtown Salt Lake City. The church's gleaming six-towered temple, constructed over a 40-year period with quartzite, copper and gold leaf, is the centerpiece of the square, which is also home to the church's administrative buildings, the dome-shaped Tabernacle, the LDS Assembly Hall and beautiful gardens that radiate with color from spring into fall.

most elevations, and then only if you're standing still for long periods of time.

Other essentials to pack or buy along the way include a good sunscreen, high-quality sunglasses, and a wide-brimmed hat if you're en route to southern Utah. If you are planning to camp in the mountains in the summer months, you'll be glad you brought along mosquito repellent. Umbrellas are generally unnecessary, unless they're intended to produce shade in the desert.

For outdoor activities, tough-soled hiking boots are more comfortable than running shoes on slickrock. Even RV travelers and those who prefer to spend most nights in motels may want to take along a backpacking tent and sleeping bag in case the urge to sleep under the starry skies becomes irresistible. A canteen, first-aid kit, flashlight and other routine camping gear are also likely to come in handy. Both cross-country and downhill ski rentals are available in resort areas during the winter. Come summer, mountain bikes replace skis in most of the rental shops. Other outdoor recreation equipment—canoes, fishing tackle, golf clubs—can be rented, too.

A camera, of course, is essential for capturing your travel experience; of equal importance is a good pair of binoculars to scan southern Utah cliffsides for dwellings, bring wildlife up close or merely pan distant landscapes from scenic overlooks. And don't, for heaven's sake, forget your copy of *Hidden Utah*.

LODGING   Utah accommodations run the gamut from tiny one-room cabins to luxury resorts that blend traditional alpine-lodge ambience with contemporary elegance. Bed-and-breakfast establishments are found in most of the larger or more tourist-oriented towns, and even in some more remote locations such as Panguitch and Vernal. Typical of the genre are lovingly restored Victorian-era mansions comfortably furnished with period decor; these usually have fewer than a half-dozen rooms.

DOLLAR-SAVING TIPS

To save money, consider avoiding ski trips during Christmas, New Year's and Presidents' weekend, or stay in more affordable lodging in Salt Lake City. Also good to know is that resorts offer multiday ticket packages that are cheaper than buying a series of day tickets, and that early-season lodging packages often offer free or reduced-price skiing privileges. Another way to save money on ski trips is to come early or late in the season. Summer is much more affordable in Utah's ski country, as accommodations are in surplus and room rates often drop to less than half the winter rates.

The abundance of motels in towns along all major highway corridors presents a range of choices, from name-brand motor inns to traditional ma-and-pa establishments that have endured for the half-century since motels became a part of American culture. While ordinary motels in the vicinity of major tourist destinations can be pricey, lodgings in small towns away from major resorts and interstate routes can offer friendliness, quietude and comfort at ridiculously low rates.

At the other end of the price spectrum, high-season (winter) rates in Park City, Snowbird and Alta can be frightfully exorbitant. These resort areas justify an "ultra-ultra-deluxe" notation on prices, as choice properties can command tariffs upwards of $1000 a night, particularly over Christmas week and Presidents' Day weekend. At the same time, a number of new hotels in Salt Lake City can deliver quite a blow to your budget, with year-round room rates starting at $150 a night and quickly moving past $200.

Zion and Bryce Canyon are the only national parks in Utah with lodges within their borders. Zion Lodge offers a fairly generic ambience, somewhat akin to a motor lodge, while Bryce Canyon Lodge is a stately, rustic building restored to its original 1920s splendor. Both offer rooms at mid-range prices, and since their locations make them highly sought-after, travelers must make reservations at least several months in advance, longer for peak dates such as the Fourth of July and Labor Day.

Whatever your preference and budget, you can probably find something to suit your taste. Just remember that rooms can be scarce and prices may rise during peak season, which is summer in most of the state, Park City and the Cottonwood Canyons during winter. Travelers planning to visit a place in peak season should either make advance bookings or arrive early in the day, before the No Vacancy signs start lighting up.

Lodging prices in this book focus on high-season rates; you can expect lesser rates during the off-season. *Budget* hostelries generally run less than $65 per night for two people and are clean but modest. *Moderate* motels and hotels range from $65–$100; what they have to offer in the way of luxury often depends on their location, but they usually have larger rooms and more attractive surroundings than their budget counterparts. For *deluxe*-priced accommodations, expect to spend between $100 and $150 for a homey bed and breakfast or a double in a hotel or resort; you'll commonly find spacious rooms, a fashionable lobby, a restaurant and often a bar or nightclub. *Ultra-deluxe* facilities, priced above $150, are among the finest in the state, offering all the amenities of a deluxe hotel, plenty of extras and great locations; these places for the most part are limited to Utah's ski resort areas and the heart of Salt Lake City's downtown.

As noted above, there are *ultra-ultra-deluxe* accommodations in Park City and at Snowbird and Alta that surpass $500 a night and can even go beyond $1000 during peak holiday seasons.

Room rates vary as much with locale as with quality. Some of the trendier destinations have no rooms at all in the budget price range. In other communities and small towns, just about every motel falls into the budget category.

DINING

Utah offers a delicious spectrum of possibilities, ranging from regional cuisine such as beef and trout to elaborate creations utilizing seafood and wild game. Most cities have Italian, Mexican and Chinese restaurants, and while you can choose from a wide selection of gourmet foods in Salt Lake City and Park City, off-the-beaten culinary treasures can be found in Torrey, the Heber Valley, St. George, Springdale, Logan and Moab. If your idea of an ideal vacation includes savoring epicurean delights, then by all means seize the opportunity whenever it arises.

In summer, many of Park City's restaurants try to drum up business by offering two-for-one coupons in the local newspaper, *The Park Record*.

One Utah staple that seems to appear on most menus is Utah trout; another is rack of lamb. In northern Utah during the summer and fall, fresh fruits and berries from the region appear in desserts.

Restaurants listed in this book offer lunch and dinner unless otherwise noted. Dinner entrées at *budget* eateries cost $15 or less. The ambience is informal, service usually speedy and the crowd often a local one. *Moderate*-priced restaurant entrées range between $15 and $25 at dinner; surroundings are casual but pleasant, the pace slower, and the menu more varied than at budget restaurants. *Deluxe* establishments tab many of their entrées from $25; presentation is typically sophisticated, decor plusher and the service more personalized than at moderate-priced restaurants.

Restaurants in resort towns often close for a period during the off-season. And because restaurants change hands often, efforts have been made in this book to include places with established reputations. Compared to evening dinners, breakfast and lunch menus vary less in price from restaurant to restaurant.

LIQUOR

Utah's conservatism has led to somewhat confusing liquor laws, in which you need a membership (essentially a cover charge good for two weeks) to enter a private club that serves hard liquor. There are "beer bars," though, where you don't need a membership to quaff a brew, and most restaurants have liquor licenses that allow you to enjoy a drink with your meal.

Wherever you drink, however, it's illegal in Utah to nurse two drinks (such as a shot of whiskey and a beer chaser) at the same time.

Smoking, which is banned in most buildings throughout Utah, *is* allowed within private clubs. As a result, you can expect a smoky environment in these establishments.

DRIVING

Utah is a rugged state and there are some important things to remember when driving. Its 84,916 square miles present a wide variety of road conditions, from Salt Lake City's heavy interstate traffic typical of that found in East and West Coast urban areas, to narrow, twisting mountain roads leading to the ski resorts, to long, straight stretches of highway through the Great Salt Lake Desert and central portions of the state that can be dangerously mesmerizing. Mountainous areas in the northern part of the state and the deserts in the southern half of the state can be potentially hazardous for inattentive or inexperienced drivers.

In the mountains, don't be surprised by the lack of guardrails separating motorists from precipitous dropoffs. The fact is, highway safety studies have found that far fewer accidents occur where there are no guardrails. Statistically, edgy, winding mountain roads are much safer than straight, fast interstate highways.

Unpaved roads are another story. While many are wide and well-graded, weather and/or the wear and tear of heavy seasonal use can create unexpected road conditions. Some U.S. Forest Service and Bureau of Land Management roads are designated for four-wheel drive or high-clearance vehicles only. If you see a sign indicating four-wheel drive only, believe it. These roads can be very dangerous in a standard passenger car without the high ground clearance and extra traction afforded by four-wheel drive . . . and there may be no safe place to turn around if you get stuck.

In the state's desert areas, thunderstorms can send deadly torrents across low-lying roads and quickly turn dirt roads into muddy quagmires or leave them as slick as ice, a dangerous situation on downhill grades.

Away from the heavily urbanized Wasatch Front, many roads—interstates and state highways alike—take you far from civilization, so be sure to have a full radiator and a tank of gas. If you're heading into the rugged outback of the San Rafael Swell or the West Desert, it's a good idea to carry extra fuel, food and water. Should you become stuck, local people are usually helpful, offering stranded vehicles assistance, but in case no one else is around, a CB radio or car phone is a handy travel companion for long backcountry drives. Don't place too much faith in cell phones, as coverage can be spotty.

Utah gets its share of snow in the winter months—upwards of 500 inches in some places. Mountain passes, not to mention stretches of high-desert highways, frequently become snow-packed or suffer from ground blizzards. Under these conditions, tire chains are always advised, even on main highways. State patrol officers may make you turn back if your car is not equipped with chains or four-wheel drive. At the very least, studded tires are recommended.

The maximum speed limit on interstate highways is 75 miles per hour, while on other roads limits typically range from 55 to 65 m.p.h., and 35 or even 25 m.p.h. in construction zones. Violators are subject to fines, of course.

You can get full information on statewide road conditions for Utah any time of the year by calling 800-492-2400. You may also contact the Utah Highway Patrol at 801-965-4505.

TRAVELING WITH CHILDREN

Any place that has cowboys and Indians, rocks to climb and limitless room to run is bound to be a hit with youngsters. Plenty of family adventures await in Utah, from tackling rivers and hiking through the backcountry to rockhounding and visiting manmade attractions. A few guidelines will help make travel with children easier.

Book reservations in advance, making sure that the places you stay accept children. Many bed and breakfasts do not. If you need a crib or extra cot, arrange for it ahead of time. A travel agent can be of help here, as well as with most other travel plans.

If you are traveling by air, try to reserve bulkhead seats, where there is plenty of room. Take along extras you may need, such as diapers, changes of clothing, snacks and toys or small games. When traveling by car, be sure to take along the extras, too. Pack plenty of water and juices to drink; dehydration can be a subtle but serious problem. Most towns, as well as some national parks, have stores that carry diapers, baby food, snacks and other essentials, though they usually close early. Larger towns often have all-night groceries or convenience stores.

The emphasis on strong family values and large families explains why Utah claims one of the largest birthrates in the United States

A first-aid kit is a must for any trip. Along with adhesive bandages and antiseptic and anti-itch creams, include any medicines your pediatrician might recommend to treat allergies, colds, diarrhea or any chronic problems your child may have.

Utah's sunshine is intense, both in the southern canyon country and the northern mountains. Take extra care by using sunscreen or sunblock with an SPF of 15 or higher, long-sleeve shirts and wide-brimmed hats. Children's skin is usually more tender than adult skin and can burn severely before you realize it.

Many national parks and monuments offer special activities designed just for children. Visitors centers' film presentations and rangers' campfire slide shows can educate children about the natural history of Utah and head off some questions. Since kids tend to wonder about a lot more things than adults have answers

for, however, be prepared and seize every opportunity to learn
more yourself.

Parts of Utah, particularly in the southern canyon country, can
be harsh and unforgiving—on pets as well as humans. While
kennels exist throughout the state for boarding your animals
overnight, and some lodgings even permit your pets in your
room, it's best to leave your pets behind at home. That said, pets
are permitted on leashes in virtually all campgrounds. In national
parks and monuments, though, pets are prohibited on trails and
in the backcountry. You are supposed to walk your dog on the
roadside, pick up after it, then leave the animal in the car while
you go hiking.

Make sure the dog gets adequate shade, ventilation and
water. Fortunately, dogs are free to run everywhere else in national forests, and leashes are required only in designated camping and picnic areas.

Wildlife such as mountain lions and coyotes can pose special
hazards in the backcountry of southern Utah. While there are no
grizzly bears in the state, there are black bears that, if sufficiently
provoked, may attack dogs. Porcupines, common in conifer
forests, are tempting to chase and slow enough to catch, but if
you dog latches on to one of them, a mouthful of quills means
painfully pulling them out one by one with pliers, or making an
emergency visit to a veterinary clinic in the nearest town.

The rugged beauty of Utah is appealing to many: the wide open
spaces stretching for miles and miles and the sprawling mountains invite people who are looking to get away from it all. It's a
state that gives people a lot of space, literally, and encourages
you to do your own thing, which allows gays or lesbian travelers to feel comfortable here.

That notwithstanding, Utah is a conservative state and has no
openly gay communities. Information and support on gay and
lesbian issues in Utah, however, can be obtained from the **Gay
and Lesbian Community Center of Utah** in Salt Lake City. ~ 361
North 300 West; 801-539-8800, 888-874-2743; www.glccu.com.

Traveling solo grants an independence and freedom different from
that of traveling with a partner, but single travelers are more vul-
nerable to crime and should take additional precautions.

While Utah's crime rate is lower than those found in more urbanized states, don't let that give you a false sense of security or
override common sense. It's unwise to hitchhike and probably
best to avoid inexpensive accommodations on the outskirts of
town; the money saved does not outweigh the risk. Bed and
breakfasts and youth hostels are generally your safest bet for

lodging, and they also foster an environment ideal for bonding with fellow travelers.

Keep all valuables well-hidden and hold onto cameras and purses. Avoid late-night treks or strolls through questionable sections of town, but if you find yourself in this situation, continue walking with a confident air until you reach a safe haven. A fierce scowl never hurts.

These hints should by no means deter you from seeking out adventure. Wherever you go, stay alert, use your common sense and trust your instincts.

If you are hassled or threatened in some way, never be afraid to scream for assistance. It's a good idea to carry change for a phone call and a number to call in a case of emergency. For more hints, get a copy of *Safety and Security for Women Who Travel* (Travelers Tales).

> In winter it is wise to travel with a shovel, gravel or cat litter for traction, blankets or sleeping bags, and a long-burning candle in your car.

SENIOR TRAVELERS   Utah is a hospitable place for older vacationers. The large number of national parks in the southern half of the state means that persons age 62 and older can save considerable money with a Golden Age Pass, which sells for a one-time fee of $10 and allows free lifetime admission into National Park Service units. Apply for one in person at any national park unit that charges an entrance fee. Many private sightseeing attractions also give significant discounts to seniors.

The **American Association of Retired Persons** (AARP) offers membership to anyone over 50. AARP's benefits include travel discounts with a number of firms. ~ 601 E Street NW, Washington, DC 20049; 800-424-3410; www.aarp.org.

Elderhostel provides educational courses that are all-inclusive packages at colleges and universities, some in Utah. ~ 11 Avenue de Lafayette, Boston, MA 02111; 877-426-8056, fax 877-426-2166; www.elderhostel.org.

Be extra careful about health matters. In Utah's changeable climate and elevation, seniors are more at risk for suffering hypothermia. High altitudes may present a risk to persons with heart or respiratory conditions; ask your physician for advice when planning your trip. Also, southern Utah's summers can be quite hot, with temperatures surpassing 100°F, so it's important to drink plenty of water and avoid hiking during the height of the day.

In addition to the medications you ordinarily use, it's a good idea to bring along the prescriptions for obtaining more. Consider carrying a medical record with you, including your history and current medical status as well as your doctor's name, phone and address. Make sure that your insurance covers you while you are away from home.

Utah is striving to make public areas fully accessible to persons with **DISABLED** disabilities. Parking spaces and restroom facilities for the handi- **TRAVELERS** capped are provided according to both state law and national park regulations. National parks, forests and monuments also post signs that tell which trails are wheelchair accessible. Additionally, the National Park Service offers a free **Golden Access Pass**, which provides free access into NPS units for disabled individuals.

There are many organizations offering information for travelers with disabilities, including the **Society for Accessible Travel & Hospitality** (SATH) at 347 5th Avenue, Suite 610, New York, NY, 10016, 212-447-7284, fax 212-725-8253, www.sath.org; and the **MossRehab ResourceNet** at MossRehab Hospital, 1200 West Tabor Road, Philadelphia, PA 19141, 215-456-9600, www.mossresourcenet.org.

For general travel advice, contact **Travelin' Talk**, a networking organization. ~ P.O. Box 1796, Wheat Ridge, CO 80034; 303-232-2979; www.travelintalk.net. **Access-Able Travel Source** provides traveling information online. ~ www.access-able.com.

Passports and Visas   Most foreign visitors need a passport and **FOREIGN** tourist visa to enter the United States. Contact your nearest U.S. **TRAVELERS** Embassy or Consulate well in advance to obtain a visa and to check on any other entry requirements.

Customs Requirements   Foreign travelers are allowed to carry in the following: 200 cigarettes (1 carton), 50 cigars or 2 kilograms (4.4 pounds) of smoking tobacco; one liter of alcohol for personal use only (you must be 21 years of age to bring in alcohol); and US$100 worth of duty-free gifts that can include an additional quantity of 100 cigars. You may bring in any amount of currency, but must fill out a form if you bring in over US$10,000. Carry any prescription drugs in clearly marked containers (you may have to produce a written prescription or doctor's statement for the customs officer). Meat or meat products, seeds, plants, fruits and narcotics are not allowed to be brought into the United States. Contact the **United States Customs Service** for further information. ~ 1300 Pennsylvania Avenue NW, Washington, DC 20229; 202-927-6724; www.customs.treas.gov.

Driving   If you plan to rent a car, an international driver's license should be obtained before arriving in the United States. Some car-rental agencies require both a foreign license and an international driver's license. Many also require a lessee to be at least 25 years of age; all require a major credit card. Seat belts are mandatory for the driver and all passengers. Children under the age of five or under 40 pounds should be in the back seat in approved child-safety restraints.

Currency   United States money is based on the dollar. Bills come in denominations of $1, $2, $5, $10, $20, $50 and $100. Every dollar is divided into 100 cents. Coins are the penny (1 cent), nickel (5 cents), dime (10 cents), quarter (25 cents), half-dollar (50 cents) and dollar, although half-dollar and dollar coins are rarely used. You may not use foreign currency to purchase goods and services in the United States. Consider buying traveler's checks in dollar amounts. You may also use credit cards affiliated with an American company, such as Interbank, Barclay Card, VISA and American Express.

Electricity and Electronics   Electric outlets use currents of 110 volts, 60 cycles. To operate appliances made for other electrical systems, you need a transformer or other adapter. Travelers who use laptop computers for telecommunications should be aware that modem configurations for U.S. telephone systems may be different from their European counterparts. Similarly, the U.S. format for videotapes is different from that in Europe; National Park Service visitors centers and other stores that sell souvenir videos often have them available in European format on request.

Weights and Measures   The United States uses the English system of weights and measures. American units and their metric equivalents are: 1 inch = 2.5 centimeters; 1 foot (12 inches) = 0.3 meter; 1 yard (3 feet) = 0.9 meter; 1 mile (5280 feet) = 1.6 kilometers; 1 ounce = 28 grams; 1 pound (16 ounces) = 0.45 kilogram; 1 quart (liquid) = 0.9 liter.

Outdoor Adventures

CAMPING

Tent or RV camping is a great way to tour Utah's national and state parks and forests during the spring, summer and fall months. Besides probably saving substantial sums of money, campers enjoy the freedom to watch sunsets from beautiful places, spend nights under spectacular starry skies, and wake up to find themselves in lovely surroundings that few hotels can match.

It's not hard to find a place to pitch your tent or park your RV. Plus, most towns have some sort of commercial RV park, and long-term mobile-home parks often rent spaces to RVers by the night. But unless you absolutely need cable television, none of these places can compete with the wide array of public campgrounds available in government-administered sites.

Federal campgrounds are typically less developed; you usually won't find electric, water or sewer hookups in campgrounds at national forests, monuments or recreation areas. However, Utah state parks feature a wide range of campsites, from rustic sites with no amenities to campgrounds with RV hookups, showers and electricity. As for national parks, there are about 650 campsites in Zion, roughly 200 in Bryce Canyon, 70 in Capitol Reef and 52 in Arches. Canyonlands National Park has a dozen campsites in the Island in the Sky District, 26 in the Needles District, and none in the Maze District, though it does allow primitive camping that requires you to hike into the backcountry. More and more parks are charging a nominal fee for backcountry camping.

National park campground reservations can be made by calling 800-365-2267, or on-line at www.reservations.nps.gov. A number of campsites are always held back for first-come, first-serve campers, and during the height of the season they are usually taken by early afternoon. As a result, plan on traveling in the morning and reaching your intended campground by early afternoon—or, during peak season at Zion, Arches or Canyonlands, by mid-morning. In the national parks, campers may find it more convenient to keep a single location for as long as a week and explore surrounding areas on day trips.

For a list of state parks with camping facilities, contact **Utah State Parks and Recreation**. ~ 1594 West North Temple, Suite 116, Salt Lake City; 801-538-7221, 800-322-3770; www.stateparks.utah.gov. For information on camping in Utah's national forests, contact **National Forest Service-Intermountain Region**. ~ 2501 Wall Avenue, Ogden; 801-625-5306; www.fs.fed.us/r4. Camping and reservation information for national parks, monuments and recreation areas is available from the parks and monuments listed in this book or from the **National Park Service–Rocky Mountain Regional Headquarters**. ~ P.O. Box 25287, Denver, CO 80225; 303-969-2000. For information on camping in public lands administered by the **Bureau of Land Management**, contact the BLM's Salt Lake office. ~ 324 South State Street, Suite 301, Salt Lake City; 801-539-4001.

Roughly 65 percent of Utah is owned by the federal government, either in the form of a national park, monument or forest, or lands overseen by the U.S. Bureau of Land Management.

Fishing, camping, boating and hunting are allowed on the roughly four-and-a-half-million-acre **Uintah and Ouray Indian Reservation** in northeastern Utah. For information and permits, contact the Northern Ute Indian Tribe's Fish and Wildlife Office. ~ P.O. Box 190, Fort Duchesne, UT 84026; 435-722-5511.

PERMITS

Tent camping is allowed in the backcountry of all national forests except in a few areas where signs are posted prohibiting it. You may need a permit to hike or camp in national forest wilderness areas, so contact specific forests for more information. Ranger stations provide trail maps and advice on current conditions and fire regulations. In dry seasons, emergency rules may prohibit campfires and sometimes ban cigarette smoking, with stiff enforcement penalties.

For backcountry hiking in national parks and monuments, you must first obtain a permit from the ranger at the front desk in the visitors center. The permit procedure is simple, although there might be a nominal fee. The permit system helps park administrators measure the impact on sensitive ecosystems and distribute use evenly among major trails to prevent overcrowding.

BOATING

Most of Utah's large lakes are surrounded by corresponding state parks, where you can find a campground and boat ramp, as well as fish-cleaning stations. State boating regulations can be obtained from the **Utah State Parks and Recreation.** ~ 1594 West North Temple, Suite 116, Salt Lake City, UT 84114; 801-538-7220; www.stateparks.utah.gov. Aside from Lake Powell in the Glen Canyon National Recreation Area, lakeside boat rentals in Utah can be hard to find, although they are available at Great Salt Lake, Utah Lake, Panguitch Lake and Flaming Gorge National Recreation Area. Two good web sites with Utah boating information are www.utahrec.com and www.boatingutah.com.

At Lake Powell, houseboats and other watercraft are booked far in advance. Take a look at Chapter Seven (Southeastern Utah) for details on how to arrange for a Lake Powell boat trip.

River rafting is a very popular sport in northeastern and southeastern Utah, notably on the Green, Yampa and Colorado rivers. Independent rafters, kayakers and canoeists are welcome once they obtain permits from the Bureau of Land Management or National Park Service, but because of the bulky equipment and specialized knowledge of river hazards involved, most adventurous souls stick with group trips offered by any of the many rafting companies located in Green River, Jensen and Moab. Rafters, as well as people using canoes, kayaks, windsurfers or inner tubes, are required by state and federal regulations to wear life jackets.

FISHING

In a land as arid as Utah, many residents have an irresistible fascination with water. During the warm months, especially on weekends, lake shores and readily accessible portions of streams are often packed with anglers. Vacationers can beat the crowds to some extent by planning their fishing days during the week.

Utah fish hatcheries keep busy stocking streams with trout, particularly rainbows, the most popular game fish throughout the West. The larger reservoirs feature an assortment of sport fish, including crappie, carp, white bass, smallmouth bass, largemouth bass and walleye pike.

For copies of state fishing regulations, inquire at a local fishing supply store or marina. Utah's regulations can also be obtained by contacting the **Utah Division of Wildlife Resources.** ~ 1594 West North Temple, Salt Lake City; 801-538-4700; www.wildlife.utah.gov.

State fishing licenses are required for fishing in national parks and recreation areas, but not on Indian reservations, where daily permits are sold by the tribal governments.

In winter, downhill and cross-country skiing are all very popular. Utah has 14 downhill ski resorts; the largest are the Park City Mountain Resort, The Canyons and Snowbasin Resort, all within an hour's drive of Salt Lake City. There are seven commercially run cross-country trail systems in the state, as well as countless miles of trails that weave through national forests. Maps and brochures are available from the **Utah State Parks and Recreation.** Information on Utah's ski resorts can be obtained from the resorts listed throughout this book, or from **Ski Utah.** ~ 150 West 500 South, Salt Lake City; 801-534-1779; www.skiutah.com, www.rideutah.com.

WINTER SPORTS

The best way to assure the reliability of the folks guiding you into the wilderness by horse, raft or cross-country skis is to choose someone who has met the standards of a statewide organization of their peers. A comprehensive list of guides, outfitters and dude ranches is available from the **Utah Travel Council.** ~ Council Hall, Salt Lake City; 801-538-1030, 800-200-1160; www.utah.com.

GUIDES & OUTFITTERS

TWO

Salt Lake Valley

Gazing out across the Salt Lake Valley today, it's hard to envision the rugged wilderness that confronted Brigham Young in late July of 1847 when he and 147 pilgrims arrived in search of a nourishing land where they could enjoy religious freedom. Where scrub-covered foothills once rambled and fingers of creeks drained out of the overshadowing Wasatch Mountains, there now stands a thriving metropolis with residential neighborhoods, a business core, industrial sectors and a supporting infrastructure of bridges and highways. Stretching north and south of Salt Lake City proper, chains of smaller communities that were once isolated islands now bind the Wasatch Front in a sea of suburbia from Ogden south through Salt Lake City and on to Provo and Orem.

While young, wiry Pony Express riders once blazed a trail westward towards Sacramento, Route 80, a ribbon of interstate highway that runs into the setting sun, now leads the way west. On its way, the interstate squeezes between the alkaline southern shores of the Great Salt Lake and the northern tip of Tooele, once a ranching and mining outpost that now serves as a bedroom community to Utah's capital, before cutting the desolate Great Salt Lake Desert and the Bonneville Salt Flats in half.

Today's metropolis of Salt Lake City in large part is testament to the industrious nature of Brigham Young and his followers. It's said that on the very day that they reached the valley—July 24, 1847—they dug into the soil and planted gardens, and soon thereafter laid out the checkerboard grid that would become their city.

Not all was milk and honey for the pilgrims, though—the U.S. Cavalry arrived in Salt Lake City during the Civil War. (President Lincoln, worried that Young, his growing church and the fledgling Utah Territory would side with the Confederates, dispatched the troops.) While the war never reached Utah, the soldiers' presence left an indelible mark on the state as they roamed into the canyons surrounding Salt Lake City in search of valuable ores. Their successes not only spawned the state's mining industry, but also lured thousands of non-LDS settlers to Utah.

These days the sprawling Salt Lake Valley harbors roughly three-quarters of Utah's 2.2 million residents, making the 84,990-square-mile state one of the nation's most urban—an ironic distinction in a land of open spaces, rugged canyons and lofty mountain peaks. The valley is home to the world-wide headquarters of the Church of Jesus Christ of Latter-day Saints and the University of Utah, the state's flagship public institution of higher education, and is *the* cultural center on the western flanks of the Rocky Mountains.

The winter of 2002 saw Salt Lake City imprint its culture, mountains and hospitality on the world's sporting community when it hosted the XIX Olympic Winter Games. The Games, ranked among the best Winter Olympics ever, branded Salt Lake and the Wasatch Range as a North American winter sports capital.

But those who call the Wasatch Front home have long recognized the recreational treasures that exist here. As much as the city and its embracing valley invest in business through hard work and entrepreneurship, more than a few of their residents make their homes here because of the recreational cornucopia that lies minutes away. Seven alpine resorts and six wilderness areas lie within an hour's drive of downtown, while the canyons gnawed into the Wasatch Range by time and weather offer some of the region's finest climbing and hiking routes. The Provo River is a renowned trout stream, one of the state's best, and the number of golf courses in the valley suggest that links, not skiing, should be the unofficial state sport.

As the rising sun's rays crest the Wasatch Mountains in north-central Utah, they illuminate the "New West" metropolis of Salt Lake City. Hard against the mountains' rumpled flanks, with the Great Salt Lake shimmering just off to the west, Utah's capital is an evolving educational, financial, technological and cultural center determined to capture and reflect the vibrancy of the Rocky Mountain West.

Salt Lake City

Salt Lake's future certainly seems boundless with the hard-work mentality that has produced one of the nation's best business climates. It's a city with an envious quality of life thanks to the surrounding mountains, visiting Broadway shows, resident ballet and symphony, and professional sports. It's a city that, after hosting the world during the 2002 Olympic Winter Games, has become a multisport winter training grounds for the western United States.

While Salt Lake City was conceived by the LDS Church, it is not a one-religion enclave. In fact, only about half of the city's population is Mormon. The rich diversity is found not only in the other religions that have footholds through churches in the city, but in the wide array of cuisines served in the city's restaurants, in the global student body population at the University of Utah, and in the cultural offerings that highlight the nightlife throughout the year.

The Salt Lake Valley can easily be split in two, with Salt Lake City a world of its own and the burgeoning southern half of the valley, with its chic ski resorts and restaurants, a land of its own.

SIGHTS

Hand-hewn from a high-desert wilderness in the mid-1800s by religious refugees seeking Zion, Salt Lake City rapidly evolved from a far-flung outpost into a bustling Western city. Between the 1850s and the early 1900s, Salt Lake City grew rapidly and beautifully as architects drew from the latest vogues sweeping the eastern half of the country. Many of these ornate and elaborate buildings remain, salted among more contemporary highrises.

HIDDEN ►

Not far north of downtown is **The Children's Museum of Utah**, a fun, hands-on museum with dozens and dozens of kid-delighting interactive exhibits. Along with more than 400 artifacts from around the state, the museum offers workshops and performances spanning the arts, sciences and humanities. Closed Sunday and Monday. Admission. ~ 840 North 300 West; 801-328-3383, fax 801-328-3384; www.childmuseum.org.

Utah's **Capitol Building** arose in 1915 and was designed to resemble the nation's capitol. The dome carries an outer layer of copper, while inside the rotunda is laid with Georgia marble. Standing within recessed alcoves in the rotunda are important figures from Utah's past, while the walls hold murals reflecting the state's trapper and explorer history. Tours are offered daily. ~ 400 North State Street; 801-538-3000.

Today, across the street to the south of the capitol, you'll find **Council Hall**. But back in 1866, when it was built to house the city council and serve as the territorial capitol, the structure was located several blocks to the south. In the 1960s the sandstone block building was dismantled and moved north to its present location. Today the 60-foot-square structure houses the **Utah Travel Council**. Information on state and national parks and forests can be obtained here. There's also a natural-history bookstore inside. ~ 300 North State Street; 801-538-1030, 800-200-1160.

A nice morning, afternoon or evening stroll can be had by heading up **City Creek Canyon** just northeast of the capitol. At the mouth of the canyon lies Memory Grove, which pays tribute to the men and women from Utah who served in the country's military forces. Individual memorials to World War I, World War II, Vietnam and other conflicts, as well as a meditation chapel, are surrounded by grassy lawns that border City Creek. Following the paved road north through Memorial Grove will take you deeper into City Creek Canyon, which offers hiking and biking trails as well as picnic grounds. The canyon is open to vehicles on even-numbered days and legal holidays, open to bikes on odd-numbered days, and opened to pedestrians every day. ~ Approximately 250 North Canyon Road; 801-483-6797.

The **Pioneer Memorial Museum**, overseen by the local chapter of Daughters of Utah Pioneers, provides a broad picture of Utah and pioneer history. While the second floor offers a wonderful collection of dolls, the basement tugs at the hearts of military his-

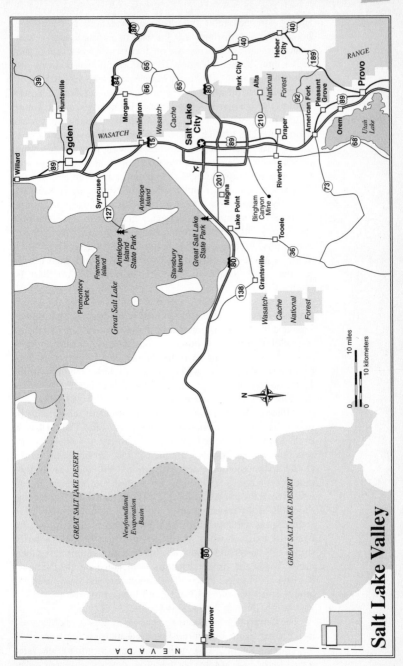

Salt Lake Valley

torians with its exhibit of uniforms and weapons. In the carriage house, reached through a subterranean passage, 19th-century wagons, sleighs and surreys are on display, as is a blacksmith shop and a late-1800s fire engine. Closed Sunday except from June through August. ~ 300 North Main Street; 801-538-1050.

A quick stroll northeast from Eagle Gate at Temple Square leads to the one-acre **Brigham Young Historic Park**, which honors Young for his work as a pioneer, settler, territorial governor and head of the LDS Church. An oval-shaped pathway circles a small grassy area and leads past exhibits showing how the Mormons tamed the arid state with innovative irrigation systems, cut rock from nearby canyons for their buildings, and funneled streams with wooden flumes to millworks. ~ 50 North 2nd Avenue.

A short walk east on 1st Avenue leads to **Mormon Pioneer Memorial Monument**, a small, tidy graveyard that is the final resting place of Brigham Young and several other Mormon pioneers and church leaders. Rising just inside the grounds is "All is Well," a statue of a pioneer husband and wife with their daughter that stands as a tribute to all Utah settlers. ~ 140 East 1st Avenue.

Societal stature wasn't overlooked in Salt Lake City, as evidenced by the stuffy **Alta Club** located across from Temple Square. Founded in 1883 by prominent Utah businessmen, the members'-only club continues to flourish. The Italian Renaissance architecture was in keeping with the style of East Coast men's clubs of the day. While the Alta Club initially excluded members of the Latter-day Saints Church, that slight vanished with the arrival of the 20th century. ~ 100 East South Temple; 801-322-1081.

Although Mormonism is Utah's predominant religion, it's by no means the only religion practiced in the state. The **Cathedral of the Madeleine**, located just a few blocks east of Temple Square, was built by the Roman Catholic Church. Construction on the church's Romanesque exterior began in 1900 and was finished nine years later; the interior, a rich Spanish Gothic environment reflective of the late Middle Ages, was completed in 1918. Lining the walls of the towering cathedral are beautiful, two-story-tall stained-glass windows made in Munich. While bat gargoyles jut from the exterior walls just below the roof line, the interior shows off masterful woodwork, frescoes and an intricate tabernacle. Today the ornate structure is included on the National Register of Historic Places. The church is open daily, and 45-minute tours are offered Friday and Sunday afternoons. ~ 331 East South Temple; 801-328-8941.

The **Governor's Mansion**, also known as the Kearns Mansion, is a Chateauesque-influenced limestone mansion built in 1902 for Thomas Kearns, who made his fortune in mining and later served in the U.S. Senate. The mansion, now the governor's official residence, is bookended by twin, three-story circular towers. Built into the home are vaults for both jewelry and wine. Tours are offered Tuesday and Thursday afternoons from April through November. ~ 603 East South Temple; 801-538-1005.

To peer into Salt Lake City's past, descend into the **Social Hall Heritage Museum**, a subterranean gallery that houses the remains of Utah's first public building—a 350-seat Greek Revival theater. Displayed behind glass walls are sections of the building's walls and other artifacts found on the site in 1990 during excavations for a walkway passing beneath State Street. The walkway is open throughout the day; tours can be arranged by appointment. ~ 39 South State Street; 801-321-8745.

Some of the West's best music can be heard in the **Maurice Abravanel Concert Hall**. The spacious hall is a lasting legacy to the memory of the Greek-born Abravanel, who long conducted the Utah Symphony. Built in 1976, the hall is renowned for its impeccable acoustics. ~ 123 West South Temple; 801-355-2787, 888-451-2787.

Downtown Salt Lake City

The **Salt Palace Convention Center** is the lifeblood of the city's convention industry and home to the **Salt Lake Convention and Visitors Bureau**. The bureau contains rack after rack after rack of brochures and pamphlets highlighting Salt Lake City's and Utah's tourist attractions, lodgings and restaurants. Also available is a walking-tour guide that encompasses the entire downtown. ~ 90 South West Temple; 801-521-2822, 800-541-4955, fax 801-534-4927; www.visitsaltlake.com, e-mail slcvb@saltlake.org.

City officials refer to it as "19th-century street furniture," but most folks see it as simply an ornate **clock**. Erected on the southwestern corner of 100 South and Main Street in 1873, the four-faced clock was initially powered by a water wheel beneath the street. Then large springs that had to be wound once a week enabled it to keep time. Finally, in 1912, the clock was wired for electricity, which continues to drive it nowadays. ~ 100 South and Main Street.

Built in 1913 to entertain growing Salt Lake City, today's **Capitol Theater** was originally known as the Orpheum Theater and trod regularly by vaudeville acts. It now hosts a variety of performances, including visits by national touring troupes. ~ 50 West 200 South; 801-355-2787, 888-451-2787; www.arttix.org.

HIDDEN ▶ In the basement of the Holy Trinity Greek Orthodox Cathedral, Utah's Greek immigrants are remembered at the **Hellenic Cultural Museum**, which documents their struggles and achievements in the state. On display is a mining exhibit, videos, ethnic costumes, letters and Greek artifacts. Open Sunday and Wednesday. ~ 279 South 300 West; 801-359-4163.

Formerly the Hansen Planetarium, the **Clark Planetarium** opened its doors in spring 2003 with a facility that includes a "Star Theater" featuring a five-story-tall screen, as well as an IMAX Theater, classrooms and a gift shop. Admission. ~ 110 South 400 West; 801-538-2104; www.clarkplanetarium.com.

It's not your typical "sight," but the $80-million **City Library** that opened in February 2003 is a sight to behold. A work of architectural art with a 600-foot crescent-shaped wall, the six-story facility boasts rooftop gardens, a 320-seat auditorium for lectures and other special events, seven specialty shops, fireplaces on each floor that are stacked three high, and, since this is a library, 500,000 books and materials. ~ 210 East 400 South; 801-524-8200; www.slcpl.lib.ut.us.

A small cultural and recreational oasis in the heart of the city, the **Gallivan Center** boasts an ice-skating rink, a pond, water fountains, grassy areas, an aviary, an outdoor chess board with three-foot-tall pieces, artworks and a 1000-seat amphitheater. During the summer, the center is the site of weekly entertainment and host to at least one festival per month. ~ 239 South Main Street; 801-532-0459, fax 801-535-6110; www.gallivanevents.com.

When riding the rails was a popular form of public transportation, the **Denver and Rio Grande Depot** was the jumping-off point in Salt Lake City. Located on the west side of downtown, this sprawling depot was designed as the crown jewel of the Denver and Rio Grande and Western Pacific railroads. A blend of Renaissance Revival and beaux-arts classicism architecture, the depot cost $750,000 when it was built in 1910. Since 1981 the depot has housed the **Utah State Historical Society**, which sponsors a permanent exhibit on Utah history and a variety of revolving exhibits. Also inside the depot is the **Utah History Information Center**, a public research facility that contains a wealth of information on Utah and the West in general. Closed Sunday. ~ 300 South 455 West; 801-533-3500 (museum), 801-533-3535 (information center), fax 801-533-3503; www. history.utah.org.

The **Gateway Center** is a pedestrian mall featuring upwards of 100 shops and restaurants on the northwestern edge of downtown. There's definitely lots to do here, including viewing the Olympic Legacy Plaza, home to a fountain with dancing jets of water and the Olympic Wall of Honor, which notes the 2002 Winter Games volunteers and donors. ~ 90 South 400 West.

One of Salt Lake City's most famous and statuesque landmarks is the **Salt Lake City and County Building**, which dates to

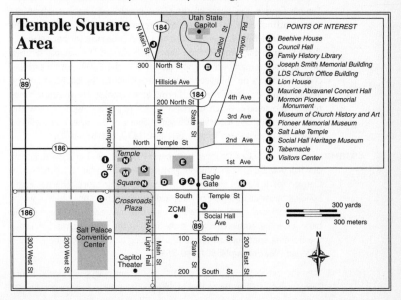

Text continued on page 50.

Temple Square

For a taste of the state's history, and to behold the beauty held in some of the most gorgeous flower gardens in Utah, nothing compares with Temple Square. In an area running just one block north to south and two blocks east to west is a rich collection of modern and beautifully restored historic buildings.

MUSEUM OF CHURCH HISTORY AND ART   This building, located across from the northwestern corner of Temple Square, is where questions about the history of the LDS Church can be answered. Inside you'll find a gallery honoring the church's past presidents, exhibits detailing the plight of Brigham Young and his followers who fled to Utah to leave behind religious intolerance, and pioneer artifacts. ~ 45 North West Temple; 801-240-3310.

FAMILY HISTORY LIBRARY   Just south of the church museum, this facility houses one of the world's best genealogical libraries. Within its extensive computerized collections are hundreds of millions of families. The collections are open to public use and guides stand ready to help you get started. Closed Sunday. ~ 35 North West Temple; 801-240-2331.

TEMPLE SQUARE   Across the street to the east of the library is historic Temple Square, the heart of the LDS Church and Utah's number-one tourist attraction. Covering ten downtown acres, the square contains the six-spired **Salt Lake Temple** and the **Tabernacle** that serves as the backdrop for the Mormon Tabernacle Choir. The temple is open only to church members in good standing. In the 8000-seat tabernacle, choir rehearsals on Thursday evenings are open to the public, as are the Sunday morning performances. Spring and summer are the best times to visit the square, which is covered with fragrant flower gardens and pools, cascades and fountains of water. Tours of the square are offered daily. ~ 50 West North Temple; 801-240-1670, 801-537-9703.

ASSEMBLY HALL   Constructed between 1877 and 1880 as a meeting hall, the hall was built from leftover granite taken from Little Cottonwood Canyon for the Salt Lake Temple. Essentially a miniature tabernacle, the building houses a 650-pipe organ. Inside the benches and columns, which are original, are made from white pine but painted, in the case of the benches, to resemble oak, and in the case of the columns, marble. Today the building continues to serve as a meeting place and host concerts. ~ 50 West North Temple; 801-240-2534.

JOSEPH SMITH MEMORIAL BUILDING   Continue east along South Temple and you'll come to this building, where more history on the LDS

Church and its followers is available. There are free, regular showings of *The Testaments,* a large-format (think IMAX) church documentary film tracing the Mormons' flight to Utah. The building was originally the Hotel Utah. The front doors open to the old hotel's massive lobby, complete with marble pillars holding up the second-floor balcony with its ornately carved railing. There is also a genealogical center for the public to research their family history. The tenth floor holds two restaurants. Closed Sunday. ~ 15 East South Temple; 801-240-1266.

LION HOUSE This adobe-block building a block and a half east of the memorial building was built in 1855 for Brigham Young and his extensive family. Young, who was married to more than two dozen women, partitioned the home according to whether his wives had children: The main floor was reserved for mothers and their children, the second for Young's childless wives, and the third for children. Young died here in 1877 from appendicitis. The home's name stems from the statute of a lion resting atop the front portico. There are no tours of the home, but a restaurant located in the building's original kitchen and dining room on the lower level is open to the public for cafeteria-style lunches (Monday through Saturday) and dinners (Friday and Saturday). ~ 63 East South Temple; 801-363-5466.

BEEHIVE HOUSE Just east and adjacent to Young's home is the Beehive House, which he used as his official residence when he was president of the Mormon Church and governor of the Utah Territory. The church used the house for its headquarters until 1917. The house's name stems from the wooden beehive that sits atop the roof as a testament to the hard-working nature of Utah's pioneers. Listed on the National Register of Historic Places, tours of the house and its pioneer furnishings are offered daily. ~ 67 East South Temple; 801-240-2671.

LDS CHURCH OFFICE BUILDING On the north end of the block, separated from the Lion and Beehive houses by lush, colorful gardens, this 28-story building has some of the best views of Salt Lake City. The base of world-wide operations for the church, the office building is the tallest structure in Salt Lake City. Observation decks on the 26th floor offer panoramic views of both the Wasatch Range and the Salt Lake Valley. Tours of the church's beautiful gardens start here. ~ 50 East North Temple; 801-240-2190.

EAGLE GATE Spanning State Street and South Temple just south of the Beehive and Lion houses, this arch was originally erected in 1859 to serve as the entrance to Brigham Young's home. The first eagle to perch atop the archway was carved from wood. The current eagle is bronze, weighs 4000 pounds and has a wingspan of 20 feet. ~ State Street and South Temple.

the early 1890s and is thought to be located on the grounds where Brigham Young and his followers first camped in 1847 when they reached the valley. Exquisitely detailed carvings of Indian chiefs, Spanish explorers and pioneers grace the building's exterior, while inside there are 40 fireplaces with polished marble hearths. In the late 1980s a massive renovation, driven by fears that the Wasatch Fault that passes beneath Salt Lake City was primed for a jolt, saw the installation of hundreds of "base isolators" that would act something like shock absorbers during a quake; the entire building had to be severed from its foundation and jacked up in order to put in the isolators. Today the building houses the offices of the mayor and the city council. Closed weekends. ~ 451 South State Street; 801-535-6333.

In an earlier day **Trolley Square** held the barns that housed the city's trolley fleet. Dating to 1907, the barns marked the beginning and the end of the day for nearly 150 trolley cars that rolled through the city, powered by overhead electrical cables. Today the site holds an eclectic array of antique shops, restaurants, boutiques and theaters. ~ 602 East 500 South; 801-521-9877.

HIDDEN ►   One of the city's most eclectic pieces of backyard art can be found at **Gilgal Garden**, which occupies a small, half-acre lot hidden away in downtown Salt Lake City. The site contains a collection of sculptures created by the late Thomas Child, an LDS stonemason who used quartz and granite to turn his yard into a memorial of sorts to the church. The likeness of Mormon founder Joseph Smith's face can be found atop a sphinx's body, while quotes from Emerson, Sophocles and Brigham Young can be seen inscribed into pavement stones. ~ 749 East 500 South.

Not far south of the heart of the downtown area lies **Liberty Park** with its 16 wooded acres, the **Chase Home Museum of**

AUTHOR FAVORITE

sights   Just as the Vatican in Rome is the spiritual center for Catholics, **Temple Square** in Salt Lake City is the heart of the Latter-day Saints religion. Located at the geographic center of the city, this is where Brigham Young's home, the church's administrative buildings, elaborate temple, tabernacle, and history and archives are located. While only faithful church members may enter the temple, the other buildings are open to visitors. The one-block by two-block area makes for a wonderful day-long or half-day tour. With five million visitors a year, Temple Square is Utah's biggest tourist attraction. Please see "Walking Tour" for details. ~ 50 West North Temple; 801-240-2534.

Utah Folkart (801-533-5760; www.folkartsmuseum.org) and the
Tracy Aviary (801-596-8500; www.tracyaviary.org). The folkart
museum offers an interesting view of Utah through the traditional arts of the state's American Indian tribes, its settlers, and
its ethnic cultures. At the aviary you'll find more than 240
species of birds from around the world on display. The park also
contains tennis courts, jogging paths, a children's playground
and a small lake with paddle boats. An unusual attraction is the
Seven Canyons Fountain, which covers an acre and depicts a section of the Wasatch Front. Each of the front's canyons is labeled
and water flowing from the fountain represents the streams that
cut the canyons. ~ 600 East 1300 South.

Franklin Covey Field just might offer the most picturesque
setting of any baseball stadium in the country. Home to the Salt
Lake Stingers of the Triple-A Pacific Coast League, the stadium
faces the craggy Wasatch Range, which must be an intoxicating
view difficult for opposing batters to ignore when they step up
to the plate. ~ 77 West 1300 South; 801-485-3800; www.stingers
baseball.com.

LODGING

From sumptuous hotels and historic bed and breakfasts to resort
complexes and chain properties, Salt Lake City and its suburbs
offer more than 17,500 hotel rooms, which translates into an
awful lot of places to lay your head. The arrival of light rail in
the downtown area in 1999 and the 2002 Olympic Winter
Games combined to spur the revival of some historic properties
and the debut of new properties.

At **Wolfe Krest Suites,** the architecture of this 1905 Georgian
Revival mansion is well worth an afternoon's inspection. As for
the baker's dozen of suites, each comes with its own fireplace and
jetted tub. Owned and designed by Kay Malone, the wife of Utah
Jazz power forward Karl Malone, the suites are plushly outfitted, as is the rest of the property. Out front there's a covered
porch where you can enjoy summer evenings; City Creek Canyon with its nature trail is a short walk away. ~ 273 North East
Capitol Boulevard; 801-521-8710, 800-669-4525; www.wolfe
krest.com. DELUXE TO ULTRA-DELUXE.

A piece of Salt Lake City's history has been preserved in the
Saltair Bed and Breakfast, a quaint Victorian home that once be-
longed to Fortunato Anselmo, an Italian vice counsel for Utah and
Wyoming. Due to his diplomatic role, Anselmo's home was considered to stand on foreign soil, and so while Prohibition shut down
most breweries and wineries in the country, he continued to make
vino in his basement. In addition to rooms in the house,
there is a two-bedroom bungalow and two cottages that sleep up
to four. Gay-friendly. ~ 164 South 900 East; 801-533-8184, 800-

◄ *HIDDEN*

Text continued on page 54.

The Great
Salt Lake

Jim Bridger thought he had reached the Pacific Ocean when he
stumbled upon the Great Salt Lake in the early 1800s. Considering
the saltiness of the water, that's probably not too surprising. A remnant
of the prehistoric Lake Bonneville that covered 20,000 square miles in
parts of today's Utah, Idaho and Nevada, the Great Salt Lake takes in the
water from four rivers and numerous creeks and streams.

Outside of the Great Lakes, the lake is America's largest inland body
of water, measuring 92 miles north to south and 48 miles east to west.
Despite its size, the lake has an average depth of just 13 feet.

Its saltiness, which makes it impossible for swimmers to sink, is
attributed to the fact that the lake has no outlets and thereby collects
all the salts and minerals washed into it by rivers and streams. Due to
fluctuations in annual precipitation and the resulting runoff from the
mountains, the lake's salinity changes from year to year. It has ranged
from a low of 5.5 percent all the way up to 27.3 percent.

The water level also varies greatly. In 1963, when the lake reached its
recorded low, eight of the ten islands were landlocked. In 1983, when
high snowfalls and rainfalls pushed the lake up 12 feet, the waters
submerged access to Antelope Island and threatened to flood portions
of Salt Lake City and Ogden. In response to the rising waters the state
installed huge pumps on the lake's western shores to shunt some of
the waters into the West Desert.

Although the rise and fall of the lake's waters have deterred development
along the shoreline, the wetlands that wrap the lake make it a key stopover for migratory birds. Between two and five million feathered creatures
enjoy the marshes, relishing the feast of brine shrimp and a variety of
insects. Among the birds you might see are white pelicans, snowy
plovers, eared grebes, bank swallows, bald eagles and peregrine falcons.

Of the lake's ten islands, **Antelope Island** is the largest, covering
28,463 acres. Reached via a seven-and-a-half-mile-long causeway

extending from Syracuse, a small community 30 miles north of Salt Lake City via Route 15, the island today is a state park with sandy beaches, rugged mountain trails and a resident herd of roughly 700 bison descended from a small number introduced in 1893. Mixing with the shaggy buffalo are mule deer, big-horn sheep and pronghorn antelope. ~ From Salt Lake City, take Route 15 north for 16 miles to Exit 335, then west 14 miles to the island; 801-773-2941.

Mormons first explored Antelope Island in 1848, a year after reaching the Salt Lake Valley. Among the initial explorers was Fielding Garr, who returned later that year to establish a ranch near freshwater springs on the southeastern edge of the island. The ranch went on to become one of the West's largest, with 10,000 sheep once roaming Antelope Island.

Today the **Garr Ranch** is a time capsule preserving late-19th- and 20th-century ranching practices. The few buildings that remain housed the ranch superintendent's family and the hired hands; during the winter months potbelly stoves and fireplaces warmed both the main house and the bunkhouse. The main house, the oldest pioneer structure in Utah still in its original location, is an interesting amalgamation of architecture, as it was built in three phases. The first two stages involved adobe bricks made on the island; the third employed concrete blocks. Nearby, the 1880s spring house kept meats and milk from spoiling under the hot summer sun. Across the yard is the blacksmith's shop, which stayed busy keeping the horses shod and the ranch equipment running. ~ 4528 West 1700 South, Syracuse; 801-773-2941; parks.ut.us/parks/www1/ante.htm.

Antelope Island offers mile after mile of cycling terrain for both road bikes and mountain bikes. The nine-mile-long White Rock Bay Loop offers a scenic ride for mountain bikers, who will curse the uphills on the way out but enjoy the downhills on the return. Road bikers are frequently seen on the seven-and-a-half-mile causeway that links the island to the mainland, and the six-mile-long loop around the northern end of the island is good for family rides. Late each summer cyclists flock to the causeway to tour "Antelope By Moonlight," an invigorating ride out and back across the causeway that starts at 10 p.m.

Twenty minutes west of Salt Lake City by car, the lake is readily accessed at both Antelope Island State Park and Great Salt Lake State Park.

733-8184, fax 801-595-0332; www.saltlakebandb.com, e-mail saltair@saltlakebandb.com. DELUXE TO ULTRA-DELUXE.

The **Anton Boxrud Bed and Breakfast** lies within Salt Lake City's historic district, just a half-block from the governor's mansion. Built in 1901, the home might be too stuffy for children, but adults enjoy the hand-woven lace works, polished wood trims and columns, and thick terry robes. Complementing seven bedrooms (five with private baths) is a parlor fireplace to relax next to, a hot tub out back surrounded by a grape arbor for slow simmering, and a covered porch in front for watching the world go by. Gay-friendly. ~ 57 South 600 East; 801-363-8035, 800-524-5511, fax 801-596-1316; www.antonboxrud.com, e-mail antonboxrud@attbi.com. MODERATE TO DELUXE.

The **Inn on Capitol Hill** dates to 1906, when it was built for a doctor who worked for the Union Pacific Railroad. A large, sprawling, four-story brick home—some would call it a mansion—on a hillside, the inn's 13 guest rooms reflect a different aspect of Utah's early days. One room honors the Ute Indians, another the state's mountain men, and still another the railroad era. A full breakfast is included. ~ 225 North State Street; 801-575-1112, 888-884-3466, fax 801-933-4957; www.utahinn.com, e-mail reservations@utahinn.com. DELUXE TO ULTRA-DELUXE.

The stately **Brigham Street Inn** is almost perfectly centered between the University of Utah and downtown Salt Lake City. Built in 1898, this mansion has nine guest rooms that are lavishly furnished with fine bedding and rich carpeting. Some rooms offer their own fireplaces, others have balconies. Room 9 has its own garden entrance as well as a private kitchen and dining area. ~ 1135 East South Temple; 801-364-4461, 800-417-4461, fax 801-521-3201. MODERATE TO ULTRA-DELUXE.

The **New Peery Hotel**, which first opened its doors in 1910 and is listed on the National Register of Historic Places, today has something of a European feel, with rich carpeting and period furnishings throughout. There are basically two varieties of

AUTHOR FAVORITE

On the north side of the city, the **Ellerbeck Mansion Bed & Breakfast** features six guest rooms in a nicely restored 1892 Victorian home just five blocks north of Temple Square. In winter you can warm yourself by one of the mansion's two fireplaces; you can relax with a book in one of the parlor's armchairs anytime. The centerpiece of the "Christmas Wishes" suite is a hand-carved walnut sleigh bed. Reserve this room and you can enjoy your own fireplace. ~ 3rd Avenue and B Street; 801-355-2500, 800-966-8364, fax 801-530-0938; www.ellerbeckbedandbreakfast.com. DELUXE.

rooms—smallish queen rooms and deluxe king, double queen and suite rooms. All rooms boast canopy beds. Hotel amenities include a workout room and two restaurants. Gay-friendly. ~ 110 West Broadway; 801-521-4300, 800-331-0073, fax 801-364-3295; www.peeryhotel.com. DELUXE TO ULTRA-DELUXE.

In 1999, the **Hotel Monaco** chain took over and restored the old Continental Bank Building, which, ironically, started out life on the first floor of another hotel, the White House. The eclectic boutique-style property decorates its 225 rooms with bold color patterns and mahogany furnishings. For lonely travelers, the hotel also offers "loaner" goldfish for the rooms. ~ 15 West 200 South; 801-595-0000, 800-805-1801, fax 801-532-8500; www. monaco-saltlakecity.com. DELUXE TO ULTRA-DELUXE.

Little America Hotel and Towers long has been a Salt Lake City mainstay. Although owned by the same company that owns the Snowbasin ski resort, the hotel and its 850 rooms and suites might be a bit much for ski vacationers. When you spend your days on the slopes, do you really need data-port phones and work desks? Still, the Italian marble baths are nice for an après-ski or -hike soak, and downstairs you'll find a full-service restaurant, coffee shop and lounge. ~ 500 South Main Street; 801-363-6781, 800-453-9450, fax 801-596-5911; www.littleamerica.com. MODERATE TO ULTRA-DELUXE.

Standing between Temple Square and the Salt Palace Convention Center, **The Inn at Temple Square** is an elegant time capsule in the heart of downtown. The 90 rooms and suites offer a mix of traditional elegance with modern conveniences. Four-poster beds are standard. Follow the staircase to the second-floor lobby and you'll find a cozy library to relax in. A plus for the health-conscious is the hotel's strict no-smoking policy; guests are asked to sign a pledge not to smoke within the hotel. ~ 71 West South Temple; 801-531-1000, 800-843-4668, fax 801-536-7272; www.theinn.com. MODERATE TO ULTRA-DELUXE.

The **Crystal Inn** is on the southern edge of the heart of downtown. Its 175 rooms are larger than most competitors' and feature either a king- or queen-sized bed. Its rates include a hot buffet breakfast, free airport shuttle, and an indoor pool with hot tub and fitness facility. Rooms are partitioned to provide a sitting area and come with microwave ovens and refrigerators. ~ 230 West 500 South; 801-328-4466, 800-366-4466, fax 801-328-4072; www.crystalinns.com. MODERATE TO DELUXE.

Got a tight budget but want to stay close to downtown but not on a park bench? Try the **Avenues Hostel**. This no-frills hostel just five blocks from Temple Square delivers warm, dry rooms with wood-frame bunks and mattresses. You can opt for a spot in the dormitory and use the shared bathrooms, or go after one of the private rooms with their own bathrooms. Beyond the sleeping space, the hostel offers two complete kitchens, an out-door kitchen with a grill, and two living rooms, one of which holds a large-screen TV and a fireplace. Not only are local phone calls free, but there's a computer with internet access for guests, and they'll pick up from the airport for just $10. Needless to say, this place is popular with the budget-conscious, and reservations are highly recommended for the winter and summer seasons. ~ 107 F Street; 801-359-3855, fax 801-532-0182; www.hostels.com/slchostel. BUDGET.

Another clean, inexpensive and generally no-frills place to hang your hat is the **International Ute Hostel**. Located in a con-verted store, the hostelry is a relatively short walk from down-town and offers free transportation from the airport, Amtrak station or Greyhound bus depot. The hostel also can arrange ski, bike or even golf club rentals for you. The dorm rooms all share a bathroom, but what did you expect for $15 a night? There's also kitchen facilities, and both smoking and no-smoking com-mon areas. ~ 21 East Kelsey Avenue; 801-595-1645; www.info bytes.com/utehostel, e-mail utehostel@infobytes.com. BUDGET.

DINING

Salt Lake City's dining scene befits a metropolitan city. In fact, while Denverites might take exception to the claim, some Salt Lake chefs will tell you that Utah's capital has become the Rocky Mountain's culinary capital. Interspersed among the traditional standard-American eateries is a highly diverse range of international fla-vors, including Middle Eastern, French, Japanese, Mexican, Chinese, Indian, Spanish and more. You can dine in elegance or show up after a day on the slopes or the golf course without changing your attire.

HIDDEN ▶

The **Blue Iguana** serves up a wide range of Mexican dishes, but is particularly known for its *moles*. Ensconced in a below-street-level nook on a back alley around the corner from the Capitol Theater, the restaurant's list of *moles* ranges from the green chile *verde* and nuts and habanero chile *amarillo* to the chocolate-based *negro* and *de almendras*, an almond *mole*. ~ Arrow Press Square, 165 South West Temple; 801-533-8900, fax 801-531-6690; www.blueiguana.citysearch.com. BUDGET TO MODERATE.

HIDDEN ▶

Easy to overlook if you're not attentive when driving through downtown is **Martine**, housed in the old, stately Utah Commercial and Savings Bank building. Inside, handsome oak woodwork and booths make an elegant setting for dinner. The menu fea-tures several varieties of tapas, and you'll often be able to find house-smoked lamb tenderloin or seared duck breast. This is a hidden gem in Salt Lake's culinary circles. ~ 22 East 100 South; 801-363-9328. MODERATE TO DELUXE.

Caffe Molise is one of those interesting Italian restaurants every city wishes it had. Local artworks hang on the walls, the dining room is simple and unpretentious, the menu is built around recipes handed down from one generation to another, and live jazz creates a romantic environment on weekend nights. The lasagna is routinely hailed the best in the city; dishes such as crab ravioli show the chef's willingness to surprise diners. ~ 55 West 100 South; 801-364-8833, fax 801-364-9678; www.caffe molise.com. MODERATE.

Vegetarian cuisine is the hallmark of the **Oasis Café**, although it also serves seafood. In addition to featuring a wide selection of imported teas and roasting its own coffee beans, the café is next door to the Golden Braid bookstore, where you can sate your literary soul. Breakfast, lunch and dinner are offered. ~ 151 South 500 East; 801-322-0404, fax 801-322-3902. MODERATE TO DELUXE.

◄ HIDDEN

Lamb's Grill Cafe is a Salt Lake City institution, dating to 1919 and thus the oldest continually operating eatery in the capital. The 1930s-style café ambience still reigns, and power lunches featuring some of the city's power elite still take place. The rice pudding is renowned. Breakfast is served here, too. The restaurant features live jazz on Tuesday and classical music on Friday and Saturday. Closed Sunday. ~ 169 South Main Street; 801-364-7166, fax 801-355-1644. MODERATE.

The dining experience at the **Market Street Grill** is a step into the past: the restaurant tries to maintain a 1930s ambience with blond-wood wainscoting, a long counter, and black-and-white checkered flooring. The menu is heavy with seafood, such as crab-stuffed shrimp, Pacific Northwest salmon and Maine lobster, all of which is flown in daily. There is also a wide selection of beef and poultry as well as pasta dishes. Breakfast and Sunday brunch are available if you're out and about early. ~ 48 Market Street; 801-322-4668, fax 801-531-0730; www.gastronomyinc. com. MODERATE TO DELUXE.

Belly dancers spice up meals on Friday and Saturday at **The Cedars of Lebanon**, where Middle Eastern and Lebanese foods crowd the menu. Tabbouleh, *baba ghanoush*, hummus and, of

NO COMPASS REQUIRED

When Brigham Young and his followers laid out Salt Lake City, they made Temple Square the city's geographic center. From the square the streets are laid out in a crisscross fashion in a numerical sequence. While the southeast corner of the square is located at "0 East 0 West, 0 North and 0 South," one block north is known as "100 North," while two blocks north would be "200 North." One block south is "100 South," while two blocks south is "200 South," and so on, moving in all compass directions.

course, baklava are served, along with chicken, lamb, beef and chicken kabobs. ~ 152 East 200 South; 801-364-4096; www. cedarsoflebanon.citysearch.com. BUDGET TO MODERATE.

Thai food with wonderful presentation and flair can be found at **Lemon Grass Thai Cuisine**. Stop here for lunch and you'll eat your fill (and then some) and save some cash, as the price is under $10. ~ 327 West 200 South; 801-596-1778. BUDGET TO MODERATE.

The end of the 20th century brought a restoration of some of Salt Lake City's historic buildings, including an extensive renovation of the Continental Bank built in 1924. While much of the building was transformed into a hotel, **Bambara** took over the lobby and quickly won local culinary awards with its American regional cuisine. The open kitchen anchors the middle of the lobby so you can watch as the chefs prepare pan-roasted and grilled meats, seafood and game dishes. Breakfast, lunch and dinner are served. ~ 202 South Main Street; 801-363-5454, fax 801-363-5888. MODERATE TO DELUXE.

With a little searching, you will find **Cucina—A Gourmet Deli**. Located in Salt Lake's historic avenues district, this Italian delicatessen offers three meals a day, imported cheeses and meats if you want to build your own meal, and incredible salads that can be a meal on their own. ~ 1026 East 2nd Avenue; 801-322-3055; www.cucinadeli.com. BUDGET.

Despite being housed in the old Salt Lake City High School building, the setting for **Baci Trattoria** is somewhat nouveau—arched ceilings, splashes of bright colors and glass artwork that stirs art-deco memories. During warm weather, tables move out onto the sidewalk. The meals, however, aren't overwhelmed by the surroundings. Go simple with pizza baked in a wood-fired oven, or choose a more elaborate Mediterranean or Italian dish.

AUTHOR FAVORITE

If you relish shellfish as much as I do, head to **L'Avenue Bistro** on the south end of the city. Just off Route 80, this French eatery serves up scrumptious mussels in a variety of sauces, ranging from wine shallot to Roquefort. The shellfish are accompanied by a large paper cone overflowing with *pomme frites*. While the mussels are enough for a meal, the bistro also serves a variety of seafood, lamb, duck and beef. The setting is as wonderful as the food, with warm hardwood flooring, etched-glass windows, mustard-colored walls, and period ceiling fans. The bar features a 1905 zinc-plated bar top brought over from a small town 200 miles outside Paris. ~ 1355 East 2100 South; 801-485-4494; www.lavenuebistro.com. MODERATE.

Closed Sunday. ~ 134-140 West Pierpont; 801-328-1500, fax 801-539-8783; www.gastronomyinc.com. MODERATE TO DELUXE.

Squatters is one of the city's popular brewpubs. Along with the handcrafted ales and lagers that stream from its taps, the pub serves up a tasty menu that ranges from munchies such as buffalo wings and black-bean nachos to the usual—burgers, steaks and sandwiches—and the unusual—spicy Thai chicken pizzas and jambalaya. ~ 147 West Broadway; 801-363-2739; www.squatters.com. MODERATE.

At the **Metropolitan**, which has been nominated for a James Beard Award, you'll find "hand-crafted new American cooking." Examples are appetizers such as fried rock shrimp with cucumber—a spicy dish that's one of my favorites—and wild-mushroom ragout, and entrées such as organic boneless chicken stuffed with sage and mezzo secco cheese or seared elk rack. The cosmopolitan ambience—clean lines, lots of glass, an open kitchen trimmed in copper—mirrors the food. ~ 173 West Broadway; 801-364-3472, fax 801-364-8671. MODERATE TO DELUXE.

Ensconced in an old church that still retains its beautiful stained-glass windows, you would expect a heavenly experience when you enter **Ichiban Sushi**, which *Gourmet* magazine calls one of the country's top sushi bars. If you love sushi, you'll understand that recognition when you sample one of the creations of chef Peggy Whiting, an American trained in Japan. The kitchen also dishes out four varieties of sukiyaki; seafood and chicken dishes; and combination platters that might mix different types of sushi, salmon or chicken teriyaki. Complementing the food is the ambience—warm wood floors and ceilings, private rooms in the loft, and, fittingly, a saltwater aquarium just inside the entrance. ~ 336 South 400 East; 801-532-7522. BUDGET TO MODERATE.

Spicy tandoori dishes, curries and other traditional Indian cuisine can be found at **Taj India**. Not far from the heart of downtown, this restaurant focuses on Northern Indian cooking such as the tandoori chicken, marinated in yogurt and roasted on a skewer in tandoor, and the *rogan josh*—cubed lamb braised in a garlic sauce. ~ 73 East 400 South; 801-596-8727. BUDGET TO MODERATE.

Although more than a century old, Salt Lake City is still evolving; evidence can be found in the neighborhoods that are sprouting their own restaurants and shopping outlets. The general area of 900 South and 900 East is one such neighborhood worth a visit.

Hidden away in a nook of the growing "9th and 9th" neighborhood, **Wasabi Sushi** has established a reputation for its "sushi to go." There's no dining-in here—just order your meal and stand by while the chefs create it. You can find a seaweed-based soup,

◄ HIDDEN

rice bowls, and a variety of sushi "rolls" similar to the California and Seattle rolls. ~ 865 East 900 South; 801-328-3474, fax 801-521-6372. BUDGET TO MODERATE.

SHOPPING   Shopping is a spectator sport in the Salt Lake Valley. Dozens of unique shops and antique stores, and even a fews malls, lie within the heart of downtown, while the suburbs offer more malls, stand-alone stores and factory outlets.

The **Gateway Center** is a sprawling one-block-wide-by-three-blocks-deep development designed to breathe life into the capital's west side. The 2.4-million-square-foot project blends retail, hotel, residential and cultural destinations into one area. Among the attractions are a 13-screen theater, restaurants, nightclubs and museums. Part of the project entailed renovating the historic Union Pacific depot, which serves as the center's entrance. Among the stores you'll find here are Abercrombie and Fitch, Banana Republic, Coldwater Creek, J. Crew, Galyan's Sporting Goods, Virgin Records and Barnes & Noble. ~ Located between North Temple, 200 South, 400 West and 500 West.

The **Mormon Handicraft Store** carries quilts and quilting supplies, candles, handicrafts, sewing supplies, soaps, cookies and fudge. ~ 15 West South Temple; 801-355-2141.

Wander into the "avenues" section just east of Temple Square and you'll find the **E Street Gallery**, which specializes in hand-made treasures: furniture, glassworks, wooden bowls, jewelry, textiles and more. ~ 82 E Street; 801-359-2979; www.estgallery.com.

For some of the best art and crafts produced in Utah, be sure to stop at **Utah Artist Hands**, a small downtown gallery. Inside you'll find paintings, photographs, pottery, woodworks and more. ~ 61 West 100 South; 801-355-0206; www.utahhands.com.

HIDDEN ►   A renowned, locally owned bookstore that sells new and used books is **Sam Weller's Books**. The shop, which has been in the Weller family since 1929, features three stories of new, used and rare books. Can't find what you want? They'll special order it. Closed Sunday. ~ 254 South Main Street; 801-328-2586, 800-333-7269; www.samwellers.com.

Rare-book hounds head to **Ken Sanders Rare Books**, which specializes in Western Americana, first editions and Mormon books. It's also a great source for old maps, prints and paper ephemera. ~ 268 South 200 East; 801-521-3819; www.ksb.com.

Salt Lake City has a wealth of antique shops that offer everything from fine furniture to cowboy artifacts and Persian rugs. **Anthony's Antiques** offers not only French Country pieces from the 17th, 18th and 19th centuries, but also fine art from local artists and Black Forest decorative items. Closed Sunday. ~ 401 East 200 South; 801-328-2231.

The 2002 Olympic Winter Games

Thanks to the Olympic movement, Walter Mitty aspirations and actual Olympic ambitions play out at the wide array of winter sports venues that make the Salt Lake City area the winter sports training ground in the western United States. In the years prior to the 2002 Olympic Winter Games, the venues tested the mettle of both world-class and recreational skiers, ice sliders and skaters. Although the Games are over, these sites and facilities are expected to remain in place and operation for years to come.

The Olympic movement has convinced quite a few of America's top athletes to move to Utah for training. Downhill queen Picabo Street is the director of skiing at the Park City Mountain Resort and top freestyle skiers Eric Bergoust and Joe Pack both live in Park City.

The dean of Utah's winter Olympic athletes, though, is Stein Eriksen, a Norwegian who in the 1950s dominated international ski racing. At the VI Winter Games in Oslo he broke with skiing tradition and, rather than making wide swings around the slalom and giant slalom gates, cut tight lines through the courses and shaved precious seconds off his runs to win the gold medals. In 1954 this golden Norseman crushed the competition at the World Championships to become the first alpine skier ever to win the giant slalom, slalom and combined events at one competition. Shockingly, despite being just 27 years old, Eriksen retired from racing and headed to the United States to teach Americans how to ski.

On winter days Eriksen, belying his 70-plus years, usually can be seen cutting graceful arcs down the slopes at the Deer Valley Resort, while his many Olympic and World Championship medals and trophies can be viewed in a display case in his namesake Stein Eriksen Lodge.

While many skiers try to emulate Eriksen's grace each winter, others challenge their speed and balance on the Olympic downhill at the Snowbasin resort east of Ogden. Nordic skiers, meanwhile, can kick-and-glide or skate-ski over the demanding Soldier Hollow Olympic course. And thanks to regular public sessions at the Ogden Ice Sheet, curling is no longer quite as odd as many folks think.

Summer doesn't bring an end to the action, either, as the Utah Olympic Park offers wheeled rides down the bobsled and luge tracks while freestyle skiers hone their tricks by flipping into a splash pool.

The **Beehive Collectors Gallery** specializes in Mormon memorabilia, books, military items, Indian art, rugs and Western photographs. Open Friday and Saturday or by appointment. ~ 368 East 300 South; 801-533-0119.

The 11,623 pipes that funnel the sound of the Tabernacle organ are made from round, hand-carved wood staves ranging in length from one-half inch to 32 feet. Organ recitals are held daily and are open to the public.

Creative and eclectic crafts and jewelry made by local and regional artists, as well as Alessi kitchenware imported from Italy, can be found at **Q Street Fine Crafts**. Closed Sunday and Monday. ~ 88 Q Street; 801-359-1899.

Metaphysical and other New Age literary works can be found at the **Golden Braid** bookstore. Texts on detoxifying your body, vegetarian diets, and Zen are among the subjects broached. ~ 151 South 500 East; 801-322-1162.

"Handmade gourmet Mexican" ingredients can be found at **Rico Mexican Market**, a thriving outlet that evolved from Jorge Fierro's peddling of pinto beans at one of Salt Lake City's farmers' markets. The market is stocked with a dozen or so salsas, chipotles, whole green chiles, jalapeño peppers, pink beans, baby lima beans, black-eyed beans, chile puya, and tortillas. Closed Sunday. ~ 779 South 500 East; 801-533-9923.

Art galleries can be found throughout the downtown area. The **Dolores Chase Fine Art Gallery** presents contemporary paintings from Utah artists. In the heart of downtown near several restaurants, it's a perfect stop before or after dinner on the two nights (Thursday and Friday) that it's open. Closed Sunday. ~ 260 South 200 West; 801-328-2787.

The **Tivoli Gallery** is one of Salt Lake City's oldest galleries, and with 25,000 square feet of display space, also one of the city's largest. American and European artworks from the 19th and 20th centuries are joined by a collection of contemporary works from Utah artists. Open Saturday by appointment. Closed Sunday and Monday. ~ 255 South State Street; 801-521-6288.

An interesting morning or afternoon can be spent shopping at the **Trolley Square** complex on the east side of Salt Lake City. On this site that once housed the city's trolley barns you'll find restaurants, a brewpub, antiques, artworks jewelry stores, Pottery Barn and Restoration Hardware outlets, a Williams-Sonoma shop and more. ~ 602 East 500 South; 801-521-9877.

Perusing the aisles at **Liberty Heights Fresh** makes me feel as if I'm in a remote village shop looking for the day's provisions. The bins are stocked with fresh fruits and vegetables, cut flowers, freshly baked breads, vinegars and olive oils. The cheese cooler is a great place to hang out while convincing the cheese monger you need to sample just one more round before making a decision. ~ 1300 South 1100 East; 801-467-2434; www.libertyheightsfresh.com.

Another pocket of Salt Lake City that has evolved its own identity is the Sugarhouse section at the south end of the capital. Visit and you'll find interesting shops bearing everything from antiques to artworks to books to even tattoos.

Mountain Body is an "Herbal Cosmetic Deli" where you can find "mountain glows" (a concoction of oils, extracts, minerals and emollients for recharging your skin), "mountain balms" (for healing chapped skin), bath additives and aromatherapy products. ~ 1155 East Wilmington, The Commons at Sugarhouse; 801-474-2331, 800-417-2365; www.mountainbody.com.

At **Ten Thousand Villages** you'll find an interesting assortment of handicrafts collected from throughout the world. The store boasts potteries, woven goods and carvings among its stock. Closed Sunday. ~ 2186 South Highland Drive; 801-485-8827.

NIGHTLIFE

Although some folks are confused by Utah's liquor laws, you can certainly have fun in the capital, with or without a drink. For starters, there usually are shows and concerts to be taken in or sporting events featuring the National Basketball Association's Utah Jazz, the International Hockey League's Utah Grizzlies, or the Pacific Coast League's Salt Lake Buzz. Beyond these options are dozens of nightclubs and saloons where you can wet your whistle and catch a touring musical act.

One thing to keep in mind about Utah's nightclubs and saloons is that many are "private clubs." Under state law, they need this distinction to be permitted to serve hard liquor. To get into these clubs, you must buy a membership. This membership can be an annual one if you visit the state frequently, or a one- or two-week-long one. Fees might range from $5 for a two-week membership to $15 or more for an annual membership. To better understand this membership process, and to save yourself some bucks by applying at one place for several Salt Lake City private club memberships, visit www.slcnightlife.com.

Throughout the fall and winter months many locals take in one or more of the performances of the **Utah Symphony**, which makes its home in the acoustically impeccable **Maurice Abravanel Concert Hall** in the heart of downtown. Guest artists such as Bernadette Peters and The Chieftans frequently perform with the symphony. During the summer months the symphony goes on the road, playing in outdoor arenas such as the Deer Valley Resort. ~ 123 West South Temple; 801-355-2787 (tickets), 888-451-2787.

Sports fans and concert enthusiasts flock to the **Delta Center** throughout the year. When the NBA's Utah Jazz isn't in action, the 20,000-plus-seat arena is center stage for some of the best in rock-and-roll and country music, as well as the occasional tractor pull. ~ 301 West South Temple; 801-325-2000.

Since Salt Lake City's lights make it hard to study the night sky, head to **Clark Planetarium**, where you'll find plenty of stars to behold during one of the planetarium's astrological shows. There's also an IMAX Theater here, which provides another brand of entertainment. Admission. ~ 110 South 400 West; 801-538-2104; www.clarkplanetarium.com.

The **Capitol Theater** may be old, but it remains a lively place. Throughout the year this theatrical grand dame is the setting for touring Broadway shows, the Utah Opera Company, Ballet West and the Ririe-Woodbury Dance Company. ~ 50 West 200 South; 801-355-2787, 888-451-2787 (tickets).

Martini bars are somewhat new to Salt Lake, but they're making inroads. **The Red Door** offers the refined drink in four "octanes." The private club also offers vodkas, cognac and wine, as well as munchies. ~ 57 West 200 South; 801-363-6030.

Two dancefloors, the latest in lighting, and deejays keep things hopping for the 20- and 30-something crowd at **Club Axis**. ~ 108 South 500 West; 801-519-2947; www.clubaxis.com

When touring acts pass through Salt Lake City, they frequently stop for appearances at **X-Scape**, which claims to be the biggest full-service nightclub in the state. ~ 115 South West Temple; 801-539-8400; www.utahconcerts.com.

Don't let the goat skull over the bar intimidate you. The **Dead Goat Saloon** has been around since 1965 as a private club that showcases regional and national rock-and-roll acts. A nominal "membership fee" (i.e., cover) gets you in. ~ Arrow Press Square, 165 South West Temple; 801-328-4628; www.deadgoat.com.

HIDDEN ►   You have to search for **The Lazy Moon**, but the hunt is worthwhile if all you want is a nice microbrew, pizza or burgers and some good tunes. This was one of the first bars I found myself in when I moved to Utah in 1993. I had a great time, but forgot to write down the address and it took me a while to find it again. Located in what once was a boiler room for the Boston and Newhouse buildings, the Lazy Moon has wonderful brick walls and exposed pipes; it's the kind of place you'd expect to

AUTHOR FAVORITE

Sports-bar fans—and bar fans in general—can find a game and a wide range of domestic and international brews at the **Port O'Call Social Club**, which employs 16 satellites to feed its 40 televisions. Pool, foosball tables and acoustic music, on occasion, are other entertainment options. Lines to get in grow long on weekends, so hope you have good timing. ~ 400 South West Temple Street; 801-521-0589; www.portocall.com.

find in a college town. There's live music; in warm weather there's a nice patio. Smoking allowed. ~ 32 East Exchange Place; 801-363-7600.

The Zephyr Club is a private club that hosts national rock acts. ~ 301 South West Temple; 801-355-5646.

At **Papiyons**, a private club, the crowd dances Thursday through Saturday from 8 p.m. to 1:30 a.m. Different nights generate different musical genres, from salsa and merengue on Thursdays to Top-40 on Fridays and hip-hop on Saturdays. ~ 145 West Pierpont Avenue; 801-328-0868.

Naked occupies two floors in a renovated warehouse; the top floor is where you rock out to the sound system, downstairs is where you recover or relax over a drink and enjoy conversation. The club, which is somewhat more upscale than Salt Lake's other nightclubs, caters to a diverse crowd. Saturday is popular with a gay clientele. ~ 326 South West Temple; 801-521-9292.

At Trolley Square is the **Green Street Social Club**, which has live entertainment, billiards and, in warm weather, a patio where you can enjoy your drink. ~ 602 Trolley Square; 801-532-4200.

For a movie and a cold brew, **Brewvies** has two 153-seat cinemas, a restaurant and a bar that serves locally brewed beers on tap as well as a collection of bottled selections. Drinks and munchies can be taken to your seat in the theater. ~ 200 West 677 South Street; 801-355-5500.

WASATCH-CACHE NATIONAL FOREST   **PARKS**
If it's not the busiest forest in the country in terms of recreation, you can be sure the Wasatch-Cache National Forest is not far from the top. Its snow-covered peaks attract skiers and snowboarders in winter, hikers, campers and climbers in the warmer months. Sprawled across 1.2 million acres from the northeastern corner of the state through the Salt Lake Valley and north to the Idaho border, the national forest on Salt Lake City's doorstep claims four alpine resorts within 30 minutes of downtown. Wilderness areas near the capital include the **Lone Peak Wilderness**, a 30,088-acre parcel in the central Wasatch Range co-managed with the Uinta National Forest; the **Twin Peaks Wilderness**, an 11,334-acre tract close to Salt Lake City; and the **Mount Olympus Wilderness**, a 16,000-acre preserve just north of the Twin Peaks Wilderness. ~ The most direct forest access from Salt Lake City is via Routes 190 and 210 southeast of the city. Millcreek, Emigration and City Creek canyons are the other main access routes from Salt Lake City. Salt Lake Ranger District: 6944 South 3000 East, Salt Lake City; 801-943-1794. Winter users can call 801-364-1581 for avalanche conditions in the forest.

▲ From Farmington and Bountiful just north of Salt Lake City to Big and Little Cottonwood canyons and a slice of the forest southwest of Grantsville, there are 18 campgrounds with 376 sites in this section of the forest, some with hookups; free to $12; most have a 14-day maximum stay.

UINTA NATIONAL FOREST 🚶 🚴 🐎 🛶 ⚓ Adjoining the Wasatch-Cache National Forest near the southern end of the Salt Lake Valley is the Uinta National Forest, which encompasses 958,258 acres of high desert, rugged canyons and lofty peaks reaching to 11,877 feet. The **Lone Peak Wilderness** along the forest's northern boundary covers 30,088 acres and attracts many day-users. Facilities include picnic areas and restrooms. ~ The major access from the Salt Lake Valley is via Route 92. Uinta National Forest: 88 West 100 North, Provo, 801-377-5780; Pleasant Grove Ranger District: 390 North 100 East, Pleasant Grove, 801-785-3563.

▲ Forest-wide, there are 29 campgrounds in the three ranger districts with 1314 RV/tent sites, some with hookups; the bulk of the sites are in the Heber Ranger District; free to $12 for individual sites; most have a 14-day maximum stay.

ANTELOPE ISLAND STATE PARK 🚶 🚴 🐎 🏊 🚤 ⛵ Antelope Island State Park not only attracts humans but is popular with hundreds of species of shorebirds and wading fowl. The island is also home to bison and a herd of bighorn sheep, which was introduced in 1997. Pronghorn antelope, which were spied on the island when explorer John C. Fremont and guide Kit Carson visited in 1845, had vanished by the 1930s; in 1993 a small herd was reintroduced by the state. Swimmers and campers head to the two miles of sandy beaches rimming Bridger Bay while hikers trek to Elephant Head, Split Rock Bay or the top of 6595-foot Frary Peak. Facilities include swimming beaches, restrooms, showers, group pavilions, a marina, hiking and mountain biking trails and concessions. Day-use fee, $8 (includes $2 causeway/wildlife fee). ~ From Salt Lake City, take Route 15 16 miles north to Exit 335, then head west 14 miles on Routes 108/127 to the island; 4528 West 1700 South, Syracuse; 801-773-2941; parks.state.ut.us/parks/www1/ante.htm.

▲ There is one campground with 26 RV sites and 30 tent sites; $10 per night; 14-day maximum stay. Reservations: 800-322-3770.

GREAT SALT LAKE STATE PARK 🏊 🎣 🚣 🚤 ⛵ Although this inland sea covers more than 2000 square miles, you won't find any fishing here since it's too salty for fish. But this doesn't deter summer crowds that come to enjoy the white-sand beaches and the steady breezes that make for good sailing. You'll find outdoor showers, restrooms, picnic crowds and a 300-slip marina. ~ Route 80, 16 miles west of Salt Lake City; 801-250-1898; parks.state.ut.us/parks/www1/grea.htm.

Salt Lake City's eastern border is a well-defined series of benches that stair-step up into the Wasatch Range thanks to the relentless tidal work of ancient Lake Bonneville. These levels make obvious building locations, as demonstrated by the homes, businesses and roads that straddle them.

The East Bench

SIGHTS

The **University of Utah,** the state's oldest university, sprawls across the lower levels of these benches. The campus includes Presidents Circle, where you'll find Kingsbury Hall and the Utah Museum of Natural History, as well as the Utah Museum of Fine Arts and Rice Stadium, which staged the opening and closing ceremonies of the 2002 Olympic Winter Games. ~ 801-581-6515.

So that the Salt Lake Games will not be forgotten, the organizing committee and the university collaborated to build the **Olympic Cauldron Park** near the south entrance to Rice Stadium. Towering over the park is the 72-foot-tall Olympic Cauldron, which flickered with the Olympic flame throughout the 2002 Winter Games. Surrounding the cauldron is a wall engraved with the names of the Games' medalists. In the years to come plans call for the park to include a visitors center with an Olympic gallery, café and gift shop.

Envisioned initially to serve the needs of the University of Utah's theatrical students, over the decades **Kingsbury Hall** has become a significant stop on the nation's cultural highway. Dedicated in 1930 and renovated in the late 1990s, the assembly hall has seen the likes of Maude Adams, Basil Rathbone, Orson Welles, Vincent Price, Sir John Gielgud and Roddy McDowell tread across its stage; Robert Frost and Carl Sandburg recite poetry; and balladeer Burl Ives sing his stories. More recently, the hall has been the backdrop for Carol Channing, pianist Michael Feinstein, Willie Nelson and other performers from the arts of mime, modern dance, ballet and opera. ~ Presidents Circle, University of Utah; 801-581-6261, 801-581-7100 (tickets); www.kingsburyhall.org.

HEAVENLY VOICES

The Mormon Tabernacle Choir claims its roots in the hardy pioneers who flocked west with Brigham Young in search of a land where they could practice their religion without persecution. At night the church members would raise their voices to the heavens around their campfires. A month after Brigham Young led his followers into the Salt Lake Valley the Tabernacle Choir was officially formed. The dome-shaped Tabernacle was first used in 1867. Its acoustics are so fine that it's said you can hear a pin dropped 170 feet away.

Dark and dusty like all good museums should be, the **Utah Museum of Natural History** displays dinosaur fossils found in Utah as well as state mammals, minerals and other natural-history topics. The main dinosaur room is crowded with towering skeletons of all manner of 'saurs, including a stegosaurus and allosaurus. Admission. ~ Presidents Circle, University of Utah; 801-581-6927, fax 801-585-3684; www.umnh.utah.edu.

Fine arts, from throughout Utah as well as from around the world, can be found at the **Utah Museum of Fine Arts**. Among the museum's holdings are paintings and sculptures from around the world. It also has a variety of rotating temporary exhibits in addition to educational programs for young and old, concerts and lectures. In addition to its many galleries, the building is home to a research center. ~ 370 South 1530 East, University of Utah; 801-581-7049; www.utah.edu/umfa.

Fort Douglas was established on a bench overlooking the city by President Lincoln in 1862 in response to the LDS Church's refusal to allow the Union Army to enlist recruits from the Utah Territory. Although the rhetoric between Brigham Young and Washington grew hot and LDS faithful, prepared to battle Union troops, no shots were ever traded. The 120-acre site served as a prisoner-of-war camp for captured German soldiers during both World Wars. Among the buildings and sites worth visiting are the **Fort Douglas Museum**, which recounts the fort's past as well as early military history in Utah; the officers' quarters located along **Officers Circle**; and the **Post Chapel**. The military grounds are just east of the University of Utah. The museum is closed Sunday and Monday. ~ 32 Potter Street, Fort Douglas; 801-581-1710.

Literally growing up the east bench of Salt Lake City, not far from Fort Douglas, is the **Red Butte Garden and Arboretum**, a 150-acre sanctuary for plants, shrubs, trees and wildlife that is the largest botanical and ecological center in the Intermountain West. Overseen by the University of Utah, the arboretum features fragrant butterfly and herb gardens, wildflower meadows, waterfalls, ponds, a whimsical children's garden complete with a 150-foot-long vegetative rattlesnake tunnel covered with ivy, and hiking trails. During the summer the garden hosts a concert series. Closed Monday from November through March. Admission. ~ 300 Wakara Way; 801-581-4747, fax 801-585-6491; www.redbutte.utah.edu.

Near the mouth of Emigration Canyon, **This Is the Place Heritage Park** lies on the east side of Salt Lake City, where it's thought that Brigham Young uttered those now-famous words, "This is the right place," when he first viewed the expansive valley. A monument marking the alleged spot can be found in the park just south of **Old Deseret Village**, a living-history park where guides in mid-19th-century garb recall the times of Young and his followers. The village, which is open Memorial Day through Labor Day weekend and then briefly in December for "Candlelight Christmas," includes an apple orchard, "shaving parlor," ice cream shop, gristmill and other pioneer shops. While entering the park itself is free, admission is charged for the village. ~ 2601 Sunnyside Avenue; 801-582-1847.

Just past the park lies **Hogle Zoo**, the home of polar bears, snow leopards, Siberian tigers, apes, Capuchin monkeys, giraffes and hundreds of other animals. Unfortunately, most of the enclosures are dusty, unimaginative crowded spaces. Admission. ~ 2600 East Sunnyside Avenue; 801-582-1631, fax 801-584-1770; www.hoglezoo.org.

Located close to the University of Utah, Red Butte Gardens and Hogle Zoo, the **Red Butte Café** specializes in quick and delicious yet unpretentious meals. On the edge of a strip mall, the café features booths and wood tables surrounded by earth-toned walls inlaid with windows that provide a somewhat airy atmosphere on sunny days. The menu is filled with Southwestern entrées as well as cold and grilled sandwiches if you're in a rush. ~ 1414 Foothill Drive; 801-581-9498. BUDGET TO MODERATE.

DINING

◀ HIDDEN

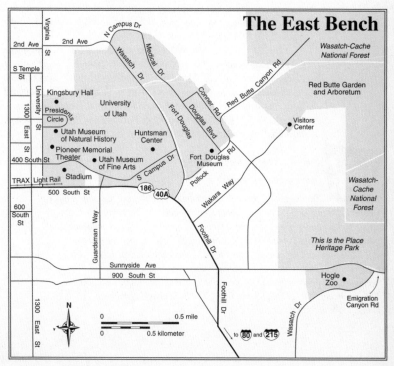

The East Bench

The **KarenJane Restaurant & Wine Bar**, which opened in 2002, offers a diverse menu. There are not too many places where you'll find red curry marinated grilled shrimp on the same menu with grilled tenderloin. But then, that's what's nice about this restaurant: you can't always predict what the chef might be up to. ~ 224 South 1300 East; 801-581-0888. MODERATE.

 HIDDEN ►

If your vision of an Italian bistro is a small, quaint eatery off the beaten path with a rich variety of pasta and meat dishes and a hearty wine list, try the **Fresco Italian Café**. Tucked away not far from the heart of downtown behind the King's English bookstore, this cozy restaurant features pasta and vegetarian dishes as well as lamb and veal. A fireplace heats the small dining room while the tables wear linen tablecloths, the walls are white plaster and the floors heavy terra-cotta tiles. Summertime is perfect for dinners served out back on the patio. Dinner only. ~ 1513 South 1500 East; 801-486-1300. MODERATE TO DELUXE.

Visually, there's nothing high-end about **Mazza**, a tidy nine-table nook that produces delicious Middle Eastern meals such as falafel patties and a variety of sandwiches as well as side dishes of hummus, *baba ghanoush* and basmati rice. So what if you have to eat it off of plastic plates with plastic utensils? While you're munching, check out the intriguing photos of 1930s "Beyrouth" or the sketches of an even earlier Beirut and Tyr. ~ 1515 South 1500 East; 801-484-9259. BUDGET.

One of the most consistent Indian restaurants in Salt Lake City is the **Bombay House**, which locals have honored with a "Best of Utah" rating. The menu is traditional, with such entrées as chicken *saag* and chicken *aloo* as well as lamb *kurma* and lamb *madras*. You'll also find some traditional Indian soups and appetizers. ~ 1615 South Foothill Drive; 801-581-0222; www.bombayhouse.com. MODERATE.

AUTHOR FAVORITE

Southeast of town near the head of Millcreek Canyon sits **Log Haven**, offering widely varied contemporary cuisine. The setting is elegantly rustic amid towering evergreens; waterfalls cascade out the front door and run past the patio in back. The restaurant lies within a log mansion built in 1920 as a wedding present from a Salt Lake businessman to his wife. Imaginative entrées such as coriander-rubbed ahi tuna and whiskey syrup–glazed prawns grace the menu. ~ Located four miles up Millcreek Canyon Road; 801-272-8255, fax 801-272-6315; www.log-haven.com, e-mail loghaven@aol.com. MODERATE TO DELUXE.

At the colorfully named **The Blue Cockatoo** gift shop you can **SHOPPING**
find local artworks such as hand-blown glass bird feeders, photography revealing southern Utah, and eclectic metal creations
featuring over-sized flies, spiders and dragonflies. There's even a
beetle of sorts whose body is a World War II soldier's helmet. ~
1506 South 1500 East; 801-467-4023.

Throughout the year plays, modern dance and concerts are pre- **NIGHTLIFE**
sented within **Kingsbury Hall** on the University of Utah campus.
The hall, which turned 70 in 2000, was renovated from top to
bottom in the late 1990s and continues to draw national acts. ~
Presidents Circle, University of Utah; 801-581-6261.

EAST CANYON STATE PARK 🚣 🚤 🛥 ⛵ Located a short **PARKS**
drive northeast of Salt Lake City in a gap in the mountains, East
Canyon State Park is known for its boating and fishing in East
Canyon Reservoir. Raptors and great blue herons are frequently
spotted near the shorelines. Open year-round, the park is popular with boaters and anglers during the warm-weather months
and ice-fishers come winter. Facilities include picnic grounds,
boat ramps, a group pavilion, showers and fish-cleaning stations.
Day-use fee, $7. ~ From Salt Lake City, head east about 5.5 miles
on Route 80 to Exit 143, then north 14 miles on Route 65 to the
park; 5535 South Route 66, Morgan; 801-829-6866; parks.
state.ut.us/parks/www1/east.htm.
      ▲ There are two campgrounds with 31 RV and 15 tent sites;
$14 per night; 14-day maximum stay. Reservations: 800-322-
3770.

The South Valley, more a suburban extension of   ▼▼▼▼▼▼▼▼▼▼▼▼
Salt Lake City than a separate entity, is best known   **South Valley and**
for being the gateway to the recreational bonanzas   **Mountain Resorts**
that lie within the steep, granitic Big and Little
Cottonwood canyons.
      Lying at the mouths of the canyons are Murray and Sandy,
towns that were developed here because of the streams that spilled
out of the canyons and the silver ore nestled within. Although
Murray, settled in 1849, got its start as an agrarian settlement, a
smelter arrived in 1869 to turn silver ore into bars and the mining
industry remained rooted in the community for nearly a century.
These days the city enjoys a mix of industrial, office and service
businesses.
      Sandy, homestead in the 1860s, enjoyed a similar start in life
as smelters rolled in to minister the ore pulled from Little Cottonwood Canyon while hotels, saloons and brothels catered to the
miners' needs and, ahem, desires. When the mining industry stum-

bled in the 1890s, the community quickly turned its efforts to agriculture, a move that kept Sandy from turning into a ghost town. Service businesses, malls and offices today feed the city's economy.

West of the cities the South Valley sweeps broadly across to the Oquirrh Mountain range, which has proven to be one of Utah's richest mining beds thanks to the long history of the Bingham Canyon mine that continues to produce copper, gold, lead, silver and other ores.

It takes only minutes to leave Murray and Sandy and head into the resorts of one or the other of the Cottonwood canyons. While Alta and Brighton date to the 1930s, Snowbird and Solitude are relative newcomers, arriving in 1971 and 1956 respectively. The four arguably enjoy the most and the best snow in Utah, as the ridgeline that divides them from the Park City resorts has a habit of stalling storms over Alta, Bright, Snowbird and Solitude.

Though Snowbird does the most year-round business, drawing a steady crowd of summer vacationers to its hiking and biking trails, Solitude is moving in that direction with the ongoing build-out of its base village; Alta and Brighton seem largely content to focus on winter.

SIGHTS

Fifteen minutes from the heart of Salt Lake City via Routes 80 and 215 lie Big and Little Cottonwood canyons, two long, west-running gorges cut into the Wasatch Range that have been perfectly sculpted for ski resorts with dramatically jutting, angular peaks, steep slopes, thick forests and intermittent meadows. Clustered on the western flanks of the Wasatch Range, the canyons' four resorts are blessed with ridiculous amounts of snow, in large part due to the prevailing winds that usually stall winter storms along the north–south ridgeline and directly over the resorts, and in part due to moisture from the Great Salt Lake that gets sucked up by these storms and then laid down in prodigious quantities of snow on the slopes.

Taking the 6200 South exit from Route 215 and then heading east, you'll first encounter Big Cottonwood Canyon, with its hiking trails, a gushing stream that roars during spring runoff, and two ski resorts.

Brighton, at the canyon's head, isn't the Wasatch's steepest resort, but its heavily forested slopes offer an intimate experience for skiers and snowboarders. There also are a few bowls that are packed with powder throughout the winter. With free skiing for kids under ten, Brighton has a solid reputation as a family-oriented resort. What this resort lacks, though, are après-ski lounges, restaurants and beds. In summer this resort sleeps, although its parking lots are used by hikers heading into the high country. ~ Route 190, 25 miles from Salt Lake City, Star Route, Brighton; 801-532-4731, 800-873-5512, fax 435-649-1787; www.skibrighton.com.

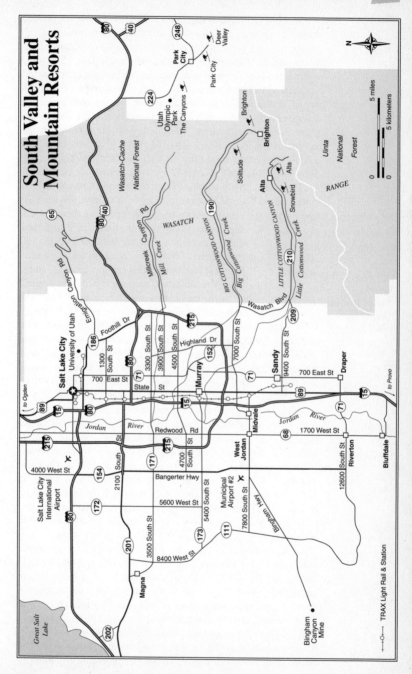

South Valley and
Mountain Resorts

TRAX Light Rail & Station

So close to Brighton that you can ski over to it is the **Solitude Mountain Resort**, a blossoming destination that somehow continues to offer, well, solitude for skiers and snowboarders; its sprawling, picturesque terrain sates the soul. A day at Solitude is a day well-spent. With so many ski options in the area, at Solitude you almost feel as if you're skiing at your own private resort. The resort base is beautifully unfolding with an intimate pedestrian village complete with an ice-skating rink, hotels, restaurants and shops. Come summertime, Solitude is popular with hikers and mountain bikers. ~ Route 210, 23 miles from Salt Lake City, 12000 Big Cottonwood Canyon, Salt Lake City; 801-534-1400, 800-748-4754, fax 435-649-5276; www.skisolitude.com.

The next canyon south of Big Cottonwood Canyon is Little Cottonwood Canyon, a name that in no way impugns the year-round recreation you'll experience there. As with Big Cottonwood Canyon, here you'll find trout streams and trailheads that lead off into the wilderness areas of Wasatch-Cache National Forest.

In 1864 a group of soldiers enjoying a picnic near the head of Little Cottonwood Canyon stumbled across silver in the area of present-day Alta.

Skiing is foremost in this canyon, though, and to skiers the **Alta Ski Lifts Company** is hallowed ground. Cradled by the mountains near the canyon's head, this skiers-only resort shuns high-tech in favor of the yesteryear romanticism of an isolated mountain resort. Lifts and tows distribute skiers around the mountain, which receives 500 inches and more of snow each year. At the base, a small handful of cozy lodges hang on the lip of the ski area, ready to provide a quaint, intimate stay for overnight guests. With lift prices far below what most destination resorts charge these days, Alta is ski country's best bargain. In summer the resort is much quieter, with hikers wandering through its forests and wildflower-strewn meadows on their way to the high country. ~ Route 210, 25 miles from Salt Lake City, Alta; 801-359-1078; www.alta.com.

Just west and adjacent to Alta is the **Snowbird Ski and Summer Resort**, which lacks its neighbor's romantic yesteryear ambience but more than makes up for it with terrain that's best suited for advanced and expert skiers and 'boarders. An expanse of terrain filled with wide, rolling bowls, steep tree-lined chutes and cruisers makes it hard to call it quits at day's end. But when quitting time does arrive, you don't need to go far to find a warm—or cold—drink and a satisfying meal. Dominating the resort base is the monolithic Cliff Lodge, which is the heart of a small, self-contained village that covers all the bases with retail shops, restaurants and even a delicatessen. Whereas Alta focuses on winter, Snowbird, as its full name implies, doesn't let summer slip away quietly. Once the snow melts from the slopes the resort opens its hiking and mountain biking trails, climbing wall, ropes course and pools. It also features summer concerts, star gazing and outdoor theater. ~ Route 210, 24 miles from Salt Lake City; 801-933-2222, 800-232-9542, fax 801-933-2298; www.snowbird.com.

Surprising only in that it took so long to arrive is a lift ticket that will get you into both Alta and Snowbird. The *Alta Snowbird Pass* lets skiers—sorry 'boarders, you're still *non gratis* at Alta—enjoy these two resorts with one lift ticket. With the pass, skiers are allowed to make tracks across the combined resorts' 4700 acres. The connection between the two resorts was made possible in 2001 when Snowbird installed a second high-speed quad lift in Mineral Basin. The lift runs to the saddle on Sugarloaf Mountain, a point that lets skiers drop down into either resort.

Outside the canyons, life for travelers mellows but doesn't totally disappear.

Not far from the mouth of Big Cottonwood Canyon is a slice of early-20th-century life. Throughout the year **Wheeler Historic Farm** stages dances, Victorian teas, wagon rides and farm and garden shows. Visitors can try their hand at milking cows or take a hay-wagon ride. School kids often camp overnight at the farm, which harbors a "haunted" woods. Admission. ~ 6351 South 900 East, Salt Lake City; 801-264-2212.

Although the western edge of the south Salt Lake Valley holds no ski resorts, it has one of the wonders of the industrial world. About the time Antelope Island was being explored, so too was a canyon 25 miles southwest of Salt Lake City. Thomas and Sanford Bingham were ranchers, but their surname has forever been linked to one of the mining industry's greatest feats: the **Bingham Canyon Mine**. The mine, nicknamed "the richest hole on Earth," got its start in 1863 when Union soldiers from Fort Douglas detected lead ore in the canyon. A decade later discoveries of gold and silver spurred a boom that ran for 20 years. Though the site was considered spent in 1893, two engineers thought the relatively sparse copper ores buried there could be profitably mined if done on a large scale. Thus open-pit mining was born.

Today the mine operated by Kennecott Utah Copper is two and a half miles wide and roughly a half-mile deep. Through the years more than 15 million tons of copper have been pulled from the mine, making it the most productive copper mine in history. In 1972 it was listed as a National Historic Landmark. On one rim of the mine sits a visitors center with mining artifacts, videos, displays of copper's effect on our lives, and 3-D microscopes for viewing ore samples. The center is closed November through March. Admission. ~ Take Route 15 south to the 9000 South exit and head west to the mine, Bingham; 801-252-3234.

Between the ski resorts on the eastern side of the valley and the Bingham Mine on the western side are two quieter attractions that provide some meditative space.

HIDDEN ►   A tribute to the world can be found at the **International Peace Gardens,** the floral centerpiece of a 21-acre park featuring botanical displays in honor of two dozen countries; it's located near the southwestern corner of Salt Lake City. Closed December through April. ~ 1060 South 900 West, Salt Lake City; 801-974-2411.

Veterans and their families are drawn to **Veterans Memorial State Park,** a 30-acre memorial commemorating those who fought for the United States. In addition to a cemetery, the grounds contain a chapel as well as a military museum. ~ 17111 Camp Williams Road, about 23 miles south of Salt Lake City via Routes 15, 71 and 68, Riverton; 801-254-9036.

HIDDEN ►   Shoppers and history buffs will find that their interests overlap at **Gardner Village,** which offers a step back into the 19th century. Located on a parcel of land where Brigham Young directed Archibald Gardner to build a gristmill in 1853, the village today contains a collection of quaint shops connected by meandering walkways. Soon after Gardner built his mill, which was fed by water from the West Jordan Canal he developed, the site grew to include a mattress factory, broom factory, blacksmith shop and general store. After the first mill burned down, Gardner replaced it in 1877. The site's only original building remaining today, the mill has been converted into a restaurant and furniture shop. There are other historic buildings on the grounds, but they were moved in from other locations in Utah. There is a museum on the grounds that opens a window on Gardner's life and times. ~ From Salt Lake City, take Route 15 south about seven miles to Exit 301 and then west on 7800 South, 1100 West 7800 South, West Jordan; 801-566-8903; www.gardnervillage.com.

LODGING   Up the Cottonwood canyons, most of the lodging possibilities surround Alta and Snowbird, although a base village arising at the bottom of Solitude Mountain Resort promises badly needed rooms. Be prepared for sticker shock during ski season; bargains are prevalent in summer.

HIDDEN ►   One of the more intriguing properties outside of the two canyons is **La Europa Royale,** a refined cross between an intimate B&B and a lavish hotel. Not far from the entrances to Big and Little Cottonwood canyons, this self-described "elegant small hotel" is surrounded by two acres of carefully tended grounds perfect for evening strolls. The nine rooms and suites feature two-person whirlpool baths and showers, fireplaces and sound-proof walls. Meals are served in the dining room, on the patio or in your room. ~ 1135 East Vine Street, Salt Lake City; 801-263-7999, 800-523-8767, fax 801-263-8090; www.laeuropa.com, e-mail tflynn@laeuropa.com. DELUXE TO ULTRA-DELUXE.

Over the ridge in Big Cottonwood Canyon, the growing base at Solitude offers another place to stay. There are a number of options at The Village at Solitude, ranging from a hotel to time-share rentals.

The Inn at Solitude offers 46 hotel rooms at the base of the slopes in a European-style structure complete with a living room and library, an exercise center, a wine cellar, a full-service spa, a heated outdoor pool and hot tub, and ski lockers. There's even a small movie theater, a club and a restaurant on the premises. ~ 12000 Big Cottonwood Canyon, Salt Lake City; 801-536-5700, 800-748-4754, fax 801-535-4135; www.skisolitude.com. DELUXE TO ULTRA-DELUXE.

During 1942 members of the 503rd Parachute Battalion practiced winter warfare in the mountains surrounding Alta.

Across the courtyard, **Creekside at Solitude** offers 16 one-, two- and three-bedroom condos that rise over the Creekside restaurant. Each of the units has a wood-burning fireplace, full kitchens, living and dining rooms, a private deck and a spot in the underground parking garage. ~ 12000 Big Cottonwood Canyon, Salt Lake City; 801-536-5700, 800-748-4754, fax 801-535-4135; www.skisolitude.com. ULTRA-DELUXE.

Close by, but not close enough to be classified as ski-in, ski-out accommodations, **The Crossings** is a collection of three- and four-bedroom townhomes. Each comes with two fireplaces, a full kitchen, a private deck, and a one-car garage. ~ 12000 Big Cottonwood Canyon, Salt Lake City; 801-536-5700, 800-748-4754, fax 801-535-4135; www.skisolitude.com. ULTRA-DELUXE.

Over at Brighton, accommodations are decidedly more spartan. There's just one lodge—the **Brighton Lodge**—and it offers just 20 rooms, of which five are essentially hostel-style rooms (yes, with ultra-deluxe price tags) with a shared bathroom down the hall. The room rates include a complimentary continental breakfast, and there's also a large jacuzzi outside for mingling with the other guests. ~ Star Route, Brighton; 800-873-5512. ULTRA-DELUXE.

The **Silver Fork Lodge Bed and Breakfast** isn't part of either Brighton or Solitude, but stands alone near these two resorts. In winter the lodge's location allows you to walk outside and hit the alpine slopes, or strap on cross-country skis or snowshoes and head into the woods. Come summer the hiking trails aren't far. The rooms have a rustic flavor with thick log bed posts and pine paneling. The windows permit killer views of Honeycomb Canyon and the Solitude resort. There is a sauna and a restaurant in the lodge. ~ 11332 East Big Cottonwood Canyon, Brighton; 801-533-9977, 888-649-9551; www.silverforklodge.com. DELUXE TO ULTRA-DELUXE.

The immediate area near Alta has a good number of properties with a wide range of ambience. Being slopeside, these accommodations are quite expensive in general. Also, there is extremely limited parking at Alta, and after storms you may find you have to dig out your rig. If you're flying into Utah for a ski vacation, it's best to take a shuttle from the airport directly to your lodge.

The Lodge at Snowbird offers a mix of condominium-type rooms, from hotel-style units to studios with lofts. All have fireplaces and full kitchens, which help contain the cost of a ski vacation, and balconies with grand mountains views. The lodge also features a heated pool and hot tub and a ground-level restaurant. ~ Little Cottonwood Canyon Road, Snowbird; 801-947-8220, 800-453-3000, fax 801-742-2211; www.snowbird.com. DELUXE TO ULTRA-DELUXE.

Snowbird provides more lodging possibilities, thanks to the **Cliff Lodge** and its outlying condominium properties. Combined, they offer more than 900 rooms at the resort base. The Cliff Lodge is an imposing ten-story structure that towers over the resort base. Outwardly, this blocky, battleship-gray concrete edifice struggles to blend in with the canyon's craggy peaks and rugged walls. But inside you'll find one of the country's most extensive oriental rug collections draped across the lobby walls, comfortable rooms, and a varied collection of restaurants. Atop the hotel is a 25-meter outdoor pool with adjoining hot tub and a spa where you can get rubbed down or wrapped in seaweed. In summer, the climbing wall that runs up the west-facing side of the lodge tests climbers' skills. ~ Little Cottonwood Canyon Road, Snowbird; 801-947-8220, 800-453-3000, fax 801-742-2211; www.snowbird.com. DELUXE TO ULTRA-DELUXE.

Conveniently located between Alta and Snowbird, for those skiers who want to sample both resorts, are the **Hellgate Condominiums**. The 12 units come with full kitchens, fireplaces, cable television and nearby laundry facilities. Outside there's a hot tub to share with the other guests. There is limited garage parking. ~ Little Cottonwood Canyon Road, Alta; 801-742-2020; www.hellgate-alta.com. ULTRA-DELUXE.

There are other lodging possibilities in Little Cottonwood Canyon. The **Blackjack Condominium Lodge**, which draws its name from an old mine, offers studio and one-bedroom units equipped with fireplaces and full kitchens. Guests also have access to exercise rooms, saunas and laundry facilities. ~ Superior Bypass Road, Alta; 801-742-3200, 800-343-0347, fax 801-742-3201; www.blackjacklodge.com, e-mail ski@blackjacklodge.com. DELUXE TO ULTRA-DELUXE.

A heated swimming pool with adjoining hot tub, situated between the **Alta Peruvian Lodge** and its ski slopes, makes for a wonderful après-ski soak. Within the lodge's walls are dorms and rooms with private and shared baths. You can warm yourself at day's end in front of several fireplaces or with hot chocolate or

Not all lodges take credit cards, so be sure to check on payment options.

apple cider. Breakfast, lunch and dinner are included in the rates. While winter is definitely the busy season, the lodge is open and less expensive during the summer months. ~ Little Cottonwood Canyon Road, Alta; 801-742-3000, 800-453-8488, fax 801-742-3007; www.altaperuvian.citysearch.com. MODERATE TO ULTRA-DELUXE.

The **Travis Home** is a modified A-frame home that comes fully furnished and stands across the street from the Alta resort. The home has three bedrooms, a loft, two baths, a complete kitchen, a fireplace and laundry facilities. ~ P.O. Box 8076, Alta, UT 84092; 801-942-5219. MODERATE TO ULTRA-DELUXE.

Open only during the ski season, the 94-room **Goldminer's Daughter Lodge** is located next to the Alta Lodge and across from the Wildcat and Collins lifts. There's no pretentiousness in this property, where tight hallways lead to rooms that come in a variety of sizes and furnishings. All rooms—except dorm rooms—have private bathrooms, television and phones. While the smaller rooms hold one double bed, the larger bedrooms feature either a king-sized bed or two double beds. Breakfast and dinner are included. ~ Little Cottonwood Canyon, Alta; 801-742-2300, 800-453-4573. MODERATE TO DELUXE.

Owned and overseen by Alta's venerable mayor, Bill Levitt, the **Alta Lodge** has been opening its doors to guests—many of them repeat visitors—for more than six decades. The rooms (refined college dormitory style is an apt description) are nothing to rave about but the breakfasts and dinners (included in your room rate) are delicious and filling. The lodge's location across from the Collins and Wildcat lifts is convenient. If you're not interested in paying full-freight for a room with bath, less-expensive dorm rooms are available. Upstairs is the Sitzmark Club, a cozy lounge with a roaring fireplace for recounting the day's war stories. A special kids' program includes après-ski activities, dinner and a movie. If the lodge is full, inquire about the two-bedroom condominium that can sleep up to six. Winter isn't the only season here. With the area's enjoyable summers and great hiking possibilities, the lodge is a good base of operations from June to October. ~ Little Cottonwood Canyon Road, Alta; 801-742-3500, 800-707-2582, fax 801-742-3504; www.altalodge.com, e-mail info@altalodge.com. DELUXE TO ULTRA-DELUXE.

The oldest and smallest lodge at Alta is the **Snowpine Lodge**, which lies across from the Albion and Sunnyside lifts. Like the Alta Lodge, the interior is simple and rustic with a mix of wood planks and stone walls dating to the late 1800s; a wall of glass lining the dining room provides a gorgeous view of the ski area. With space for just 50, the lodge definitely has an intimate feel; it's a place where you get to know your fellow guests. The rooms (some with private baths) are cozy and clean and carry a Western motif with exposed wood and Western art. There is an outdoor hot tub, and you'll also find a sauna on the grounds. Unlike some of its neighboring lodges, Snowpine shuts down for the summer. ~ Little Cottonwood Canyon, Alta; 801-742-2000, fax 801-742-2244; www.thesnowpine.com. MODERATE TO DELUXE.

Next door to the Snowpine is **Alta's Rustler Lodge**, an eight-floor complex ready to pamper one after a powder day. If the heated pool and jacuzzi don't get out the kinks, try a spell in the eucalyptus steam room. There's also a fitness center if the slopes didn't provide enough of a workout. As with the other lodges, the 87 rooms range in size and furnishings, while the common areas offer comfortable chairs and couches. Breakfast and dinner are included in the room rates. During the summer, this lodge caters to groups only. ~ Little Cottonwood Road, Alta; 801-742-2200, 888-532-2582, fax 801-742-3832; www.rustlerlodge.com. DELUXE TO ULTRA-DELUXE.

A number of high-end condominium and townhouse properties in the canyon, ranging from one-bedroom units to sprawling five-bedroom houses, are managed by **Canyon Services**. ~ P.O. Box 920025, Snowbird, UT 84092; 801-943-1842, 800-562-2888, fax 801-943-4161; www.canyonservices.com. ULTRA-DELUXE.

DINING

Although not quite as mature as those found in the heart of Salt Lake City, dining options in this part of the valley are growing quite nicely, thank you.

HIDDEN ►

On the border of Salt Lake City and the south end of the Salt Lake Valley is **Café Madrid**, where you'll find authentic Spanish cuisine, not some Americanized knock-off or Mexican hybrid, thanks to the chef who hails from Spain. Don't let the surrounding shopping center fool you. Inside the café you'll find a menu with potato-onion frittatas, squid in ink, chicken marsala and a paella that must be ordered a day ahead. There are also nearly four dozen Spanish wines to choose from. Dinner only. Closed Sunday. ~ 2080 East 3900 South, Salt Lake City; 801-273-0837. MODERATE.

Outside of the canyons, one of the valley's best Italian restaurants is **Tuscany**. The restaurant feels like a northern Italian hunting lodge, and the flagstone patio garden, interspersed with towering conifers, offers some of the best dining seats in the summer. One of the most interesting dining rooms is the aptly called Log Room, made from hand-peeled logs. There's a gorgeous river-rock fireplace here, too; ask for a seat next to it when you make your reservation. Linguini with clams in garlic sauce, oven-roasted pesto-crusted salmon filet and various meat dishes are among the menu items. Dinner nightly; no lunch Saturday through Monday. ~ 2832 East 6200 South, Salt Lake City; 801-277-9919, fax 801-277-0980. MODERATE TO DELUXE.

At **Market Street Grill, Cottonwood**, you'll find fresh sea-food, steaks, chops and chicken. The open-air deck on the second floor is a nice touch, with gorgeous views up into Big Cottonwood Canyon. ~ 2985 East 6580 South, Salt Lake City; 801-942-8860.

The atmosphere at **Lone Star Taqueria** is decidedly Tex-Mex: The wooden split-rail fence that rims the restaurant's patio proudly bears hubcaps and cowboy boots while the interior is festive with colorful banners streaming from the ceiling. Some say the best fish tacos in the Salt Lake Valley are found here; you'll have to be the judge of that. If tacos aren't your thing, you'll also find overstuffed burritos crammed with beef, roasted pork, broiled chicken or vegetables. ~ 2265 East Fort Union Boulevard, Salt Lake City; 801-944-2300. BUDGET TO MODERATE.

The ambience is rich and the food French at **La Caille**, where ◄ HIDDEN
the setting is a replica of a French chateau and the food is served by waitresses and waiters in 18th-century costumes. Located just beyond the mouth of Little Cottonwood Canyon, the restaurant grounds features a winery; in the warm months peacocks stroll the yards. ~ 9565 Wasatch Boulevard, Sandy; 801-942-1751, fax 801-944-8990. MODERATE TO DELUXE.

At **The Mayan** you get a show along with your dinner. This seemingly out-of-place theme restaurant features cliff divers, a tropical rainforest setting, imitation Mayan ruins, talking animals, and tables high in the trees. The menu is decidedly Mexican: fiesta *pollo*, honey-lime chicken, broiled burritos, mahimahi à la *Veracruzana* and the like. ~ 9400 South State Street, Sandy; 801-304-4600. BUDGET.

In the canyons, since all of the lodges at Alta offer meal plans for their guests, the lack of demand for independent restaurants has resulted in the existence of just one in the immediate vicinity of the resort. Snowbird, meanwhile, offers eight sit-down eateries at the base and one mid-mountain, although not all are open year-round.

Alta's lone independent, the **Shallow Shaft**, is a cozy affair, living proof that one shouldn't judge a book by its cover. Some consider the restaurant's interior, which is lined with mining memorabilia, a bit funky, but the food belies the setting. Once known for its Southwestern fare, the Shallow Shaft's menu now reads like one out of downtown Salt Lake, with appetizers such as stuffed mushrooms and smoked-salmon-and-avocado quesadillas followed by rack of lamb, house-smoked Atlantic salmon with a honey-lime-chipotle glaze and fresh grapefruit, and linguini with pesto. ~ Alta Road, Alta; 801-742-2177, fax 801-742-2914; www.shallowshaft.com, e-mail tgarling@shallowshaft.com. MODERATE TO DELUXE.

During the hiking season, the Kickstand, a sandwich and snack kiosk, opens for business in the parking lot below the Albion Basin.

Down the road at Snowbird the options run from steaks and seafood to pizza and Southwestern.

The **Steak Pit** is the resort's steak house. Beef shares the menu, however, with Alaskan king crab, Australian lobster tail and other denizens of the deep. As befits a steakhouse, the ambience is rustic. The cedar-plank walls are lined with photos of the resort and its mountains, as well as celebrities such as former NFL great Steve Young, while diners are seated around oak tables in booths. ~ Snowbird Center Level 1, Snowbird; 801-933-2260. MODERATE TO DELUXE.

Skiers and shredders in a hurry graze at **The Rendezvous**, a cafeteria that features a variety of hot and cold entrées for a quick meal. Open in winter only. ~ Snowbird Center Level 2, Snowbird; 801-742-2222 ext. 4086. BUDGET.

Fast-food burger joints haven't yet surfaced in the canyons, but there's a **Pier 49 San Francisco Pizza** outlet at Snowbird where you can build a gourmet pizza. ~ Snowbird Center Level 2, Snowbird; 801-742-3222. BUDGET.

During its 19th-century boom days Alta proudly laid claim to 26 bars on its main street.

A relaxed, family-friendly atmosphere reigns at **The Forklift**, where breakfasts can be built around pancakes or omelets, and lunches over burgers or pasta dishes. Located across from the tram dock, the restaurant offers patio dining during the summer months. ~ Snowbird Center Level 3, Snowbird; 801-933-2240. BUDGET TO MODERATE.

High atop the Cliff Lodge rests **The Aerie**, the resort's top-of-the-line restaurant, where the meals are nearly as intoxicating as the views. Game, beef and seafood are splashed across the menu in forms such as crab-salad cake and jumbo shrimp, rabbit ravioli, filet mignon and seared ahi tuna, while in the adjoining lounge one can order sushi. ~ Cliff Lodge, Level 10, Snowbird; 801-933-2160. MODERATE TO DELUXE.

The **Atrium** offers quick summer breakfast buffets and hearty winter lunch buffets, along with a large espresso bar sure to keep the energy levels up. ~ Cliff Lodge, Level B, Snowbird; 801-933-2140. BUDGET TO MODERATE.

Sushi with a view. That's what you get at the **Aerie Sushi Bar**. Facing the mountain, this is the perfect place for an après-ski get-together. Fresh sushi, the wizardry of the chefs, comfy digs and great views—this combination is hard to beat. ~ Cliff Lodge, Level 10, Snowbird; 801-933-2175. BUDGET TO MODERATE.

You'd be wise to keep a cold beverage by your side while eating at **Keyhole Junction**, where spiciness is a mainstay of its Southwestern and Mexico dishes. If you need proof, try the grilled flank steak. Vegetarians will enjoy the wild-mushroom enchiladas, which are topped with *queso fresco*, roasted chiles, onions and cilantro. Margarita lovers will find a soul mate in the Twisted Shrimp, which are doused in a tequila, garlic and lime marinade. ~ The Cliff Lodge, Level A, Snowbird; 801-933-2025. BUDGET TO DELUXE.

Over at The Lodge, the **Lodge Club Bistro** whips up entrées ranging from meats such as beef tenderloin and rack of lamb, to fowl, seafood and pasta dishes. Through the restaurant's windows you can watch the Snowbird tram crawl across the sky to the top of the resort. Inside, flower-filled vases sit atop the white linen–covered tables. In summer, the tables are moved out onto the patio. ~ The Lodge at Snowbird, Pool Level, Snowbird; 801-933-2145. MODERATE TO DELUXE.

The Iron Blosam Lodge is home to the **Wildflower Ristorante,** where candlelit meals are served. Mediterranean fare, such as olive-crusted duck breast, molasses-cured double thick pork chops, and pastas dressed with lobster, grace the menu. ~ Iron Blosam, Level 3, Snowbird; 801-933-2230. MODERATE TO DELUXE.

If you don't want to leave the mountain for a meal, head over to the **Mid-Gad Restaurant,** found on the mountain right off the aptly named Lunch Run in the Gad Valley. Meals are quick, revolving around sandwiches, burgers, pizzas and chili. ~ Gad Valley, Snowbird; 801-933-2245. BUDGET.

SHOPPING

Malls and furniture stores dominate the shopping scene in the region, but there are a few exceptions.

In a state where recreation ranks high, it's no surprise that Salt Lake City includes a **Patagonia** outlet store stocked to the rafters with fleece goods, sweaters and other outdoorsy apparel. ~ 3267 South Highland Drive, Salt Lake City; 801-466-2226.

The **Cottonwood Mall,** Utah's first indoor mall, claims more than 140 stores and a theater. ~ 4835 South Highland Drive, Salt Lake City; 801-278-0416.

With skiing, hiking, biking, boating and camping luring countless Utahns out of doors, there's an REI store where you can buy the latest gear or rent some for a weekend outing. ~ 3285 East 3300 South, Salt Lake City; 801-486-2100.

The **Fashion Place Mall** offers more than 100 stores, including 15 food outlets. ~ 6191 South State Street, Murray; 801-265-0504.

Gardner Village mixes history with shopping. Located on the grounds where a grist mill was erected in 1877 at the request of Brigham Young, the village today is a cluster of quaint shops selling everything from fudge to metalworks. Throughout the year the village stages a number of events such as Easter egg hunts, gardening workshops and scarecrow festivals. ~ 1100 West 7800 South, West Jordan; 801-566-8903; www.gardnervillage.com.

The **South Towne Center** claims not only chain department stores under its roof but also more than 70 specialty stores and a ten-screen cinema. There's also a food court. ~ 10450 South State Street, Sandy; 801-572-1516; www.southtownecenter.com.

Roughly three dozen factory outlet stores, including Adidas, Samsonite and Bass Shoes, exist at the **Factory Stores of America** complex 13 miles south of Salt Lake City in Draper. ~ 12101 South Factory Outlet Drive, Draper; 801-571-2933.

NIGHTLIFE Live entertainment ranging from bluegrass to rock can be found at the **Hog Wallow Pub** Thursday through Saturday nights. ~ 3200 East Big Cottonwood Canyon Road, Salt Lake City; 801-733-5567.

With Salt Lake City's nightclubs and theaters a short ride north, the southern end of the valley is not particularly known for its after-dark activities. However, **The Comedy Circuit** showcases some of the country's top comedians. The shows, offered Wednesday through Saturday at 8 p.m., with two shows on Friday, run two hours and are for adult audiences. ~ 7720 South 700 West, Midvale; 801-561-7777.

At **New Sandy's Station** the crowd tends toward Southern interests, with live bands and deejays playing country-and-western tunes, a crowd that enjoys line dancing, and televised sports such as World Wrestling Entertainment and football. ~ 8925 South 255 West, Sandy; 801-255-2078; www.sandystation.com.

Tooele and the Great Salt Lake Desert

Utah is actually considered to be an urban state since the bulk of its population is clustered around the Wasatch Range, but you don't have to head too far west before wide open spaces become the dominant landscape. Tooele County, just 15 miles west of Salt Lake City, represents the last bastion of humanity before the Nevada border is reached, and its population is roughly 20,000.

Tooele and Grantsville, which sit side by side in a small valley bordered on the east by the Oquirrh Mountains, on the west by the Stansbury Mountains and on the north by the southern shore of the Great Salt Lake, are small, sleepy agricultural towns that increasingly are becoming bedroom communities for Salt Lake City.

Just west of Tooele and Grantsville, the Stansbury Range rises to 11,031 feet and then quickly gives way to the Great Salt Lake Desert, which not only holds a bombing range for the Air Force but also the Salt Flats that sate Hollywood's need for desolate landscapes and race-car drivers' need for speed.

The county's only other substantial town huddles on Utah's far western border in the form of Wendover, another sleepy town that is overshadowed by its sister community of Wendover, Nevada, which thrives with its casinos and nightclubs.

Settled by ranchers in 1849, Tooele County landed on the map in 1864 when soldiers found profitable silver, lead, zinc and gold ores in the Rush Valley, just south of Tooele. The initial discovery led to 500 claims being logged in the first year alone. While the town of Ophir's population climbed to roughly 6000 in the boom days of the 1870s, Mercur's population once hit 10,000.

Today the mining towns have mostly vanished; those that remain do so largely as ghost towns. The major economic impetus comes from the military, which arrived during World War II and erected an air base in Wendover, next to the Nevada border, where the *Enola Gay* was hangered before making its infamous bombing run on Hiroshima. The Tooele Army Depot was also established during the war and served as a supply, storage and repair center. The Dugway Proving Grounds, built in a remote area of Tooele County in 1942 to serve as a testing grounds for weaponry, gained controversy during the Vietnam War when it functioned as a biological and chemical warfare center.

The Great Salt Lake Desert, born some 20,000 years ago when prehistoric Lake Bonneville began to recede, remains today like it almost always has—a large, mostly barren stretch of flat land interrupted by a few wrinkles of mountains.

SIGHTS

Despite its out-of-the-way location, the town of **Tooele** and the county of the same name hold interesting insights into the hardy souls who settled this part of Utah, those who forged their way across the state en route to presumably greener pastures in California, and those who came to develop America's military might.

When the **Benson Gristmill** earned a spot on the National Register of Historic Sites in 1972, it was said to be the most significant structural landmark between Salt Lake City and Reno, Nevada. The structure's integrity comes from 24-inch beams that were held together with wooden pegs pounded into holes lined with "green" leather; when the leather dried out, it shrank and provided a tight fit for the pegs. Handmade nails were used to secure the wooden planks onto the building's exterior. The two-story mill was built in 1854 to grind grain grown by Tooele County's settlers. A year later the growing community around the mill was named "Richville," which served as the county seat until 1861. Open Tuesday through Saturday from May 1 to Labor Day. ~ About eight miles north of Tooele at the junction of Routes 138 and 36, Stansbury Park; 435-882-7678.

Even some native Utahns have trouble pronouncing Tooele, which is pronounced "Too-WILL-ah." The name is thought to have been derived from the name of a Goshute Indian chief.

A whirlwind of activity usually can be found at the **Deseret Peak Complex,** a growing recreation center that currently boasts baseball fields, a demolition derby arena, a horse track, a BMX bike track, an outdoor pool and soccer fields. Plans call for a fine-arts center, an archery park and a convention center to be added in the years ahead. ~ 2930 West Route 112, Tooele; 435-843-4000.

Tooele County's mining past comes alive at the **Barrick Mining Museum,** where a visitors center at the Deseret Peak Complex displays ore cars, tools and other items from Barrick's mining past. Closed Labor Day to Memorial Day. ~ 2930 West Route 112, Tooele; 435-843-4000.

The railroad played a central role in Utah, hauling freight, mail and people across the sprawling state. At the **Tooele County Railroad and Mining Museum** a piece of railroading history exists in the form of a steam engine, some cabooses and a dining car. A miniature railroad on the grounds provides rides for kids on Saturday, while the museum details some of the county's mining history. Closed Sunday and Monday, and from Labor Day to Memorial Day. ~ Broadway and Vine Street, Tooele; 435-882-2836.

A tiny rock building in downtown Tooele houses the **Daughters of Utah Pioneers Museum,** which contains pioneer artifacts and early-day photos of the region. Along with the unique 1867 building is an 1855 log cabin. ~ 35 East Vine Street, Tooele.

Eight miles northwest of Tooele via Route 112 lies **Grantsville,** another agrarian outpost that contains a few surprises for travelers. For instance, remnants of an ill-fated group of pioneers who struggled across the Great Salt Lake Desert and then perished in the High Sierra can be found in the **Donner-Reed Museum.** A limited number of guns, furnishings and other items the California-bound settlers tossed out onto the desert in an effort to lighten their wagons' loads are housed in the museum along with other pioneer and American Indian artifacts. Tours by appointment. ~ Corner of Cooley and Clark streets, Grantsville; 435-884-3411.

HIDDEN ►   Sharks in Grantsville? They can be found at the **Bonneville Seabase,** a diving center that operates out of natural hot springs that bubble to the surface just south of the Great Salt Lake. Scuba diving and snorkeling are allowed in the springs, which also teem with shrimp, puffers, angel fish and other salt-water denizens. Open Thursday through Monday and by appointment. ~ Route 138, five miles northwest of Grantsville; 435-884-3879, 800-840-3874.

Heading west toward the Nevada border from Grantsville on Route 80, the Great Salt Lake Desert quickly fills the windshield, and then some, sparkling alkali white to the south, west and north. Sharp-eyed motorists along Route 80 will spy the 85-foot-HIDDEN ►   tall "Tree of Life," also known as "The Tree of Utah" and "The Metaphor," rising above the glaringly white salt flats on the north side of the interstate 26 miles east of Wendover. The unusual artwork arose in 1981 under the direction of Karl Momen, a Swedish artist who couldn't resist using the flats as his palette. Littering the flats beneath the tree are several "leaves" appearing to have fallen from the tree. Parking is not allowed along the interstate. ~ Route 80, 59 miles west of Grantsville.

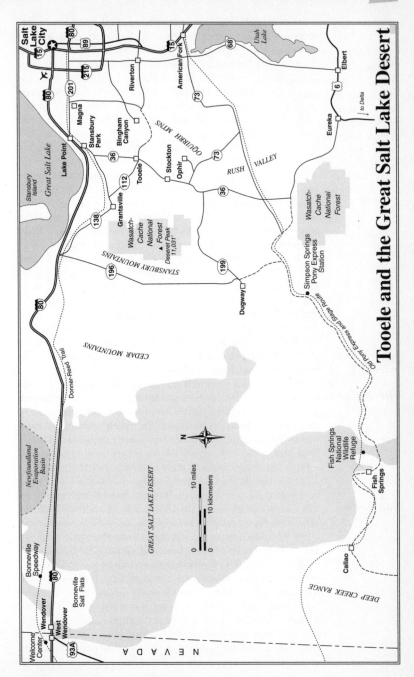

Tooele and the Great Salt Lake Desert

On Route 80, closing in on the Utah–Nevada border is a rather strange but famous spot. Hollywood often visits the **Bonneville Salt Flats** for its movie-making needs. Both *Independence Day* and *Con-Air* shot some scenes there. The flats also attract car racers intent on setting land-speed records down the seven-mile-long Bonneville Speedway. The flats, made up of a sodium compound similar to common table salt, cover more than 30,000 acres in extreme western Utah, just east of Wendover. They typically rejuvenate themselves each year through a succession of flooding from the Great Salt Lake and evaporation; gusting winds keep the surface flat. The racing season on the Bonneville Speedway is usually July through October, when the surface of the salt flats is particularly hard. ~ Route 80 Exit 4, ten miles east of Wendover; for information, contact the U.S. Bureau of Land Management; 801-977-4300; www.ut.blm.gov/recsite.html.

The first unofficial land-speed record established on the Bonneville Salt Flats came in 1914 when Teddy Tetzlaff drove his *Blitzen Benz*: 141.73 mph.

Today the **Wendover Army Air Field** is a military ghost town, but in 1945 it was a top-secret facility where the crew for the *Enola Gay* trained for the nuclear bombing run on Japan. During World War II the base was home to nearly 20,000 soldiers and airmen. The air field's deserted buildings are on the grounds of the Wendover (Utah) Airport found on the south end of town. Brochures for self-guided tours of the airbase can be picked up at the Nevada Welcome Center off Exit 410 of Route 80. ~ To reach the airbase, head south on 2nd Street in Wendover.

HIDDEN ►

Fifty-one miles southwest of Tooele on the Old Pony Express and Stage Route lies the **Simpson Springs Pony Express Station**, a replica of the original station here on the southeastern edge of the Great Salt Lake Desert. Due to the remote and isolated location of Simpson Springs, the setting is pretty darn near what existed back in the 1860s when the Pony Express was in business. ~ From Tooele, go south 25 miles on Route 36 then head about 26 miles west on the Old Pony Express and Stage Route.

HIDDEN ►

Located 42 miles west of Simpson Springs and almost 93 miles southwest of Tooele, the 18,000-acre **Fish Springs National Wildlife Refuge** is the most isolated national wildlife refuge in the lower 48 states. Due to the fact that it's the only wetland of any size within 30 miles, it's long been a desert oasis for humans and wildlife. While pre-Columbian Indian tribes frequented the area, the Pony Express maintained a station here in 1860–61; the transcontinental telegraph line also came through the area, as did the Lincoln Highway when it was constructed in the early 20th century. These days birds are the main visitors, with nearly 270 species having been spotted at the refuge. An 11-mile-long auto route follows the dikes around the refuge's nine ponds and offers great views of some of the rookeries. ~ Head south from Tooele 25 miles on Route 36, then west on the gravel Old Pony Express and Stage Route for 63 miles; 435-831-5353.

Tooele is an overnight waystation for Route 80 travelers, and as such offers two chain motels, an independent and not much more in the way of lodgings.

LODGING

The **Oquirrh Motor Inn** along Route 80 north of Tooele has 41 rooms. Nothing fancy here, just clean, comfortable rooms. ~ Route 80, Lake Point; 801-250-0118. MODERATE.

The **Best Western** in town offers 31 traditional motel rooms equipped with phones and a swimming pool. ~ 365 North Main Street, Tooele; 435-882-5010, 800-448-5010. MODERATE.

Just up the street is the **American Inn and Suites**, which has 60 rooms, an outdoor pool and a hot tub. A continental breakfast comes with the rates. ~ 491 South Main Street, Tooele; 435-882-6100. MODERATE.

Being so close to Salt Lake City, it's not surprising that Tooele doesn't have much in the way of dining, but if you don't want to make the drive to the capital you surely won't go hungry. Don't, however, expect dazzling settings.

DINING

Mexican cuisine, along with some steaks and ribs, is served at **La Frontera**, where you can build your dinner from an à la carte menu featuring enchiladas, tostadas, burritos and tacos. The ambience is much what you would expect in a modest small-town restaurant—colorful blankets and sombreros on the walls with diners seated at tables and in booths. ~ 494 South Main Street, Tooele; 435-882-0000. BUDGET TO MODERATE.

Since 1970 the kitchen at **Sun Lok Yuen** has been treating locals to a wide variety of Chinese entrées as well as burgers, sandwiches, steaks and chops. Among the specials is Four Treasures, a combination of chicken, scallops, shrimp and vegetables served in a hash-brown basket with rice. You'll also find Peking spareribs, Hong Kong steak and seafood, chicken and vegetable platters. Inside, Chinese artworks adorn the walls while the seating ranges from booths and tables with Chinese motifs to a banquet area. ~ 615 North Main Street, Tooele; 435-882-3003. BUDGET.

◄ HIDDEN

FISH SPRINGS NATIONAL WILDLIFE REFUGE 🚶 🚲 Established in 1959, this 18,000-acre refuge is centered around a remote wetland that lures birds from miles around. The refuge attracts the most birds during the fall, but in the spring and summer there's a greater variety of species; during the winter bald eagles call the wetlands home. Young birds begin hatching in early summer, with ducklings and goslings easily viewed from dike

PARKS

◄ HIDDEN

roads. Common species certain to be seen in spring and early summer include pied-bill grebes, Canada goose, snowy egrets (which nest on the refuge) and redhead ducks.

Ten millennia pass between the time rain/snow falls in the Fish Springs area, seeps underground and resurfaces through the springs—making the water there some of the purest you'll find.

Also present are a variety of mammals, reptiles and amphibians, including long-tailed weasels, antelope, collared lizards, Great Basin sagebrush lizards and striped whipsnakes. A small kiosk contains brochures and interpretive panels describing the refuge and the birds you might see. While there is a small picnic ground, no camping is allowed on the refuge. There is, however, primitive (no facilities) camping permitted on public lands a quarter-mile away. ~ Take Route 36 25 miles south of Tooele and then head west on the Old Pony Express and Stage Route for 63 miles; 435-831-5353; fishsprings.fws.gov.

Outdoor Adventures

Salt Lake City is a recreationalist's nirvana. With seven ski resorts and six wilderness areas within an hour of downtown, one never has to travel far to find something to do in the out-of-doors.

FISHING

Despite its incredible size, the Great Salt Lake is barren of fish due to its salinity. But there are plenty of other streams, lakes and reservoirs to try your luck. For information on fishing seasons, fees and hot spots, contact the **Utah Division of Wildlife Resources**. ~ 1594 West North Temple, Salt Lake City; 801-538-4700; www.wildlife.utah.gov.

Near Salt Lake City, **Big and Little Cottonwood** creeks as well as **Mill Creek** have been known to produce trout. The **Jordan River**, meanwhile, carries trout, catfish, walleye and bass. West of Salt Lake City are a few reservoirs near Tooele, Grantsville and Vernon that have been productive trout fisheries. Located about 40 miles northeast of Salt Lake City via Routes 80 and 65, **East Canyon Reservoir** offers rainbow and brown trout as well as kokanee salmon.

Outfitters Flyfishing is the specialty at **Western Rivers Flyfishers**. Not only can they outfit you with the right gear, but they can lead you to fish in the Provo and Green rivers as well as in the streams along the south slope of the Uinta Mountains. ~ 1071 East 900 South, Salt Lake City; 801-521-6424, 800-545-4312; www.wrflyfisher.com. Guiding trips to the Provo River, as well as Strawberry Reservoir with its renowned trout fishery, is **Wilderness Trout Expeditions**. ~ P.O. Box 17382, Salt Lake City, UT 84117; 800-939-2680; www.wildernesstrout.com. Along with guiding trips to the Provo River, the folks at **Spinner Fall Fly Shop** can take you on a float trip on the Green River in northeastern Utah. ~ 2645 East Parleys Way, Salt Lake City; 801-201-2066, 877-811-3474; www.spinnerfall.com.

With paddling possible on the Great Salt Lake, Utah Lake, Echo Reservoir, the Jordan, Provo and Weber rivers, there are plenty of canoeing and kayaking options in the area. Wildlife watchers will get their fill of birds at these areas, particularly the Great Salt Lake, which is a major migratory stop for shorebirds and waterfowl that winter along the Gulf Coast and further south while heading north to Canada for the summers. Great blue herons are easily spotted at Echo Reservoir, while the Provo and Weber rivers, both stellar fisheries, attract bald eagles and moose. **CANOEING & KAYAKING**

At **Wasatch Touring** they can sell you a canoe or rent you a one-or two-person kayak. ~ 702 East 100 South, Salt Lake City; 801-359-9361; www.xmission.com/~wtouring.

In search of a new canoe, kayak or whitewater raft? Or do you just need some paddling equipment? Whatever your needs, stop by **Sidsports**, which also carries sailing equipment. ~ 265 East 3900 South, Salt Lake City; 801-261-0300; www.sidsports.com.

With the Wasatch Range so close, climbing opportunities abound in the Salt Lake area. There are climbing schools to instruct you on the finer points of scaling mountains, boulder fields near the bottom of Little Cottonwood Canyon where you can practice bouldering, and even indoor climbing centers. **CLIMBING**

For help in deciding where to climb in the area, contact the **Salt Lake Climbers' Alliance**. They publish a nice map pointing to various climbs close to Salt Lake. ~ www.saltlakeclimbers.org.

Scale 45-foot-tall walls and practice your belays and free climbing at the **Rockreation Sport Climbing Center**. Lessons are available. ~ 2074 East 3900 South, Salt Lake City; 801-278-7473.

Exum Utah Mountain Adventures, which is affiliated with the Exum Mountain Guides that lead climbs to the top of the Grand Teton in Wyoming, takes climbing, ice climbing and mountaineering classes into the Wasatch Range. ~ 2070 East 3900 South, Salt Lake City; 801-550-3986; www.exum.ofutah.com.

Not to be overlooked is the **Cliff Lodge** at the Snowbird Resort. One wall of this ten-story hotel has been turned into a climbing wall for would-be speed climbers. ~ Little Cottonwood Canyon, Snowbird; 801-933-2147.

Outfitters Climbing shoes for excursions into canyons or at Cliff Lodge can be rented at **Wasatch Touring**. ~ 702 East 100 South, Salt Lake City; 801-359-9361; www.xmission.com/~w touring.

The folks at **International Mountain Equipment** can outfit you and direct you to the best climbing in the area. They also offer rentals. ~ 3265 East 3300 South, Salt Lake City; 801-484-8073; www.imeutah.com.

**SKIING &
SNOW-
BOARDING**

Although there are 14 alpine ski resorts scattered about Utah, the heart of the state's ski country lies in the Wasatch Range that runs along Salt Lake City's eastern border. Two of the canyons found here—Big and Little Cottonwood—together claim four resorts, not to mention countless acres of backcountry terrain open to skiers and snowboarders if they've got the leg muscle and lung capacity to reach them, or the fat wallets to join a heli-skiing trek. If the roads are clear, any of the four can be reached within 40 minutes from downtown Salt Lake City.

The skiing at **Alta Ski Lifts Company** is arguably Utah's best, but it's had since 1938 to perfect its dizzying powder chutes, steep, powder-choked bowls, and rolling intermediate terrain. Nine slow-speed lifts and five surface tows serve 2200 skiable acres and a vertical drop of 2020 feet. More than 40 marked runs and steep bowls are graced with 500 inches of snow, on average, each winter. Snowboarders are not allowed on the slopes here. However, Alta hauls skiers and snowboarders into Grizzly Gulch, a snow-choked canyon adjacent to the resort, for guided off-trail skiing and 'boarding on 325 acres with a 1500-foot vertical drop. Frankly, the price is pretty steep—$200 for five runs; if you get to Alta early after a storm you can find the same deliciously deep and fluffy powder on the resort's landscape. ~ Route 210, Alta; 801-359-1078; www.altaskiarea.com.

Next door to Alta Ski Lifts Company, **Snowbird** is a relative newcomer on the block. Renowned for steep pitches and chutes that rim Peruvian Gulch, Snowbird contains more than 2500 skiable acres for skiers and 'boarders, and a vertical drop of 3240 feet that is reached via a 125-passenger tram and nine chairlifts; it also has natural as well as manmade halfpipes. In summer the resort lures hikers, mountain bikers, and climbers who assault the world-class climbing route that runs up the side of the ten-story Cliff Lodge. ~ Route 210, Snowbird; 801-933-2222, fax 801-933-2298; www.snowbird.com.

Over the granitic ridge to the north lies Big Cottonwood Canyon with its two resorts. **Brighton**, long a favorite with snowboarders, offers about 500 inches of snow each winter and a variety of terrain across its 850 skiable acres found near the canyon's headwall. Seven lifts move skiers and 'boarders around the 64 marked trails on two mountains. Those under 10 ski or 'board free with adults, and if you're over 70, you can ski free, too. ~ Star Route, Brighton; 801-532-4731, 800-873-5512, fax 435-649-1787; www.skibrighton.com.

Solitude, next door to Brighton, long has matched the definition of its name, but a growing base village and marketing are changing that. Along with 1200 skiable acres, a vertical drop of 2047 feet, 450 inches of snow annually and seven lifts, the resort has some of the most striking scenery in the Wasatch cut by 63 designated trails and three broad bowls shared by skiers and 'boarders. A lift in craggy Honeycomb Canyon allows you to enjoy run after run through the wide bowls and tree runs hidden in the canyon. ~ 12000 Big Cottonwood Canyon, Salt Lake City; 801-534-1400, 800-748-4754, fax 435-649-5276; www.ski solitude.com.

Skinny ski fanatics have a few options in the Wasatch Range. The **Solitude Nordic Center** offers 20 kilometers of groomed track right next door to its downhill cousin, and they're some of the toughest trails in the state. Accessories, rentals and lessons are available. ~ 12000 Big Cottonwood Canyon, Salt Lake City; 801-536-5774; www.skisolitude.com/nordiccenter.cfm.

Just east of Salt Lake City via Route 80 lies **Mountain Dell**, a golf course that doubles as a cross-country ski center when snow covers the fairways. ~ 3287 Cummings Road, Salt Lake City; 801-582-3812.

Those who detest lift lines charter a ride with **Wasatch Powderbird Guides**, a helicopter-oriented ski and snowbird experience that flies to backcountry slopes in the Wasatch Range. ~ P.O. Box 920057, Snowbird, UT 84092; 801-742-2800; www.heliski wasatch.com.

Ski Rentals   While you can rent your gear at any of the resorts, there are numerous rental shops in Salt Lake City. **Utah Ski & Golf** has a handful of outlets in the Salt Lake area, ranging from two valley locations (134 West 600 South, 801-355-9088; 2432 East Fort Union Boulevard, 801-942-1522, 800-858-5221; www. utahskigolf.com) to two shops at the Salt Lake City International Airport (Terminals 1 & 2; 801-539-8660). Another shop with multiple outlets is **Ski-N-See** (135 West 500 South, Bountiful, 801-295-1428; 1339 East Fort Union Boulevard, 801-733-4477;

AUTHOR FAVORITE

The **Alta Ski Lifts Company**, cradled at the head of Little Cottonwood Canyon, dates to 1938 when a group of Salt Lake City businessmen paid for the first ski lift. These days the resort retains much of its early-day charm: snowboards are banned, lift prices are far below those charged at most of the state's other resorts, and the snow continues to pile up deeper than anywhere else in Utah. The terrain is dazzling, ranging from vertigo-inducing steeps and powder chutes to long cruisers, bowls and novice territory. See page 92 for more information.

2420 East 7000 South, 801-943-1970; 2125 East 9400 South, 801-942-1780; 772 East 9400 South, Sandy, 801-571-2031; 800-722-3685; www.skinsee.com), which rents skis and snowboards. Yet another possibility is **Breeze Ski Rentals**. ~ 2354 South Foothill Drive, Salt Lake City; 801-485-4850.

When the Alta ski resort opened on January 15, 1939, skiers paid 25 cents for one lift ride and $1.50 for an all-day pass.

If you need gear for Nordic skiing or snowshoeing during your visit, **Wasatch Touring** carries rentals in both areas, as well as lots of free advice on where to go. ~ 702 East 100 South, Salt Lake City; 801-259-9361; www.wasatchtouring.com.

Wild Rose Mountain Sports can also outfit you with Nordic skis or snowshoes, either as a purchase or a rental. ~ 702 East 3rd Avenue, Salt Lake City; 801-533-8671, 800-750-7377.

GOLF

With plenty of golf courses and mild winters, it's not impossible to swing the club on any given day of the year in the Salt Lake Valley. Due to the valley's avid duffers, reservations are suggested at every course.

The nine-hole **Jordan River Golf Course** not far from the Salt Lake airport carries a par of 27 over its 1170 yards and makes for a quick round. ~ 1200 North Redwood Road, Salt Lake City; 801-533-4527. Also close to the airport is the par-72, 18-hole **Rose Park Golf Course**. Relatively flat, the course covers 6696 yards and offers a driving range. ~ 1386 North Redwood Road, Salt Lake City; 801-596-5030.

At the airport, the **Wingpointe** course stretches its 18 holes out over 7200 yards. There's also a driving range. ~ 3602 West 100 North, Salt Lake City; 801-575-2345.

A quick nine holes can be played without leaving the city at the **University of Utah**'s nine-hole course, where the par over the 2500 yards is 33. ~ Central Campus Drive and Federal Way, Salt Lake City; 801-581-6511.

The **Bonneville Golf Course**, near the mouth of Emigration Canyon where Brigham Young first saw the Salt Lake Valley, has plenty of hills and a creek that make its par-72, 6824-yard course interesting. Be forewarned, though: this is a popular course and tee times are hard to come by. Reservations can be made a week in advance. ~ 954 Connor Street, Salt Lake City; 801-583-9513, reservations 801-484-3333.

On the east side of the city, the **Forest Dale Golf Course** is the oldest golf course in the state—and possibly the Rockies—dating to 1903 when it debuted as the Salt Lake Country Club. It offers nine holes with a par of 36 over the 2970 yards. ~ 2375 South 900 East, Salt Lake City; 801-483-5420.

The **Fore Lakes Golf Course** is dotted by many lakes. Its 18 holes are broken into two nine-hole courses, one an executive nine hole. There is a driving range. ~ 1285 West 4700 South, Salt Lake City; 801-266-8621.

Ups and downs, lots of them, make the **Old Mill Golf Course** one of the area's tougher courses. The 6303-yard course is a par 71. ~ 6080 South Wasatch Boulevard, Salt Lake City; 801-424-1302.

To escape the valley's heat, the **Mountain Dell** course is roughly ten minutes east of Salt Lake City via Route 80. The 36-hole course rises and falls across a scenic mountain setting and overlooks the Mountain Dell Reservoir. ~ Parley's Canyon, Salt Lake City; 801-582-3812.

Just a little south of Salt Lake City, the **Murray Parkway** course is user-friendly with wide fairways and spacious greens over the 18-hole, 6800-yard course, which includes a driving range. ~ 6345 Murray Parkway Avenue, Murray; 801-262-4653.

The 18 holes at **Riverbend Golf Course** are split in half—nine holes run along a bluff overlooking the Jordan River, nine at the bottom of the bluff. Water hazards are frequent both top and bottom. ~ 12800 South 1040 West, Riverton; 801-253-3673.

RIDING STABLES

Despite Utah being part of the West and with mountains nearby, horses are not the preferred mode of recreational travel in the Salt Lake Valley. Still, you can find a place to ride if need be.

At **Sunrise Riding Stables** south of Salt Lake City you can rent a steed, or sign up for Western riding lessons. ~ Route 15, roughly 16 miles south of Salt Lake City; 17000 South 1300 West, Bluffdale; 801-254-1081.

Trail rides are offered throughout the summer months at the **Deer Valley** (800-558-3337), **Park City** (435-645-7256), **The Canyons** (435-615-3412) and **Sundance** (801-225-4107) resorts.

BIKING

While the Wasatch Range is renowned for its hiking possibilities, mountain bikers know there are more than a few good paths to take into the mountains.

SALT LAKE CITY City Creek Canyon is popular with hikers and bikers. The six-mile paved trail runs out of the city and into the foothills of the Wasatch Range. To balance foot and pedal traffic in the canyon, cyclists are only allowed on odd-numbered days and never on holidays.

In Bountiful, five miles north of Salt Lake City, the 13.5-mile **Mueller Park Trail** runs from the Mueller Park Picnic Grounds on the east side of Bountiful up into the Wasatch to Rudy's Flat. Most of the trail can be handled by beginners and intermediates, though there are a few steep and rocky stretches that might turn some riders into walkers.

EAST BENCH Along the East Bench, the **Emigration Canyon Road** that runs east from the Hogle Zoo and This Is the Place

Heritage Park offers a scenic, eight-mile-long ride up into the hills. The road is narrow and curvy, though, which can make for some interesting moments when traffic passes. Near Little Mountain Pass there are views of Lookout Peak and the Mountain Dell Reservoir.

For an easier ride, the **Bonneville Shoreline Trail** runs along the benches on the east side of Salt Lake City and offers a more moderate pedaling experience. The route, which provides nice views of the Great Salt Lake, Antelope Island and downtown Salt Lake City, can be accessed via City Creek Canyon as well as just east of This Is the Place Heritage Park. Since the trail is popular with hikers and joggers, it can get congested, and Salt Lake City's diehard riders can close quickly, and quietly, upon more leisurely cyclists.

On the southeastern edge of Salt Lake City, the **Millcreek Pipeline Trail** runs six and a half miles one way along an old water pipeline right-of-way up to the head of Millcreek Canyon. The ride, which starts at Rattlesnake Gulch just past the fee station at the mouth of the canyon, rolls through thick forest and across open slopes; a steep uphill welcomes riders. To avoid this drive to the end of the canyon and access the trail at the Elbow Fork trailhead and pedal downhill through the canyon, although without a shuttle car a return uphill trip will be required. Millcreek Canyon is reached by taking Wasatch Boulevard to 3800 South and then heading east.

SOUTH VALLEY AND MOUNTAIN RESORTS In Big Cottonwood Canyon, the **Solitude Mountain Resort** offers lift-served mountain biking and rents mountain bikes. A five-and-a-half-mile loop trail provides access to both Lake Solitude and Silver Lake.

Across the ridge in Little Cottonwood Canyon, beginners, or flatlanders unaccustomed to Utah's elevation, should consider the **Albion Basin Summer Road** as a good starting point for a cool summer ride. Starting at an elevation of roughly 9000 feet, the two-mile-long road runs from the base of the Alta Ski Area up into the wildflower-dappled Albion Basin inside the Wasatch-Cache National Forest.

In the winter months **Grizzly Gulch** is popular with back-country skiers and snowboarders, but come summertime the mostly uphill, four-and-a-quarter-mile trail that runs into it is preferred by mountain bikers. The trailhead is found between the Shallow Shaft and Our Lady of the Snows Center in Alta.

The **Snowbird Ski and Summer Resort** turns many of its mountain maintenance roads into mountain bike trails once the snow has melted. While you can pedal uphill for an incredible workout, it's also possible to ride with your bike to the top of

Hidden Peak on the resort's tram and cycle downhill. Stop at the Activity Center located off Entry Level 2 for a trail map.

The **Wasatch Crest Trail**, part of the Great Western Trail that runs from Canada to Mexico, cuts north and south through the mountains just east of Salt Lake City. Hikers and bikers know it as a quick retreat from suburbia. Experienced cyclists in search of a strenuous workout, and intermediates looking to improve their ability, pedal a 20-mile out-and-back section accessed from the end of Millcreek Canyon. The single-track route follows the Big Water Trail to its junction with the Great Western Trail, which in turn leads to the Wasatch Crest Trail. Along the way to the turnaround point near the head of Big Cottonwood Canyon, the narrow path provides sweeping views of the Park City side of the Wasatch. Due to high demand from hikers and bikers, cyclists can only access the trail from Mill Creek Canyon on even-numbered days.

While the mountains overshadowing the Salt Lake Valley just to the east average 500 inches of snow each winter, the valley floor receives an average of 59 inches of snow.

TOOELE AND THE GREAT SALT LAKE DESERT   In the Tooele area, the **Copper Pit Overlook** is a 19-mile out-and-back mountain bike ride that gains nearly 4000 feet in elevation as it climbs into the Oquirrh Mountains on the way to a great view down into the Bingham Canyon Mine. The strenuous nature of the ride's first leg quickly weeds out novice cyclists. The trail, which starts with four miles of asphalt before turning to dirt and gravel, begins at the Tooele County Museum (Broadway and Vine Street).

A shorter, not-as-steep ride runs 12 miles roundtrip from the junction of Route 73 and the Ophir Canyon Road south of Tooele to **Ophir Canyon** and the site of this one-time boom town. Along the route are old mining-car rail beds and some mine-related ruins.

The **Jacob City Trail** that starts in Stockton runs eight miles one way to the ghost town of Jacob City. As with the Copper Pit Overlook and Ophir Canyon rides, the hardest part of this ride is on the way out to Jacob City, as you gain 3140 feet in elevation. But the ruins of Jacob City, the views of Rush Valley and the Deseret Peak Wilderness Area to the west, as well as the exhilarating downhill return trip, make this a fun ride. The ride starts at Bryan's Service Store in Stockton at 29 North Conner Avenue.

The **Butterfield Canyon-Middle Canyon Road** runs across the Oquirrh Mountains between Salt Lake City and Tooele and offers a great view of the Bingham Copper Mine.

Mountain biking is possible on **Stansbury Island**, just north of Tooele in the Great Salt Lake. A nine-mile loop starts from a parking lot almost seven miles up Stansbury Island Road (stay left at the first junction three and a half miles up the road, then straight past a stop sign located two miles past the junction; another mile will bring you to the parking area). The ride starts with a series of steep switchbacks, but it levels out somewhat as it navigates the slopes above Tabby's Canyon before throwing several downhill stretches at riders. Summer can be an unbearably hot time for this ride.

Bike Rentals   For trail information, bike sales or repairs, try **Canyon Sports**. ~ 1844 East 7000 South, Salt Lake City; 801-942-3100. **Guthrie's Bicycle** has been selling bikes for nearly a century and also carries a wide range of books and guides. ~ 731 East 2100 South, Salt Lake City; 801-484-0404, 888-480-0404.

Another source of information and repairs is **Golsan Cycles**. ~ 4678 South Highland Drive, Salt Lake City; 801-278-6820. **Bingham Cyclery**, on Salt Lake's east side, also sells, repairs and informs. ~ 1370 South 2100 East, Salt Lake City; 801-583-1940; www.binghamcyclery.com. **Wild Rose Mountain Sports** can outfit you, repair your bike or sell you a mountain bike. ~ 702 East 3rd Avenue, Salt Lake City; 801-533-8671.

Bingham Cyclery also has a shop in Midvale, south of Salt Lake City, and Sandy. ~ 707 East Fort Union Boulevard, Midvale, 801-561-2453; 1300 East 10510 South, Sandy, 801-571-4480.

Mountain bikes can be rented, purchased and repaired at **Wasatch Touring**. ~ 702 East 100 South, Salt Lake City; 801-359-9361; www.wasatchtouring.com.

HIKING   With canyons riddling the Wasatch Range, it doesn't take long to find a trailhead. Many of the ski resorts have excellent hiking trails within their boundaries, and some offer lift-served hiking, too. Flatlanders need to keep in mind the quickly rising elevation, which runs from 4330 feet in downtown Salt Lake City to above 11,000 feet on some of the peaks just outside the city. Rattlesnakes can be common along the trails during hot summer months, too. A great resource is the *Hiking the Wasatch* map. Compiled by the Wasatch Mountain Club and sold at most Salt Lake outdoors stores, the map clearly lays out trailheads, hiking routes and mileages. Any questions that might arise over hiking in the Wasatch probably can be answered by the folks at the **Public Lands Information Center**. ~ REI outlet, 3285 East 3300 South; 801-466-6411. All distances listed for hiking trails are one way unless otherwise noted.

SALT LAKE CITY   Not to be overlooked is Antelope Island, with its handful of hikes. One of the island's longer hikes runs from **White Rock Bay to Split Rock Bay** (6.5 miles), weaving together a leg of the White Rock Bay Loop and the Split Rock Loop. Not far from the trailhead the well-worn trail crosses a grassy basin before clambering along the western flanks of Frary Peak and then dropping to the beach. While bison and antelope can occasionally be spotted in the basin, chukars, a game bird, flutter across the rocks. A short spur runs to the point of **Elephant Head** (1 mile). Not only does the hike give spectacular views of the Great Salt Lake, it passes horse corrals ranchers formed out of rock walls in the 1870s. In summer, heat and insects conspire against hikers, making this trek better done in spring or fall.

The salt contained in the Great Salt Lake is not totally worthless. Several companies, including Morton, take salt from the lake to make table salt and water softeners.

Grandeur Peak (3 miles), located 3.2 miles up Millcreek Canyon just minutes from downtown, is an unassuming summit but one that gives panoramic views of the Salt Lake Valley and the Great Salt Lake. Located on the southeastern edge of the city, the trail runs not quite three miles from the Church Fork picnic area parking lot to the summit, climbing through old-growth forest, aspen groves and wildflower meadows before topping out on a rocky outcrop at 8299 feet.

At 9026 feet, **Mount Olympus** (3 miles) is not the tallest peak fronting Salt Lake City, but its imposing presence over the city makes it a desirable hike for many. It also happens to be one of the more grueling hikes, thanks to the steady diet of switchbacks that swing the trail back and forth up the mountain. The trailhead can be found at a parking lot just above Wasatch Boulevard.

While most above-treeline trails involve scrambles across talus slopes, that's not the case with the hike to **Lookout Peak** (3.5 miles). This hike, which starts in Affleck Park, a Salt Lake County park found five miles up Route 65 from Route 80 Exit 134, runs a short way through forest before cruising through scattered scrub oak stands and then breaking completely out into the clear. The summit, reached 3.5 miles from the trailhead, offers good views of downtown Salt Lake City and the Great Salt Lake.

SOUTH VALLEY AND MOUNTAIN RESORTS   Little Cottonwood Canyon, along with being home to the Alta and Snowbird ski resorts, is chockfull of hikes that lead into the Twin Peaks and Lone Peak wilderness areas. The walk to **Red Pine Lakes** (3 miles) quickly leaves the canyon floor from the White Pine Trailhead on its way to the 30,088-acre Lone Peak Wilderness. Climbing up through a narrow side canyon, the trail runs through dense stands of conifer with aspen sprinkled liberally throughout before the trees give way near the trail's end to rugged boulder fields and two lakes puddled beneath glacial cirques. Towering above and just west of the boulder fields is the 11,326-foot Pfeifferhorn, a triangular-shaped peak that hardy hikers can reach via a ridgeline scramble.

You can reach a gorgeous alpine cirque if you head up the **Maybird Lakes Trail** (3.75 miles). This trail shares the same trailhead as Red Pine Lakes, but for some reason few people use it.

◄ HIDDEN

The turnoff is 1.63 miles above the trailhead. After crossing a bridge over a small creek the trail heads west and uphill into Maybird Gulch for another 1.19 miles. It's strenuous at times, but the payoff is a beautiful cirque with three little lakes shimmering beneath the dramatic Pfeifferhorn, which some know as the Little Matterhorn. Along the way you'll likely come across ruffed grouse that make their homes on the mountain.

The **Dog Lake Trail** (2 miles) is a nice hike for families, as it's relatively short and ends up at a small lake (or big pond), where you can relax on a log and have a pleasant lunch. The hike begins at the Mill D Trailhead in Big Cottonwood Canyon. It winds through a pretty aspen and conifer forest on the way to the lake.

If the Dog Lake hike isn't enough of a workout for you, then head to **Desolation Lake** (3.5 miles). This trail shares the same trailhead as Dog Lake. One and a half miles up the trail you come to a junction; go straight and you'll continue on to Dog Lake, bear right and the trail runs for another two miles to the lake. I like this trail for workouts because it offers a nice mix of uphills and flats for trail running, as well as spectacular views.

TOOELE AND THE GREAT SALT LAKE DESERT   About 43 miles west of Salt Lake City lie the Stansbury Mountains and the Deseret Peak Wilderness, which sprawls below 11,031-foot **Deseret Peak** (6 miles). The trail is reached via the South Willow Canyon road south of Grantsville. Along the way it crosses a stream and throws a spur to Willow Lakes. From the summit there are sweeping views of the Salt Flats to the west and the Wasatch Range to the east.

A view into Nevada is offered from the summit of King Top, an 8350-foot mountain top in the Confusion Range of Utah's West Desert. Getting to the trailhead is half the job, as it lies roughly 62 miles west of Delta via Route 6. The **King Top Trail** (6 miles) hike through Cat Canyon is not particularly tough since the elevation gain is just 2100 feet. But there's no water out there and in the summer this place gets hot. Quiet, watchful hikers just might see some of the region's wild horses.

GOOPY WHEN WET

Tempting as they are for off-road driving in the spirit of those land-speed racers, the Salt Flats are to be avoided. Ruts along Route 80 testify to the many cars and pickups that get mired in the mud beneath the salty surface crust that gets goopy when wet. When wet, the salty surface solution can short-out your rig's electrical system.

Transportation

Salt Lake City is like the center of a wheel, with two major interstate highways and numerous state routes running like spokes through Utah's capital. While **Route 80** runs east and west through the state, passing through Salt Lake City, **Route 15** runs north and south, also passing through the city. **Route 215** is the belt route that encircles the city and ties into spur **Route 190** and **Route 210** that lead into the Cottonwood Canyons southeast of Salt Lake City as well as **Route 201**, which runs west of the capital to Magna.

CAR

AIR
Nearly a dozen airlines—America West, American, Continental, Delta, Frontier, jetBlue, Northwest, Skywest, Southwest and United—fly into **Salt Lake City International Airport**, which is located seven miles west of the capital. ~ 776 North Terminal Drive, Salt Lake City; 801-575-2400; www.slcairport.com.

BUS
Greyhound Bus Lines makes regular stops in Salt Lake. *Note*: Salt Lake officials have announced plans to build a sprawling mass transit center at 600 West 200–300 South. The entire complex isn't expected to be completed until 2007. However, officials hope to have a small station in place for Greyhound and Amtrak by fall 2003. ~ 160 West South Temple, Salt Lake City; 801-355-9579, 800-231-2222; www.greyhound.com.

TRAIN
Amtrak stops in Salt Lake City to and from the West Coast. ~ 801-531-0188, 800-872-7245; www.amtrak.com.

CAR RENTALS
Car-rental companies that have offices nearby or at the Salt Lake City International Airport include **Avis Rent A Car** (801-575-2847), **Budget Rent A Car** (801-363-1500), **Dollar Rent A Car** (801-575-2580), **Enterprise Rent a Car** (801-537-7433), **Hertz Rent a Car** (801-575-2683), **National Car Rental** (801-575-2277) and **Thrifty Car Rental** (801-595-6677).

There are also a number of shuttle companies that run vans or buses to and from the airport. For information, contact one of the airport's two transportation desks, located in the terminals near the baggage carousels. ~ 801-575-2477.

PUBLIC TRANSIT
The **Utah Transit Authority** operates dozens of routes through Salt Lake City and the surrounding communities. A Free Ride Zone exists in the heart of the downtown commercial district. ~ 801-743-3882.

The core of the Salt Lake Valley is cut by the TRAX **Light Rail** system, which is operated by the Utah Transit Authority and runs from the downtown area south into Sandy. ~ 801-743-3882.

The **Pioneer Trolley** runs during the summer months in the heart of Salt Lake City surrounding Temple Square. The trolley, which is guided and makes a 15-minute loop of the area, is free. If you can't spot one of the "Pioneer Trolley Stop" signs near the Joseph Smith Memorial Building, call for stop locations. ~ 801-743-3882.

TAXIS   Taxi service is available throughout the Salt Lake Valley. In Salt Lake City is the **City Cab Company**. ~ 801-363-5550. Also operating in the capital is **Yellow Cab**. ~ 801-521-2100. There's also **Ute Cab**. ~ 801-359-7788. The **Murray Cab Company** also serves the valley. ~ 801-328-5704. So does the **South Salt Lake Cab Company**. ~ 801-328-5704. Still another option is **FreshTraks**. ~ 801-288-1330, 888-840-1330; www.freshtraks.net.

THREE

Northern Utah

Northern Utah has long been a Western crossroads, serving as both a meeting place and a thoroughfare. Long before settlers arrived, the Blackfoot, Shoshone, Paiute and Ute tribes regularly passed through the mountainous area that marks the eastern edge of the Great Basin. They came no doubt to enjoy the warm waters of the many hot springs that bubble up along the Wasatch Fault, which runs north and south through the region, and to stalk the plentiful game that roamed the forests. So revered was the Cache Valley to the Shoshone that they referred to it as "the house of the great spirit." They also called it "Willow Valley," a reference to the thick willow stands that still exist there.

Spanish explorers had little more than a passing interest in the area, arriving in the 1770s from southern Utah in search of routes to the West Coast. While they made some maps, they didn't stay for long.

It was the arrival of the mountain men in the early 1800s, however, that made a lasting impact on the region; they left their names behind in settlements that slowly grew and tamed the wilderness. A young Jim Bridger, at the time just 20 years old, was one of the first mountain men to reach the Cache Valley. While chasing beaver pelts along the Bear River the trapper, working for the Rocky Mountain Fur Company, made it all the way to the Great Salt Lake, which, upon tasting, he decided must be the Pacific Ocean. The practice of trappers such as Bridger to hide, or "cache," their pelts until they could be sold at rendezvous inspired the naming of the Cache Valley and Cache County.

It was a mountain man, Miles Goodyear, who built Utah's first white settlement. The year was 1846 when Goodyear figured he could make more money running a fort than tending to his traps. So he erected Fort Buenaventura near present-day Ogden.

The region literally became a crossroads on May 10, 1869, when two steam-belching locomotives, the Central Pacific Railroad's "Jupiter" and the Union Pacific's "No. 119," met cattle guard to cattle guard at Promontory Summit not far from the northern shore of the Great Salt Lake, marking the completion of the nation's first transcontinental railroad and the beginning of the end of the "wild West."

These days the region, which remains more rural than urban, continues as a crossroads, both literally and figuratively. Interstate highways that shuttle travelers north and south through Utah and Idaho cut through the region, while smaller routes meander east and west along the contours of the landscape to Wyoming and Nevada. More figuratively, the region stands at something of an economic and societal crossroads. While Cache Valley communities like Logan, Brigham City, Wellsville and Garden City continue to tightly embrace their agricultural heritage, Ogden has been transformed into a diverse metropolitan area with its business fingers dipped into the aerospace, industrial and financial sectors.

With much of the sparsely populated region either under the waters of the Great Salt Lake or preserved by the Wasatch-Cache National Forest, it's not surprising that tourism and outdoor recreation are integral parts of the economy. Just look across the landscape. Where the fresh waters of the Bear River spill into the Great Salt Lake on the northern shores of Willard Bay they nourish a sprawling bird refuge that teems with millions of birds during their spring and fall migrations. Northeast of Brigham City, Wellsville Mountain rises nearly 5000 feet straight up to create the country's steepest range while buttressing behind it a pocket of wilderness reminiscent of that which confronted Bridger.

Liberally sprinkled across the region are state parks, bejeweled high-country lakes and sprawling valley lakes and reservoirs that conspire with the forests and mountains to create a year-round outdoor lover's dream.

▼▼▼▼▼▼▼▼▼▼
Ogden Area

Overshadowed by the prominence of Salt Lake City 35 miles to the south, but certainly not lost in that shadow, Ogden has a long, colorful history dating to the mountain men who roamed the West in the mid-19th century. Trappers regularly held rendezvous in the area; in fact, the city took its name from Peter Skene Ogden, a brigade leader for the Hudson Bay Fur Company. The valley went on to claim Utah's first white settlement, which arose in 1846 when trapper Miles Goodyear, deciding life would be easier as a merchant, built a fort and trading post near the confluence of the Weber and Ogden rivers.

Some 80 years later, it's said that gangster Al Capone found Ogden a bit too rough for his liking and boarded a train back to Chicago, where his chosen career flourished. Boxer Jack Dempsey apparently didn't mind the street life, which was colored by the city's thriving red-light district, and pummeled quite a few opponents on his climb up the heavyweight ladder.

These days Ogden is a more sophisticated city with strong industrial and financial centers. Home to Weber State University and Hill Air Force Base, the city also claimed a share of the 2002 Olympic Winter Games with its ice sheet for curling and the Snowbasin Ski Resort for downhill, Super G and combined ski races, as well as the alpine events for the 2002 Paralympic Winter Games.

SIGHTS

Stretching along the western foothills of the Wasatch Range, Ogden holds an envious position among the state's metropolitan com-

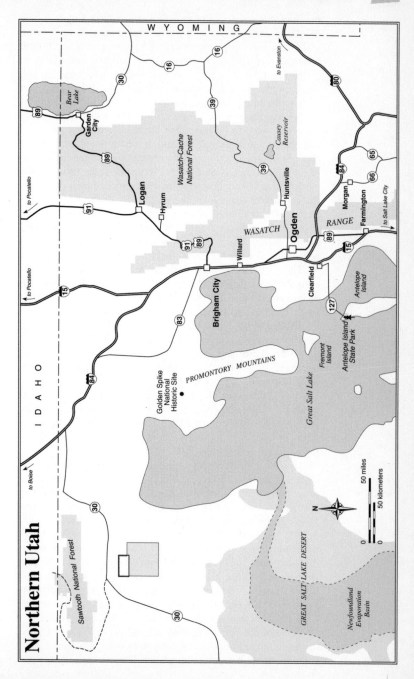

Northern Utah

munities. It's not as big or crowded as Salt Lake City, nor does it have to share the limelight with an adjoining city, as do Provo and Orem. No, Ogden enjoys a modest population of 77,000 and beautiful surroundings of mountainous national forest lands to the east and the Great Salt Lake to the west. A farming and railroad community in its youth, today Ogden blends historical sites with a vibrant industrial sector and nearby recreational outlets.

For a glimpse of the Ogden's colorful past as a 19th-century rail town, head to **Historic 25th Street**, a two-block stretch of downtown that is nearing the end of a long restoration project that has returned the luster the street enjoyed during the heyday of the United States' railroad era. So proud of the revitalization work are the street's businesses that they created their own website to tout the area: www.historic25.com. Today this National Historic District boasts interesting shops, antique stores, restaurants and hotels in beautifully restored buildings scattered among private clubs and a few weary structures in need of restoration. See the "Walking Tour" below for more details.

The anchor of Historic 25th Street is **Union Station**, a cavernous railroad depot that dates to the 1920s. You'll find a clutch of interesting museums that let you peek into Northern Utah's past. While trains no longer stop here, the building also houses the **Ogden/Weber Convention and Visitors Bureau** information center, a great place to learn about the valley's history and stock up on brochures and maps as well as souvenirs and Olympic merchandise. ~ 2501 Wall Avenue, Ogden; 801-627-8288, 866-867-8824; www.ogdencvb.org.

Utah claims two theaters tied to the Egyptian revival that swept the nation in the 1920s. One is in Park City, the other here in Ogden. The fully restored 1924 **Peery's Egyptian Theater** continues to host plays and films. ~ Historic 25th Street and Washington Boulevard, Ogden; 801-395-3227, 800-337-2690.

Historic 25th Street isn't the only unique part of downtown Ogden. In the early 1900s a number of wealthy families who would HIDDEN ▶ prove prominent in Utah history settled in what is now the **Eccles Historic District**. Among the houses here is one that Leroy and Myrtle Eccles built at 2509 Eccles Avenue for more than $100,000 in 1917. A lavish home reflecting Italian Renaissance architecture, today it serves as a backdrop for weddings and receptions. A stucco home built in the Old English Cottage style, with a steeply pitched roof broken by dormers, can be found at 2580 Eccles Avenue. A brochure guiding you through this district is available at the visitors center in Union Station. ~ Bordered by 25th and 26th streets and Van Buren and Jackson avenues.

Some of the best local, regional and national art in Ogden can be found at **Eccles Community Art Center**. The center itself is a work of art, housed in a handsome 1893 Victorian sandstone

Ogden Area

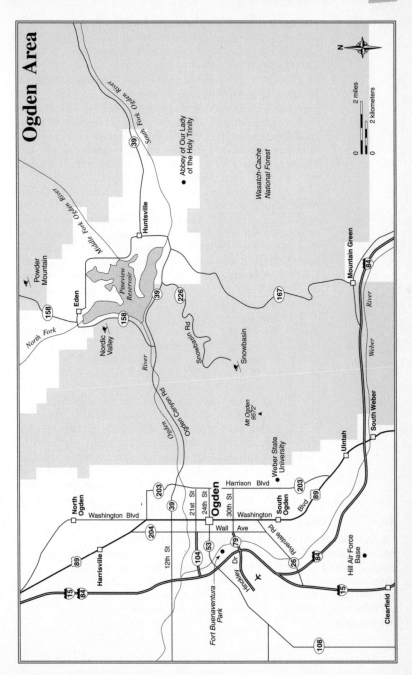

N

South Fork Ogden River

39

• Abbey of Our Lady
of the Holy Trinity

Huntsville

Wasatch-Cache
National Forest

2 miles

2 kilometers

0

0

Powder
Mountain

Middle Fork Ogden River

158

Eden

Pineview
Reservoir

39

226

167

Mountain Green

84

North Fork

Nordic
Valley

158

158

River

Snowbasin Rd

Snowbasin

Weber River

South Weber

Ogden Canyon Rd

Mt Ogden
9572'

Uintah

89

203

203

Weber State
University

•

Harrison Blvd

North
Ogden

Washington Blvd

39

21st St

24th St

Ogden

30th St

Washington

South
Ogden

Blvd

84

204

Wall Ave

Riverdale Rd

Hill Air Force
Base   •

89

Harrisville

12th St

104

53

79

Hinckley Dr

26

84

15

15

84

Fort Buenaventura
Park

15

Clearfield

108

mansion and now listed on the national and state registers of historic places. The adjacent Carriage House Gallery displays more works and has a small gift shop. ~ 2508 Jefferson Avenue, Ogden; 801-392-6935.

Youngsters can't avoid having fun in the **Treehouse Children's Museum**, an interactive museum that focuses on reading. The treehouse is crammed with things for kids age 2-to-12 to do and explore. They can read a book, be read to, roam through Storybook Village with its props for storytelling, or perform in the museum's theater, which stages its presentations on the last Thursday of the month. Admission. ~ 455 23rd Street, Ogden; 801-394-9663; www.treehousemuseum.org.

There's no need to leave town to enjoy nature—the **Ogden Nature Center** provides a wild touch to the city. This 127-acre wildlife sanctuary offers nature trails for summer strolls or winter cross-country ski outings as well as ponds, wetlands and more than 10,000 trees. Each year the center also tries to rehabilitate injured or orphaned birds. The treehouse is sure to delight the kids. Closed Sunday and from Christmas to January 2. Admission. ~ 966 West 12th Street, Ogden; 801-621-7595; www.ogden naturecenter.org, e-mail info@ogdennaturecenter.org.

Fort Buenaventura Park, found on 88 acres along the Weber River in West Ogden, recalls the days of the 1840s when trapping and mountain men were on their way out and settlers were slowly colonizing the West. Miles Goodyear built his trading post here in 1846, and while the original structure no longer exists, a replica based on historical records was erected on 32 acres in 1980 and includes cabins, a trading post and a visitors center. Just like the original stockade, wooden pegs, not nails, were used to hold the log walls in place. Goodyear had high hopes for his trading post, as it was located along the Hasting's Cutoff, a route that led to California. One of the wagon trains that stopped at his trading post on the way to California carried the ill-fated Donner Party, which met an untimely disaster when it became ma-

RIGHT ON TRACK

Kids get a kick out of the **Utah State Railroad Museum**, housed in downtown Ogden's Union Station. Inside the museum the Wattis-Dumke Model Railroad Exhibit features an HO-scale model railroad layout with a dozen trains in motion. The layouts depict the construction of the railroad through the West, with scenics of the Great Salt Lake as well as the Wasatch and Sierra Nevada ranges. ~ 2501 Wall Avenue, Ogden; 801-629-8535.

rooned in the heavy snows of the Sierra Nevada Range. ~ 2450 A Avenue, Ogden; 801-399-8099.

With two rivers coursing through town, the three-mile-long **Ogden River Parkway** should come as no surprise. The parkway runs along the Ogden River from the mouth of the six-acre Ogden Canyon into the heart of downtown. The prehistoric past rises out of the parkway in the form of the **Ogden Eccles Dinosaur Park,** which features more than 100 life-size dinosaur models such as archaeopteryx (a reptilian bird), tyrannosaurus rex and triceratops. There's also a hands-on fossil display, a museum and a paleontological laboratory. While the parkway and museum are open year-round, the outdoor dinosaur park is only open April through October, weather permitting, so call ahead. Admission. ~ 1544 East Park Boulevard, Ogden; 801-393-3466; www. dinosaurpark.org, e-mail dinopark@ci.ogden.ut.us.

One of the town's claims to fame isn't within Ogden's borders, but rather towers over it. A knock-off of **Ben Lomond Peak,** which rises 9717 feet high on Ogden's eastern skyline, is flashed daily across television and movie screens throughout the world as the logo for Paramount Pictures.

Although you might need to enlist to stroll through the heart of Hill Air Force Base, ordinary civilians can tour the vintage aircraft and missiles on display at the **Hill Aerospace Museum**. Sprawling across 50 acres near the northwest corner of the airbase, the museum displays a wide array of jet- and propeller-driven warplanes, among them an F-15 fighter, a B-52 bomber, a Soviet MIG and an SR-71C "Blackbird" spy plane. Air Force uniforms are also among the exhibits. ~ 7961 Wardleigh Road, Hill Air Force Base; 801-777-6868; www.hill.af.mil/museum/info/museum.htm.

One of America's oldest amusement parks, **Lagoon** dates to 1886, when it was known as Lakeside Park, a popular swimming resort then located on the shore of the Great Salt Lake. Its colorful history includes a period in the 1960s when rock-and-roll stars such as the Beach Boys and Rolling Stones performed at the park. Today Lagoon is known as the largest amusement park between Kansas City and the Pacific Ocean, with more than 40 rides and four roller coasters, including "Colossus the Fire Dragon," which shuttles screaming riders through 65-foot diameter loops at speeds up to 55 m.p.h. Nearby is "Lagoon A Beach," six acres of watery fun, ranging from waterfalls and fountains to towering "hydrotubes" and a meandering manmade river. The park also has a 15-acre re-creation of a frontier village, complete with gun shooters and live entertainment. Open daily Memorial Day through Labor Day, and weekends in April, May and September. Admission. ~ Route 15 Exit 327, 17 miles south of

Text continued on page 112.

Historic 25th Street

In late-19th-century Ogden, the railroad was the city's lifeblood. From Union Station, today the undisputed hallmark of Historic 25th Street, prosperity swept through the front doors and rolled like a wave up 25th Street. Hotels, saloons and shops in tasteful architectures quickly arose to capture the attention, and business, of those who got off the trains.

Many of those buildings remain, in many cases housing unique businesses that continue, as did their forefathers, to try to attract shoppers. A free self-guiding brochure available at the visitors center in Union Station traces the history of not just the street, but also the city.

UNION STATION   Union Station, a sprawling, Mediterranean Colonial–style depot reminiscent of America's early-20th-century love affair with railroads, is the third to stand in this location. The first depot, a small, unassuming facility, arose just after the golden spike was driven at Promontory Summit. In 1889 a more lavish, Victorian-style building replaced it. However, it burned to the ground in 1923 and was succeeded by the present building. Although trains no longer stop here, today the building retains a grand, cavernous lobby with sprawling **murals** at each end of the lobby depicting the completion of the transcontinental railroad. Outside, a cobblestone courtyard surrounds a water fountain while locomotive displays bookend the building. Kids particularly enjoy clambering over steam locomotive 4436 on the north end and peering inside its caboose. Union Station is also home to the Utah State Railroad Museum and The Natural History Museum, as well as a gift shop and the Union Grill. The **Myra Powell Gallery** displays both local and nationally known artists. One hallway displays artworks honoring Utah's railroad legacy in the form of paintings depicting locomotives at work in various settings around the state. Admission for museums. ~ 2501 Wall Avenue; 801-629-8444, 800-255-8824, museums 801-629-8535; www.theunion station.org.

UTAH STATE RAILROAD MUSEUM   The state railroad museum sprawls both inside and outside of Union Station. Outside in the station's yards you can inspect a handful of retired locomotives and their cars and clamber inside a caboose. Inside the depot, tour the Wattis-Dumke Model Railroad Exhibit with its HO-scale model railroad. Eight different HO layouts depict how turn-of-the-20th-century crews cut through mountains as they laid tracks through the Wasatch Range, around the Great Salt Lake, and into the Sierra Mountains.

BROWNING LEGACY   Upstairs, more than a century of firearms history is on display at the **Browning Firearms Museum**, which stores the legacy of John M. Browning, an Ogden resident. The first edition of the Browning Automatic Rifle, which served the U.S. military well for 80 years, is on display, as are an assortment of machine guns. Back downstairs at the **Browning/Kimball Car Museum** you can marvel over horseless carriages from the early 1900s. Among the favorites is a 1931 Pierce Arrow once owned by Chicago mobsters who had it fitted with gun holsters.

MURPHY BLOCK   Back on Historic 25th Street, a series of shops stand on the spot where George Murphy, a Civil War veteran, developed the "Murphy Block" in 1887. Initially, Murphy ran a tobacco and cigar shop on the first floor of the "Murphy Building," while the second floor housed the Windsor Hotel. Over the years the structure fronted businesses ranging from a grocery and confectionery to a curio shop. During World War II troops were entertained by the USO here.

SENATE SALOON   Next door to the "Murphy Building" George Murphy erected the Senate Saloon in 1889, a grandiose structure festooned with elaborate cornices and moldings that are hallmarks of Italianate architecture. Today it houses a variety of shops. ~ 105–111 Historic 25th Street.

ASPEN STUDIO   Across the street stands the Aspen Studio, a two-story structure built around 1903 to house a saloon and grocery on the main floor and rented rooms on the second. The Grand Saloon took over the main floor in 1913 and was frequented by the region's sheepherders. Prohibition transformed the saloon into a billiard hall. Today the building, which has a corbeled upper cornice and a panel inscribed with "Aspen Studio," is home to a taxidermy and fine-arts shop. ~ 136 Historic 25th Street; 801-399-9052.

LONDON ICE CREAM PARLOR   One of the oldest buildings on Historic 25th Street, and perhaps one of the most architecturally significant, is the London Ice Cream Parlor. The two-story brick building carries a Greek Revival facade with pediment roof and pilasters, as well as some Italianate influences in its Roman-arched windows and bracketed cornice. Today it's home to The Athenian, a Greek-American restaurant. During its highly colorful past it had a second-floor boarding house that evolved into the "K.C. Rooms," a lively bordello. ~ 252–254 Historic 25th Street.

KANSAS CITY LIQUOR HOUSE   Directly across the street stands the Kansas City Liquor House, a two-story building built around 1890. Less decorative than others on the street, the building has square windows and no ornate stone- or brick-work. Although the location housed businesses that sold Chinese goods and furniture over the years, today it is home to a business more fitting to the building's name—Rooster's, a brewpub. ~ 253 Historic 25th Street; 801-627-6171.

Ogden; 801-451-8000, 800-748-5246; www.lagoonpark.com, e-mail info@lagoonpark.com.

HIDDEN ►   Got a hankering for some creamed honey with a dollop of spirituality? Then visit the **Abbey of Our Lady of the Holy Trinity**, a trappist monastery nestled on 1800 acres of rich farmland. After a stop in the gift shop, where you'll find 14 flavors of creamed honey prepared by the white-robed monks, attend one of their prayer sessions or listen to their Gregorian chants. ~ About 15 miles east of Ogden in Huntsville via Route 39.

LODGING   A modest variety of lodging possibilities is available in Ogden, ranging from highway chains and historic hotels to thematic bed and breakfasts.

HIDDEN ►   It might seem hokey to some, but others will find the ruggedness of the **Alaskan Inn** a wonderful escape from standard motel and hotel rooms. Located four miles up Ogden Canyon, the lodge offers 12 rooms and 11 cabins; each, through their furnishings and decor, evokes a particular flavor of Alaska, such as the Northern Lights, the Iditarod or the Mother Lode. ~ 435 Ogden Canyon Road, Ogden; 801-621-8600, 888-707-8600; www.alaskaninn.com, e-mail mail@alaskaninn.com. DELUXE.

The **Ogden Plaza** can be found in the historic Eccles Building, which rose above downtown Ogden in 1914. Inside this eight-story hotel you'll find 137 rooms, including eight suites. Nico's Grille and Lounge is also located within the hotel, so you don't have to go far for something to eat or a nightcap. In addition, the hotel offers a 24-hour business center and fitness center, just in case you can't sleep. ~ 2401 Washington Boulevard, Ogden; 801-394-9400, fax 801-394-9500. MODERATE TO DELUXE.

The **Best Rest Inn** and its 101 standard roadside-motel rooms can be found on the west side of Ogden just off Route 15 Exit 346. Close by you'll find not only the Ogden Nature Center but also the Ogden Raptors baseball stadium. ~ 1206 West 2100 South, Ogden; 801-393-8644, 800-343-8644. BUDGET.

Another quick, reliable option is the **Holiday Inn Express**, across from Comfort Suites. Along with 75 rooms and an indoor pool, hot tub and fitness center, the motel offers a business center where you can finish that report or fax a letter. ~ 1200 West 2245 South, Ogden; 801-392-5000, 800-465-4329. MODERATE.

At the **High Country Inn**, a Best Western property, the 111 rooms are supported by a heated outdoor pool, an exercise facility and rooms equipped with Nintendo machines to keep the kids happy. ~ 1335 West 12th Street, Ogden; 801-394-9474, 800-594-8979, fax 801-392-6589; www.bestwestern.com/highcountryinn. MODERATE TO DELUXE.

HIDDEN ►   Themes run through **Wright's Getaway Lodge**, a bed-and-breakfast establishment 15 miles northeast of Ogden near Eden.

Located on four acres of heavily treed land in a canyon above the Nordic Valley ski resort, the lodge has three suites equipped with surround-sound, jetted tubs, gas fireplaces, two-headed marble shower stalls and hand-painted murals. You can choose from the Aloha Suite, with a waterfall jacuzzi and 250-gallon salt-water aquarium; the Moonlight Rendezvous, with its black lights and 60-inch TV screen; and the Wild Kingdom, with its steam shower and "under bed" sound system. ~ P.O. Box 247, Eden, UT 84310; 801-745-4848; www.getawaylodge.com. DELUXE.

Venture east of Ogden towards Huntsville and a wonderful stay can be found at the **Snowberry Inn**. The seven guest rooms are housed in a beautiful hand-peeled log cabin that has wonderful views of Pineview Reservoir and the surrounding mountains. All rooms offer private baths and queen-sized beds. There's a common area in which you can relax with a game of cards, while outside there are broad porches and a hot tub. Breakfasts are vegetarian. ~ 1315 North Route 158, Eden; 801-745-2634, 888-334-3466, fax 801-745-0585; www.snowberryinn.com, e-mail snowberryinn@aol.com. MODERATE TO DELUXE.

DINING

Ogden's various heritages come to bloom in the wide array of eateries. Along with Mexican and hearty American fares you can find Italian, traditional German dishes and even Louisiana 'gator served up regularly in town.

Inside the historic Union Pacific Railroad Depot you can not only visit some interesting museums, but you can also grab a bite to eat at the **Union Grill**. The menu is tasty and diverse, ranging from bowls of chili and sandwiches to seafood and beef entrées. ~ 2501 Wall Avenue, Ogden; 801-621-2830. BUDGET TO MODERATE.

Locals often crowd **Karen's Café** for the breakfast and lunch specials that are rolled out each week. Just about everything is homemade, even the hamburger buns. While the lunch menu often features roast beef and chicken-fried steak, the breakfast

ARMING THE NATION

Many of the 19th-century firearms that were used to tame the West (and hold up stagecoaches and passenger trains, for that matter) can be traced to John M. Browning, the father of the Browning Arms Company. Browning lived and worked in Ogden, where he and his employees designed and built many of the weapons that carried the Winchester, Remington and Colt labels. The company remains in business today. The Browning Firearms Museum in Union Station displays various models built by the company over the years.

burrito is usually a hit. No dinner. ~ 242 Historic 25th Street, Ogden; 801-392-0345. BUDGET.

Not far up the street is **Rooster's,** a brew pub that operates out of the historic Kansas City Liquor House. Pizzas aren't run of the mill here, carrying everything from rock shrimp and asparagus to smoked salmon. The menu also includes portobello mushroom and chicken-breast sandwiches, as well as jambalaya, beer-battered fish-and-chips, and Alaskan king salmon. Among the house brews are Golden Spike Ale, Two-bit Amber, Junction City Chocolate Stout and Bee's Knees Honey Wheat. ~ 253 Historic 25th Street, Ogden; 801-627-6171, fax 435-627-1353; www.roostersbrewingco.com. BUDGET TO MODERATE.

The **La Ferrovia Ristorante** is a mom-and-pop Italian eatery that dates to 1988, when Giuseppina and Rita Iodice arrived from Naples, Italy, and moved into a space at Union Station; in fact, the restaurant's name ("the iron road") is a result of that original location. Today located in a storefront on Historic 25th Street, the restaurant features *cannellone, cotoletta alla bolognese* and *bistecca all capricciosa*. Of course, you'll also find spaghetti, lasagna, pizza and calzones. During warm weather ask for a table on the back patio. Closed Sunday and Monday. ~ 234 Historic 25th Street, Ogden; 801-394-8628. BUDGET TO MODERATE.

HIDDEN ►

An authentic taste of Louisiana's bayou country can be found at the **Cajun Skillet,** where chef Thomas Jackson flies his alligator and crawdads—and just about all his ingredients—in fresh from his home state. How your alligator is prepared depends on how you want it: fried, stewed, blackened. The 26-item menu also features seafood and steaks if you're not up for 'gator. ~ 2550 Washington Boulevard, Ogden; 801-393-7702. BUDGET TO MODERATE.

Jeremiah's consistently serves up one of the best breakfasts in town, both from a taste and price vantage point. The "Break of Dawn" special is an all-you-can-eat feast with eggs and bacon,

AUTHOR FAVORITE

To me, atmosphere is as important as an outstanding menu, and **Bistro 258** on Historic 25th Street combines the two perfectly with its crisp table linens, warm wood floors, historic brick walls, smartly dressed waiters and creative menus. The only problem is choosing an entrée—the *linguini alla bucaniera* is a wonderful dish of shrimp, scallops, clams and salmon drizzled with a saffron cream, but it's hard to pass up hand-cut filet mignon served with a creamed stoneground mustard demi sauce. Closed Sunday. ~ 258 Historic 25th Street, Ogden; 801-394-1595. MODERATE.

French toast, pancakes and more. Lunch and dinner, meanwhile, revolve around burgers, sandwiches, fajitas and fish. During your meal you can check out the area's trail network, which is laid out on the place mats. ~ High Country Inn, 1307 West 1200 South, Ogden; 801-394-3273. BUDGET.

Mexican, not Southwestern, cuisine is served up at **El Matador**, which is famous for its "Vera Cruz Combination." Featuring two cheese enchiladas, two jumbo shrimp and one beef taco, the combo isn't likely to leave you hungry. ~ 2564 Ogden Avenue, Ogden; 801-393-3151. BUDGET.

Rich Teutonic dishes crowd the menu at the **Bavarian Chalet**, a traditional German restaurant where the wiener schnitzel comes in veal, pork or turkey. You'll also find sauerbraten, beef *rouladen* and *schlachtplate*. If you're uncertain, try the King Ludwig Sampler, which includes wiener schnitzel, *jaeger schnitzel*, sausages and vegetables. If that's too hearty, Chef Wolfgang Stadelmann also offers steaks, fish and vegetarian dinners. Dinner only. Closed Sunday and Monday. ~ 4387 South Harrison Boulevard, Ogden; 801-479-7561; www.bavarian-chalet.com. MODERATE.

Off the beaten path near the junction of Valley Drive and Canyon Road lies **The Greenery**, a long-time Ogden favorite that's part of Rainbow Gardens (see "Shopping" below). The menu is diverse, finding room for clam chowder and vegetable soup next to crab salad and turkey sandwiches as well as halibut steaks. The setting is airy and the service prompt. ~ 1851 Valley Drive, Ogden; 801-392-1777. BUDGET.

◀ HIDDEN

Thematic businesses aren't restricted to lodgings in the Ogden area. The **Timbermine** offers dining in the surroundings of an old underground mine, complete with well-worn timbers and ore cars. Steak and prime rib are the motherlode here, although the menu also includes lobster, shrimp, halibut and salmon. Dinner only. ~ 1701 Park Boulevard, Ogden; 801-393-2155; www.timbermine. com. MODERATE TO DELUXE.

◀ HIDDEN

Not to be outdone by some creaky mine, the **Prairie Schooner** is a steakhouse that circles the wagons for dinner. Meals are served inside covered wagons reminiscent of Oregon Trail days. Along with steaks, the menu features prime rib, seafood and chicken. Lunch is also served, but not in the wagons. ~ 445 Park Boulevard, Ogden; 801-392-2712. MODERATE TO DELUXE.

There are a number of restaurants to be found outside Ogden's limits that are good places to stop when hunger strikes.

Although it started out in 1912 as a summer home, the **GrayCliff Lodge Restaurant** has been feeding folks since 1945. Tables can be found throughout the house in what used to be the family room as well as on a long covered porch that offers beautiful views of Ogden Canyon's forests and an airy meal during the summer months. Located five miles up Ogden Canyon, the restaurant specializes in lamb, steak, poultry and local trout. Dinner only; brunch is served Sunday. Closed Monday. ~ 508 Ogden Canyon, Ogden; 801-392-6775, 800-879-6775; www. grayclifflodge.com. MODERATE TO DELUXE.

HIDDEN ▶

Some say the country's best hamburger, the Star Burger, can be found in **The Shooting Star Saloon** in tiny Huntsville, just eight miles east of the Snowbasin resort. Along with the usual hamburger patty, this burger boasts a piece of bratwurst. This hole-in-the-wall watering hole also happens to be Utah's oldest continually operating bar, dating to 1879 when it was known as "Hoken's Hole" after its proprietor, Hoken Olsen. Of particular note besides the hamburgers is the stuffed bust of a 300-pound St. Bernard. ~ 7350 East 200 South, Huntsville; 801-745-2002. BUDGET.

HIDDEN ▶

At **Eats of Eden**, nine miles northeast of Ogden in a gap within the Wasatch Range, you'll find sandwiches built upon home-baked breads, hand-crafted pizzas, pastas, soups and burgers. Located unobtrusively in a small storefront shop along Route 162 next to Eden's post office, this café lures in locals with its manicotti (made with three-cheese crêpes instead of pasta) and bread pudding. ~ 2595 North Route 162, Eden; 801-745-8618. BUDGET.

SHOPPING

Along with charming architecture, **Historic 25th Street** offers intriguing shopping in the form of many antique and specialty shops.

Young's General Store carries an incredible potpourri of items, ranging from fine and costume jewelry to silverware, antique bottles and toys, watches, guns and oak furniture. ~ 109 Historic 25th Street, Ogden; 801-392-1473.

Aaron Lily, an antique shop, focuses on jewelry, custom clothes, furniture and artworks. ~ 111 Historic 25th Street, Ogden; 801-392-8023.

Next door, the **Painted Lady** proffers Victorian furnishings, china, clocks and lamps among the crowded stock within its walls. ~ 115 Historic 25th Street, Ogden; 801-393-4445.

Artworks and stuffed animals share the space at **Aspen Studio and Gallery**, which is housed in the historic Aspen Studio. Inside are bronze works, sculptures, watercolors, photos and mounted wildlife. ~ 136 Historic 25th Street, Ogden; 801-399-9052.

At **Needlepoint Joint** you can find Beatrix Potter, Danforth Pewter and Winnie the Pooh collections as well as all your yarn and needlepoint thread needs. Closed Sunday. ~ 241 Historic 25th Street, Ogden; 801-394-4355.

Looking for that hard-to-get kitchen gadget? Try **Pan Handlers**, where kitchenware and crockery are king. In fact, they claim to have everything the cook needs. ~ 260 Historic 25th Street, Ogden; 801-392-6510.

One of the oldest Western-wear shops in the Intermountain West can be found at **Cross Western Wear**. Step inside this shop and you'll find cowboy hats, boots, buckles and clothing as well as hand-made saddles and chaps. They'll also consider buying your old saddle if you have one to get rid of. ~ 2246 Washington Boulevard, Ogden; 801-394-5773; www.crosswestern.com.

Book lovers head to **The Bookshelf**, which stocks the latest titles as well as comic books, Japanese magazines and unusual journals. ~ 2432 Washington Boulevard, Ogden; 801-621-4752.

What started out as a spa at the mouth of Ogden Canyon is now self-described as "Western America's Largest Gift Emporium." **Rainbow Gardens** offers more than 20 departments packed with such items as scented soaps and candles, baskets, picture frames, silk flowers, greeting cards and children's games. The operation dates to 1890, when a real estate developer made plans to turn the existing hot springs into the Ogden Canyon Sanitarium. A hotel and bathhouse finally arrived in 1903, and by 1906 trolley cars were ferrying folks from downtown Ogden to the spa. While the spa went out of business in 1972, the operation saw its first gift shop open in 1970 and the owners have never looked back. When you descend into the "Gift Garden" you are actually stepping down into one of the old spa's bathing pools. ~ 1851 Valley Drive, Ogden; 801-621-1606.

◀ HIDDEN

NIGHTLIFE

An early-20th-century classic, **Peery's Egyptian Theater** has hosted a dozen Utah premières, one U.S. première, and even a world première. Weber State University's Department of Performing Arts frequently stages its plays here. Each January the theater also shows some of the films appearing at the Sundance Film Festival. ~ Historic 25th Street and Washington Boulevard, Ogden; 801-395-3227.

> Ogden early on was known as "Junction City," a reference to its railroading fame.

For a ten-week run each summer local musicians show off their skills at **Talent in the Park** shows held Wednesday nights in Ogden's Municipal Garden amphitheater. ~ Historic 25th Street and Washington Boulevard, Ogden; 801-629-8242.

Concerts, ballet and dramatic presentations are often offered in the Ogden area. The **Utah Musical Theater**, which stages its performances in Peery's Egyptian Theater, offers a mix of Broadway classics such as *The Unsinkable Molly Brown* and *1776*. ~ 2415 Washington Boulevard, Ogden; box office 801-626-8500.

The **Ogden Symphony Ballet Association** brings the Utah Symphony, Ballet West and the Utah Opera Company to town and holds its performances in the Browning Center at Weber State University as well as the Egyptian Theater. ~ 638 East 26th Street, Ogden; 801-399-9214.

For a few chuckles, check out **Wise Guys,** which schedules stand-up comics Thursday through Saturday. Cover. ~ 208 Historic 25th Street, Ogden; 801-622-5588.

Billiards, darts, pizza and rock-and-roll share the scene at **Brewski's,** one of three private clubs owned by the same management. What's the advantage of joint ownership? Well, one membership fee gets you into all three. ~ 244 Historic 25th Street, Ogden; 801-394-1713; www.brewskisonline.net.

Teaser's Sports Bar & Grill is a private club that books live rock bands on weekends and offers other entertainment midweek. ~ 366 36th Street, Ogden; 801-395-1517.

PARKS

FORT BUENAVENTURA PARK Located on the site of the first permanent white settlement in the Great Basin, the focal point of this 88-acre park is a replica of the 1846 fort mountain man Miles Goodyear built with hopes of drumming up business with the wagon trains heading West. Today guides in period dress recount the fort's history, while exhibits delve into the lives of the mountain men and American Indians who lived in the region. There also are picnic grounds, canoe rentals, restrooms and fishing along the Weber River. Day-use fee, $5. ~ 2450 A Avenue, Ogden; 801-621-4808.

▲ There are 12 campsites; $10 per night. Reservations: 801-625-3850.

HIDDEN ▶

OGDEN WHITEWATER PARK The careful placement of rock created this kayak "rodeo arena" on a short stretch of the Weber River that flows past Ogden. Running along 200 yards of river that streams under the Wilson Lane Bridge at 24th Street, the free whitewater park challenges kayakers with waves they can surf and play in. ~ Wilson Lane and 24th Street, Ogden.

WASATCH-CACHE NATIONAL FOREST The Ogden District, northern tier, of the 1.2-million-acre Wasatch-Cache National Forest cuts north-to-south through northern Utah. Squeezed between the Great Salt Lake and the Wyoming border, this section of forest offers Ogden res-

---

GETTING PHYSICAL

In town and looking for a workout? Head over to the **Mount Ogden Exercise Trail.** The loop actually consists of two paths—a dirt path for bicycles, the other covered with bark chips for joggers and walkers. The two follow a rolling route around Mount Ogden park and golf course and offer access to the Bonneville Shoreline Trail, Waterfall Canyon and Taylor's Canyon.

idents and visitors a quick escape from the urban landscape into the mountains' dense forests, hiking trails and ski areas. The forest is home to the Snowbasin Ski Resort, the host of the downhill and Super G races of the 2002 Olympic Winter Games, as well as seemingly endless hiking, biking and equestrian trails. ~ Many trails in the national forest have trailheads in Ogden, while Route 39 eastbound runs six miles through Ogden River Canyon to numerous access points around Pineview Reservoir, as well as continuing 16 miles farther east to the Monte Cristo Range; Ogden Ranger District, 507 25th Street, Suite 103, Ogden; 801-625-5112; www.fs.fed.us/wcnf.

▲ The Ogden District of the Wasatch-Cache National Forest contains 326 campsites in 14 developed campgrounds; $5 to $12 per night; 7-day maximum stay at developed campgrounds, 14 days at undeveloped sites.

The transcontinental railroad put Brigham City on the map when the rails were joined at nearby Promontory Summit, but the rich agricultural

Brigham City Area

lands that surround the community keep it going. Members of the LDS Church arrived in the area late in 1851 and quickly laid out their farms the following spring. Despite attacks by the Shoshone tribes that lived in the area, Brigham Young was determined to see a community hacked out of the wilderness. In 1854 he sent out 50 Salt Lake City families with hopes they could get the job done. Their arrival gave what had been a small, rustic settlement the makings of a more formal community—one named Brigham City in honor of the church leader.

Agriculture was the wellspring of Brigham City's economy. In 1855 a settler returned from Salt Lake City with 100 peach stones and planted them around town. The resulting harvests were so bountiful that in 1904 the town started its annual harvest festival, Peach Days.

While the area held onto its agrarian roots for more than a century, in 1957 Brigham City's economy got a decided boost when Thiokol Chemical Corporation, in search of a somewhat remote yet easily accessible area, selected Box Elder County for the home of its solid fuel rocket propellant plant. Located 27 miles west of Brigham City, the Thiokol plant not only became the biggest employer in the country but nearly doubled Brigham City's population with its employees.

While Thiokol continues to be a major cog in the local economy due to its work with NASA's shuttle program, Brigham City and surrounding Box Elder County continue to rely on the agricultural sector, which produces crops such as corn, tomatoes, alfalfa, potatoes, onions and fruit as well as cattle and sheep. If you drive on Route 89 between Brigham City and Ogden, you'll find numerous opportunities to buy fresh fruit and produce during the growing season.

Also dear to Brigham City's heart is the Bear River Migratory Bird Refuge. Proof of this endearment is the archway that frames Main Street and proclaims to all: "Brigham, Gateway—World's Greatest Game Bird Refuge."

SIGHTS

HIDDEN ►

On the way from Ogden to Brigham City (a distance of 21 miles) you'll come upon **Willard,** and if you bypass this tiny town you'll overlook one of the most unique collections of stone houses in Utah. Willard's dozen or so stone houses, built in Gothic and Greek Revival styles, date to the late 19th century and reflect the fine craftsmanship, as well as the professions, of some of the Mormon missionaries who settled here near the edge of the Great Salt Lake. One, for instance, was the home of a composer, who personalized his home by having wooden notes carved into the eaves. These structures were built by Welshman Shadrach Jones, who designed them after those in his native Wales. So architecturally and historically significant are the homes that in the 1970s a 12-block swath of Willard was listed in the national and state historic registers. For information on a walking tour, available April through October, call 435-734-8315. ~ Route 15 Exit 360, 12 miles south of Ogden.

Just across Route 15 from the town of Willard is **Willard Bay State Park,** a popular swimming, boating and waterskiing spot during the summer months, a reliable fishing hole year-round, and a favorite with eagles during the winter months. The freshwater bay, created by an impoundment that separates the bay from the salty lake, covers 9900 acres on the eastern edge of the Great Salt Lake. ~ Take Route 15 and get off on Exit 360, 900 West 650 North #A, Willard; 435-734-9494, 800-822-3770.

Once you reach Brigham City, you'll discover that the blending of history, rocketry, agriculture and natural resources have left the area blessed with a wide range of attractions. For a taste of that history and a primer on the area, stop by the **Chamber of Commerce** offices inside the **Old City Hall and Fire Station.** The two-story building was erected in 1909; the fire department took up the ground floor, city offices the second. A jail cell was fitted into the building's southeastern corner, while a "hobo apartment" was situated in the basement. The fire department eventually moved into its own building in 1935, the police department left in 1966, and the rest of the city offices in 1973. ~ 6 North Main Street, Brigham City; 435-723-3931.

The **Brigham City Pioneer Co-op** across the street from the chamber opened for business in 1891. However, it didn't stay open for long. A fire damaged the building in late 1894 and the business never recovered. Down through the years the restored building has housed a bank, a furniture store, a post office, a mortuary and a variety of other businesses. In 1990 the structure was placed on the National Register of Historic Places. These days a bank occupies the building, which sports beautiful brickwork on the wall facing the street and a north-facing wall of rock. ~ 5 North Main Street, Brigham City.

One of Utah's oldest manufacturing businesses exists in the form of the **Baron Woolen Mill,** which first produced wool products in 1870 when it was part of the Brigham City Mercantile

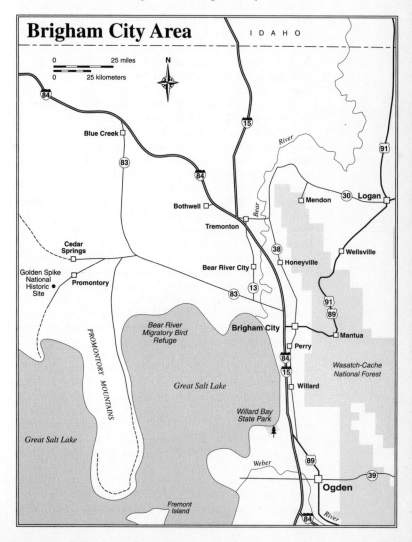

Brigham City Area

Cooperative. The building housing the mill is actually the fourth to bear the company's name: the first burned down in 1877, the second in 1907, and the third in 1949. While the mill's looms were idle from 1990 to 1993, it reopened in 1995 for a few years to produce Virgin American Wool and cotton blankets with its century-old equipment. Though the operation shut down early in 1999, the community is working to restore the mill and open it as a museum. ~ 56 North 500 East, Brigham City.

Just a bit east of Main Street is the **Grist Mill**, which dates to 1856 and was intended to serve as the northeastern corner of a rock wall that would encircle Brigham City for defense against Indians. For a while the mill actually functioned as a guardhouse of sorts, with men stationed on the upper floors to watch for trouble. A monument company took over the flour mill around 1890 and it continues operations there today. ~ 327 East 200 North, Brigham City.

Brigham City's love for the nearby bird refuge is reflected by the **Welcome to Brigham City Arch** erected over Main Street in 1928 shortly after the refuge was designated. The original arch, which was replicated in 1984 with the archway now spanning the street, stood nine feet high and 33 feet wide. Foot-high letters spelled out "Welcome to" while 30-inch letters added "Brigham." Sprawled across the bottom of the original sign were the words, "Gateway to the World's Greatest Game Bird Sanctuary." Images of flying ducks topped the sign, which carried more than 350 lights to illuminate it at night. ~ Spanning Main Street between Forest Street and 100 South.

Most Utah communities in the late 1800s featured tithing offices, where LDS Church members would contribute one-tenth of their annual earnings to the church. In many cases the contributions were in the form of goods and produce if cash wasn't available. Brigham City's two-story **Tithing Office** dates to 1877. The basement contained storage rooms for dairy products and meat, while outside a rock wall, long-since removed, surrounded the building to corral livestock tithed to the church. These days the building contains rental apartments. ~ 66 South 100 West, Brigham City.

When Brigham Young visited Brigham City in the 1860s he selected "Sagebrush Hill," the highest spot on Main Street, as the site for the **Box Elder LDS Tabernacle**. Although construction began in 1868, the limestone and sandstone building wasn't completed until October 1890. A fire gutted the building six years later, but it was rebuilt and rededicated in 1897. The LDS Church closed the tabernacle, which was placed on the National Register of Historical Places in 1971, from 1986 to 1987 to restore it. Guided tours are available in the summer months. ~ 251 South Main Street, Brigham City; 435-723-5376.

Northern Utah and southern Idaho are the traditional lands of the Shoshone tribe, specifically the **Northwest Band of the Shoshone Nation**. Today you can get information on the tribe at its headquarters' office in Brigham City. In the not-so-distant future, though, the tribe hopes to move its headquarters to the American West Heritage Center near Logan. Closed weekends. ~ 862 South Main Street, Brigham City; 435-734-2286.

Although the **Brigham City Train Depot** is not open for rail business, Amtrak trains shoot by the historic building twice a day, and town officials hope someday a short-line railroad will chug between the depot and Promontory Summit. When it was opened by the Union Pacific Railroad in 1906, freight trains arrived with coal shipments from central Utah's coal mines while outgoing trains carried fresh and canned fruit and vegetables. In 1994 the railroad turned over the depot to Box Elder County, which immediately deeded it to the Golden Spike Association. A small railroad-related museum is open in the depot Monday, Tuesday, Thursday, Friday and Saturday from 1 p.m. to 5 p.m. Closed Wednesday and Sunday; shortened hours in winter. ~ 833 West Forest Street, Brigham City; 435-723-2989.

Fifteen miles west of town via Forest Street lies the **Bear River Migratory Bird Refuge**, which has been luring hundreds of feathered species for centuries to the marshlands created around the mouth of the Bear River. When explorer John C. Fremont came upon the area in 1843 he wrote that "the waterfowl made such a noise like thunder . . . as the whole scene was animated with waterfowl." Encompassing 74,000 acres, the watery refuge regularly lures more than 200 bird species, including tundra swans, white-faced ibis and Western grebe. White pelicans can be seen most of the year. ~ Bird Refuge Road, 15 miles west of Brigham City; 435-723-5887, fax 435-723-8873.

Fragments of America's aerospace history can be glimpsed at the **Thiokol Rocket Display**, just five miles north of the Golden Spike National Historic Site. Thiokol, which is headquartered in Ogden, bought 11,000 acres in northern Utah in 1956 with visions of a sprawling rocket plant. In 1958 the U.S. Air Force

ALL ALONG THE FRUITWAY

Northern Utah is known for its fresh fruits, so much so that the stretch of Route 89 between Willard and Brigham City is referred to as "the Fruitway." The highway winds through orchards that have long provided produce for northern Utah. During the harvest season roadside hawkers sell just-picked apples, peaches, pears, pumpkins, corn and other produce from their stands.

hired the company to build the first stage of their Minuteman intercontinental ballistic missile. Since that first project Thiokol has worked on "Poseidon" and "Trident" missiles for the Navy as well as the Air Force's "Peacekeeper" nuclear missile. The display, located on the west side of the plant, includes some of the solid rocket motors used by NASA. ~ Route 83, 26 miles west of Brigham City.

HIDDEN ►

One of the best known examples of "earthwork," a late-1960s art genre in which artists used the landscape as their palettes, can be found just beneath the surface of the Great Salt Lake not far from Promontory Point. The **Spiral Jetty** was created by Robert Smithson in 1970 using earth and black basalt to form a 1500-foot-long coil that runs counterclockwise out into Rozel Bay. Unfortunately, the Great Salt Lake was at a very low level when Smithson, who died in 1973, built the jetty. Since then the lake has risen and submerged the jetty, which usually is very difficult to find. However, summer 2002 saw the lake's level drop enough to expose the jetty. Stop at the visitors center at Golden Spike Historic Site for a detailed map to the jetty since the route crosses unmarked roads and private lands.

If you head 15 miles north of Brigham City on Route 38, you'll find that the area is more than just birds, trains and rockets. For centuries the region's hot springs were a source of rejuvenation for weary travelers. Long used by Shoshone and Bannock Indians who wintered in northern Utah, **Crystal Springs** has been soothing bathers' muscles commercially since 1901 when an Ogden entrepreneur opened the hot springs to the public. During World War II the operation flourished; bands even played in the evening. Today the resort offers hot tubs, an Olympic-sized pool, water slides and a lap pool. The adjoining campground offers 130 campsites with full hookups. Admission. ~ 8215 North Route 38, Honeyville; 435-279-8104.

sights

AUTHOR FAVORITE

East met West, as the saying goes, at Promontory Summit 32 miles west of Brigham City on May 10, 1869, when the locomotives from the Union Pacific and the Central Pacific railroads met head-on. Today at the **Golden Spike National Historic Site** visitors can learn about the laying of the rails that tied the country together and view vintage railroad films. Also on location are replicas of the "Jupiter" and the "119," the two trains involved. See "The Golden Spike" on page 126 for more information. ~ Route 83, 32 miles west of Brigham City; 435-471-2209, fax 435-471-2341; www.nps.gov/gosp.

Marble Park is an intriguing slice of Americana. Located   ◄ HIDDEN
about 25 miles north of Brigham City in Bothwell via Route 15,
the park was once a weed-choked gravel pit. From the wasteland
Boyd Marble has created sculptures from old wagon-wheel rims,
milk cans, tractor seats and whatever other scraps of farm equipment he could lay his hands on. While some of the exhibits reflect historic farm implements, other sculptures honor American
Indians, mountain men, cowboys and even the Mormon Temple
in Salt Lake City. Away from the sculptures, the park has room
for picnics and family reunions. ~ 11150 West 11200 North,
Bothwell; 435-854-3740.

Minutes away from Marble Park along Route 102 is the largest
private collection of horse-drawn wagons in the West. **Eli Ander-**   ◄ HIDDEN
son's Wagons range from handcarts and Conestoga wagons to
horse-drawn hearses and hook-and-ladder trucks. Showings are
by appointment only. ~ 8790 West Route 102, Bothwell; 435-
854-3760.

Lodging possibilities are few and modest in Brigham City, al-   **LODGING**
though with Ogden just 21 miles away you shouldn't have trouble finding a bed if the local options are sold out.

Located along Box Elder Creek, **Creekside Bed & Breakfast**
offers only two rooms, but they're a welcome change from typical chain-motel rooms. The Bunk House Room comes with a
queen-sized log bed, while the Romantic Cottage Room has a
queen-sized brass bed. Stay here and you'll get to enjoy a fire in
the sitting room or a relaxing dip in the hot tub outside. Both
rooms can be reserved to serve as a two-bedroom suite. Each
morning a hearty country breakfast is available. ~ 526 North
500 West, Brigham City; 435-723-3333. BUDGET TO DELUXE.

The most rooms in one place in Brigham City can be found
at the **Crystal Inn**, which offers 52 as well as a swimming pool
and a continental breakfast. The rooms are comfortable, a bit
larger than most motel units, with TVs, phones, microwaves and
small refrigerators. ~ 480 Westland Drive, Brigham City; 435-723-
0440, 800-408-0440; www.crystalinn.com. MODERATE.

If all you need is a warm, dry place to lay your head, then try
out the **Galaxie Motel**. There are 29 rooms here but no pool. ~
740 South Main Street, Brigham City; 435-723-3439, 800-577-
4315. BUDGET.

For "chain reliability," head to the **Howard Johnson Inn** in the
heart of town. Not only is the motel a half hour from Golden Spike
National Historic Site and 15 minutes from the Bear River Migratory Bird Refuge, there's an indoor pool and jacuzzi on site and
a golf course across the street. ~ 1167 South Main Street, Brigham
City; 435-723-8511, 800-446-4656. BUDGET TO MODERATE.

Text continued on page 128.

The Golden Spike

"We have got done praying. The spike is about to be presented."

That message raced across the nation's telegraph lines on May 10, 1869, just before the final, golden spike was used to bind together America's first transcontinental rail line at Promontory Summit, 32 miles west of Brigham City. The joining of the rails laid by the Central Pacific and Union Pacific railroads brought the "Jupiter" and the "119," the respective railroads' locomotives, nose to nose and kicked off a heady celebration. Although a golden spike, engraved with the names of the CP's directors and the notation, "the last spike," on its head, was briefly dropped into a hole bored into a finely polished tie hewn from California laurel to symbolize the joining of the rails, an ordinary iron spike was driven into the tie with powerful strokes that reverberated across the country via the telegraph wires attached to it.

With the line complete, emigrants would no longer need to follow dusty wagon trails that meandered across the Western landscape to reach the fabled lands of California and Oregon. Trains had conquered the prairie and would turn what had been months'-long treks into comparatively short journeys.

Today you can stand at Golden Spike National Historic Site on the rolling ground near Promontory and gaze across a landscape that has hardly changed since the rails were joined. While ramshackle collections of saloons, hotels and bordellos sprang up along the line east and west of Promontory as the rail workers brought the two lines towards each other, they just as quickly evaporated after the lines were joined and the workers moved on. Not even the "Jupiter" and "119" enjoyed their fleeting fame; the "Jupiter" was scrapped for its iron in 1901, and the "119" met a similar fate in 1903.

Sadly, trains don't clickity-clack past the summit anymore. In 1904 the 123-mile-long Promontory Branch was lost to obscurity when the Lucin Cutoff, a 12-mile-long route built on trestles across the Great Salt Lake, diverted train traffic away from Promontory. In 1942 most of the iron rails were removed from the area to help fuel America's efforts in

World War II. As for the golden "last spike," it resides at Stanford University, California.

For a hint of the excitement that spread out from Promontory Summit on May 10, 1869, try to visit the historic site on May 10 to take in a re-enactment of the joining of the rails. The first re-enactment of the driving of the last spike was held in 1948, and in 1957 the 2735-acre historic site was created by Congress.

Start your visit by checking the activities board in the visitors center to see if any talks are scheduled. During summer months, living-history presentations are often on tap. Also, the "Jupiter" and "No. 199" replicas come out several times a day between mid-April and mid-October to blow their stacks while chugging back and forth on nearly two miles of track that were relaid in the 1960s by the National Park Service. Youngsters between 8 and 12 should sign up for the Junior Engineer Program, which uses a workbook to help them learn more about America's rail history.

A self-guided tour leads you by foot along the "Big Fill Walk," which covers a mile and a half of the original Central Pacific and Union Pacific grade, while the "Promontory Trail" is a nine-mile-long auto tour that retraces part of the historic railroad grade.

More ambitious visitors strike out along the Transcontinental Railroad National Back Country Byway, a 90-mile route that follows the original railroad grade. There are no services along the route, so be sure to fill up your gas tank, pack water, and see that your spare tire is inflated (old spikes occasionally surface on the route and puncture tires).

The visitors center is open daily, offering a glimpse of the past through slide shows, films and exhibits. While the annual Railroader's Festival is held the second Saturday in August, during the last week in December the locomotives chug out into the cold winter air for steam demon-strations. Visitors can also tour the engine house. Admission. ~ From Brigham City, drive 32 miles west on Route 83 to reach Golden Spike Historic Site, P.O. Box 897, Brigham City, UT 84302; 435-471-2209; www.nps.gov/gosp.

DINING

Hearty and plentiful menus are the hallmark in the Brigham City area, and considering the agricultural heritage of the area, that should come as no surprise.

HIDDEN ►

Just eight miles south of Brigham City lies Perry and the **Maddox Ranch House**, one of the best steak houses in all of Utah. The restaurant dates to World War II, when Irv Maddox opened a seven-stool counter café on Main Street in Brigham City. In 1949 Maddox and his wife Wilma bought a small piece of property in Perry, which at the time was in the middle of nowhere. The Maddoxes realized the remoteness of the location at the time and therefore built a small log restaurant that was mounted on skids—easily moved if business dictated. Today the restaurant remains in the exact location and continues to feature family-style dinners. You don't even need to leave your car for a meal as the restaurant features a drive-in section where servers come to your car to take your order of burgers, sandwiches, hot dogs, fries and the like. Closed Sunday and Monday. ~ 1900 South Route 89, Perry; 435-723-8545, 800-544-5474. BUDGET TO MODERATE.

HIDDEN ►

Since 1937 locals have headed to **Peach City Ice Cream** for sweet desserts as well as hamburgers, sandwiches and one of the 30 flavors of milkshakes (including peach, of course). Good luck downing the Walt Mann Special, a confectionary delight that swells with six scoops of ice cream and your choice of toppings. ~ 306 North Main Street, Brigham City; 435-723-3923. BUDGET.

Lunch and dinner at **Ricardo's Restaurant**, which is housed in a rustic-style café that blends Mexico with the American West, revolve around Mexican dishes like enchiladas, tostadas, burritos, *rellenos* and tacos. Closed Sunday and Monday. ~ 131 South Main Street, Brigham City; 435-723-1811. BUDGET.

Surrounded by a festive atmosphere of dangling piñatas, pottery and bright pastel colors, regular diners at **Melina's Mexican Restaurant** have made favorites out of the fish tacos and beef, chicken and shrimp fajitas. Closed Sunday. ~ 40 West 700 South, Brigham City; 435-723-6000. BUDGET.

HIDDEN ►

Located in the heart of downtown, **The Idle Isle Café** has been feeding souls since May 1, 1921, when P. C. Knudson and his wife Verabel opened an ice cream and candy store. With its classic marble soda fountain counter and wooden booth tables, the café has weathered good times and bad with consistent, reliable service, a home-style menu and prices that have developed a strong local following. The name was the result of a local contest. Closed Sunday. ~ 24 South Main Street, Brigham City, 435-734-2468. BUDGET.

Another Main Street stalwart is **Bert's Café**, which opened for business a decade after the Idle Isle. Not a place to watch your cholesterol, this eatery is known for its meaty breakfasts, ranging from bone-in ham and chicken-fried steaks to omelettes—all of which come with eggs and homemade hash browns. While the sign says the café doesn't open until 6 a.m., caffeine fiends can get a mug of joe by 5:30 a.m. ~ 89 South Main Street, Brigham City; 435-734-9544. BUDGET.

SHOPPING

Shopping options are meager in Brigham City. Main Street stays busy with office-supply stores, copy centers, insurance offices, real-estate office and not much more. As a result, most locals drive to Ogden for serious shopping binges.

There are, however, souvenirs and curios to be found at the **Brigham City Train Depot**. ~ 833 West Forest Street, Brigham City; 435-723-2989.

NIGHTLIFE

Aside from the movie theater on Main Street and the playhouse south of town, there's not a heckuva lot to do in Brigham City when the sun sets. The **Capitol Theatre** has two screens. It's open Monday through Friday at 6:30 p.m., and Saturday at noon with matinees. Closed Sunday. ~ 53 South Main Street, Brigham City; 435-723-3113.

For a cold beer mixed with some local color, head to **B&B Billiards**, a half-block south of Main Street on Forest Street. Just be forewarned that the atmosphere can be smoky and the jukebox loud. ~ 21 West Forest Street, Brigham City; 435-734-1682.

At the **Heritage Theater** near Perry, local troupes offer some touch-notch productions, with actors coming from Utah State University's theatrical department as well as surrounding communities. Performances are on Friday, Saturday and Monday. ~ 2505 South Route 89, Perry; 435-723-8392.

PARKS

WILLARD BAY STATE PARK A 9900-acre freshwater lake separated from the Great Salt Lake by dikes, Willard Bay offers year-round fishing for walleye, crappie, wiper and catfish, as well as a playground for waterskiers. The state park is divided into a north and a south marina. The north marina has restrooms, showers, boat slips and rentals, and sandy beaches. The south marina features restrooms, showers and boat

BOBBING FOR LOBSTERS

Live lobsters in Utah? You'll find them at **Belmont Hot Springs**, 31 miles north of Brigham City. The crustaceans are raised along with tropical fish in the 95° water churned out by Belmont Hot Springs. If you're not in the mood for lobster, you can still swim, golf and even scuba dive at the resort. No swimming mid-October to April. ~ 19200 North 5600 West, Plymouth; 435-458-3200.

ramps. Day-use fee, $6. ~ 900 West 650 North #A, take Route 15 to Exit 354 for the south marina or 15 miles north to Exit 360 for the north marina; 435-734-9494; parks.state.ut.us/parks/www1/will.htm.

▲ The north marina has 62 tent sites and 101 RV sites; $14 to $20 per night; 14-day maximum stay; open year-round. The south marina has 12 tent sites and 30 RV sites; $14 per night; 14-day maximum stay; open April through October. Reservations: 800-322-3770.

WASATCH-CACHE NATIONAL FOREST The Logan District of the 1.2-million-acre Wasatch-Cache National Forest lies less than five miles east of Brigham City, providing a quick getaway for outdoors lovers. A dozen miles northeast of the city lies the **Wellsville Mountains Wilderness Area,** which covers 23,750 acres of incredibly rugged land. The western edge of the wilderness area is shored up by Wellsville Mountain, which, due to its narrow base and 5000-foot rise from the valley floor, is considered the steepest mountain in the country. Once heavily logged, the wilderness area is returning to what it was when 19th-century trappers made their way through the Rocky Mountain West—dense forests cut by streams and broken by wildflower-dappled meadows and small alpine lakes. Moose, mountain lion and occasionally bighorn sheep can be seen here. ~ From Brigham City, Routes 38 and 89/91 offer quick access to the wilderness area; Logan Ranger District, 1500 East Route 89, Logan; 435-755-3620; www.fs.fed.us/wcnf.

▲ Within this section of the forest are 234 sites in 16 developed campgrounds; $6 to $12 per night; seven-day maximum stay. Reservations: 877-444-6777; www.reserveusa.com.

SAWTOOTH NATIONAL FOREST A tiny slice of the 2.1-million-acre, Idaho-based Sawtooth National Forest extends into Utah just to the northwest of the Great Salt Lake and about 90 miles west of Brigham City. Known as the **Raft River Division,** the forest's peaks rise to 9600 feet and, on clear

---

TAKEN FOR A RIDE

Capitalists built this country, and proof can be found in the annals of the transcontinental railroad. While the Central Pacific and Union Pacific railroads were hired by Congress to build the line, they took some liberties with the contract, which paid them according to the amount of rail they laid. With hopes of squeezing a few extra dollars out of the federal government, the two railroads actually laid two parallel grades alongside each other for more than 200 miles.

days, offer sprawling views of the Great Salt Lake to the south, the Snake River Plain and the Sawtooth Mountains to the north, and Nevada to the west. Much of this section of forest is sparsely wooded, although there are some heavy stands of piñon and juniper. ~ From Brigham City, take Route 84 49 miles north to Snowville, then follow Route 30 west 41 miles to the forest. The Raft River Division is managed by the Minidoka Ranger District of the Sawtooth National Forest, 3650 South Overland Avenue, Burley, ID 83318; 208-678-0430; www.fs.fed.us/r4/sawtooth.

▲ This division has one campground with 14 sites; no fee; 14-day maximum stay. Closed November through May.

BEAR RIVER MIGRATORY BIRD REFUGE 🚲 ⤸ Dating to 1928, this bird sanctuary was nearly wiped out in 1983 when heavy snows and rainfall raised the level of the Great Salt Lake and inundated the freshwater marshlands near the mouth of the Bear River. The lake's encroaching saline waters killed many of the refuge's trees and pond vegetation that waterfowl had relied upon and destroyed all of the refuge buildings. Although the refuge had attracted as many as 60,000 tundra swans to its waters prior to the flood, after the flood those numbers dropped to 259 in 1984 and just three the following year. By 1989 the lake's level receded to the point where the refuge's dikes could be rebuilt. As the lake's level dropped the marshlands regained their health. Today they once again attract millions of birds during the spring and fall migrations, including tundra swans, white pelicans, great blue herons, black-crowned night herons, snowy egrets and black-necked stilts. If you're in the area in late spring or early summer, check on the dates for the annual Bear River Bird Festival, which offers tours of normally closed sections of the refuge as well as photography and sketching workshops. Year-round, visitors can take a 12-mile auto tour along the dikes that wind through the marshes. ~ From Brigham City, head west 15 miles on the Bear River Refuge Road; 435-723-5887, fax 435-723-8873; www.mountain-prairie.fws.gov/bearriver.

Logan Area

Twenty-five miles northeast of Brigham City via Route 89/91 lie Logan and the Cache Valley, two of Utah's most picturesque and charming valleys thanks to the mountain ranges that wrap it to the east and west and the bucolic lifestyle that still dominates more than 150 years after the valley was settled. Before white settlers reached the valley in the mid-1800s the region was home to several American Indians tribes—Bannock, Blackfoot and Shoshone. One Shoshone tribe established its village along the Logan River, which the Indians referred to as *Kwagunogwai*, or "river of the cranes," a reference to the plentiful sandhill cranes found here.

Early in the 19th century mountain men such as Jim Bridger and Jedediah Smith traversed the length of Logan Canyon in search of beaver, trapping their way to the Great Salt Lake where they wondered whether they had reached the Pacific Ocean. And it was a trapper, Ephraim Logan, whose name stuck on the town that was founded in 1859. Settlers dispatched to the region by the LDS Church arrived at the 15-mile-wide-by-60-mile-long valley in 1855 and soon appreciated the rich soils and long growing season that would turn the Cache Valley into Utah's fruit basket. Along with Logan, the communities of Wellsville, Providence, Mendon, Smithfield and Richmond were founded by these settlers. The valley's agricultural heritage made it the logical site for Utah State University, which in 1888 was established in Logan as Utah's land-grant university. While agriculture remains king in the Logan area, the university has diversified its curriculum, offering classes from agriculture to space technology for its 20,000 students.

Although it lies 40 miles northeast of Logan, Bear Lake has long been linked to the Cache Valley, harkening back at least to the gregarious lakeside rendezvous staged in the late 1820s by the Rocky Mountain Fur Company for trappers and Indians alike. These gatherings offered the trappers a time to come down out of the mountains, renew old acquaintances, swap goods and, frankly, wash away months of solitude with whiskey and carrying on.

Modern-day explorers continue to head to Bear Lake, northern Utah's premier watery vacation spot, where they can camp on the shores and boat on the lake. In August, the Raspberry Festival draws thousands to the lake and surrounding raspberry patches. The ride from Logan to the lake runs through spectacular Logan Canyon, where the canyon's mile-high variegated limestone walls are covered with lush vegetation and hold trailheads ready to lead you high into the backcountry.

SIGHTS   After leaving Brigham City, but before you get to Logan, is the turnoff to Route 101 and the **Hardware Ranch**, which has been around since 1945 when it was established to provide critical winter habitat for wildlife and to serve as a feeding ground for elk. Each winter the ranch is home to roughly 600 elk. Wagon rides are popular during the summer months; in winter, when weather allows, sleighs pulled by Clydesdales haul visitors through the refuge for an up-close look at the elk. On winter weekends you can sign on for both a sleigh ride and an all-you-can-eat chicken or rib barbecue dinner at the ranch headquarters. During the spring, summer and fall you can fish the 15 miles of streams that run through the ranch's 14,000 acres if you have the requisite license. ~ Located 25 miles southeast of Logan and 18 miles east of Hyrum at the head of Blacksmith Fork Canyon on Route

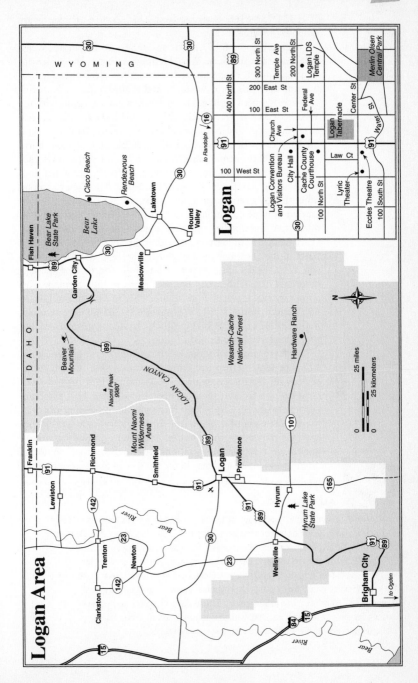

Logan

WYOMING

Merlin Olsen Central Park

300 North St
Temple Ave
200 North St
Logan LDS Temple

400 North St
89
200 East St
100 East St
Federal Ave

Church Ave
Logan Tabernacle

91
City Hall
Law Ct

100 West St
Logan Convention and Visitors Bureau
Cache County Courthouse
100 North St

Lyric Theater
Eccles Theatre
100 South St

30

Center St
Water St
91

Logan Area

IDAHO

to Randolph

Cisco Beach
Rendezvous Beach
Laketown

Fish Haven
Bear Lake State Park
Bear Lake
Round Valley

Garden City
Meadowville

30
89
16

N

Hardware Ranch

Wasatch-Cache National Forest

Beaver Mountain
89

Naomi Peak 9980'
LOGAN CANYON

Mount Naomi Wilderness Area
89

25 miles
25 kilometers
0
0

Franklin
91
Richmond
Smithfield
Logan
Providence
165

101

Lewiston
142
91
Hyrum
91
89
Hyrum Lake State Park

Bear River
23
30
Wellsville

Clarkston
Trenton
Newton
142
23

Brigham City
91
89

to Ogden

84
15

Bear River

15

101; 435-753-6168; www.hardwareranch.com, e-mail hardware
ranch@sisna.com.

Back on Route 89/91 north on the way to Logan lies Wellsville and the **American West Heritage Center**. The American
West has long been glamorized and continues to be heralded for
its wide open spaces, frontier life and rugged mountains. At this
160-acre Western heritage center you can come to grips with the
West between the years 1820–1920. A small pioneer village, with
two "dugouts" and two log cabins, is in place, as is a general
mercantile, an opera house, a livery stable and an oxen barn.
Late in 2002 the center launched an ambitious "Dream Catcher
Campaign" that is intended to fund a 15-to-20-year expansion.
Through the campaign, the heritage center would gain, among
other things, a replica fur-trading fort, an Indian village, a military encampment, a pioneer settlement, a frontier town, and an
interactive multimedia center. The expansion would also provide
space for the headquarters and cultural center of the Northwest
Band of the Shoshone nation. During the Festival of the American West, held each summer in late July and early August, a
mountain man rendezvous site, an American Indian village, and
a military encampment come to life. ~ Six miles south of Logan,
4025 South Route 89/91, Wellsville; 435-245-6050, box office
800-225-3378, fax 435-245-6052; www.americanwestcenter.
org, e-mail awhc@cc.usu.edu.

Under the auspices of the American West Heritage Center, the
127-acre **Jensen Historical Farm** captures a slice of early-20th-
century life. At the living-history museum the long days of 1917
farm life are recounted throughout the summer by Utah State
University students, from barn raising to sheep shearing and even
the re-enactment of a turn-of-the-20th-century wedding. Visitors
can take part in churning butter, gathering eggs and harvesting
apples, or watch demonstrations on candlemaking, spinning,
quilting and blacksmithing. In the fall a corn maze is open to the

sights

AUTHOR FAVORITE

Forty miles northeast of Logan on Route 89 lies **Bear Lake**, a
112-square-mile body of water that straddles the Utah–Idaho border. Donald
Mackenzie, an explorer for the North West Fur Company, discovered the
lake in 1819 and named it Black Bear Lake, although years later the "black"
was dropped. The popular **Rendezvous Beach**, part of Bear Lake State
Park, carries its name from the gatherings fur trappers and Indians held
there in 1827 and 1828 to trade goods. These days sailboats and power-
boats play on the water's surface, while swimmers splash along its
beaches and scuba divers explore the eastern shoreline.

public, while sleigh rides are offered around Christmas time. Closed Sunday. Admission. ~ 4025 South Route 89, Wellsville; 435-245-6050 or 435-245-4064.

From Wellsville, **Logan** is just six miles to the north in the sprawling Cache Valley, which is nestled between the Wellsville Mountains to the west and the Bear River Range to the east. A college town, Logan has much more going on than Brigham City, yet it retains much of its charm as a pastoral community.

If you're traveling with children, or just love animals, stop by Logan's **Willow Park Zoo**, where you'll see monkeys and eagles, coyotes, kangaroos and more. While you set up your picnic the youngsters can feed the ducks and geese. ~ 419 West 700 South, Logan; 435-750-9893.

Logan still has that small-town feel, thanks to preservation efforts that have kept many of the town's old buildings in shape. The **Dansante Building**, which holds the administrative offices and box office of the Utah Festival Opera Company, has long ties to entertainment. Built in 1900, the building early on housed a roller skating rink. It was later converted into a dancehall that stayed in business for nearly 30 years, drawing upwards of 3000 revelers on major holidays. Although two clothing companies occupied the building for a time, in the mid-1990s the opera company bought the building, restored it and expanded it for the festival. Today it harbors a 124-seat recital hall, rehearsal halls and prop, costume and scenery shops. ~ 59 South 100 West, Logan; 435-750-0300.

Theatrical renovations are a habit in Logan. The **Capitol Theater**, Logan's fourth opera house when it opened for business in 1923, arose on the spot where the Thatcher Opera House had stood until it burned down on April 17, 1912. The Capitol Theater dominated the Cache Valley's performing-arts circle for 30 years before performances were halted in the 1950s and the theater fell into disrepair. But a multimillion-dollar restoration project allowed the neoclassical-style theater to reopen in 1993 as the **Ellen Eccles Theater**. Inside you'll find not only a state-of-the-art theatrical system, but plush red seats, a grand foyer, sweeping balconies and impeccable acoustics that serve touring Broadway productions, musicals, ballet and symphonies. ~ 43 South Main Street, Logan; 435-752-0026 or 435-753-6518.

The **Bluebird Restaurant** is one of the oldest and busiest historical sites in Logan. Operating as a restaurant since 1914, the Bluebird boasts a marble soda fountain where you can still get an ice cream float. Head to the rear of the restaurant and you'll find a mural painted in the 1960s that not only depicts Cache Valley's past, but also guesses how it might appear in the future, with spacecraft buzzing about Logan. ~ 19 North Main Street, Logan; 435-752-3155.

Another Logan theater has been restored to its original elegance—the 1913 **Caine Lyric Theater**, now the home of the Old Lyric Repertory Theater and, thespians swear, to a ghost clothed in Elizabethan garb topped by a fool's hat. Charm exudes from this Victorian-style proscenium-arch playhouse that can seat 388. During the summer months a mix of professional and aspiring actors join forces to stage comedies, musicals and dramas. ~ 28 West Center Street, Logan; 435-797-1500.

Actors don't tromp the stage at the **Utah Theater**, which instead focuses on celluloid presentations. Still, the old art-deco appearance of this movie theater warrants a peek if you're into unique architecture. Of course, you also can catch a movie here. ~ 18 West Center Street, Logan; 435-752-3072.

If genealogy sparks your interest, be sure to stop at the **Logan Tabernacle** before leaving town. Opened in 1891 after 25 years of volunteer laboring, the tabernacle is recognized as home to the second largest genealogy library in Utah, just behind the Family History Museum in Salt Lake City. The librarians claim that if you can give them an hour, they'll locate the records of one of your ancestors. In the 1870s and 1880s the local women's Relief Society used the tabernacle to make hats, baskets, brooms and sewing projects. Tours are scheduled throughout the summer. The tabernacle also is the backdrop for free entertainment during the summer, when pianists, violinists, cellists, singers and flutists perform. ~ 50 North Main Street, Logan; 435-755-5594.

One of Logan's earliest federal buildings, the **Hall of Justice** is now home to the **Logan Convention and Visitors Bureau** as well as the Cache Valley Tourist Council offices. These offices can answer questions about the Cache Valley and load you up with brochures, maps and ideas. Also available is a pamphlet that lays out a 45-minute walking tour of historic Main Street. ~ 160 North Main Street, Logan; 435-752-2161, 800-882-4433, fax 435-753-5825; www.tourcachevalley.com, e-mail tourism@tour cachevalley.com.

The **Daughters of Utah Pioneers** have squeezed their museum into what used to be the building's courtroom. Inside are displays of the days of the mountain men as well as early pioneer artifacts. Perhaps the most unusual display is that of an intricate "hair wreath" 18-year-old Elizabeth Cook Dalton wove in 1878 with strands of hair from her parents, relatives, and her own head. Open Monday afternoon and Tuesday through Friday from June through September; by appointment the rest of the year. ~ 160 North Main Street, Logan; 435-752-5139 (summer), 435-753-1635.

Kitty-corner from the Convention and Visitors Bureau is the **Cache County Courthouse**, which was built in 1883 and continues to house county offices, giving it the distinction of being the oldest county building in the state still used for its original purpose. ~ 179 North Main Street, Logan.

Ensconced on a terrace left behind by prehistoric Lake Bonneville, the **Logan LDS Temple** looks out across the Cache Valley. Built during a seven-year-period between 1877 and 1884, the limestone temple is an example of modified Gothic architecture. Only LDS Church members can enter the building, but the architecture and the view are worth a visit. ~ 200 North 200 East, Logan; 435-752-3611.

Logan is home to Utah's land-grant college, **Utah State University**. Huddled on the northeastern edge of town, the university sits atop a hill overlooking Logan. Founded in 1888, the university boasts eight colleges and roughly 20,000 students. Although its roots are in agriculture, the school has a rich array of degree programs, ranging from agronomy to rocketry. ~ Utah State University, Logan; 435-797-1000; www.usu.edu.

One of northern Utah's best art museums is the **Nora Eccles Harrison Museum of Art** on the university campus. Inside the museum is a rich collection from throughout the Intermountain region. You'll find not only Western pieces but also international works, American Indian artworks, and regional crafts. Closed weekends. ~ 650 North 1100 East, Logan; 435-797-0163.

As one of the largest cheese-producing regions of the country, the Cache Valley has more than its share of dairy product outlets. Much of the valley's cheese finds its way onto the hamburgers churned out by Burger King and McDonald's. Beyond cheese, Utah State University played a role in pioneering the production of ice cream. You can sample the product—**Aggie Ice Cream**—at the university's Nutrition and Food Science Building. Closed Sunday. ~ 750 North 1200 East, Logan; 435-797-2109.

Despite the rolling agricultural land and forests that surround Utah State University, not all the work done there revolves around agriculture. The university's **Space Dynamics Laboratory** has played a research and development role in the U.S. space program since the early 1960s and currently is recognized as a leader in

MOUNTAIN MEN MEETINGS

Northern Utah was a popular place for rendezvous in the early 1800s. In 1826 the mountain men gathered near the mouth of Blacksmith's Fork Canyon, near Hyrum. In 1827 and again in 1828 the gathering was moved to the south end of Bear Lake. After two years in Wyoming, the annual rendezvous was moved back to the Cache Valley in 1831. Late each May, the Cache Valley Renaissance Rendezvous is held near Hyrum and recalls the heady days of trappers.

space instrumentation and research. As a result, the university has placed more experiments on space shuttles than any other university. To learn about the lab's involvement in U.S. exploration of Mars, call ahead to arrange a tour of the facility. ~ 1695 North Research Park Way, Logan; 435-797-4600.

Although the 2002 Salt Lake Olympic Winter Games didn't feature any events in Logan, the **Eccles Ice Center** built in 2001 gained the attention of Olympic teams from Russia, France, China, Slovakia and Switzerland, which practiced there before heading to Salt Lake. You can try to imitate their moves during public skating hours. Admission. ~ 2825 North 200 East, Logan; 435-787-2288; www.ecclesice.com.

Formed by an earthquake 28,000 years ago, Bear Lake has a unique aquamarine color created by the sunlight refracting off limestone particles suspended in the water.

For a good primer on the area's geology and human history before heading into the mountains east of Logan, stop at the **Logan Ranger District Office** of the Wasatch-Cache National Forest. Not only can you find maps and guidebooks here, but outside at the Lady Bird Overlook there's an exhibit that outlines the geological processes that affected the Cache Valley. Other panels touch on the Shoshone Indians and mountain men. ~ 1500 East Route 89, Logan; 435-755-3620.

A short 1.3-mile hike away from Route 89 leads you to **Wind Caves**, which some know as Witch's Castle. A small cave and three arches have been gnawed into the limestone outcropping by wind, rain and time. From the cave site you have a good view of the **China Wall**, a band of limestone threaded through Logan Canyon. ~ Located 5.2 miles up Logan Canyon.

It's not often that animals get historical markers, but when you're reputed to be the biggest grizzly ever killed in the continental United States, well, you deserve more than just a hole in the ground. Be forewarned, however: it's a five-and-a-half-mile hike to **Old Ephraim's Grave**. For the curious, Old Ephraim was named after a grizzly in California that was regaled in a story by P.T. Barnum. "Eph," as he was often called, roamed the mountains east of Logan. He stood nine feet, eleven inches tall and was killed by sheep rancher Frank Clark on August 22, 1923, with six shots from Clark's .25-35 caliber rifle. While Eph was buried after being skinned, local Boy Scouts later dug up the grizzly's skull and shipped it to the Smithsonian Institute, where it was displayed for a while. The massive skull was returned to Utah in 1978 and is on display at Utah State University's Merrill Library. ~ The trailhead is 9.2 miles up Logan Canyon at the end of Right Hand Fork Road.

Not far from the trail to Old Ephraim's resting place is the **Jardine Juniper**, which, at an estimated 1500 years old, is believed by some to be the world's oldest juniper tree. A four-and-a-half-mile hike takes you to the old gnarled tree, which is sadly slipping away, a victim of age and disease. ~ The trailhead is found at the Wood Camp turnoff a dozen miles up Route 89 from Logan.

"Tourists" have been visiting **Bear Lake** for hundreds of years, and with good reason. In this arid region the sparkling waters are a welcome sight. The lake bed was sculpted 28,000 years ago by earthquakes, and the unusual aqua-blue color of the waters is the result of calcium carbonates (limestone particles) suspended in the water. The lake was first called Black Bear Lake by trapper Donald MacKenzie, who came upon it in 1819 while scouting the region for beavers for the North West Fur Company. The lake's popular **Rendezvous Beach** was named for the rendezvous of trappers and Indians held there during the summers of 1827 and 1828. **Cisco Beach** is popular for the seven-inch-long Bonneville cisco, a member of the white fish family, that swim to shore to spawn in mid-winter. Anglers easily scoop these fish up in nets. ~ Route 89, Garden City.

A stone's throw from the western shore of Bear Lake, **Garden City** is a small outpost along Route 89 that dates to 1864. One of the lake's more fertile spots, the town of less than 300 is home to several raspberry farms, motels and Bear Lake State Park and marina. Each August the town is overrun by berry lovers in town for the annual Bear Lake Raspberry Days Festival.

LODGING

Between Logan and Bear Lake, there are quite a few lodging possibilities. Look hard enough and you can find bed-and-breakfast operations in wonderfully historic homes, or you can settle for a shoreside resort setting at Bear Lake. Naturally, you'll also find a range of roadside chain motels.

◄ HIDDEN

Two miles south of Logan, the **Providence Inn Bed & Breakfast** was initially built by settlers in the mid-1800s as a meeting house. Within its historic walls you'll find a sweeping staircase, vaulted ceilings and Palladian windows. The 17 rooms (15 in the main building, two in an adjacent Arts and Crafts bungalow) are decorated in either Early American, Georgian or Victorian style. While the parlor sports a roaring fireplace, each room has a private bath and TV. ~ 10 South Main, Providence; 435-752-3432, 800-480-4943; www.providenceinn.com, e-mail provinn@providenceinn.com. MODERATE TO ULTRA-DELUXE.

The **Baugh Mansion** dates to 1899, when the Victorian home was built for an English family that had moved to Logan in the late 1800s. The best of the three guest rooms is the Master Bedroom, which comes with a four-poster queen-sized bed and a gas fireplace. Local musicians occasionally stop by to jam in the living room, where you'll find a baby grand piano. A full English breakfast is included. ~ 164 West 100 North, Logan; 435-750-5860; www.baughmansion.com. MODERATE TO ULTRA-DELUXE.

Among Logan's stately Victorian homes is the **Logan House Inn,** a historic mansion that boasts its own ballroom and fine Arts and Craft workmanship, such as the stained-glass window over the grand staircase. A private residence for many years, today the turn-of-the-20th-century Greek Revival/Georgian Manor home serves as a bed and breakfast. Most of the six guest rooms feature fireplaces as well as jetted tubs. A favorite is The Library, which holds more than 500 books in its cherrywood cabinets. Breakfasts range from pancakes or french toast stuffed with almond cream filling and almond raspberry sauce to simple continental fare. ~ 168 North 100 East, Logan; 435-752-7727, 800-478-7459, fax 435-752-0092; www.loganhouseinn.com, e-mail loganinn@loganhouseinn.com. MODERATE TO ULTRA-DELUXE.

The view alone is worth a stay at the **Bear Lake Garden Gate Inn.** But step inside anyway after gazing at Bear Lake shimmering below; this modern Victorian-influenced lodging provides 15 comfortable rooms, each with its own jetted bathtub, phone, TV and queen- or king-sized bed. A dozen of the rooms also feature gas fireplaces, so be sure to ask for one of those when making a reservation. Outside, in addition to the lake, you'll find a hot tub and lap pool. Continental breakfast included. ~ 26 North Christa Circle (a half mile west of the Garden City Junction on Route 89), Garden City; 435-946-8300; www.bearlakegardengateinn.com, e-mail info@gardengateinn.com. MODERATE TO DELUXE

At the **Bear Lake Motor Lodge** your pets can join you on vacation. Half of the 20 rooms have kitchenettes, although there is a restaurant on the grounds if you don't want to bother with cooking. The lodge also comes with a beachfront perfect for after-dinner strolls or a mid-day swim. ~ 50 South Bear Lake Boulevard, Garden City; 435-946-3271. BUDGET TO MODERATE.

There are 14 beachfront cabins and eight condo units at the **Blue Water Beach Resort** down the street. Although the cabins are on the rustic side, you'd be hard-pressed to beat the location. The resort also has an RV park, pitch-and-putt golf, an outdoor

AUTHOR FAVORITE

History and comfort cross paths at the **Providence Inn Bed & Breakfast,** which is part of the "Old Rock Church" built between 1869 and 1871. Stones for the original building were carved from a nearby quarry. In 1926 a much larger wing was added to the church and it evolved into the bed and breakfast; the entire building is listed on the National Register of Historic Places. Room 307 is my favorite: Located in the attic above the church, the room features exposed support timbers, a four-poster canopy bed, and a free-standing tub. See page 139 for more information.

swimming pool and a hot tub. ~ 2126 South Bear Lake Boulevard, Garden City; 435-946-3333, 800-756-0795. MODERATE TO DELUXE.

Not only is the **Canyon Cove Inn** a short walk from the lake shore, it's surrounded by some of the raspberry patches that provide the crucial ingredients for the raspberry shakes that are famous in Garden City. This two-story motel offers five varieties of rooms, ranging from budget-oriented one-bedroom units to suites with a private bedroom and a living area with a couch, refrigerator and microwave. If it's too cold for a swim in the lake, the motel has an indoor pool. ~ 315 West Logan Highway, Garden City; 435-946-3565, 877-232-7525; www.canyoncove.com, e-mail info@canyoncove.com. MODERATE TO DELUXE.

Overlooking Bear Lake from a spot just north of Garden City, the **Harbor Village Resort** offers one of the most complete lodging packages at the lake. The 40 modest but comfortable rooms are supported by an on-site restaurant, exercise facilities, a spa, laundry facilities and an indoor/outdoor pool. ~ 900 North Bear Lake Boulevard, Garden City; 435-946-3448. MODERATE TO ULTRA-DELUXE.

Logan hardly bursts with culinary treasures, but there are a few.

DINING

Pier Antonio Micheli had a sure hit when he decided to open **Le Nonne** in Logan. Pier, who hails from Tuscany, borrowed many of the recipes his grandmother used in Italy for the family's restaurants there. Enter his café-style eatery and you'll find hearty northern Italian flavors in the homemade pastas such as spinach-and-ricotta ravioli or chicken ravioli and seafood dishes such as salmon with lemon capers or charbroiled swordfish topped with fresh diced tomatoes, garlic and basil. This easily is my favorite Italian restaurant in northern Utah. No lunch on Saturday. Closed Sunday. ~ 132 North Main Street, Logan; 435-752-9577. BUDGET TO MODERATE.

If you want to eat where the locals do, head to the **Copper Mill Restaurant**, where meals come with fresh-baked rolls and homemade raspberry jam. You'll find prime beef on the dinner menu. Closed Sunday. ~ 55 North Main Street, Logan; 435-752-0647. BUDGET TO MODERATE.

For that old-time, soda fountain feeling, try the **Bluebird Restaurant**, a landmark since 1914. You can still sit at the marble soda fountain bar and gorge yourself on a banana split. Dinners run the gamut, from prime rib and steak to the restaurant's signature "Bluebird Chicken," which has an Asian flavor. ~ 19 North Main Street, Logan; 435-752-3155. BUDGET TO MODERATE.

Take a stroll down Federal Avenue to **Caffé Ibis**, perhaps the most popular coffee shop in Logan. Barely more than a niche in a storefront, the café's dozen or so tables serve a steady line of customers. Along with freshly ground espressos, cappuccinos, lattes and straight coffee, you'll find a pleasing array of teas, fruit smoothies, deli items, baked goods, quiches and creative sandwiches. ~ 52 Federal Avenue, Logan; 435-753-4777. BUDGET.

Modern-day ice cream production was pioneered at Utah State University, and you can sample the results at **Aggie's Ice Cream Shop**, where some of the best ice cream in northern Utah is scooped out. The ice cream is made at the university's Dairy Science Building and delivered right to Aggie's. ~ 750 North 1200 East, Logan; 435-797-2109. BUDGET.

Italian dishes, steaks and chicken dominate the menu at **Gia's Restaurant**. Utah State University students head to meet friends in the basement pizzeria, while the upstairs dining room offers more formal table service. ~ 119 South Main Street, Logan; 435-752-8384. BUDGET TO MODERATE.

You want a steak, Western decor, and some live entertainment? **Cabin Fever** has local musicians Wednesday through Saturday and the food is dependably good. ~ 180 West 1200 South, Logan; 435-753-2667. BUDGET.

For a sit-down meal with a romantic view, the **Harbor Village Restaurant** overlooks the lake. ~ 785 North Bear Lake Boulevard, Garden City; 435-946-3448. MODERATE.

SHOPPING   Being a college town as well as the only major outpost in extreme northern Utah, Logan offers an eclectic and diverse shopping experience. In downtown, Federal Avenue and Church Street harbor antique stores, art galleries and craft shops while 100 East is popular for bicycles as well as collectibles and gardening supplies.

Antiques, country crafts and American Indian pieces can be found at **Country Village Antique and Craft Mall**, where independent dealers stock booths under one roof. ~ 730 South Main Street, Logan; 435-753-1707.

AUTHOR FAVORITE

Nothing tastes better during a mountain hike than fruit and vegetables. You can find some of the freshest produce in Utah every Saturday from mid-May through October at the **Cache Valley Gardener's Market**. Stop by the stands for lush blueberries, raspberries and blackberries, some of the best green beans I've ever tasted, sweet corn, melons and more. Crafts, herbs, flowers and gardening advice from the experts at Utah State University also are offered from time to time. ~ Garff Wayside Park, 150 South Main Street (behind Tony Roma's Restaurant), Logan.

Federal Avenue is undergoing a small renaissance, architecturally: the city has installed decorative streetlamps and hopes to encourage some storefront remodeling.

Earthly Awakening is the kind of bohemian shop you'd expect to find in a college town, with its herbal remedies, potpourris and crystals. ~ 21 Federal Avenue, Logan; 435-755-8657.

Down the street at **On the Avenue** are local crafts such as painted furniture, whimsical dolls, candles, garden sculptures and stained-glass items. ~ 34 Federal Avenue, Logan; 435-753-1150.

Chocoholics can't resist the **Blue Bird Candy Company**, which has been making hand-dipped chocolate candies since 1914. Closed Sunday. ~ 75 West Center Street, Logan; 435-753-3670.

Browse through shelf after shelf of contemporary fiction and children's books at **Chapter Two Books**, which is housed in an elegant Victorian house. Closed Sunday. ~ 130 North 100 East, Logan; 435-752-9089.

Smiling Moon is a toy store that believes that toys should be powered by kids, not batteries. Located in a nicely restored Victorian, the house offers wooden blocks, wooden trains and, naturally, wooden Lincoln Logs. You'll also find wooden puzzles, kites, hand and finger puppets and, for the older folks, brain puzzlers. ~ 146 North 100 East, Logan; 435-752-0055.

To focus your shopping in one contained area, visit the **Cache Valley Mall** on the north end of town. Here more than 40 shops, including a few chain department stores, are clustered together under one roof. Surrounding the mall are restaurants and theaters. ~ 1300 North Main Street, Logan; 435-753-5400.

Not far from downtown is **Gossner Foods**, a family-owned   ◄ HIDDEN
company where you can stop by and sample and purchase cheeses, Aggie ice cream and gourmet milks, such as root beer–flavored milk. If that's not to your liking, they also have chocolate, strawberry, mocha and banana. Closed Sunday. ~ 1000 West 1051 North, Logan; 435-752-9365.

For something sweet, visit **Cox Honeyland and Gifts**. Owned by a family whose honey production goes back five generations, the shop offers pure honey as well as creamed honey spreads containing fresh fruit such as raspberries, oranges and apricots. ~ 1780 South Route 91, Logan; 435-752-3234.

Can't leave Utah without a cowboy hat? Well, there's a good chance you'll find one that fits at **Smithfield Implement**. This family-owned ranch supply business dates to 1914. Inside the walls are not only cowboy hats but Dutch ovens, jeans and many other things you'd only need if you were a rancher. Closed Sunday. ~ 99 North Main Street, Smithfield; 435-563-3211.

The Bear Lake region is renowned for its raspberries, so it's not surprising that there are several raspberry farms and outlets in

Garden City that are open to the public and offer everything from fresh berries to jellies and even ice pops. Hours vary, so call in advance. Among them are **Calder's** (600 West 650 South; 435-946-2306), **Hildt's Berry Farm** (80 East 75 North; 435-946-3229) and **Price's Bear Lake Berry Farm** (96 West Route 89; 435-946-8850).

NIGHTLIFE During the summer, warm, dry evenings come alive at the **Sherwood Hills Summer Theater**, where actors bring melodramas to life on an outdoor stage. A bonus for guests is the chuckwagon suppers that precede the shows. Closed Sunday through Wednesday. ~ Route 89/91, Wellsville; 435-245-5054, 800-532-5066; www.sherwoodhills.com.

Looking for a burger or sandwich paired with a beer or refreshing drink amid a younger crowd? The **White Owl** is the college hangout in Logan, complete with a pool room. In summer they open the rooftop deck to dining. ~ 36 West Center Street, Logan; 435-753-9165.

Wind Cave, a series of grottos cut by erosion, is one of the highlights in the Logan District of Wasatch-Cache National Forest.

Opera is not out of the question in Logan during the summer, when the **Utah Festival Opera Company** stages a four-week season in the Ellen Eccles Theatre, an 1100-seat playhouse built in 1923. Since the productions, which might include *Carmen*, *Julius Caesar* or *The Mikado*, are performed in a revolving repertory, several shows can be seen over the course of three days. ~ 59 South 100 West, Logan; 800-262-0074; www.ufoc.org, e-mail opera@ufoc.org.

The Eccles Theatre is also the backdrop for touring Broadway shows and concerts throughout the year.

Open during summer months is the **Old Lyric Repertory Theatre**, which stages dramas, comedies and even musical revues. ~ 28 West Center Street, Logan; 435-752-1500.

Tucked amid the interesting Federal Avenue shops is **Mulligan's Social Club**, where you can take a break for a cold beer or other libation. ~ 33 Federal Avenue, Logan; 435-752-5511.

For those staying at Bear Lake, the **Pickleville Playhouse** stages musical melodramas during the summer. ~ South Bear Lake Boulevard, Garden City; 435-946-2918 or 435-755-0961.

PARKS   **WASATCH-CACHE NATIONAL FOREST** East of Logan lies the northern tip of the Wasatch-Cache National Forest and the 44,964-acre **Mount Naomi Wilderness Area**. Within its boundaries, moose, elk and beaver, in addition to five species of flowers unique to the area, thrive. Also found in the national forest is the "Jardine Juniper" (at an estimated 1500 years old it's one of the oldest juniper trees in the world) and countless miles of hiking trails. ~ Trailheads to Wind Cave and the Jardine Juniper are located off Route 89 heading east through Logan Canyon. Logan Ranger District, 1500 East Route 89, Logan; 435-755-3620; www.fs.fed.us/wcnf.

▲ Within this section of the forest's Logan District are 234 campsites in 16 developed campgrounds; $6 to $12 per night; seven-day maximum stay. Reservations: 877-444-6777; www.reserveusa.com.

BEAR LAKE STATE PARK

Thanks to its shimmering turquoise waters, Bear Lake is often referred to as the Caribbean of the Rockies. Stretching 20 miles north to south and eight miles east to west, the lake and its sandy beaches are a popular summer retreat for boaters, sailors, scuba divers, anglers, cyclists and campers. You'll find a 45-mile cycling loop that wraps the lake, state-owned beaches, campgrounds and marina, and seven boat ramps located along its shores. Bear Lake State Park is broken into three units: the marina on the west shore with its 377 boat slips and a five-lane boat ramp, Rendezvous Beach on the south shore, and Eastside/Cisco Beach on the east side. Day-use fee, $6. ~ Route 89, 41 miles east of Logan; 435-946-3343; parks.state.ut.us/parks/www1/bear.htm.

▲ There are 220 lakeside campsites at Rendezvous Beach, 25 campsites at Bear Lake Eastside, and 13 campsites at the marina; $14 to $20 per night; 14-day maximum stay. Reservations: 800-322-3770.

Among private campgrounds, **Bear Lake KOA Campground**, located one mile north of Garden City, has 150 sites, some with full hookups, and 7 cabins; $18 to $45 per night. There's also a heated swimming pool, tennis courts and bike rentals. Closed October through April. ~ 485 North Bear Lake Boulevard, Garden City; 435-946-3454, 800-562-3442.

HYRUM LAKE STATE PARK Southeast of Logan along Route 101, this tiny state park is wrapped around a 450-acre lake that provides fishing and small boating opportunities. There are restrooms and showers. Sixteen miles farther east on Route 101 lies the **Hardware Ranch** (see "Logan Sights" above), which is a winter feeding ground for elk. Day-use fee, $5. ~ Route 165, eight miles south of Logan, 405 West 300 South, Hyrum; 435-245-6866; parks.state.ut.us/parks/www1/hyru.htm.

▲ There are 32 campsites; $14 per night; 14-day maximum stay. Reservations: 800-322-3770.

Although you won't catch any fish in the Great Salt Lake (because there are none!), there are endless miles of streams and a good number of reservoirs and high-country lakes in the mountains of northern Utah to keep anglers occupied throughout the fishing season.

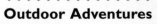

Outdoor Adventures

FISHING

OGDEN AREA   Streams rushing out of the mountains just east of Ogden are full of fish. While the **Ogden, Weber** and **South Fork** streams are reliable trout fisheries, Rocky Mountain whitefish occasionally can be hooked in the South Fork. Smallmouth bass are stocked in the lower Weber River on the west side of Route 15.

Young anglers are often found at the **21st Street Pond** in Ogden. Found just off the Route 15 freeway ramp at 21st Street, the pond is popular with families and productive in spring and winter.

Just ten miles east of Ogden via Route 39 shimmers **Pineview Reservoir**, a warm-water fishery rich in bass, catfish, crappie, bluegill, yellow perch and tiger musky. Not even winter slows the fishing since the reservoir freezes over and draws ice fishermen.

Trout anglers head to **Causey Reservoir**, a deep, narrow reservoir about 30 miles east of Ogden on the South Fork of the Ogden River. Cutthroat, rainbow, brook and brown trout have been pulled from the reservoir, which sees the best action in spring and fall.

HIDDEN ►   **BRIGHAM CITY AREA**   Bluegill anglers should head to **Mantua Reservoir** along Route 89/91 in Wellsville Canyon. Along with bluegill, it is stocked with bass and trout.

Some of northern Utah's best dry flyfishing can be had along Route 101 in Blacksmith Fork Canyon east of Hyrum. While stone fly and salmonfly hatch between mid-May and June, from July through September grasshoppers are the bait of choice.

Mountain Valley Trout & Llama Farm is a privately owned retreat that allows fishing for various trout species. You can pay $10 per hour to fish with catch and release in mind, or keep your catch and pay $2.99 per pound (cleaned). ~ 1471 West Route 218, Smithfield; 435-563-3647; www.northernutah.com/mvtrout.

LOGAN AREA   What would fishing be without tall tales of the one that got away? Well, they say a 40-pound trout was once pulled from the **Logan River** in Logan Canyon. The river's fishing is at its best from June into August. Farther up Logan Canyon lies **Tony Grove Lake**, which is stocked with rainbow trout. To get there, head 19 miles up the canyon on Route 89, then take the turnoff seven miles to the lake.

Bear Lake is a vibrant trout fishery, renowned for its cutthroat stock. The Idaho record cutthroat, weighing 19 pounds, was pulled from this lake. Also found in the waters are lake trout and Bonneville whitefish, which can be hooked from shore in the late fall. Trolling and jigging are most productive in the winter and spring months. Bonneville cisco, thought to exist only in the lake, are a member of the whitefish family. These seven-inch-long fish run at the end of January and early February, drawing hundreds to the lake shores with dipping nets.

Outfitters Tackle, but no guides, can be found at **Al's Sporting Goods** in Logan. ~ 1617 North Main Street, Logan; 435-752-5151. **Willow Valley Sportsman** can lead you to fish in northern Utah. ~ 42 South Main Street, Logan; 435-755-6800; www.willowvalley.net. **Bear River Basin Outfitters** can take you to extreme northern Utah and southeastern Idaho. They guide along the Bear River system, Bear Lake and in some private lakes in the mountains above Laketown. ~ 2123 South Bear Lake Boulevard, Garden City; 435-946-2876.

Where there are mountains in Utah, there usually are lakes are reservoirs that capture the spring runoff and provide places to fish or swim during the summer months.

WATER SPORTS

OGDEN AREA With 2879 surface acres, **Pineview Reservoir**, ten miles east of Ogden via Route 39 (Ogden Scenic Byway), is a popular retreat for boaters, windsurfers and waterskiers.

Diamond Peak rents sit-on-top kayaks, inflatable kayaks and canoes for use on the reservoir. ~ 2429 North Route 162, Eden; 801-745-0101.

BRIGHAM CITY AREA Although it covers just 554 acres, waterskiers still manage to enjoy themselves on **Mantua Reservoir**, located on Route 89 east of Brigham City. Possibly due to its small size, the reservoir is often overlooked. As a result, boaters sometimes find that they have Mantua to themselves, even on summer weekends.

◄ HIDDEN

LOGAN AREA Snug in the mountains eight miles south of Logan, **Hyrum State Park** offers a 450-acre reservoir perfect for canoeing and swimming. ~ 405 West 300 South, Hyrum; 801-245-6866.

Just west of downtown Logan shimmers the **Cutler Wetlands**, a watery oasis created by irrigation dams along the Bear River. Here are approximately 10,000 acres of open water, wetlands and uplands. There are three buoy-marked trails canoeists can follow—the North Marsh Canoe Trail, the Logan River Canoe Trail and the Little Bear River Canoe Trail—as well as two unmarked trails. ~ 200 North and approximately 4800 West, Logan; www.bridgerlandaudubon.org/wetlands maze for maps and information.

Along Cutler Wetlands' canoe trails you may spot such birds as sandhill cranes, ring-necked pheasants, northern harriers, short-eared owls, and black-crowned night herons.

Other places to launch your canoe along the Bear River include the **Upper Bear River Recreation Area** (approximately 3000 North and 2900 West), **Benson Marina** (3000 North and approximately 4800 West) and **Cutler Canyon Recreation Area** (Route 23 and about 6200 North). A private marina where you can rent a canoe or arrange a shuttle is the **Muddy Road Outfitters Marina**. ~ 435-753-3693.

Just looking for a place to take a dip? Try the **Logan Aquatic Center**. Across the street from the Cache Valley Fairgrounds, the outdoor complex features two water slides, a lap pool and a kiddie pool. Admission. ~ 451 South 500 West, Logan; 435-716-9266.

The 160-square-mile **Bear Lake**, the state's second largest freshwater lake, is *the* destination for water-sports enthusiasts in northern Utah. Power boaters, sailors, windsurfers, scuba divers and plain old swimmers are also lured by the water and the white-sand beaches that rim the lake.

There are plenty of boat ramps to go around, although they fill up quickly in summer. Bear Lake State Park has a 305-slip marina and rentals, while several other businesses in the area rent watercraft. **Bear Lake Sails** rents sailboats, power boats and canoes. ~ 2141 South Bear Lake Boulevard, Garden City; 435-946-2994. Watercraft rentals also can be made at **Bear Lake Funtime**. ~ 1217 South Bear Lake Boulevard, Garden City; 435-946-3200.

CLIMBING   Nearly 300 climbing routes, ranging in difficulty, have been blazed up the limestone and quartzite cliffs in Logan Canyon east of Logan, and roughly 230 of these are bolt-protected. Check with the Logan District Ranger Office to see which climbs have been closed to protect threatened or endangered plant species. Available in many Logan bookstores, *Logan Canyon Climbs* by Tim Monsell details the canyon's climbs.

Aspiring climbers can work on their techniques at **Adventure Sports Rock Gym**, an indoor facility perfect for getting used to hanging onto rocks with your fingers and moving across rock faces. Gear is also sold here. ~ 51 South Main Street, Logan; 435-752-8152; www.bittersweetgear.com.

DOWNHILL SKIING & SNOW-BOARDING   Although northern Utah can't claim as many alpine resorts as the Salt Lake City and Park City areas, this doesn't mean that those you will find are any less worthy. In fact, if you want to avoid crowds, this just might be the part of Utah to consider.

OGDEN AREA   **Nordic Valley** doesn't pretend to be one of Utah's big boys when it comes to skiing, instead offering a low-key family experience. With just 85 skiable acres, a vertical drop of but 960 feet and only two lifts, this tucked-away area 15 miles east of Ogden is open nightly for night skiing, and Friday through Sunday for day skiing. ~ Located 15 miles east of Ogden off Route 158, 3567 Nordic Valley Way, Eden; 801-745-3511 (seasonal).

Overlooked when compared to Wasatch Range resorts, **Powder Mountain** offers access to 5500 acres of skiing, of which 2800 acres are lift-served and the rest accessed by Snowcat or return shuttle. Nineteen miles east of Ogden, the resort offers four lifts and three surface tows that haul skiers and boarders around the 70-

plus downhill runs. ~ Route 158, 19 miles east of Ogden and located just past Nordic Valley; 801-745-3772; www.powder mountain.com.

The 2002 Olympic Winter Games pumped badly needed life into **Snowbasin**, which faced a "mom-and-pop" existence until the Salt Lake Organizing Committee decided the resort, operating since 1939, should host the Games' downhill and Super G ski races. The resort added two beautiful rock-and-timber on-the-mountain day lodges, as well as a sprawling lodge at the base with restaurant and lounge. Skiers and snowboarders alike use the resort's nine lifts to get around the 3200 skiable acres. The base reformation is a work in progress, but once done expect an upscale ski-and-golf resort in the mold of Sun Valley. ~ Routes 39 and 167, 17 miles east of Ogden, Huntsville; 801-399-1135; www.snowbasin.com.

Diamond Peaks Heli-Ski Adventures uses helicopters, not lifts, to reach the slopes. The company has access to 12,000 acres of backcountry skiing and snowboarding with a vertical drop of 2800 feet. ~ P.O. Box 12302, Ogden, UT 84412; 801-745-4631; www.diamondpeaks.com.

LOGAN AREA A family operation since 1939, 664-acre **Beaver Mountain Ski Area** caters to skiers and snowboarders with some of the best powder in northern Utah. Tucked away near the head of Logan Canyon, the resort has a 1600-foot vertical drop and five lifts. There's also a tubing hill. ~ Route 89, 27 miles east of Logan, Logan Canyon; 435-753-0921, 435-753-4822 (ski report); www.skithebeav.com.

Most of the cross-country ski opportunities in northern Utah require you to work a little harder at the sport as you'll more than likely have to break trail, although there is a resort in the Logan area that offers groomed trails.

CROSS-COUNTRY SKIING

AUTHOR FAVORITE

The consummate mom-and-pop resort, operated by the same family since 1939, **Beaver Mountain Ski Area** is a diamond in the rough—this is one of my favorite resorts for a low-key day spent in an incredibly beautiful location. No mega-seat high-speed lifts here, no ritzy restaurants, no trophy homes littering the mountain—just 664 acres of some of the best powder skiing and boarding in northern Utah. See above for more information.

OGDEN AREA   No need to leave Ogden to get a decent cross-country workout: the 127-acre **Ogden Nature Center** found on the city's west side off of 12th Street has hiking trails that skiers can use in the winter.

Out of town, the **Maples Nordic Loop** at the Snowbasin Ski Area features a gently rolling 6.2-kilometer-long ski trail with only a moderate elevation gain of 6360 feet to 6500 feet. ~ Head 17 miles east of Ogden via Route 39 and 167 to the Snowbasin Ski Area and the campground.

Going nearly 30 miles east of Ogden via Route 39, the trail leading from the **South Fork Campgrounds** runs four kilometers and has a negligible elevation rise. ~ Route 39.

Another popular area with cross-country skiers is **North Fork Park** along **Avon-Liberty Road**. To get there, from Ogden head 15 miles toward the Nordic Valley ski area and take the left fork onto North Ogden Divide Road. How far you ski down the road is up to you.

LOGAN AREA   Not far from Logan, **Sherwood Hills** offers 20 kilometers of groomed trails that wind through the forests in the Wellsville Mountains. Lessons, rentals and even night skiing are also available. ~ Located on the south end of Wellsville along Route 89/91, Wellsville; 435-245-5054, 800-532-5066.

OTHER WINTER SPORTS   The awarding of the 2002 Olympic Winter Games brought a bevy of winter sports facilities to Utah's Wasatch Range. In Ogden, the **Ice Sheet**, next to the Dee Events Center, is used by ice hockey leagues as well as the city's curling and figure skating clubs. Learn-to-curl classes are held weekly at the facility. Time is also set aside for the general public to skate on the rink. ~ 4390 Harrison Boulevard, Ogden; 801-399-8750.

The **21st Street Pond** usually freezes over during the winter months and is popular with ice skaters. If you go, check the ice before heading out across the pond. ~ East of Route 15 on 21st Street, Ogden.

ALL IN FUN

Based 30 minutes east of Ogden in Huntsville, **Red Rock Ranch and Outfitters** mixes work with fun. The century-old working ranch still offers livestock for sale and entertains tourists with a taste of the Old (and the new) West. While snowmobile tours and sleigh rides are offered during the winter months, come summer wagon rides, hay rides, Dutch-oven dinners, guided horseback rides and even overnight pack trips are the way of life. ~ Huntsville; 801-745-4305, 801-745-6393; www.redrock ranchandoutfitters.com.

Golf is more popular than skiing in Utah, which explains the countless courses. During mild winters, golf can be a year-round sport.

OGDEN AREA **The Barn**, a 6000-yard, 18-hole public golf course named after a white barn that is now used for the course lounge, is nestled on farmland in Ogden's northern foothills. A relatively flat, tree-lined course, three duck-filled ponds add to the natural hazards. ~ 305 West Pleasant View Drive, Ogden; 801-782-7320.

The **Ben Lomond** golf course spreads its 18 holes over 6200 yards. Like The Barn, this par-72 course is also fairly flat, but the holes are longer. Its relatively low elevation enables this course to be one of the first to open in the spring. ~ 1600 North 500 West, Ogden; 801-782-7754.

If you're pressed for time, the **El Monte Golf Course** features nine holes cradled in the mouth of Ogden Canyon. This course features rolling hills and water that occasionally lure moose. Located across from the Eccles Dinosaur Park, this course can be demanding when the dinosaurs roar as you're getting ready to tee off. ~ 1300 Valley Drive, Ogden; 801-629-8333.

The **Mount Ogden** course on Ogden's East Bench is one of the more challenging 18-hole courses in the region thanks to its dramatic elevation changes and narrow, heavily treed fairways. Several dog-leg holes make it impossible to see the pin from the tee. ~ 1787 Constitution Way, Ogden; 801-629-8700.

No time for 18 holes? Try **Mulligan's Golf & Games**, which offers a short 9-hole course, a lighted driving range, and two 18-hole miniature courses. ~ 1690 West 400 North, Ogden; 801-392-4653.

If your short game needs work, head to the **Pleasant Valley Golf Center**, which boasts an 18-hole natural grass putting course as well as a driving range. ~ 5600 South 500 East, Ogden; 801-475-4787.

Views of the Great Salt Lake and Antelope Island might distract you when you're putting around the 18-hole, 6800-yard public course at **Schneiter's Bluff**. ~ 300 North 3500 West, West Point; 801-773-0731.

The **Wolf Creek Resort** offers an 18-hole, 7000-yard public course that is hilly and very challenging due to its sand and water traps, roughs and long holes. This is one of the state's most scenic mountain courses, thanks to the nearby ski resorts and Pineview Reservoir; wildlife in the form of moose, elk and fox often crop up. ~ 3900 North Wolf Creek Drive, Eden; 801-745-3365.

The **Valley View Golf Course** is often the backdrop of amateur tournaments. Its 18-hole, 6800-yard course is par 72. ~ 2501 East Gentile, Layton; 801-546-1630.

BRIGHAM CITY AREA The 18-hole, 6769-yard **Eagle Mountain Golf Course** in Brigham City is supported by a driving range, a putting green and a chipping area. Built onto the side of a mountain, this par-71 course, which provides sweeping views of the Great Salt Lake, requires precise drives. ~ 960 East 700 South, Brigham City; 435-723-3212.

Brigham City's other course is **Brigham Willow Golf Course**, a 2650-yard, par-37, nine-hole course that can challenge beginning players while giving more experienced duffers someplace to work on their shots. ~ Junction of Routes 89 and 30, Brigham City; 435-723-5301.

LOGAN AREA In Smithfield four miles north of Logan, the 18-hole, 6877-yard **Birch Creek Golf Course** is set on the side of the Bear River Range, offering sweeping views of the Cache Valley and providing challenging greens. ~ 600 East Center Street, Smithfield; 435-563-6825.

Located in Sardine Canyon just a dozen miles southwest of Logan on Route 89/91 is the **Sherwood Hills Golf Course**, a modest nine-hole course that spans 3315 yards and features narrow, heavily treed fairways. ~ Located on the south end of Wellsville along Route 89/91, Wellsville; 435-245-6055, 800-532-5066.

Thanks to its tight fairways and scenery the 18-hole, 6502-yard **Logan River Golf Course** is viewed not only as one of Utah's top ten courses but as one of the top 500 in the country. Built in 1993, the par-71 course flows in and out of groves of trees along the Logan River. ~ 550 West 1000 South, Logan; 435-750-0123.

It's not as challenging as the courses on the west side of the mountains, but the **Bear Lake Golf Course** offers a nice respite from boating on Bear Lake. The nine holes cover 3400 yards and overlook the lake. ~ 2176 South Bear Lake Boulevard, Garden City; 435-946-8742.

RIDING STABLES The Wasatch Range that dominates northern Utah offers countless areas for riding horseback.

Logan Canyon is great to ramble through on horseback, with its gorgeous canyons and forests. **Beaver Creek Trail Rides** can get you into the mountains east of Logan with one-hour, three-hour or custom rides. ~ Route 89, 12 miles west of Garden City near Beaver Mountain, P.O. Box 139, Millville, UT 84326; 435-946-3400.

During the summer months horseback rides can be arranged through the **Sherwood Hills Resort**. These rides, which run one and two hours and are suitable for beginners, head off into the Wellsville Mountains. ~ Route 89/91, on the south end of Wellsville; 435-245-5054, 800-532-5066; www.havilandsoldwestadventures.com.

There's no lack of riding terrain in northern Utah, although, as with other parts of the state, you will be expected to earn the mileage as the mountains result in a lot of elevation in most rides.

OGDEN AREA   In the Ogden area, mountain bikers looking for a full day's ride like the **Skyline Trail**, which starts from the west side of Pineview Reservoir one and a half miles from the dam, from the Willard Basin or from North Ogden Divide. The trail, which ranges from 6184 feet to 8100 feet, runs for 22 miles and is also used by horseback riders, motorbikes and hikers.

Beus Canyon offers a shorter ride, one covering seven miles. Access can be found at the Snowbasin Ski Area. It, too, is part of the Great Western Trail and also is used by horseback riders and hikers.

A more level ride is along the **Running Water Jeep Loop**, which runs 9.2 miles along forest roads. Access is via Forest Road 192 or Forest Road 144 from the Curtis Creek Road. While no hikers or horseback riders use this loop, which begins at an elevation of 8200 feet and ends at 8600 feet, you may be sharing it with ATVs.

The **Ben Lomond Trail** is one of the most popular riding trails in the area, and the reason is obvious: on clear days from the top of 9712-foot Ben Lomond Peak you can see for 100 miles. Of course, the 7.6-mile ride to the top is long and strenuous, as the climb from the trailhead at the North Fork Park Campground covers nearly 3000 vertical feet. The trail is open to hikers and horseback riders, so be careful on your way down.

For a rundown on both mountain- and road-bike rides in the Logan area, stop by the Cache Valley Tourist Council offices or one of Logan's bike shops for a brochure that pinpoints trailheads and offers trail descriptions.

A nice ride that's often overlooked because of its location on the east end of the Ogden Valley is the **Skin Toe/Baldy Ridge Trail**. The trailhead can be found on the north side of Causey Reservoir near the Boy Scout Camp. While the Skin Toe Trail runs only 1 mile, the Baldy Ridge component of this ride goes on for another 9.5 miles. While the Skin Toe Trail runs around the reservoir, the Baldy Ridge Trail climbs into the mountains. The upper portion can be rocky at times, but the views are gorgeous.

BRIGHAM CITY AREA   Hard-core mountain bikers will enjoy pedaling down **Willard Peak Road**. Running 12 miles one way, this out and back route begins at the LDS Church on the south side of Mantua and climbs 4200 feet on the way to Inspiration Point near Willard Peak. Wildlife such as deer, moose and elk are often seen. From Inspiration Point are great views of both the Wasatch Mountains and Great Salt Lake.

A longer but less grueling ride in terms of elevation is the 32-mile route between **Brigham City** and **Golden Spike National Historic Site**. Traversing paved state and county roads, the jaunt is pretty flat, outside of the short climb to Promontory Summit. Along the way to the historic site the path winds through irrigated farmland, wetlands and the Thiokol Rocket Manufacturing Plant. Access in Brigham City is at the Willows Golf Course parking lot at the junction of Routes 38 and 13. In the summer this can be a long, hot ride, with temperatures near 100 degrees possible.

LOGAN AREA Bird lovers will appreciate the **Bear River Bird Refuge Road**. The 12-mile-long refuge loop runs along dikes built to create ponds for waterfowl. During the spring this ride provides views of dozens of bird species, and possibly a fox or two. You can pick up a bird checklist at a kiosk near the entrance to the refuge.

To better appreciate the bucolic nature of this part of Utah, try the 28-mile loop for road bikes that runs from **Richmond to Cornish** and back to Richmond. This route traverses some gorgeous rolling farmland and passes through the small towns of Trenton, Cornish, Lewiston and Richmond.

Another road-bike tour that leads past marshlands where you might spot white-faced ibis, great blue herons, and flocks of ducks is the 24-mile **Little Pyrenees** loop. The ride starts in Logan on Route 165 and heads south to Hyrum, where you'll pass Hyrum Reservoir before turning back north toward Wellsville and Mendon. At Mendon the route cuts through marshes of the Little Bear River and crosses the Logan River before leading you back to Logan.

Locals rate the **Cowley Canyon/Logan Peak** mountain-bike ride very difficult, and for good reason: the trail climbs more than 4000 feet over 13 miles. But the payoff is great views of both the Bear River Range and the Wellsville Mountains. The trailhead is at the Lodge Campground 11 miles east of Logan on Route 89.

A more moderate but equally scenic ride for mountain bikers is the 16-mile out-and-back route that runs into **Smithfield Canyon**. The trail is an old gravel and dirt road that starts in Smithfield but soon leads you into the Wasatch-Cache National Forest. The ride runs along Summit Creek (so you might spot wildlife if you're attentive) and ends at the Mt. Naomi Wilderness boundary. There are quite a few camping opportunities along the route, including a Forest Service campground, so you can easily turn this into a relaxing overnight ride.

Mountain bikers in the Bear Lake area often frequent **Hodge's Canyon Road**, which runs from the western shores of Bear Lake at Pickelville to a 10-mile loop that winds through aspen groves and past the South Sinks area, where the landside is indented by sinks caused by water eroding the limestone beneath the earth's surface. Another popular ride—one that's a bit easier and suitable for beginners—involves a 15-mile loop that runs from Meadowville to Route 30 on the western shore of Bear Lake, south to Laketown and then back west into Round Valley before returning to Meadowville. Along the way you'll pass a pioneer cemetery as well as a ghost town.

One of the most popular rides along Bear Lake is on the 4.3-mile **Garden City Bicycle and Pedestrian Trail.** The 10-foot-wide asphalt strip lures, hikers, joggers, rollerbladers and skateboarders, too. The 45-mile **Bear Lake Loop Bicycle Trail** offers not only a more strenuous workout but a geology primer on the lake and surrounding landscape through interpretive signs.

Mountain bikers like the 4.5-mile **Swan Creek** loop trail, accessed off Route 89 near Lakota just north of Garden City. A more grueling ride goes 15.5 miles from the Bear Lake Summit to Meadowville.

Bike Rentals   In Ogden, **Kent's Sports Store** sells bikes and services all brands of bikes. ~ 307 Washington Boulevard, Ogden; 801-394-8487. **Diamond Peak** rents bikes for cycling around Pineview Reservoir. ~ 2429 North Route 162, Eden; 801-745-0101. If you need bike rentals or repairs in Brigham City, try **Loveland's Cycle.** ~ 352 North Main Street, Brigham City; 435-734-2666. In Logan, you can find repairs and sales at **Sunrise Cyclery.**~ 138 North 100 East, Logan; 435-753-3294.

With national forests blanketing the mountains due east of Logan, Brigham City and Ogden, hiking opportunities in the area overflow. From short morning or afternoon treks to multiday excursions into the mountains, the options are many. All distances listed for hiking trails are one way unless otherwise noted.

HIKING

OGDEN AREA   The **Bonneville Shoreline Trail** runs north and south along the Wasatch Front. In the Ogden area, it is a major artery that provides access to all the trails climbing up Mount

HELPFUL HIKING HINTS

Looking for cascading waterfalls or dense groves of juniper and cedar? Searching for panoramic views or a quiet alpine lake for a few hours of fishing? All these possibilities and more can be found in northern Utah's forests. Although you will come across streams in the mountains, it's best to pack your own water or carry a good water filter to avoid slurping down bacterial parasites that could make your life miserable once you return to civilization. Also, realistically judge your ability before setting out. Not only are many of the trails steep and strenuous, many trailheads are found at an elevation of 5000 feet, which means surprisingly thin air for those coming from near sea level.

Ogden. Trailheads can be found at 22nd Street and 46th Street. Between 22nd Street and 46th Street, which crosses the mouth of Beus Canyon, the trail crosses Taylor's, Waterfall and Strong's canyons.

The **Indian Trail** (4.3 miles) begins near the east end of Ogden's 22nd Street and runs to the mouth of Ogden Canyon, quickly rising from 5000 feet to 6000 feet and offering nice, if at times precipitous, views. Its name relates to the American Indians who used the route when high water made Ogden Canyon impassable. A spur located a half mile up the Indian Trail wends two miles to **Hidden Valley**.

Families with youngsters not ready for the rigors of mountain hiking will enjoy the **North Arm Wildlife Viewing Trail** (1 mile) that runs along the north side of Pineview Reservoir east of Ogden. The trailhead can be found along Route 162 on the north side of the reservoir.

The **Beus Canyon Trail** (6 miles) climbs more than 4000 feet from 46th Street towards the 9572-foot summit of Mount Ogden. It's popular with hikers, mountain bikers and equestrians, but is highly challenging due to the grade. Cresting at a saddle just below the summit, the route continues down the eastern flanks of Mount Ogden towards Snowbasin.

For a quick, moderate hike, the **Strong's Canyon Trail** (.5 mile) offers a short trek through trees along Strong's Creek. The trailhead is found at 36th Street and follows the Mount Ogden Exercise Trail for a short distance veering upstream.

The short, steep **Waterfall Canyon Trail** (1 mile) begins at 29th Street and climbs 1000 feet to Malans Falls. Along the way to the falls, the trail parallels a cascading stream and offers nice views of Ogden and Great Salt Lake. The trail passes through a mix of scrub oak, aspen and conifer forest.

BRIGHAM CITY AREA   You won't find as many hiking options in the immediate vicinity of Brigham City as you will around Logan and even Ogden, mainly because of the in-your-face steepness of the Wellsville Mountains, but if you look, there are some possibilities. If you take Route 91/89 around to the eastern side of the mountains and then head roughly seven miles north on Route 23 to Mendon you'll find two trails that climb up into the mountains. The **Deep Canyon to Wellsville Ridge and Stewart Pass** (5 miles), thanks to the pitch of the Wellsville Mountains, can be strenuous; in summer this hike takes you through nice wildflower meadows. The trailhead is along the north end of 300 North in Mendon.

Another route to Stewart Pass can be reached via the **Maple Bench Trail** (7 miles). This out-and-back course is another tough uphill climb into the Wellsville Mountain Wilderness Area. It runs two miles up to Stewart Pass, and then continues for another one and a half miles to Stewart Peak. The trailhead can be found at the end of Forest Service Road 86 located south of Mendon.

LOGAN AREA   Around Logan, hikers almost instinctively head up Logan Canyon and its many jumping off points to get away from it all. The trailhead to **Old Ephraim's Grave** (5.5 miles) can be found off Right Hand Fork Road found 9.2 miles up Logan Canyon. The hike is a good one, and the elevation rises only 1600 feet along the way. At the gravesite stands an 11-foot-tall stone, which some say represents the bear's height, although others put him closer to ten feet.

Wind Cave Trail (1.3 miles) is another popular destination for hikers, although it's steep and can be brutally hot in the summer because there's little shade along the way. A relatively short hike, the trail leads to the cave, which is actually a series of small caverns and arches sculpted by ice and wind. Watch for snakes in summer. The trailhead can be found across from the Guinavah-Malibu Campground 5.3 miles up Logan Canyon from Logan.

A relatively quick jaunt that gets you to the highest point in the Bear River Range is the **Naomi Peak Trail** (2.9 miles), which starts at the Tony Grove Lake Parking Area and leads into the Mt. Naomi Wilderness Area. The trail is rocky and steep in places on the way to the summit of 9980-foot Naomi Peak. The turnoff from Route 89 in Logan Canyon to the parking area is located 19 miles from Logan. Once you turn off the highway, it's another seven miles to the parking area.

A good hiking guide to the Logan area is available at the Logan Ranger District office or the Cache Valley Tourist Council office.

A nice but longer alternative to the Naomi Peak Trail is the **High Creek Trail** (10 miles). Running from the Tony Grove parking lot, this is a great overnight hike. As you gain 4200 feet in elevation you pass through forestlands cut by a gushing mountain stream (early in the season) before entering a glacial valley and subalpine meadows. Among the payoffs are cascading waterfalls along the last two miles.

Another pleasant hike out of the Tony Grove parking lot leads to **White Pine Lake** (3.4 miles). The path cuts through stands of fir, spruce and aspen, meadows of dazzling wildflowers, and ends at a gorgeous glacial lake set in a cirque.

Set off down the **Limber Pine Nature Trail** (1 mile roundtrip) and you'll head through a thick stand of limber pine trees. Among them is a gigantic limber pine—actually five separate trees that have grown together. Its age? An estimated 560 years. This short loop also boasts views of Bear Lake and offers interpretive signs that help youngsters understand forest ecology and wildlife. The trailhead can be found 30 miles east of Logan next to the Sunrise Campground along Route 89.

A wonderful path near the mouth of Logan Canyon is the **Riverside Trail** (4.2 miles), which, as its name implies, follows the Logan River. Moose frequent the river corridor, so watch out for them. There are six areas where you can jump onto the trail: near the canyon mouth across Route 89 from the national forest boundary sign; at the Red Bridge turnoff on the right side of the road about a mile up the canyon; at the Bridger Campground; at the Gus Lind Dispersed Campground; at the Spring Hollow Campground; and at the Guinavah Campground.

How can hardened hikers ignore the Wellsville Mountains? They can't. One way to get to the top of this steeply pitched range is via the **Deep Canyon/Wellsville Ridge** trail. It's only a 10-mile roundtrip to Stewart Pass, but it's a tough haul, gaining nearly 3000 feet in elevation. The payoff? Great views, beautiful wildflowers in summer, and raptors (Stewart Ridge is along a major flyway). The trailhead is at the west end of 300 North in Mendon, a small town just west of Logan.

Transportation

CAR

Interstate **Route 15** is the major thoroughfare through northern Utah, passing right by Ogden and Brigham City. Logan is a bit off the beaten path, requiring a jaunt up **Route 89** from Brigham City.

Other key roads in the region include **Route 39**, which heads east from Ogden and works its way into Wyoming, and interstate **Route 84**, which leads west from Wyoming to Ogden. At Ogden, Route 84 overlaps Route 15 north to Tremonton, where the two part ways, with 84 continuing northwest towards Twin Falls, Idaho, and 15 continuing north towards Pocatello, Idaho.

AIR

See Chapter Two for information about **Salt Lake City International Airport**, the closest airport serving these parts.

In Ogden, **Mountain Valley Transportation** offers shuttles from area hotels to Salt Lake City International Airport as well as to Powder Mountain and Snowbasin. ~ 877-834-3456. **Utah Shuttle Services**, meanwhile, runs six times a day between the airport and the Ogden Intermodal Terminal at 2329 Wall Avenue. ~ 801-393-5438.

In Logan, **Cache Valley Limo Airport Shuttle** (435-563-6400, 800-658-8526) provides rides to Salt Lake International.

BUS

Greyhound Bus Lines (800-231-2222; www.greyhound.com) has regular service through northern Utah. In Ogden the bus stops at 2501 Grant Avenue, 801-394-5573; in Logan at 754 West 600 North, 435-752-2877; and in Brigham City at the Trailside General Store at 38 East 100 South.

CAR RENTALS

Many of the major car-rental agencies have offices in Ogden, including **Avis Rent A Car** (3110 Wall Avenue; 801-621-2980) and **Enterprise Rent A Car** (36th and Riverdale; 801-399-5555). **Hertz**

Rent A Car is located in the heart of downtown Ogden. ~ 2805 Washington Boulevard, Ogden; 801-621-6500.

Hertz Rent A Car can also be found in Brigham City. ~ 816 North Main Street, Brigham City; 435-723-5255.

Rental cars can be obtained at a number of Logan locations. **Hertz Rent A Car** has an office in the Comfort Inn. ~ 447 North Main Street, Logan; 435-752-9141. **Enterprise Rent A Car** has its own offices on Main Street. ~ 1849 North Main Street, Logan; 435-755-6111.

Travel around Ogden is made easy by **Utah Transit Authority**, which makes countless stops around town. ~ 801-621-4636.

PUBLIC TRANSIT

In Brigham City, **Utah Transit Authority** offers service within the city as well as a route to Ogden. ~ 435-734-2901

Within Logan, LTD **Bus Service** provides free transportation between 6:15 a.m. and 9:45 p.m. Monday through Friday; on Saturday, service runs from 9:30 a.m. to 6:30 p.m. No service on Sunday. ~ 435-752-2877.

Both Ogden and Logan have taxi services; Brigham City does not.

TAXIS

For getting around town, try **Yellow Cab Company**. ~ 1450 Washington Boulevard #52, Ogden; 801-394-9411.

Cache Valley Cab (435-752-4555) offers taxi service in Logan, as does **Logan Taxi** (435-753-3663).

FOUR

Northeastern Utah

From world-class ski resorts to sandstone cliffs rife with dinosaur fossils, no part of Utah is as diverse—in appearance, in economics, in lay of the land—as the state's northeastern corner. The region defines diversity, from the tony ski resort community of Park City with its multimillion-dollar homes, chic restaurants and crisp mountain air to the sleepy and bucolic feel of Heber Valley with its ranches and slower pace to blue-collar Vernal with its tidy neighborhoods, fast-food eateries and dusty landscape.

Just as diverse as the communities' walks of life are their backgrounds. Park City, ever the epitome of nonconformity in generally strait-laced Utah, gained foothold as a boomtown in the mid-1800s when silver was plucked from its mountains by Union soldiers on a mission to lure outsiders into the dominion of the Church of Jesus Christ of Latter-day Saints. They succeeded grandly—Irish, Chinese, Scandinavians, English, Swedes and others poured into Park City to feast upon silver's succor.

Most mining booms, however, tend to bust, and Park City's was no exception. At one time arguably the richest mining camp in the world, by the early 1900s the town's economy was in a state of collapse. It was a condition that wasn't really righted until the ski industry arrived for good in the 1960s and brought with it a certain cachet that enticed the rich. By the 20th century's end, this mountain playground had lured not only the rich but also lower classes who work in Park City's service industry and middle-class commuters who head daily to the Salt Lake Valley to work. An offshoot of the town's gentrification—some might call it snobbishness—and the resulting division between the haves and have-nots is the ongoing clash over the town's future. How much growth is enough? How much is too much? Is the community in truth merely a commodity available to the highest bidder? These are questions that continue to spur debate.

The same can't be said of the communities found farther east, in the eye-blink towns of Heber City, Duchesne, Roosevelt and Vernal and within the 3.3-million-acre Uintah and Ouray Indian Reservation. Heber City tries to snare its share of

Park City's winter market, although with rolling cross-country courses and hot springs instead of alpine resorts. In summer the town caters to anglers, hikers and campers heading to nearby state parks or into the high country of the Uinta Mountains or the Wasatch Range.

In Vernal and the Uintah and Ouray Indian Reservation, without ski slopes running to their doorsteps, most residents eke a gritty living from the landscape, toiling on ranches, farms, mines and oil and gas wells. Some have also turned to the natural resources for a living, guiding customers down the rivers, into the mountains and across the riddled landscape in search of pictures, history and wildlife.

If there's one thing that knits this far-flung region together, it would be the rumpled mountains and their playgrounds. From the Wasatch Range that cradles three ski resorts in and around Park City to the towering Uinta Range that attracts backcountry skiers, hikers, anglers and campers to its canyons and high-country lakes, northeastern Utah's geography lends itself to human exploration and recreation.

Major John Wesley Powell left his mark on the land in 1869 when he and a small, gritty band of men pushed their wooden dories into the Green River in southwestern Wyoming and rode the river south through today's Flaming Gorge and Dinosaur National Monument to its confluence with the Colorado River outside Moab and farther south through the Grand Canyon. A predecessor of today's whitewater cowboys who ply the bucking rivers for a living, Powell marveled at the fantastic scenery time had cut into the land, a scenery that remains just as amazing and breathtaking today.

Park City Area

Park City, nestled in a small, north–south running valley on the backside of the Wasatch Range 31 miles east of Salt Lake City on Route 80, is Utah's only true ski town. Nowhere else in the state, which boasts 14 alpine resorts, will you find such a vibrant, pulsating town curled up right at the bottom of the slopes.

It wasn't always so. The town stumbled into life as a rough-and-tumble outcast, a place decidedly out of step with the rest of the pious state. Union troops, stationed in Salt Lake City during the Civil War to ensure that Brigham Young and his Latter-day Saints didn't try to wrest the territory from the United States, were encouraged to prospect in the Park City area with hopes that a strike would lure hundreds of non-LDS prospectors into the territory. Silver was finally found in the thickly timbered mountains above town in 1868 and the boom was on, drawing thousands of Irish, Swedish, Finnish, Cornish, Chinese, Scottish and Yugoslavian miners, who in turn gladly patronized the 27 saloons and a notoriously popular red-light district. The prevalence of alcohol in the town was a strong pull even in pious Salt Lake City, which from time to time would see its thirsty citizens head east to Park City for a little libation.

During Park City's mining heyday, its ore beds produced 23 millionaires, including George Hearst, grandfather of newspaperman William Randolph Hearst. All told, more than $400 million in silver was hauled from the mountains. Today memories of the miners drift through more than 1200 miles of tunnels that remain within the mountains. At one point the boom made Park City the country's richest mining camp, with silver, lead, gold and zinc reserves boasting a gross value of $2.5 billion. Still, the boom was relatively short-lived. The town's mines were wallowing by 1907 when a recession shuddered through the country.

While Prohibition left most towns across the country dry, the good times continued to roll in Park City, where officials looked the other way. However, when Prohibition ended, the town's economy, already struggling with the slumping mining industry, plummeted further. And while Park City dabbled with skiing from the 1920s onward, it wasn't until the 1960s when the town truly realized the figurative gold mine buried in the heavy snows that often inundated Park City.

In 1962, in a bid to mine that potential windfall, a delegation from the Utah Press Association, during lunch at the White House with President Kennedy, broached the topic of a ski resort and boldly inquired about federal funding for the project. The following year Park City qualified for a federal loan through the Area Redevelopment Agency and the Treasure Mountain Resort was born, opening on December 31, 1963, with a gondola, chairlift and two J-bars.

Since that small step, the town's ski industry has steadily grown. So reliable is the skiing that the "White Circus," the World Cup ski tour, stops here each fall to race at the Park City Mountain Resort.

The 2002 Salt Lake City Olympic Winter Games helped solidify Park City's growing reputation as a winter playground. With three Olympic venues in the mountains overlooking the town, and boisterous nightlife along its historic Main Street, Park City gained international exposure and acclaim. While the Winter Games likely won't return to Park City for the foreseeable future, their athletes will come to compete in World Cup skiing, snowboarding, ski jumping and sliding competitions. In fact, the 2003 World Freestyle Championships were held at the Deer Valley Resort, and the 2005 World Luge Championships are slated to be staged at the Utah Olympic Park.

SIGHTS   Does Park City today evoke the quaint, yesteryear mining town image that city tourism officials would have you believe? Not entirely. Outside of Main Street, a half-mile-long stretch of pavement buttressed by shops and restaurants housed in an architectural amalgamation of 19th-century and present-day motifs, the town appears much like any other resort community chasing the almighty dollar. Although locals hate comparisons with Aspen,

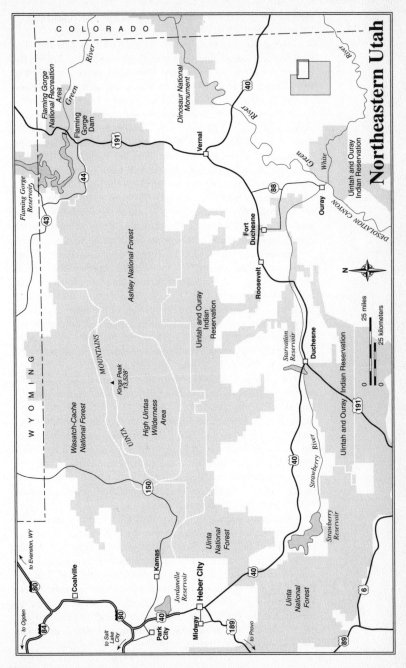

their town is rife with developers studding the hillsides with "starter castles"; real estate prices rocket ever upward.

On the way to Main Street, visit the **Park City Chamber Bureau Visitors Center,** located inside the Jess Reid Building on the corner of Kearns Boulevard and Route 224 at the north end of town. Inside are maps of both the immediate area and the region as well as reams of brochures. There's also a brief description—in words, pictures and memorabilia—of Park City's mining and skiing heritage. ~ 750 Kearns Boulevard, Park City; 435-658-4541, 800-453-1360, fax 435-649-4132; www.parkcityinfo.com.

Adjacent to the Jess Reid Building lies Park City's **Olympic Welcome Plaza,** where some of the Salt Lake Games' memories are preserved. On columns that rise above the plaza are the names of the medalists from the three Park City–area venues. The 60-foot-tall Olympic Way Finding Tower is one of the venue towers that was used during the Games. The plaza also sports columns bearing commemorative posters from previous Olympic Winter Games.

The soul of Park City's **"Old Town,"** or original core, is **Main Street,** particularly the stretch sandwiched between 9th Street at the bottom and Daly Avenue at the top. This is the town's tourist hub, with restaurants, bars, art galleries and shops. An afternoon could easily be spent drifting up one side of the street and down the other, browsing in shops, admiring the early-20th-century architecture, and stopping for a bite to eat. Plaques erected on 45 buildings provide detail on historic structures. Please see "Historic Park City Walking Tour" for more details.

Few original buildings remain from the town that was incorporated in 1884, though, since a fire that broke out in the American Hotel in the pre-dawn hours of June 19, 1898, crackled through Old Town. The flames left more than 200 businesses and homes in ashes and 500 folks homeless. Among the buildings lost was the town's $30,000 opera house, which had been open for just three months. A call to arms throughout Utah produced a workforce that reconstructed the town in just 18 months; in keeping with Park City's ribald reputation, among the first businesses to be rebuilt was a saloon.

For a quick primer on historic Park City, and to pick up a $1 brochure outlining a walking tour of the historic district, stop at the old **City Hall.** Today this two-story brick and masonry building, which was erected in 1895 and rebuilt after being mostly destroyed by the fire, houses a small visitors center as well as the **Park City Museum and Territorial Jail.** There are exhibits on Park City's mining past and, in the basement, four dank cells that constituted the Utah Territorial Prison. One of the exhibits explains how Utah's "Silver Queen," Susanna Bradford, made her millions. ~ 528 Main Street, Park City; 435-649-6104.

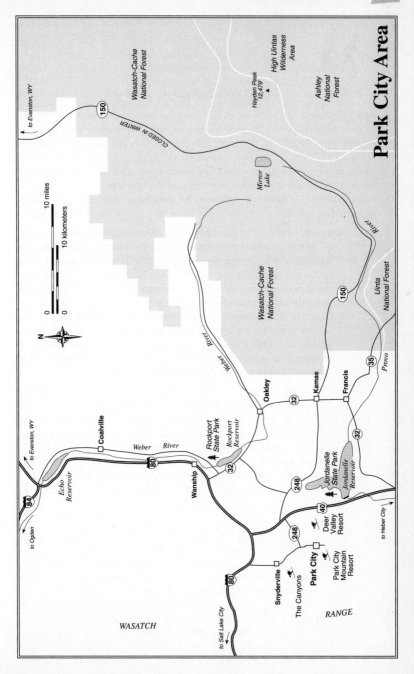

Park City Area

to Evanston, WY

150

Wasatch-Cache National Forest

High Uintas Wilderness Area

Hayden Peak 12,479 ▲

Ashley National Forest

CLOSED IN WINTER

Mirror Lake

10 miles

10 kilometers

0   0

N

Wasatch-Cache National Forest

Weber River

150

Uinta National Forest

River

35

Provo

to Evanston, WY

Coalville

Weber   River

Oakley

32

Kamas

Francis

80

Rockport State Park

Rockport Reservoir

32

32

Echo Reservoir

Wanship

248

Jordanelle State Park

Jordanelle Reservoir

32

84

40

to Ogden

to Heber City

248

Deer Valley Resort

to Salt Lake City

80

Snyderville

Park City

Park City Mountain Resort

The Canyons

WASATCH

RANGE

Historic Park City

Park City arose as the antithesis of Salt Lake City. Union soldiers were encouraged by their officers to look for silver in the mountains surrounding the town with hopes a strike would lure thousands of non-LDS miners into the state. The strike made in 1872 not only put Park City on the nation's map as arguably the richest silver camp around, it also saw Park City become one of the few Utah communities founded by non-Mormons. The richness of the boom brought prosperity to town, as well as 27 saloons, a number of bordellos, and some magnificent buildings that you can admire during an hour or so walk up and down Main Street.

THE IMPERIAL HOTEL   By starting in front of this building at the top, or south end, of Main Street, your tour will be downhill. Located on the west side of Main Street, the hotel arose in 1904 as the Bogan Boarding House and remains as one of just four historic boarding houses for miners that exist in the Park City area today. When it first opened, the boarding house's steam-heated rooms were rented by the day, week or month. In 1918, when a flu epidemic swept the area, the building became an emergency hospital. After a fire gutted the structure in 1940, it languished until 1987, when it was restored as the Imperial Hotel. Today it does business as the "1904 Imperial Hotel." ~ 221 Main Street; 435-649-1904, 800-669-8824; www.1904imperial.com.

THE EGYPTIAN THEATER   Head a block south and onto the east side of the street and you'll find that Park City's hankering for the arts is not a come-lately desire. After the 1898 fire the Dewey Theater was built on the site of a livery stable and equipped with 600 wooden opera chairs and a floor that could be tilted toward the stage during shows or laid flat for parties and dances. When heavy snows collapsed the theater's roof in 1916, just hours after a show, the Egyptian Theater arose like the proverbial phoenix from the rubble a decade later. Architecturally re-

Towering over the southern end of Main Street (and town, for that matter) is **Deer Valley**, one of Park City's three ski resorts. The resort is renowned for its magnificent lodgings, expensive second homes, and delectable menus. The skiing's not bad, either. In summer the resort is a haven for mountain bikers and outdoor-concert enthusiasts. ~ From Main Street, head south one mile on Deer Valley Drive; 435-649-1000; www.deervalley.com.

A short walk north (downhill) from City Hall brings you to the Olympic Walkway linking Park City's Transit Center and Main Street. Here on the sidewalk is **Franz the Bear**, a life-size

flective of the "Egyptian Revival" style that swept the country in the 1920s, the 400-seat theater offered Park City's first "talkies," as well as vaudeville acts. Since 1981 the theater has been the home of Egyptian Theater Company. ~ 328 Main Street; 435-649-9371.

350 MAIN   A few doors below the Egyptian Theater is a landmark of America's department store history. In the early 1900s when J.C. Penney opened his first department store in western Wyoming, it was known as the Golden Rule Mercantile Co. In 1909 the chain arrived in Park City on Main Street and remained a mainstay until the 1930s, when the store moved out and a pharmacy moved in. Through the decades the building's evolution continued and went on to house a grocery, a popular bar and restaurant and, today, the 350 Main New American Brasserie. ~ 350 Main Street; 435-649-3140.

BELL TOWER   Not quite two blocks south, on the same side of the street, stands the remains of not only Park City's first city hall but also its first fire alarm. After the 1898 fire, city officials realized they needed more than a constable discharging his revolver to alert residents to a fire, so they erected a three-story wooden bell tower that ran up the south wall of City Hall and remains there today. Though a 1500-pound bell initially was used as the alarm, in 1905 it was replaced by an electric siren that doubled, until 1980, as a 10 p.m. curfew signal for minors. ~ 518 Main Street.

PARK CITY MORTUARY   A half-block farther south on the street is the site of one of the town's shrewdest merchants. From his two-story building on Main Street that was rebuilt after the 1898 fire, Bill Fennemore operated a small grocery as well as Park City's first mortuary, which he promoted with a small casket-shaped sign. A more enterprising mortician, George Archer, assumed the business in 1921 and supplemented his income in alcohol-dry Utah by driving his hearse 52 miles to Evanston, Wyoming, where he loaded it with bootleg liquor that he would sell to Park City bar owners. Today a Japanese restaurant, Kampai, occupies the main floor. ~ 586 Main Street; 435-649-0655.

bronze critter relaxing on a park bench. During the Salt Lake Games an estimated 500,000 visitors traversed the walkway. Many stopped to sit next to Franz for a unique keepsake picture.

Near the bottom (north end) of Main Street you can find an expansive collection of local and regional art at the **Kimball Art Center**, which is housed in a restored, 1940s-era, service station. ~ 638 Park Avenue, Park City; 435-649-8882; www.kimball-art.org.

In the late 1990s, with the Salt Lake Games on the horizon, development extended the commercial portion of Main Street farther north beyond Heber Avenue. Initially slow to take off, this area blossomed with the Olympic movement and has delivered a clutch of restaurants, shops and lodgings worth perusing. It's also the terminal location of Park City Mountain Resort's Town Lift, a chairlift that ferries skiers from downtown Park City to the top of the mountain. So that skiers and snowboarders don't have to take off their skis or 'boards to cross Park Avenue on their way back down the mountain and into Old Town, a "ski bridge" now spans the street.

On the north side of Heber Avenue just a block east of Main Street extends an arm of Park City's trails system. The paved pathway runs along Poison Creek to **City Park**, which is constantly in motion during the warm-weather months with a wide variety of sports. There's also a pavilion there for barbecues, picnic areas and a playground for younger children, as well as a sprawling skateboard park. ~ Vehicle access to City Park can be made off Park Avenue between 13th and 14th Streets.

Just northwest of Main Street sprawls the **Park City Mountain Resort**, the granddaddy of the city's ski scene. One of Utah's largest ski areas in winter, in summer the hills are open to hikers and mountain bikers; kids love the alpine slide and the Ziprider, a harrowing 2300-foot cable ride deemed the world's steepest. ~ From Park Avenue, take Lowell Drive a half-mile to the resort base; 1310 Lowell Avenue, Park City; 435-649-8111, 800-222-7275; www.parkcitymountain.com.

HIDDEN ► Beginning (or ending, depending on your direction of travel) in Park City, the **Historic Union Pacific Rail Trail State Park** winds for 28 miles along a narrow railroad corridor between Park City and Echo Reservoir to the east. Rail service along the corridor began in 1880, when Park City's burgeoning silver mines brought freight trains into town. During the mid-1970s passenger service was offered with hopes that skiers would provide steady winter business, but it never caught on. In the mid-1980s freight service to Park City also ended. When the Union Pacific Railroad abandoned the line in 1989, the Utah Division of Parks and Recreation moved to convert it into a recreational trail. In 1992, the rail trail was dedicated and became the first non-motorized trail in the state. ~ The trailhead is on the east side of Park City and can be accessed from the parking lot on the south side of Prospector Avenue; Prospector Square, Park City.

Find a hilltop near Park City's eastern boundary and you can almost see **Jordanelle State Park**, where a shimmering 3300-acre reservoir dances with some two million trout and bass. With Deer Valley Resort providing an alpine backdrop to the west and groves of scrub oak, juniper, pine and aspen studding the surrounding rolling hillsides, the state park that opened in 1995 is nestled in a valley that was homesteaded for ranching in 1864. ~ Route 40, four miles east of Park City.

Just beyond Park City's northern boundary lies **The Canyons,** a burgeoning all-season recreational empire. With more than 6000 skiable acres in the resort's future, this property stands to become one of the largest ski resorts in North America. As with Park City's other two resorts, hiking and mountain biking are big here in the summer, while a small amphitheater at the base of the resort occasionally offers concerts. The folks at NBC were so smitten with The Canyon's setting that they broadcast "The Today Show" during the Olympics from the Grand Summit Resort Hotel at the resort's base complex. ~ The Canyons is located five miles north of Park City off Route 224, 4000 The Canyons Resort Drive, Park City; 435-649-5400, 888-226-9667; www.thecanyons.com.

Large Spring Camp, a quarter-mile beyond Mormon Flat along East Canyon Road, was used by emigrants as an overnight stop.

You can relive the glory of the Salt Lake Games with a visit to the **Utah Olympic Park** north of Park City. Here you'll find the ski jumps and bobsled and luge track used during the Games, as well as the wonderful **Alf Engen Museum,** which chronicles much of the Games through enlarged newspaper displays, photos and interactive exhibits. The museum also is home to the **Intermountain Ski Hall of Fame,** which honors Rocky Mountain sporting greats. Admission. ~ 3000 Bear Hollow Drive, Park City; 435-658-4200.

For peace and quiet, visit the **Swaner Nature Preserve** about seven miles north of Park City along Route 80. In the spring and late summer or early fall you'll share the open meadows with sandhill cranes that arrive during their migrations. A privately owned nature preserve that's open to the public, Swaner's more than 1050 acres offer a growing trail network for hiking, cross-country skiing and snowshoeing as well as birding. A nature center similar to the one found at Rock Cliff in Jordanelle State Park is planned for the park. ~ Route 80, seven miles north of Park City; 801-363-4811; www.swanernaturepreserve.

◄ *HIDDEN*

About ten miles north and west of Park City lies **East Canyon,** which was a popular route for mid-19th-century travelers heading West. Through the canyon passed the ill-fated Donner-Reed Party in 1846, and in July 1847 Mormon pioneers led by Brigham Young came through on what became the Mormon Trail. **Mormon Flat** is the spot where Young and his followers rested and prepared for the final push into the Salt Lake Valley. For the next 22 years an estimated 200,000 travelers—trappers, Mormons, '49ers, freight wagons, stagecoaches and even Pony Express riders—came down the east side of the canyon and exited over Big Mountain Pass, which was the steepest sustained climb on the 1300-mile-long Mormon Trail, rising 1400 feet in just four miles. ~ To visit the site and adjacent Large Spring Camp, head west from Park City on Route 80 and take Exit 143 to the Jeremy Ranch sub-

◄ *HIDDEN*

division. At the bottom of the exit ramp, turn right, then left at the four-way stop. Take the first right, Jeremy Road, which leads about a mile through the subdivision to the mouth of East Canyon. From here, East Canyon Road, a dirt road that is not maintained during the winter, runs four miles to Mormon Flat.

Above the left side of the road just before you reach Mormon Flat you can make out two rock "**breastworks**" built into the hillside. These were erected by the Utah Militia in the fall of 1857 to guard Salt Lake City against U.S. troops summoned to squelch the so-called Mormon Rebellion that never arose.

Tales of Spanish gold, dense forests of conifer and aspen, and rugged mountains dotted with sparkling lakes lie just 13 miles east of Park City on Route 150 in the **Wasatch-Cache National Forest**. The forest's western gateway is in **Kamas**, a small ranching town that launches the Mirror Lake Highway (Route 150) up into the Uinta Mountains, which is the only major range in the country that runs east–west instead of north–south.

The Uintas are Utah's tallest range of mountains, rising above 13,000 feet, stretching 100 miles between Kamas and Flaming Gorge, and covering 3500 square miles. While summer is the busiest season in the national forest, when thousands engage in fishing, camping and hiking, in winter snowmobiles, cross-country skiers and even dogsleds skim through the snow-covered parcel. In the very heart of the national forest is the **High Uintas Wilderness Area**, a 456,705-acre swath of wild, rugged backcountry that appears today much as it always has.

Perhaps more intriguing than the forest's recreational possibilities is the legend of lost gold that dates to the mid-1800s. As the story goes, Spanish explorers who some think first reached the Uintas in the mid-1600s spent much of their time mining for gold as well as looking for caches of gold that they believed were hauled there and hidden by Aztecs. When Brigham Young and his Mormon followers arrived in Utah in 1847, they were virtually penniless. However, a Ute Indian chief offered to supply Young with gold. Supposedly, the gold the chief gave the Mormons came from mines left behind by the Spaniards, and some believe many caches remain today.

Although far less crowded than the Wasatch Range closer to the Salt Lake Valley, the Uintas seduce more and more people each year and summer weekends often mean crowded campgrounds; if you head down one of the backcountry trails you'll escape most of the hordes. ~ Wasatch-Cache National Forest, Kamas Ranger District, 50 East Center Street, Kamas; 435-783-4338.

LODGING   With 21,500 rentable beds in Park City, finding a place to stay isn't a terribly hard task. However, it can be an expensive one if you wait until the last minute during the middle of the ski season.

Conversely, during the shoulder seasons of May and June and September and October bargains are easily found. Depending on your taste, during the high season you can pay less than $100 a night for a clean and comfortable motel room, or as much as $4000 for space in one of the sumptuous lodges at Deer Valley.

There are only 20 rooms and suites at the Austrian-influenced **Goldener Hirsch Inn**, so you know they must be something special. Each of the large rooms (located mid-mountain at the Deer Valley Resort) features hand-painted and hand-carved furniture imported from Austria. You'll find king-sized beds, wood-burning fireplaces and, in most rooms, a private balcony. Amenities include a mini-bar, a humidifier, dataport phones and cable TV. Downstairs there's an award-winning restaurant. ~ 7570 Royal Street, Deer Valley; 435-649-7770, 800-252-3373; www.goldenerhirschinn.com. MODERATE TO ULTRA-DELUXE.

There is a small handful of bed-and-breakfast establishments in town and they're much in demand. The historical **Old Miner's Lodge** was built in 1889 as a boarding house for miners. Originally, much of the lumber that went into the lodge was salvaged from area mines. Today the lodge's dozen rooms and suites have been restored to their late-1800s best, and furnished with antiques and down comforters and pillows. Downstairs in the cozy living room is a large fireplace. There's also an outdoor hot tub. Full breakfast is included. Gay-friendly. ~ 615 Woodside Avenue, Park City; 435-645-8068, 800-648-8068, fax 435-645-7420; www. oldminerslodge.com, e-mail stay@oldminerslodge.com. MODERATE TO ULTRA-DELUXE.

Less than two blocks away is the frilly **Angel House Inn**, which takes its name from archangels who, if you believe in such things,

AUTHOR FAVORITE

The royal blood in me relishes the sheer opulence and slopeside elegance of the **Stein Eriksen Lodge**, with its 59 suites and 111 rooms. Named in honor of the great Norwegian skier of the 1950s, the lodge lies mid-mountain at the Deer Valley Resort and features elegant restaurants, a spa, a slopeside ski locker room, and a rustic atmosphere that evokes Scandinavia. In the main lobby, a display case glows with Stein's many medals and trophies. Among the amenities are wood-burning fireplaces, balconies overlooking the slopes, and full kitchens. Of course, you'll pay dearly for them. ~ Head about three-quarter-mile south on Deer Valley Drive to Royal Street and follow it to 7700 Stein Way, Deer Valley; 435-649-3700, 800-453-1302, fax 435-649-5825; www.steinlodge. com, e-mail info@steinlodge.com. ULTRA-DELUXE.

play a role in romance or pleasures of the natural world. Some of their names grace the Victorian inn's nine guest rooms. Follow a day on the slopes (one of which runs adjacent to the inn) or knocking about town with a plate of hors d'oeuvres and a book in front of the parlor's fireplace. ~ 713 Norfolk Avenue, Park City; 435-647-0338, 800-264-3501; www.angelhouseinn.com, e-mail info@angelhouseinn.com. MODERATE TO ULTRA-DELUXE.

The **1904 Imperial Hotel**, like the Old Miner's Lodge, has history on its side, but a decidedly more colorful history. Like the lodge, the Imperial Hotel started out as a boarding house for miners. Over the years, though, it also logged time as a brothel. The ten rooms bear the names of historic area mines and include phones and color televisions. Downstairs, the hot tub sits in a room used for wine-making during Prohibition. ~ 221 Main Street, Park City; 435-649-1904, 800-669-8824, fax 435-645-7421; www.1904imperial.com, e-mail stay@1904imperial.com. MODERATE TO ULTRA-DELUXE.

HIDDEN ►   Perhaps the town's most unobtrusive abode, yet one with turn-of-the-20th-century elegance and charm, is the **Mary E. Sullivan House**, located high up on Main Street. A reclaimed mining shack dating to 1892, today the two-story Victorian home features three bedrooms, a kitchen and sitting room, a family room and game room, and a formal parlor. The hand-stenciled borders, clawfoot tubs and artworks dating to the late 19th century harken to a simpler time, while the outdoor hot tub makes you glad to be alive in the 21st century. Closed mid-April to mid-November. ~ 146 Main Street, Park City; 800-803-9589; www.thistlesprings. com. ULTRA-DELUXE.

The **Blue Church Lodge** started out in 1897 as a Mormon church. Today the lodge, which is on the National Register of Historic Places, and its associated townhouses are a short walk from both Main Street and the Town Lift that provides access to the Park City Mountain Resort. Ambience in the rooms and condos ranges from country elegant to rustic mountain lodge, and you'll find full kitchens, fireplaces and spas. Closed mid-April to

STILL IN SESSION

The **Washington School Inn**, with its limestone block walls, withstood the fire of 1898. Once laid out with three large classrooms, the school later served as a social hall for the Veterans of Foreign Wars before becoming an inn in 1984. Inside are a dozen rooms and three suites, while outside the original carved-wood bell tower still caps the building. ~ 543 Park Avenue, Park City; 435-649-3800, 800-824-1672. MODERATE TO ULTRA-DELUXE.

mid-November. ~ 424 Park Avenue, Park City; 435-649-8009, 800-626-5467, fax 435-649-0686; e-mail bcl@ditell.com. DELUXE TO ULTRA-DELUXE.

Just down the hill from the Park City Mountain Resort lies the **Old Town Guest House** with four rooms. Country decor graces the home from top to bottom, from the lodgepole-pine furniture to the flannel robes in each room. The sitting room has a fireplace, and outside there's a hot tub. Two rooms share a shower and phone. ~ 1011 Empire Avenue, Park City; 435-649-2642, 800-290-6423 ext. 3710; www.oldtownguesthouse.com, e-mail info@oldtownguesthouse.com. MODERATE TO DELUXE.

A good number of hotels are scattered throughout Park City. Many countries' ski teams call **The Yarrow** home during the annual World Cup ski races at the Park City Mountain Resort due to its handy location. Situated on the northern end of town, the 181-room hotel is located next to a grocery store, ski shops and movie theater; inside the hotel is a cozy lounge with a fireplace, outside there's a bus stop for Park City's free shuttle buses. ~ 1800 Park Avenue, Park City; 435-649-7000, 800-927-7694; www.yarrow resort.com. DELUXE TO ULTRA-DELUXE.

The **Park City Marriott** opened in 1999 after investing millions in a makeover of the former Olympic Park Hotel. Along with 199 standard rooms the upgrade added a fitness center to go along with the indoor pool. You'll also find a ski and snowboard rental shop on the property as well as a lift-ticket outlet. ~ 1895 Sidewinder Drive, Park City; 435-649-2900, 800-234-9003; www.parkcityutah.com. DELUXE TO ULTRA-DELUXE.

Close to the slopes and located in the center of Park City Mountain Resort's village is **The Lodge at the Mountain Village**. Options here range from a room for two to a four-bedroom condo that can sleep ten people. Amenities include an indoor/outdoor heated pool, an exercise room with a sauna and steam room, and laundry facilities. You're also close to resort activities as well as to the city's free shuttle bus. ~ 1415 Lowell Avenue, Park City; 435-649-0800, 888-727-5248; www.thelodgepc.com. BUDGET TO ULTRA-DELUXE.

Staying at the **Silver King Hotel** means you have to walk across Lowell Avenue to reach the lifts at the Park City Mountain Resort—not as good as walking out your door, but it's still a lot better than dealing with traffic and parking in the winter. Rooms here run the gamut from nicely furnished and appointed studio units to three-bedroom condos that feature full kitchens, fireplaces and laundry facilities. There's no pool here, but there is a hot tub. ~ 1485 Empire Avenue, Park City; 435-649-5500, 877-664-5464; www.silverkinghotel.com. MODERATE TO ULTRA-DELUXE.

The **Grand Summit Hotel** rises luxuriously above the base of The Canyons resort, offering you the closest beds to the resort's lifts. You're also in the center of après-ski life, as restaurants, clubs and the resort village's open-air amphitheater are a short walk away. Well-appointed rooms range from one-bedroom units to suites, and most come with fireplaces and balconies. If you ever tire from skiing or snowboarding, there's an outdoor heated pool, health club and spa. ~ 4000 The Canyons Resort Drive, Park City; 435-615-8040, 888-843-2269; www.thecanyons.com. DELUXE TO ULTRA-DELUXE.

There are thousands of other rooms to be rented in Park City, and for help in tracking one down try **Central Reservations of Park City** (435-649-6606, 800-570-6296; www.parkcityski.com/cci.html), **Deer Valley Lodging** (435-649-4040, 800-453-3833; www.deervalleylodging.com) or **David Holland's Resort Lodging and Conference Services** (435-655-3315, 888-727-5248; www.888parkcity.com).

DINING

With roughly 7000 residents, Park City easily has the most culinary options per capita in Utah. Heck, the town even boasts that it has more chefs per capita than Paris! Not surprisingly, the more than 100 restaurants and bars that are shoe-horned into town guarantee that your toughest choice come meal time is not *what* to eat, but *where*.

The 2002 Salt Lake Winter Games complicated dining in Park City, but in a good way. Long-time restaurants spruced up, newcomers offered more choices, and competition overall brought the best out of everyone. Stroll Main Street, where the bulk of the town's restaurants reside, and you'll find French, Mexican, Southwestern, Italian, Thai, Vietnamese, Chinese, Japanese and "roadside America" eateries. Elsewhere you'll find German, Austrian and Swiss menus.

Caution: During the height of ski season, reservations are mandatory at most restaurants. Also take note that during the shoulder seasons—late spring and early fall—some restaurants close to give their staffs a rest, refresh their menus, and occasionally spruce up their interiors, so call ahead. If you visit in summer, pick up the *Park Record* newspaper and look for two-for-one coupons that many restaurants offer to drum up business during this somewhat slow season.

While the skiing at Deer Valley is among the world's best, a strong argument can be made that food is the resort's forte, thanks to the many fine restaurants you'll find in and around the resort. Rich, hearty Teutonic meals are served at the **Goldener Hirsch Inn**, where Austrian elegance reigns. The Black Forest sandwich combines European breads and hams; the weinerschnitzel features Bayerishes kraut, apple soufflé and parsley brown butter. ~ 7570 Royal Street, Deer Valley; 435-649-7770; www.goldener hirschinn.com. MODERATE TO DELUXE.

Also in Deer Valley and nestled amid evergreens and aspens, **The Glitretind** in the Stein Eriksen Lodge treats eating as a celebration of life. Choosing an entrée at the restaurant (named after the "Shining Peak," Norway's highest mountain) requires that you first decide whether to eat "Western," with the grilled beef tenderloin or be a bit more adventurous with the pink-peppercorn-and-caper-crusted Pacific tuna seared rare. Oenophiles will appreciate the voluminous wine list. ~ 7700 Royal Street East, Stein Eriksen Lodge, Deer Valley; 435-649-3700 ext. 83, 435-645-6455; www.steinlodge.com. DELUXE.

Swiss fare is on the menu at **La Pasch**, another of the upscale ◀ HIDDEN eateries that surround the Deer Valley Resort. On the menu are fondue, alpine stews, foie gras, fresh seafood and more. Your meal will be enhanced by the restaurant's eye-catching stone fireplace. ~ 8200 Royal Street (inside the Stag Lodge), Deer Valley; 435-649-8300. MODERATE TO DELUXE.

Perhaps the most intimate dining experience at the Deer Valley Resort is at the **Mariposa**, a 22-table restaurant that only serves dinner. My wife and I head here for those special dinners—anniversaries, birthdays, etc.—or whenever the urge for a romantic setting strikes. Meals before a flickering fireplace might include sautéed tiger prawns with lime butter, or the Mariposa mixed grill that includes lamb chop, venison filet and wild boar sausage. Dinner only. ~ Silver Lake Lodge, Deer Valley; 435-645-6715. DELUXE.

Back in Park City proper, top-notch restaurants line Main Street. Deciding which to try could depend entirely on how far up the street (there's a steady uphill grade as you head south) you want to walk.

At the top of Main Street, when you enter the **Grappa Italian Restaurant** it's almost as if you've walked into a Tuscan farmhouse. Underfoot are heavy tiles, while the walls are a combination of plaster and heavy beams. Garlic-rich aromas waft steadily

AUTHOR FAVORITE

Growing up on the East Coast, fresh seafood was an integral part of my diet. Fortunately, living in the Rockies doesn't mean I have to go without. The Seafood Buffet the Deer Valley Resort serves up in its **Snow Park Lodge** during the ski season allows me an opportunity to gorge myself on shellfish, Dungeness crab, yellowfin tuna, New Zealand clams and other seafood flown in fresh on a daily basis. Of course, the prime rib and barbecued babyback ribs make sure I don't forget I'm in beef country. ~ Snow Park Lodge, Deer Valley; 435-645-6632. DELUXE.

from the kitchen. The center of the two-story building is open, allowing diners on the second-floor to gaze down on those on the first, and in summer you can dine on the patio. Depending on the chef's whims, you could start with seafood crêpes before an entrée of boneless salmon steak crusted in horseradish, garlic and herbs served with fettuccini. ~ 151 Main Street, Park City; 435-645-0636; www.grapparestaurant.com. DELUXE.

The **Wasatch Brew Pub**, dating to 1986, owns the distinction of being the state's first modern-day microbrewery. Largely a sports bar that draws its share of ski bums and resort employees once the slopes close, the pub serves up surprisingly good rack of lamb on occasion, tasty Utah trout, among other dishes, and an array of microbrews. As the pub's owner likes to say, "We drink our share . . . and sell the rest!" This is a great place to find out where the locals are skiing. ~ 250 Main Street, Park City; 435-649-0900; www.wasatchbeers.com. MODERATE TO DELUXE.

Though the **Eating Establishment** doesn't exactly stand out in this town of high-end eateries, since 1972 locals have known it as a reliable, and reasonably priced, place for breakfast, lunch and dinner. ~ 317 Main Street, Park City; 435-649-8284. BUDGET TO MODERATE.

The **350 Main Street New American Brasserie** prepares showy presentations of beef, seafood and poultry. You can be cautious by ordering the basil roasted chicken breast, or more daring with the Pacific ahi, which is rolled in Hawaiian seasonings, charred and served rare, and accompanied by octopus and taro sauté with conch fritters. The building, which began life in the early 1900s as a department store, has a marvelous copper ceiling as well as an airy deck out back for warm summer evenings. ~ 350 Main Street, Park City; 435-649-3140; www.350main.com. MODERATE TO DELUXE.

MAMA'S MUNCHIES, MARGARITAS AND MORE

Where do Park City locals go for a casual dinner? Well, if they like Southwestern cuisine they head to **Nacho Mama's**, which can be found in a nondescript building about a five-minute drive from Main Street. Traditional Mexican favorites are available, as are less traditional entrées such as *carne adovada* (a dish of sliced pork baked with three different chiles) and grilled chicken topped with pecans and pineapple salsa. Also known for its margaritas, the eatery has a pool table, foosball, a bar and TVs to stay on top of Sunday afternoon's (or Monday night's) game. ~ 1821 Sidewinder Drive, Park City; 435-645-8226; www.nacho mamas.com. MODERATE.

Zona Rosa serves "nuevo Latino" cuisine that melds traditional Southwestern dishes with a splash of the ocean deep in a cantina atmosphere. Entrées might include barbecued prawns glazed with honey and served with seared greens and rice as well as grilled salmon, shrimp-and-pesto quesadillas, calamari and nightly specials. You'll also find fresh fruit margaritas here. ~ 501 Main Street, Park City; 435-645-0700. BUDGET TO MODERATE.

During his two visits to Park City, former President Bill Clinton would regularly turn up at the **Main Street Deli** for a cup of coffee and something to munch on. Thankfully, you don't need a Secret Service detail to get into this Main Street mainstay that serves up budget-priced breakfasts, lunches and dinners. ~ 525 Main Street, Park City; 435-649-1110. BUDGET.

Arguably, the best and most consistent food in town is available at the **Riverhorse Café**, a "loft" restaurant that requires a hike up a steep staircase to reach the dining room. Make the trek, though, and you'll be rewarded with a fine meal, a local pianist or guitarist, and a menu with everything from Alaskan halibut and grilled Utah red trout to grilled sea scallops and a 17-ounce steak. Housed in the Old Masonic Hall, this eatery offers a balcony for watching Main Street's comings and goings, as well as a private dining room with a hidden "celebrity entrance" that allows the likes of Robert Redford, Brad Pitt, Tom Cruise and Bette Midler to come and go unseen. Dinner only. ~ 540 Main Street, Park City; 435-649-3536. MODERATE TO DELUXE.

You have to go underground to find **Bangkok Thai**, but I assure that you'll enjoy the experience. Amid a setting of white linen and crystal and warm wooden booths you'll taste some of the best Thai food in the Rockies. From the lobster and mango spring rolls to the curry dishes of pork, chicken, beef or shrimp, you can't go wrong. ~ 605 Main Street, Park City; 435-649-8424. MODERATE.   ◄ *HIDDEN*

The **Easy Street Brasserie** is a saucy French restaurant that touts the fact that it's "French, without all the France." Inside this private club (a modest membership fee will get you in) you'll discover a "country cuisine" menu and family-style dining. Entrées might include scallop and shrimp with pastis, red wine–braised lamb shanks, and paillard of veal with capers and lemon. Outside there's a heated patio that, if the weather isn't too severe, permits outdoor dining year-round. Being a private club, the restaurant also houses a bar with its own menu that opens at 2 p.m. and closes at 1 a.m. ~ 201 Heber Avenue, Park City; 435-658-2500; www.easystreetbrasserie.com. MODERATE TO DELUXE.

Zoom, Robert Redford's "roadhouse grill," is situated inside an old train depot. This two-story restaurant, a reliable spotting ground for celebrities during the Sundance Film Festival, features a relaxed roadhouse-style dining room and bar on the lower level, while the upper floor contains a much more comfortable and spacious dining room. During summer, a sunken patio wrapped with flower gardens just off the main floor offers the best al fresco dining in Park City. With a menu offering ribs with cornbread and coleslaw, Black Angus steaks with french fries, and maple-cured pork chop with cranberry stuffing, this is not the place to count calories. ~ 660 Main Street, Park City; 435-649-9108. MODERATE.

Meander farther south on Main Street and you'll enter "lower Old Town," a somewhat recent commercial addition that continues to grow and gain attention with shoppers and diners. A short walk east of Main Street leads to a nice pedestrian plaza lined by shops and restaurants.

You'll smell the kitchen before you enter **La Casita**, a brightly colored and delicious Mexican restaurant that offers breakfast, lunch and dinner. The wonderful aromas, and the sign over the door promising "110 Mexicano," are clues to the traditional dishes you'll find on the menu: *bistec a la Mexicana, camarones Monterrey* and *coctel de camarones.* ~ 710 Main Street, Park City; 435-645-9585. MODERATE.

Sushi lovers won't leave **Mikado** disappointed. In fact, the Zagat 2002 guide said the simply decorated restaurant had the best sushi in town. You'll also find tempura and teriyaki dishes as well as surf and turf. ~ 738 Main Street, Park City; 435-655-7100. MODERATE.

Don't confine your epicurean excursions to Old Town, as there are a handful of worthy restaurants located off Main Street to sample.

HIDDEN ▶

Tough to find if you're not looking for it, but definitely worth the search, is **Chez Betty**, which occupies a floor in the Copper Bottom Inn just off Park Avenue. Consistently hailed for its service, the menu is one of the best in Park City. Appetizers range from sautéed Pacific curry oysters to saffron and scallion risotto with seared medallions of filet mignon, and entrées might include grilled beef tenderloin on a crispy potato pancake and grilled portobello mushroom served with sap sago risotto. A table by the double-sided fireplace is an elegant way to wind down the day. ~ 1637 Short Line Road, Park City; 435-649-8181; www.chezbetty.com. DELUXE.

Windy Ridge is off the beaten path but worth finding for a relaxing meal that won't bust your budget. Breakfasts feature egg dishes and griddle favorites, while lunch revolves around hot sandwiches, grill items and pastas. Dinners get a bit more creative with roasted game hen, pan-seared perch and seared Atlantic salmon. The wine and beer menu isn't too shabby for this small

Skiing at Your Doorstep

Park City arguably offers the most accessible skiing in the United States, thanks to the proximity of Salt Lake City International Airport just 36 miles away. Travelers on either coast can board a morning flight and be skiing by early afternoon. Between them the Deer Valley Resort, Park City Mountain Resort and The Canyons offer nearly 50 lifts and, at last count, 8550 skiable acres cut by more than 300 designated trails.

The terrain varies greatly, from easy, almost melancholy runs to steep chutes down precipitous cliffs. There are thickly treed mountainsides for skiers and boarders to weave through, wide-open bowls to see how many turns you can link through knee-deep powder without stopping, and long cruisers for testing your stability at high speeds.

Accessibility aside, what makes the skiing so heady is the snow. Each year, on average, more than 29 feet of snow bury the Park City resorts. It's snow with a ridiculously low moisture content thanks to the atmospheric "wringing" that takes place as storms born in the Pacific cross the Sierra Nevada and Great Basin before slamming into the Wasatch Front. While resorts in other parts of the country generally see snow with an 11 or 12 percent moisture content, Utah's snow typically has a water content of just 4 percent.

Although they're competitors, the three resorts realized that if one brings customers to town, those customers will likely try out the other two resorts. This thinking resulted in the "Silver Passport," which allows the holder to ski all three resorts with an interchangeable lift ticket.

The passport, which can only be purchased in conjunction with a lodging package, comes in four varieties: one version is good for four days of skiing over a five-day period, another for five days out of six, a third good for six days of skiing in seven days, and a fourth for seven days of skiing in a nine-day period.

However, Deer Valley still does not allow snowboarders, and this pass won't get shredders onto that mountain.

restaurant, and in summer you can dine on the patio. ~ 1250 Iron Horse Drive, Park City; 435-647-0880. MODERATE.

HIDDEN ► When I don't want to drive all the way into Park City for a meal, I head to **Sage Grill**, a comfortable eatery located about eight miles north of town. Easy to overlook in a commercial complex salted with banks, department stores, groceries and shops, the restaurant offers Park City cuisine at a reduced price and without the downtown parking hassles. California-inspired entrées range from house-made linguine topped with clams (still in their steamed-open shells) to grilled balsamic pork chop served with porcini mashed potatoes and glazed carrots. ~ 6300 North Sagewood Drive, Park City; 435-658-2267, fax 435-658-2270. MODERATE TO DELUXE.

Guests at The Canyons resort don't need to leave the resort for dinner. At the **Westgate Grill** entrées aren't as steeply priced as they are in downtown Park City. The live jazz can be nice, but sometimes it also can make conversation tough. The tables are placed a bit too close together for me, but the dinners, particularly the seared sea scallops stuffed with crab and the swordfish accompanied by clams and mussels, are sumptuous. ~ 3000 The Canyons Resort Drive, Park City; 435-655-2260. MODERATE.

HIDDEN ► East of Park City by 13 miles lies Kamas, and in this tiny cow town is a great little restaurant that's been resurrected by a chef who once worked at the Deer Valley Resort. Once upon a time the **Gateway Grill** would have worn the "greasy spoon" moniker, but Sean Wharton has introduced the locals to butternut squash soup, smoked shrimp quesadilla, succulent steak and fresh seafood, not to mention a modest wine list. Burgers and fries are still possible, too. ~ 215 South Main Street, Kamas; 435-783-2867. MODERATE.

If you head into the Uinta Mountains east of Park City for a hike, it's almost mandatory that you stop at **Dick's Drive In** on your way back to Park City. This welcome waystation harkens back to the days when you placed your order for a burger and they actually cooked it in front of your eyes, rather than pulled one out from under a warming light. Dick's has great shakes and floats, too. The signs on the wall proudly proclaim that it'll take time to make your meal, as Dick's is not in the fast-food business. ~ 235 East Center Street, Kamas; 435-783-4312. BUDGET.

SHOPPING   **Main Street**, with its interesting and unique locally owned shops squeezed into clapboard- and brick-fronted buildings—some historic, some replicas—is shopping central in Park City. While many resort towns these days are being overrun by national chains, Park City has, so far, dug its heels in against this move. If there is an Achilles heel to Main Street, it's the disturbing number of real estate offices that have surfaced on this pedestrian-heavy street.

You often have to search for the most interesting shops and bargains, and that can be said for the fine furniture and accessories at the **Pyras Collections**. Hidden on the second floor of the Treasure Mountain Inn at the top of Main Street, this shop features antique Chinese tables, armoires and more. ~ 255 Main Street, Suite 7, Park City; 435-615-1262; www.pyrascollections.com.

◄ *HIDDEN*

Rock and Silver, one of the oldest Main Street businesses, offers insight into the minerals and gems to be found inside both Utah's mountains and mountains the world over with its collections of gemstones and mineral deposits. ~ 312 Main Street, Park City; 435-649-5427.

Southwestern-influenced jewelry can be found, along with clothing and home furnishings, at **Nativo**, which shares its address with Rock and Silver. ~ 312 Main Street, Park City; 435-645-8088.

Photographer Thomas Mangelsen perhaps is best known for his picture of an Alaskan brown bear snatching a fish out of mid-air, but he's taken quite a few other incredible wildlife pictures during his lengthy career. You can find many of them at **Images of Nature**. ~ 364 Main Street, Park City; 435-649-7598.

Berets were the fashion rage of the Salt Lake Games, and while they aren't being made anymore, stop in at the **Roots** store for T-shirts, sweatshirts and other Games leftover. As the official supplier to the United States Olympic Committee through 2012 at least, Roots will be churning out more stylish U.S. team clothing in the years to come. ~ 408 Main Street, Park City; 435-615-1166; www.roots.com.

Park City Jewelers has a team of artisans who design and manufacturer jewelry on-site. Among the unique material it works with are polished dinosaur fossil bones, which really generate conversation over cocktails. ~ 430 Main Street, Park City; 435-649-6550; www.parkcityjewelers.com.

At the **Expanding Heart** you'll find an eclectic and metaphysical collection of books, aromatherapy products, massage

AUTHOR FAVORITE

Dolly's Book Store is an Old Town fixture and the town's best when you're in search of regional books and guides as well as national bestsellers and contemporary music selections. I love perusing the shelves, as the stories they hold can take me around the world. Dolly's shares its building with the Rocky Mountain Chocolate Factory, so you can feed your sweet tooth and your literary soul at the same time. ~ 510 Main Street, Park City; 435-649-8062.

oils, bath salts, crystals, candles, incense, jewelry and CDs. ~ 505 Main Street, Park City; 435-649-1255.

Local artworks and organic teas can be found at the **Queen of Arts Tea Room and Gallery**. Take time to order a cup of steaming tea while you study the paintings, potteries and other creations. ~ 515 Main Street, Park City; 435-647-9311.

With Donny and Marie hailing from Utah, is it any wonder there's an **Osmond General Store** in Park City? It's crammed with merchandise ranging from candles and kitchen linens to Hollywood memorabilia. Where else in Utah can you buy an original *Star Wars* movie poster signed by George Lucas, Harrison Ford, Mark Hamill and Carrie Fisher? ~ 541 Main Street, Park City; 435-658-2302; www.osmondgeneralstore.com.

What could be Park City's largest collection of wooden skis and snowshoes can be found at **Southwest Indian Traders**, where there's also a wide variety of turquoise jewelry and Western antiques. ~ 550 Main Street, Park City; 435-645-9177.

Mountain Woods Furniture seems to exist so you can take a piece of the mountains home with you. From log-constructed bunkbeds and office tables to unique coat racks, mirrors, lamps and pillows, this shop has something for everyone who likes the rustic look. They'll even custom-design something for you. ~ 591 Main Street, Park City; 435-658-0005.

It doesn't matter what season it is: you can find U.S. Olympic Team memorabilia and outerwear at the **U.S. Olympic Spirit Store**. ~ 751 Main Street, Park City; 435-655-7597.

I love the gourmet foods, fine cheeses, breads, meats and organic produce carried at the **Mountain Rose Market**. They're the perfect ingredients for a picnic or trail snack. There's also a deli on-site. ~ 2001 Sidewinder Drive, Park City; 435-649-9525; www.mountainrosemarket.com.

Some of the best deals are actually found about eight miles north of town in the **Factory Stores at Park City**, with more than 60 outlet shops ranging from Bose to Nike to OshKosh B'Gosh. ~ 6699 North Landmark Drive, Park City; 435-645-7078.

A worthy stop if you're heading into the Uintas is the **Samak Smoke House and Country Store** on the Mirror Lake Highway (Route 150). My dog and I can vouch that they make and sell Utah's best smoked jerky (in beef, turkey and trout). They also carry maps, fishing supplies, dry goods and sodas and rent snowshoes. ~ 1937 East Mirror Lake Highway, Kamas; 435-783-4880.

NIGHTLIFE   Park City has a refreshing dose of year-round activity. When the snow finally runs off and the mud dries (usually by mid-June), the mountains come alive with outdoor concerts, an international jazz festival and a "Concerts in the Park" series. Many summer weekends find local musicians performing on the Town Lift square on lower Main Street. Early August delivers a three-day arts festival, which overruns Main Street with dozens of booths offering everything from oil paintings and bronze sculptures to pottery and wooden crafts. Throughout the year you can usually find performances at both the Eccles Center for the Performing Arts or the community-run Egyptian Theater.

The **Deer Valley Resort** on the south end of town brings music to the mountains with the likes of Lyle Lovett, Kenny Loggins, B. B. King and Doc Severinsen. ~ 2250 Deer Valley Drive South, Park City; 435-649-1000, 800-424-3337.

The **Eccles Center for the Performing Arts** presents concerts, ballet, modern dance, comedy and avant-garde theater. In mid-January the center is given over to the Sundance Film Festival for screenings. ~ 1750 Kearns Boulevard, Park City; 435-655-3114.

Local thespians tromp the stage at the refurbished **Egyptian Theater** on Main Street, and during the Sundance Film Festival you'll find films screened here as well. ~ 328 Main Street, Park City; 435-649-9371.

You don't need to be hungry to head to **The Spur Bar & Grill**, where you can while away the night sitting in front of the fire while listening to live jazz, blues, bluegrass or acoustic rock-and-roll. ~ 350½ Main Street, Park City; 435-615-1618.

Along with being a popular restaurant, **Mileti's** also lures locals and visitors to its bar, particularly on weekends. ~ 412 Main Street, Park City; 435-649-8211.   ◀ HIDDEN

Harry O's is where the frisky twenty-something crowd rocks on weekends, sometimes to live acts, sometimes to deejays. ~ 427 Main Street, Park City; 435-647-9494.

Across the street is the **Phat Tire Saloon**, which rocks to live music most nights until 1 a.m. Located below street level beneath a Chinese restaurant, the Phat Tire also offers pool tables if you're not into dancing. ~ 438 Main Street, Park City; 435-658-2699.

One of Main Street's oldest buildings today houses the **No Name Saloon**, which jumps through the night and early into the next morning. ~ 447 Main Street, Park City; 435-649-6667.

LIGHTS, CAMERA, FAME

Park City is overrun each January when Robert Redford brings his **Sundance Film Festival**, the country's most prestigious independent film festival, to Park City for ten usually snowy days of premieres, competitions and haggling between Hollywood studios and, in many cases, young and upcoming directors. Among the productions that gained fame at Sundance were *The Blair Witch Project, sex, lies and videotape* and *The Brothers McMullen*. ~ 801-328-3456.

Mother Urban's Ratskeller takes its name from one of Park City's infamous madams. Housed in the basement of a Main Street building, this bar draws a lively crowd as well as live entertainment. Beware: the smoke can get thick. ~ 625 Main Street, Park City; 435-615-7200.

Renee's Bar and Café is a delightfully refreshing trendsetter in Utah—the first private club to ban smoking! Just a block away from Main Street, this welcome addition to Park City's nightlife offers a lengthy wine list, local beers on tap, light fare, vegetarian munchies and live entertainment that attracts young and old. ~ 136 Heber Avenue #107, Park City; 435-615-8357.

> The "Friday Night Strolls" of Main Street's art galleries, held on the first Friday of every month from 6 p.m. to 9 p.m., begin at the Kimball Art Center.

Sports fans will feel at home at the **Broken Thumb Sports Grill**, which claims to be Park City's original sports grill. Whether that's true is debatable, but you will find two big-screen televisions here, as well as foosball and pool tables, Utah microbrews, chicken wings that come in spicy temperaments, sandwiches and burgers. ~ 1200 East Little Kate Drive (inside the Racquet Club), Park City; 435-647-3932.

Many restaurants and bars have some form of entertainment during the ski season, whether it's in the form of a pianist or guitarist. On occasion live jazz can be found in some establishments. To see who's playing where, check *The Park Record*, Park City's local newspaper, or, if you're computer-capable, log onto www.parkcityinfo.com to see who's playing where and when.

PARKS

CITY PARK Naturally, there's a park in Park City. City Park occupies one of the few stretches of flat ground in town. With soccer fields, a softball diamond, a playground, basketball courts and sand volleyball courts, the park is constantly busy during the warm-weather months. A quarter-mile bike path runs the length of the park alongside Poison Creek. ~ Accessed via Sullivan Lane between 13th and 14th streets along Park Avenue.

WASATCH-CACHE NATIONAL FOREST Drawing its name from both American Indians and mountain men, the Wasatch-Cache National Forest stretches across 1.2 million Utah acres, from the northeastern corner through the northern end of the state all the way to the Idaho border. While "Wasatch" is a Ute word meaning "high mountain pass," "cache" comes from the mountain men who would "cache," or store, their pelts in pits or caves until they could be traded at a rendezvous. One of the most heavily utilized forests in the country, the Wasatch-Cache sees most of its recreational pressures centered around the craggy granite peaks that harbor four alpine resorts southeast of Salt Lake City and along the northern and western slopes of the Uinta Range east of Park City and northeast of Heber City. Summer brings anglers, hikers, backpackers, biking, boating and horseback riding to the Kamas, Mountain View and Evanston districts; winter sees skiers, snowshoers and snowmobilers. Forest highlights include the **High Uintas Wilderness**, a 456,705-acre tract east of Park City and north of Vernal. Day-use fee, $3 per vehicle. ~ Route 150 runs through the forest from Kamas, Utah, to Evanston, Wyoming; Kamas Ranger District, 50 East Center Street, Kamas, UT 84036; 435-783-4338. Winter users can call 801-364-1581 for information on avalanche conditions in the forest.

▲ In the forest's Kamas, Mountain View and Evanston ranger districts northeast of Park City there are 38 campgrounds with 904 designated campsites (no hookups); free to $14; most have a 14-day maximum stay. Reservations: 877-444-6777.

JORDANELLE STATE PARK

Jordanelle State Park's 3300-acre reservoir and its close proximity to the Wasatch Front make this park one of the state's busiest, particularly in the summer when the mercury tops 100 degrees in Salt Lake City. While boaters, anglers and swimmers converge on the water, the park's perimeter trail attracts hikers, mountain bikers, horseback riders and even Nordic skiers. The mixture of water, woodlands and sage meadows is a favorite with birders. Finches, sparrows, hawks, owls, kestrels, woodpeckers and golden eagles frequent the **Rock Cliff area**, while waterfowl such as grebes, pelicans and loons enjoy the marshlands and open waters. The **Hailstone area** often attracts mountain bluebirds, western meadowlarks and northern flickers; since Hailstone lies along a major raptor migration route, in the spring turkey vultures, golden eagles and a variety of hawks often can be seen drifting overhead. Fishing is excellent for rainbow trout, cutthroat trout and smallmouth bass, while the Provo River that fills the reservoir is a brown trout fishery. Facilities include two developed recreation sites, picnic grounds, beaches, restrooms, showers, boat launches, day-use cabanas, laundry facilities, a marina and a restaurant. The park also has a 12-mile-long trail that circles the reservoir and draws hikers, bikers, equestrians and Nordic skiers. The trail ties into the Historic Union Pacific Rail Trail State Park, making it possible to ride, hike or jog from Park City to Jordanelle. In the future, officials hope to develop a trail system that will connect Jordanelle to the nearby Deer Creek, Rockport and Wasatch Mountain state parks. Day-use fee, $9 per vehicle. ~ The Hailstone entrance is located off Exit 8 of Route 40, just four miles from the Park City exit, while the Rock Cliff entrance is eight miles from Route 40 on Route 32; Hailstone visitors center, 435-649-9540; Rock Cliff, 435-783-3030; parks.state.ut.us/parks/www1/jord.htm.

▲ Four campgrounds have 236 sites, 103 equipped with RV hookups; $14 to $17 per night; 14-day maximum stay. Reservations: 800-322-3770.

ROCKPORT STATE PARK 🏃 🏠 ⛵ 🛶 🚤 ⛴ 🎣 One of the most overlooked of Utah's parks, possibly due to its dearth of shade, Rockport State Park lies 27 miles east of Park City. The park revolves around a manmade reservoir created by damming the mouth of a canyon. The surrounding hillsides are covered mostly with scrub oak and brush, although the campgrounds have some trees to provide a modicum of shade. Rockport is popular with boaters, anglers, waterskiers and swimmers. In winter months cross-country skiers skim across the reservoir's frozen surface. Facilities include campgrounds, picnic areas, restrooms and showers. Day-use fee, $7 per vehicle. ~ 9040 North Route 302, Peoa; 435-336-2241; parks.state.ut.us/parks/www1/rock.htm.

▲ There are 86 tent sites and 36 RV sites with hookups; $8 to $17 per night. Reservations: 800-322-3770.

HIDDEN ► **HISTORIC UNION PACIFIC RAIL TRAIL STATE PARK** 🏃 🚴 🐎 🏠 Hikers, mountain bikers, equestrians, joggers and, in winter, cross-country skiers all work out at the Historic Union Pacific Rail Trail State Park, which is nothing more than a 28-mile-long, 125-foot-wide corridor. Early morning or early evening treks might produce sightings of mule deer, elk or even moose. The trail runs through lands with significant geological, archaeological and paleontological significance. In the 1960s an excavation not far from the trail corridor unearthed fossilized remains of both mastodons and sabertooth cats. No facilities. ~ Trail access in Park City is along either Prospector Avenue or Cochise Court; 435-649-6839; parks.state.ut.us/parks/www1/hist.htm.

▼▼▼▼▼▼▼▼▼▼▼

Heber City Area

Heber City is one of those towns we all want to move to. In stark contrast to the bustling, increasingly high-tech 21st-century personality of the Wasatch Front communities of Ogden, Salt Lake City, Provo and Orem, Heber City and its namesake valley on the Wasatch Back reflect the state's less hectic, bucolic demeanor. Eastbound Route 40, which divides the town of 7500 in half, shuttles you past sheep, cattle, llamas and, on occasion, some bison grazing alongside the highway. Overhead, golden eagles and redtail hawks wheel on the air currents.

The Provo River, Utah's best-known blue-ribbon trout fishery, meanders through the valley, luring both anglers and raptors, while deer, elk, moose and black bear roam the rimming mountains. Sandhill cranes browse the fields bordering the river during their migrations, and rare whooping cranes have occasionally been spotted there, too.

Although intent on retaining its rural roots, Heber City is not bashful about keeping in step with the economic times. Just 40 miles east of Salt Lake City via Route 80 and Route 40, and 24 miles from Provo by way of Route 189, Heber City is a growing bedroom community for those cities.

It doesn't take long to negotiate this four-stoplight town. While there's talk of rerouting Route 40 around the heart of town, for now it still doubles as Heber City's Main Street, cutting straight through the business district.

Farming and ranching remain integral parts of the Heber Valley's lifeblood, although tourism and recreation are gaining prominence. Cradled in the valley's western corner is Soldier Hollow, a portion of Wasatch State Park where the biathlon and Nordic events of the 2002 Winter Olympic Games were staged. Headquartered on the western edge of town, the steam-powered Heber Valley Historic Railroad stands ready to haul you back to a simpler time, if for only a few hours.

SIGHTS

If you arrive in Heber City from the north via Route 40, stop first at the **Heber Valley Chamber of Commerce Visitors Center**. Not only can you bone up on the valley's—and city's—history here, the center is a gold mine of information on Heber City's lodgings and eateries, as well as area attractions. ~ 475 North Main Street, Heber City; 435-654-3666; www.hebervalleycc.org, e-mail hebercc@shadowlink.net.

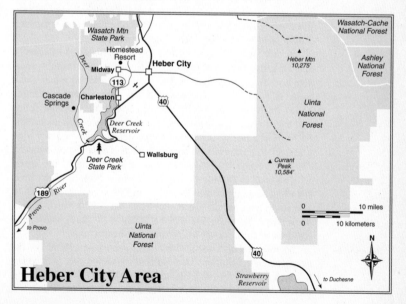

Heber City Area

One of the oldest buildings in town is the **Wasatch Stake Tabernacle,** which the LDS Church built in 1889. Today this structure, built from red sandstone quarried just east of Heber City, houses the city offices. A small museum on the first floor recounts some of the history of Wasatch County. Hanging on one wall is a quilt made in 1996 by the Daughters of Utah Pioneers that depicts some of the county's barns in fine stitchwork. ~ 75 North Main Street, Heber City; 435-654-0757

Departing Heber City on a regular basis throughout the year is the **Heber Valley Historic Railroad,** which uses steam locomotives and an occasional diesel to haul passengers across the valley and past Deer Creek Reservoir into Provo Canyon. These 17-mile trips, featured daily through the summer and mid-fall, run three and a half hours roundtrip. Shorter trips to Soldier Hollow or the Deer Creek Dam are offered on winter weekends as well as throughout the warmer months. Special rides involving evening barbecues, murder mystery plays and even fiddlers are available throughout the year. During the Christmas season the railroad offers a trip that revolves around narration of Chris Van Allsburg's *The Polar Express,* as well as a visit by Santa Claus. Reservations for all trips are highly recommended. ~ 450 South 600 West, Heber City; 435-654-5601, fax 435-654-3709; www.hebervalleyrr.org, e-mail hebervalleyrr@shadowlink.net.

Heber City can't be discussed without mention of its neighbor, **Midway,** located just three miles to the west. This lilliputian town in the afternoon shadow of the Wasatch Range is even more rustic than Heber City, with its homes and few businesses land-locked by ranches, farms and mountains.

In this Swiss-flavored hamlet lies **The Homestead Resort,** a stately, turn-of-the-20th-century retreat built up around a massive hot spring that soothed the weary muscles of miners who toiled all week in the silver mines of Park City. There aren't many places in the country where you can spend the morning skiing and the afternoon scuba diving, but Midway is one thanks to the 65-foot-deep hot spring at The Homestead. Entombed in a towering, 55-foot mound of minerals deposited over the millennia by the hot spring's mineral-laden waters, the inside of the crater with its watery pool is perfect for learning how to scuba dive, spending some time snorkeling, or simply swimming. Instruction and equipment rentals are available on site. ~ 700 North Homestead Drive, Midway; 435-654-1102, 800-327-7220; www.homesteadresort.com, e-mail info@homesteadresort.com.

HIDDEN ►   **Memorial Hill** rises abruptly from the pastureland on the eastern edge of Midway. A road that corkscrews its way to the hilltop leads to a memorial dedicated to the county's war veterans, though brass plaques honoring them were stolen from the rock memorial atop the hill. Still, the ride to the top is worth it—the 360-degree view of Midway, Heber City, the Heber Valley and Mount Timpanogos is outstanding. ~ About 300 North on River Road, Midway.

The best way to leave the valley and get into the mountains, at least during the warmer months of the year, is to visit **Cascade Springs** via a spur of the Alpine Loop Scenic Backway. Cascade Springs is actually a series of springs that spill down the mountainside through a string of limestone pools and terraces, only to disappear back into the mountain. The U.S. Forest Service has installed boardwalks around the springs. In the summer, lush patches of vegetation surround the springs. Look closely for trout in the springs. Fishing is not allowed here, though. ~ The 24-mile loop runs from near Timpanogos Cave National Monument (see Chapter Five), up through a mountain pass on the end of the Mount Timpanogos Wilderness Area, past the Sundance Resort and down the Provo River Canyon to Orem and then back north to the monument. Coming from Heber City, take Route 113 west to Midway, where it bends to the south. After about three miles on 113 you'll come to Tate Lane, where you turn to the west. Another quarter-mile or so brings you to Cascade Springs Road (a dirt lane that may be impassable in muddy weather), which runs for seven miles to the springs.

◀ *HIDDEN*

Cascade Springs pump out seven million gallons of water each day.

Within 15 minutes of Heber City's Main Street you'll find three state parks. Which to visit depends on whether you want to fish or play golf during the warmer months or ice-fish or cross-country ski during the winter months. **Jordanelle State Park** (see "Park City Area") north of Heber City is primarily a boater's paradise since the main feature is a 3300-acre reservoir, but there are hiking trails and campgrounds to enjoy, too. **Wasatch Mountain State Park** to the west offers something for most outdoors lovers, with a sprawling golf course, hiking trails, campgrounds and cross-country skiing come winter. **Deer Creek State Park** southwest of Heber City makes its living entertaining anglers with its fishing and boaters who flock here for skiing and windsurfing.

Quaint and removed from the bustling Salt Lake Valley, the Heber Valley has a small collection of accommodations for travelers.

LODGING

For local color, the **Swiss Alps Inn** on Main Street features a working, life-size glockenspiel clock atop the main building. Inside you'll find clean and unassuming rooms. There's also an indoor spa and outdoor heated pool. ~ 167 South Main Street, Heber City; 435-654-0722; www.swissalpsinn.com, e-mail alps@swissalpsinn.com. BUDGET TO MODERATE.

The ubiquitous **Holiday Inn Express** has standard rooms. ~ 1268 South Main Street, Heber City; 435-654-9990. MODERATE.

Drifting asleep to the sound of splashing water is possible at the **Johnson Mill Bed & Breakfast**, along the eastern boundary of Midway. Occupying a century-old flour mill, the inn sits on 35 acres next to the Provo River. You can walk from your room onto the covered wraparound porch and then down to spring-fed ponds and streams crowded with German brown and rainbow trout and a family of swans. There's even a gazebo in one pond accessed by a wooden pier. And, of course, the natural waterfall that once powered the grist mill remains. The rooms are large and comfortable, with fireplaces, vaulted ceilings and private balconies. ~ 100 North Johnson Mill Road, Midway; 435-654-4466, 888-272-0030, fax 435-657-1454; www.johnsonmill. com. DELUXE TO ULTRA-DELUXE.

The **Inn on the Creek** reflects the valley's Swiss heritage by recreating the feel of a small mountain village. In the spring colorful bursts of wildflowers erupt around the inn's main building, which has eight rooms for adults. Outlying chalets can handle families or larger groups and feature kitchens for when you don't feel like heading to the inn for your meals. There's also a heated pool for recouping after a hard ski or day on the links, or you can relax before your room's fireplace. ~ 375 Rainbow Lane, Midway; 435-654-0892, 800-654-0892, fax 435-654-5971; www. innoncreek.com. DELUXE TO ULTRA-DELUXE.

Directly across from Wasatch Mountain State Park and just two miles from Soldier Hollow, site of the Salt Lake Games' cross-country, biathlon and Nordic combined events, the **Blue Boar Inn** holds just 14 rooms, but they come with fireplaces, full bathrooms and televisions if you can't find enough to do outdoors. Meals—breakfast is included in your room charge—is served downstairs in the dining room. ~ 1235 Warm Springs Road, Midway; 435-654-1400, 888-650-1400, fax 435-654-6459; www.theblueboar inn.com. ULTRA-DELUXE.

For pure indulgence in the Heber Valley, stay at **The Homestead Resort**. After a day of hiking or skiing in Wasatch Mountain State Park or the surrounding mountains, or perhaps sailing or windsurfing on either Deer Creek or Jordanelle reservoirs, you can squirrel yourself away in one of the executive cottages, a family-style room, or even the Virginia House, a Victorian-style structure that operates like a B&B. While relaxing in your room you can even sate your sweet tooth with the complimentary fudge. ~ 700 North Homestead Drive, Midway; 435-654-1102, 800-327-7220; www.homesteadresort.com. DELUXE TO ULTRA-DELUXE.

Daniels Summit Lodge, 16 miles southeast of Heber City ◀ *HIDDEN*
along Route 40, is the gateway to more than 200 miles of snowmobile trails, which in the summer turn into mountain bike routes.
You'll also find some cross-country ski trails here. The log and
stone lodge offers 42 lodge rooms and eight cabins, most equipped
with fireplaces and jetted tubs. You'll also find an indoor pool
and spa, a restaurant, a general store and a gift shop, as well as
snowmobile rentals and guided tours in winter and guided horseback rides in summer. ~ P.O. Box 490, Heber City, UT 84032; 800-
519-9969, fax 435-548-2982; www.danielssummit.com. MOD-
ERATE TO ULTRA-DELUXE.

Unlike Park City, Heber City is not exactly a culinary hotbed, but   **DINING**
you can find some surprisingly good meals in the area.
    You can find Mexican dishes in both Midway and Heber
City at **Don Pedro's**, a locally owned eatery featuring the usual
Mexican fare. ~ 1050 South Main Street, Heber City, 435-657-
0600; 42 West Main Street in Midway, 435-654-0805. BUDGET
TO MODERATE.
    Not far from Main Street in Heber City is the **Snake Creek**   ◀ *HIDDEN*
Grill, a locals' favorite where the meals are on par with those
served in Park City but at roughly two-thirds the cost. The grill
is housed in a clapboard building right out of the Old West.
Inside you'll find a truly eclectic dinner menu that includes entrées such as blue cornmeal–crusted trout, ten-spice salmon with
red curry–Japanese noodle stirfry, and zucchini-tomato risotto
with spice-grilled white shrimp. Reservations suggested. ~ 650
West 100 South, Heber City; 435-654-2133; www.snakegrill
creek.com. MODERATE.
    The Homestead Resort offers the formal **Simon's Restaurant**
for dinner and Sunday brunch throughout the year, and **Fanny's**
Grill, which serves three meals a day in a more casual atmosphere.
Housed inside the main building, the restaurants carry a country
atmosphere befitting the resort's location. Simon's is decidedly
the more expensive of the two, although the Sunday brunch is well

AUTHOR FAVORITE

If you're just passing through Heber City on the way to some-
where else and it's hot out, the incredibly thick and rich milkshakes at
Granny's will cool you down and fill you up at the same time.
Choosing one of the 44 flavors could take some time. ~ 511 South
Main Street, Heber City; 435-654-3097. BUDGET.

worth it, with multiple stations offering made-to-order omelets, french toast, pastries, cereals, meats and desserts. Fanny's menus offer somewhat more traditional—and heartier—country fare, such as ribs, chops and fried chicken dishes for dinner and burgers and steak sandwiches, as well as pastas, for lunch. ~ 700 North Homestead Drive, Midway; 435-654-1102, 800-327-7220; www. homesteadresort.com. MODERATE TO DELUXE.

Located virtually next door to The Homestead Resort lies the **Inn on the Creek,** a laid-out European resort whose restaurant is dominated by a large fireplace. Dinner entrées here might include lobster ravioli with seared scallops, grilled pork chops or lamb stew. ~ 375 Rainbow Lane, Midway; 435-654-0892, 800-654-0892, fax 435-654-5871; www.innoncreek.com. MODERATE TO DELUXE.

SHOPPING   When it comes time for serious shopping in Heber City, most locals head to nearby Park City or even Provo. But this doesn't mean the town and nearby Midway are entirely devoid of intriguing shops. At **Old Heber Town,** a small cluster of shops housed in buildings out of the Old West, you'll find restaurants, antique shops, craft stores and even an art gallery. ~ 650 West 100 South, Heber City.

Just minutes away is **Water From the Moon,** an eclectic shop with clothing, sterling silver items, and gifts for the home. ~ 118 South 500 West, Heber City; 435-654-2267.

Books and Beyond is not your typical bookstore, located in a 1700-square-foot converted garage. Walls segregate the genres and create some interesting quiet spaces where you can read. There's also an espresso café. ~ 511 West 100 South, Heber City; 435-657-2665.

Whimsy Cottage caters to quilters with fabrics and patterns. ~ 350 South Main Street, Heber City; 435-657-7137; www. whimsycottage.com.

Pinto Pony Designs carries not only furniture and home furnishings but wildlife, Western and American Indian artworks. ~ 261 South Main Street, Heber City; 435-654-5555.

Rural landscapes dominate the collections at the **Edeleiss Gallery** in Midway. Closed Sunday and Monday. ~ 65 East Main Street, Midway; 435-654-1335.

Photography of the mountains and settings around Heber City and Midway, as well as from as far away as Canada, can be found inside **Rustic Elegance,** where you can even arrange your own photograph. ~ 210 East Main Street, Suite E-4, Midway; 435-654-2583.

A wide array of gifts and home accessories, as well as some winter sports antiques such as snowshoes, skates and skis, await at **All That Stuff in the Barn**. ~ 128 West 100 North, Midway; 435-654-5889.

Olson Galleries in the Glockenspiel Haus specializes in fine-art originals and prints as well as finely detailed pen and ink drawings. ~ 101 West Main Street, Midway; 435-654-3725; www. olsongalleries.com.

NIGHTLIFE

They don't roll up the streets in Heber City come nightfall, but it can certainly seem like it. If you don't mind smoke and are only looking for a cold beer and possibly a game of pool, head to **The Other End** at the northern edge of town. ~ 1223 North Route 40, Heber City; no phone.

For a movie, try **Reel Theatres**. ~ 94 South Main Street, Heber City; 435-654-1181.

Or, you can roll a game or two at **Holiday Lanes**. ~ 515 North Main Street, Heber City; 435-654-0372.

PARKS

UINTA NATIONAL FOREST 🚶 🚴 🏇 🏕 ⛴ 🛶 🎣 Within its 958,258 acres the Uinta National Forest claims high desert, rugged canyons and lofty peaks reaching to 11,877 feet. It also contains three wilderness areas and the Mount Timpanogos Cave National Monument, which is administered by the National Park Service. Also in the forest and not far from Heber City are the **Strawberry Reservoir Recreation Area** (23 miles south of Heber City via Route 40; 435-548-2321) and the **Currant Creek Reservoir Recreation Area** (head 40 miles south of Heber City on Route 40 to Currant Creek Road, a dirt road that runs 17 miles to the reservoir). Elk, black bear, cougar, moose, mountain goats, bighorn sheep and mule deer are often spotted in the forest. The Provo River that runs between the Jordanelle and Deer Creek reservoirs and then on through Provo Canyon west of Heber City to Provo is an outstanding trout fishery. Facilities include picnic areas, restrooms, a ski resort and cross-country ski trails. Two major highways, Route 189 between Provo and Heber City and Route 40 between Heber City and Fruitland, bisect portions of the forest. ~ Heber Ranger District, 2460 South Route 40, Heber; 435-654-0470.

In Soldier Hollow, at the southern end of Wasatch Mountain State Park, you can kick-and-glide or skate-ski along the same routes Olympic athletes competed on during the Salt Lake Games in 2002.

▲ Forest-wide, there are 26 campgrounds in the three ranger districts with 1314 RV/tent sites, some with hookups; the bulk of the sites are in the Heber Ranger District; free to $12 for individual sites; most have a 14-day maximum stay. Reservations: 877-444-6777.

WASATCH MOUNTAIN STATE PARK 🚶 🚴 🏇 🏕 Cradled in the nook of the eponymous mountain range, the 22,000-acre

Wasatch Mountain State Park offers both finely manicured fairways of a USGA-sanctioned golf course and rugged mountains for hiking and mountain biking. The golf course boasts 27 holes and ten lakes waiting to swallow your drives. Beyond golf, you'll find wonderful hiking opportunities and plenty of campsites complete with picnic tables and grills. In fall, which usually begins to show its colorful hand in early September, the park's forests ignite in a blaze of crimson, orange, yellow and brown leaves of maples, aspen, scrub oaks and serviceberry. Things don't slow down in winter, when storms bury the golf course and surrounding hillsides and meadows under snows perfect for cross-country skiing. Facilities at the park include a visitors center, restrooms and showers, and a group picnic pavilion as well as a ranch-style building (complete with kitchen) known as the "chalet" that groups can rent summer and winter. Day-use fee, $5. ~ Routes 113 and 224, about six miles northwest of Heber City; 435-654-1791 (visitors center), 435-654-3961 (campground); parks.state.ut.us/parks/www1/wasa.htm.

▲ There are four campgrounds with 139 RV and 57 tent sites; $11 to $20 per night; 14-day maximum stay. Reservations: 800-322-3770.

DEER CREEK STATE PARK 🚶 🚵 🛶 🎣 ⛵ 🚤 🏊 ⛴ Created by the damming of the Provo River at the head of Provo Canyon, Deer Creek State Park is built around a sprawling reservoir designed to quench Wasatch Front water needs. Within its 3260 acres, you'll find tremendous fishing and reliable breezes for windsurfing and sailing. Facilities include a concrete boat launch, fish-cleaning stations, a restaurant and marina (which rents boats and sells gas), restrooms, showers and a group picnic pavilion. Day-use fee, $9. ~ Route 189, about five miles southwest of Heber City; 435-654-0171; parks.state.ut.us/parks/www1/dear.htm.

▲ There are 72 campsites, 58 for RVs and 14 for tents; $14 to $20 per night; 14-day maximum stay. Reservations: 800-322-3770 (May through September).

Vernal Area

Connecting Park City, Heber City and Vernal likes dots on a connect-the-dots puzzle is Route 40. This sturdy, two-lane highway that climbs through mountains and races across the plains is the key artery across northeastern Utah. From Heber City it runs 128 miles to Vernal, passing through majestic, pine-covered mountains as well as tedious scrublands along the way.

At first glance, Vernal seems little more than a drab waystation between Salt Lake City and Denver. Indeed, cruising down Route 40 from point A to B, Vernal materializes through the windshield as little more than a humdrum rural community that somehow ekes out a living from a barren, custard-colored landscape. Pause for a moment, though, and take note of your surroundings. Northeast of town lies the rugged sandstone maze that is Dinosaur National Monument; to the north rise the snow-capped Uinta Mountains, the Rocky Mountains' only range that runs east to west; while to the south sprawls the roughly 3.3-million-acre Uintah and Ouray Indian Reservation.

These "playgrounds" make Vernal a perfect jumping-off point for a diverse array of recreational options: hiking, fishing or cross-country skiing in the Ashley National Forest that drapes across the canyon-riddled flanks of the Uintas, floating down the nearby Green or Yampa rivers, wading through the geologic wonderland known as Fantasy Canyon, tracing prehistoric history in Dinosaur National Monument. You'll also find museums that recall the days of Butch Cassidy and the Sundance Kid as well as the towering dinosaurs that once trod across the land here.

So smitten, in fact, is Vernal with its proximity to Dinosaur National Monument that it's known as the heart of "Dinosaurland," a common moniker for this corner of Utah. Enter town from the west on Route 40 and you'll be greeted by a towering

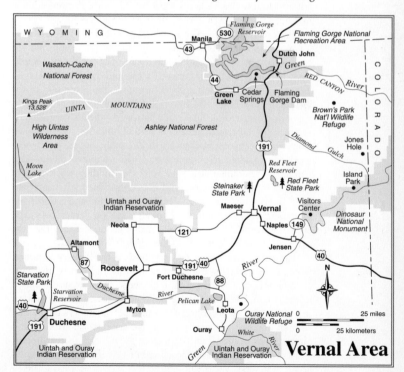

Vernal Area

replica of a tyrannosaurus rex, while from the town's eastern gateway you'll encounter "Dinah," an outrageously pink Barney lookalike.

SIGHTS   Water is a precious resource in northeastern Utah's high-desert landscape. The U.S. Bureau of Land Management realized just how important water in the Uintah Basin was to wildlife in the early 1970s when the agency spotted waterfowl living in Pariette Draw, which is 48 miles southwest of Vernal. BLM biologists realized they could multiply the benefit of the draw's water by developing 20 ponds and other waterways along the draw. Since its

HIDDEN ►   completion in 1975, the **Pariette Wetlands** have become a waterfowl magnet as well as the BLM's largest waterfowl management area in Utah. Each year nearly 2000 ducks are born and reared in the wetlands, which also attract geese and shorebirds such as avocets and black-necked stilts as well as white pelicans and herons during the summer months. ~ To reach the 9033-acre preserve, just west of Myton turn south off Route 40 and onto the Sand Wash–Green River access road. After 1.7 miles of paved road you'll come to Nine Mile–Sand Wash Junction, where you turn left and follow the wetlands signs for 23 miles. For more information, call the BLM's Vernal office at 435-781-4400.

Back on Route 40, about 130 miles east of Heber City is **Vernal**, a town of about 7100 people. Once in Vernal, you'll find the town's most handsome building in the form of the **Vernal Temple**. Built by the LDS Church between 1900 and 1907 as the Uintah Tabernacle, the temple's architecture is a simpler version of the Georgian New England Church design. During the nearly eight years of construction, financially strapped officials shrewdly assembled the tabernacle at a cost of $37,000. Logs were hauled from nearby canyons, bricks were made locally, and the pine woodwork was painted to resemble oak while wooden pillars were painted to resemble marble. In 1992 the building was closed to the public because of structural concerns. Three years later the LDS Church embarked on a $7 million renovation and transformed the tabernacle into a temple. Though non-church members can't enter the temple, they can stroll the tidy grounds and admire the exterior of the building. ~ 170 South 400 West, Vernal.

Across the street from the tabernacle is the **Pioneer Museum**, which is open during the summer months and run by the local chapter of Daughters of the Utah Pioneers. The museum is housed in the original **Vernal Tithing Building**, a rock building erected in 1887 and used to collect farm products members of the LDS Church donated to the church. Inside are historic artifacts and photographs of the Uinta Basin from the mid-1800s that impart a taste of life in the West. Closed Labor Day through May. ~ 200 South 500 West, Vernal; no phone.

A must-stop on your way to Dinosaur National Monument (see "Dinosaur National Monument" below), which lies 20 miles east of town, is the **Utah Field House of Natural History State Park**. Located on Main Street two blocks from the center of Vernal, this facility is a catalog of eastern Utah's geologic past and natural history. Outside on the park grounds you'll find a kid-pleasing "dinosaur garden" stocked with 18 life-sized replicas of prehistoric nasties such as tyrannosaurus rex and utahraptor, a voracious carnivore whose fossilized remains were discovered not too long ago in central Utah's outback. The replicas depict a wide slice of dino life, coming from periods ranging from 65 million to 150 million years ago. Kids can experience their own fossil "dig" in a sandbox containing casts of actual bones. Inside, the field house exhibits more recent history—artifacts from the Fremont and Ute cultures that once roamed the region as well as geology displays that chronicle 600 million years of life. Before you leave the museum, stop in the adjoining travel information center to pick up a free Dinosaur Hunting License. Ground was broken in 2002 for a new museum building to house this incredible collection; it is scheduled to open in spring 2004. Admission. ~ 235 East Main Street, Vernal; 435-789-3799; parks.state.ut.us/parks/www1/utah.htm.

Next door to the field house in a corner of the Uintah County Library is the **Ladies of the White House Doll Collection**, a doll-lover's display of First Ladies in their inaugural ball gowns. Done in conjunction with the country's bicentennial celebration, the exhibit includes pictures of the Vernal-area women who made the dresses as well as short histories on the First Ladies. The library is closed Sunday. ~ 155 East Main Street, Vernal; 435-789-0091.

◄ HIDDEN

Bits and pieces of Uintah County's outlaw past are on display at the county-owned **Western Heritage Museum**, which not only touches on Butch and Sundance's Wild Bunch Gang but also has extensive exhibits on the Old West and American Indians. A mockup of a general store stands in one corner of the museum, while elsewhere in the hall you'll find hammers, pliers, nails and horseshoes from a blacksmith's shop, saddle and rifle collections,

AUTHOR FAVORITE

sights **Dinosaur National Monument** sates not only my curiosity about ancient reptiles but also renews my appreciation for nature's power when I see how the once-level landscape was twisted into a dome and then cut in half by the river. See page 204 for more information.

Fremont Indian arrowheads and woven baskets, and even the 25 pounds of medical tools and drugs that one of Vernal's first doctors toted about in his black bag. Closed Sunday. ~ 300 East 200 South, Vernal; 435-789-7399.

As evidenced by Dinosaur National Monument, the Uintah Basin is a treasure trove of dinosaur fossils. You can also find **dinosaur tracks**, if you know where to look. One good area is **Red Fleet State Park** found ten miles north of Vernal. More than 200 three-toed tracks belonging to a bipedal dinosaur are frozen in stone on the shore of Red Fleet Reservoir across from the boat ramp. ~ Route 191, ten miles north of Vernal, Vernal; 435-789-4432.

HIDDEN ►   The **Dry Fork Petroglyphs** ten miles north of town via 3500 West and the Dry Fork Canyon Road are a dazzling display of the Fremont Culture's artistry. The 1200-to-1600-year-old rock art, most of which is composed of trapezoidal figures, covers a 200-foot-high Navajo sandstone cliff. Some of the pictures are nine feet tall. Next to the parking area is a replica of a saloon as well as a general store. ~ 3500 West, located ten miles north of Vernal.

While the bizarre rock formations of southern Utah are well-known and preserved in the form of national parks, there's a canyon about 27 miles south of downtown Vernal that also bears otherworldly rock configurations worth visiting. Although the

HIDDEN ►   area is not actually a canyon, it's known as **Fantasy Canyon** due to its fragile sandstone formations. These formations, between 38 million and 50 million years old, were created by sediments that filled the prehistoric Lake Uintah that once inundated the region. One of the more unusual minerals found in Fantasy Canyon is gilsonite. This shiny black mineral exists in a one-inch wide vertical vein. Thicker, commercially mined veins of gilsonite are found near Bonanza and Ouray. A fossilized turtle shell can also be seen in the canyon. ~ To reach Fantasy Canyon, head south of Vernal on Route 45 for 21 miles, then turn right onto Glen Bench Road and take it 18 miles to the canyon. For a map, stop at the BLM office at 170 South 500 East; 435-781-4400.

Fantasy Canyon's strange, delicate compositions have inspired another nickname for this natural wonder: "Nature's China Shop."

Thirty-six miles north of Vernal lies **Flaming Gorge National Recreation Area**, a 207,363-acre playground for boating, hiking, camping and some of the world's best lake-trout fishing. The gorge was named in 1869 by Major John Wesley Powell, who was enchanted by the way the setting sun reflected off the canyon's red-rock cliffs. Part of the landscape was submerged, though, in 1964 when the Flaming Gorge Dam was completed. A close-up look at the area's twisted and folded rock formations can be had on the 11-mile **Sheep Creek Geologic Loop**, a scenic drive that most vehicles can handle. In the fall, kokanee salmon enter Sheep Creek from the reservoir to spawn. The "Drive through the Ages" runs from Vernal to the national recreation area, using a series of interpretive signs to highlight 80 million years of geology. From Vernal, the drive along Route 191 to the visitors center at Dutch John takes about an hour as the highway darts and jogs up and over the Uinta Mountains before reaching the **Flaming Gorge Dam.** Erected in 1964, the 502-foot-high hydroelectric dam created a reservoir that runs 91 miles north into Wyoming. See "Parks" below for more information about Flaming Gorge National Recreation Area.

Although it's roughly 40 miles northeast of Vernal by a questionable road in the best of weather or 77 miles via a roundabout way on better roads, the **John Jarvie Ranch Historic Site** next to **Brown's Park National Wildlife Refuge** lets you step back into the late 1800s. The area in general was a favorite with the Blackfoot, Sioux, Cheyenne, Arapaho and Navajo nations, who enjoyed the area's relatively mild winters. Later, notorious outlaws like Butch Cassidy and the Sundance Kid would hole up in the park between robberies. For them, the coming together of the states of Wyoming, Colorado and Utah made it easy to flee law officers whose jurisdiction ended at the state line. The 35-acre ranch itself is in Utah, although the wildlife refuge is in Colorado.

◀ *HIDDEN*

Jarvie, a Scot, settled here in 1880 to run a ferry across the Green River. He later added a general store and post office. Today four of the original structures, each more than a century old, remain in place. Although the general store is a replica of the one built in 1881, inside you'll find many of the artifacts from Jarvie's life, as well as a safe that was robbed on the night Jarvie was murdered. Tours of the property are offered daily from May through October. ~ If the weather is good and dry, head east from Vernal on Brown's Park Road for 25 miles to a signed turnoff to the north. This 16-mile-long dirt road passes through some spectacular country. If the weather is questionable, take Route 191 north for 55 miles to the Wyoming border, then east 22 miles along Clay Basin Road, a maintained gravel road; 435-885-3307; www.blm.gov/utah/vernal/rec/john.html.

The remote setting of the 13,455-acre wildlife refuge, which straddles the Colorado–Utah border just downstream of the Flaming Gorge Dam, provides lush habitat for mule deer, elk, pronghorn antelope, marsh hawks, American kestrels and about 12,000 waterfowl during peak migrations. The fishing in the Green River is pretty good, too.

Southwest of Vernal by 32 miles via Routes 191/40 and 88 is one of three wildlife refuges nurtured by the Green River. As with the other two—Seedskadee in Wyoming and Brown's Park along the Colorado–Utah border—**Ouray National Wildlife Refuge** is a nesting ground for waterfowl. It also plays a special role in efforts by the U.S. Fish and Wildlife Service to recover dwindling populations of the Colorado pike minnow and the razorback sucker. It's roughly a 90-minute drive from Vernal to this 11,987-acre preserve. ~ To reach the refuge, head 15 miles west of Vernal on Route 191/40 and then south 17 miles on Route 88; 435-545-2522 or 435-789-0351; www.r6.fws.gov/ouray.

LODGING   Cruise Vernal's Main Street and you'll quickly be surrounded by familiar names: Weston, Best Western, Days Inn, Econo Lodge. For reliable accommodations, you can't really go wrong with one of these outfits, but if you look a bit farther afield you'll find comfortable establishments that offer a more personalized touch.

The **Landmark Inn** blends a part of Vernal's past with a taste of the countryside. Originally the setting for the Landmark Missionary Baptist Church, the two-story building was converted in 1996 into a bed and breakfast by two brothers from North Carolina who brought the flavor of a country inn west with them. Each of the three suites and eight bedrooms carry their own character; some have four-poster beds, others rough-hewn log bed frames. The suites offer jetted tubs, large-screen TVs and fireplaces. Not far from the heart of downtown, the Landmark Inn is just a block south of the Utah Fieldhouse. ~ 288 East 100 South, Vernal; 435-781-1800, 888-738-1800; www.landmark-inn.com, e-mail landmark@easilink.com. MODERATE TO ULTRA-DELUXE.

If you're planning to split your time between Dinosaur National Monument and the Flaming Gorge National Recreation Area, there are two lodges not far from Flaming Gorge that offer quieter, prettier mountain settings than you can find in Vernal.

Located 39 miles north of Vernal on the shores of a 20-acre lake in the Ashley National Forest just ten miles from Flaming Gorge Reservoir, the **Red Canyon Lodge** has been catering to tourists since 1930 with a variety of cabins. Surrounded by thick forest, the lodge is a great base of operations for hiking, biking,

FIT FOR A KING

The sport of kings—falconry—continues to be practiced in Utah at **Falcon's Ledge**, a unique lodge hidden away in Altamont, a small town 15 miles north of Duchesne. The lodge's reputation stems largely from its fly-fishing opportunities, but from September through March falconry comes to roost. Birding also fills the lodge's time during those months, while fly-fishing dominates the schedule from April through October, with time for gold panning tossed in. ~ At Duchesne, turn north off Route 40 and onto Route 87 for 15 miles; Box 67, Altamont, UT 84001; 435-454-3737, 877-879-3737, fax 435-454-3392; www.falconsledge.com. ULTRA-DELUXE.

fishing or boating. There's a range of cabins to meet most budgets, from simple units offering just beds with a central shower house and restroom a short walk away all the way up to luxury cabins that can sleep four, boast two queen beds, kitchenettes and full bathrooms. All cabins have free-standing wood stoves. Kids have their own trout pond at the lodge. Along with accommodations, the lodge offers boat rentals for East Greens Lake, mountain bike and cross-country ski rentals, horseback riding, fly-fishing lessons and its own tackle shop. Open April to early October, and weekends only during the winter. ~ 790 Red Canyon Road, Dutch John; 435-889-3759, fax 435-889-5106; www.redcanyonlodge. com, e-mail info@redcanyonlodge.com. BUDGET TO DELUXE.

Just seven miles from Red Canyon Lodge and 38 from Vernal is the **Flaming Gorge Lodge**. There are no charming log cabins here, but rather a variety of motel and condominium units. However, unlike the cabins at Red Canyon, the rooms have televisions, VCRs and telephones just in case you don't want to stray too far from civilization. The 24 one-bedroom condos can sleep four and come with kitchens. The 21 motel rooms feature two double beds. There's a dining room and café on the property, as well as a general store and gas station, a tackle shop, a liquor store, and raft and bike rentals. Winter days at the lodge revolve around snowmobiling and cross-country skiing. ~ 155 Greendale Road, Route 191, Dutch John; 435-889-3773, fax 435-889-3788; www.fglodge. com, e-mail lodge@fglodge.com. MODERATE TO DELUXE.

Another option, one farther afield but worth the trip if you like mountains and solitude, is the **U Bar Wilderness Ranch**. On the fringe of the 460,000-acre Uinta Wilderness Area in the Uinta Mountains, the ranch is the stepping-off point for horse trips and fishing excursions. You can head into the forest for several days by yourself or with a guide, or with a guide, or be content with a cabin at the ranch. The six nicely preserved cabins, some nearly 70 years old, are beautifully hand-hewn and feature beds with hand-made duvets and log furniture. A bathhouse is a short walk away. Meals are in the main lodge, which has a sitting room with a fireplace. ~ Along Route 118, 26 miles north of Roosevelt; 435-645-7256, 800-303-7256; www.rockymtnrec.com. DELUXE.

DINING

Vernal is chockfull of eateries, but most are of the fast-food genre. Cruise Main Street and Route 40 on either end of town and you'll find plenty of burger, Mexican and pizza joints, as well as rib restaurants and an occasional Chinese diner.

The **Curry Manor**, however, offers fine dining in a two-story brick home built in 1910. Meals are served in five (three upstairs, two down) elegant dining rooms draped with lace curtains and filled with antiques. Chicken, pasta, beef and seafood can be found on the lunch and dinner menus, which might include three-cheese tortellini, king crab legs and Maine lobster. ~ 189 South Vernal Avenue, Vernal; 435-789-2289. MODERATE TO DELUXE.

At **La Cabana** the menu is dominated by Mexican fare—burritos, tacos and fajitas, as well as 22 combination platters—but you also can find hamburgers and steaks. Closed Sunday. ~ 56 West Main Street, Vernal, 435-789-3151. BUDGET.

Need a quick dose of caffeine, looking for a book, or just want to check your e-mail? Then drop by **Reader's Roost,** where you'll be able to order a cup of coffee, read a novel or cruise cyberspace via the internet stations. Oh yeah, if hunger strikes you can order from their deli menu. Closed Sunday. ~ 27 West Main Street, Vernal; 435-789-8400.

On your way out to Dinosaur National Monument, be sure to stop at the **Dinosaur Quarry Gift Shop**. You'll find a nice snack bar with hamburgers, hot dogs, pizza, sandwiches and more. ~ 3017 South 500 East, Vernal; 435-789-8804.

SHOPPING   The state of shopping in Vernal is about what you'd expect from a ranching and mining community: you can find lots of overalls and work boots, but beyond that the pickings are pretty slim.

An exception is the **Fullbright Studio**. Inside this Main Street shop you'll find beautiful jewelry made by owner and goldsmith Randy Fullbright, who also has a good collection of gemstones and fossils. ~ 216 East Main Street, Vernal; 435-789-2451; www.fullbrightstudio.com.

The **Dinosaur Quarry Gift Shop** carries T-shirts and dinosaur souvenirs. ~ 3017 South 500 East, Vernal; 435-789-8804.

If you're in a need of a pair of cowboy boots or a saddle, stop by the **Bull Ring**. ~ 1801 West Route 40, Vernal; 435-789-9474.

BRICK BY BRICK

In 1916 it cost quite a bit in freight to haul textured bricks from Salt Lake City into the Uintah Basin by rail. While the bricks sold for only seven cents apiece, hauling them to Vernal ran 28 cents each, a price banker William Colthart couldn't stomach. Being an ingenious sort, though, Colthart realized that the U.S. Postal Service only charged 52 cents to send a 50-pound parcel from Salt Lake to Vernal. So, he had the 80,000 bricks packed in 50-pound bundles and mailed to Vernal. You can see the result of his craftiness—the so-called "**Parcel Post Bank**"—on the southwest corner of Vernal Avenue and Main Street in the form of the Zion National Bank. ~ 3 West Main Street, Vernal.

When the sun goes down in Vernal, about the best thing to do in this sleepy town is head for your lodging's pool or hot tub, find a good book to read or turn on the television. **NIGHTLIFE**

At the **Gateway Saloon and Social Club** you can find a game of darts if you don't mind the country-and-western tunes chugging out of the jukebox or the smoky atmosphere. ~ 773 East Main Street, Vernal; 435-789-9842.

ASHLEY NATIONAL FOREST 🚶 🚲 🐎 🏕️ 🚤 Visible from Vernal but requiring a short drive to reach is the Ashley National Forest. Draped across the southern half of the Uinta Mountains and dipping south of Vernal, the national forest shelters alpine high country that offers a cool respite from the dry, dusty summers that descend on most of northeastern Utah. The forest shelters the headwaters of a vast watershed that flows all the way down through Nevada and into California via the Green and Colorado rivers. Within its 1.4 million acres (of which 1.3 million lie in Utah) are thick stands of forest dotted by high-country lakes, Utah's highest point (13,528-foot Kings Peak), more than half of the 456,705-acre High Uintas Wilderness Area and the Flaming Gorge National Recreation Area. Mountain goats, elk, moose and black bears can be found in the forest, which draws more than 2.5 million visitors a year for boating, fishing, camping, hiking, backpacking, horseback riding, cross-country skiing and snowmobiling. ~ From Vernal, Route 191 runs north into Ashley National Forest; along the way it provides numerous access routes to the forest. Access can also be gained via 2500 West and 3500 West out of Vernal; 435-789-1181; www.fs. fed.us/r4/ashley. **PARKS**

▲ The forest, which also spills into southwestern Wyoming, has 46 campgrounds with 1216 sites, most of which are in the immediate area of Flaming Gorge National Recreation Area; free to $14; 14-day maximum stay. Reservations: 877-444-6777.

FLAMING GORGE NATIONAL RECREATION AREA 🚶 🚲 🐎 🎣 ⛵ 🚤 Straddling the Utah–Wyoming border, the Flaming Gorge National Recreation Area is centered around a 91-mile-long reservoir but offers a wide range of activities, from boating and fishing to hiking, camping and cross-country skiing. There are two designated swimming areas—the Sunny Cove beach is near the Mustang Ridge campground just north of the dam, while the Lucerne beach is one mile west of the Lucerne campground; no lifeguards. Day-use fee, $2 per vehicle. ~ Off Route 191, 41 miles north of Vernal; P.O. Box 279, Manila, UT 84046; 435-784-3445; www.fs.fed.us/r4/ashley/fg_ html_aw.html.

Text continued on page 206.

Dinosaur National Monument

Twenty miles east of Vernal via Routes 40 and 149, Dinosaur National Monument would rightly be a national park if it weren't so remote. Within its 210,000 acres you can retreat into prehistory while studying the world's largest Jurassic period fossil quarry, lose yourself on a float down the Green or Yampa rivers, or stand atop a sandstone cliff overlooking a deep river gorge.

Standing amid the monument's serrated sandstone and sage landscape, it's hard to, in your mind's eye, superimpose a broad expanse of savannah, one with a shallow, nourishing ribbon of river running through it. Such a setting did exist here, though it was hundreds of millions of years ago when dinosaurs stalked the earth, when today's sandstone was only sand. The sand not only evolved into the rich sandstone ridges and cliffs that today define the region's geography, but it also preserved in rock a veritable Jurassic Park of fossilized dinosaurs.

For this maze of land, left rumpled when the Earth's occasional upheavals tilted the ancient savannah on its side, it's probably best that the landscape lies within a monument, not a national park. Without the more prestigious "park" distinction, the preserve enjoys a largely obscure existence, one that ensures visitors solitude throughout most of the year, aside from the high season of June through August.

Whether it's your first or last stop during a trip to Dinosaur, the fossil quarry is definitely a must-see. Although paleontologists no longer chip away at the famous hillside Earl Douglass, a paleontologist sent fossil-hunting by Pittsburgh's Carnegie Museum, discovered in 1909 when he spied eight tail vertebrae of an Apatosaurus sticking out of the ground, exhibits and life-sized models in the quarry's visitors center recount the prehistoric history. Between 1909 and 1924 more than 350 tons of fossils—plants, crocodiles, clams, dinosaurs—and their surrounding rock were plucked from the ridge.

Today at the visitors center, which was built over the fossil-rich ridge Douglass uncovered, more than 2000 fossilized bones remain embedded in the 200-foot-long wall. Leg bones, back bones, ribs and even toothy skulls can be seen on the rock face from the visitors center's walkway. While the skulls can be difficult to spot, peer through the small length of pipe mounted on the railing and you'll easily make out the skull of a Camarasaurus.

Most of the bones were from vegetarian sauropods—better known to most of us as brontosaurs—although some meat-eating theropods are also represented in the quarry.

While paleontologists halted work on the rock face in 1991, these days they are busy at work on digs elsewhere in the monument. From time to time you can find them cleaning specimens in the visitors center's paleontology lab, which you can peer into through large windows on the lower level of the visitors center.

Although it's known as the "dinosaur" national monument, the landscape has more to offer than just a dinosaur graveyard. The Green and Yampa rivers flow through the monument, of which almost two-thirds lies in Colorado, and carry hundreds of paddlers downstream during the summer months. Through most of the year self-guided auto tours can take you away from the dinosaur quarry and the monument headquarters in Dinosaur, Colorado, and deeper into the monument, past jagged ridges of sandstone stained orange, yellow, red, brown and grey from various mineral deposits, to the cabins of early homesteaders and to pictographs and petroglyphs ancient American Indians left behind.

The 22-mile-long **"Tour of the Tilted Rocks"** auto tour starts near the quarry's visitors center. It winds past petroglyphs, hiking trails and the historic Josie Morris homestead, all the while revealing the monument's twisted geology. If you enter the monument in Colorado, the 62-mile-long **"Journey through Time"** leads across the Blue Mountain Plateau, offering spectacular overlooks of the Green and Yampa rivers. Booklets detailing these drives can be purchased at both the dinosaur quarry visitors center and the monument headquarters at Deerlodge, Colorado.

Though there are few established long-distance hiking trails in Dinosaur, with a good map and compass skills you can venture off the beaten path. There are six campgrounds within the monument, including two near the quarry. Admission. ~ The monument's dinosaur quarry is located seven miles north of Jensen via Route 149; monument headquarters is located two miles east of Dinosaur, Colorado, along Route 40; 970-374-3000; www.nps.gov/dino.

▲ There are 20 campgrounds, including 4 boat-in sites; $6 to $18 per night; 16-day maximum stay. Reservations: 877-444-6777.

RED FLEET STATE PARK 🚶 🚤 ⛵ 🚣 🛥 🛶 Three towering fins of Navajo sandstone that jut up from the Red Fleet Reservoir inspired the name for Red Fleet State Park, since from the air they look like a fleet at sail. The 650-acre reservoir is a favorite of local boaters, in large part due to its sandstone cliffs and remote sandy beaches hidden in side canyons. Along with water sports, the park offers a fishery noteworthy for rainbow and brown trout as well as bluegill and bass. The park's campground sprawls across a hillside that provides great views of the reservoir. The park gained fame in 1987 when a dinosaur trackway with more than 200 tracks was discovered on the shore directly across from the boat launch. Facilities include modern restrooms, fish-cleaning stations, barbecue grills and picnic tables. Day-use fee, $5 per vehicle. ~ Route 191, ten miles north of Vernal; 435-789-4432; parks.state.ut.us/parks/www1/redf.htm.

▲ There are 38 tent/RV sites and 29 for RVs; $11 per night; 14-day maximum stay.

STEINAKER STATE PARK 🚶 🚤 ⛵ 🚣 🛥 🛶 Just five and a half miles north of Vernal via Route 191 is Steinaker State Park, which is wrapped around a reservoir. In the middle of summer the waters warm to 70 degrees, making the park popular with water lovers. Off-highway-vehicle areas are nearby; one can be accessed from the park grounds, while another is just two miles away. Facilities include restrooms, picnic grounds and a boat ramp. Anglers like the reservoir for its rainbow trout and largemouth bass fisheries. Day-use fee, $5. ~ 4335 North Route 191, five and a half miles north of Vernal off Route 191; 435-789-4432; parks.state.ut.us/parks/www1/stei.htm.

▲ There are 31 tent/RV sites; $11 per night; 14-day maximum stay.

OURAY NATIONAL WILDLIFE REFUGE Thirty-one miles southwest of Vernal lies the 12,000-acre Ouray National Wildlife Refuge, a squat tract of land that started out in 1960 as a waterfowl breeding grounds. Today it lures hundreds of mule deer, elk, bald eagles in addition to more than 200 species of birds. It's also the backdrop for the Ouray National Fish Hatchery that works to help the endangered Colorado pike minnow and the razorback sucker rebound from the brink of extinction. These two unusual residents are hard to spot, for they live in the Green River's murky waters; they were doomed by the dams that sprang up throughout the Colorado River Basin in the 1960s and created a cooler, clearer river flow than the fish prefer. Now, efforts to bolster their numbers have resulted in increasing seasonal flows from the dams to replicate spring floods, allowing the flooding of some bottomlands to provide spawning grounds for the fish, and controlling winter flows from the dams so they don't scour the river bottoms or break up any ice caps that form. ~ To reach the refuge, head 15 miles west of Vernal on Route 191/40 and then south 17 miles on Route 88; 435-789-0351; www.r6.fws.gov/ouray.

Chockfull as northeastern Utah is with mountains, national forests and state parks, you don't need to look far for something to do in the outdoors no matter what season you visit.

▼▼▼▼▼▼▼▼▼▼▼▼▼▼

Outdoor Adventures

FISHING

Park City and Heber City's best fishing arguably can be found in the **Provo River**, both in the sections above and below **Jordanelle Dam** and farther south below **Deer Creek Dam**. Brown and rainbow trout are plentiful in both areas. Most anglers tend to overlook the stretch of the river that flows into the Jordanelle Reservoir near the state park's Rock Cliff area, so you can often find a more solitary, yet just as productive, fishing experience.

If you prefer lake fishing, both Jordanelle and Deer Creek reservoirs near Heber City feature boat ramps, fish-cleaning stations and sizeable populations of rainbow and cutthroat trout as well as smallmouth bass. Just off Route 40, 26 miles southeast of Heber City is **Strawberry Reservoir**, another popular fishing spot in summer and winter.

> The Green River below Flaming Gorge Dam is an outstanding trout fishery, where as many as 22,000 trout per mile have been counted.

While the Wyoming portion of the **Flaming Gorge National Recreation Area** is predominately high desert, the Utah section offers pristine mountain scenery covered by thick forests of piñon pines and junipers and cut by steep canyons. While the reservoir holds bass and catfish, most anglers come for the lake trout, which can top 50 pounds. German trout weighing more than 30 pounds have also been pulled from the reservoir, as have rainbow trout over 25 pounds.

Other reliable reservoirs in the region include **Starvation Reservoir** west of Duchesne and **Steinaker** and **Red Fleet reservoirs** north of Vernal. **Pelican Lake**, off Route 88 south of Vernal, is a popular bluegill and bass fishery. Many of the trails in the Uinta, Wasatch-Cache and Ashley national forests lead to pristine mountain lakes stocked with trout, including rare Colorado cutthroats.

Outfitters & Guides A few Park City–based guide services can lead you to fish. **Jan's Mountain Outfitters** offers free fly-casting lessons in the summer and guides trips to the Provo, Green and Weber rivers, as well as to lakes in the Uinta Mountains. ~ 1600 Park Avenue, Park City; 435-649-4949, 800-745-1020; www.jans. com. The **Park City Fly Shop** offers year-round guide service, fishing the Provo and Upper Green rivers. ~ 2065 Sidewinder Drive, Park City; 435-645-8382, 800-324-6778; www.pcflyshop.com.

Trout Bum 2 stalks the Provo, Green and Weber rivers, as well as high-country lakes. ~ 4343 North Route 224, Suite 101, Park City; 435-658-1166, 877-878-2862; www.troutbum2.com.

The **Four Seasons Fly Fishers** can lead you to some of the Wasatch Range's streams into southwestern Wyoming or, if you have the time, down to Argentina! ~ 44 West 100 South, Heber City; 435-657-2010, 800-498-5440; www.utahflyfish.com.

Flaming Gorge National Refuge Area outfitters include **Conquest Expeditions,** which also guides on the Green Reservoir. ~ P.O. Box 487, Manila, UT 84046; 435-784-3370. **Trout Creek Flies** also serves the area. ~ P.O. Box 247, Dutch John, UT 84023; 435-885-3355, 800-835-4551.

BOATING

While both Deer Creek and Jordanelle state parks revolve around their respective reservoirs, Jordanelle is the bigger of the two and therefore offers more play space on the water. Muscle-powered boats usually enter the reservoir in the long, watery arm near Rock Cliff, while power boats and other fuel-powered water toys and sailboats enter at Hailstone on the western shore of Jordanelle. The marinas at both state parks have rentals.

In Park City, try **Peak Experience,** which rents kayaks. ~ 875 Iron Horse Drive, Park City; 435-645-5366. Canoes, kayaks and fishing boats can be rented in Heber City from **Daytrips Out-fitters.** ~ 625 North Main Street, Heber City; 435-654-8294, 888-654-8294.

At Flaming Gorge, boat rentals can be found at two local marinas. **Lucerne Marina,** which also rents fishing equipment and houseboats, is roughly 63 miles north of Vernal and seven miles east of Manila via Routes 191, 44 and 43. ~ P.O. Box 10, Manila, UT 84046; 435-784-3483, 888-820-9225. **Cedar Springs Marina,** about 45 miles north of Vernal and two miles west of Flaming Gorge Dam on Route 191, rents boats and offers guided tours. ~ P.O. Box 337, Dutch John, UT 84023; 435-889-3795.

CANOEING, KAYAKING & RIVER RUNNING

Most of the lakes in the Uinta Range are either too small or too hard to reach for paddling, although **Washington Lake, Trial Lake** and **Mirror Lake** along Route 150 east of Kamas and the **Smith and Morehouse Reservoir,** reached via State Route 213 north of Kamas, are all large enough and easily accessible for hours of canoeing fun.

Most of northeastern Utah's rivers are too small for paddling anything other than kayaks, and then only early in the floating season, although the Green, Yampa and White rivers to the north, east and south of Vernal have outstanding reputations with paddlers of kayaks, canoes and rafts. How experienced you are dictates which river you can handle on your own; you'd be best advised to sign on with one of the region's commercial outfitters.

The seven-mile stretch of **Green River** between the Flaming Gorge Dam and Little Hole makes a great day for an unguided trip and does not require permits. The rapids are timid, the views fantastic, and fishing incredible. Experienced paddlers can continue all the way to the Colorado border, stopping at campsites along the way. While the eight miles between Little Hole and Indian Crossing may contain Class III rapids, the 11-mile stretch between Indian Crossing and the Colorado border is gentle. For more information, contact the Flaming Gorge Ranger District. ~ Ashley National Forest, P.O. Box 279, Manila, UT 84046; 435-784-3445.

> Many of the wildlife and avian species, such as mule deer, ring-necked pheasant, cinnamon teal ducks and great blue herons, that you can spy at Ouray were present when John Wesley Powell explored the Colorado River Basin in the late 1800s.

The Green and Yampa rivers through Dinosaur National Monument are popular with whitewater enthusiasts and are plied by a number of commercial companies. At high water, a Class IV rapid occasionally can be found on the Green River near the Gates of Lodore, although for the most part these two rivers feature Class III and lesser rapids through Dinosaur. For paddlers who aren't interested in commercial trips but are experienced with Class III waters, a nice daytrip through the monument begins at Rainbow Park and concludes about nine miles downstream at the Split Mountain campground. Permits from the National Park Service are required for both commercial and private trips; applications can be obtained either from Dinosaur National Monument's river office or from the agency's website. ~ 970-374-2468; www.nps.gov.dino/river/index.htm.

Outfitters   Paddlers can obtain river flow information by calling 800-277-7571. For a booklet outlining Utah's river outfitters, call the **Utah Travel Council**. ~ Council Hall, Salt Lake City, UT 84114; 801-538-1030, 800-200-1160; www.utah.com.

There are a number of raft companies that run these rivers.

Adrift Adventures plies the waters of the Green and Colorado rivers. ~ P.O. Box 192, Jensen, UT 84035; 435-789-3600, 800-824-0150; www.adrift.com.

Chapoose Canyon Adventures, owned by a member of the Ute Tribe, floats sections of the Green River and provides American Indian narration to areas considered sacred by the tribe. ~ P.O. Box 766, Fort Duchesne, UT 84026; 435-722-4072, 877-722-4001; www.chapoose.com.

Dinosaur River Expeditions navigates the Green and Yampa rivers through Dinosaur National Monument. ~ P.O. Box 3387, Park City, UT 84060; 435-649-8092, 800-247-6197; www.dino adv.com.

Trips down the Colorado, Green and Yampa rivers can be arranged through **Sheri Griffith Expeditions**. ~ 2231 South Route 191, Moab; 435-259-8229, 800-332-2439; www.griffithexp.com.

Sections of the Colorado, Green and Yampa rivers are run by **Hatch River Expeditions**. ~ P.O. Box 1150, Vernal, UT 84078; 435-789-4316, 800-342-8243; www.hatchriver.com.

Holiday Expeditions can arrange trips down the Colorado, Green, San Juan and Yampa rivers. ~ 544 East 3900 South, Salt Lake City; 801-266-2087, 800-624-6323; www.bikeraft.com.

Since 1985 **Centennial Canoe Outfitters** has offered a variety of multiday canoe trips down the Green and Colorado rivers. ~ P.O. Box 3365, Centennial, CO 80161; 303-755-3501, 877-353-1850; www.centennialcanoe.com.

DOWNHILL SKIING & SNOW-BOARDING

Utah is second only to Colorado when it comes to the top ski states in the U.S., and much of the state's credit goes to the resorts in the Park City area. A testament to the Park City resorts' challenging terrain are the 2002 Winter Olympic Games, which turned to the resorts for some of the Games' venues.

Salt Lake City gave its name to the 2002 Winter Olympic Games, but Park City lent its ambience, not to mention some pretty darn good skiing. From the middle of Main Street you can gaze south and see the manicured slopes of Deer Valley, which hosted the slalom, mogul and aerial events during the Games, while to the west rise the runs of the Park City Mountain Resort, which hosted the giant slalom and snowboarding events.

The **Park City Mountain Resort**, with 750 acres of bowls and 100 trails snaking down 3300 acres of skiable terrain, arguably offers more uphill capacity than any other in the state with 14 lifts, four of which can haul six skiers or snowboarders at a time. You won't find the steepest terrain or the deepest powder in Utah here, but there is something for everyone, from first-time skiers to long-toothed experts and shredders. For snowboarders, the Eagle Superpipe (the massive rider-swallowing halfpipe used during the Olympics) is a permanent fixture for those who want something tougher than the regulation-sized PayDay halfpipe. It also added three new terrain parks in 2002, and boosted its snowmaking system to offset Mother Nature's whims. I avoid lift lines by skiing mid-week or, during busy weekends, dashing over to McConkey's high-speed six-seater for tremendous tree and bowl skiing. While the Motherlode Lift is slow, it, too, is usually overlooked and uncrowded and the terrain it serves super. ~ 1310 Lowell Avenue, Park City; 435-649-8111, 800-222-7275; www.parkcitymountain.com.

Separated from the Park City Mountain Resort by just a narrow ridgeline of trees, the **Deer Valley Resort** epitomizes the elegance of alpine skiing. Green-clad hosts stand ready to unload your skis when you drive up to Snow Park Lodge at the base of the Bald Eagle Mountain or to take them from you at Silver Lake when you stop for a bite of lunch, and 35 to 50 percent of the terrain is manicured, seemingly with a fine-tooth comb, every night during the season. Nineteen lifts service 88 trails and six bowls spread across 1750 acres. While the resort, which bans snowboards, has long been frowned upon for lacking heart, that reputation is overcooked. Daly Chutes, Daly Bowl and Anchor Trees in Empire Canyon challenge the most experienced skier. If you like deep powder, head straight to Empire Canyon early in the day for first tracks after storms. Sometimes you can find untracked powder in the trees here a day or two after storms strike. Ontario Bowl, reached via Quincy Express, is another powder cache. ~ 2250 Deer Valley Drive South, Park City; 435-649-1000, 800-424-3337; www.deervalley.com.

Winter definitely, and rightly so, receives top billing in Park City. The U.S. Ski and Snowboard Association (435-649-9090; www.usski team.com) calls Park City home.

Five miles north of Park City off Route 224 lies the area's other downhill ski and snowboarding area, **The Canyons**, which has blossomed into a year-round destination resort. Encompassing eight mountains, the resort spans 3500 heavily treed acres with 144 trails and a number of bowls reached via 16 lifts. The resort's commitment to snowboarders explains its 18-acre "CIA Terrain Park." Located off the Redhawk lift, the park boasts 25 rails and boxes for a total of 30 features. There also are two half-pipes here, lighting for night use, and a state-of-the-art sound system. You can also find some natural terrain pipes off the Saddleback Express, Snow Canyon Express, and Super Condor Express lifts. Skiers can enjoy tree skiing in "The Pines" off the Saddleback Express and in the glades surrounding "99-90," a sprawling bowl that offers bumps and cruising as well. Novices and intermediates aren't ignored: the terrain threading below the Dreamscape Lift is designed for them. ~ 4000 The Canyons Resort Drive, Park City; 435-649-5400, 888-226-9667; www. thecanyons.com.

If the youngsters couldn't care less about skiing and snowboarding but want to gain some speed on snow, take them over to **Gorgoza Park**, a tubing hill affiliated with the Park City Mountain Resort. Located about eight miles north of Park City just off Route 80, Gorgoza Park offers lift-assisted tubing for kids three and older. There's also a terrain park here with rails, tables and jumps where skiers and snowboarders can practice their jibbing skills. ~ 3863 West Kilby Road, Route 80 Exit 143; 435-658-2648.

Powder skiing without lifts? Hitch a ride—albeit an expensive one—with **Park City Powder Cats** and spend a day on 20,000 acres in the Uinta Mountains, knee-deep or higher in some of Utah's famously dry snow. After each run a comfy Snowcat hauls you back to the top of the mountain. ~ 1647 Short Line Road, Park City; 435-649-6596, 800-635-4719; www.pccats.com.

Five resorts, one day, one pass. It's possible with the **Ski Utah Interconnect Tour**, which leads higher-level skiers through the backcountry from the Park City Mountain Resort to Solitude, Brighton, Alta and Snowbird before calling it a day. Reservations recommended. ~ 801-534-1907; www.skiutah.com.

Ski Rentals If you forgot your skis or snowboard, need a new ski jacket or helmet, or simply want to check out the latest gear, you have a number of options. In addition to suppliers at the various resorts, you can try **Bahnhof Sport** (838 Main Street, Park City; 435-615-9077), **ColeSport** (which has several Park City locations, the main number is 435-649-4800), **Destination Sports** (875 Main Street, Park City; 435-940-0140) and **Jan's Mountain Outfitters** (which has several Park City locations, the main number is 435-649-4949).

CROSS-COUNTRY SKIING

Skinny-ski fanatics have long used the meadows and mountains found throughout northeastern Utah for their exercise. While there's not an abundance of groomed cross-country resorts, the ones that exist are wonderful. The region's mountains offer mile after mile of ungroomed terrain for Nordic skiers.

PARK CITY AREA Cross-country-ski fans in the Park City area have only one choice for groomed trails—the **White Pine Touring Center**, which takes over the Park City Municipal Golf Course once the snow flies. There are 18 kilometers of groomed track for both classic and skate skiers; the ski shop handles rentals, sales and accessories. ~ Park Avenue, Park City; 435-615-5858.

The **Norwegian Outdoor Exploration Center** can arrange an ambitious cross-country nature tour into the Uinta Mountains. A less strenuous guided twilight snowshoe tour in the mountains surrounding Park City is also available. ~ 333 Main Street, Park City; 435-649-5322, 800-649-5322; www.outdoorcenter.org.

HEBER CITY AREA The **Soldier Hollow** area of Wasatch Mountain State Park on the western edge of the Heber Valley offers 31 kilometers of trails for a wide variety of abilities. Most of the ter-

BACK ON THE LOOSE

Until 1981 the black-footed ferret, a small, weasel-like animal, was thought to be extinct. But then a ranch dog near Meeteetse, Wyoming, lugged one home. Wyoming wildlife officials, in a bid to boost the numbers of what then was considered to be the rarest mammal in North America, embarked on a captive-breeding program that has since produced more than 2000 ferrets. As part of the effort to return the mammals to their historic habitat, about 70 ferrets were released into the Coyote Basin about 30 miles southwest of Vernal in fall 1999. Spotting them can be tricky, though, as the ferrets are largely nocturnal creatures.

rain is designed to test world-class athletes, however, so expect a tough workout. In addition to the ski trails, of which 10 kilometers are designed specifically for us mere mortals, the facility boasts a 1000-foot-long tubing hill and some snowshoe trails. You'll find both ski and snowshoe rentals on site in the day lodge. You also can test your skills in biathlon—a mix of cross-country skiing and target shooting. ~ Routes 113 and 224, Heber City; 435-654-2002; www.soldierhollow.org.

The U.S. Forest Service also maintains ski trails in the Wasatch-Cache and Uinta forests. The **Beaver Creek Trail**, found along the Mirror Lake Highway east of Kamas in the Wasatch-Cache Forest, is an easy, mostly flat trail ideal for beginners or a quick workout. You need to go through Wyoming to get there, but south of Evanston, Wyoming, on Route 150 in Utah lies the **Lily Lake Trails** system that offers some great cross-country skiing and snowshoe trails. Meanwhile, the Little South Fork Trail in the Uinta forest southeast of Heber along Route 35 is more demanding with rolling terrain. You'll also find some groomed cross-country ski trails around Strawberry Reservoir south of Heber City. Trailheads can be found near the visitors center on West Strawberry Road off Route 40.

VERNAL AREA   In the Vernal area there are no groomed courses such as those in the Park City or Heber City areas, although there are eight defined backcountry routes that range in length from 2.5 miles to 12.5 miles. The **Canyon Rim Trail**, although lengthy at 12.5 miles roundtrip, is relatively level and can be handled by novices and provides fantastic views of Red Canyon and the Uinta Mountains as well as the chance to spot moose and elk. More experienced skiers will like the **Dowd Mountain Trail**, a ten-mile loop that mixes flat and steep terrain and offers breathtaking vistas of Flaming Gorge, Red Canyon and the Uintas. Brochures describing these routes and providing directions to them can be obtained from the Dinosaurland Travel Board. ~ 25 East Main Street, Vernal; 435-789-6932, 800-477-5558; www.dinoland.com.

Ski in the winter, golf in the summer. What better way to exercise in northeastern Utah? Obviously, more than a few souls share this sentiment, as evidenced by the many golf courses that can be found in the region.

GOLF

PARK CITY AREA   Already well-known for its skiing and snowboarding, Park City is slowly but steadily building a reputation as a duffer's paradise. The thin air at the relatively high elevation of 7000 feet adds distance to drives and summer days never get unbearably hot.

The 18-hole **Park City Municipal Golf Course** is popular with locals who didn't splurge on the pricy memberships required at the Jeremy Ranch Golf Course or the Park Meadows Country

Club. The par-72 municipal course is located near the base of the Park City Mountain Resort and has 6400 yards of rolling terrain dotted with small lakes, aspens and firs. ~ 1541 Thaynes Canyon Drive, Park City; 435-615-5800.

A 20-minute drive northwest of Park City via Routes 224 and 80 lies **Mountain Dell**, a rolling, 18-hole, 6787-yard course that's nestled in Parley's Canyon between the interstate and the mountains. ~ 3287 Cummings Road, Salt Lake City; 801-582-3812.

HEBER CITY AREA The Heber City–Midway area has two golf courses. **The Homestead** offers an 18-hole, par-72, 7000-yard course with a sweeping view of the Heber Valley. ~ 700 North Homestead Drive, Midway; 435-654-1102, 800-327-7220. **Wasatch Mountain State Park**'s 36 holes are laid out in a fashion that allows duffers to play mountain, valley or lake courses. ~ Routes 113 and 224, Heber City; golf course 435-654-0532.

VERNAL AREA The 6780-yard, par-72 **Dinaland Golf Course** features 18 holes against a backdrop of the Uinta Mountains. ~ 675 South 2000 East, Vernal; 435-781-1428. In Roosevelt, the 18-hole **Roosevelt Golf Course** offers an array of land and water hazards, and features one hole where the green is on an island. ~ 1155 Clubhouse Drive, Roosevelt; 435-722-9644.

RIDING STABLES

Through winter and summer, on designated trails and across mountain meadows, riding on the back of a horse is a great way to get to know a place. Horseback trips into the Uinta Mountains, either for fishing or just to enjoy the scenery, are available through a number of outfitters. For a thorough directory of those who lead trips into the Uintas, contact the **Utah Travel Council**. ~ Council Hall, Salt Lake City; 801-538-1030, 800-200-1160; www.utah.com.

Experienced riders can gallop through the mountains surrounding Park City with **Wind in Your Hair Riding**. ~ 2565 South State Road 32, Wanship; 435-336-4795, 435-901-4644; www.windinyourhair.com.

Horse rides can also be arranged through the **Rocking "R" Ranch** on its 2000-acre spread, or at the Deer Valley Resort or Park City Mountain Resort. ~ 435-645-7256, 800-303-7256; www.rockymtnrec.com.

BIKING

While you'll find a few road-bike fanatics pedaling across northeastern Utah when warm weather arrives, far and away mountain bikes are the preferred mode of travel for those who like to ride. With ski resorts turning into mountain biking resorts in the summer, and the endless miles of trail in national forests, this comes as no surprise.

PARK CITY AREA In the Park City area, mountain bikes replace skis on the tops of locals' cars when the snow melts, and for good reason. Each of the three Park City resorts has miles and miles of lift-served bike trails, and the surrounding national forests and public lands offer single-track trails as well as forest roads that are perfect for exploring on bike. Maps of the biking possibilities in the Park City area can be found at the town's bike and ski shops.

A popular, 20-mile, out-and-back trail with locals (and one of the most picturesque in the area), is the **Ridge Trail**, aka the **Wasatch Crest Trail**. This breathtaking—both due to the views as well as the uphills—single-track route follows the ridgeline from the Deer Valley Resort, across the top of the Park City Mountain Resort and past The Canyons.

The **Deer Valley Resort** boasts one of the best mountain bike schools in the West, and has miles of trails to support it. Cyclists can either ride a chairlift to the top of Bald Mountain and follow one of numerous single- or double-track trails that wind their way back to the base, or slog it uphill from the bottom to the top and then back down.

The **Historic Union Pacific Rail Trail** runs 28 miles from Park City to Echo Junction and makes for a fun ride, although it tilts downhill a bit heading to Echo, making the return trip something of a grunt if the day is hot. During late summer, wild currants, chokecherries and service berries ripen along the trail, making it easy to stop for a while and munch.

Round Valley offers a six-mile-long route on the east side of Park City that is easy enough for beginners yet challenging enough to keep more experienced riders happy. Starting near the National Ability Center's equestrian center on Route 248, the trail follows a relatively level path to Trailside Park.

Advanced bikers gut their way up the **Sweeney Switchbacks**, a two-mile-long series of switchbacks that cuts back and forth through aspens and evergreens as it climbs uphill. The trail, which starts near the south end of Lowell Avenue in Park City, connects to the Park City Mountain Resort trail system.

VERNAL AREA In the Vernal area, numerous hiking/biking trails wind through the Ashley National Forest. In Dinosaur

HOT-AIR BALLOONING

Winter is the busy time for drifting above Park City's mountains in a colorful hot air balloon, although trips are possible throughout the year. Try **ABC Hot Air Balloons**. ~ 514 Main Street, Park City; 435-649-2223, 800-820-2223. Also offering trips above Park City is **Park City Balloon Adventures**. ~ P.O. Box 1344, Park City, UT 84060; 435-645-8787, 800-396-8787.

National Monument, a 20-mile loop stitches together paved roads, dirt roads and even a section of slickrock for mountain bikers.

A 21.5-mile route through **Dry Fork Canyon** ten miles north of Vernal via the Dry Fork Canyon Road is perfect for road bikers and leads to dramatic displays of petroglyphs. The gentle grade makes this a good family ride.

Views of Flaming Gorge Reservoir and the Uinta Range are blended with Western history at the historic **Swett Ranch**. A six-mile mountain bike loop that follows graded roads around the ranch property, which contains a collection of old farm implements and offers some insight into pioneer life, winds through aspen groves and crosses streams.

Bike Rentals In the Park City area, bike rentals, repairs and sales can be found at **ColeSport** (1615 Park Avenue; 435-649-4806), **Jan's Mountain Outfitters** (1600 Park Avenue; 435-649-4949) and **White Pine Touring** (1685 Bonanza Drive; 435-615-6869, 435-649-8710).

Holiday Expeditions, a Salt Lake City–based outfitter that leads river and mountain bike adventures, offers a two-day ride that takes you into Dinosaur National Monument. ~ 544 East 3900 South, Salt Lake City; 800-624-6323; www.bikeraft.com.

More trail information and rentals in the Vernal area can be found at **Altitude Cycle**. ~ 510 East Main Street, Suite 8, Vernal; 435-781-2595. Or try **Basin Saw and Cycle**. ~ 450 North Vernal Avenue, Vernal; 435-781-1226.

HIKING The Wasatch-Cache, Uinta and Ashley national forests all offer incredible backcountry trails that quickly lead you into the aspen and conifer forests that blanket the mountains. All distances listed for hiking trails are one way unless otherwise noted.

The Mirror Lake Highway (Route 150), that runs 80 miles between Kamas and Evanston, Wyoming, is the quickest way to get into the Uinta Mountains. Shared by the three forests, the Uintas offer everything from developed campgrounds that are overrun just about every summer weekend to primeval forest.

AUTHOR FAVORITE

The one-mile **Stewart Falls Trail** is an enjoyable, kid-friendly hike in the Uinta National Forest that starts at the Sundance Resort and roams through the forests below Mount Timpanogos to a gorgeous waterfall that's most furious in the early summer as snowmelt spills off the mountain. The trail follows a gentle grade through aspen and evergreens before reaching the moss-covered base of the 40-foot-tall waterfall.

Close to Kamas, the **Yellow Pine Trail** (4 miles) starts off Route 150 six miles east of Kamas and runs to Yellow Pine Lakes; it's a steep trail in places that quickly tests your stamina. The reward is a wonderful subalpine setting bursting with wildflowers in mid-summer.

Across the road from the Yellow Pine parking area is the **Beaver Creek Trail** that parallels its namesake creek. Offering a wonderful, not-too-strenuous hike for youngsters, during the winter months this trail is perfect for classic skiing, leading skiers through aspen groves and thick pockets of conifers. How far you ski is up to you, although a 4-mile out-and-back ski is perfect for a half-day outing.

The **Shingle Creek Trail** (5 miles) is found only about three miles east of the Yellow Pine trailhead and follows its namesake creek north towards Shingle Creek Lake. While it starts out somewhat rugged in terms of steepness and rocks, the trail soon begins to parallel the creek while climbing gently through thick forest. In winter, this is a wonderful place to retreat with snowshoes.

A half-day hike or multiday expedition can be made out of the **Notch Mountain Trail**. Located near Milepost 25 on the Mirror Lake Highway, the trail slowly winds through forest before popping out at Wall Lake. From the lakeshore you get a nice view of the notch in the mountain. Once you reach the notch (a three-mile hike), you can either turn around and head back to your car or continue down into a backcountry of forest and lakes.

Bald Mountain (2 miles) towers over the Uinta Mountains . . . at least the eastern portion of the range. You'll quickly realize how the mountain, 30 miles east of Kamas, got its name once you see it. Climbing to the top is relatively quick, and from the summit you get a spectacular view of the surrounding countryside. One thing that's always amazed me are the great number of lakes you can spy from this vantage point.

Kids like the **Mirror Lake Shoreline Trail** (1.5 miles), found 31 miles east of Kamas along Route 150. Circling the lake, it offers countless opportunities for tossing stones into the water or fishing; adults like the views of Bald Mountain and Hayden Peak.

Thirty-four miles east of Kamas is the **Highline Trail** (60 miles), which runs along the roof of the Uintas, crossing the headwaters of many drainages along the way. From the trailhead along Route 150 it takes just a mile to reach the High Uintas Wilderness boundary. Seven and a half miles from the trailhead you reach Rocky Sea Pass, a rocky, above-treeline pass cluttered with huge boulders that inspired the area's name. The trail is for the most part a nice hike, rising only 1200 feet and passing several small lakes along the way, although the final push to the pass is over steep, rocky terrain.

Forty-six miles east of Kamas along Route 150 lies the trail to **Christmas Meadows** (2.5 miles), passing willow thickets that are favorites with moose and aspen forest before climbing uphill along a cascading creek. Six miles from the trailhead lies **Amethyst Lake**, a shimmering high-country lake with several prime campsites.

Kings Peak, the highest point in Utah at 13,528 feet, can be reached from the **Henry's Fork Trailhead**, which is reached by taking the Route 80 business loop that runs through Evanston, Wyoming, and then heading south to Mountain View, where you need to take Route 410 to the trailhead. The hike to Kings Peak through Gunsight Pass runs 12 miles one way and gains 4200 feet.

In the Uinta National Forest, the 11,788-foot summit of **Mountain Timpanogos Trail** (6 miles) starts from either the North Fork in Provo Canyon or the Timpooneke Campground in American Fork Canyon.

In the Ashley National Forest, one of the best routes into the High Uintas Wilderness is via the **Uinta Canyon Trailhead**, also known as the Uinta River Trailhead, found near the U-Bar Ranch 18 miles north of Neola via Route 121. Three miles down the trail lies the wilderness area's boundary; 12 miles in lies Lake At-wood, a sprawling lake scooped out of the landscape by long-gone glaciers.

Two popular hikes in Dinosaur National Monument are the treks to Jones Hole and Harper's Corner. The short **Harper's Corner Trail** (1 mile) provides great geology lessons and fantastic views into the canyons created by the Green and Yampa rivers. The hike into **Jones Hole Trail** (4 miles) starts at the Jones Hole National Fish Hatchery, located about an hour's drive from the dinosaur quarry via the Brush Creek Road and Diamond Mountain Road. This trail passes by various faults and formations and mixes in prehistoric rock art. About 1.8 miles down the trail lies the **Island Park Trail**. Just a quarter-mile up this trail is a nice waterfall surrounded by Douglas fir and birch trees, something you wouldn't expect from the more desert-like surroundings in the rest of the monument. A third of a mile past the waterfall is a fork in the trail—the left fork runs 7.5 miles to the historic Ruple Ranch in Island Park, the right-hand fork runs another two or three miles into a series of box canyons known as the Labyrinths.

Transportation

CAR

Routes 80 and 40 are the main travel corridors through northeastern Utah. While 80, an interstate freeway, heads east past Park City before entering western Wyoming near Evanston, 40 dips south near Park City and then veers east through Duchesne, Roosevelt and Vernal before entering Colorado.

Route 191 runs north from Vernal, past Flaming Gorge National Recreation Area and on to Rock Springs, Wyoming, and south to Price, Green River and eventually Moab. Route 150 runs northeast from Kamas through the Wasatch-Cache National Forest to Evanston, Wyoming.

For road and travel information, call 801-964-6000.

The **Salt Lake International Airport** is 36 miles west of Park City off Route 80. See Chapter Two for more information.

Commuter service via **Skywest** (800-453-9417) is available from Salt Lake International to Vernal Municipal Airport.

AIR

Greyhound Bus Lines (800-231-2222; www.greyhound.com) serves northeastern Utah from Salt Lake City. It operates on a flag stop basis through Park City, Heber City and Duchesne, with a station stop in Vernal.

Lewis Brothers Stages serves Park City from Salt Lake City. ~ 549 West 500 South, Salt Lake City; 801-359-8677, 800-826-5844; www.lewisbros.com.

BUS

Rentals in Park City can be arranged through **All-Resort Car Rental** (435-649-3999), **Budget Rent A Car** (435-645-7555, 800-527-0700) and **Park City Car Rentals** (435-658-0403, 800-724-7767).

In Heber City, **Daytrips Outfitters** can line you up with a car or four-wheel-drive vehicle. ~ 675 North Main Street, Heber City; 435-654-8294, 888-654-8294. **Avis Rent A Car** (800-331-1212) has a desk at the municipal airport in Vernal.

CAR RENTALS

Park City has a free shuttle bus system that operates within the city limits. Between Memorial Day and Labor Day the buses run daily between 7:30 a.m. until 10:30 p.m. During the ski season the schedule shifts slightly to 7 a.m. to 1 a.m.

PUBLIC TRANSIT

Among the taxi companies serving Park City are **Park City Taxi** (435-658-2227), **Powder for the People** (435-649-6648) and **Ace Cab Company** (435-649-8294). In Heber City, you can catch a ride from **Daytrips Transportation**. ~ 675 North Main Street, Heber City; 435-654-8294, 888-654-8294. When in Vernal, **Vernal Cab** can move you about town. ~ 44 West Main Street, Vernal; 435-790-1212.

TAXIS

FIVE

Central Utah

The official world center of the Mormon faith may be in Salt Lake City, but in terms of everyday culture and lifestyle, it lies in Provo and in the rural valleys to its south. Nearly 100 percent white, middle-class and politically conservative—and Mormon, of course—this region has not experienced the same outside influences as greater Salt Lake. As a result, many restaurants and visitor attractions are closed on Sunday.

Provo, a city of 110,000 some 45 miles south of the Utah capital, focuses around Brigham Young University, one of the world's largest private church-supported universities. Flanked east and north by the high Wasatch Range and on the west by Utah Lake, the state's largest freshwater lake, Provo is surrounded by enviable natural beauty. No doubt that's been a factor in the late-20th-century movement of numerous high-tech software firms into the Utah Valley, complementing the traditional economic mainstays of farming, mining and steel production.

Provo's sister city is Orem, which borders the university town to the north. If you don't pay attention to signs, you easily can move from one to the other without knowing it.

Southeast of Provo, across the Wasatch, the town of Price is the hub of a region famed for its fossils and fossil fuels. The Cleveland-Lloyd Dinosaur Quarry, on the edge of the San Rafael Swell south of Price, has been the most productive Jurassic bone park on earth. The advent of the railroad in the 1880s made coal mining productive throughout the region.

Due south of Provo, the valleys of the Sanpete and Sevier rivers are sprinkled with quiet, historic agricultural communities in the Mormon tradition. The magnificent temple in Manti and remnants of the Fremont Indian heritage, including hundreds of petroglyphs south of Richfield, are highlights.

Anchoring central Utah is Capitol Reef National Park, a spectacular geological area straddling the Fremont River. Earth wrinkled by the forces of nature, Capitol Reef is a melange of domes and cliffs, spires and other amazing rock formations tossed together in a beautiful jumble.

The Fremont Indians, counterparts of the Anasazi, inhabited central Utah for five centuries, between about A.D. 800 and A.D. 1300. Numerous archaeological sites remain today, the most notable of which are hundreds of petroglyphs carved into canyon rocks and cliff ruins that blend so well into the cliffs that they're nearly invisible. The Fremont were succeeded in the region by Ute Indians in the mountains and river valleys, Goshiutes in the desert west.

The first white men to visit this region of North America were not Mormons at all, but Catholic priests. In September 1776, fathers Francisco Silvestre Velez de Escalante and Francisco Atanasio Dominguez, en route from Santa Fe to California, set foot in the valley of Utah Lake and found it populated by villages of Ute Indians who called themselves the Timpanogotzis, or "Fish Eaters." Velez de Escalante noted in his journal that climate was favorable, pastureland abundant, and that irrigation would support two or three sizeable communities in the valley.

Sporadic Spanish trade expeditions, in addition to fur trappers, followed the trail of Dominguez and Velez de Escalante into the Utah Valley in subsequent decades. In October 1824, a party of French Canadian trappers entered the valley from the north. Along the Jordan River they were ambushed by a group of Snake Indians, who killed eight of the trappers. Etienne Provost, who was leading the band, survived the attack and went on to establish trading posts on the shores of Utah Lake. Provo was named after the trapper.

Other groups passed through central Utah, including mountain man Jedediah Smith in 1826 and John C. Fremont in 1843. The first white settlement, a Mormon colony located along the Provo River called Fort Utah, was established in March 1849 when church leader Brigham Young sent John Higbee south with a contingent of 30 pioneer families. Welcomed by the Utes, the Mormons built a fort and planted 225 acres with corn, rye and wheat. A dozen more colonies quickly followed.

Not all was harmonious with the Indians, however. The most serious conflict was the Walker War, which lasted from 1853 to 1854. Touched off by a trade dispute in the Springville area, a series of clashes led by Ute Chief Walkara raged for more than a year in central Utah, leaving 20 Mormon settlers dead before a treaty was signed.

Following the winter of 1857–58, when Mormons threatened to rebel against the U.S. government, 3500 federal troops were stationed at Camp Floyd, west of Utah Lake about 40 miles from Provo. The rebellion never materialized, but troops remained at Camp Floyd until the outbreak of the Civil War in 1861, comprising the largest military encampment in the U.S.

In 1858, the Overland Stage Route was established through Fairfield, and an inn, stagecoach stop and Pony Express station were built. Within a few years, the transcontinental railroad was operating through northern Utah, extending to Provo and central Utah by 1875 and boosting the economy, with minerals and agricultural products being shipped to coastal markets.

During the 1920s, and especially during World War II, numerous steel mills were built in the Utah Valley to take advantage of the ready supply of ores; today, one mill remains. Since the 1980s, a high-technology revolution has attracted such computer software companies as Novell.

▼▼▼▼▼▼▼▼▼▼▼
Provo Area

Provo is the core of an area of roughly 330,000 people, extending 34 miles from Lehi to Santaquin on the east side of freshwater Utah Lake. The 40-mile-long Jordan River connects Utah Lake with the Great Salt Lake to its north, much as the biblical Jordan River flows from the freshwater Sea of Galilee into the saltwater Dead Sea. East of the metropolitan area rise the Wasatch Mountains, topping out at 11,750-foot Mount Timpanogos in the north and 11,877-foot Mount Nebo in the south.

Provo's main attraction is Brigham Young University, an institution as well known for its strict moral and dress codes as for its academic programs, museums, cultural events and spectator sports. Established in 1875 by Brigham Young himself to train teachers for Mormon schools, it has become the intellectual center of the Mormon Church. About one-fourth of Provo's population is BYU students, and scores of other residents are employed by, or provide services to the university.

SIGHTS

Anchoring downtown Provo is the historic Utah County Courthouse, a Classical Revival building constructed of Manti limestone in the 1920s; paintings adorn the Gothic-style rotunda of this stunning three-story building. Within is the **Utah Valley Convention and Visitors Bureau**, which dispenses free copies of the "Provo Historic Buildings Tour" booklet. ~ 51 South University Avenue, Provo; 801-370-8394, 800-222-8824; www.utahvalley.org/cvb.

A collection of more than 4000 dolls, begun in 1910 by Laura McCurdy Clark and continued by her descendants, is exhibited in the **McCurdy Historical Doll Museum**. Permanent and rotating exhibits explore themes such as women of the Bible, American Indians, folk dresses of the world, toy soldiers and U.S. first ladies. Dolls are used in children's storytelling and as models for crafts classes. There's even a doll-repair shop and 47 rooms of miniature furniture. Closed Sunday and Monday. Admission. ~ 246 North 100 East Street, Provo; 801-377-9935.

BRIGHAM YOUNG UNIVERSITY   This church-sponsored university has more than 32,000 students and a well-earned reputation for moral rectitude. Young himself told the first two dozen students in 1876: "I want you to remember that you ought not to teach even the alphabet or the multiplication tables without the spirit of God." Modern students must subscribe to a strict code of honor, which demands that they abstain from lying, alcohol, tobacco, caffeine, non-prescription drugs and pre-marital sex, and that they dress neatly and modestly (no shorts, even in summer) and groom themselves carefully (no beards). Degrees are offered in 150 undergraduate programs and 57 graduate departments. Languages are an academic strength here: 45 tongues are

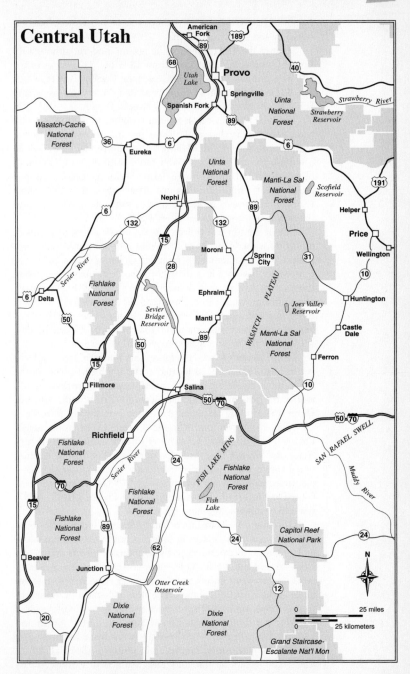

Central Utah

American Fork
189
89
68
Utah Lake
40
Provo
Springville
Strawberry River
Uinta National Forest
Strawberry Reservoir
Spanish Fork
89
Wasatch-Cache National Forest
36
6
Eureka
6
Uinta National Forest
Manti-La Sal National Forest
Scofield Reservoir
191
Nephi
132
89
Helper
132
Price
6
Moroni
Spring City
31
Wellington
28
Sevier River
Fishlake National Forest
15
10
Ephraim
Joes Valley Reservoir
Huntington
Sevier Bridge Reservoir
Manti
WASATCH PLATEAU
Castle Dale
6
Delta
50
89
Manti-La Sal National Forest
Ferron
50
10
15
Fillmore
Salina
50
70
50
70
SAN RAFAEL SWELL
Richfield
Fishlake National Forest
Sevier River
24
FISH LAKE MTNS
Fishlake National Forest
Muddy River
70
15
Fishlake National Forest
Fish Lake
Fishlake National Forest
Capitol Reef National Park
24
89
Fishlake National Forest
24
Beaver
62
Junction
Otter Creek Reservoir
12
N
0   25 miles
0   25 kilometers
20
Dixie National Forest
Dixie National Forest
Grand Staircase-Escalante Nat'l Mon

taught to help train young Mormons to serve two-year international missions for the church.

Most of the 450 campus buildings are modern, although six Lower Campus buildings date from 1884 to 1912. Focus of the 646-acre campus is the 52-bell **Centennial Carillon Tower**, which can be heard throughout campus at daily intervals.~ Academy Square, 500 North and University streets, Provo.

The 66,000-seat **Cougar Stadium** is home to the BYU football team that produced several all-star pro quarterbacks, including Steve Young and Jim McMahon. Other campus facilities include a motion-picture studio, TV and radio stations, a mountaintop observatory and an 837-acre farm. Performances by campus music, theater and dance groups attract thousands of Utahns. Free guided campus tours are offered twice daily on weekdays (reservations recommended). ~ 801-378-4678.

One of the top five collections of Jurassic dinosaur fossils in the world is the highlight of the BYU **Earth Science Museum** opposite Cougar Stadium. Fully mounted skeletons of tyrannosaurus, camptosaurus, allosaurus, diceratops and deinosuchus are among those on display, along with the massive nine-foot shoulder blade of an ultrasaurus, a 150-million-year-old dinosaur egg, dinosaur footprints and a petrified tree trunk. Visitors may watch as paleontologists clean more than 100 tons of fossils. Closed Sunday. ~ 1683 North Canyon Road, Provo; 801-378-3680.

The **Museum of Art**—the largest art museum between Denver and San Francisco—is located at the southwest corner of the BYU campus beside the Harris Fine Art Center. More than 14,000 works are exhibited, including pieces by Rembrandt, Albrecht Dürer and Honoré Daumier. An orientation theater introduces the collection to visitors, who see a range of art from ancient Etruscan to 17th- and 18th-century European and 19th-century American West. Other galleries display a fascinating international variety of musical instruments and contemporary works— paintings, sculpture and ceramics—by BYU faculty and students. Closed Sunday. ~ 492 East Campus Drive, Provo; 801-422-8287; www.byu.edu/moa/museum/index.

The **Monte L. Bean Life Science Museum** has two floors of natural-history displays that include mounted and preserved mammals, reptiles, birds and eggs, fish, mollusks, insects and plants from around the world. One room complements the heads of large African game animals with computer views of the same animals in their natural habitats. The Bean is located in the southwest campus, about 300 yards north of the Museum of Art near the Marriott Center arena. Closed Sunday. ~ 1430 North and Lambert Lane, Provo; 801-378-5051; www.byu.edu/mlbean.

The BYU **Museum of Peoples and Culture** in Allen Hall chronicles 50,000 years of humanity with artifacts of various Ameri-

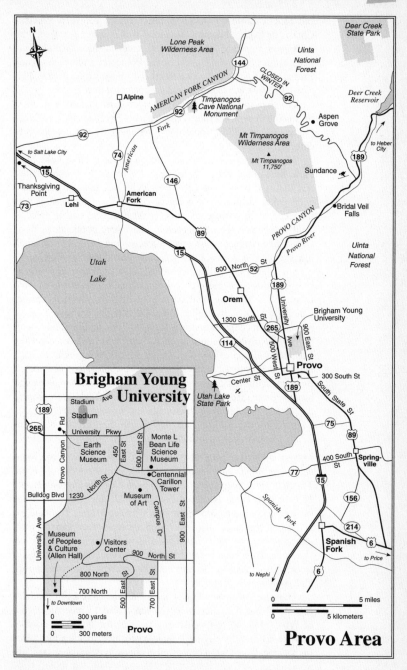

Provo Area

can Indian cultures, including the Fremont Anasazi, Mexican Chiapa de Corzo, Navajo, Shoshone and Zoque. Special emphasis is given to the Mayas of Central America. Also displayed are items from Colombia, Egypt, Israel, Polynesia and Syria. Closed Saturday and Sunday. ~ 700 North 100 East Street, Provo; 801-378-6112; www.byu.edu/anthro/mopc/main.htm.

Overlooking the BYU campus from Provo's northeast foothills is the **Provo Mormon Temple**, whose gold spires were completed only in 1972. Non-church members are not permitted to enter the temple.

The best place to approach Utah Lake is at **Utah Lake State Park**, four miles west of downtown Provo. At 139 square miles, this remnant of ancient Lake Bonneville is Utah's largest freshwater lake. Although the water is shallow (average depth is nine feet) and often murky, it's popular with anglers and boaters. A small museum at the visitors center offers park publications along with information on native fish species and some of the lake's history. ~ 4400 West Center Street, Provo; 801-375-0731.

Suburban Springville, six miles south of Provo, is home to Utah's oldest art museum, the **Springville Museum of Art**. Launched in 1903 by local artists who donated works to Springville High School, the collection grew over the years; in 1937, it moved into its current Spanish Mission–style building, built with Works Progress Administration funding and now listed on the National Register of Historic Places. Six galleries present the permanent collection of late-19th- and 20th-century works by Utah painters, sculptors and printmakers; a variety of changing exhibitions rotate through five other galleries. The Utah Photographic Art Reference Archives document the history of art in Utah. Closed Monday. ~ 126 East 400 South, Springville; 801-489-2727; www.shs.nebo.edu/museum/museum.html.

PROVO CANYON AND THE ALPINE LOOP   Two scenic highways combine to make a pleasant day's loop drive out of Provo. The first of the pair, **Provo Canyon Scenic Byway**, follows Route 189 through Uinta National Forest for 32 miles to Route 40 at Heber City, winding along the south side of Mount Timpanogos and along the Provo River through a steep-walled canyon that, although heavily treed, has a significant history with winter avalanches. This river is famed among fly fishermen for its wild trout. At the head of the canyon is Deer Creek Reservoir, a popular spot for water sports.

En route, the byway passes beautiful **Bridal Veil Falls**, six miles past the Route 52 junction at Olmstead and 15 miles northeast of Provo. Hiking trails skirt the base of the 607-foot double-cataract falls, and a city park maintained by Provo is a nice place for a picnic. Come winter, ice climbers flock to the frozen waterfall.

Provo Canyon is linked to the city of American Fork, north of Provo, via narrow, winding Route 92, the 20-mile **Alpine Loop** that circles **Mount Timpanogos**, an 11,750-tall battleship-gray crag that is Utah's best impression of a Swiss Alp. It's also the centerpiece of the 10,518-acre Mount Timpanogos Wilderness Area. So steep is this road and so tight are its curves that trailers are absolutely prohibited; the route is closed in winter. Yet two major attractions, the Sundance Resort and Timpanogos Cave National Monument, make this trip a "must" for most travelers to the region, and other lesser diversions—viewpoints, hiking trails, fishing streams, a side trip to Cascade Springs—easily take up a full day. The highway is at its most impressive in autumn, when colorful foliage decorates every panorama.

Just a couple of miles after climbing out of Provo Canyon, Route 92 passes the entrance road to **Sundance Resort**, actor/director Robert Redford's mountain domain. Redford bought a tiny Uinta National Forest ski area here in 1969, renamed it for the character he played opposite Paul Newman in the movie *Butch Cassidy and the Sundance Kid,* and guided its environmentally conscious evolution into an arts community, ski resort and personal home.

Yet Sundance has maintained a smaller, quieter, more tasteful family ambience than other Wasatch resorts. Rental condominiums and restaurants invite visitors to linger and participate in activities that range from skiing in the winter to mountain biking, horseback riding, backpacking and flyfishing, as well as summer theater and concerts. ~ From Provo, head about nine miles east on Route 189 through Provo Canyon to the Sundance turnoff at Route 92, then two miles to the resort; 801-225-4100, theater 801-225-4107; www.sundanceresort.com.

sights

AUTHOR FAVORITE

Thanksgiving Point is a legacy of Alan Ashton, who made his fortune as co-founder of WordPerfect Corp. Located in a natural terrain bowl outside Lehi, Thanksgiving Point has thriving, expansive gardens that are Utah's most impressive, a championship golf course and a petting zoo. The 55-acre gardens are a magical collection of themes, including a traditional rose garden, a colorful Monet Garden, a scented Butterfly Garden, a Secret Garden and a Waterfall Garden. The Parterre Garden features a life-size carousel with floral topiary ponies. Kids delight in the outdoor garden railroad, possibly the largest in the world. Admission. ~ 3003 North Thanksgiving Way, Lehi; 801-768-2300, 888-672-6040; www.thanksgiving-point.com.

Beyond Sundance, Route 92 descends to American Fork Canyon and **Timpanogos Cave National Monument**. From a visitors center on the canyon floor, a steep one-and-a-half-mile paved trail climbs 1065 feet to the cavern entrance at 6730 feet. Actually three adjacent limestone caves, 1800 feet long and connected by manmade tunnels, Timpanogos Cave is considered a "live" or "wet" cave because its dripstone is still in formation. Prevalent are impressive stalagmites and chandelier-like stalactites, helictites and aragonite crystals, colorful flowstone in subtle hues, and rimstone formed by calcium carbonate in the groundwater. Bring a jacket; the cave maintains a constant 43-degree temperature and humidity is nearly 100 percent. An orientation film is presented several times daily at the visitors center, which also has exhibits and a bookstore. Plan 45 to 60 minutes to explore the cave; add several extra hours to tour the visitors center, make the hike to the cave entrance, and wait your turn for the tour. Tickets must be purchased at the visitors center (or up to two weeks in advance). Tours, limited to 20 persons, are offered on a first-come, first-serve basis every 10 to 20 minutes. They do sell out, sometimes by mid-morning, so it's wise to arrive early, especially on Saturdays and holidays. Open daily Memorial Day through Labor Day. Admission. ~ Route 92, seven miles east of American Fork; visitors center 801-756-5238, park headquarters 801-756-5239; www.nps.gov/tica.

En route from American Fork back to Provo, a distance of 19 miles, consider a detour to **Lehi**, a small town 16 miles north of Provo on the west side of Route 15 that is home to one of Utah's oldest museums. **John Hutching's Museum of Natural History**, a family hobby starting in 1913, has evolved into an eclectic collection of fossils, shells, minerals, pioneer and Indian artifacts, and items from the modern computer industry. The late founder's sons frequently greet visitors to the museum, housed in a 1920 Spanish Revival–style building that once was a Carnegie library

LIGHT AT THE END OF THE TUNNEL

The first of the three caves at Timpanogos Cave National Monument, Hansen Cave, was discovered by Martin Hansen in 1887 as he tracked a mountain lion. A Chicago onyx company later stripped the cave's walls of mineral deposits in the 1890s. After the other two caves were discovered— Timpanogos Cave in 1914 by two teenage boys as they awaited relatives on a private tour of Hansen Cave, Middle Cave in 1921 by Martin Hansen's son and grandson—an active cry was raised to preserve this unique natural area. Response was rapid: The national monument was established and the cave electrically lighted in 1922.

and a World War I memorial. Closed Sunday. Admission. ~ 55 North Center Street, Lehi; 801-768-7180.

Jurassic Park comes to life at the **North American Museum of Ancient Life** that's part of Thanksgiving Point. Arguably the country's largest museum dedicated to dinosaurs, the facility covers more than 122,000 square feet. Inside you'll find more than 60 mounted dinosaur fossils, many set in natural settings. Among the highlights are a 120-foot-long supersaurus, the longest of its kind in the world, as well as two T. Rexes locked in battle. Kids enjoy the numerous hands-on exhibits; a favorite is a digging quarry where they can search for fossils. The museum even stages "DinoSnore" adventures in which kids from the fourth grade on up can have sleep-outs in the museum among the dinosaurs. If that's not enough, there's also a towering three-dimensional projection theater. Admission. ~ Take Exit 287 off Route 15.

WEST OF UTAH LAKE   From Lehi, Route 73 continues west 25 miles to **Fairfield**, a tiny community that boomed in mid-1858 as a supply point for nearby Camp Floyd. Its population of settlers, merchants and gamblers reached 7000; supplying food and goods provided a steady income. Camp Floyd was the largest Army camp in the United States until the 3500 troops, under General Albert Sidney Johnston, were recalled to the East upon the outbreak of the Civil War in July 1861.

The old fort site is preserved in **Camp Floyd–Stagecoach Inn State Park**, one-half mile west of Fairfield via Route 73. Of 400 original structures, all that remain are an old commissary building and a cemetery where 84 soldiers were buried. Also here is the restored 1858 Stagecoach Inn, once a two-story adobe-and-frame hotel for the Overland Stage and rest stop for Pony Express riders, now a museum with pioneer artifacts and period decor. Open Easter weekend to mid-October. Admission. ~ 18035 West 1540 North, Fairfield; 801-768-8932.

To complete the loop, head west 45 miles on the old stage route to Ibapah. From this tiny town near the Utah–Nevada border, a paved road runs 60 miles north to the casinos in the Nevada border town of Wendover; Route 80 continues another 120 miles east to Salt Lake City to complete a 366-mile loop drive. Intrepid travelers undertaking this long journey must be aware that no gas is sold along the 218-mile stretch from Lehi to Wendover, and water is scarce.

Although there's a surprising lack of B&B options in the Provo/Orem area, that doesn't mean you won't be able to find a room. It simply means that you'll most likely wind up in a chain motel or hotel.   **LODGING**

One of Provo's more unique lodgings is the **Hine's Mansion**, built in 1895 for Russell Spencer Hines, whose fortunes were tied to mining and real estate. It was intended as a showplace, as its size and fine woodwork attest. Today it holds ten largely Victorian bedrooms equipped with two-person jetted tubs, and king- and queen-sized beds. ~ 383 West 100 South, Provo; 801-374-8400, 800-428-5636, fax 801-374-0823; www.hinesmansion. com. DELUXE TO ULTRA-DELUXE.

Provo's biggest and most luxurious place to stay is the **Provo Marriott Hotel and Conference Center**. This nine-story downtown hotel has 331 comfortable rooms, the uppermost of which offer picturesque views of the Wasatch Range or Utah Lake. Each of the tastefully appointed rooms has a coffeemaker, an honor bar and cable TV; in-room refrigerators and nonsmoking rooms are available on request. Mingles restaurant offers fine dining; Seasons is a private lounge for hotel guests. Other amenities include indoor and outdoor swimming pools, a whirlpool, sauna and fitness room, as well as a business center, coin laundry, gift shop and covered parking. ~ 101 West 100 North, Provo; 801-377-4700, 800-777-7144, fax 801-377-4708; www.marriott.com. DELUXE.

Brigham Young University visitors can stay three blocks from campus at the pleasant **Best Western CottonTree Inn**. The two-story motor inn overlooks foot and bicycle paths along the Provo River greenbelt and has bikes rentals. All 80 rooms have cable TV; some are equipped with microwave ovens and refrigerators. Facilities include a swimming pool, a whirlpool and coin laundry. ~ 2230 North University Parkway, Provo; 801-373-7044, 800-662-6886, fax 801-375-5240; www.cottontree.net. MODERATE.

The **Provo Travelodge** is a completely nonsmoking hotel, a nice touch that the rest of the travel industry should pay attention to. Another twist at this hotel are rooms designed for families—they come with three beds, so little Johnny doesn't have to be forced to sleep on the couch. ~ 124 South University Avenue, Provo; 801-373-1974. MODERATE TO DELUXE.

HIDDEN ►

In nearby suburban Springville, the historic Kearns Hotel—built as a home in 1892 and converted to a hostelry in 1909—has been impressively restored and reopened as the **Victorian Inn Bed and Breakfast**. The seven rooms include two full-size suites and two mini-suites with jacuzzi tubs; all are furnished with antiques and reproductions from the late 19th century, including hand-carved queen beds. Five rooms have whirlpools. Morning light filtering through original stained-glass parlor windows adds atmosphere to the full breakfast. For a delicious start to your day, try the crème brûlée french toast topped with blackberry sauce. ~ 94 West 200 South, Springville; 801-489-0737, 888-489-0737, fax 801-489-8875. MODERATE TO DELUXE.

The **Sundance Resort** has a wide range of mountain accommodations. More than 100 cottages and mountain homes, from one to five bedrooms, are magnificently situated on the slopes of a canyon at 6000 feet elevation. Alpine views are impressive from the original "Mandan" cottages; the "River Run" units sit beside a creek near the base of the ski lifts, while "The Pines" are in Sundance Village itself. All feature rustic handcrafted furniture, American Indian artwork, stone fireplaces and outdoor decks; they are stocked with Sundance's own environmentally gentle bath products. Most units have fully equipped kitchens and whirlpool baths. This is not the place for skimpy bank accounts, but if you can afford it, you'll never forget Sundance's solitude and striking beauty. ~ RR 3, Box A-1, Sundance, UT 84604; 801-225-4107, 800-892-1600, fax 801-226-1937. ULTRA-DELUXE.

At the **Best Western Timpanogos Inn** you can choose from 59 rooms and wake up to a complimentary breakfast of fresh buttermilk pancakes made from flour purchased locally from the historic Lehi Mill. Located north of Provo and Orem, this inn lets you avoid the congested downtown area and be close to Thanksgiving Point. There's an indoor pool and hot tub, as well as laundry facilities. ~ 195 South 850 East, Lehi; 801-768-1400, 866-444-1218. MODERATE TO DELUXE.

The **Quality Inn and Suites Hotel** along Route 15 at American Fork is less expensive than hotels and motels in downtown Provo, yet is centrally located between Brigham Young University, Thanksgiving Point and Timpanogos Cave National Monument. Located in the Utah Valley Business Park, the motel does not offer the best setting, but it's accessible and offers an indoor pool and spa. ~ 712 South Utah Valley Drive, American Fork; 801-763-8383, 800-228-5151, fax 801-763-8380; www.afqualityinn.com. MODERATE.

DINING

You wouldn't expect to find Brazilian cuisine this far north, but its popularity can be traced to **Tucanos Brazilian Grill**. Among

HAVE HORSE, WILL DELIVER

The Pony Express is inscribed in American legend although it operated for only 19 months between 1860 and 1861. A relay of some 80 jockey-sized riders covered the 1400-mile trail between St. Joseph, Missouri, and Sacramento, California, in just ten days, exchanging horses every 12 miles or so. The best-preserved section of the **Pony Express Trail and Old Stage Route** that begins just west of Fairfield runs 133 miles west from the Stagecoach Inn through the arid terrain of western Utah. Now a graded sand-and-gravel road maintained by the Bureau of Land Management, the trail has interpretive signs at most of the 16 former stations from Camp Floyd to Ibapah (Deep Creek), near the Nevada state line.

the favorites are Tucanos *churrasco*. ~ 4801 North University Avenue, Suite 790, Provo; 801-224-4774. MODERATE.

When Provo families go out for steak and seafood, they frequently wind up at **Magleby's**, in the Village Green neighborhood on the north side of the city. There's a "welcome home" ambiance here—antiques and collectibles complement lace curtains and old-fashioned upholstery. Menu items include Black Angus ribeye steak, prime rib, chicken, fresh fish and breaded shrimp. An all-you-can-eat Friday-and-Saturday-night buffet draws throngs of locals, who often finish their meal with Lenora's Famous Deep-Dish Apple Pie. Closed Sunday. ~ 1675 North 200 West, Provo; 801-374-6249. MODERATE TO DELUXE.

A variety of excellent ethnic choices is available in the BYU campus area. Budget-conscious students gather at **The Brick Oven**, a Provo staple for decades. Besides great pizza, the Oven serves spaghetti and lasagna. Closed Sunday. ~ 111 East 800 North, Provo; 801-374-8800. BUDGET.

A Sikh chef prepares curries, breads and tandoori-baked meats at the **Bombay House**. You can also order beer to go with your meal. Closed Sunday. ~ 463 North University Avenue, Provo; 801-373-6677. BUDGET.

A twist on traditional American favorites can be found at **Papa Lee's Island Grill**, which serves up "Cheeseburgers in Paradise" as well as coconut shrimp, Jamaican chicken and other seafood and chicken entrées. There's also an array of specialty drinks that evoke warmer climes and a splash of ocean. ~ 117 North University Avenue, Provo; 801-375-2654. BUDGET TO MODERATE.

The Sundance Resort has two fine restaurants. **The Tree Room** is a rustically elegant, candlelit dining room adorned with Western and American Indian art from Robert Redford's personal collection. Creative menus combine seasonal ingredients—vegetables and fruits, locally grown herbs and edible flowers—while drawing upon various culinary traditions. Game farms provide buffalo,

AUTHOR FAVORITE

One of the most authentic Italian restaurants in the Rocky Mountain region is a family business in downtown Provo. **La Dolce Vita** is the domain of Giovanni Della Corte, who emigrated to Utah from his native Naples in 1980 and put all three generations of his family to work in this unpretentious cafe. The fare is pasta, pizza and calzone, generous portions of which are served with savory homemade sauces, salad and warm bread. Desserts, including tiramisu and spumoni, are a house specialty. Beer, wine and espresso drinks are served. Closed Sunday. ~ 61 North 100 East, Provo; 801-373-8482. BUDGET.

venison, antelope and elk to accompany beef, chicken and fresh seafood, including Utah trout. The restaurant's name stems from the tree that Redford built the restaurant around. Although it died long ago, its trunk still rises through the dining room. Reservations are recommended. ~ Sundance Resort; 801-225-4107. DELUXE.

The less-formal **Foundry Grill** applies regional accents to Southwestern cuisine in a ranch-house setting with big picture windows looking out on Mount Timpanogos. Most dishes are prepared in a wood oven or over a wood-fired grill and rotisserie. If Redford is at the resort and dining here, you'll likely miss him since he prefers a smaller, more intimate dining room off the main dining room. Reservations are recommended. ~ Sundance Resort; 801-225-4107. MODERATE.

Head out to Lehi and you'll find a sumptuous Mexico meal at **Cocolito's**, where the burritos, chimichangas, enchiladas, tacos and fajitas are made fresh daily. Be sure to save room for desserts such as fruit chimis and fried ice cream. ~ 102 West Main Street, Lehi; 801-766-8161. BUDGET TO MODERATE.

SHOPPING

At **Riverwoods**, a collection of shops at the mouth of Provo Canyon, you'll find everything from A (Abercrombie & Fitch) to Y (Yankee Candle Company), and quite a bit in-between. ~ 4801 North University Avenue, Provo; 801-802-8430.

To sample regional artworks, stop by **The Window Box**, which offers not only fine artworks but also custom framing. ~ 62 West Center Street, Provo; 801-377-4367.

If you've ever seen a copy of the mail-order *Sundance Catalog*, you'll recognize the inventory at the Sundance Resort's expansive **General Store**. Its stock of handmade Southwestern-style clothing, outdoor apparel, American Indian arts and jewelry, furniture and gift items were the inspiration for the catalog. ~ Sundance Resort; 801-225-4107.

Candy lovers of all ages are delighted by **Peppermint Place**. Launched in the 1970s as a home business, this 500-product factory is in the north Provo suburb of Alpine. Large windows provide a bird's-eye view of the floor where candy is made and decorated. A short video details the entire process of making candy canes. Closed Sunday. ~ 155 East 200 North, Alpine; 801-756-6916 ext. 600, 801-756-7400.

Pecan pie bars, homemade sweets such as baked apple pudding cake and chocolate peanut-butter bars, and freshly ground sacks of flour, oats, buttermilk mixes and more can be found at **Lehi Mill**, which has been grinding out products since 1906. ~ 833 East Main Street, Lehi; 801-768-4401; www.lehimill.com.

American folk art is on display at **Dowdle Folk Art** at Thanksgiving Point. Inside the store you'll find calendars, prints, puzzles, original artworks, and gifts. ~ 3003 North Thanksgiving Way, Suite 1776, Lehi; 801-766-5656.

If you're looking for a little something to go with your mountain retreat back home, check out **Moonbeams and Cabin Dreams**. The furniture here leans to the "rustic custom" style, which is fully evident in the free-standing, wood-carved display case topped by the carved image of a longhorn steer head. ~ 446 West 800 North, Orem; 801-227-0100.

NIGHTLIFE   When it comes to after-dark activity, Provo is a very quiet city. The main entertainment venue is Brigham Young University. The BYU **Theater** has a year-round schedule of student performances. ~ 801-378-4322.

It should not be surprising that, in a town dominated by the Mormon faith, alcoholic beverages are hard to come by. Tipplers might head to **Seasons**, a private club in the Provo Park Hotel. ~ 101 West 100 North; 801-377-4700.

With rare exceptions, nightclubs are alcohol-free, including **Club Omni**, a Tuesday-to-Saturday dance club. Cover. ~ 150 West 100 South Street; 801-375-0011; www.clubomni.com.

Jokes are the staple at **ComedySportz**, an improvisational nightclub that often features two teams of comedians going head-to-head for your laughter. Performances are staged Fridays and Saturdays, as well as the second and fourth Thursdays of the month. Cover. ~ 36 West Center Street, Provo; 801-377-9700.

Laughter is the medicine doled out at **Johnny B's Comedy Club**, were comics and hypnotists perform in a smoke- and alcohol-free environment. Cover. ~ 177 West 300 South, Provo; 801-377-6910.

Sundance Resort is smaller than Provo but often livelier. **The Owl Bar**, which Butch Cassidy and his Hole-in-the-Wall Gang frequented in the 1890s, has been moved from Thermopolis, Wyoming, and restored. The highlight of this gathering place for locals and resort guests to recount their day's adventures and listen to live bands is the rosewood bar that dominates one wall. Look hard for the bullet hole that remains from the bar's rowdier days in Thermopolis. ~ Sundance Resort; 801-225-4107.

A bigger draw is the **Sundance Summer Theater**, situated in a beautiful natural amphitheater surrounded by firs with a mountain backdrop. Each season, extending mid-June to August, three or four productions are presented, typically including family musicals (nightly except Sunday) and children's matinees (Thursday to Sunday). ~ Sundance Resort; 801-225-4100.

Sundance guests gain free admission to the **Sundance Institute Screening Room**, presenting a year-round calendar of foreign and independent films, movie classics and documentaries. ~ Sundance Resort; 801-225-4107.

UTAH LAKE STATE PARK 🏊 ⛵ 🎣 🚣 🛶 🚤 ⚓ The main point of water-sports access to Utah's largest freshwater lake, a 96,600-acre body of water between the Wasatch Range and the Lake Mountains, this 308-acre park has four boat-launching ramps and a 30-acre marina. Other marinas can be found nearby in Lindon and American Fork. Although the average depth of the often-murky lake is only ten feet, it's a great place to catch trophy-size walleye and bass, channel catfish and various panfish, including yellow perch. Windsurfing and waterskiing are also popular on the lake. Winter doesn't slow visitation, as there's ice-fishing on the lake. A visitors center and museum serve the state park. Day-use fee, $6. ~ 4400 West Center Street, four miles west of downtown Provo; 801-375-0731.

PARKS

At Sundance Resort, Robert Redford launched the famous Sundance Film Festival, which soon outgrew its first home and relocated to Park City (but kept its name).

▲ There are 54 sites; $17 per night. Reservations: 800-322-3770 (April 15 to October 15).

CAMP FLOYD–STAGECOACH INN STATE PARK American history is the focus of this park. You won't find any swimming, fishing, boating or hiking here, but you will find a restored military outpost that, in pre–Civil War America, was the largest post in the country. Roughly 3500 troops were dispatched here to ward off a possible rebellion by Mormons, only to be called back in 1861 as the Civil War broke out. On the grounds today are a cemetery and commissary building; nearby is the Stagecoach Inn, a stopover along the Pony Express route. You can tour the inn with its original period furnishings. Day-use fee, $5 per vehicle. ~ 18035 West 1540 North, Fairfield; 801-768-8932.

UINTA NATIONAL FOREST 🥾 🚴 🏇 🎿 🏕 🏊 ⛵ 🎣 🚣 🚤 ⚓ Extending in several parcels to the south, east and north of Provo, this 1484-square-mile national forest combines high, forested mountains and open rangeland. Two alpine wilderness areas are in the far north—Lone Peak and Timpanogos, the latter surrounding 11,750-foot Mount Timpanogos—while the Mount Nebo Wilderness is in the south near Nephi. Circling 11,877-foot Mount Nebo is the Mount Nebo Loop Scenic Byway (see "Nephi-Manti Area," below), providing access to numerous trailheads for hiking and horseback riding. Another popular forest recreation area is Strawberry Reservoir, about 50 miles east of Provo via Heber City and Route 40, renowned for its trout fishing and sailing. ~ Forest access can be found throughout the region, particularly along Route 189 between Provo and Heber City, Route 92 east of American Fork, and the Hobble Creek Road running east from Springville; 801-377-5780; www.fs.fed.us/r4/uinta.

▲ There are 38 campgrounds with 1994 sites, 360 for tents only; $12 per night. Reservations: 877-444-6777.

Price Area

First settled by Mormon farmers on a tributary of the Green River 80 miles southeast of Provo via Route 6 and named for a bishop of their faith, Price boomed in the 1880s with the discovery of coal and the advent of the railroad. Deposits of natural gas, uranium and helium were subsequently found in the area, helping the community to grow to a population of about 9000.

Today the community is the gateway to a vast recreational playground in central Utah. While Nine Mile Canyon, with its incredible collection of petroglyphs and pictographs, lies directly northeast of Price, directly south stretches the rough and beautiful maze of canyon country known as the San Rafael Swell.

An egg-shaped piece of Utah outback running 65 miles long by 40 miles wide, the swell rose above the landscape 60 million years ago as a bulging blister of sedimentary rock. So rugged is the landscape that in the mid-1700s Spanish explorers detoured around the canyon-riddled land in their search for a route from Sante Fe to California. Even mountain men saw the land as too difficult to bother with, although in the late 1800s Butch Cassidy and the Sundance Kid loved this rocky maze for eluding posses. Today the swell is overseen by the U.S. Bureau of Land Management and is open to camping, hiking and, during spring runoff, paddling along the San Rafael River.

Since the 1920s, the San Rafael Swell has produced prodigious numbers of dinosaur skeletons, making it a treasure trove for paleontologists. West of Price is the largest parcel of Manti-La Sal National Forest, which maintains its headquarters here.

SIGHTS

Route 6 runs southeast of Provo through a gap in the Wasatch Range to Helper, Scofield and Price, towns that started life as gritty, blue-collar outposts.

Before you reach Helper, 61 miles southeast of Provo, you'll come across Route 96, a small state highway that runs roughly 16 miles south to the boom-and-bust coal-mining town of **Scofield**. Fewer than 50 people now live here, but in the early 1920s the population exceeded 6000. In the old Scofield cemetery on a hillside east of town, 199 tombstones give testimony to the most serious mine disaster in U.S. history when on May 1, 1900, the No. 4 mine in Winter Quarters Canyon exploded.

Just above town is popular **Scofield State Park** on Scofield Reservoir, created by a dam built in the 1940s. ~ Located 11 miles south of Route 6 and five miles north of the town of Scofield.

Coal and rail gave a name to the small town of **Helper**, seven miles north of Price on Route 6. In order to carry heavily laden coal trains over 7477-foot Soldier Summit, between here and

Provo, the Denver & Rio Grande Railroad required extra engines to push. A terminal for these "helper" locomotives was built here. Today, the entire downtown is a National Historic District reflecting the ethnic and religious diversity of its immigrant miners. Town history is well documented at the **Western Mining & Railroad Museum** in the heart of the historic district. As one might expect, there are extensive displays of 19th-century coal-mining tools and railroad equipment, along with old photos, a collection of Depression-era art, and the wooden steps of the old Pleasant

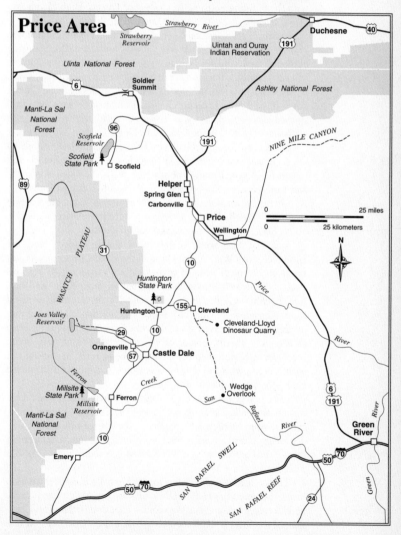

Price Area

Valley Coal Co., which Butch Cassidy and his gang robbed in 1897. ~ 294 South Main Street, Helper; 435-472-3009.

Route 6, which joins Route 191 just north of Helper, rolls into Price from the west, offering several exits into town while skirting the city to the south. Early-20th-century historic sites in downtown Price include the Depression-era **Price Municipal Building**, its main foyer wrapped in a 200-foot-long mural that depicts regional history; it took three years for artist Lynn Fausett to complete it. The city library is in the building, which shares a wall with the building housing the College of Eastern Utah's Utah Prehistoric Museum. ~ 100 East Main Street, Price.

Nearby is the Classical Revival–style **Price Theater**, which was known as the Star Theater when it was built in 1923, featuring masks of Greek muses around its second-story exterior. Movies still run nightly; admission is just $2. ~ 20 East Main Street, Price.

Two blocks north, the **Notre Dame de Lourdes Catholic Church** dates from 1918. The church, small but ornate with beautiful stained-glass windows, was financed with help from French Catholics who lived in the area. ~ 210 North Carbon Avenue, Price.

The Byzantine-style **Hellenic Orthodox Church** was built by Greek immigrant miners in 1916. It has ornate woodwork and portraits of saints lining the interior walls. Services, weddings and funerals are still performed. ~ 61 South 200 East, Price.

Literature on a walking tour is available from the **Carbon County Travel Bureau**. ~ 155 East Main Street, Price; 435-637-3009, 800-842-0789; www.castlecountry.com.

You can find some members of Butch Cassidy and the Sundance Kid's Wild Bunch Gang in the **Price City Cemetery**, located on the north side of town. Among those buried here include "Gunplay" Maxwell, who died in a gunfight in Price; Johnny Walker, killed by a posse outside of Green River; and Matt Warner, who rode with Butch and Sundance for a number of years, only to leave his life of crime behind and work in Price as a deputy sheriff, justice of the peace and night patrolman. John Herring, who died from wounds he suffered in a shoot-out with a posse who thought he was Butch Cassidy, is also buried here. ~ 595 East 400 North, Price.

Price is also home to the **College of Eastern Utah**, a two-year community college that opened in 1937 as Carbon College. Today catering to more than 3000 students, the college offers associate-degree programs in areas such as mining, nursing, engineering, theater and graphic arts. ~ 451 East 400 North, Price; 435-637-2120; www.ceu.edu.

The college is well-known for its **Utah Prehistoric Museum**. Inside the museum's Hall of Dinosaurs are eight complete Jurassic and Cretaceous dinosaur skeletons—including Utahraptor, considered the fiercest of all carnivores—and the world's largest collection of dinosaur-track casts, primarily from nearby coal mines. Meanwhile, the Hall of Archaeology exhibits Fremont Indian artifacts, including the Pilling figurine collection (clay ornaments at least 800 years old), and collections of minerals and fossils. Information about self-guiding tours to American Indian petroglyphs in Nine Mile Canyon is also available. ~ 200 East Main Street, Price; 435-637-5060; museum.ceu.edu.

Harboring more blasts from the past, **Nine Mile Canyon** exhibits thousands of prehistoric etchings. Also up this canyon (which is actually about 40 miles long), on Bureau of Land Management terrain, are old homesteads, stagecoach stops and other historic sites. Brochures and maps are available from BLM or regional tourist offices. The canyon's name may have been derived from a 19th-century mapmaker who made a nine-mile triangulation drawing when charting the area. ~ From Price, head nine miles east on Route 6/191 to Wellington, and then head north on Nine Mile Canyon Road, which is paved for the first 13 miles before turning into a gravel road. The mouth of the canyon is about 25 miles northeast of Wellington; BLM information 435-636-3600.

Most of the College of Eastern Utah's paleontological exhibits came from the **Cleveland-Lloyd Dinosaur Quarry**, a National Natural Landmark administered by the Bureau of Land Management. About 12,000 bones from at least 70 different animals of 14 species have been recovered from this quarry, the most productive Jurassic-period source in the world. About 147 million years ago, this area was a shallow freshwater lake with a muddy bottom that trapped both plant-eating dinosaurs and their carnivorous predators. The accumulating skeletons were covered with volcanic ash after the lake bottom dried; subsequent rivers and shallow seas deposited further layers of sand and mud. Then water and wind eroded the landscape to again expose the now-fossilized bones.

◄ HIDDEN

AUTHOR FAVORITE

One of the most amazing museums I've ever been in has no roof or walls. You can find it in **Nine Mile Canyon**. Located northeast of Price, the canyon is actually closer to 40 miles long. Sometimes called "the world's longest art gallery," it contains thousands of panels of Fremont Indian rock art in addition to ruins of their civilization, which may have been established here as early as A.D. 300. Earlier artifacts found here have been dated as far back as 12,000 years. See above for more information.

The allosaurus, largest of the Jurassic flesh-eaters, was by far the most common dinosaur found here. A complete, reconstructed skeleton greets arrivals at the quarry's visitors center, along with the only stegosaurus footprints ever found. Other animals found here are also introduced, including the common plant-eating camarasaurus and camptosaurus.

More than 60 museums around the world have casts and original skeletons from the Cleveland-Lloyd Dinosaur Quarry, which also produced several dinosaur eggs, one of which contained a fossilized embryo.

Work-in-progress can be viewed in an adjacent covered building; the self-guided Rock Walk Nature Trail winds through the boulder-strewn landscape. Since work began in 1929, scientists from the College of Eastern Utah, Brigham Young University, University of Utah and Princeton University have all dug here. Open daily in summer, weekends at other times. Admission. ~ Dinosaur Quarry and Flat Top Road (216 Road); from Route 155 off Route 10, 25 miles south of Price, follow signs east on a graded, unmarked road; 435-820-8485.

Fourteen miles south of the Cleveland-Lloyd Dinosaur Quarry along Route 10 is the little coal-mining town of Castle Dale, where more dinosaur skeletons are on display in the **Museum of the San Rafael**. The geology and natural history of the San Rafael Swell area (once a popular hideout for outlaws) is also presented here, along with various Indian relics. Among the relics is the "Sitterud Bundle," which was found in the high desert surrounding Castle Dale. Closed Saturday and Sunday. ~ 96 North 100 East, Castle Dale; 435-381-5252.

You can enter the **San Rafael Swell** either by dropping south from the Cleveland-Lloyd quarry or heading east from Castle Dale via dirt roads that crisscross the swell. It's a vast and rugged countryside, so be sure you're prepared with a good spare tire, a tankful of gas, and plenty of drinking water. Don't let the remoteness scare you off: this part of Utah is well worth the effort of exploration. Drive out to the top of the Wedge Overlook and not only will you be able to peer down into the goosenecks the San Rafael River has carved, you also can camp out under one of the most spectacular star shows on earth.

Elsewhere in the swell are side canyons named Little Wild Horse, Crack and Penitentiary; erosion has sculpted some beautiful arches if you have the time to find them. There are numerous panels of American Indian artworks in the form of petroglyphs and pictographs; some date 3000 years old. Among the most notable is the Buckhorn Wash Panel, which lies a bit northeast of the Wedge. For maps and information on the swell and all it offers, stop at the BLM office in Price. ~ 125 South 600 West, Price; 435-636-3600.

Just west of downtown Price stands the **Holiday Inn Hotel &**
Suites, a welcome waystation after driving down from Salt Lake
City. The hotel offers 151 rooms, a restaurant and lounge, and
an indoor heated pool the kids will love. There's also a game
room, and you can get a workout in the exercise room. The rooms
come complete with internet access. ~ 838 Westwood Boulevard,
Price; 435-637-8880, fax 435-637-7707. MODERATE.

A long-time favorite with many travelers in this region is the
Greenwell Inn, which combines 125 comfortable rooms with a
Mexican restaurant, a private club and a slew of other amenities.
The two-story motel has an indoor swimming pool, a hot tub, a
fitness room, coin laundry and more. Refrigerators are available
on request; a complimentary continental breakfast is served.
Nonsmokers, disabled visitors and pets are all accommodated. ~
655 East Main Street, Price; 435-637-3520, 800-666-3520, fax
435-637-4858; www.greenwellinn.com. MODERATE.

The **Best Western Carriage House Inn** has a swimming pool
and whirlpool both indoors and out. Forty-one rooms have standard furnishings; eleven family units incorporate a refrigerator
and microwave oven. Kids 12 and under stay free. ~ 590 East
Main Street, Price; 435-637-5660, 800-228-5732, fax 435-637-
5157. MODERATE.

For a more rustic experience, look to the **Nine Mile Ranch
Bunk n Breakfast** at the foot of Nine Mile Canyon. A non-
smoking cabin and a two-unit bunkhouse are available year-
round; in summer, guests are invited to stay in tepees. There's
also a campground. Activities here include hay rides, mountain
biking, Dutch-oven dinners and guided canyon tours; a country
store provides essentials. ~ Nine Mile Canyon Road; 435-637-
2572, 435-613-9794; www.ninemilecanyon.com, e-mail ninemile
ranch@yahoo.com. BUDGET TO MODERATE.

Thirty-two miles south of Price in Castle Dale, the two-story
Village Inn offers 21 clean and comfortable rooms. These simple
accommodations come with a queen- or king-sized bed, cable TV,
phones, microwaves and mini-refrigerators. ~ 375 East Main
Street, Castle Dale; 435-381-2309, fax 435-381-5121. BUDGET.

Gourmet sandwiches, pizza and "comfort food" entrées complement handcrafted beers at **Grogg's Pinnacle Brewing Co.** in the
old railroad town of Helper. Pale ale, raspberry wheat, amber ale
and porter are among the alcoholic selections at this brewpub. ~
1653 North Carbondale Road, Helper; 435-637-2924. BUDGET
TO MODERATE.

Farlaino's Cafe serves up good portions of homemade Italian
cuisine three meals a day. In the evening, pasta shares the spot-
light with seafood and steaks. Midday diners look for homemade

soup and daily specials. At breakfast, skillet dishes and a concession to Mexico—a burrito smothered in green chili—hold forth. ~ 87 West Main Street, Price; 435-637-9217. MODERATE.

Moussaka? Dolmas? Baklava? The **Greek Streak** has 'em all. Full Greek meals, including soup, salad and honey-drenched pastries, are the fare at lunch and dinner. Lamb roast or stew is often on the menu, and there are gyros for those who want something lighter. Closed Sunday. ~ 30 West 100 North, Price; 435-637-1930. BUDGET TO MODERATE.

Bagels, deli sandwiches and premium coffees are the fare at **Rosie's Deli & Bakery**. A wide choice of different breads, meats and cheeses go into a variety of hoagies and calzones. Salads, soups and pastries are also available. ~ 61 South 700 East, Price; 435-637-6743. BUDGET.

When visitors to the **Cowboy Club & Country Kitchen** aren't kicking up their heels and dancing to live country-and-western music, they're enjoying homestyle meals. All food at this establishment is made from scratch, including soups and breads. Steak and seafood dishes dominate the menu. ~ 31 East Main Street, Wellington; 435-637-8606. MODERATE.

PARKS

MANTI-LA SAL NATIONAL FOREST Of the three mountain blocks that comprise 1.3-million-acre Manti-La Sal National Forest, the largest—the Manti Division—lies west of Price. Narrow canyons, alpine meadows and broad rolling ridges cloaked with aspen and spruce are characteristic of this region. There is fine trout fishing in creeks and small lakes; the only boat ramp is at Joe's Valley Reservoir, west of Castle Dale, but Ferron and Electric Lake reservoirs are also popular. Skyline Drive, a scenic 87-mile route that follows the high crest of the Wasatch Plateau between Mount Nebo and the San Rafael Swell, runs south from Tucker to Route 70. Narrow, rough and unpaved, the road is open mid-July through September only and should not be attempted in foul weather. ~ Located west of Price, the forest can be accessed via Routes 264 near Scofield and 31 west of Cleveland; 435-637-2817.

▲ There are 10 campgrounds with 181 sites, 16 for tents only, in the Manti Division; $6 to $15 per night. Reservations: 877-444-6777.

SCOFIELD STATE PARK This park, set low on the eastern flanks of the Wasatch Plateau just outside the Manti-La Sal National Forest, revolves around a 2800-acre reservoir located at 7616 feet elevation. The reservoir is renowned for boating and fishing. Rainbow and wild cutthroat trout are prolific; brown trout are also caught in Fish Creek, served by a hiking trail. Boat rentals are available at the Mountain View unit on the east side of the lake. The day-use Lakeside unit has a fishing platform for disabled visitors. Day-use fee, $6. ~ Route 96, Scofield, ten miles southwest of Colton Junction (Route 6); 435-448-9449 (summer), 435-637-8497 (winter).

▲ There are 34 sites at Mountain View, 40 group sites at Madsen Bay; $11 to $14 per night. Closed November through April. Reservations: 800-322-3770.

HUNTINGTON STATE PARK 🚶 🚴 ⚓ 🏊 🛥 🛶 ⛵ Thanks to its landscaping, this 237-acre park at the base of the Wasatch Plateau has the feel of a tidy, well-kept city park, not that of a rugged national park. Amid this pleasant setting the park has a wide range of water sports, including trout and bass fishing. Picnic areas, restrooms with shower facilities, a boat ramp and a group-use pavilion can be found on the grounds. Hiking and biking trails also meander throughout the park. Day-use fee, $5. ~ Route 10, one mile northeast of Huntington; 435-687-2491.

▲ There are 22 sites; $12 per night. Reservations: 800-322-3770 (April 15 to October 15).

MILLSITE STATE PARK 🚴 ⚓ 🏊 🛥 🛶 ⛵ The focal point of the park is Millsite Reservoir, a secluded 435-acre lake at the mouth of Ferron Canyon. The canyon climbs in a series of terraces up into the mountains that rise to 11,000 feet on the western skyline above the park. The reservoir, formed in 1971 when the Mill Site Dam was constructed at the canyon mouth, is skirted by rugged canyon walls and a towering butte that soars up above the north shore. It offers excellent year-round fishing for rainbow and cutthroat trout; an attractive sandy beach lures swimmers. Adjacent is a nine-hole golf course; mountain biking and off-road vehicle trails depart nearby. Day-use fee, $5. ~ Ferron Canyon Road, four miles west of Route 10 near Ferron; 435-687-2491.

▲ There are 20 sites; $14 per night. Reservations: 800-322-3770 (April 15 to October 15).

sights

AUTHOR FAVORITE

When I need a quick jolt of southern Utah's canyon country but don't have the time to drive to Zion or Canyonlands national parks, I head to the **San Rafael Swell**. This sprawling public-lands playground features vast gorges, patches of slickrock, box canyons and arches and countless hiking and camping opportunities. Wild horses and bighorn sheep also roam this land located south of Price. A lazy summer day can even be spent tubing down the San Rafael River, which cuts a canyon so deep and beautiful through the heart of the swell that it's known as the Little Grand Canyon. For more information, see page 240.

▼ ▼ ▼ ▼ ▼ ▼ ▼ ▼ ▼ ▼ ▼ ▼
Nephi-Manti Area

Driving south of Provo along Route 15 the landscape begins to open up as the Wasatch Range dwindles in size and the urban setting around Provo gives way to agriculture. The valleys on either side of the southern Wasatch Range, including the Mount Nebo area and the Sanpete Valley, are as traditionally Mormon as anywhere else in the world. Inhabited until about A.D. 1300 by Fremont Indians, who left various reminders of their residence, the region subsequently became home to Utes and (in the western desert) Goshiutes. Although explored by Spanish expeditions and fur trappers, the region was not settled by non-Indians until the Mormon arrival in the 1850s.

Today the countryside is little changed from 100 years ago. Small towns popular with artisans are scattered here and there, a bucolic atmosphere reaches in all directions, and country charm can be found just about everywhere you look. You can roar past this backcountry by staying on Route 15 heading north or south, but if you enjoy poking along through an agrarian landscape and taking the time to investigate Utah's back roads, follow the meanders of Route 89. You won't be disappointed.

SIGHTS

HIDDEN ►

Northwest of Nephi about 40 miles on Route 6 is the old silver-mining town of **Eureka**. Between 1869 and 1976, this community—high in the 8000-foot Tintic Mountains—was the center of the Tintic Mining District, which produced 16.6 million tons and $570 million in base and precious metals. Head frames and mine dumps still rise above Eureka's narrow, twisting streets. There once were hundreds of mines here; most are now ghost towns but their names live on: Eureka Hill, Bullion Beck, Blue Rock and Gemini. Ruins can be toured on a backroads driving tour; a self-guiding brochure can be obtained at the Tintic Mining Museum in Eureka.

The excellent **Tintic Mining Museum** documents and preserves much of the region's history; a highlight is a three-dimensional scale model of the inside of a silver mine. Spread throughout two buildings, the museum chronicles mining life in the region. One building, the old Eureka City Hall that was built in 1899, contains displays of mining tools, historic photos, living quarters of a typical miner's home, and the town's old court room. Next door in the old railroad depot is a nice mineral exhibit, a representation of the early mining days in Eureka, and a saloon mockup. Tours by appointment. ~ 241 West Main Street, Eureka; 435-433-6842.

A sandy reminder of ancient Lake Bonneville, the 124-square-mile **Little Sahara Recreation Area** was created from deposits the Sevier River left behind on its way to emptying into Lake Bonneville. Along with providing off-road-vehicle opportunities, this natural playground contains a 9000-acre preserve for plants and animals that is off-limits to vehicles. ~ Route 132, 31 miles west of Nephi.

Before arriving at Nephi on Route 15 you can't miss **Mount Nebo**, a hulking 11,877-foot-high mountain visible from much of central Utah. The southernmost mountain of the Wasatch, it is surrounded by the Mount Nebo Wilderness. Extending around the east flank of the mountain, through Uinta National Forest between Nephi and Payson, is the 38-mile **Nebo Loop Scenic Byway** (closed in winter).

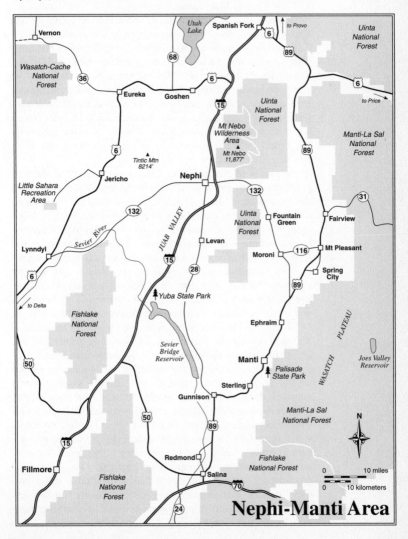

Nephi-Manti Area

The broad streets of the quiet town of **Nephi** (population 4000), nestled at the foot of Mount Nebo, are a prime example of the well-ordered grid street system prescribed for all 19th-century Mormon communities. The town, named for the first of several prophets who wrote the Book of Mormon, was established on Salt Creek in 1851 and became an important livestock shipping center after a railroad line was stretched south from Salt Lake City in the 1870s. One early building that recalls Nephi's heyday is the **Juab County Jail**, built in 1892 and in use until 1974. ~ 4 South Main Street.

From Route 132 about three miles east of Nephi in Salt Creek Canyon, the byway winds through a miniature Bryce Canyon known as the **Devil's Kitchen** due to the spires and other eerie forms whittled out of a dazzling reddish natural amphitheater similar to those found at Bryce Canyon National Park. Also along the byway is **Payson Lakes Recreation Area**, a picturesque high-country setting in the Uinta National Forest perfect for a little fishing or a quiet hike in the woods, ending 12 miles farther north in downtown Payson. Views from the road are breathtaking, especially when accented by fall colors; large herds of elk and deer are often seen.

Southeast of Nephi, Route 132 crosses a saddle in the Sanpitch Mountains and descends into the **Sanpete Valley**. Somewhat sheltered from modern influences because they are bypassed by interstate freeways, the valley's bevy of small towns (none larger than 3000 people) are steeped in Mormon tradition. Its agricultural economy is noted for its sheep ranches, turkey farms and sugar-beet fields. The town of Sanpete is Utah's geographic center.

Fifty Mormon families—220 people—established the first settlement here in November 1849, following an invitation from Ute Chief Walker to build a community among Chief Sanpeetch and his tribe. Numerous other communities were created in the 1850s and the Utah Mormons were soon joined by hundreds of Mormon converts from Denmark, Sweden and Norway. The valley became known throughout Utah as "Little Scandinavia."

At the head of the Sanpete Valley, at the junction of Routes 89 and 31, is Fairview, settled in 1859. Its main point of tourist interest is the **Fairview Museum of History and Art**, lodged in an old schoolhouse. The eclectic collection includes a replica of a Columbian mammoth, discovered in 1988 at Huntington Reservoir in the mountains east of town; other exhibits focus on geology, natural history, Indian and pioneer history, thousands of miniature wood carvings, and early farm equipment (on the outside grounds). A sculpture by Avard Fairbanks, "Love and Devotion," honors Peter and Celestia Peterson, lifelong Fairview residents whose 82 years of marriage is believed to be unsurpassed. ~ 85 North 100 East, Fairview; 435-427-9216.

Mount Pleasant, six miles south of Fairview, has the best-preserved Main Street from late-19th-century Utah, when this was the most prosperous sheep-ranching center in the state. Two blocks of two- and three-story commercial buildings extend off Route 89, east from its junction with Route 116. Oldest is the 1875 **Liberal Hall,** on the south side of Main; it was built as the first home of the Wasatch Academy, established by Presbyterians as an alternative school for disaffected Mormon youth. The academy moved to a new home, two blocks south, in 1888; all 20 of its buildings, including Lincoln Hall (1893), the President's House (1895) and Indiana Hall (1900), are listed on the National Register of Historic Places. Now among Utah's most prestigious private academies, Wasatch attracts students from all over the United States. ~ Second West and First South, Mount Pleasant; 435-462-2411.

The Old Spanish Trail, blazed by Spaniards seeking a route from Sante Fe to Los Angeles, cuts through central Utah. Heading west from Green River the trail passed through the San Rafael Swell on its way to the Wasatch Plateau.

The entire village of **Spring City,** four miles south of Mount Pleasant on Route 117, is a National Historic District. The agrarian hamlet of fewer than 1000 residents, founded in 1852, boasts at least 60 late-19th-century stone, adobe and brick houses. The earliest are of Federalist and Greek Revival styles, typical in Mormon pioneer settlements. Scandinavian immigrants built one-story "pair houses" of two rooms linked by a central entrance. Around the turn of the 20th century, the gingerbread ornamentation of Victorian houses made an appearance; these were succeeded by bungalows between 1910 and 1930. Historical home tours are offered annually on Memorial Day Saturday, or by appointment. ~ 187 North Main Street, Spring City; 435-462-2211.

◄ *HIDDEN*

In the heart of the Sanpete Valley is **Ephraim,** 14 miles south of Mount Pleasant and 29 miles southeast of Nephi on Route 89. Its **Snow College** has been a regional cultural center since 1888. Named not for climate but for two early Mormon church leaders, the college became a state institution in 1932. Its 2000 students come from all over Utah, many to attend the school's acclaimed theater and music departments. ~ 150 East College Avenue, Ephraim; 435-283-7000.

Snow College also operates the **Great Basin Environmental Education Center,** nine miles up Ephraim Canyon at the base of Haystack Mountain. Built by the U.S. Forest Service between 1912 and 1914, this historic station was the first in the United States to study the ecology of range management. The college has preserved its dozen-or-so buildings as a conference center, including the original laboratory, and has established a museum. The center offers a variety of field programs for the public, ranging from Dutch-oven cooking to the geology of central Utah and

Central Utah's Heritage Highway 89

Nearly forgotten when Route 15 was cut through Utah from the Idaho border in the north to Nevada in the south, Route 89 slowly meanders across a page of yesteryear, a two-lane ribbon of asphalt dotted by quaint, largely agricultural communities. While the entire 250-mile route from Fairview in Sanpete County to Kanab in Kane County can be traversed in four or five hours, you could spend a day or two alone following the highway from Fairview to Marysvale, a distance of just 105 miles.

LITTLE DENMARK   Fairview was settled by Scandinavians, whose influence on the area is apparent in the architecture and agrarian lifestyle that remains today. Crops and livestock continue to feed the economy, along with artisans and quaint bed-and-breakfast establishments in homes reflecting the fine craftsmanship of the settlers. Starting in Fairview, the **Fairview Museum of History and Art** (page 246) opens a window on the immigrants through both artifacts and artworks. Southbound Route 89 leads ten miles to Mount Pleasant, where a short spur runs to **Spring City** (page 247), with its architecturally unique buildings and artisans. The farms surrounding **Moroni**, eight miles west of Spring City, produce turkeys that are the focus of countless Thanksgiving dinners around the country, while **Manti** (page 249), 18 miles south of Spring City, is home to one of the LDS Church's most beautiful temples. Your next stop is Salina, about 25 miles south of Fairview.

SEVIER VALLEY   At the heart of the Sevier Valley is **Salina**, one of Utah's most obvious ties to the Old West, as the area is rich in Old West lure

mythology of the night sky. Open in summer only. ~ Forest Route 8; 435-283-7261.

The Greek Revival–style **Ephraim Co-op Building** was constructed of native limestone in 1872. It is a rare surviving example of a 19th-century Mormon cooperative merchandising enterprise. The Ephraim United Order Co-operative Store occupied the main floor; the second floor was used for meetings and cultural events, and Snow College's first classes. The building was restored and reopened in 1990 as a crafts outlet for local artisans. An inscription on the north wall reads "Ephraim U.O. Mercantile Institution," with an adjacent beehive encircled by the words, "Holiness to the Lord." ~ 96 North Main Street, Ephraim; 435-283-6654.

Next door, an old mill has been turned into the **Central Utah Art Center.** ~ 80 North Main Street, Ephraim; 435-283-5110.

and rural life. Modern-day cowboys still head to Salina, where Route 89 meets Route 70, to order a saddle or a pair of boots from **Burns Saddlery** (page 261), which has been filling orders for a century. Though not actually on Route 89, five-mile-long **Fish Lake** is about 40 miles below Sigurd via Routes 24 and 25. Here the fish bite reliably and **Fish Lake Lodge** (page 259) contains countless stories about the ones that got away. Opened in 1932, the lodge continues to serve anglers anxious to hook into one of the lake's mackinaw trout. From Sevier, **Fremont Indian State Park** (page 258) with its ruins and displays is about six miles west along Route 70.

THE HEADWATERS Almost 38 miles south of Salina on Route 89 lies the **Big Rock Candy Mountain Resort** (page 260), which gained fame through its namesake song popularized in the 1940s, '50s and '60s by the late Burl Ives. Today between mid-April and mid-November the resort offers cabins and lodge rooms not far from the Sevier River, where you can enjoy raft trips. This portion of the Heritage Highway actually runs far south of Marysvale to Orderville, but the Marysvale area five miles south of Big Rock Candy Mountain offers several worthwhile stops. **Moore's Old Pine Inn** (page 260) is the historic hotel where writer Zane Grey worked on one of his books and where Butch Cassidy allegedly rested up between robberies. Several ghost towns in the **Tushar Mountains** just west of town stand testament to the mining craze that swept the region in the late 1800s. If rag rugs interest you, stop in at **Lizzie and Charlie's Rag Rug Factory** (page 261), where they will demonstrate their craft on antique looms.

The **Canute Peterson House** was the home of a Norwegian immigrant who became the stake president for all Mormon churches in the Sanpete Valley in the 1860s. The 1869 rock home was built with two "polygamy pits"—hiding places beneath the dining-room floor and beside the kitchen—to conceal two of Peterson's three wives from federal marshals. ~ 10 North Main Street, Ephraim.

Just seven miles south of Ephraim on Route 89 lies **Manti**. The first Mormon settlement in the Sanpete Valley, today Manti is famous for its handsome temple. Overlooking the north side of town from a hilltop, the **Manti Temple** was dedicated by Brigham Young himself in 1877 and completed in 1888. Built of native limestone quarried at the site, it was given two towers by architect William Folsom. Although the building appears to face west toward the town, its east-facing tower is slightly higher—oriented (as per Mormon tradition) to greet the resurrected Christ coming from that direction. Its unique design blends Gothic, French Renaissance and French Second Empire styles, giving it an almost castle-like appearance. Only Mormon Church members are permitted to enter the temple, but slide shows of the interior and free guided tours of the grounds are offered at an adjacent visitors center. ~ Temple Hill, off Route 89 North; 435-835-2291.

Every late June, the temple draws a cast of thousands and an audience of tens of thousands for the **Mormon Miracle Pageant**. This colorful program tells the history of the Mormon faith, from its pre-Columbian origins to the 19th-century trek to Utah. ~ 435-835-3000.

Also in Manti are two small museums; both open limited hours and by appointment. The **Manti Art Museum** presents regional paintings, many oils and some watercolors. It contains everything from "primitive" works to professional pieces by local artists—many of which outline a history of the valley. Closed Saturday and Sunday. ~ 50 South Main Street, Manti; 435-835-2962.

The **History House on Heritage Corner** displays a wide variety of exhibits, from pioneer artifacts to a hat collection owned by a local woman who was behind the early directing of the Mormon Miracle Pageant. Open 4 p.m. to 8 p.m. on Friday, Saturday and Monday. ~ 401 North Main Street, Manti; 435-835-5841.

LODGING

Lodging in the area is largely restricted to small mom-and-pop motels, although there are also some nice bed-and-breakfast operations where you'll find a comfortable room and a good meal.

The one-story **Safari Motel** wraps around a cool central swimming pool with a shaded lawn. Some of the 28 rooms have refrigerators. ~ 413 South Main Street, Nephi; 435-623-1071, fax 435-623-2436. BUDGET.

Out in the Sanpete Valley, the little **Iron Horse Motel** has ten friendly rooms near Snow College. The non-smoking accommodations welcome pets and have TVs and phones. ~ 670 North Main Street, Ephraim; 435-283-4223. BUDGET.

HIDDEN ►

Just west of Main Street lies **Yardley Inn**, a Victorian reminder of an earlier, more relaxed day. Kept in the manner of an old English Country inn, the Yardley's four bedrooms sport either four-poster or brass beds. The Moonlight and Roses Room features a jacuzzi next to a marble fireplace. Full gourmet breakfasts are served either in the home's dining room or in the garden room, while romantics can book a horse-drawn carriage ride through the neighborhood. ~ 190 South 200 West, Manti; 435-835-1861, 800-858-6634, fax 435-835-1863; www.ut-biz.com/yardleyinn. MODERATE TO DELUXE.

When Manti Temple construction workers needed a comfortable place to stay in 1880, the **Manti House Inn** was born. Constructed of native stone, it was fully restored in 1985 and is today an elegant B&B. Fully furnished with period antiques, the house has six individually decorated rooms with private baths and quilted beds. Meals are served in the lovely dining room, adjoining a parlor that features a piano still boasting century-old sheet music. A hot tub is available to all. An ice-cream parlor is open summer afternoons. ~ 401 North Main Street, Manti; 435-835-0161, 800-835-7512, fax 435-835-0161; www.mantihouse.com. MODERATE.

The **Legacy Inn** has only four rooms, but they're among the most charming you'll find in the area. The Victorian master suite has a queen-sized four-poster high plantation bed set in front of a fireplace. The Tower Room boasts a beautiful mahogany queen-sized bed in an octagonal-shaped room that features four stained-glass windows that offer sweeping views of Manti. For families, there's a suite that links a private room with a queen-sized mission-style bed to a large family room with two twin beds and a futon. This room also has a fireplace. ~ 337 North 100 East, Manti; 435-835-8352; www.sanpete.com/legacyinn. MODERATE.

In the same town is the **Manti Motel & Outpost,** which has 12 pet-friendly, non-smoking rooms and a half-dozen RV slots. Some have kitchens; all have refrigerators, microwaves, TVs, VCRs and phones. ~ 445 North Main Street, Manti; 435-835-8533. BUDGET.

Nearby, **Manti Country Village** has 23 large rooms with all amenities; the two-story motor inn also has a coffee shop, a whirlpool and an exercise bike. ~ 145 North Main Street, Manti; 435-835-9300, 800-452-0787, fax 435-835-6286. MODERATE.

The hills above Spring City are where you'll find the **Wind Walker Guest Ranch,** with 21 comfortable rooms, a stable of

AUTHOR FAVORITE

Step into yesteryear at the **Ephraim Homestead Bed & Breakfast**, where owners McKay and Sherron Andreasen have preserved a slice of the mid-1800s. Their authentic 1860s log cabin is furnished in Mormon pioneer style; guests can view slides and old photo albums, or browse through heritage magazines. The bedroom is on the second floor; downstairs is a living room with a fireplace, a cast-iron stove, and a bathroom with clawfoot tub. There are also two rooms in a traditional barn. In adhering to Mormon tenets, guests are asked not to drink or smoke on the premises. ~ 135 West 100 North, Ephraim; 435-283-6367; www.sanpete.com/homestead. MODERATE.

horses, and 900,000 acres that allow you to get closer to the Western landscape and the wide open skies. The rooms all have private bath (some with jacuzzi tubs) but no phones or TVs. Meals are included and are served in the main building, which has a soothing fireplace. You can learn how to ride, fish in one of the ranch's lakes, or go for a hike; there's also a pool and hot tub on the ranch. Youngsters can be kept busy with craft programs, archery, table tennis, volleyball and kites. Rates are based on multiday stays. While June–September offer three-night minimum packages, the rest of the year has a two-night minimum stay. ~ 11550 Pigeon Hollow Road, Spring City; 435-462-0282, 888-606-9463; www.windwalker.org. ULTRA-DELUXE.

If you're looking for something a bit more realistic when it comes to ranches, call the folks at the **Hansen Family Ranch**. They'll be happy to put you to work with the cowboys driving sheep on their spread. At night you can bed down in a 1930s-era sheep wagon or in a bit more modern 27-foot-long trailer. Meals are cooked in Dutch ovens. ~ 685 West 200 North, Fountain Green; 866-211-4691; www.hansenfamilyranch.com. MODERATE.

DINING

A traveling salesman was the founding force behind **J. C. Mickelson's Restaurant**, whose longevity is challenged by few other eateries south of Utah Lake. The decor is contemporary Americana roadside—a counter ringed by stools dominates the center of the restaurant while booths line the walls. Now in a second generation of Mickelsons, the establishment that pulls tourists offer the nearby interstate still focuses on good basic American "road food"—country-fried steak, burgers, seafood—three meals a day. Homemade pies are baked daily and revolve around apples, blueberries, pecans and cherries. ~ 2100 South Main Street, Nephi; 435-623-0152. BUDGET.

The **Horseshow Mountain Restaurant** has something of a Southern-plantation feel, with its wraparound covered deck for summer dining, fireplaces, ample use of polished oak inside, and manicured lawns. Away from the maddening pace of Route 15 in scenic Mount Pleasant, the restaurant dishes up poultry, seafood, pasta and beef. Closed Sunday. ~ 850 South Route 89, Mount Pleasant; 435-462-9533. MODERATE TO DELUXE.

Elsewhere in the Sanpete Valley, budget restaurants abound. Worth stopping at is the **Backroads Restaurant**, locally renowned for its charbroiler, serving three meals daily. ~ 70 North State Street, Mount Pleasant; 435-462-3111. BUDGET.

Away from hectic Route 15, locals enjoy the relaxed setting of the **Satisfied Ewe Cafe** in the heart of Ephraim. Nothing fancy here—plastic tablecloths topped by candle centerpieces hide the folding table in the main dining room, which also sports a small, seven-stool counter, while bench-table combinations attached to the walls can be found in the back room. Serving three meals daily, the café lures locals at breakfast with the "Grand Ram"— three dollar-sized pancakes accompanied by an egg of your choice, bacon and sausage—while dinners are pretty much what you'd expect in the country—hamburger steak with onions. ~ 350 North Main Street, Ephraim; 435-283-6364. BUDGET.

SHOPPING

David and Jenni Smith at **The Claysmiths** make stoneware pottery such as bowls, plates and cups, as well as ironwork items such as wine holders and fireplace tools. They also produce candles and soaps. ~ 16 East 100 South, Fairview; 435-427-9307; www.theclaysmiths.com.

Hand-crafted Mormon pine furniture (cupboards, chests, beds) can be found in Mount Pleasant at **Peel Furniture Works**. Although they call the pieces "reproductions," they're handmade by local craftsmen the same way Mormon pioneers made them 150 years ago. ~ 565 West Main Street, Mount Pleasant; 435-462-2887.

All the furniture at Peel Furniture Works is made from trees (Douglas fir, spruce and ponderosa pine) taken from the surrounding mountains.

Antique hunters in Mount Pleasant usually head for **Heart of Utah Antiques**. ~ 146 West Main Street, Mount Pleasant; 435-462-2644.

Utah is filled with the unexpected. How else would you explain the violins made by **Paul Hart**, who practices his craft in a late-19th-century pharmacy that's been restored for his trade? Hart stays busy and devoted to his work, cranking out about a dozen violins a year. ~ 36 West Main, Mount Pleasant; 435-462-0301.

Joseph Bennion, one of Utah's best potters, lives in Spring City, and you can buy his works at his shop, **Horseshoe Mountain Pottery**. ~ 278 South Main Street, Spring City; 435-462-2708.

Hand-sewn quilts and other cottage crafts are sold at the historic **Ephraim Co-operative Mercantile Association**. Next door in its old mill, the **Central Utah Art Gallery** proffers works by local artists. ~ 80 North Main Street, Ephraim; 435-283-5110.

For more than 20 years **S.R. Johnson** has been making award-winning knives for hunters and collectors. If you're interested in seeing how he fashions his knives, or want to place a custom order, give him a call. ~ 202 East 200 North, Manti; 435-835-7941.

PARKS

LITTLE SAHARA RECREATION AREA 🚶 🚵 Nearly 125 square miles of shifting dunes make this BLM-administered area the most popular recreation area for off-road vehicles in the state of Utah. The steep sandy slopes challenge drivers of four-wheelers, dune buggies, motorbikes and other vehicles. Non-camping RVers enjoy hiking or playing in the sand; special areas are set aside for picnicking and nature study. Day-use fee, $8. ~ Off Route 6, four miles west of Jericho Junction; 31 miles west of Nephi via

Route 132 and paved County Road to Jericho Junction; 435-433-5960.

▲ There are four campgrounds with 583 sites; no fee.

PAYSON LAKES RECREATION AREA. 🏃 ⛵ 🎣 🚣 Located 12 miles south of Payson along the 38-mile Nebo Loop Scenic Byway, this parcel in the Uinta National Forest is nestled in the high country and surrounded by aspens, conifers and cottonwoods. Hiking trails wind through the forest and lead into the nearby Mount Nebo Wilderness Area, while the lakes comfort the souls of anglers, canoeists and swimmers. Facilities include water and toilet facilities. The scenic byway is closed in winter. Day-use fee, $6. ~ The recreation area is found 12 miles south of Payson on the Nebo Loop Scenic Byway accessed from Route 15 at Santaquin.

▲ There is one campground with 88 sites for both tents and trailers; $11 to $22 per night. Reservations: 877-444-6777 (reservations recommended).

YUBA STATE PARK ⛵ 🛶 🚴 🎣 🏊 🚤 🚣 Outdoorspeople love this park on Sevier Bridge Reservoir, which offers year-round fishing for walleye and yellow perch. The reservoir is something of an oasis in this high-desert landscape. There are three units—the main developed area at Oasis; a primitive camping area beside a boat ramp on the east side of the lake; and the East Beach, which is restricted to boat-in camping. Petroglyphs and pictographs can be found on the rocks just north of the park's Painted Rocks area located on the southeastern side of the reservoir. Day-use fee, $7. ~ The Oasis area is two miles south of Route 15, 30 miles south of Nephi, the Painted Rocks area is 15 miles south of Levan on Route 28; 435-758-2611.

▲ There are two campgrounds with 46 sites (7 for tents only); $8 to $14 per night. Reservations: 800-322-3770 (April through October).

PALISADE STATE PARK 🏃 🚴 ⛵ 🎣 🚣 🚤 Nestled on the western slope of the Manti Range in lower Manti Canyon just past a residential subdivision south of Manti, on a small reservoir

---

FOWL PLAY

The polygamous practices of the Sanpete Valley's Mormons were aggressively prosecuted by the federal government in the 1870s and '80s and many church members went into hiding. Local legend claims that when federal officers ordered a small boy to take them to a polygamist, he cautiously led them to a chicken run and pointed out a rooster.

amid sagebrush-covered hills, is this nicely landscaped 70-acre park popular with families. Canoe and paddleboat rentals are available beside a sandy swimming beach; motorized vessels are not permitted on the lake. The park is located just east of Sterling, a picturesque farming community. Hiking and biking trails extend from the park up Sixmile Canyon. Day-use fee, $5. ~ Palisade Road, Sterling, two miles east of Route 89; 435-835-7275.

▲ There are 53 sites; $14 per night. Reservations: 800-322-3770 (April 1 to September 15).

Richfield Area

Two interstate highways—southbound Route 15 from Salt Lake City and westbound Route 70 from Denver—join in central Utah. Before coming together, however, they run parallel for about 40 miles, divided by the 9000-foot-high Pahvant Mountains. West of the Pahvant peaks, the highway borders the Great Basin, its few small historic towns finding footholds in a semi-arid climate. East of the mountains, the Sevier River has provided a lush and modestly populated valley for farming.

The virtues of this region were not lost on Fremont Indians, who inhabited the flanks of the Pahvant Range for about 800 years. Their mark—particularly myriad rock paintings and etchings—can be seen in a great number of ruins. The Mormon pioneer heritage is also strong, especially on the west slope.

SIGHTS

Situated between Nephi and Richfield, the town of Delta is located on the eastern edge of Utah's West Desert. An arid, largely barren expanse of land, the West Desert is renowned with rockhounds for the gems it yields.

◀ HIDDEN

One of the best spots for rockhounding is located 40 miles northwest of Delta in the form of 7113-foot-tall **Topaz Mountain**. Located on the southern end of the Thomas Mountain Range, this rhyolite mountain is a veritable treasure chest of semiprecious stones such as topaz, garnet and red beryl. Topaz, Utah's state gemstone, comes in shades of amber, although most are clear as a result of sunlight exposure; amber topaz formed six to seven million years ago by liquids deposited within cavities of rhyolite, a volcanic rock, can be found by hardy searchers who spend hours breaking open rock with hammers and pry bars. The mountain is within U.S. Bureau of Land Management lands and is open to amateur collectors. Red beryl, a rare gemstone, and garnet can also be dug up in the mountain, but not as frequently as topaz. One of the mountain's most popular and productive areas is known as Topaz Cove, or Topaz Valley, which is located on the south end of the mountain and is easily accessed by a dirt road. ~ Take Route 174 west 40 miles to the BLM-administered rock-hounding area.

Closer to Delta lies a stark reminder of Americans' paranoia during World War II, when more than 8000 Japanese Americans from the San Francisco Bay Area were interned at the **Topaz Relocation Center** from 1942 to 1945. Located 17 miles northwest of Delta, Topaz was one of ten such camps in the western United States. Although more than 30 square miles were set aside, a 42-block core held most of the camp's 623 buildings. During the height of the war the relocation center was one of the largest cities, population-wise, in Utah. It featured homes, schools, gardens and even a hospital in addition to a barb-wired perimeter and guard towers. After the war most of the buildings were dismantled or moved to other locations. Today only a few foundations and traces of streets remain. A monument erected in 1976 by the Japanese-American Citizen League marks the site. ~ West 4500 North Street; from Delta, take Route 6 west eight miles to 7000 West Street, north six miles to West 4500 North, then west about four miles to Topaz; no phone.

The town of **Delta**, on Routes 6 and 50, is off the beaten path for anyone not en route to or from Nevada's Great Basin National Park. Nevertheless, this agricultural town of 3000—founded in 1907 after dams on the Sevier River provided water for irrigation—has an interesting history best recounted at the **Great Basin Museum**. Antique farming equipment, pioneer and interment-camp artifacts, an old telephone switchboard, photos and documents recall bygone eras. Closed Sunday. ~ 328 West 100 North, Delta; 435-864-5013.

Eleven miles southwest of Delta is **Fort Deseret**; like Cove Fort, it was constructed in the mid-1860s as protection against Indians. Unlike sturdy Cove Fort, Fort Deseret was hastily built, its ten-foot-high adobe walls completed in fewer than ten days by 98 men divided into two teams in a speed competition. Ironically, the 550-foot-square fort never had to withstand an Indian attack, and eventually came to be used by the Indians themselves. Its walls have long since been disintegrating, but the ruins are sheltered within **Fort Deseret State Park**, which, due to its primitive, un-maintained status, is not publicized by the state. ~ Route 257, two miles south of the town of Deseret.

HIDDEN ►

Millard Fillmore, 13th president of the United States, isn't a national leader who garnered a lot of acclaim . . . or, for that matter, name recognition. Yet Fillmore, whose brief term of office (1850–52) coincided with early Mormon settlement, may be the the most honored president in Utah place names. The little town of **Fillmore** (population 2000) just off Route 15 was designated capital of the Utah Territory as it was being built in 1851 because of its central geographical location. The government operated from here until 1858, when it was moved 150 miles back north to the population center in Salt Lake City. Fillmore is now a farming center and the seat of Millard County, Utah's third largest.

Fillmore's old capitol is preserved as **Territorial Statehouse State Park**. Elaborately designed by Truman O. Angell, architect of the Salt Lake City Temple, it was intended to have four wings and an imposing dome. Only the south wing was completed, however; it housed the legislature from 1856 to 1858. The capitol was subsequently used as a social center, an office building, a

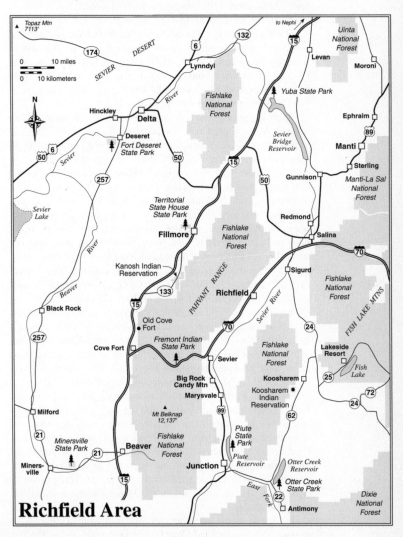

Richfield Area

school, a jail and a theater. It was restored by the Daughters of Utah Pioneers in the 1920s, and is now open as a museum. Visitors can tour the assembly room, jail and schoolhouse, and see Indian and pioneer artifacts and historic documents. Admission. ~ 50 West Capitol Avenue, Fillmore; 435-743-5316.

Salina is the first town of the region encountered by many travelers. It's at a crucial highway junction—a strip of motels, gas stations and fast-food restaurants where southbound Route 89 from the Sanpete Valley meets westbound Route 70.

Richfield, 16 miles south of Salina on Route 118 via Route 70, is a bustling little town of 5600 that appears relatively affluent compared to many others of the region. Sitting on the eastern flank of the Pahvants in the valley of the Sevier, it is a gateway to many of the finest Fremont Indian sites in Utah. Find out how to find them from the **Richfield Chamber of Commerce**. ~ 250 North Main Street; 435-896-4241.

More developed than Fort Deseret State Park is **Fremont Indian State Park**, on Clear Creek southwest of Richfield. In 1983, the largest-known Fremont village was discovered by interstate highway construction crews. Dubbed Five Finger Ridge Village, it contained more than 100 separate buildings that may have housed 300 people. Construction work was postponed while several tons of artifacts, including pottery, arrowheads and grinding stones, were removed; they are now displayed or stored at the park's museum, established near the site. Exhibits trace the history of the Fremont culture, from its rise around A.D. 500 to its disappearance around A.D. 1300. Park trails lead to 769 panels of painted pictographs and etched petroglyphs, as well as smaller archaeological sites. Admission. ~ 11550 West Clear Creek Canyon Road, 21 miles southwest of Richfield off Route 70 Exit 17; 435-527-4631.

Southeast of Richfield in the Fishlake National Forest, you can get a glimpse of how forest rangers lived nearly a century ago by visiting the early-20th-century **Koosharem Guard Station**, which has been restored to its original condition. ~ Located eight miles west of Koosharem and Route 62, the station is along Forest Road 068, which is reached via Forest Road 076.

Six miles south of the multicolored rock formations of **Big Rock Candy Mountain** (named for the rocky slope's yellowish coloration that stems from the area's iron oxide deposits), the canyons running east from 12,139-foot Mount Belknap including Deer Creek and Beaver Creek contain numerous American Indian **petroglyphs** predating the birth of Christ. Trails are unmarked, but are easily located off the Paiute ATV Trail and other backcountry roads. ~ Via Route 89, 24 miles south of Richfield, near Marysvale.

It's not so much coincidence as the well-studied choice of a strategic location that led **Cove Fort** to be constructed in 1867 at virtually the same point where Routes 15 and 70 join today. Erected between Richfield (39 miles northeast), Fillmore (33 miles north) and Beaver (27 miles south) to protect travelers from Indian attacks, this dark basalt fort—100 square feet with walls 18 feet high—is the only bastion preserved from that era. Mormon Church docents lead tours of 12 rooms adorned with 19th-century furnishings, including "rolling pin" beds and double-oven stoves. The fort served as a stage station and telegraph office; though built for defense, no hostile shots were ever fired here. Also on the grounds is a small pioneer settlement with a livestock barn, a blacksmith shop and an icehouse. ~ Route 161, one mile north of Exit 1 off Route 70 or two miles south of Exit 135 off Route 15; 435-438-5547; www.covefort.org.

South of Cove Fort along Route 15, **Beaver**—like other Mormon communities in central and southern Utah—began as an agricultural colony. But non-Mormon miners descended upon the community in the late 19th century when gold and silver were discovered in the mountains to its west. The Mormons didn't much care for the coarseness of the newcomers, and the U.S. Army was induced to build Fort Cameron to allay tensions between the two groups.

Elsewhere in Beaver, more than 200 historic structures have architectural appeal. Among them is the **Old Beaver County Courthouse**, an ornate building that is now a historical museum. Visitors can view pioneer and mining exhibits, as well as the original courtroom and a dungeon-like basement jail. ~ 90 East Center Street, Beaver.

Standing on the shores of Fish Lake since 1931, **Fish Lake Lodge** oversees almost 50 cabins of varying accommodations. While "rustic" cabins might be 70 years old and offer only a bed, or a bed, bath and kitchen, "deluxe" cabins are much newer and sport wood-burning stoves and color televisions along with full kitchens. Inside the lodge, built with thick spruce logs taken from nearby Pelican Canyon, is a restaurant serving three modest meals

LODGING

TREASURE HUNT

Utah is renowned by rockhounds for the treasures its landscape holds. Some of the best rockhounding territory lies in the West Desert. While topaz gems are readily found near Topaz Mountain, the ground around Antelope Springs yields trilobites while geodes can be dug up not far from Dugway. For information on rockhounding, and these sites, contact the BLM's Fillmore office. ~ P.O. Box 778, Fillmore, UT 84631; 435-743-3100.

a day, a gift shop and a small grocery. Out on the shore you'll find a marina where you can rent a 15-foot skiff to go in search of one of the lake's legendary Mackinaw trout. ~ HC 80, Route 25, Richfield; 435-638-1000; www.fishlake.com. BUDGET TO ULTRA-DELUXE.

Several good franchise motels are on the main strip through Richfield, the best of which may be the two-story **Best Western Apple Tree Inn**. Its 62 rooms include five family-size suites; all have ceiling fans and cable TV. There's a swimming pool and hot tub; pets are accepted with a small deposit. ~ 145 South Main Street, Richfield; 435-896-5481, 800-231-0749, fax 435-896-9465. BUDGET TO MODERATE.

The resort that gained fame via a song sung by the late Burl Ives still operates today. However, **Big Rock Candy Mountain Resort** has been upgraded since the 1940s when it first landed on the map. Six of the original cabins remain, along with one more-recent hand-peeled log cabin. There are also nine lodge rooms in a number of "flavors": the Butterscotch Room, Carmel Room, Chocolate Fudge Room, etc. Closed mid-November to mid-April. ~ Route 89, five miles north of Marysvale; 888-560-7625; www.marysvale.org/brcm. BUDGET TO MODERATE.

> Outlaw Butch Cassidy used to lay low between robberies at the old Pine Hotel (now Moore's Old Pine Inn), and Zane Grey wrote part of his classic *Riders of the Purple Sage* while staying there.

"Butch Cassidy and Zane Grey slept here!" claim the owners of **Moore's Old Pine Inn**, a charming historic hotel on Route 89 south of Richfield. Built in 1882, the inn offers four regular rooms that share two bathrooms, three suites with private baths, and two cabins. All are decorated with antiques or Western furnishings, original art and hand-loomed rugs; some have fireplaces and jacuzzi tubs. Guests may relax in the television room, peruse a historic photo gallery, and wander four acres of grounds abutting Bullion Creek and the Paiute ATV Trail. Full breakfast is served; smoking is not allowed. ~ 60 South State Street, Marysvale; 435-326-4565, 800-887-4565; www.marysvale.org/pine/oldpine.html. MODERATE TO DELUXE.

Built around a pond at the south end of the town of Beaver, the charming, 20-room **Sleepy Lagoon Motel** is a tranquil, old-fashioned refuge that predates the modern interstate highways. Rooms are simple, but all have phones and TVs; the swimming pool is refreshing on hot summer days. ~ 882 South Main Street, Beaver; 435-438-5681. BUDGET TO MODERATE.

DINING

Colorful streetside flower boxes are your first hint of the warm, cozy atmosphere inside the **Little Wonder Café**. Three times a day American home cooking is served here, including soups, salads and great burgers. Dinners revolve around chicken, steak, seafood and pasta. ~ 101 North Main Street, Richfield; 435-896-8960. BUDGET TO MODERATE.

Mexican dishes—enchiladas, burritos, tacos and the like—along with sandwiches and salads are dished out at **Pepperbelly's** amid a "roadside deco" decor of old highway signs, service station signs, license plates and even some of those old glass gasoline pumps. Closed Sunday. ~ 680 South Main Street, Richfield; 435-896-2097. BUDGET.

Talk about tradition: **Arshel's Cafe** has been holding forth on Utah's main north–south corridor since the 1930s when it started out as little more than a hot dog stand. Now three simple home-cooked meals are prepared and served in this roadside home daily. The setting is somewhat like that of a country kitchen—four stools line the counter while a small number of tables and booths handle the rest of the space demanded by repeat customers and referrals. Start with the soup of the day, dive into a chicken-fried steak with real potatoes and gravy, and save room for the peach cobbler. ~ 711 North Main Street, Beaver; 435-438-2977. BUDGET.

SHOPPING What's special about this part of Utah? Rocks. Fossil hunters and rockhounds can go crazy on this eastern edge of the Great Basin. The **West Desert Collectors** displays and sells a wonderful selection of minerals found locally, including agate, quartz, garnet, topaz, obsidian, red beryl, pyrite, petrified wood and trilobite fossils. The folks here can direct you to great rockhounding sites, including Topaz Mountain (41 miles northwest via Route 174) for topaz and Antelope Springs (21 miles west via Notch Peak Loop off Route 6/50) for trilobites. ~ 278 West Main Street, Delta; 435-864-2175; www.westdesertcollectors.com.

◀ HIDDEN **Burns Saddlery** has been hammering out saddles, boots and other leather goods since 1898. It also carries Western wear and has a nice exhibit of antique guns, saddles and spurs. ~ 79 West Main Street, Salina; 435-529-7484, 800-453-1281; www.burns saddlery.com.

Dried flowers are fused into candles, pictures, greeting cards and glassware at **Pressed Petals**, where they dry the flowers they use on the site. ~ 47 South Main Street, Richfield; 435-896-9531.

Rag rugs, made in the traditional fashion passed down from artisans in Denmark, are hand-woven on antique looms at **Lizzie and Charlie's Rag Rug Factory** in Marysvale. The shop doubles as a working museum; weaving demonstrations are offered to visitors. ~ 210 East Bullion Avenue, Marysvale; 435-326-4213.

FISHLAKE NATIONAL FOREST 🏃 🚲 🐎 ⛷ 🏕 🏊 🎣 **PARKS** 🚤 🛶 ⛵ Encompassing the Pahvant Range west of Richfield,

Text continued on page 264.

Great Basin
National Park

Just west of the Utah border in Nevada, **Great Basin National Park** embraces rugged high-alpine terrain very different from Utah's red-rock canyonlands. Encompassing 120 square miles of high-desert country, it includes the spectacular Lehman Caves, the stunning Lexington Arch, and towering 13,063-foot Wheeler Peak. A visitors center is located on the road toward the caves near the turnoff for Wheeler Peak Scenic Drive. Admission. ~ Route 488, Baker; south of Route 6, 106 miles west of Delta; 702-234-7331; www.nps.gov/grba.

Like many other great cave systems, the **Lehman Caves** formed in a limestone reef, made thousands of feet thick by the accumulated skeletal remains of marine creatures deposited by a shallow inland sea that covered the Great Basin 550 million years ago. Over the last 20 million years, calcite-laden water percolating through the Snake Mountains eroded the limestone; on the roofs and floors of the caves, the calcite deposits began to form stalactites and stalagmites, flowstone, cave popcorn, helictites, argonite crystals, shields and draperies.

Discovered by Absalom Lehman in 1885, the caves maintain a constant, year-round temperature of 50 degrees Fahrenheit. From the park's visitors center, rangers lead regular 90-minute tours that wind six-tenths of a mile through the main cave, taking in such features as the Grand Palace, Gothic Palace and Cypress Swamp. Other tours include a candlelight trip and a two-and-a-half-hour "spelunking" tour of rarely seen side caverns; the latter may require crawling through tight passages and use of special caving equipment.

Below Lehman Caves, the **Wheeler Peak Scenic Drive** ascends 12 miles to a parking area at 10,161 feet elevation on the northern flank of Wheeler Peak. Here departs a strenuous, five-mile (one-way) summit trail, the last three miles of it above timberline. The summit of Wheeler Peak, named for a 19th-century surveyor, provides a stunning, 360-degree panoramic view of waves of desert mountain ranges extending through two states to the east and west.

Lexington Arch is worth the 30-mile detour required to get there from Lehman Caves. A natural limestone arch—quite unlike the red sandstone arches of Utah—Lexington Arch stands 75 feet high and spans 120 feet. Geologists dispute whether the arch is actually a natural bridge or the eroded remnant of an ancient cave passage. ~ From Baker, at the junction of Route 488, take Route 487 southeast 8 miles to Garrison, Utah; then Route 21 southwest 4.5 miles; then well-marked Arch Canyon Road 12 miles to a parking area. A one-mile hike brings you to the arch.

There are four campgrounds within Great Basin National Park. Baker Creek, south of the visitors center, has 32 units. Along the Wheeler Peak Scenic Drive, Lower Lehman Creek has 11 spaces, Upper Lehman Creek has 24 spaces, and the Wheeler Creek Campground (at 9950 feet) has 37 spaces.

Of the four campgrounds, only one—Lower Lehman—is open year-round. The rest are usually open from late spring through September or October. No reservations are taken for the sites, which will cost you $7 a night. Facilities in the campgrounds are fairly primitive, with pit toilets and water available only in the summer.

While Lehman Caves is one of the most popular attractions of the park, if you stay above ground for a while you'll walk past some of the oldest living things on Earth—the **Great Basin Bristlecone Pine trees**. These gnarled and twisted trees routinely live past 1000 years, and one cut down from Wheeler Peak in 1964 was estimated as being older than 4900 years. While you can find some bristlecones on the lower reaches of Wheeler Peak, most grow between 9000 and 11,500 feet in harsh conditions where they face little, if any, competition from other trees. A relative of the Great Basin Bristlecone Pine, the Rocky Mountain Bristlecone Pine can be found growing on the northern lip of Cedar Breaks National Monument in Utah.

the Canyon Mountains northeast of Delta, the Tushar Mountains east of Beaver and the Sevier Plateau east of Richfield to Capitol Reef National Park, this 2241-square-mile national forest that was once a mining hotbed now offers a wide range of recreational opportunities. Highlights include the **Beaver Canyon Scenic Byway** (Route 153), which extends through avenues of aspen, spruce and fir to the Elk Meadows ski area; the **Paiute ATV Trail**, a 250-mile backcountry boulevard for all-terrain vehicles; and glacially gouged, five-mile-long **Fish Lake**, famous for its mackinaw and rainbow trout fishing. ~ Route 70 cuts east–west through the forest's two arms, providing access at Sevier, Elsinore and Richfield, while Route 89, which runs north–south between the arms, offers many access points between Salina and Junction. Main office, 115 East 900 North, Richfield; 435-896-9233.

▲ There are 20 campgrounds with 381 sites, 70 for tents only, 43 with hookups at Fish Lake; $11 to $13 per night. Reservations: 877-444-6777.

FREMONT INDIAN STATE PARK 🏃 🚵 🏇 🛶 ⚓ Established to preserve Clear Creek Canyon's treasure trove of ancient petroglyphs, pictographs and archaeological sites, this 1120-acre park helps visitors trace Fremont culture between A.D. 500 and A.D. 1300. A video presentation in the visitors center introduces this prehistoric Indian group to novices, and artifacts found in nearby sites are exhibited. A dozen interpretive trails lead to 769 rock-art panels. Day-use fee, $5. ~ 11550 West Clear Creek Canyon Road, Sevier, 21 miles southwest of Richfield off Route 70; 435-527-4631.

▲ There are 31 sites, 16 for tents only; $11 per night. Reservations: 800-322-3770 (April through October).

PIUTE STATE PARK 🚲 ⚓ ⚓ ⚓ ⚓ ⚓ One of Utah's few "primitive" parks that has not been overly developed with modern restrooms or picnic grounds, Piute State Park is in an envi-

LIFE AND CRIMES IN BEAVER

Beaver's main claim to fame is as the birthplace in 1866 of Robert Leroy Parker, a good Mormon boy better known to Old West history as Butch Cassidy. With his gang of outlaws dubbed The Wild Bunch, Cassidy robbed banks and trains and generally wreaked havoc throughout the Rocky Mountain West in the 1890s. The maze-like badlands of Utah's canyonlands made ideal hiding places from the long arm of the law. Actor Paul Newman played Cassidy in the 1969 movie *Butch Cassidy and the Sundance Kid,* a fairly accurate version of his life of crime (albeit with poetic license).

able setting—backed against the cliffs of the Sevier Plateau to the east and facing the heavily forested Tushar Mountains that rise more than 12000 feet to the west. Boating and year-round trophy trout fishing are reasons why Utahns trek to this location, where the Sevier River has been dammed to create 3360-acre Piute Reservoir. There's also rockhounding in the area. Facilities are primitive. Day-use fee, $5. ~ Just east of Route 89, 5 miles north of Junction and 12 miles south of Marysvale; 435-624-3268.

▲ There are primitive tent sites; $8 per night.

OTTER CREEK STATE PARK 🚲 🎠 ⚓ ⚓ ⚓ ⚓ ⚓ Built by farmers in the 1890s on a Sevier River tributary at 6400 feet, the long and narrow Otter Creek Reservoir—seven miles long and three-quarters-mile wide—now has this increasingly popular state park at its southern end. Located within the Pacific Migratory Bird Flyway, the reservoir lures waterfowl, raptors and a variety of songbirds during the spring and fall migrations. There's a good beach here, and anglers catch large rainbow and cutthroat trout year-round. Day-use fee, $5. ~ Route 22, 4 miles northwest of Antimony and 12 miles east of Junction; 435-624-3268.

▲ There are 30 beachfront sites (6 for tents only); $11 to $14 per night. Reservations: 800-322-3770 (April 15 to October 15).

MINERSVILLE STATE PARK ⚓ ⚓ ⚓ ⚓ ⚓ This 207-acre park is situated on a finger of the Escalante Desert between the Mineral and Tushar mountains. It takes its name from the mining of ore deposits in the Mineral Mountains that lured settlers to the area in search of silver and lead. The desert setting and overall lack of trees make this a hot park come summertime, so visits are best done in the spring and fall before the desert heats up. Still, the drainage and repair of the Rocky Ford Dam on the Beaver River has turned the 1130-acre Minersville Reservoir into a prime smallmouth bass fishery that's hard to ignore no matter what the weather. Plus, the reservoir is a nice place to cool off when the temperature climbs. Day-use fee, $5. ~ Route 21, 12 miles southwest of Beaver; 435-438-5472.

▲ There are 47 sites (29 with hookups; 18 for tents only); $17 per night. Reservations: 800-322-3770 (April through November).

The southern edge of central Utah serves almost as a line of demarcation for the state's magnificent canyon

Capitol Reef National Park

country. Found here, straddling a 100-mile-long by three-mile-wide geologic oddity known as the Waterpocket Fold, is Capitol Reef National Park. Farther south, Zion and Bryce national parks (see Chapter Six) are the hallmarks of southwestern Utah, while

Canyonlands and Arches national parks (see Chapter Seven) preserve the unique features of southeastern Utah.

The landscape in this part of Utah reflects the transition from the somewhat lusher northern half of the state and the decidedly more arid southern section. Thick conifer forests prevalent in the mountains above Salina, Richfield and Beaver give way to sparse stands of juniper and cedar around Bicknell, Teasdale and Torrey. The lack of vegetation makes the landscape more susceptible to wind and water erosion, highly creative forces that have sculpted whimsical geologic formations such as those found in remote Goblin Valley State Park (see Chapter Seven).

Capitol Reef is easily Utah's least-visited national park, thanks to its remoteness, although the arrival in recent years of chain motels along Route 24 just beyond the park's western border is no doubt boosting visitation. Even so, the park's main attraction is a rugged, isolated desertscape of oddly crafted sandstone formations—dusty washes that can turn into frothy torrents during a summer rainstorm—and stone arches and bridges—some easily spotted, others treasures discovered only by the relentless. While mule deer frequently show up at the Fruita orchards near the visitors center, patient visitors might spy golden eagles overhead, bighorn sheep in the rugged backcountry, and lush hanging gardens growing in canyons where rainfall spills down the cliffs.

In this seemingly desolate terrain there are no major towns, just isolated outposts, and few residents. Although bleak-sounding, benefits of this lack of humanity are sprawling vistas that appear much as they always have, and, at night, a spectacular and poignant ceiling of stars like none you've ever seen.

SIGHTS

Route 24 southeast of Richfield weaves across two mountain ridges before descending into the valley of the Fremont River at **Loa**, a small ranching community nestled among rolling hills. Known as the Rabbit Valley, this high-altitude (7000 feet) dale was first settled in the 1870s by Mormon colonists, who raised livestock and grew feed crops. East of Loa are a string of other tiny, rustic and unpretentious towns: Lyman, Bicknell, Teasdale and Torrey.

Before you reach Torrey and Capitol Reef National Park you pass through the eye-blink town of **Bicknell**, which receives its proverbial 15 minutes of fame each summer with an international film festival dedicated to campy B films.

Before you know it, you're past Teasdale, a tiny ranching community, and upon Torrey, the western gateway to **Capitol Reef National Park**.

A national park since 1971, Capitol Reef's domed cliffs—reminiscent of the Capitol rotunda in Washington, D.C.—prompted early explorers to christen it thusly. Maritime men were reminded of barrier reefs by the cliffs of the Waterpocket Fold, a 100-mile

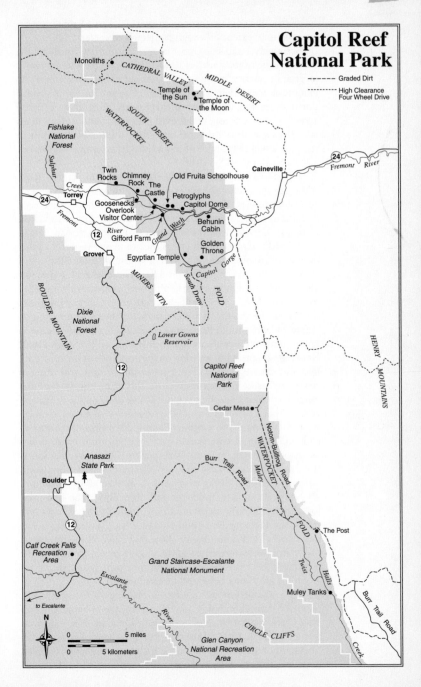

Capitol Reef National Park

- - - - - Graded Dirt
· · · · · · · High Clearance Four Wheel Drive

Monoliths

CATHEDRAL VALLEY

MIDDLE DESERT

Temple of the Sun

Temple of the Moon

WATERPOCKET

SOUTH DESERT

Fishlake National Forest

Sulphur

Creek

24

Caineville

Fremont River

Twin Rocks

Chimney Rock

The Castle

Old Fruita Schoolhouse

Petroglyphs

Torrey

Goosenecks Overlook Visitor Center

Capitol Dome

Fremont

Grand Wash

Behunin Cabin

12

River

Gifford Farm

Egyptian Temple

Golden Throne

Grover

MINERS MTN

Capitol Gorge

South Draw

FOLD

BOULDER MOUNTAIN

Dixie National Forest

Lower Gowns Reservoir

12

Capitol Reef National Park

HENRY MOUNTAINS

Cedar Mesa

Notom-Bullfrog Road

WATERPOCKET

Anasazi State Park

Burr Trail Road

Muley

Boulder

FOLD

12

The Post

Calf Creek Falls Recreation Area

Grand Staircase-Escalante National Monument

Twist

Halls

Burr Trail Road

Escalante

Muley Tanks

to Escalante

N

0   5 miles

0   5 kilometers

River

CIRCLE CLIFFS

Glen Canyon National Recreation Area

Creek

bulge that blistered up through the earth's crust 65 million years ago and now extends through the park's epicenter.

Seemingly small since most people arrive from Torrey on the western edge of the park via Route 24, stop at the visitors center at Fruita and then continue east and out of the park after traveling little more than a dozen miles. Capitol Reef is a slender, north–south ranging preserve that covers more than 240,000 acres. No lodges or restaurants exist in the park, and perhaps that's why folks spend so little time here. With a bit of effort, some of the park's wonders are easily, and quickly, accessed. Admission. ~ Route 24; 435-425-3791.

Elevations range from 4000 to 8200 feet in Capitol Reef. Although the national park is mostly wilderness, it has several accessible aspects. To the south, fossilized sand dunes have been buckled upward by the Waterpocket Fold. Near the center is lush Fruita, with its gardens and orchards that date to the late 1800s. At the park's remote north end is the grand and peaceful Cathedral Valley, a landscape of towering sandstone monoliths.

One of the blessings of Capitol Reef National Park is that just a few hours and a short side-trip off Route 24 are all that is needed to see some of the park's highlights, both geological and historical.

When entering the park from the west, the first four miles on Route 24 bring you to **Panorama Point**, where the late-afternoon light is kind to the mummy-like formations and landmark **Castle Rock**, a monumental formation on the north side of the road that, if you squint your eyes and tilt your head just right, resembles an Arthurian castle. You can walk up the short **Goosenecks Trail** (0.1 mile) overlooking gurgling Sulphur Creek or sit on the bench and gaze at Boulder Mountain and the Aquarius Plateau to the southwest. An 0.3-mile trek to Sunset Point yields a view of the soaring cliffs and bulging domes that dominate the heart of the park as well as a good look at the amazing **Waterpocket Fold** that reaches southward toward Lake Powell and eastward to the Henry Mountains. At sunset, Capitol Reef's wild beauty bursts in all its splendor.

Nearly seven miles inside the park from Torrey, the 12.5-mile-long **Scenic Drive** branches south off Route 24 to a visitors center on the Fremont River and continues as a paved road a few miles farther to **Fruita**. A slide show that explores the formation of Capitol Reef is presented at the visitors center, along with the artifacts of the American Indians who grew corn, beans and squash along the river long before white men arrived.

When the Mormons appeared in the late 19th century, they planted beautiful orchards on the banks of the Fremont and Sulphur Creek in a settlement they first called Junction. The name was then changed in 1902 to Fruita because of the prolific orchards. This hardy little community made its living by selling its apples, pears, peaches, cherries and apricots to communities as far away as Richfield and Price. The orchards remain today, tended by park service crews and picked by visitors.

Fruita also harbors several reminders of the past: an 1895 one-room log schoolhouse, a circa-1900 blacksmith shop, and the 1908 **Gifford Farm** homestead. The pioneer Gifford home added electricity only in 1948 and was lived in until 1969. Guided tours are offered. ~ Located along the Scenic Drive about a mile south of the visitors center.

Back on the scenic drive and just a few miles south of the visitors center you can branch off into Grand Wash. However, this unpaved mile-long spur through the dusty, narrow wash should be avoided if any kind of threatening weather is detected, as flash floods can quickly inundate the wash. Burrowed into the hillside on the north side of the road near the mouth of the wash are two shafts into the long-abandoned **Oyler Uranium Mine**. These pits were dug in 1904 when uranium was used in some medicines. Today gates prevent people from entering the mine.

Once inside the wash, the **Cassidy Arch Trail** (1.75 miles) soon appears on the north side of the road. Named for Butch Cassidy, a famous 19th-century outlaw thought to have used Grand Wash to hide from pursuing posses, the trail entails a healthy climb from the floor of the wash to a cliffside viewpoint above this arch.

After returning to the scenic drive and heading south, roughly four miles later you'll come to the end of the paved drive and find another unpaved spur that runs into **Capitol Gorge,** a sinuous, mile-long canyon, and the yellow sandstone monoliths of the **Golden Throne Trail** (2 miles), which leads you from the bottom of the gorge to the clifftops for some great views of the Golden Throne formation as well as the surrounding park.

From the visitors center, if you head east on Route 24 about a mile you'll reach the **Old Fruita Schoolhouse**, a one-room log cabin built in 1896 (although it didn't welcome its first "official" class until 1900) that saw its last class in 1941. Today it's well-preserved by the National Park Service and listed on the National Register of Historic Places. South of the schoolhouse across the road are acres of orchards set against the backdrop of a red-rock-cliff;

RIPE FOR THE PICKIN'

In Fruita, visitors can harvest cherries, apricots, peaches, apples and pears throughout the summer, with cherries ripening first, usually by mid-June, and apples last, usually by early September. You can eat as much as you want within the orchards, and take as much as you want for a nominal fee. No charge is assessed on the mule deer who also gorge themselves on the fruit.

in spring when the trees are blooming this makes a wonderful late-afternoon photograph.

Farther east along this route (six miles from the visitors center), you can step back in time at the **Behunin Cabin**, a one-room, dirt-floored, sandstone structure that was home to a family of ten when it was built in 1882.

Adventurous souls shouldn't be so fast to leave the park behind, as backroads that creep and crawl away from paved Route 24 lead to some intriguing vistas and, in today's hectic world, precious solitude.

HIDDEN ▶ Those with time on their hands and a stout rig to carry them can embark down the 56-mile four-wheel-drive **Cathedral Valley Road** that branches north off Route 24 five miles west of Caineville, beyond the park's east entrance. The steep winding road, including a ford of the Fremont River, pays big dividends for travelers appropriately equipped. Red-sandstone monoliths with names like **Temple of the Sun** and **Temple of the Moon**, two pyramidal towers that have staved off erosion, rise 500 feet or more above the surrounding landscape and dwarf visitors.

While the sheer bulk of the park's acreage lies south of Route 24 in Capitol Reef's "Waterpocket District," getting to it—aside from the scenic drive that runs past Fruita—is no easy task. Just beyond the park's eastern boundary the dirt-based Notom-Bullfrog Road heads south off Route 24 into something of a no-man's land riddled with canyons, outstanding views and, during rainy periods, lush hanging gardens. It runs roughly 22 miles before re-entering the park just northeast of the primitive Cedar Mesa campground with its five sites, picnic tables, fire grills, pit toilets . . . and no water.

South of the campground the road runs roughly 12 miles before intersecting the **Burr Trail Road**, which enters the park from the west and climbs in a somewhat diabolical fashion 800 feet up, via a series of switchbacks, to the top of the Waterpocket Fold. From this point, the Burr Trail Road, known to some as the Notom-Bullfrog Road, exits the park to the east and continues on 25 miles to Bullfrog Marina in Glen Canyon National Recreation Area.

OUT OF SCHOOL

Hiking trails run a short distance east of the Old Fruita Schoolhouse along the Fremont River to **petroglyph and pictograph panels**. Chipped into and painted onto the rock by the Fremont culture thought to have lived here from A.D. 700 to A.D. 1250, the art depicts odd-shaped humanistic forms, squiggles and animals, possibly bighorn sheep.

There are quite a few good hikes, which are best done in the spring or fall due to the deliriously hot summer weather, located off the Notom-Bullfrog and Burr Trail roads. From The Post, located three miles south of the Notom-Bullfrog and Burr Trail Road junction, the **Lower Muley Twist** trail offers a 15-mile loop into the arid canyon country. A good overnight trip into canyons that harbor colorful hanging gardens in spring can be found along the **Halls Creek Narrows Trail**. From the trailhead at Halls Overlook, found just outside the park's eastern border on a spur road about three miles west of the Notom-Bullfrog Road, you can hike the 21.9-mile long Halls Creek Narrows loop trail that passes through the Halls Narrows, one of the region's classic slot canyons.

If you prefer not to hike, or it's the middle of summer and concern for staying alive convinces you not to hike, you can stitch these roads together to make a 125-mile loop tour by car of Capitol Reef, one that offers sweeping views of the Waterpocket Fold. To do so, head east of the visitors center to the Notom-Bullfrog Road and follow it south 34 miles to the Burr Trail Road junction. Heading west 37 miles on the Burr Trail Road brings you to Boulder, where you need to turn right, or north, onto Route 12. From Boulder the Capitol Reef Visitors Center at Fruita is 47 miles away.

If there's such a thing as rustic luxury, **The Lodge at Red River Ranch** is the place to find it. Matt Alexander built and opened the three-story log lodge in 1994 on land his family has ranched since 1978. Each of the 15 guest rooms is furnished with a different antique theme (honeymooners love the Vintage Room and its skylit bath); every room has hardwood floors, a wood-burning fireplace and a balcony or patio, but no phone or TV. The marvelous living room, dubbed the Great Room, is modeled after a classic hunting lodge; decor is Western and American Indian and includes Navajo rugs. Bisected by the Fremont River, the ranch offers great trout fishing and horseback riding. Hearty American breakfasts and Southwestern-style wild-game dinners are available for an additional charge. Closed October through March. ~ 2900 West Route 24, Teasdale; 435-425-3322, 800-205-6343, fax 435-425-3329; www.redriverranch.com. DELUXE.

LODGING

In tiny Teasdale just west of Torrey, south of the main highway and backed against a cliff, **Muley Twist Inn** offers five rooms in an intoxicating high-desert setting of piñon pine. Located on the second floor, the rooms all have queen beds and private baths; some have trundle beds that accommodate youngsters. Downstairs is a large living room for relaxing with a book or board game and the airy dining room. The wraparound porch is perfect for watching the sunrise or rocking away after dinner. A short drive away is Capitol Reef National Park. Full, hearty breakfasts and afternoon snacks are included; lunch and dinner can be arranged.

◄ HIDDEN

Closed November through March. ~ 125 South Street, Teasdale; 435-425-3640, 800-530-1038, fax 435-425-3641; www.go-utah. com/muleytwist. MODERATE.

Capitol Reef Inn & Café provides more than its simple facade would suggest. Ten spacious guest rooms with two double beds and a working area are welcome to those toting a lot of high-country gear. There's a communal hot tub and, as the name implies, a restaurant. But the walls can seem a little thin, depending on who your neighbors are. Closed November through May. ~ 360 West Main Street, Torrey; 435-425-3271; www.capitolreefinn. com, e-mail cri@capitolreefinn.com. BUDGET.

You only have two choices at the **Torrey Pines Bed & Breakfast Inn,** but that doesn't necessarily make your decision easy. The charming two-bedroom cottage with wraparound porch has an upstairs bedroom with a king-sized bed and a nice but small balcony, as well as two twin beds and a full kitchenette downstairs. Your other option is a condo unit outfitted with a king-sized bed, sleeper couch and a jacuzzi. In addition, there's a kitchenette and laundry facilities. Both cottage and condo have phones and TV. ~ 250 South 800 East Route 12, Torrey; 435-425-3401; www. torreypinesinn.com. MODERATE TO DELUXE.

Cheerful local art dresses up the 50 rooms at **Wonderland Inn,** atop a hill at the edge of Torrey. All rooms have views; artificial-wood furniture is the only detractor. Guests can enjoy an indoor/outdoor pool and jacuzzi. There's also a three-meals-a-day coffee shop. ~ Route 12 and 24, Torrey; 435-425-3775, 877-854-0184, fax 435-425-3212; www.capitolreefwonderland.com, e-mail wndrland@color-country.net. BUDGET TO MODERATE.

HIDDEN ►   **SkyRidge** is more than a hilltop B&B inn near the entrance to Capitol Reef National Park. It's also a gallery of locally produced art, most of it Southwestern in motif. Without question, this is one of the finest lodgings in all of southern Utah. All six nonsmoking rooms are comfortable affairs boasting Southwestern decor, large beds, and plenty of windows from which to savor the surrounding rockscape. All have private baths; two have their own jacuzzis, and there is also a large outdoor hot tub. The library is well stocked with books, videos and compact discs. In addition to breakfast, hors d'oeuvres are served nightly near the big living-room fireplace. Wonderful views extend across Rabbit Valley. ~ 590 East Route 24, Torrey; phone/fax 435-425-3222; www.skyridgeinn.com. DELUXE TO ULTRA-DELUXE.

For peace, quiet and log walls, check into **Cowboy Homestead Cabins.** Located about three miles south of Torrey on Route 12, these four charming cabins are set on a 160-acre spread that is surrounded by undeveloped public lands. The cabins themselves aren't sprawling, but they're clean and tidy with comfortable queen-sized beds and kitchenettes outfitted with microwaves, refrigerators and dishes. Outside your door there's a barbecue you can fire up to cook your dinner. ~ 2100 South Route 12, Torrey; 435-425-3414, 888-854-5871; www.cowboyhomesteadcabins. com. BUDGET TO MODERATE.

DINING

Dining options, not too surprisingly, are few in this remote area, but what options do exist are surprisingly good.

You will want to try the steaks and Mexican dishes, but pies are the specialty of the house at **Sunglow Family Restaurant,** which is located in Bicknell eight miles west of Torrey. Pinto-bean pie, fruit pies and a renowned pickle pie outclass other standard diner fare at this friendly eatery. Closed Sunday. ~ 63 East Main Street, Bicknell; 435-425-3701. BUDGET.

Specializing in locally raised foods, the **Capitol Reef Café** likewise surprises with its fresh approach to cooking. Utah rainbow trout, vegetarian dishes, homemade soups and heaping gardens of salad are the order of the day, along with hearty breakfasts. Espresso and café au lait are nice touches. The café is often busy, so be prepared to wait for a table. Closed November through May. ~ 360 West Main Street, Torrey; 435-425-3271. MODERATE.

For a quick snack, try **Brink's Burgers.** In addition to cheeseburgers, they serve good fries and thick, old-fashioned milkshakes. Closed November through February. ~ 165 East Main Street, Torrey; 435-425-3710. BUDGET.

SHOPPING

The store at the **Capitol Reef Inn** has plenty of good guidebooks, maps and trinkets of the area. Closed November through May. ~ 360 West Main Street, Torrey; 435-425-3271.

Fresh takes on desert landscapes can be found at **Gallery 24,** which displays the contemporary works of four local artisans along with occasional guests. Sharing the same address, **The Old**

AUTHOR FAVORITE

In 1995, former Utah "chef of the year" Gary Pankow and his wife Jane, a pastry chef, opened **Café Diablo** at the west end of Torrey; its innovative Southwestern cuisine seems startlingly out of place in this rural location. House specialties include rattlesnake cakes with ancho-chile aioli, pumpkin seed–crusted trout with cilantro lime sauce, and pork ribs in chipotle sauce with sweet-potato fries. Jane's desserts are killer, especially the Double Diablo cake with crème anglaise. On the walls, intermingled with Mexican-style masks, are original paintings for sale by local artists. There's also a children's menu. Dinner only; licensed for beer only. Closed mid-October to mid-April. ~ 599 West Main Street, Torrey; 435-425-3070; www.cafediablo.net. MODERATE TO DELUXE.

Cedar Tree is an interesting shop with rocks and fossils collected from the Utah desert, as well as pottery and jewelry. Both are closed November through March. ~ 135 East Main Street, Torrey; Gallery 24, 435-425-2124; Old Cedar Tree, 435-425-3992.

Paintings, sculptures and photographs by such notables as David Muench and John Telford, as well as Navajo rugs in a variety of sizes and designs, are among the fine arts at the **Torrey Gallery**, located in a small, attractive clapboard building. ~ 80 East Main Street, Torrey; 435-425-3909; www.torreygallery.com.

You can find American Indian–style flutes and other unusual gifts from the desert at **The Flute Shop**, which is located about four miles south of Torrey on Route 12. ~ 2650 South Route 12, Torrey; 435-425-3144.

Undoubtedly the region's best place to shop for authentic handmade items is the **Gifford Homestead & Gift Shop** in Capitol Reef National Park. Local artisans reproduce the same utensils and household tools used by early Mormon pioneers, demonstrating and selling them at this historic site. Look for boot jacks, butter churns and hand-dipped candles. ~ Scenic Drive, Fruita; 435-425-3791.

PARKS

CAPITOL REEF NATIONAL PARK 🏃 🚵 🐎 🏕 ⛵ Covering 376 square miles of contorted desert, this national treasure is veined by roads and hiking trails that lead past the region's sculptured rock layers to vista points, deep canyons and remote waterfalls. The park features a visitors center, campfire programs, a paved scenic road and restrooms. Swimming in the Fremont River is inadvisable due to a deceiving undertow. Day-use fee, $5, payable at station south of Fruita on Scenic Drive. ~ Route 24, 11 miles east of Torrey; 435-425-3791.

▲ There are 72 sites at Fruita and 10 sites in two Cathedral Valley campgrounds; $10 per night at the Fruita campground, no charge at Cathedral Valley.

▼▼▼▼▼▼▼▼▼▼▼▼

Outdoor Adventures

FISHING

PROVO AREA Anglers snare rainbow, German brown and cutthroat trout in the **Provo River**, as well as Rocky Mountain whitefish. Elsewhere in the Provo area, **American Fork Creek** yields browns and rainbows, while shallow **Utah Lake** harbors carp, catfish, yellow perch, trophy-size bass and walleye pike. ~ The Provo River runs along Route 189 through the Provo Canyon northeast of Provo, while Utah Lake is due west of Provo.

PRICE AREA In the Price area, **Scofield Reservoir**, located 11 miles south of Route 6, is stocked with rainbow trout; native cutthroat also inhabit the reservoir and tributary streams. Rainbows and cutthroat also populate **Ferron, Huntington Canyon, Joe's**

Valley and **Millsite reservoirs**; flyfishermen catch good-sized brown trout in the **Huntington River** and **Ferron** and **Cottonwood creeks**. Fishing licenses can be purchased at **Gart Brothers** in Price, or at the BLM office. ~ Ferron Reservoir is located almost 24 miles west of the town of Ferron via Ferron Canyon Road and Forest Service Road 022; Huntington Reservoir is 4 miles west of Cleveland via Route 155; Joe's Valley Reservoir is 16 miles west of Castle Dale via Routes 57 and 29; and Millsite Reservoir is located 4 miles west of Ferron.

RICHFIELD AREA South of Richfield, **Piute**, **Otter Creek** and **Johnson Valley reservoirs** are excellent for rainbows and cutthroats; ice-fishing is popular in winter. There's also good trout fishing near Beaver at **Kent's Lake**, located roughly 15 miles east of Beaver via Route 153 and Forest Service Road 137, and **Minersville Reservoir**, found eight miles west of Beaver via Route 21. The state park is located 11 miles south of Route 6 and 5 miles north of the town of Scofield. Native brown trout, and stocked mackinaw (lake trout), rainbow trout and splake, are the catches at large **Fish Lake**, which is 40 miles southeast of Richfield via Routes 119, 24 and 25; as deep as 85 feet and covering 2500 acres, this lake requires boats for the most successful angling. ~ Piute Reservoir is 4 miles south of Marysvale along Route 89; Otter Creek Reservoir is 8 miles southeast of Marysvale via Routes 89 and 22; and Johnson Valley Reservoir is 48 miles southeast of Richfield via Routes 119, 24 and 25.

> The Provo River has been rated one of ten "blue ribbon" flyfishing streams in the American West by *Field and Stream* magazine.

CAPITOL REEF AREA The Boulder Top area is one of the great brook trout fisheries in North America. Located south of the Rabbit Valley and west of Capitol Reef National Park, its numerous small lakes—such as **Fish Creek Reservoir**, **Blind Lake**, **Pear Lake** and **Donkey Reservoir**—are on the northeastern edge of the timbered Aquarius Plateau, which reaches above 11,000 feet. A state-record seven-and-one-half-pound brookie was hooked here; catches in the five-pound range are common. Flyfishermen also snag cutthroat and rainbow trout. The ice-free season extends from mid-May to early November. ~ The Boulder Top area is roughly eight miles south of Teasdale and reached via Forest Service Road 521 from Teasdale and Forest Service Road 179 from Grover.

Outfitters **Alpine Angler** offers guided trips to these lakes, accessible only by four-wheel-drive, horseback or foot. ~ 310 West Main Street, Torrey; 435-425-3660, 888-484-3331; www.fly-fishing-utah.net. **The Outdoor Source** conducts flyfishing and float-tubing clinics from base camps at Boulder Top. ~ HC 61 Box 230, Fremont, UT 84747; 435-836-2372; www.outdoorsource.net.

BOATING   Many of the lakes throughout this expansive region have boat ramps that lure motorboaters and waterskiers; numerous others encourage use of non-motorized vessels. Largest is 150-square-mile **Utah Lake**, with its 144-slot marina and numerous launch ramps for Provo-area residents and visitors. Also in the vicinity is **Deer Creek Reservoir**, found a dozen miles northeast of Provo along Route 189 at the head of Provo Canyon. Elsewhere in central Utah, most recreation-oriented reservoirs are contained within state parks—among them **Scofield, Huntington, Millsite, Yuba** (Sevier Bridge), **Palisade, Piute, Otter Creek** and **Minersville reservoirs**. Others worth considering are **Mona Reservoir**, nine miles north of Nephi via Route 41, **Gunnison Reservoir** seven miles south of Manti via Route 89 and **Johnson Valley Reservoir**, 48 miles southeast of Richfield via Routes 119, 24 and 25. At **Fish Lake**, 40 miles southeast of Richfield via Routes 119, 24 and 25, boats are available for rent from Fish Lake Lodge. ~ Scofield Reservoir is located along Route 96, 11 miles south of Route 6; Huntington Reservoir is 4 miles west of Cleveland via Route 155; Millsite Reservoir is 4 miles west of Ferron via Ferron Canyon Road; Yuba (Sevier Bridge) Reservoir is 2 miles south of Route 15 via Route 202, 30 miles south of Nephi via Route 28; Palisade Reservoir is 2 miles east of Route 89 and Sterling; Piute Reservoir is 4 miles south of Marysvale along Route 89; Otter Creek Reservoir is 8 miles southeast of Marysvale via Routes 89 and 22; and Minersville Reservoir is found 8 miles west of Beaver via Route 21.

For a unique cross-country ski experience, try skiing by lantern at the Sundance Nordic Center. The flickering lanterns and star-filled skies combine for an unforgettable experience.

RIVER RUNNING   On the Sevier River south of Richfield, a four-mile stretch through Marysvale Canyon is popular with novice rafters and tubers. Rentals can be arranged through **Big Rock Raft**. ~ Route 89, north of Marysville; 435-326-4321.

SKIING   **Sundance Resort** may not have the high profile of Park City, Deer Valley or Snowbird, but actor-director Robert Redford's environmentally sensitive resort community situated above Provo Canyon is a world-class destination in its own right, rich in light powder snow. Seven chairlifts serve 41 trails and bowls that cater to skiers of all abilities, with a vertical drop of 2150 feet from a top elevation of 8250 feet. Sundance also has a **Nordic Center** (801-223-4170) one and a half miles north of its main entrance, with 15 kilometers of cross-country trails, some of them lit for night skiing. ~ Route 92, 17 miles northeast of Provo; 801-225-4100, 800-892-1600; www.sundanceresort.com.

   Elk Meadows Ski Resort in the Tushar Mountains is the region's other full-service ski area. Its base area is the highest in Utah at 9200 feet. Five chairlifts serve 30 runs for downhill skiers; 10

kilometers of marked and groomed cross-country ski trails cater to Nordic enthusiasts. The ski school is excellent. At presstime, the resort was closed for possible construction; call to check on its status. ~ Route 153, 19 miles east of Beaver; 435-438-5433, 888-881-7669; www.elkmeadows.com.

CLIMBING

With all of its craggy mountaintops and granite outcrops, this part of Utah, like much of northern Utah, is renowned for its rock-climbing possibilities. While Big and Little Cottonwood canyons southeast of Salt Lake City attract most of the attention, American Fork Canyon north of Provo and Rock Canyon east of the city are also popular.

If you need climbing instruction or are interested in a guided trip, call Doug Hansen at **High Angle Technologies**. He leads clients into both American Fork and Rock canyons, as well as on excursions into the Tushar and Mineral mountains. Ice-climbing up Bridal Veil Falls in Provo Canyon can also be arranged. ~ 759 North State Street, Orem; 801-221-0398, cell 801-376-5200.

To equip yourself for climbs, or simply for a backpacking trek, you probably can find what you need at **High Adventure Specialties**, which sells alpine mountaineering equipment as well. ~ 1799 North State Street, Orem; 801-226-7498; www.highad venturespecialties.com.

RIDING STABLES & PACK TRIPS

Much of central Utah is isolated backcountry, inaccessible by road. It's a rugged, picturesque landscape easily reached while astride a horse. Of course, there are also areas nearby resorts that make perfect day rides, too. If a day on horseback interests you, there are outfitters ready to accommodate you.

Equestrians in the Provo area can ride at **Sundance Resort**, which offers guided day trips into the mountains that sprawl below Mount Timpanogos. Wranglers also offer lessons in the resort's arena. ~ Route 92, 17 miles northeast of Provo; 801-225-4100, 800-892-1600; www.sundanceresort.com.

South of Price, **Winn's Wild West Trail Rides & Cattle Drives** offers one-and two-day trips into the San Rafael Swell during the spring and fall, while the Manti-La Sal Mountains are the destination during the summer. ~ P.O. Box 246, Ferron, UT 84523; 435-384-2592; www.winnwildwest.com.

The **Johnson Cattle Company** offers multiday pack trips as well as day-long trail rides into Fishlake National Forest. ~ P.O. Box 122, Aurora, UT 84620; 435-529-3227.

Backcountry packing is a great way to see the off-road attractions of Capitol Reef National Park. **Hondoo Rivers & Trails** offers horse trips with a minimum of two nights and three days. You can rough it and camp out in the backcountry, or sign on for one of their inn-to-inn trips. ~ 90 East Main Street, Torrey;

435-425-3519, 800-332-2696; www.hondo.com. Shorter expeditions ranging from one hour to a full day can be arranged through the **Best Western Capitol Reef Inn**. ~ Route 24 east of Torrey; 435-425-3761.

GOLF

As you travel north to south in Utah, the golf season lengths, much to the delight of duffers who marvel at the added driving power they enjoy in the state's higher altitude and thinner air (when compared to sea-level courses). In central Utah, you never need to look far for some links.

PROVO AREA The **East Bay Golf Course** near Utah Lake has 27 holes, a majority of them with water hazards, all with waterfowl hazards. ~ 1860 South East Bay Boulevard, Provo; 801-379-6612. The **Seven Peaks Resort** course, with 18 holes spread over 3328 yards, is located a few blocks from Brigham Young University. ~ 1450 East 500 North, Provo; 801-375-5155.

Surrounded by orchards, one of the busiest courses in the area is the par-35, nine-hole **Cascade Fairways**. ~ 1313 East 800 North, Orem; 801-225-6677. The par-72 **Tri-City Golf Course**, between American Fork, Lehi and Pleasant Grove, has 18 holes nestled near the foot of Mount Timpanogos. ~ 1400 North 200 East, American Fork; 801-756-3594. The 18 holes at **Thanksgiving Point Golf Course** were designed by Johnny Miller, who stretched the course to 7728 yards to accommodate big drivers. ~ 2095 North West Frontage Road, Lehi; 801-768-7400.

Picturesque 18-hole **Hobble Creek Golf Course** and its 6315 yards occupies a narrow canyon east of Springville. ~ Hobble Creek Canyon Drive, seven miles east of Route 15 Exit 263; 801-489-6297. The 18 holes of **Spanish Oaks Golf Course** are spread across 6386 yards located in Spanish Fork Canyon beneath Dominguez Hill, where missionaries first entered the Utah Valley in 1776. ~ 2300 Powerhouse Road, four miles east of Route 15 Exit 261, Spanish Fork; 801-798-9816. The **Gladstan Golf Course** is actually two nine-hole courses tucked against the Wasatch Range. The back nine is closer to the mountains and decidedly hillier. ~ 1 Gladstan Drive off Route 15 Exit 254, Payson; 801-465-2549.

PRICE AREA The par-70, 18-hole **Carbon Country Club**, an easy, pleasant course built in the late 1940s, is the oldest golf course in the eastern half of Utah. ~ 3055 North Route 6, Price; 435-637-2388. Other central Utah courses all have nine holes. **Millsite Golf Course**, set among arid hills at the foot of the Wasatch Plateau, is one of the state's most distinctive thanks to the surrounding buttes. ~ 3000 West Canyon Road, four miles from Ferron; 435-384-2887.

NEPHI-MANTI AREA Canyon Hills Golf Course, a par-36, nine-hole course is scenically located at the mouth of Salt Creek Can-

Earning
Your Views

Bikers in search of a hardcore, multiday expedition need look no further than the **Notom Road-Burr Trail-Boulder Mountain Loop**. Extending 80 miles one-way from Boulder, 32 miles south of Torrey on Route 12, to the east entrance of Capitol Reef National Park on Route 24, it is even strenuous for advanced riders.

The historic Burr Trail runs east from Boulder Mountain through the Circle Cliffs of Grand Staircase-Escalante National Monument, joining Notom Road at Oyster Shell Reef on the Waterpocket Fold. It then proceeds north up the Strike Valley on the east side of the Fold. Most of the route is graded dirt and sand. Riders who eschew a shuttle have a return of 50 miles on paved roads to Boulder.

A somewhat shorter ride at roughly 60 miles (but one that loops back on itself and returns you to your starting point) is the **Burr Trail-Wolverine Loop ride**. Starting in Boulder, this ride leads you east of Boulder to the Wolverine Petrified Forest, a high-desert tableau scattered with slices of petrified wood that appear to have been sawed from a tree. About 16 miles down the Burr Trail you turn right onto the Wolverine Loop, which runs to the petrified forest. You can either backtrack from there to the Burr Trail and Boulder, which would shorten the overall ride, or continue on down the dirt road and back to the Burr Trail and back west to Boulder.

Shuttles are available from **Hondoo Rivers & Trails**. ~ 90 East Main Street, Torrey; 435-425-3519; www.hondoo.com. Also offering shuttle service and bike repair and rentals is **Wild Hare Expeditions**. ~ 2600 East Route 24, Torrey; 435-425-3999, 888-304-4273; www.color-country.net/~thehare.

yon. ~ 1200 East 100 North, Nephi; 435-623-9930. **Sunset View Golf Course**, a nine-hole, par-36 course that runs 3102 yards, is surrounded by sagebrush plains and is the most inexpensive public golf course in Utah. ~ Route 6, two miles north of Delta; 435-864-2508. The par-72, 18-hole **Palisade Golf Course** at Palisade State Park has wide fairways, few hazards and well-maintained greens covering 6360 yards. ~ Two miles east of Route 89, five miles south of Manti; 435-835-4653.

RICHFIELD AREA   Cove View Golf Course, a nine-hole, par-36 course spread over 2988 yards, is inexpensive, uncrowded and flat. ~ Off Route 70 Exit 37, one and a half miles southwest of Richfield; 435-896-9987. The par-34 **Canyon Breeze Golf Course**, another nine-hole course, is located on the site of old Fort Cameron at the mouth of Beaver Canyon. It plays over 2746 yards. ~ Route 153, two miles east of Beaver; 435-438-2601.

BIKING   In outdoor-rich Utah, muscle power is the preferred form of locomotion for many residents. This explains the state's many trails for cyclists. Here in the mountainous central portion of the state, however, riders need to be prepared for steep hill climbs and descents.

PROVO AREA   A short but rewarding ride follows the **Provo River Parkway Trail** 13 miles from Utah Lake through Provo and up Provo Canyon, where it runs along the swift-running river. It continues past Bridal Veil Falls to Vivian Park, a nice place for a lunch break or just a rest before turning around.

Road bikers appreciate the **Utah Lake Loop**, an informal 100-mile circuit around Utah's largest freshwater lake. A fairly level ride, its most rewarding stretch is the 34 miles of Route 68, which affords marvelous views of the Wasatch Mountains from the west side of the lake between Lehi, on Route 73, and the orchard town of Elberta, on Route 6.

Mountain bikers seeking a workout often head to **Squaw Peak Road**, which runs 35 miles from Route 189 just north of Provo south into Provo Canyon, where it hooks up with a fork of Hobble Creek Canyon. The up-and-down mix of asphalt road and dirt trail roams through aspen and maple forests and is capped by a precipitous downhill.

PRICE AREA   In summer, when desert temperatures peak, bikers head for the cool heights of the Wasatch Plateau in Manti-La Sal National Forest. A popular route, about 60 miles long but often done in segments, extends from **Scofield State Park to Joe's Valley Reservoir**; most of the route is above 7000 feet elevation. From the state park, follow Route 96 south through Scofield, turning west on Route 264, the Eccles Canyon Scenic Byway. The road winds uphill to Route 31, which coincides with Skyline Drive near

Lower Gooseberry Reservoir. Past Huntington Reservoir, turn off Route 31 and continue south on Miller Flat Road through Scad Valley, beneath Bald Mountain and Bald Ridge, to Upper Joe's Valley and Route 29 near Joe's Valley Reservoir. Riders will need shuttle service to execute this beautiful alpine ride one-way; otherwise, numerous forest trails make possible loop trips with little backtracking.

Spring and fall are the best seasons to undertake trips up **Nine Mile Canyon** or into the San Rafael Swell. The intermediate, one-way ride up the length of Nine Mile Canyon is 40 miles long. The ride begins on the east side of Wellington, where you turn north off Route 6/191 and onto Nine Mile Canyon Road, which is paved for the first 13 miles before changing into a gravel road. The mouth of the canyon is about 25 miles northeast of Wellington.

The eight-mile **Sheep Canyon** route, a novice ride, begins 24 miles up Nine Mile Canyon and takes in impressive petroglyphs. The 23-mile **Prickly Pear/Harmon Canyon Loop**, beginning 33 miles up Nine Mile Canyon and suitable for advanced bikers, ascends and descends 2000 vertical feet of desert mountains and offers great views of the Badland Cliffs.

The Sevier Bridge Reservoir can rise to cover 10,000 surface acres when filled to capacity.

The **Buckhorn Flat Railroad Grade** through San Rafael country was built along the base of Cedar Mountain in the early 1880s, but ties and rails were never laid as the railroad owners chose another route. Today, the 11-mile, one-way road is a smooth, level thoroughfare; Fremont pictographs and petroglyphs may be seen in side canyons. The trailhead is reached from Cleveland or Huntington via the Lawrence to Tan Seeps Road (BLM Road 322) or from Castle Dale via the Green River Cutoff (BLM Road 401). A southern branch from the same trailhead leads to **The Wedge Overlook** via BLM Road 405; it's an easy 10-mile ride along the rim of the canyon, with marvelous views of the Little Grand Canyon of the San Rafael River.

NEPHI-MANTI AREA   East of Route 89 and the Sanpete Valley, **Skyline Drive** (Forest Road 150) follows the crest of the Wasatch Plateau from north to south. This 87-mile, mostly unpaved route is closed to motorized travel except from mid-July through September. Most riders begin at the rail siding of Tucker, west of Soldier Summit on Route 6, and continue south through Manti-La Sal and Fishlake national forests, between Mount Nebo and the San Rafael Swell, all the way to Route 70 Exit 71, east of Salina. Skyline Drive is rated moderate to strenuous for bikers; much of the route is above 10,000 feet altitude, and the southern section of the road, in particular, is rough and narrow.

RICHFIELD AREA   Mountain bikers enjoy the **Paiute ATV Trail** as much as do off-road vehicle enthusiasts. The 250-mile circuit through Fishlake National Forest can be tackled in any number of segments and loops in the Pahvant Range, Tushar Mountains and Sevier Plateau. Two of the most popular are the **Marysvale-Beaver Creek Trail** section, climbing for 20 miles up the east side of Mount Belknap in the Tushars, and the **Trail Mountain Loop**, a relatively level, scenic, 15-mile run from Route 13 west of Fremont Indian State Park.

Mytoge Mountain, overlooking the southeastern shore of Fish Lake, offers a 25-mile advanced-intermediate loop featured in an annual autumn "fat tire festival." Beginning and ending at Fish Lake Lodge on Route 25, the route circles the lake on Forest Road 046 and adjoining roads. The single-track descent past a pair of small crater lakes is steep and wild.

CAPITOL REEF NATIONAL PARK   The national park—and adjacent national forest and BLM land—offer some of the most varied and interesting terrain in the Southwest, from red-rock canyons to cool, tree-shaded oases. These are some of the most popular rides in and near the park: Novice bikers can ride out (and back in) the 12.5-mile **Scenic Drive** from the visitors center. Ten miles of the route are paved; two-mile (roundtrip) extensions to Capitol Gorge and Grand Wash are dirt and gravel.

A good family ride is the four-mile **Twin Rocks** trail, an easy, rolling, dirt-and-gravel track that begins and ends on Route 24. From a turnout on the south side of the highway, six miles west of the visitors center, it achieves fine views of Waterpocket Fold and Boulder Mountain.

The **Velvet Ridge** trail runs north from Torrey into Fishlake National Forest, around the flank of 11,306-foot Thousand Lakes Mountain. Nine miles one-way (many bikers request a shuttle), the moderate track starts where Forest Service Road 146 joins Route 24. The route follows a jeep trail of dirt and gravel, with rocky and sandy spots best avoided in wet weather. A acclivitous final pitch rewards with spectacular views.

A moderately strenuous trail for intermediate and advanced riders begins well outside the national park, on the flank of Boulder Mountain, and runs past **Lower Bowns Reservoir and Tantalus Flats** to Scenic Drive. From Dixie National Forest Road 181 (30 miles from Fruita), at 8500 feet near the Wildcat Ranger Station, it descends 3000 feet sometimes steeply past the reservoir, across Tantalus Flats, and into the park via South Draw Road across Pleasant Creek. En route, riders endure dirt, sand and shale, and cross creeks. The length is 12 miles to Scenic Drive or 22 miles back to Fruita. Most riders arrange a shuttle to the trailhead.

The challenging, 56-mile **Cathedral Valley Loop** is recommended for advanced riders. Running up Caineville Wash from

Route 24 at Caineville, 17 miles east of Fruita, it accesses remote and arid Cathedral Valley, with its red-sandstone monoliths towering 500 feet above desert washes; the loop returns to Route 24 five miles west of Caineville. This is a strenuous ride: bikers encounter steep hills, stretches of deep sand, muddy wash crossings, tight switchbacks, and a ford of the Fremont River. Carry water.

Bike Rentals When you're in Price and in need of a bike, an excellent shop offering sales, rentals and repairs of mountain bikes is **Decker's Bicycle Shop**. ~ 77 East Main Street, Price; 435-637-0086. Ask here about the annual mid-May San Rafael Mountain Bike Festival.

Central Utah offers a delightful and interesting mixture of hiking opportunities, ranging from trails that wind up and down through thick forests and rise above 10,000 feet to desert hikes that don't feature varied elevation but often meander through canyons and past intriguing sandstone formations. Common sense dictates that desert hikes, particularly in the hot summer months, require you to carry plenty of water since you won't find much in this landscape.

HIKING

All distances listed are one way unless otherwise noted.

PROVO AREA One of the most popular trails in the entire state of Utah is the ascent of **Timpanogos Peak** (9.4 miles). Beginning from Aspen Grove, 6900 feet elevation on Alpine Loop Road (Route 92) just past Sundance Resort, it climbs to the snow-capped summit of the 11,750-foot peak, passing numerous waterfalls and gem-like Emerald Lake (6.9 miles from Aspen Grove). Strong hikers can make the climb in three hours, although most people require five to six hours to peak and another three to four hours to descend. Sometimes on summer weekends, as many as 500 hikers may share the trail at once. An easier trail, beginning from Sundance Resort, is **Stewart Falls Trail** (1.5 miles) to a series of cascades on a mountain stream.

PRICE AREA In Manti-La Sal National Forest, **Fish Creek National Recreation Trail** (11 miles) descends from Jones Ridge, on

GETTING LOST IN THE ROCKS

South of Route 24 on Scenic Drive, the splendid Waterpocket Fold ridge seems to go on forever. A logical first stop is the flat **Grand Wash** (2.3 miles), which cuts through towering thrones en route through the fold. The trail leads into narrow canyons and past pockmarked rocks. A short, steep detour off Grand Wash to **Cassidy Arch** (1.75 miles) traverses canyon depths to cliffs. Late-19th-century outlaw Butch Cassidy is said to have hidden out in these honeycombs.

Skyline Drive (Forest Road 150), to Scofield Reservoir. The gentle **Left Fork Huntington Trail** (3 miles) at Huntington Campground (Route 31) follows Scad Valley Creek. The moderate-grade **Bristlecone Ridge Trail** (1 mile) is a nature trail with viewpoints at Price Canyon Recreation Site (Route 6 north of Helper).

NEPHI-MANTI AREA   The strenuous, 5000-foot ascent of the south summit of **Mount Nebo** (6 miles) begins on the mountain's eastern flank at Ponderosa Campground, ten miles northeast of Nephi off Route 132. The view from the top extends for hundreds of miles northeast through the Wasatch Range, east to the Wasatch Plateau and west across the Great Basin. Further trail information can be obtained from the Uinta National Forest office. ~ 740 South Main Street, Nephi; 435-623-2735.

The Navajo people called Surprise Canyon the "Land of the Sleeping Rainbows."

RICHFIELD AREA   The **Fish Lake Mountains Trail** (12 miles) traverses the glaciated, 11,000-foot Fish Lake Hightop Plateau from Pelican Overlook. The moderate hike, with marvelous views, is generally accomplished as an overnight trek.

CAPITOL REEF NATIONAL PARK   Hikes in Capitol Reef's backcountry are best conducted in the spring and fall months, as summertime temperatures can easily and quickly climb past 100 degrees. If you do hike in summer, park officials recommend 1.5 gallons of water per person per day, and you'll likely have to carry most of that in with you as there are few reliable water sources in the backcountry. Finally, wood collecting is prohibited in the park, so be sure to have a reliable cook stove and enough fuel for it.

Trails at Capitol Reef range from easy to steep, offering so much unexplored backcountry that hikers can disappear for days. Rock cairns mark some trails, while other routes are located by studying topographic maps.

Near Route 24 is **Hickman Bridge Trail** (1 mile), a self-guided, family-oriented nature hike to a 133-foot rock rainbow with a gentle elevation gain (400 feet). Skirt past the Capitol Dome with its white mounds of Navajo sandstone capping the rock. Continuing up the rim takes you past triple-decker ice cream cone–colored rocks to the overlook (2.3 miles).

From the **Chimney Rock Trail** (1.75 miles), three miles west of the visitors center on a trail with petrified wood, this path winds past the sandstone up switchbacks. (Remember, no specimens may be collected in national parks.)

The **Lower Spring Canyon Route** (9 miles), which skirts chocolate-brown canyons, begins at Chimney Rock Trail; it negotiates two 10-foot dry falls and crosses a river. Some of the path is on a river bed that is a flash-flood risk in threatening weather.

From Burr Trail (see "Earning Your Views"), a rugged road shaves over two miles off the **Upper Muley Twist** (5.5 miles) hike, which offers drama in the form of Saddle Arch and narrows within Waterpocket Fold. Access is one mile west of the Burr Trail switchbacks.

Lower Muley Twist (12 miles) boasts areas that are steep and narrow enough to "twist a mule pulling a wagon." The colorful route traverses Waterpocket Fold. Start from Burr Trail west of Notom Road. Much easier but still spectacular hiking amid sheer walls and similar scenery is **Surprise Canyon** (1 mile), north of The Post turnoff.

The **Halls Creek Narrows Trail** (21.9 miles roundtrip) is found just beyond the southeastern corner of the park via a spur road roughly 3 miles west of the Notom-Bullfrog Road. It quickly dives into the park via a steep series of switchbacks that drop you 800 feet, and 1.2 miles to Halls Creek. From the bottom it's 7.5 miles to the mouth of the Narrows, a three-mile-long slot canyon cut through Navajo sandstone by a year-round flowing creek. After you exit the slot, it's 1.5 miles back to the beginning of the Narrows via the Hall Divide, 7.5 miles back to Halls Creek, and 1.2 miles to the trailhead.

Outfitters **Wild Hare Expeditions** provide expert guides for backcountry hiking and backpacking. ~ 116 West Main Street, Torrey; 435-425-3999, 888-304-4273.

Transportation

CAR

The north–south interstate highway, **Route 15**, is the main byway through central Utah, connecting Salt Lake City with Provo, Nephi, Fillmore and Beaver en route to Cedar City and St. George. It is intersected between Fillmore and Beaver by another interstate, **Route 70**, which extends east through Richfield and Salina en route to Green River and Denver.

Other important highways in central Utah include **Route 6**, which runs east from Nevada through Delta to Spanish Fork, then southeast through Price to Route 70. **Route 89** parallels Route 15 to the east, linking Springville to the Sanpete Valley, Manti, Richfield and Marysvale. **Route 24** runs southeasterly from tiny Sigurd, between Salina and Richfield, to the towns of the Rabbit Valley and Capitol Reef National Park.

Be prepared for snow and ice in winter and early spring. For road reports, call 800-492-2400 from anywhere within Utah.

AIR

Small airports at Provo, Spanish Fork, Price, Cleveland, Nephi, Mount Pleasant, Manti, Salina, Richfield, Delta, Fillmore, Beaver and Loa (for Capitol Reef) serve charters and private planes, but most air traffic to central Utah arrives at **Salt Lake City International Airport** (801-575-2400); see Chapter Two for more information. **Executive Charter** operates a shuttle service 365 days a year, 24 hours a day, using luxury sedans and Suburbans. Based in Orem, their drivers can pick you up at the Salt Lake airport and take you anywhere in the state. Rates begin at $50 an hour. ~ 922 North 700 East, Orem; 801-434-8945, 800-787-0507, fax 801-434-8946; www.executivecharter.cc.

Xpress Shuttle, which serves Orem, Provo, Lehi, Lindon, Springville and Spanish Fork, has desks at the Salt Lake airport. ~ 801-375-5533, 800-397-0773; www.xpressshuttle.com.

TRAIN

Amtrak serves Provo with four scheduled departures daily: eastbound to Chicago, westbound to San Francisco ("California Zephyr") or Los Angeles ("Desert Wind"). The depot is located at 600 South and 200 West. All trains also stop in Helper, near Price, coming to or from Chicago; the "Desert Wind" pauses twice daily in Milford, west of Beaver. ~ 800-872-7245; www. amtrak.com.

BUS

Greyhound/Trailways (800-231-2222; www.greyhound.com) plies major routes, with stops in towns along primary highways throughout the region. In central Utah, Greyhound stops in Provo at 124 North 300 West, 801-373-4211; in Price at 277 North Carbondale Road, 435-637-7153; in Fillmore at Caleb Country Grill, 590 North Main Street, 435-743-6876; and in Beaver at El Bambi Café, 935 North Main Street, 435-438-2229.

CAR RENTALS

Most travelers in need of rental cars will have already claimed their wheels in Salt Lake City. Nevertheless, several major auto-rental agencies have outposts in Provo. They include **Budget Rent A Car** (800-237-7251), **Hertz Rent A Car** (801-3434-4520, 800-654-3131), **National Car Rental** (801-373-2114, 800-227-7368) and **Payless Rent A Car** (801-374-9000, 800-729-5377).

Larger towns elsewhere in the region are represented by local rental agencies. Price, for instance, has **Lo Cost Rent A Car** at Mountain View Motors. ~ 1355 South Carbon Avenue; 435-637-0110. Another place is **Community Motors**. ~ 354 South Route 55; 435-637-1972, 800-944-0219. Or you can try **E Z Rent A Car**. ~ 396 South Carbon Avenue; 435-637-4200, 800-789-2271.

PUBLIC TRANSIT

The only community in this region with a public transportation system is its largest, Provo. The **Utah Transit Authority** has a dozen or so routes in metropolitan Provo, extending south to Payson and north to Lehi, with connections to Salt Lake City. Buses run from 6 a.m. to 7 p.m. Monday through Saturday. ~ 801-375-4636.

TAXIS

Only Utah's largest towns have taxi companies, and in this region of the state that means Price and Provo. In Price, call the **Carbon Cab Company**. ~ 435-637-8222. When you're in need of a ride in Provo, summon **Yellow Cab**. ~ 801-377-7070.

SIX

Southwestern Utah

 A child's jumbo-size crayon box couldn't contain all the pastels, reds, violets, greens and blues found in the unspoiled lands of southwestern Utah. What's most striking about this country is not only that it has managed to avoid the grasp of developers but also that it's been seemingly skipped by the hands of time. This region puts the letter "p" in pristine.

For starters, consider national parks like Zion, established in 1919, and Bryce, officially designated a park in 1928. Ever popular, these preserves draw hoards of visitors. Added to these treasures, not more than a few hours away, are national monuments like Cedar Breaks and Grand Staircase–Escalante, and state parks like Goblin Valley, Snow Canyon and Coral Pink Sand Dunes.

The area we call southwestern Utah is bordered roughly by the Henry Mountains to the east, Vermilion Cliffs and Beaver Dam Mountains to the south and the arid Great Basin to the west. A unique topographic variety is contained within these lands, as high mountain lakes and forests overlook the twisted rock found in Goblin Valley. Ever-evolving sculptured rock pinnacles in Bryce coexist adjacent to bristlecone pines, thought to be the oldest living things on earth.

Generally low humidity and rainfall in the lower elevations provide a favorable growing climate for the rare Joshua trees, sagebrush and yucca, while up high aspen and pine trees, oaks and juniper flourish.

Until recently, the powers in charge appeared to be in no hurry to sell this land. That is really no surprise. Despite being a primary connector, scenic Route 12 between Escalante and Torrey was paved only in the late 1980s. The rugged Henry Mountains were the last range in this country to be charted, and herds of buffalo still roam freely as do bighorn sheep, antelope and bear. The little town of Boulder, northeastern gateway to the Grand Staircase–Escalante National Monument, was the very last place in the 45th state to switch over to modern carriers after having its mail delivered by mule team for half a century.

Promotional efforts have begun to expand the possibilities for "Color Country," yet even the construction of skyscrapers couldn't detract from the rainbow-hued rocks, endless forests, lush gardens and those many, many waterways.

287

Southwestern Utah offers lakes and creeks like Panguitch, Gunlock and Quail brimming with fish not fishermen, hiking trails crying out for someone to traipse over them, ski areas with volumes of snow and biking areas that aren't akin to freeways. Ghost towns have probably stayed that way for a reason.

Working ranches have not yet disappeared, and some towns appear to have more horses than people. The area has managed to remain true to its Western heritage as rodeos are a popular diversion in the summertime. The rugged terrain is well suited to these sturdy equines. Probably the most famous quote about the area was made by 19th-century pioneer Ebenezer Bryce, who, upon seeing the peculiar landscape that today carries his name as a national park, remarked, "It's a hell of a place to lose a cow."

Among the landowners there's still a certain genuine country courtesy that can be traced to their Mormon traditions and culture rooted in a strong work ethic and family values. The accommodations and eateries reflect this same simplicity in which clean air and water, a good church community and schools are reason enough to celebrate life. But don't be concerned that everything here is rustic. In the resorts and larger cities such as St. George and Cedar City, there are plenty of comfortable places to stay as well as a range of decent places to eat.

Mind you, in the outlying areas, at times you're better off sleeping under the stars and using the local grocery for meals. But isn't there a certain beauty in this contrast?

Nor should you fear that this is a cultural wasteland. The Utah Shakespearean Festival, based in Cedar City, draws more than 150,000 theater-lovers to the region each summer. And the internationally acclaimed American Folk Ballet calls Cedar City home as well. Concerts, plays, dance companies and more are booked into large convention complexes and tiny high school auditoriums alike. Both Dixie State College in St. George and Cedar City's Southern Utah University are known for their academic excellence.

Still, it's the church that remains the heart of the area. Brigham Young, the Mormon prophet himself, sent 309 families to colonize this corner of Utah in the winter of 1861. While those settlers were less than enthralled by their move to a wilderness, Young envisioned sprawling communities. St. George and Cedar City today are the realization of his dream. And despite some of the misgivings of the settlers, structures such as the towering St. George Temple or more modest Mormon Tabernacle serve as testament to the hard-working and dedicated pioneers who tamed the land with their newfound-irrigation techniques and made the desert bloom.

American Indians once claimed title to this land, beginning with the Desert Gatherers, who were thought to inhabit southwestern Utah about the time of Jesus. These American Indians used gardening skills and built small settlements and crafted pottery. A later medieval culture, the Anasazi, were agriculturalists who built homes into the rock.

Historians believe the Indians of the desert evolved into the Fremont culture, which disappeared from the area during the 1200s. The modern-day Paiutes now live in small reservations, having relinquished their territory to early white settlers.

Lately, snowbirds and retirees have latched onto Utah's Dixie (so called because the area first served as a cotton mission for the Mormon Church, and the warm,

Text continued on page 292.

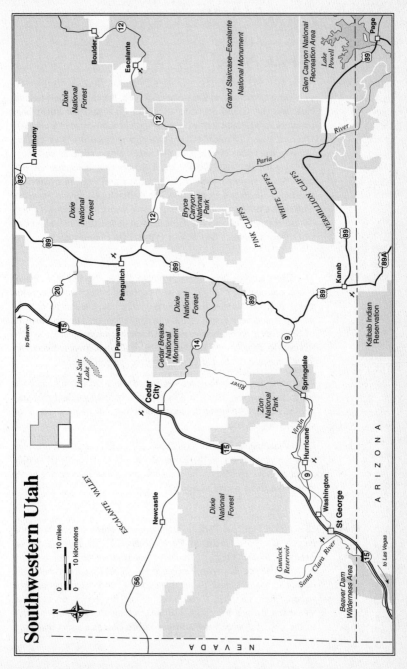

Southwestern Utah

0   10 miles

0   10 kilometers

N

NEVADA

ARIZONA

Boulder

Escalante

Antimony

Dixie National Forest

Grand Staircase–Escalante National Monument

Glen Canyon National Recreation Area

Page

Lake Powell

Paria

River

WHITE CLIFFS

VERMILLION CLIFFS

PINK CLIFFS

Bryce Canyon National Park

Panguitch

Dixie National Forest

Kanab

Kaibab Indian Reservation

Parowan

Little Salt Lake

to Beaver

Cedar Breaks National Monument

Dixie National Forest

Cedar City

Zion National Park

Springdale

Virgin River

Hurricane

Washington

St George

ESCALANTE VALLEY

Newcastle

Dixie National Forest

Gunlock Reservoir

Santa Clara River

Beaver Dam Wilderness Area

to Las Vegas

Three-day Weekend

A Red-rock Primer

The close proximity of Zion National Park, Bryce Canyon National Park and the Grand Staircase–Escalante National Monument begs travelers to visit all three in one swing, as each portrays a uniquely different aspect of southwestern Utah. Standing on the floor of Zion Canyon, the rocky ramparts of the state's oldest national park soar ever upward. At Bryce Canyon, most visitors peer *down* into the colorful bowls studded with rocky hoodoos and goblins masterfully created by erosion's many faces. The undeveloped Grand Staircase monument offers a more primitive look into the Southwest's high desert, revealing only to the most determined visitors its serpentine slot canyons, delicate arches, and 19th-century homesteads.

Day 1   The **Zion Lodge** (page 309), although not in the rich heritage of stately national park lodges, is a well-centered base of operations for a stay at **Zion National Park** (page 303). Board a shuttle outside the lodge and head north to the end of the canyon and the **Temple of Sinawava**, an impressive red-rock amphitheater. Stroll down the **Riverside Walk** and into the mouth of **Zion Canyon Narrows** for a glimpse into the park's most impressive slot canyon.

After returning from the narrows, board the shuttle and head back south to **Weeping Rock** and its beautiful hanging gardens that stay lush and colorful even at the height of summer. It's a great place for you to cool off, too.

From Weeping Rock return to Zion Lodge and cross the footbridge over the Virgin River to the **Emerald Pools** trailhead. It takes only about an hour to hike to the waterfalls and three shimmering pools that make this a parkie's favorite.

Day 2   Leave Zion National Park through the east entrance and head for **Bryce Canyon National Park** (page 323), 86 miles away via Routes 9, 89 and 12. If you haven't made advance reservations for a room in **Bryce Canyon Lodge** (page 329), which normally is a must, check at the desk to see if any cancellations have opened up a room. After securing a room, either in the lodge or at **Best Western Ruby's Inn** (page 328) just outside the park, drive south to the end of the road at **Rainbow Point**. There's a short trail here that winds through a small bristlecone grove, and from the lip of the overlook you can gaze into the Grand Staircase monument.

On your way back to the lodge, stop at **Sunset Point** for some beautiful pictures.

After dinner, take in the rodeo across from Ruby's Inn.

Day 3   Rise early and, after a hearty breakfast, take the park shuttle bus to **Bryce Point** (page 324). After admiring the view, hike a short way down the **Under the Rim Trail** to gain some perspective of the towering hoodoos and goblins.

After lunch, leave Bryce Canyon and head east on Route 12. At Cannonville, 13 miles from the park, veer south onto **Cottonwood Canyon Road** (page 327). Over the course of the next 46 miles you'll pass **Kodachrome Basin State Park**, **Grosvenor Arch**, **the Cockscomb** and **Cottonwood Narrows**, each worthy of at least a short stop.

At the end of Cottonwood Canyon Road, turn right (west) onto Route 89 and head toward Kanab. In almost 16 miles you'll come to a dirt road on your right that heads north to the **Old Paria** (page 308) movie set and the historic **Pahreah Town Site** (page 308). After a stop here, continue on to Kanab and a night at the **Parry Lodge** (page 310). The next morning you can either head south to the Grand Canyon, or work your way back north to Salt Lake City.

dry, almost subtropical climate reminds many of the South). Their varied backgrounds and interests have infused the region with new life and a desire to grow.

Local city leaders, realizing the region's natural beauty is its greatest resource, work to attract small industry to the area to create jobs that will keep the younger generation here as well. They even *boast* of the "golden arches" along main thoroughfares. Until the 1980s, few national franchises thought enough of southwestern Utah to try their luck. But in less than a decade, cities like St. George have doubled in size.

But no matter how much growth you find, it only takes a few moments to step back in history. The old courthouses located in Panguitch, Kanab and St. George reflect the best of pioneer architecture. Historic Hurricane Valley Pioneer Park captures the essence of the region's unique history, and hamlets such as Santa Clara, Pine Valley and Leeds are filled with pioneer homes and churches, arranged in traditional grid patterns with the church as the epicenter.

St. George Area

St. George (pop. 50,000) is not only a winter resort for snowbirds and retirees but also a key gateway to Zion National Park, Dixie National Forest and Snow Canyon State Park. The area is also a historical gold mine, full of restored homes, buildings from the 1800s and fascinating ghost towns.

The city began when, in 1861, Brigham Young sent some 300 families from the comparatively lush land of northern Utah to the southern Utah desert. Young envisioned a huge cotton mission that could supplement the West's supply during the Civil War, which had cut off shipments from the South.

Though initially successful, the cotton mission (and others to grow wine grapes and silkworms as well) ultimately failed because of an inability to compete in the marketplace after the Civil War. However, a warm climate and bevy of recreational activities eventually made St. George the fastest-growing city in the state.

SIGHTS

Any tour of the city should begin at the **St. George Chamber of Commerce**, located in the Old Washington County Courthouse. The brick-and-mortar building, completed in 1876, and originally used as a schoolroom and courtroom, today serves as a museum and information center. It contains panels of original glass alongside the entrance doors, original wall paintings of Zion and Grand canyons in the upper assembly room, an old security vault and much more. ~ 97 East St. George Boulevard, St. George; 435-628-1658, fax 435-673-1587; www.stgeorgechamber.com, e-mail hotspot@stgeorgechamber.com.

The courthouse serves as first stop on the **St. George Walking Tour**. The six-square-block trek points out 27 sights including some of the city's finest pioneer buildings. Pick up a map at the Chamber of Commerce.

The best way to see St. George, if you're visiting between June and Labor Day, is with a two-hour tour called **Historic St. George:**

Live. You'll travel by bus as a guide in 19th-century costume escorts you to old homes to meet actors impersonating such legendary former residents as Brigham Young. Tours begin at 9 a.m. and 10:30 a.m., Tuesday through Saturday. Fee. ~ Departs from the St. George Art Museum, 200 North Main Street, near the post office; 435-628-1658.

Next door to the courthouse is the **Daughters of Utah Pioneer Museum,** where you'll see a vast collection of community artifacts, including a dress made entirely of locally produced silk, as well as spinning wheels, quilts and Brigham Young's bed. ~ 145 North 100 East, St. George; 435-628-7274.

The **Pioneer Center for the Arts,** located next to the restored 1875 St. George Opera House, exhibits permanent and rotating collections of paintings, vintage photographs, local artworks, pottery and sculpture. Closed Sunday. ~ 47 East 200 North, St. George; 435-634-5942.

At the **Brigham Young Winter Home,** a guided tour showcases beautiful furnishings and memorabilia owned by the second president of the Mormon Church from 1869 until his death in 1877. Fruit, nut and mulberry trees (fodder for those silkworms) still cover the grounds. ~ 89 West 200 North, St. George; 435-673-2517, 435-673-5181 (temple visitors center).

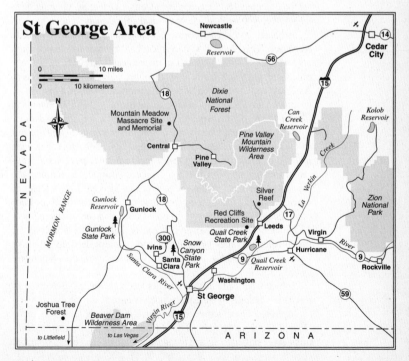

Stop 16 on the St. George walking tour is **Judd's Store**, a turn-of-the-20th-century mercantile with a working soda fountain that dishes up welcome treats on those hot Utah days. Closed Sunday. ~ 62 West Tabernacle Street, St. George; 435-628-2596.

It took 13 years to complete the **Mormon Tabernacle** in St. George. Tour guides show off the building with pride, telling how the limestone for three-foot-thick basement walls was hand quarried and the red sandstone blocks were hand cut stone by stone from a nearby site. Take special note of the intricate, plaster-of-Paris ceiling and cornice work. Glass for the windows was shipped to California by boat and then hauled by wagon team to St. George. ~ 18 South Main Street, St. George; 435-628-4072.

Pine Valley's picturesque, satin-white chapel, believed to be the oldest Mormon chapel, is still in continuous use.

Only card-carrying members of the Mormon Church may tread through the sparkling-white **St. George Temple**, built in 1877, but an on-site visitors center provides a pictorial history of the temple's construction and other background on the Church of Jesus Christ of Latter-day Saints. ~ 300 East 490 South, St. George; 435-673-5181.

Also in St. George is the **St. George Area Convention & Visitors Bureau**, which can provide information on the entire region. ~ Dixie Center, 1835 Convention Center Drive, St. George; 435-634-5747, 800-869-6635; www.utahsdixie.com.

Adjacent to the convention center is the **Rosenbruch Wildlife Museum**. This 25,000-square-foot facility features more than 200 wildlife species exhibited in their natural habitats. A quarter-mile-long pathway leads you through parts of Africa, North America and Asia. Two waterfalls plummet down a two-story mountain inside the museum. Admission. ~ 1835 Convention Center Drive, St. George; 435-656-0033; www.rosenbruch.org.

If you're a real history buff, you might want to venture out to **Old Fort Pierce**, east of St. George. The adobe fort was built in 1866 to protect settlers. Only a few remnants and partial walls remain at the site, but there is a nice monument explaining the history of the fort. While there, you can also explore a series of **dinosaur tracks** (three-toed impressions left in the mud millions of years ago). ~ Getting to Old Fort Pierce and the tracks requires a high-clearance vehicle and dry roads. Follow 700 South to the east until it becomes River Road and take another left on Stake Farm Road (1450 South) through Washington Fields. Then follow the signs.

Johnson Farm Dinosaur Tracks has a sprawling collection of tracks left behind by at least two meat-eaters, dilophosaurus and ceolophysis. These surfaced early in 2000 while land was being cleared for development. The tracks, imbedded in a three-foot-thick layer of bedrock, are thought to date to the Jurassic Period.

Closed Sunday. ~ 2000 East Riverside Drive, St. George; 435-674-5757; www.dinotrax.com.

Elsewhere, a short (200-yard) walk takes adventurous souls to more **dinosaur tracks**. Drive to the heart of **Washington**, a few miles east of St. George, and turn north on Main until you pass under Route 15. Follow the dirt road north and turn right at the road that goes up the hill to the pink water tank. Park here, then walk up the road to a chained cable gate. Turn right and walk northeast to a deep wash. Go down into the wash and follow it downstream until you find a flat, greenish slab of rock. Here you'll find the foot-long tracks from another age.

◄ HIDDEN

Three miles west of St. George sits the rural community of **Santa Clara**. Settled by Swiss immigrants, Santa Clara lays claim to the house built by noted missionary, Indian agent and colonizer Jacob Hamblin. Built in 1862, the rough-hewn, red sandstone **Jacob Hamblin Home** clearly demonstrates the sturdiness of frontier construction designed to withstand Indian attack and showcases a number of furnishings and tools from that period including old no-springs beds, Indian rugs and a wagon. ~ Route 91, Santa Clara; 435-673-2161.

Heading north from St. George on Route 18, you'll approach **Snow Canyon State Park**. A small park, the canyon itself is a white-and-red mix of Navajo sandstone covered with black lava beds. Elevations range from 3100 to 4875 feet atop the volcanic cinder cones. Grasses, willows, cacti and other shrubbery peer through cracks. Evidence of early man's impressions of Snow Canyon can be seen at a petroglyph site within the park. Admission. ~ Snow Canyon Road, off Route 18; 435-628-2255; parks.state.ut.us/parks/www1.snow.htm.

Twenty-five miles north of St. George on Route 18 is the town of Central and the turnoff to the mountain hamlet of **Pine Valley**. Along the way are numerous extinct volcanic cones and lava fields, many beckoning to be explored. Nestled in the Dixie National Forest, surrounded by 10,000-foot peaks and ponderosa pine, is the Pine Valley Mountain Wilderness Area and reservoir with numerous picnicking areas. ~ Forest Road 035.

Make the five-mile drive to Pine Valley and you'll find the **Pine Valley Chapel**, which holds the distinction of being the oldest LDS chapel still in use. Built in 1868 by Ebenezer Bryce, the chapel looks somewhat like an overturned ship. Inside you'll find a winding staircase that leads to the attic, where you can marvel at the open-beam construction. Closed Labor Day to Memorial Day.

Just north of the Pine Valley turnoff is a stone marker and memorial for the **Mountain Meadow Massacre Site and Memorial**. Here, in 1857, a group of emigrants—120 men, women and children—en route to California was slaughtered by Mormons and Indians. The event is considered a dark period in Mormon history and one the church has tried to live down ever since. ~ Route 18.

LODGING

Located midway between Salt Lake City and Los Angeles, St. George is awash in hotels, motels and bed and breakfasts. Virtually every major chain is represented, making it simple to find one that meets your requirements and pocketbook.

HIDDEN ▶

No one walks away unsatisfied from the **Seven Wives Inn**, perhaps one of the nicest accommodations in St. George. Deluxe in every way except price, the 13-room bed and breakfast is graciously decorated in Victorian antiques. Some rooms boast fireplaces, woodburning stoves, or jacuzzi tubs, and most have outside doors to porches or balconies. All have private baths. Rates include a huge gourmet breakfast in the elegant dining room and use of the swimming pool. ~ 217 North 100 West, St. George; 435-628-3737, 800-600-3737, fax 435-628-5646; www.seven wivesinn.com. MODERATE TO DELUXE.

There's a lot of bang for the buck at **Ranch Inn**. More than half the 52 units are classified "kitchenette suites," meaning they house a microwave oven, refrigerator, conversation-and-dining area, plus fully tiled bath with mirrored vanity. An indoor jacuzzi, guest laundry and heated pool round out the amenities. Continental breakfast is included. ~ 1040 South Main Street, St. George; 435-628-8000, 800-332-0400, fax 435-656-3983; www.ranch inn.net. BUDGET.

Holiday Inn Resort Hotel likes to think of itself as a complete recreational facility. Besides the 164 well-appointed rooms, restaurant and atrium-style lobby (with mini-waterfall), guests are treated to a large indoor/outdoor heated swimming pool (you can actually swim in and out of the hotel), whirlpool, tennis court, putting green, mini-gym, gameroom, video arcade, gift shop and children's play area. ~ 850 South Bluff Street, St. George; 435-628-4235, 800-457-9800, fax 435-628-8157; www.holidayinnstgeorge.com. MODERATE.

The Bluffs Inn & Suites has 61 accommodations (24 of them apartments with full kitchens), exceptionally well decorated in soft tones with large bathrooms and a living-room area. There's also an outdoor heated pool and jacuzzi. Complimentary continental breakfast is offered in the sunny lobby. ~ 1140 South Bluff Street, St. George; 435-628-6699, 800-832-5933, fax 435-673-8705; www.bluffsmotel.com. BUDGET.

A collection of nine restored pioneer homes makes up **Greene Gate Village**, a unique bed-and-breakfast complex designed to intrigue and delight. Surrounded by a flower-laden courtyard, manicured lawns, swimming pool and garden hot tub, the village has elegant decor—wallpapered rooms, duvets, antique furnishings, plump pillows—and a conscientious staff. Six rooms have large whirlpool tubs. A delicious country breakfast completes the picture. ~ 76 West Tabernacle Street, St. George; 435-628-6999, 800-350-6999, fax 435-628-6989; www.greenegatevillage.com. MODERATE TO DELUXE.

Situated off the main drag, **Ramada Inn** offers quiet refuge. An expansive lobby provides portal to 136 rooms, each with desk and upholstered chairs. The hotel also has one of the prettiest swimming-pool settings with palm trees surrounding the site. Free continental breakfast is included. ~ 1440 East St. George Boulevard, St. George; 435-628-2828, 800-228-2828, fax 435-628-0505; www.ramadainn.net. MODERATE TO DELUXE.

Due to the number of settlers originally from the South, St. George was—and still is—known as Utah's "Dixie."

The streamlined architecture of **Best Western Coral Hills Motel** is reminiscent of *The Jetsons*, but the 98 rooms are more down-to-earth with carpeting, upholstered chairs and dark woods. Indoor and outdoor swimming pools, a children's wading pool, spas, putting green and exercise room are bonuses. A continental breakfast is included. ~ 125 East St. George Boulevard, St. George; 435-673-4844, 800-542-7733, fax 435-673-5352; www.coralhills.com. MODERATE.

St. George has no lack of choices when it comes to places to eat. Besides the requisite chains (and none, it seems, are missing), there are plenty more eateries that offer a hearty meal at a reasonable cost.

DINING

J. J. Hunan Chinese Restaurant appears to be the area's choice for Asian cuisine, serving more than one style of Chinese fare. Seafood, chicken, beef, duck, pork—it's all here, presented in a gracious manner and in a fairly intimate setting. Upstairs, the **Painted Pony** serves delicious Southwest fare. Closed Sunday. ~ 2 West St. George Boulevard, St. George; J.J. Hunan 435-628-7219, Painted Pony 435-634-1700. BUDGET TO MODERATE.

Breakfast and lunch are the specialties at the **Bear Paw Coffee Company**. ~ 75 North Main Street, St. George; 435-634-0126. BUDGET.

Fajitas are tops at **Pancho & Lefty's**, a busy, fun Mexican restaurant with colorful wall murals. The menu also features tostadas, burritos and tacos. ~ 1050 South Bluff Street, St. George; 435-628-4772. BUDGET TO MODERATE.

Service is erratic, but **The Palms Restaurant** can be a good option for family dining in a pleasant setting. Besides an extensive salad bar with homemade soups and breads, dinner fare range from roast turkey to shrimp scampi to chicken teriyaki. Sandwiches, hamburgers and salads comprise the lunch menu, while breakfast includes omelettes and griddle items. The Palms also offers Sunday brunches. ~ Holiday Inn, 850 South Bluff Street, St. George; 435-628-4235. MODERATE TO DELUXE.

Text continued on page 300.

Ghost Towns of Color Country

While much of Utah's history is neatly preserved in museums and restored homes, a more fascinating (and sometimes poignant) look can be found in the ruins eroded by time, nature and man. One of the most popular and representative ghost towns of southwestern Utah is **Silver Reef**, which took its name from a sandstone formation that resembles an ocean reef, 18 miles north of St. George and only three miles off the freeway.

"Silver!" was the cry that brought more than 1000 fortune-hunters to Silver Reef more than a century ago. According to newspaper accounts, Silver Reef was the only spot in the Utah States where silver was discovered in sandstone. John Kemple is credited with the 1866 find, and the town boomed into a notorious camp of 1500 non-Mormon miners. Citizens of nearby Mormon communities were warned not to mix with the rowdy populace rumored to participate in brawls, shootings and lynchings. With 29 mines scattered over two square miles, Silver Reef proved bountiful, yielding $9 million in silver from 1877 to 1903.

Today, separate cemeteries for Protestants and Catholics remain, along with abandoned mine sites. Area historians are slowly working to restore community. Fittingly, the **Wells Fargo & Co. Express Building**, constructed in 1877 of sandstone blocks and metal doors, survived the ravages of time. It now houses the **Silver Reef Museum**. Authentic mining tools, maps, clothing and other historical paraphernalia fill shelves and glass cases. Old newspapers recount Silver Reef's heyday, and town plats show how vast the boomtown spread. Visitors can even walk into the original Wells Fargo bank vault.

Half the Wells Fargo building is used by Western bronze sculptor Jerry Anderson as a **studio and gallery**. Both his work and that of other prominent local artists are displayed and sold, along with a good assortment of books recounting Utah's ghost towns. Closed Sunday. ~ 2002 Wells Fargo Drive; 435-879-2254.

Nearby is a small structure that once served as the Powder House. Today, the building houses the **Silver Reef information center** with models of the original township and more original plats.

It only takes a few minutes to drive around and look at the nearby store ruins scattered among a new neighborhood development. At the site of the **Barbee and Walker Mill** all that remains are rock walls. The same is true of the drugstore and the Chinese laundry.

In the virtual ghost town of Silver Reef, there's a surprisingly popular restaurant. **The Cosmopolitan Steakhouse** serves beef, chicken and seafood Thursday through Saturday nights. Groups of ten or more can arrange dinner Monday through Wednesday. ~ 1915 Wells Fargo Drive, Silver Reef; 435-879-2978. MODERATE TO DELUXE.

While most Utah ghost towns lie in a stark desert environment, **Grafton** is an exception. Amid vast fields, mulberry trees and rambling cattle, the abandoned settlement sits beside the Virgin River near the red-rock cliffs of Zion National Park. Today work is under way by the Grafton Heritage Partnership Project to preserve the few historic log and adobe buildings that remain from the settlement that got its start in the 1850s as part of the region's "Cotton Mission."

Five Mormon families settled Grafton in 1859, naming the town after a Massachusetts community. Assisted by then-friendly Paiute Indians, the families dammed the Virgin River for irrigation, hoping to plant cotton. In 1861, a flood ravaged the entire area and swept away homes, barns and fields. Survivors moved their settlement to higher and safer ground, digging a system of canals and ditches. Besides cotton, they planted corn, wheat and tobacco. By 1865, 200 acres were cultivated.

Later, Indian attacks disrupted community life. Settlers were killed in alarming numbers, and Grafton residents were forced to work the fields in armed bands. Occasionally, the entire town was evacuated. After the Indian threat eased in the 1870s, the settlers obtained Brigham Young's permission to plant mulberry trees and grow silkworms.

Grafton headed toward ghost town status after 1907, as persistent problems became too much for the settlers to face. But the quaint village charmed Hollywood, and since 1950 many films, including scenes from *Butch Cassidy and the Sundance Kid*, have been filmed here. Several of the buildings still stand, including a few woodframe homes and the one-room, brick schoolhouse with small belltower. All are open for exploring.

To get to Silver Reef, go northeast from St. George on Route 15 for 18 miles to the Leeds exit. Head east one mile through town to a sign marked "Silver Reef." Turn north under the freeway and drive about two miles.

For Grafton, take Route 9 (the road to Zion National Park) to the town of Rockville. Turn south on Bridge Lane, which crosses the Virgin River. After crossing the bridge, head west and backtrack along a rutted, dirt-and-gravel road for several miles. Note that in some sections you are crossing or bordering private land so don't abuse the privilege.

SHOPPING   Shopping in this region is evolving as local retailers become more conscious of tourists' buying power. Malls, however, remain the primary outlet for shoppers.

Your best resource for guidebooks and maps on southwestern Utah and its national parks, state parks and national monuments is the **Interagency Information Center**, run by the U.S. Bureau of Land Management. Closed Sunday. ~ 345 East Riverside Drive, St. George; 435-688-3200 or 435-688-3246.

Ancestor Square, located in the St. George Historic District, offers art galleries and other shops. ~ Main Street and St. George Boulevard, St. George.

One place of note in Washington is the **Artist Gallery**, which carries works by more than a dozen regional artists. Closed Sunday. ~ 95 East Telegraph Street, Washington; 435-628-9293.

In Ivins, a short drive northwest of St. George, is **Xetava Gardens**, a Southwestern-style New Age bookstore/café with a 16-ton sandstone boulder that sits like a massive paperweight in the middle of the store. ~ 815 Coyote Gulch Court, Ivins; 435-656-0165.

NIGHTLIFE   As renown grows for St. George's wonderful year-round climate, it draws more and more crowds. Standing ready to entertain those crowds when the sun goes down is a surprisingly impressive clutch of cultural attractions.

World-class entertainers are spotlighted through the **Celebrity Concert Series** at Dixie State College, which opened in 1911 as St. George State Academy and was supported in part by the LDS church until 1933, when it became a state-run institution. ~ Dixie State College, Avenna Center, 225 South 700 East, St. George; 435-652-7800.

The **Southwest Symphony**, a community orchestra, and the **Southwest Symphonic Chorale** perform throughout the year in the M. C. Cox Auditorium. ~ Dixie State College, Avenna Center, 225 South 700 East, St. George; 435-652-7800.

Dixie State College Theater offers plays and musicals during the school year. ~ 225 South 700 East, St. George; 435-652-7800.

Musicals are the forte of the **St. George Musical Theater**. ~ 212 North Main Street, St. George; 435-634-5942; www.sgmt.org.

The **Blarney Stone** is a beer bar serving a lively crowd. There's karaoke on Wednesday. ~ 64 North 800 East, St. George; 435-673-9191.

Tuacahn Amphitheater for the Performing Arts, an open-air theater set amid the burning red-rock just ten minutes northwest of St. George, presents a series of plays throughout the summer and a Christmas festival in the winter. *Annie Get Your Gun* and *Joseph and the Amazing Technicolor Dreamcoat* were the feature shows for the summer of 2002. ~ 1100 Tuacahn Drive, Ivins; 435-652-3201, 800-746-9882; www.tuacahn.org.

SNOW CANYON STATE PARK 🏃 🚴 🐎 Black lava rock crusted over red Navajo sandstone make for a striking visual effect in this colorful canyon. Several volcanic cones welcome visitors to the northern end of the 5738-acre park, considered a treat for photographers. The park features a covered group-use pavilion, picnic areas, restrooms and hot showers. Day-use fee, $5. ~ Off Route 18: take Snow Canyon Parkway six miles and make a right on Snow Canyon Road. Snow Canyon Road leads directly into the park; 435-628-2255; parks.state.ut.us/parks/www1/snow.htm.

▲ There are 35 sites (including 14 with partial hookups); $14 to $17 per night; reservations recommended in spring and fall. There's a sewage disposal station. Reservations: 800-322-3770.

GUNLOCK STATE PARK 🚶 🛶 🚤 Fifteen miles northwest of St. George, the heart of this state park is a 240-acre reservoir that lies in the rugged ravine of the Santa Clara River. Surrounding the shimmering waters are red-rock hills dotted with green shrubbery. Superb year-round boating, waterskiing and bass fishing abound. There are toilets. ~ Old Route 91, 16 miles northwest of St. George; 435-628-2255; parks.state.ut.us/parks/www1/gunl.htm.

▲ Primitive camping allowed within the park; $8 per night. Note: Bring your own drinking water.

QUAIL CREEK STATE PARK 🚶 🚣 🛶 🚤 Stark rock escarpments surround a 600-acre reservoir with a state park set on its west shore. Quail Creek attracts anglers eager to reel in bass, trout, crappie and bluegill. Besides being an ideal site for camping and picnicking, Quail Creek Reservoir is noted for its waterskiing, boating and windsurfing. There are picnic areas and

PARKS

❖❖❖

ON THE BORDER

Heading south on Route 91 over the summit to the Beaver Dam Slope, you'll be driving toward the Arizona border. Along the way you'll pass the 1040-acre, desert-like **Joshua Tree Natural Area**, claimed to be the farthest north these picturesque trees grow. Route 91 connects with Route 15 at Beaver Dam, Arizona. Head north back toward St. George and drive through the **Virgin River Gorge**, a giant gash in the rocky earth where the Virgin River heads out of Utah through Arizona and into Nevada. It took 12 years to build this 23-mile stretch of spectacular highway.

restrooms. Day-use fee, $6. ~ Just off Route 9, 14 miles north of St. George; 435-879-2378; parks.state.ut.us/parks/www1/quai.htm.

▲ There are 23 sites; $11 per night.

RED CLIFFS RECREATION SITE 🚶🚴 Maintained by the Bureau of Land Management, this camping area is a red-rock paradise at the foot of the Pine Valley Mountains. Desert trees and plants crowd every campsite. Facilities include picnic tables, pit toilets and drinking water. Day-use fee, $2. ~ From St. George go north on Route 15 about 17 miles to the Leeds exit. From there, drive south two and one half miles and west two miles; 435-688-3200; www.ut.blm.gov/st_george/play.html.

▲ There are ten sites; $6 per night.

RED CLIFFS DESERT RESERVE 🚶🚴🐎 This 61,000-acre preserve just north of St. George is devoted to the desert tortoise, but there's lots of room for humans to play, too. In fact, there are 130 miles of trail open to hikers, equestrians, and mountain bikers. ~ The reserve borders St. George's city limits. Route 18 heading north of St. George runs right through the preserve; 435-688-3200.

Zion Area

If you've got rocks in your head, you've come to the right place. This is not to question your sanity but rather to underline the spectacular rock formations found here. From canyon walls to monuments to cliffs, the Zion area has it all. Coupled with this are some neat historic buildings and movie-set towns that have been featured in hundreds of films.

SIGHTS Halfway between St. George and Zion National Park on Route 9 lies the town of **Hurricane** (pronounced hur-i-kun), a rural community that often attracts the overflow from Zion into its motels and restaurants. In the center of town lies **Hurricane Valley Heritage Park**. The museum and information center stands amid a grassy lawn filled with pioneer-era wagons and farm machinery. The museum depicts the history of the town and displays pioneer items including an authentic kitchen. ~ 35 West State Street, Hurricane; 435-635-3245.

Nearby, the historic Bradshaw Hotel is now the **Heritage House Museum**, whose collection includes a pioneer schoolhouse and doctor's office and a fine doll exhibit. ~ 95 South Main Street, Hurricane; 435-635-3402; www.ci.hurricane.ut.us.

A relaxing break from the rigors of the road may be found at **Pah Tempe Mineral Hot Springs**, a large grouping of five soaking- and swimming-pool areas. Rustic but congenial, Pah Tempe resembles a '60s commune with a tiny bed and breakfast, lodge and campsites. Bathing suits are required. Massage therapy programs, facial packs and other services can be arranged. Admission. Note: A conflict with the local water district has diverted Pah Tempe's water flows; the hot springs are closed until that is resolved. ~ 825 North 800 East, Hurricane; 435-635-2879.

ZION NATIONAL PARK Carved almost singlehandedly by the Virgin River for over 13 millions years, **Zion National Park**, grandfather of Utah's national parks, is a breathtaking, 147,551-acre natural gallery of vividly colored cliffs, sheer-rock walls, massive stone monoliths and unique formations. Cottonwoods, willows and velvet ash trees line the river, which flows along the canyon floor, providing an ever-changing kaleidoscope of colors as one season follows another. Skittering, flitting and ambling throughout the park are mountain lions, mule deer and more than 250 species of birds, including golden eagles and rarer peregrine falcons and Mexican spotted owls.

Featuring towering cliffs, narrow slot canyons, and a wide variety of hiking trails geared to all abilities, this "heavenly city of God" is a park for all people—and lots of them. To really avoid the crowds and traffic, gear your visit to November through April, although this season can see a lot of snow in the park's upper reaches. Cars have been prohibited in Zion Canyon from March through October because of the world-class traffic jams. Only those with reservations at Zion Lodge are allowed to drive up the canyon; others must take a free, continuously running shuttle system that conveniently and quickly hauls visitors back and forth between the town of Springdale and nine stops along Zion

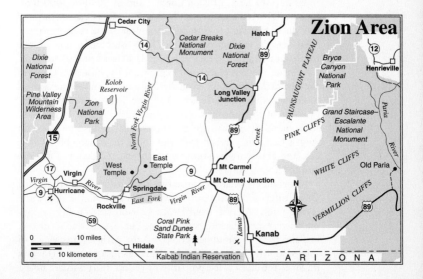

Canyon Scenic Drive. Outside of the canyon floor, the rest of the park is open to vehicle traffic.

Depending on time and specific interest, you can take the shuttle, bicycle or walk through Zion Canyon. But don't miss out on the fabulous sights that await just off the roads. Zion is best appreciated close-up, and you'll miss the true majesty of the park if you don't wander around and stare up, or down, at this awesome geology.

Be sure to stop at the **Visitor Center** (435-772-7616), where park rangers are happy to provide maps, brochures and backcountry permits. Specific dates and times for naturalist guided walks, evening programs and patio talks are posted at the center. You'll also find a wealth of maps, books and trail guides in the center. Admission. ~ Main entrance: Route 9, Springdale; 435-772-3256; www.nps.gov/zion.

Youngsters ages six through twelve can get down and dirty with nature at the **Zion Nature Center** through the Junior Ranger Program. From June through Labor Day, park rangers and the Zion Natural History Association conduct a variety of outdoor-adventure and environmental-science programs that acquaint the younger set with everything from the flight pattern of a golden eagle to the difference between a Utah beavertail cactus and a maidenhair fern.

Among the first things you'll encounter is **The Watchman**, a 2555-foot monolith of sandstone and shale that stands guard over the park entrance.

Zion Canyon Scenic Drive takes visitors about six and a half miles into the heart of Zion Canyon and its 2000-to-3000-foot-high walls carved inch-by-inch by the Virgin River cutting through the Markagunt Plateau. Just past the entrance you're likely to spot **West Temple**, the highest peak in Zion's southern section. Notice the delineated strata of rock as it rises 4100 feet from base to peak.

One of the first places you might want to pause at is **Court of the Patriarchs** viewpoint. From here you can see reverently named monuments like the Streaked Wall, the Sentinel, the Patriarchs (a series of three peaks called Abraham, Isaac and Jacob), Mt. Moroni, the Spearhead and the sheer-walled sandstone monolith Angels Landing, perched 1500 feet above the canyon bed. To the east and above are two other monuments, Mountain of the Sun and the Twin Brothers.

Emerald Pools parking area, two and a half miles up the Scenic Drive, offers access to a trail network serving both the Upper and Lower pools. A creek from Heaps Canyon sends water cascading down waterfalls into pools below. Yucca, cacti and scrub oak line the trail to the upper pool, and the path affords views of shaded, north-facing slopes rich with ponderosa pine and Douglas fir. Since the creek is fed primarily by runoff, the pools are fullest

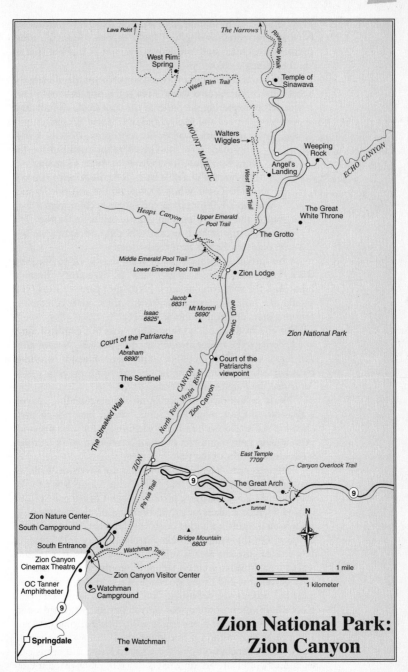

Lava Point

The Narrows

Riverside Walk

West Rim Spring

Temple of Sinawava

West Rim Trail

MOUNT MAJESTIC

Walters Wiggles

Weeping Rock

ECHO CANYON

Angel's Landing

West Rim Trail

Heaps Canyon

Upper Emerald Pool Trail

The Great White Throne

The Grotto

Middle Emerald Pool Trail

Lower Emerald Pool Trail

Zion Lodge

Jacob 6831'

Mt Moroni 5690'

Isaac 6825'

Scenic Drive

Zion National Park

Court of the Patriarchs

Abraham 6890'

CANYON

North Fork Virgin River

Zion Canyon

Court of the Patriarchs viewpoint

The Sentinel

The Streaked Wall

ZION

East Temple 7709'

Canyon Overlook Trail

9

The Great Arch

9

Pa rus Trail

tunnel

N

Zion Nature Center

South Campground

South Entrance

Zion Canyon Cinemax Theatre

Bridge Mountain 6803'

0   1 mile

0   1 kilometer

OC Tanner Amphitheater

Watchman Trail

Zion Canyon Visitor Center

Watchman Campground

9

Springdale

The Watchman

Zion National Park:
Zion Canyon

in spring and early summer, and dwindle as summer wears on, barring a torrential downpour. If you happen to visit Zion between mid-October and late November, this is a prime spot to see the changing colors.

A little over a half mile away to the northeast, paralleling the Scenic Drive, **The Grotto Picnic Area** is the perfect spot to take a break from exploring the park. In the cool shade of broadleaf trees and gambel oak you'll find fire grates, picnic tables, water and restrooms. Directly across the road from the Grotto is the trailhead for the West Rim Trail, which leads to Angel's Landing.

A quarter of a mile later along the same road you'll spot **The Great White Throne** on the east side. Notice how this 2400-foot monolith ranges in color from a deep red at the base to pink to gray to white at the top. The color variations arise because the Navajo sandstone has less iron oxide at the top than the bottom.

A bit farther is a short, paved walk that leads to **Weeping Rock**, where continuous springs "weep" across a grotto. Even on a hot day, the spot remains cool. Like other parts of Zion, you should see lush, hanging cliff gardens thick with columbine, shooting-stars and scarlet monkeyflower.

The end of the road, so to speak, comes at **Temple of Sinawava**, perhaps the easiest area in the park to access. Named after the Paiute wolf spirit, the huge natural amphitheater is formed by sheer, red cliffs that soar to the sky and two stone pillars—the Altar and the Pulpit—in the center.

Take a minute here to gaze up at the surrounding canyon walls and you just might spy some human flies testing their climbing skills. Zion's cliffs are world-famous for their demanding climbing routes, and you can spot climbers at work on these walls most months of the year.

Beginning near Temple of Sinawava is the **Riverside Walk**, an easy, mile-long paved path that follows the Virgin River to the mouth of the Zion Narrows, providing views of the massive slot canyon. Hardcore hikers tackle the 16-mile route through the Narrows from the north, entering on private land outside of the park. *Caution*: Off the path, the rocks may be slippery with algae; in July and August, the area is subject to flash floods. If a 16-mile walk through water seems a bit much, continue north into the river beyond the end of the Riverside Walk. In late summer and early fall, water levels are usually low enough to allow you to explore a half-mile or more up the canyon beyond the paved walk; you'll occasionally find waterfalls with their hanging gardens, and a place or two for a picnic lunch.

Route 9 branches off of Zion Canyon Drive and heads east from Zion National Park on what is called the **Zion–Mount Car-**

Pay close attention and you might spot the tiny Zion snail, a creature found in Zion National Park and nowhere else.

mel Highway. Considered an engineering marvel of its day (1930), the 13-mile road snakes up high precipices and around sharp, narrow turns before reaching the high, arid plateaus of the east. And, if you've ever ridden Disneyland's Matterhorn, you'll love the mile-long, narrow, unlit **tunnel**. Rangers control traffic through the darkened tube, stopping drivers when an oversized truck or recreational vehicle is passing through. Even with delays, the tunnel is a treat—huge, window-like openings allow sunlight to stream in every so often, affording unparalleled views of the vermilion cliffsides.

On the east side of the tunnel lies the park's "slickrock" territory. It's almost like a time warp from one country to another.

Canyon Overlook is a moderately easy, half-mile self-guided walk on the Zion–Mount Carmel Highway just east of the long tunnel. Unlike the lush Zion Canyon floor, this area showcases plants and animals that make rock and sand their home. The overlook itself provides views of lower Zion Canyon, including the Streaked Wall with its long, black marks sharply contrasting with the red canyon walls; West and East Temples, giant stone monoliths with temple-like edifices perched on top; and the massive, multicolored cliff called Towers of the Virgin.

Don't miss **Checkerboard Mesa**, a prime example of sandstone etched over time with horizontal lines and vertical fractures to resemble a mountainous playing board. ~ Stay on Route 9 out of Zion National Park to connect with Route 89 and head south toward the Arizona border.

EAST OF ZION   Thirteen miles east of Zion National Park in the tiny town of Mount Carmel lies the **Maynard Dixon Home**, a   ◀ HIDDEN log cabin and nearby studio where Dixon, an early to mid-1900s Western landscape painter who enjoyed national acclaim for his sweeping vistas and American Indian profiles, spent his summers. Walk the hillside trails behind the home and you're likely to pass the spot where Dixon's ashes were spread. Tours by appointment. Admission. ~ Mount Carmel; 435-648-2653, 800-992-1066; www.maynarddixon.com.

All that's missing is the surf at **Coral Pink Sand Dunes State Park**, but those who prefer sand to water will revel in the inviting dunes. This is Mother Nature's sandbox just aching to be frolicked in by young and old alike. Some of the dunes reach 100 feet in height. A resident park ranger is on hand to answer questions about this unusual area, and there are a few interpretive signs as well. A boardwalk trail leads to a vista point of the main dunes. Admission. ~ Sand Dunes Road, 12 miles south of Route 89 between Mt. Carmel Junction and Kanab; 435-648-2800.

Continuing on Route 89, you'll pass what looks like an Anasazi cliff dwelling. That's **Moqui Cave**, which claims the largest collection of dinosaur tracks in the Kanab area. Other displays include Indian artifacts, foreign money and fluorescent minerals. Closed Sunday. Admission. ~ Route 89, five miles north of Kanab; 435-644-8525; www.moquicave.com.

Farther south, Route 89 heads toward the base of the colorful Vermillion Cliffs and **Kanab**, the gateway to the Grand Staircase–Escalante National Monument and a town known as "Little Hollywood" for the more than 200 movies, most of them B-grade Westerns, filmed in the area in the mid-1900s. Today, Kanab is a crossroads for travelers headed to Lake Powell, the Grand Canyon or Bryce and has numerous motels and restaurants.

Some movie-set towns are still evident throughout the area. Because most sit on private property, check with the **Kane County Travel Information Center** to see which are open to the public. ~ 78 South 100 East, Kanab; 435-644-5033; www.kaneutah.com.

In Kanab, a bit like the Universal Studios tour is **Frontier Movie Town**, a replica of a Wild West movie set that caters to groups but lets individuals tag along. Here, marshals in white hats battle black-hatted villains during mock gunfights. You can walk along the boardwalk and peer into the false storefronts. Shops, a snack bar and historic exhibits are also on-site. ~ 297 West Center Street, Kanab; 435-644-5337, 800-551-1714.

Heritage House, located at 100 South Main, is an 1893 restored pioneer mansion built of brick and red rock and one of seven homes making up the Kanab walking tour. You can find brochures at the house or at Kane County Travel Information Center. ~ 100 South Main Street, Kanab; 435-644-2843.

Thirty miles east along Route 89 takes you to the **Old Paria** turnoff. Here, fans will find the West of their imaginations come alive on a falsefront movie-set town that's open to the public and was once used for the *Gunsmoke* television series. Films made here include Clint Eastwood's epic Western, *The Outlaw Josie Wales, Sergeants Three, The Outriders* and *Bandelero*. Nearby on the east side of the Paria River are the remains of the old **Pahreah Town Site**, established by a Mormon mission in 1870. The town began to vanish in the mid-1880s due to a series of floods that

GIVEN SHELTER

Homeless, abandoned and abused pets throughout the country find a welcome home at the **Best Friends Animal Sanctuary**, where 1800 or more animals live on the grounds on any given day. Here they are sheltered and cared for before they are passed on to adoptive families. Stop for a tour and you'll be introduced to Horse Pastures, TLC Cat Club, Dogtown, Bunny House and Feathered Friends. ~ 5001 Angel Canyon Road, Kanab; 435-644-2001; www.bestfriends.org.

swept through it, though in 1911 prospectors came looking for gold. By the mid-1930s, it was entirely deserted.

Massive vermilion cliffs surround **Zion Lodge**, set in the heart of the park. A huge lawn and shade trees welcome guests to the property, which is actually a replica of the original property. That Zion Lodge burned down in 1966 and was quickly (within 100 days) replaced by the current facility, which includes motel-style rooms, suites and cabins. While standard furnishings are the norm, location is everything. Cabins afford more privacy and feature fireplaces and private porches. A dining room, snack bar and gift shop are on-site. ~ Zion National Park; 435-772-3213; reservations 303-297-2757, fax 435-772-2001; www.zionlodge. com. MODERATE TO DELUXE.

LODGING

Cliffrose Lodge and Gardens has clean, comfortable rooms as well as five acres of lawn, gardens and shade trees along the Virgin River. A pool and jacuzzi amid the gardens create an oasis in this dry desert landscape. ~ 281 Zion Park Boulevard, Springdale; 435-772-3234, 800-243-8824; www.cliffrose-lodge.com. DELUXE.

Rooms at **Flanigan's Inn** range from okay to very nice indeed. Those on a budget might opt for the smaller, somewhat plain rooms. If you place a value on spaciousness, splurge on the larger, suitelike spaces done in oak furnishings with tile baths, bent-willow wall hangings and ceiling fans. Regardless of your room, guests can partake of the swimming pool and continental breakfast. ~ 428 Zion Park Boulevard, Springdale; 435-772-3244, 800-765-7787, fax 435-772-3396; www.flanigans.com. MODERATE TO ULTRA-DELUXE.

American and English antiques fill **Under the Eaves**. Constructed of sandstone blocks from nearby canyon walls, the 1929 home resembles a cheery English cottage. Three rooms have private baths, another two share. There's also a large suite upstairs with vaulted ceilings, a wood-burning stove, and a sitting room. Full breakfast is served each morning. ~ 980 Zion Park Boulevard, Springdale; 435-772-3457; www.under-the-eaves.com. MODERATE TO DELUXE.

Located in a quiet neighborhood, **Harvest House Bed & Breakfast** is sure to please even the most demanding. All four rooms are exquisitely decorated; all have private baths. Expect bright, airy spaces full of wicker furniture and plush carpeting; balconies offer an unparalleled view of Zion National Park. Beverages are available anytime from the dining room wet bar, and there's an extensive library of art and cookbooks. Stargazing from the backyard hot tub is a great way to end the day. A gourmet breakfast is included. ~ 29 Canyon View Drive, Springdale; 435-772-3880, fax 435-772-3327; www.harvesthouse.net, e-mail harvesthouse_utah@yahoo.com. MODERATE.

◄ HIDDEN

If you can't fall asleep without reading a good book, stay at the **Novel House Inn**, which is surrounded on three sides by Zion National Park. Each of the ten rooms is named after a famous writer and decorated in a fashion they might have approved. Downstairs in the well-stocked library you'll find works by Twain, Whitman, Tolstoy, Kipling, Dickens and others. Outside is a great view of The Watchman. ~ 73 Paradise Road, Springdale; 435-772-3650, 800-711-8400, fax 435-772-3651; www.novelhouse.com. MODERATE TO DELUXE.

John Wayne, Sammy Davis, Jr., Glen Ford, Dean Martin, Charlton Heston, Barbara Stanwyck, Ava Gardner and many more stayed at the Parry Lodge when they were working on films.

Nothing fancy, but good home cooking and warm hospitality are hallmarks of **Zion House Bed and Breakfast**. Two guest rooms offer private baths; two others are shared. All rooms have terrific views; one has a private garden area. Guests can swap tales of park adventures in the comfortable communal sitting room. A complimentary family-style breakfast is served. ~ 801 Zion Park Boulevard, Springdale; phone/fax 435-772-3281, 800-775-7404, fax 435-772-3281; www.zionhouse.com. BUDGET TO MODERATE.

Tree-shaded lawns and gardens mark the **Driftwood Lodge**. Forty-seven oversized rooms bring the outdoors inside with oak furniture and Southwestern artwork. A gift shop, a numbingly cold outdoor swimming pool and complimentary continental breakfast are nice pluses. ~ 1515 Zion Park Boulevard, Springdale; 435-772-3262, 888-801-8811, fax 435-772-3702; www.driftwoodlodge.net, e-mail drftwood@inforwest.com. MODERATE.

Most of the rooms are on the small side, but you can't beat the history when you stay at the **Parry Lodge** in Kanab. Built in 1929 to accommodate the film industry when it came to southern Utah for its red-rock backdrop, the lodge served as the hang-out for such film stars as John Wayne, Glen Ford, Charlton Heston, Barbara Stanwyck and Ava Gardner. Small plaques over various rooms point out which actor/actress slept where. The lodge also has a small pool to ward off the desert heat, a restaurant and the Old Barn Playhouse, where melodramas play out throughout the summer. ~ 89 East Center Street, Kanab; 435-644-2601, 800-748-4104, fax 435-644-2605. MODERATE.

DINING

Located right in the heart of Zion National Park, **Zion Lodge Restaurant** satisfies every appetite with bountiful breakfasts, hearty lunches and tasty dinners that revolve around Southwestern fare and beef. Hamburgers, salads, seafood, chipotle barbecued chicken and steak are pleasantly presented amid the beauty of Zion. Dinner reservations are recommended. ~ Zion National Park; 435-772-3213. BUDGET TO MODERATE.

HIDDEN ►

The rustic cantina appearance of **Bit and Spur Saloon and Mexican Restaurant** belies what many consider Utah's best

Mexican restaurant. The dinner menu focuses on traditional cuisine like *flautas*, tostadas, *rellenos* and burritos. You'll also find chili stews and creative Southwestern chicken dishes. In summer and early fall, reservations are a must. There's also a small bar with a pool table if you're just looking for a place to escape from the heat. Closed December. ~ 1212 Zion Park Boulevard, Springdale; 435-772-3498. MODERATE.

At the **Switchback Grill** you can marvel at the national park's dramatic scenery while enjoying breakfast, lunch or dinner. Dinner entrées range from prime filet and spit-roasted chicken to Utah trout or pizza. Located just outside Zion's south entrance, the grill brings the park indoors via its floor-to-ceiling windows. ~ 1149 Zion Park Boulevard, Springdale; 435-772-3700, 877-948-8080. MODERATE.

You'll get outstanding Italian-style fare along with Utah microbrews at the **Zion Pizza & Noodle Co.** Housed in a former church building in the heart of Springdale, the restaurant has indoor and patio seating and an adjacent gift shop and outdoor gear store. The menu is "eclectic Italian": traditional pizza with cheese and tomato sauce, Thai chicken pizza with peanut sauce. Dinner only Thursday through Sunday in December. Closed in January and February. ~ 868 Zion Park Boulevard at Paradise Road, Springdale; 435-772-3815; www.zionpizzanoodle.com. BUDGET.

For a jolt of caffeine visit the **Mean Bean Coffee House**. Of course, if coffee isn't what you need, there are Italian sodas, natural sodas, juices, teas (including chai) and fruit smoothies, as well as pastries and granolas. ~ 932 Zion Park Boulevard, Springdale; 435-772-0654. BUDGET.

For three healthy meals a day, **Oscar's Cafe** is the place to go. Breakfast burritos, mesquite-smoked chicken salad sandwiches and shredded beef enchiladas are served in this casual eatery. Be forewarned, though: this is not the place to go if you're in a hurry, as the kitchen can be painfully slow. ~ 948 Zion Park Boulevard, Springdale; 435-772-3232. BUDGET TO MODERATE.

You can't miss at **Flanigan's Inn Restaurant**. The bright, airy establishment serves creative Southwestern cuisine. Entrées might range from halibut with chipotle chili aioli to tournado of beef tenderloin with smoked tomato chutney. With a 2000-bottle wine celler, pairing a bottle with your dinner should be easy. Flanigans also houses the Spotted Dog Café, where you can get a cold draught or a quick lunch. Dinner reservations are recommended. ~ 428 Zion Park Boulevard, Springdale; 435-772-3244, 800-765-7787; www.flanigans.com. MODERATE TO DELUXE.

SHOPPING

Although short in stature, downtown Springdale boasts an eclectic shopping scene, one that offers crafts and paintings from regional artists, antiques, and the expected national park mementoes.

Step off the street and into the **Worthington Gallery** to find the efforts of nearly two dozen local artists. Pulled together by Greg Worthington, the artists produce wind chimes, pottery, and dazzling paintings. ~ 789 Zion Park Boulevard, Springdale; 435-772-3446, 800-626-9973; www.worthingtongallery.com.

Intricately beaded "offering bowls" the Huichol culture has been making out of gourds for hundreds of years can be found inside **Regalo Beads, Gifts and Gallery**. They also sell bead supplies if you want to work on your own designs. ~ 932 Zion Park Boulevard, Springdale; 435-772-0616.

The lawn of **Canyon Offerings** sprouts dozens of lawn ornaments in the form of hummingbirds, kokopellis, turtles and half-moons. Inside the eclectic shop are jewelry, kaleidoscopes, T-shirts, leather products, unique watches shuttered within wooden boxes, and more. ~ 933 Zion Park Boulevard, Springdale; 435-772-3456, 800-788-2443.

Enter the **Lazy Lizard Boutique** and you might think you've stumbled into a psychedelic throwback from the late 1960s. Tie-dyed shirts, dresses, sarongs and hats hang from the racks, while kites depicting dragonflies dangle from the ceiling. A psychic often offers readings in the back rooms. ~ 948 Zion Park Boulevard, Springdale; 435-772-3050.

Heavy, intricately carved wooden doors that date to the mid-1800s can be found along with cowboy and American Indian antiques at **Frontier Plunder**. Throughout the adobe building's rooms cowboy boots, saddles and spurs are joined by wooden snowshoes, American Indian pottery, and books detailing the West. ~ 1200 Zion Park Boulevard, Springdale; 435-772-3045.

Rockhounds can spend hours at **Zion Rock and Gem**, in business since 1981. Tables, shelves and boxes are stacked full of petrified wood, Moqui Marbles, snowflake obsidian, geodes, Utah picture sandstone and even fossilized shark's teeth. ~ 1416 Zion Park Boulevard, Springdale; 435-772-3436 or 435-772-3110.

AUTHOR FAVORITE

There's nothing better than working your way to the top of an overlook and then enjoying the view with a crisp apple, a crusty loaf of bread, and some cheese. I find these hiking "necessities" at **Springdale Fruit Company Market**. Nestled against the edge of an orchard, the market lies within a post-and-beam barn-influenced building and carries fresh, organic produce, as well as nuts, fresh-baked breads, dried fruits, bottled water, sodas and more. Closed December through February. ~ 2491 Zion Park Boulevard, Springdale; 435-772-3822, 877-772-3822; www.springdalefruit.com.

From May through September "Saturday Night Live" means live **NIGHTLIFE** music at the **O. C. Tanner Amphitheater** near the south entrance of Zion National Park. Depending on which Saturday you head to the arena you might encounter a symphony, bluegrass or maybe even a modern dance exhibition. Admission. ~ 300 West Lion Boulevard, Springdale; 435-652-7994.

Across Zion Park Boulevard, the **Zion Canyon Cinemax Theatre** presents two 45-minute-long movies daily on a six-story-high giant screen. *Zion Canyon Treasure of the Gods* offers an interpretive look at the legends of Zion Canyon. Admission. ~ 145 Zion Park Boulevard, Springdale; 435-772-2400, 888-256-3456.

The local hangout for drinks and occasional live music on weekends is the **Bit and Spur Saloon**. Cover for live music. ~ 1212 ◀ *HIDDEN* Zion Park Boulevard, Springdale; 435-772-3498.

ZION NATIONAL PARK 🚶 🚲 🐎 🛶 A true gem. Sheer, **PARKS** towering cliffs surround the verdant floor of Zion Canyon as lush hanging gardens and waterfalls stand in marked contrast to the desertlike terrain of stark rock formations and etched redrock walls. There are guided walks, and a hiker shuttle service can be arranged through the on-site visitors center. Facilities here include picnic areas, a restaurant, a snack bar, a gift shop and restrooms. No driving in the park allowed between June and October unless you're staying at Zion Lodge; the shuttle bus system is handy, reliable and relaxing. The $20 vehicle fee is good for a week (oversized vehicles pay a higher fee). ~ The main entrance is one mile north of Springdale via Route 9. The east entrance is 13 miles west of Mount Carmel Junction along Route 9. A one-mile tunnel connects Zion Canyon with plateaus on the east. Buses and many recreational vehicles are too large to navigate the tunnel in two-way traffic, so traffic may be temporarily halted; 435-772-3256; www.nps.gov/zion.

▲ There are about 350 sites in the Watchman and South campgrounds near the visitors center; $10 to $14 per night. Primitive camping is allowed in the six-site Lava Point Campground and in the backcountry with a $5 permit available from the visitors center; no water; no fee. Reservations: 800-365-2267; reservations.nps.gov.

CORAL PINK SAND DUNES STATE PARK 🚶 The beach comes to Utah at this expansive site of coral-pink sand dunes. Visitors here are encouraged to play in the six square miles of sand, ride offroad vehicles or build a sand castle or two. There are restrooms and showers. Day-use fee, $5. ~ Sand Dunes Road, 12 miles south of Route 89 and about 25 miles northwest of Kanab; 435-648-2800; parks.state.ut.us/parks/www1/cora.htm.

▲ There are 22 sites; $14 per night.

▼▼▼▼▼▼▼▼▼▼▼▼
Cedar City Area

Though now called "Festival City" because of its ties to the Utah Shakespearean Festival, it was iron that initially brought Mormon pioneers to Cedar City. Early Utah settlers worried about the lack of iron ore, and when deposits were discovered in the mountain 15 miles west of what is now Cedar City, an iron mission was established in 1851. Despite initial success, the foundry closed a mere seven years later, but Cedar City managed to survive and today hosts numerous cultural and sporting events.

SIGHTS

Young people know Cedar City as the location of 104-acre **Southern Utah University**, a 6000-student liberal-arts school that celebrated its centennial in 1997. Many leading cultural events, including the Utah Shakespearean Festival and American Folk Ballet (see "Nightlife" below), are presentations of this four-year school, as are the Utah Summer Games (435-865-8421, 800-367-8824), an Olympic-style sporting event that draws 7000 athletes from the state of Utah to compete in 40 events every June. SUU's **Braithwaite Fine Arts Gallery** (435-586-5432) presents a variety of visual-art exhibits throughout the year. It's on the east side of campus, just south of Old Main and northeast of the library. ~ 351 West Center Street, Cedar City; 435-586-7700.

One of the best ways to explore Cedar City is via a self-guided **Historical Tour**, as presented in a brochure distributed by the **Iron County Tourism and Convention Bureau**. The tour features 19 sites—14 of them markers and monuments—spread throughout the town. The chamber also offers advice on what to do in the area. ~ 581 North Main Street, Cedar City; 435-586-4484, 800-354-4849.

The highlight of the historical tour is **Iron Mission State Park**, whose museum tells the story of early Cedar City with a diorama of its original foundry. There are also three pioneer cabins (one of them dating from 1851, said to be the oldest log cabin in southern Utah) and a half acre devoted to antique farm machinery. The show stopper is the Gronway Parry Collection of horse-drawn vehicles. Spanning the period from 1870 to 1930, it contains all manner of coaches and wagons, including buggies, surreys, mail carts, sleighs, a bullet-scarred stagecoach, a white hearse and a water-sprinkling wagon. All are in tiptop shape; some have been featured in Western movies. Closed Sunday from November through February. Admission. ~ 585 North Main Street, Cedar City; 435-586-9290; parks.state.ut.us/parks/www1/iron.htm.

Town residents built the **Cedar City Rock Church** during the Great Depression with native materials and donated labor. Red cedar adorns the interior and benches of the chapel, while the colorful stones on the exterior—including various ores mined from such areas as Cedar Breaks and Bryce Canyon—were carefully matched. Free guided tours are offered daily in summer. ~ 75 East Center Street, Cedar City; 435-586-6759.

Sixteen miles north of Cedar City on Route 15, the small community of **Parowan** (southern Utah's oldest town) evokes a Western atmosphere with a strong heritage. Gateway to Brian Head Ski Area and Cedar Breaks National Monument, Parowan has a few motels and restaurants among many examples of original pioneer architecture.

For a quick primer on Parowan's history, visit the **Rock Church Museum**. Built between 1863 and 1867 and modeled after the Salt Lake City Tabernacle, the church underwent restoration in the 1940s and today keeps track of Parowan's past. ~ On the Town Square between Center Street and 100 South, Parowan.

Another museum exists in the **Jesse N. Smith Home**, which was built from red adobe brick in 1857 and restored in the 1970s. ~ 35 West 100 South, Parowan.

Old Irontown, 25 miles west of Cedar City on Route 56, still displays remnants of open-pit mining operations of the late 1800s. A beehived-shaped coke oven, foundry and blast furnace are on-site.

In sharp contrast to the manic crowds at the main section of Zion National Park, the **Kolob Canyons** entrance is virtually deserted. Arches, cliffs and mountains point like fingers to the sky in this part of the park, which claims one of the world's largest free-standing arches. A small visitors center offers backcountry

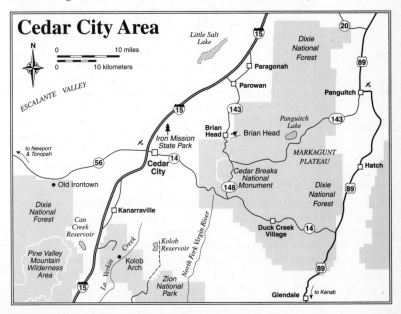

permits and information including an invaluable interpretive auto-drive pamphlet that guides you to ten stops along the five-and-a-half-mile road into the Finger Canyons of the Kolob. Deeply colored cliffs of vermilion and goldenrod mark Kolob Canyon, a markedly different section of Zion. A huge rock scar just left of Shuntavi Butte is the result of a cataclysmic break of the cliff from the rock face in 1983. ~ Just off Route 15 at Exit 40, 17 miles south of Cedar City; 435-586-9548; www.nps.gov/zion.

Kolob Canyons Viewpoint provides the ideal spot from which to view the canyon walls of massive Navajo sandstone laid down as windblown dunes 150 million years ago that now extend as fingers into the edge of the high terrace. ~ Located at the end of Kolob Canyons Road.

Though a product of the same natural forces that shaped Zion and Bryce, **Cedar Breaks National Monument** clearly holds its own. You head east from Cedar City along Route 14 then turn north on Route 148. The drive through huge glades of evergreen forest doesn't adequately prepare the viewer for the grandeur of the brilliant rock amphitheater. The jaded may surmise they've driven to 10,350 feet for nothing until they look out the huge glass windows of the visitors center. Closed October through May. Admission. ~ Route 148; 435-586-9451; www.nps.gov/cebr.

Like the coliseum of ancient Rome, Cedar Breaks is expansive and wide. Only here, visitors gaze upon a natural gallery of stone spires, columns and arches instead of warring gladiators. The sheer cliffs reveal a candy store of colors—lavenders, saffrons and crimsons—all melted together and washed across the rocks.

In marked contrast to the flowers are the bristlecone pines, called the "Methuselah" of trees. Small stands grow on the relatively poor limestone soil that is within and along the rim of the amphitheater. One gnarled and weatherbeaten pine that can be seen from the Wasatch Ramparts Trail near Spectra Point on the breaks' rim is estimated to be more than 1600 years old.

A five-mile road accesses the park's main attractions. Four scenic overlooks, trailheads and all visitor services are on or near the road.

MISTAKEN IDENTITY

Paiutes referred to the amphitheater we know today as Cedar Breaks National Monument as "un-cap-i-un-ump," which means "circle of painted cliffs." Nineteenth-century settlers, however, referred to areas that were too steep for wagons as "breaks," and thought most of the trees growing in the area were cedars (they're actually junipers) and so coined the name "Cedar Breaks."

When five-star chef Scott Wallace decided to forsake a big salary for quality of life, he settled in Cedar City and opened the **Heartland Café**. Located in the oldest commercial building in the city's restored downtown area, the café serves up American bistro-style cooking for lunch and dinner. While the lunch menu focuses on homemade soups, salads and designer sandwiches, dinners revolve around innovative chicken, beef and seafood, all at reasonable prices. Call for hours. ~ 155 North Main Street, Cedar City; 435-865-9191. BUDGET TO MODERATE.   ◄ *HIDDEN*

Milt's Stage Stop is just a short, five miles up Route 14 in Cedar Canyon, and the locals head there regularly for the juicy steaks, lobster and crab. A roaring fire heightens the atmosphere during the winters, when the surrounding mountains are cloaked in white. Dinner only. ~ Five miles up Route 14, Cedar City; 435-586-9344. MODERATE TO DELUXE.   ◄ *HIDDEN*

At the Brian Head ski area, Cedar Breaks Lodge's **Double Black Diamond Steak House** offers an intriguing menu that ranges from the expected steak and chicken to unusual wild game, pheasant and seafood in a business-casual atmosphere. Dinner only. Open Friday and Saturday only; closed mid-October to mid-November and mid-April to mid-May. ~ 223 Hunter Ridge Road, Brian Head; 435-677-3000. MODERATE TO DELUXE.

Also at the Cedar Breaks Lodge, the **Columbine Cafe** serves only breakfast standards while the adjacent **Pinnacle Breaks** cooks up steaks, chicken, seafood, burgers, quesadillas and pastas for dinner. Closed mid-October to mid-November and mid-April to mid-May. ~ 223 Hunter Ridge Road, Brian Head; 435-677-3000. BUDGET TO MODERATE.

Spring 2000 saw Cedar City embark on an ambitious, downtown restoration project intended to create a quaint **Towne Square** area that would recall the city's historic ambience with retro-architecture while establishing a natural gathering place in town. Efforts to give the two-block area from Center Street to 200 North along Main Street a unified "feel" led to a mixture of restoring old facades and building new ones to mirror the old. A main cog of the restoration project is the 1000-seat Heritage Center, a performing-arts theater. There's also a small outdoor amphitheater with a fountain that delights kids when it's hot.   **SHOPPING**

Among the shops involved in the community project is **Mountain West Books**, which is worth a look for maps and literature. ~ 77 North Main Street, Cedar City; 435-586-3828.

Bulloch Drug and Main Street Soda Fountain reaches out to the past with its soda fountain, where kids can enjoy a malt or banana split while you search for sundries. There's also a well-stocked candy counter. ~ 91 North Main Street, Cedar City; 435-586-9651.

NIGHTLIFE   Those visiting Cedar City between late June and late August should take in a performance at the renowned **Utah Shakespearean Festival**. Six plays rotate afternoons and evenings at both the Adams Theater, an authentic open-air re-creation of London's Globe Theatre, and the modern indoor Randall L. Jones Theater on the campus of **Southern Utah University**. Even if you can't attend a performance, an authentic re-creation of the Tiring House Theater of Shakespeare's era has production and literary seminars during the festival season in the foyer of the Southern Utah University Auditorium. ~ 351 West Center Street, Cedar City; 435-586-7880.

Those wishing to really get in the spirit of the evening may dine in the tradition of the Old English great halls at the King's Pavilion, located across the street north from the Festival Box Office. The **Royal Feaste** offers entertainment, fanfares, lively humor and winsome serving wenches. Reservations required; tickets available at the box office. ~ 351 West Center Street, Cedar City; 435-586-7878, 800-752-9849.

Southern Utah University plays host to a variety of cultural attractions year-round. The **University Theater Arts Department** (435-586-7746) schedules plays in the fall and spring. **American Folk Ballet** (435-586-7746), a dance troupe that combines ballet with folk dancing, performs annually at the SUU Centrum. National and international talent spanning dance, opera, classical music and country perform on campus throughout the year.

The **Summer Evening Concert Series** (435-586-5483), held at the Randall L. Jones Theater on Sunday evenings during July and August, features jazz, classical, country and more. ~ Southern Utah University: 351 West Center Street, Cedar City; 435-586-7700.

Regional and national artists make stops in Cedar City throughout the year courtesy of **Cedar City Music Arts**. ~ 435-865-1812.

A college crowd likes to hang out at **Sportsmen's Lounge**, where there is live music or a deejay kicking out the jams. Cover

HISTORICAL GRAFFITI

If you venture 12 miles northwest from Parowan on an all-season gravel road, you'll discover the **Parowan Gap Petroglyphs**. More than 1000 years of American Indian cultures—Fremont peoples, Anasazi, southern Paiute and others—inscribed such designs as snakes, lizards, bear claws and obscure geometric patterns on the smooth-surfaced walls of this 600-foot notch in the Red Hills. The site is protected by the Bureau of Land Management. ~ Head north on Main Street in Parowan, turn left at 400 North and drive for ten and a half miles; 435-865-3053.

Wednesday, Friday and Saturday. ~ 900 South Main Street, Cedar City; 435-586-6552.

The country-music set two-steps at **The Playhouse,** which features live music on Friday night. Cover on Friday. ~ 1027 North Main Street, Cedar City; 435-586-9010.

Quality bands come from near and far to play at the **Pinnacle Breaks Club** in the Cedar Breaks Lodge during the ski season. ~ 223 Hunter Ridge Road, Brian Head; 435-677-3000.

At the **Parowan Community Theater** you'll enjoy community-produced plays and musicals throughout the year. ~ 27 North Main Street, Parowan; 435-477-8732.

ZION NATIONAL PARK–KOLOB CANYONS 🚶🐎 Less widely known than Zion Canyon, 49,150-acre Kolob remains relatively untrodden yet provides as much colorful scenery as its more famous counterpart. Jackrabbits, snakes, lizards, cougars and mule deer are commonly seen; piñon, juniper and cottonwood trees abound. You will find a visitors center, a picnic area and restrooms; water is only available at the visitors center so it's a good idea to bring your own. The $20 entrance fee is good for a week. ~ Off Route 15 at Exit 40, 17 miles south of Cedar City; 435-586-9548; www.nps.gov/zion.

🔺 Backpack camping permitted with a $5 permit available from the visitors center.

CEDAR BREAKS NATIONAL MONUMENT 🚶 🚲 🏞 Millennia of erosion and uplift have carved one of the world's greatest natural amphitheaters, filled with stone pinnacles, columns, arches and canyons of soft limestone three miles from rim to rim and 2500 feet deep. Some call it a Bryce Canyon in miniature. Surrounding Cedar Breaks is a sub-alpine environment with evergreen forest of bristlecone pine, spruce and fir trees, flower-laden meadows and tall grasses. Sorry, no cedars. The Mormon settlers confused them with the gnarled juniper trees found throughout. The monument features a visitors center, a picnic area and restrooms. Services and roads are usually closed from mid-October to mid-May due to heavy snows, though snowshoeing, cross-country skiing and snowmobiling are allowed. Day-use fee (summer only), $3. ~ Located 21 miles east of Cedar City via Route 14 (turn north on Route 143 for the last three miles) or take Route 143 south two miles from Brian Head; 435-586-9451; www.nps.gov/cebr.

🔺 There are 30 sites (no hookups); $12.

PARKS

▼▼▼▼▼▼▼▼▼
Bryce Area

A couple of wonderful parks (surprise) await you here along with historic towns and one of the prettiest byways in the West. And for a bonus you can see the log cabin of Ebenezer Bryce, namesake of the region's stunning national park.

SIGHTS   The handsome architecture in the historic town of **Panguitch**, settled in 1864, is evidence of its early pioneering spirit. Around the turn of the 20th century, a communal brick kiln was supervised by an English potter who was sent here by Brigham Young to be the company's craftsman. Part of the workers' weekly salaries was paid in bricks! That accounts for the great number of stately, brick homes still found in Panguitch. English and Dutch influences are also evident in the buildings' Dixie dormers, delicate filigree and Queen Anne windows.

A short walking tour through the center of town gives you a chance to see the best of what's left. Begin the tour at the **Garfield County Courthouse**, built for just over $11,000 in 1906. ~ 55 South Main Street, Panguitch.

Cross to the **Houston home**, which was constructed in 1906 of extra-large brick fired in a Panguitch kiln. The home's lumber and shingles came from a local sawmill. ~ 72 South Main Street, Panguitch.

The building called **Southern Utah Equitable** at 47 North Main Street is a classic bit of architecture. It has housed just about every kind of business you can think of, from general merchandise to furniture, groceries and now a gift shop and restaurant.

Prominent on Center Street is the **Panguitch Social Hall Corporation**, which was first built in 1908 but burned shortly thereafter. On the same spot, using some original materials, another social hall was built. ~ 35 East Center Street.

Next door is a former library (now an antique shop) that was built in 1908 thanks to a generous donation from philanthropist Andrew Carnegie. ~ 75 East Center Street.

Finally, the city's **Daughters of Utah Pioneer Museum** is a lovely, brick monolith on the site of the old bishop's storehouse. Back in the mid-19th century, members of the Mormon Church paid their tithes with cattle and produce that were kept on this lot. Now, visitors trace the region's history here. Closed November through April. Closed Sunday. Call for hours. ~ Center Street and 1st East, Panguitch; 435-676-2365.

Before you leave Panguitch be sure to stop by the **Paunsagaunt Wildlife Museum**, which is housed in the historic old high-school building. The museum features more than 400 animals from North America in their natural habitats. Other displays include exotic game from Africa, India and Europe, a large butterfly collection, rare birds of prey and American Indian artifacts, tools, pottery and weapons. There are also a number of gift shops in the building. Closed November through March. Admission. ~ 250 East Center Street, Panguitch; 435-676-2500 (summer), 702-877-2664 (winter).

Driving south from Panguitch on Route 89 takes you to the start of one of the most scenic byways in the West. After passing a few souvenir shops and cafés near the highway junction, Route 12 starts to wind through rock tunnels. That's when you know you're in **Red Canyon**. A Dixie National Forest **visitors center** on the road's north side offers information about the small recreation area that's usually bypassed by people hurrying toward Bryce Canyon. Pink and red rocks stand amid huge pines in this compact and user-friendly park.

BRYCE CANYON NATIONAL PARK   It's another ten miles on Route 12 to the Bryce Canyon National Park turnoff. Bryce is a national park on the jagged edge of the Paunsaugunt Plateau that really does defy superlatives. Even the gigantic summertime crowds can't distract from the natural amphitheaters carved into the Pink Cliffs of southern Utah. Who would have ever thought there were this many shades of red or shapes of rock? The limestones and sandstones of Bryce, some softer than others, have been sculpted by eons of erosional forces. These rock forms come in countless profiles, which have been named "hoodoos"; they are ever-changing because of rain and snow seeping into the cracks of the rock, freezing and thawing to wear away the layers. For a quick primer on the park, stop at the visitors center, which houses a wealth of geologic information on this rugged gem of the park system as well as a nice museum that chronicles the region's human and wild life. Admission. ~ Bryce Canyon Scenic Drive, Route 63; 435-834-5322, fax 435-834-4102; www.nps.gov/brca.

Bryce offers 14 huge bowls of Creamsicle-colored spires and pinnacles. Located between 7500 and 9100 feet above sea level, the 35,000-plus acres of Bryce receive more than their fair share

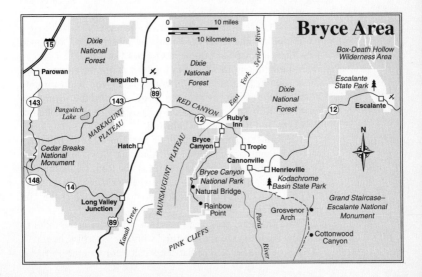

of snow during the wintertime. Some say that the rocks covered with dollops of snow are at their most beautiful in winter.

Fifty to sixty million years ago the area was covered by an inland lake. Rivers and streams carried silt and sediments from throughout the region to the lake, and the sediments settled at the bottom. With climatic changes, the lake disappeared and the sediments left behind slowly turned to rock. Later, a major regional uplift exposed the old lake deposits to the forces of erosion; colorful layers took shape as a result of this process. Red and yellow hues are due to iron oxides. The purples come from manganese. White reveals an absence of minerals in that part of the rock.

At sections of the park like Silent City and other natural amphitheaters, the rock figures resemble chess pieces, a preacher, a woman playing the organ or faces that belong on Easter Island.

Bryce Canyon's nooks and crannies are best explored on foot. For those who want to sit back and enjoy the views, a shuttle system that debuted in mid-2000 carries visitors to the mid-section of the park. The shuttle, which operates from mid-May through September, travels from Fairyland Point to Bryce Point, as well as from the northern visitors center. Unlike the Zion Park shuttle, this one is not mandator, but why not give your car a rest and enjoy the ride?

For those who want to drive on their own and if time is a factor, it's wise to drive to the overlooks on the 18-mile park road for a sweeping look at the big picture. Start at the **Fairyland Point** lookout about two miles north of the visitors center to see the imaginary creatures, the looming **Boat Mesa** and mysterious **Sinking Ship** in Fairyland Canyon. The rather strenuous Fairyland Loop Trail also begins here.

For a concentrated collection of formations, travel to the park's nucleus and either the **Sunrise** or **Sunset Point** lookouts to view the chess set–like people in **Queen's Garden**.

Walking along the Rim Trail, which skirts the canyon edge for a roundtrip distance of 11 miles, takes you to **Inspiration Point** and the eerie army of stone "people" called the **Silent City**. From the Rim Trail at this point it's possible to see the **Wall of Windows** and the majestic **Cathedral**.

The Rim Trail continues south for another one and a half miles to **Bryce Point,** which allows breathtaking views of the whole Bryce Amphitheater. Three hiking trails, the Rim, Under-the-Rim and Peekaboo Loop, may be accessed from here. Horses share the Peekaboo Loop and take riders past profiles such as the **Alligator** and **Fairy Castle**.

From the main park road continue south for seven miles to **Farview Point** to gaze at the natural wonders stretching hundreds of miles outside Bryce. The flat-topped landform to the northeast

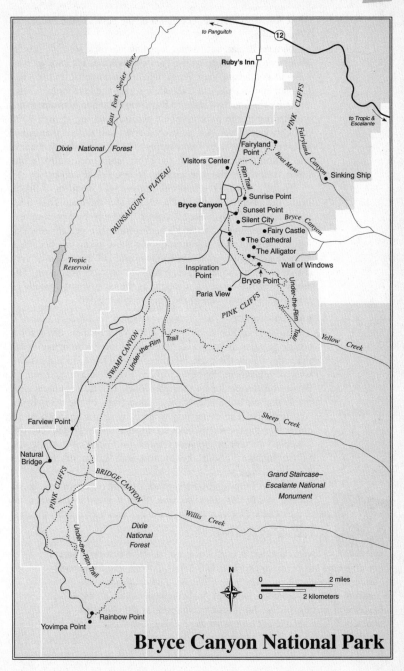

to Panguitch

12

Ruby's Inn

East Fork Sevier River

Dixie National Forest

PINK CLIFFS

to Tropic & Escalante

Fairland Canyon

Fairyland Point

Visitors Center

Rim Trail

Boat Mesa

Sinking Ship

PAUNSAUGUNT PLATEAU

Sunrise Point

Bryce Canyon

Sunset Point

Silent City

Fairy Castle

Bryce Canyon

The Cathedral

The Alligator

Tropic Reservoir

Inspiration Point

Wall of Windows

Bryce Point

Paria View

Under-the-Rim Trail

PINK CLIFFS

Yellow Creek

SWAMP CANYON

Under-the-Rim Trail

Farview Point

Sheep Creek

Natural Bridge

Grand Staircase– Escalante National Monument

PINK CLIFFS

BRIDGE CANYON

Under-the-Rim Trail

Willis Creek

Dixie National Forest

N

0 ——— 2 miles

0 ——— 2 kilometers

Rainbow Point

Yovimpa Point

Bryce Canyon National Park

is the **Aquarius Plateau**. Southeast of the park are the distinctive **White Cliffs**.

Natural Bridge, with a huge opening in a rock, stands distinctly about two miles south of the Farview lookout. It's another four miles to **Ponderosa View Point**, where you can pick up the Agua Canyon connecting foot trail while seeing the lovely pink cliffs.

Drive the final two miles to **Rainbow Point** and **Yovimpa Point** and end up at the park's highest points, towering at over 9000 feet above sea level. A little more barren and rugged than other sections of Bryce, these two overlooks serve as trailheads for several hiking paths. It's worth the short jaunt on the **Bristlecone Loop Trail** to see the rare, gnarled trees up close and personal.

To fully explore the multimillion-year-old wonders of Bryce, begin the at-times arduous 22-mile **Under-the-Rim Trail** from here and travel north on a two- or three-day backpacking excursion. Camping in the park's backcountry is especially rewarding, as the stars tend to put on quite a show in this rarefied, high altitude air. However, in late summer and fall water can be very scarce in the backcountry, requiring you to carry your own. The added weight is worth it, though, as the beauty and solitude of this seldom-visited side of the park is spectacular.

EAST OF BRYCE   The closest real town to Bryce Canyon is Tropic—where Ebenezer Bryce, a native Scotsman, lived for a couple of years. Bryce was a Mormon pioneer who helped settle the valley below the park. Neighbors called the beautiful canyon west of his ranch "Bryce's Canyon." There is a back route to Bryce from Tropic for foot travelers only. This trail connects with the Peekaboo Loop and Navajo Loop trails of the main Bryce Amphitheater. The easier way to go is by returning to Route 12 and traversing the ten miles or so through lovely **Tropic Canyon**. You need a sharp eye to spot the natural bridge on the east side of the highway about three-tenths mile north of the Water Canyon Bridge.

Once in Tropic, stop for a snack or to stretch your legs in this special village that remains true to its name. Flowers seem to

AUTHOR FAVORITE
I love to wander through slot canyons, which rushing waters over time have left delicately and colorfully fluted. **Cottonwood Narrows** is especially wonderful, particularly with kids since it's easily accessible and a treasure chest of vegetation, birds and finely tumbled stones. It's especially nice on hot days when the shaded canyon feels as if it's been air-conditioned. ~ Located about four miles south of the Grosvenor double arch.

dance in the gardens, and old trees stretch their limbs languor-ously. At the south end of town is **Ebenezer Bryce's old log cabin**, which houses American Indian artifacts.

Another few miles east on Route 12 is **Cannonville**, a town about half the size of Tropic that offers travelers basic services. Best known as the northern gateway to Kodachrome Basin State Park and the Grand Staircase–Escalante National Monument, Cannonville is also the jumping-off point for little side trips through slot canyons on the northern end of the monument.

Before embarking into the Grand Staircase, get oriented at the **visitors center**. Inside this striking, native-stone building you'll find details on the monument's geology and recreational oppor-tunities. Closed mid-November to mid-March. ~ Route 12, Cannonville; 435-679-8981.

The **Cottonwood Canyon Road** forks about three miles south of Cannonville: the left fork continues on to Kodachrome Basin State Park, while the right fork leads to Skutumpah Road and slot canyons on **Willis Creek** and **Bull Valley Gorge**.

About five and a half miles down Skutumpah Road you'll ar-rive at Willis Creek, and roughly three more miles deliver you to Bull Valley Gorge. Whereas the Willis Creek slot canyon is a nice family hike through not-terribly-narrow slots that vary in height and width, the Bull Valley Gorge slot canyon is for experienced canyoneers due to its much narrower passages and rock walls that must be negotiated. The hearty can piece together a 16-mile hike by going south through Bull Valley Gorge, up Sheep Creek and out Willis Creek. Look for signs on the gravel and dirt road south of Cannonville. Drivers should be careful as these roads can be-come treacherous during storms.

Heading south on the only road out of Cannonville in that direction, Cottonwood Canyon Road, you'll travel seven miles to **Kodachrome Basin State Park**, another wonderful Utah park with red-rock figures and slender chimneys. Spires, or "sand pipes," jut toward the sky, and natural arches beckon. Is it a surprise that Kodak is the park's official film? Quiet beauty and serenity are abundant in this out-of-the-way gem. Stop at the Trail Head sta-tion, a little store, for maps and advice. Admission. ~ Cottonwood Canyon Road, seven miles south of Cannonville; 435-679-8562.

An amazing feat of nature about ten miles south of the park boundary via rough Cottonwood Canyon Road is the **Grosvenor double arch**. The delicate colors of the monolith, coupled with a bluebird sky, must be seen to be believed. Petrified wood may be seen in the arch's vicinity.

When the road is in good condition, those with sturdy vehicles can continue south on the road to Cottonwood Canyon past two manmade circles of alabaster stones named **Gilgal**. Vaguely rem-iniscent of Stonehenge, the concept for Gilgal is biblically rooted and meant to symbolize the modern-day pilgrims who make an annual trek to this area in celebration of the summer solstice.

The jagged rampart that parallels Cottonwood Road here is known as **The Cockscomb**, a ridge of rock that divides the monument in half, with the Kaiparowits Plateau to the east and the Grand Staircase to the west.

The entire stretch of road south of Cannonville to Route 89 crosses the Kanab fault several times and offers unusual scenery and fossils plus opportunities for exploring on foot. The road then continues a few miles to the western boundary of Glen Canyon National Recreation Area. The full region is part and parcel of **Grand Staircase–Escalante National Monument**, 1.9 million acres of dramatic desert land declared a national monument in September 1996 by President Clinton. No services are available inside the monument, although more and more are becoming available in the adjacent communities. It is administered by the Bureau of Land Management, which offers topographical maps and information on road and trail conditions from its interagency offices in Kanab, Cannonville, Paria, Big Water and Escalante. ~ 435-644-4600, 435-679-8981; www.ut.blm.gov/monument/default.htm.

LODGING   Cheap, clean and very basic describes the **Color Country Motel** with its flowered bedspreads and scenic vistas on the walls. There are 26 rooms; facilities include a swimming pool and spa. ~ 526 North Main Street, Panguitch; 435-676-2386, 800-225-6518, fax 435-676-8484; e-mail bobbie@color-country.net. BUDGET.

A step up in quality—and price—is the 55-room **Best Western New Western Motel**. The housekeeping is spotless and there is a cool pool and (warm) jacuzzi for those toasty summer days. ~ 180 East Center Street, Panguitch; 435-676-8876, 800-528-1234, fax 435-676-8876 ext. 165. BUDGET.

Six rooms that evoke different flavors—the Northwoods, ranch life, and Southern comfort, to name three—can be found within the historic red brick walls of the **Red Brick Inn**. Families can be accommodated in one of two suites that combine either two or three of the rooms. Multinight discounts are available. ~ 161 North 100 West, Panguitch; 435-676-2141, 866-733-2745; www.redbrickinnutah.com. MODERATE TO DELUXE.

For a more historic sleep, try the **William Prince Inn**, a bed and breakfast in Panguitch where you'll find clawfoot tubs, a working Victrola, and the always comfortable rocking chairs. Three of the five rooms have their own bathrooms. Both full and continental breakfasts are offered. ~ 185 South 300 East, Panguitch; 435-676-2525, 888-676-2525; www.onlinepages.net/williamprince. MODERATE.

There's nothing like a full-service resort when you really feel like getting away from it all. **Best Western Ruby's Inn** operates as a world of its own, with a general store, restaurants, a liquor store, a campground complete with tepees, mountain bike rentals and shuttles, a laundromat, an auto repair shop and gas station, a helicopter pad, riding stables—even its own post office on site! Cross the street and you'll find Ruby's summer rodeo grounds, petting farm, chuckwagon rides, trail rides, and a replica of an Old West town. An international clientele can be found anytime. Rooms are decorated in Southwestern decor, and the staff remains friendly even after a long tourist season. ~ Route 63, Bryce Canyon; 435-834-5341, 800-468-8660, fax 435-834-5265; www. rubysinn.com. MODERATE.

Cottages, motel rooms and mini-suites with kitchens and fireplaces are available for guests at **Bryce Canyon Pines Motel**. Set in a grove of ponderosa pines, the motel complex also offers an RV park, restaurant, indoor pool and spa, and horseback rides. ~ Route 12, six miles northwest of the Bryce Canyon entrance; 435-834-5441, 800-892-7923, fax 435-834-5330; www.bryce canyonmotel.com, e-mail bcpines@color-country.net. BUDGET TO MODERATE.

The **Buffalo Sage Bed & Breakfast** looks like just another log cabin as you get ready to enter Tropic on Route 12. Inside, though, are four tastefully decorated rooms that feature queen- or king-size beds. There's also a cozy living room with a fireplace. The property's location atop a hill guarantees great views in all directions. ~ 980 North Route 12, Tropic; 435-679-8443, 866-232-5711; www.buffalosage.com. MODERATE.

Another very comfortable residence is the **Bryce Point Bed and Breakfast**, found about eight miles east of Bryce in the per-

AUTHOR FAVORITE

The **Bryce Canyon Lodge**, listed on the National Register of Historic Places, is the only survivor of the original lodges built by the Union Pacific Railroad at Bryce, Zion and the North Rim of the Grand Canyon. Its four types of rooms—suites, cabins, doubles and studios—fit most budgets and tastes. Splurging on a suite is a treat: these rooms ooze romance, from the white-wicker decor to Cleopatra chairs to the makeup mirror. Quaint log cabins have gas fireplaces, porches and dressing areas. Standard rooms are furnished in Southwest style. Book your reservations early; the lodge tends to book well in advance. If you arrive in the area without a reservation, check for a cancellation. Closed November through March. ~ Bryce Canyon National Park; 435-834-5361, fax 435-834-5464; www.brycecanyonlodge.com. MODERATE TO DELUXE.

petually flowering little town of Tropic. Guests enjoy a private entrance and private baths. Each of the five rooms features hand-made oak cabinets and picture windows to the garden. Out back there's a cabin where a couple can enjoy some privacy. The wraparound porches are perfect for enjoying the sunsets, and there's a hot tub for erasing any kinks that arise on the trail. Closed November through February. ~ 61 North 400 West, Tropic; 435-679-8629, 888-200-4211; www.brycepoint lodging.com. MODERATE.

The Bulberry Inn's deck provides a wonderful view of Bryce Point, Sunset Point, Inspiration Point and The Sinking Ship.

At the **Bullberry Inn**, the full breakfasts are served with ample quantities of Granny's Bullberry Jelly, which is made from the bullberries that grow in the area. The inn's five rooms offer queen-sized beds set in log frames, private bathrooms and televisions. ~ 412 South Route 12, Tropic; 435-679-8820, 800-249-8126. MODERATE.

Bryce Pioneer Village offers 62 clean motel rooms as well as an RV park with full hookups, and a restaurant featuring Dutch-oven dinners. ~ 80 South Main Route 12, Tropic; 435-679-8546, 800-222-0381; www.bpvillage.com. BUDGET TO MODERATE.

HIDDEN ►

Well off the beaten path lies the **Stone Canyon Inn**. So far off Route 12 is this gorgeous property that you'd never find it unless you knew where to look. The centerpiece of an 80-acre plot that backs up to Bryce Canyon National Park, the stone-built inn offers five well-appointed rooms that come with jacuzzi bath-tubs, TV/VCRs, and telephones. The living room and dining room share a fireplace whose rock chimney rises between the rooms to the vaulted ceiling. Owner Mike Burbidge will regale you with some of his cowboy poetry. ~ 1220 West Stone Canyon Lane, Tropic; 435-679-8611, 866-489-4680; www.stonecanyoninn.com. MODERATE TO DELUXE.

DINING

If the aroma of the mesquite grill doesn't lure you into **Cowboy's Smoke House**, the quaint rustic decor and continual strains of country-and-western music surely will. Barbecued ribs and other meats, homemade bread and Utah's best peach cobbler highlight the menu. Closed Sunday. ~ 95 North Main Street, Panguitch; 435-676-8030. MODERATE.

When it comes time to settle down and have a semi-fancy meal, there's little doubt that the top choice in this area is the beautiful old log restaurant in the **Bryce Canyon Lodge**. Service is quick and attentive though hardly fussy, the cuisine Continental but not generic. Delicious breads and Levi-busting desserts complement the generously portioned entrées. Dinner reservations are re-quired. ~ Bryce Canyon National Park; 435-834-5361. MODERATE.

Equipped to serve large groups, the **Cowboy Steakhouse and Buffet** presents satisfying meals, though surely not imaginative fare, in its spacious dining room. The Continental cuisine features steaks and chops for dinner. The dining room can be a little noisy when large groups converge. ~ Best Western Ruby's Inn, Route 63, Bryce Canyon; 435-834-5341. BUDGET TO DELUXE.

During the busy summer months, the **Canyon Diner**, adjacent to the Cowboy Steakhouse and Buffet, is a convenient spot for quick and tasty on-the-go meals. ~ Best Western Ruby's Inn, Route 63, Bryce Canyon; 435-834-5341. BUDGET.

The booths are inviting, the coffee steaming and the pies and soups fresh and delicious at **Bryce Canyon Pines**, which also offers specials every evening. Closed November through February. ~ Route 12, six miles northwest of Bryce Canyon entrance; 435-834-5441. BUDGET TO MODERATE.

Had a local not made the recommendation, we'd have never stumbled onto the very modest **Pizza Place**. A wisecracking chef ◄ HIDDEN
kept the starving wolves at bay, appeasing our ravenous hunger with an order of wonderfully gooey mozzarella cheese sticks, before the main event—a hefty, generously topped, sweet-crusted pizza that could be the tastiest pie this side of Chicago. Closed Sunday. ~ 21 North Main Street, Tropic; 435-679-8888. BUDGET.

Doug's Place is really a number of places under one roof: a grocery store, a general store, a gas station, a restaurant and a motel. The restaurant, **Hoodoo's**, offers simple roadside fare: ribeye steaks, chicken, chops and trout for dinner, burgers and sandwiches for lunch, pancakes and steak and eggs for breakfast. ~ 141 North Main Street, Tropic; 435-679-8633. BUDGET.

Thunder Horses Mercantile in Panguitch is a general mercantile   **SHOPPING**
and gift shop. ~ 47 North Main Street, Panguitch; 435-676-8900; www.buffalojava.com.

A handsome brick complex houses the **Panguitch Drug Co.** and the **Old West Cowboy Store**, which sell hats, T-shirts, postcards and convenience-store items for travelers. ~ 95 East Center Street, Panguitch; 435-676-2577; www.drugstorewest.com.

It may seem corny, but you gotta love the **Old Bryce Town**, filled with shops and services. Among them, the **Canyon Rock Shop** has a huge selection of polished stones, fossils and petrified wood, plus a place to pan for gold! Stop in the **Christmas Store** to stock up on ornaments and decorations. The **Western Store** has a great selection of pseudo-Stetsons so you can set out on the range and not feel like a total city slicker. Old Bryce Town is open from mid-May through September. ~ Route 63, across from Ruby's Inn, Bryce Canyon; 435-834-5337.

Wind chimes and chile *ristras* line the front porch, while Navajo rugs and baskets are omnipresent inside the **Bryce Canyon Trading Post**, a good place to pick up the requisite postcard, T-shirt or turquoise stones. You can even find jewelry made by local

American Indian craftsmen, film and a free cup of coffee. ~ Routes 12 and 89; 435-676-2688.

You can't miss the colorful **Red Canyon Indian Store**, a member of the Indian Arts and Crafts Association, found on Route 12 as you leave Panguitch en route to Bryce Canyon. Inside this adobe-influenced building are Navajo rugs, Indian jewelry, moccasins, reproductions of Indian artifacts such as peace pipes, pottery, Western wear and a rock shop. ~ 3279 Route 12, Panguitch; 435-676-2690; www.redcanyon.net.

NIGHTLIFE Don't be surprised if angry Indians come a'chasing when you are riding in the covered chuck wagon train en route to a hoedown and sing-along. The **B-Bar-D Covered Wagon Company** operates out of the Ruby's Inn complex during the summer season. Expect a huge country supper served from a Dutch oven amid the pines before kicking up your heels in the foot-stompin' hoedown. It's a hoot. ~ Route 63, Bryce Canyon; 435-254-4452 before mid-May, 435-834-5202 after mid-May; www.brycecowboycookout.com.

Rodeos featuring local talent are held nightly except Sunday through the summer at the **Rodeo Grounds** across from Ruby's Inn in Bryce Canyon. Barrel racing, bull wrasslin', roping and riding make for a full evening. ~ Route 63, Bryce Canyon; 435-834-5341.

PARKS **PANGUITCH LAKE** 🚶 🚲 ⛵ One of the top fishing areas in the region, 1250-acre Panguitch Lake in Dixie National Forest offers fishing along its ten-mile shoreline and in boats for rainbow, cutthroat and brown trout. There are boat rentals as well as tourist cabins, a general store and a snack shop. ~ Route 143, about 17 miles southwest of Panguitch; 435-865-3200; www.fs.fed.us/dxnf.

▲ There are three national forest campgrounds nearby. Panguitch Lake North has 49 sites; $10 per night. North of the lake, Panguitch Lake South has 17 primitive sites; $8 per night. Whitebridge campground offers 29 sites; $10 per night. There are also several privately owned campgrounds in the area. Closed mid-October to Memorial Day.

TROPIC RESERVOIR AND KING'S CREEK CAMPGROUND 🚶 ⛵ Also in the 1.9-million-acre Dixie National Forest, this recreation site is a nice place for a picnic, a walk past sawmill remains or just a place to fish for stocked trout and relax in the shade of ponderosa pines. Above the south side of the reservoir is the east fork of Sevier River. The only amenities here are restrooms and drinking water. ~ Turn south off Route 12, down the east fork of the Sevier River on Forest Road 087, about ten miles west of Bryce Canyon junction; 435-676-8815.

▲ There are 37 sites; $8 per night.

RED CANYON 🚶 🚲 A lovely collection of sculptured pink, red and scarlet rocks sit in the shadow of Bryce Canyon. Because its neighbor is so well known and considerably larger, Red Canyon tends to be overlooked by visitors. Take advantage and explore the trails of this scenic but compact U.S. Forest Service property, dotted with towering ponderosa pines and red and white juniper. If you scan the skies, you may glimpse golden and bald eagles. Pay more attention to the ground and you might spy seven plant species unique to the Claron geologic formation that runs through the area. A visitors center and restrooms are located about a half-mile down the road. ~ Route 12, about four miles east of Route 89; 435-676-8815.

▲ There are 37 sites; $10 per night.

BRYCE CANYON NATIONAL PARK 🚶 🚲 🐎 ⛺ Famous for its stupendous rock formations that seem to change color within the blink of an eye, Bryce contains a maze of trails that wind in and around its many wonders. Areas are named according to prominent "inhabitants" and structures: Fairyland, Cathedral, Queen's Garden. The 35,000-plus-acre park features its own lodge, a restaurant, a visitors center, nature walks, campfire programs, a general store, laundry, restrooms and showers. (Facilities are mainly seasonal; the visitors center is open year-round.) The $20 vehicle fee is good for a week. ~ The entrance is located two miles south of Route 12 on Route 63, eight miles northwest of Tropic; 435-834-5322, fax 435-834-4102; www.nps.gov/brca.

Kodachrome Basin State Park is chock full of petrified geyser holes (65 at last official count) believed to be freaks of nature and unique to this area.

▲ Permitted at North Campground and Sunset Campground (summer only). More than 200 campsites are open during the summer; $10 per night. There are also several backpacking campsites ($5 permit required) for those looking to escape the crowds and see the park from a different perspective.

KODACHROME BASIN STATE PARK 🚶 🐎 Vividly colored sandstone chimneys, towering rock spires and arches fill this untouched, 2240-acre park that the National Geographic Society named for its photographic value. Facilities include picnic area, a general store, restrooms and hot showers. Day-use fee, $5. ~ Located seven miles south of Cannonville off Cottonwood Canyon Road; 435-679-8562; www.parks.state.ut.us/parks/www1/koda.htm.

▲ There are 27 sites; $14 per night.

Escalante Area

Nature's beauty, wildlife, prehistoric reminders and a region rich in the Indian and Mormon heritage await you in the Escalante area along scenic Route 12. Here you'll find a petrified forest, intriguing rock formations, orchards, dinosaur fossils and, for a wonderful surprise, buffalo. While the arrival of the Grand Staircase–Escalante National Monument in 1996 drew increased attention to Escalante and Route 12, the area didn't need the monument to convince adventurous travelers in search of intriguing, off-the-beaten-path destinations to find it.

SIGHTS

Route 12 climbs from red rock to lush forest and back again to a semi-arid setting. Begin just southwest of the town of Escalante, which was settled in 1876 by Mormon ranchers, in the **Escalante State Park**. It's a showcase for petrified wood, fossilized dinosaur bones and remnants from the Fremont Indian Village thought to be 1000 years old. You don't have to be an athlete or even reasonably fit to find and appreciate the petrified wood in this small park, which has trails to suit everyone. Admission. ~ 435-826-4466.

Huge petrified logs in a spectrum of colors, dinosaur bones and nature trails help to explain the evolution of the 160-million-year-old wood and bones turned to stone that became rainbow-colored by the earth's minerals. It is thought that ancient trees were buried in the sand, causing the logs to become petrified. Millions of years later the natural weathering process exposed the wood from its rough outer shell.

Hole in the Rock Road, a Mormon pioneer passage, zigs and zags its way to Lake Powell from its starting point just southeast of Escalante. Along the historic, 62-mile road you'll see landmarks such as Chimney Rock, Dancehall Rock and the Broken Bow Arch. An annual pilgrimage retraces the steps of the first settlers.

Route 12, the high-altitude road linking Bryce to Capitol Reef through Escalante, Boulder and Torrey, has been called one of the most **scenic drives** in America as it weaves past deep canyons, fossilized sand dunes and over aspen- and conifer-studded Boulder Mountain. So scenic and dramatic is the landscape along the highway that the U.S. Department of Transportation in 2002 designated Route 12 an "all-American road." There are several campgrounds and dirt roads leading to mountain lakes along the way, plus opportunities to view vistas of the Henry Mountains, San Rafael Reef and distant shale deserts.

In tiny **Boulder**, the last town in the United States to receive its mail by mule team, is **Anasazi State Park**. It's located on the site of a former Anasazi community said to have been nearby between A.D. 1050 and 1200 before mysteriously disappearing. Here you'll find excavated village Indian artifacts, a self-guided trail through the site and a museum showing informative movies and filmstrips. Admission. ~ Route 12; 435-335-7308; www.parks.state.ut.us/parks/www1/anas.htm.

Running east from Boulder to Capitol Reef National Park (see Chapter Five) is the **Burr Trail Road**, which runs through a rugged and seemingly barren land of long-forgotten uranium mines. While 31 miles of the road from Boulder to the park are paved, there are numerous unpaved spurs that dart off into the outback. One such spur, about 16 miles east of Boulder, is known as the Wolverine Loop Road and runs south to the **Wolverine Petrified Wood Area**. Here lies an incredible collection of petrified wood, seemingly cut in slabs by a chainsaw. This area falls within the Grand Staircase–Escalante National Monument, so you can't take any petrified wood home with you, but you can take pictures of it.

◀ *HIDDEN*

LODGING

Linoleum-floored bathrooms, a credenza and a desk contribute to the comforts of the **Padre Motel**. Small but tidy. Closed November through February. ~ 20 East Main Street, Escalante; 435-826-4276. BUDGET.

It's nothing fancy, but **Rainbow Country B&B** has four clean, cozy rooms as well as a hearty breakfast to start your day. There's also a hot tub outside from which you can take in the gorgeous countryside. ~ 586 East 300 South, Escalante; www.color-country.net/~rainbow. BUDGET TO MODERATE.

Grand Staircase Bed & Breakfast/Inn has five decent-sized rooms that boast skylights, have private bathrooms, and are furnished with log furniture and handmade quilts. ~ 280 West Main Street, Escalante; 435-826-4890, 866-826-4890; www.escalante bnb.com. BUDGET TO MODERATE.

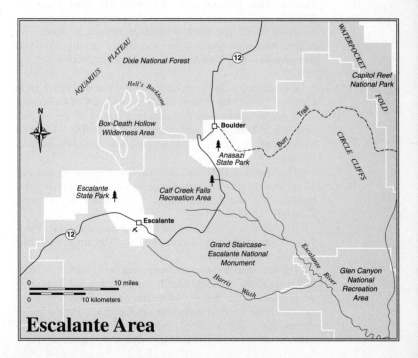

Escalante Area

The **Prospector Inn** is Escalante's largest motel, with 50 rooms. All units feature two double beds, color TV and phones. ~ 380 West Main, Escalante; 435-826-4653; BUDGET.

If you're packing a tent, or happy to settle for a simple cabin for the night, **The Bunkhouse at Escalante Outfitters** might be able to help you out. ~ 310 West Main Street, Escalante; 435-826-4266, fax 435-826-4388; www.aros.net/~slickroc/escout. BUDGET.

The **Circle D Motel** has clean rooms at budget rates. ~ 475 West Main Street, Escalante; 435-826-4297, fax 435-826-4402; www.utahcanyons.com/circled.htm. BUDGET.

A 12-acre wetland bird sanctuary provides a backdrop for **Boulder Mountain Lodge,** a beautiful multibuilding complex at the foot of the Aquarius Plateau. Twenty very spacious rooms have high vaulted ceilings with exposed timber beams and country quilt decor. In the main building, the Boulder House, you'll find a warming fireplace and a nice library. The lodge's restaurant should be your first stop in the morning and last at night. ~ Route 12, Boulder; 435-335-7460, 800-556-3446, fax 435-335-7461; www.boulder-utah.com. MODERATE TO DELUXE.

DINING

Lunch and dinner, as well as meals to go, can be found at the **Cowboy Blues Restaurant.** ~ 530 West Main Street, Escalante; 435-826-4577.

Fancy meals you won't find in downtown Escalante, but hearty American food is in abundance at the **Circle D Restaurant.** ~ 475 West Main Street, Escalante; 435-826-4251. BUDGET.

A similar menu and price is found nearby at the **Golden Loop Café.** ~ 39 West Main Street, Escalante; 435-826-4433. BUDGET.

If you're just looking for pizza or a cup of coffee, or even chai, stop at **Esca-Latte Coffee Shop and Pizza Parlor.** ~ 310 West Main Street, Escalante; 435-826-4266; www.aros.net/~slickroc/escout.

The **Trailhead Café** has lattes, cappuccinos and regular coffee as well as fruit smoothies, made-to-order deli sandwiches, burgers, and box lunches to go. ~ 100 East Main Street, Escalante; 435-826-4714.

For decent sandwiches, try the seasonal **Escalante Frosty Shop**. Closed October through March. ~ 40 East Main Street, Escalante; 435-826-4488. BUDGET.

The best meal in the region comes out of the kitchen at **Hell's Backbone Grill**, an independently owned restaurant located on the grounds of the Boulder Mountain Lodge. Featuring an organic menu of Southwestern, Western Range and Pueblo Indian recipes, the grill offers beef from area ranches, Utah rainbow trout, poultry, seafood and fresh herbs and vegetables. You'll find tortilla soup with free-range chicken; quiche with spinach and goat cheese in a handmade cornmeal crust; and chile-rubbed New York strip steak. There's also an impressive wine list. Breakfasts include fresh fruit, french toast, egg dishes, organic yogurt and blue-corn pancakes. Lunches offer lighter, but equally creative, fare built largely around sandwiches, soups and salads. ~ Route 12, Boulder; 435-335-7460, 800-556-3446, fax 435-335-7461. BUDGET TO MODERATE.

SHOPPING

For jeans and T-shirts, but more important, to stock up on backpacking and camping supplies and maps before meeting the wilderness, stop at **Escalante Outfitters**. ~ 310 West Main Street, Escalante; 435-826-4266.

David Delthony Sculptured Furniture carries unique carved chairs, ceramics, pottery and rocks. ~ 1540 West Route 12, Escalante; 435-826-4631.

If paintings are more to your liking, **Scotty Mitchell Utah Landscapes** has pastel landscapes. ~ Boulder; 435-335-7303; www.scottymitchell.com.

PARKS

ESCALANTE STATE PARK 🏃 🚴 🐎 🛶 ⚓ 🎣 🚤 🛥️ 🚣 ⚓

Trails in this well-known though tiny (it's two square miles) park lead to outcroppings of petrified wood that date back 140 million years. Wide Hollow Reservoir, which is included within the park boundaries, is a good picnicking spot; anglers try for largemouth bass, bluegill, and rainbow and cutthroat trout. There's also an interpretive trail here as well as a visitors center and restrooms. Day-use fee, $5 per vehicle. ~ Located one mile west of Escalante north of Route 12; 435-826-4466; parks.state.ut.us/parks/www1/esca.htm.

▲ There are 22 sites; $14 per night. Reservations: 800-322-3770.

In the Paiute language, *Panguitch* means "big fish," *Paunsaugunt* is "place of the beavers," and *Paria* translates into "muddy water" or "elk water."

GRAND STAIRCASE–ESCALANTE NATIONAL MONUMENT 🏃 🚴 🐎 🚣 🛥️ 🚤

As yet undeveloped, the nation's largest national monument, established in 1996, comprises 1.9 million acres (more than 2600 square miles) of unsullied desert lands between Route 12 and Glen Canyon National Recreation Area. It is named for the colorful and geologically intriguing series of plateaus and precipices that descend like steps from central Utah to the Colorado River, through the Pink, Gray, White, Vermilion and Chocolate cliffs. Those who explore via four-wheel-drive vehicle, horseback or even foot will find awesome vistas everywhere, as well as slot canyons, natural bridges and arches, cliff dwellings and petroglyphs, even prehistoric fossils. No services are available inside the monument, which is administered by the Bureau of Land Management. Information on road and trail conditions, as well as topographical maps of the region, can be obtained from the Escalante Interagency Office. ~ 755 West Main Street, Escalante; 435-826-5499.

▲ Primitive campsites are located throughout the national monument; no charge. You must supply your own water.

CALF CREEK FALLS RECREATION AREA 🏃 🛶 ⛵ Gorgeous gorges and a waterfall that rushes down 126 feet over sandstone cliffs are reached after a moderate walk. The lush setting of cottonwood trees makes Calf Creek a cool place to dine outdoors. There are restrooms. Day-use fee, $2 per vehicle. ~ Route 12, about 15 miles east of Escalante; 435-826-5499.

▲ There are 13 sites; $7 per night.

Outdoor Adventures

FISHING

Rainbow, brook, cutthroat and German brown trout are plentiful, while bass, crappie, catfish and bluegill can be found in a few bodies of water. More than a dozen reservoirs, as well as natural lakes, creeks and rivers in southwestern Utah, are stocked for fishing. Remember to get a state fishing license; nonresidents 14 and over pay $21 for seven days, $46 for a full year, while residents pay $15 for a week, $21 for a year.

ST. GEORGE AREA   The two most popular lakes among anglers are in state parks. **Gunlock Reservoir**, 16 miles northwest on the Santa Clara River, has year-round fishing for bass and crappie. **Quail Creek Reservoir**, 11 miles northeast near the Hurricane exit from Route 15, is good for rainbow trout, bass and bluegill. For more information, licenses and tackle, try the **Hurst Sports Center**. ~ 160 North 500 West, St. George; 435-673-6141.

ZION AREA   The Virgin River running through the park is stocked with trout, but anglers report a distinct lack of success. Better to try **Kolob Reservoir**, 21 miles north of Virgin via North Creek and Kolob Terrace Road.

CEDAR CITY AREA   **Parowan Creek**, flowing northward from Brian Head, and **Yankee Meadow Lake**, on Bowery Creek southeast of Parowan, are likely trout locations. Among the reservoirs within an hour's drive of Cedar City that offer dependable trout fishing are **Baker, Duck Creek, Enterprise, Kolob** and **Pine Valley**. Area lakes worth dipping your line in include **Navajo Lake**. **Ron's Sporting Goods** has information on where to catch fish and get a license. ~ 138 South Main Street, Cedar City; 435-586-9901.

BRYCE AREA   Trout-rich **Panguitch Lake** is nearly as popular in the winter for ice fishing as it is as a summer resort. Boats, bait, tackle and licenses can be secured on Panguitch Lake through the venerable **Aspen Cove Resort**. ~ 225 North Shore Road, Panguitch Lake; 435-676-8339, 866-497-5581; www.aspencoveresort.

com. Also offering rentals on the lake is **Deer Trail Lodge**. ~ Clear Creek Canyon Road; 435-676-2211, 866-676-2211; www.deer trail.com.

Just west of Bryce Canyon, south of Route 12, **Tropic Reservoir** offers excellent trout fishing. Northeast of the national park, **Pine Lake** is another fine angling destination. **J.F. Park Flyfishing** can lead you to trout near Bryce Canyon or in Boulder Mountain's lakes. ~ P.O. Box 245, Orderville, UT 84758; 435-648-2868; www.jfparkerflyfishing.com. Also guiding in the Tropic and Bryce Canyon area is **Mecham Outfitters**. ~ P.O. Box 71, Tropic, UT 84776; 435-679-8823. Rods for sale and rent, tackle, guides— even a room in their refurbished early 1900s farmhouse—can be found at **Panguitch Anglers**. ~ 21 North Main Street, Panguitch; 435-676-8950; www.panguitchanglers.com.

Sevier River is the only river in the U.S. that runs *entirely* south to north.

ESCALANTE   The Boulder Mountain lakes north and west of Escalante and Boulder contain a world-class brook trout fishery, as well as rainbow, cutthroat and German brown trout. Many of them, however, are inaccessible except by four-wheel-drive vehicle, foot or horseback. Among the most accessible are **Barker Reservoir**, **Posey Lake** and **Lower Bowns Reservoir**.

Steve Stoner of **Boulder Mountain Flyfishing** knows were the trout are biting in the streams on and surrounding Boulder Mountain. ~ 110 West 300 North, Boulder; 435-335-7306, 435-691-0368; www.bouldermountainfly-fishing.com.

Virtually in the town of Escalante itself is 30-acre **Wide Hollow Reservoir**, at Escalante Petrified Forest State Park. The lake has fine rainbow trout, bluegill and bass fishing: ice fishing is popular in winter. **Alpine Angler** operates fishing camps and a knowledgeable guide service throughout the Escalante Area. ~ 310 West Main Street, Torrey; 435-425-3660.

WATER SPORTS

Is it any surprise, with southern Utah's hot summers, that more than a few folks head out in search of water? Although watering holes are somewhat few and far between, they can be found with a little effort.

There is a modest degree of boating at New Castle and Upper Enterprise reservoirs, west of Cedar City; at Gunlock and Quail Creek reservoirs, north of St. George; at Panguitch and Navajo lakes, on either side of Cedar Breaks National Monument; at Tropic Reservoir and Pine Lake, in the Bryce Canyon area; and at Wide Hollow Reservoir in Escalante. Gunlock, Quail Creek and Wide Hollow are especially popular among waterskiers and windsurfers.

CLIMBING

Zion National Park's rock faces are a favorite destination of technical climbers. Backcountry permits are required for overnight climbs, but are available at no cost from the visitors center. Some areas may be closed for reasons of safety or resource management, so climbers are advised to consult park rangers before beginning a trip. Climbing at Bryce Canyon and Cedar Breaks, while they may be inviting, is not permitted. The sandstone in these amphitheaters is too soft to be safe for climbing.

WINTER SPORTS

While primarily a summer destination, more and more people are discovering how beautiful southwestern Utah is once the snow falls.

ZION AREA Sledding and tubing are popular at **Coral Pink Sand Dunes State Park**. ~ Twelve miles south of Route 89 between Mount Carmel Junction and Kanab; 435-648-2800.

CEDAR CITY AREA **Brian Head Ski Resort**, 12 miles southeast of Parowan, is renowned for the volumes of light, dry snow it receives: well over 30 feet a year. Catering to both alpine skiers and snowboarders, Brian Head's six chairlifts serve mostly intermediate terrain on two separate mountains. There's a 1300-foot vertical drop from the mountain's summit at 10,920 feet. Full equipment rentals and ski-school instruction are available. Cross-country skiers like to glide to colorful Cedar Breaks and beyond. About 25 miles of trails extend from the resort center; lessons and rentals are available, but there is no trail-use charge. ~ 329 South Route 143, Brian Head; 435-677-2035, fax 435-677-3883; www.brian head.com.

Catch ski fever just by walking into **George's Ski Shop & Bikes**, where you've probably never seen so much merchandise crammed into a single chalet. Past season's gear is discounted for those who really don't care about this year's colors. A variety of skis plus knowledgeable advice make this the ski shop of choice at Brian Head. They offer biking gear during the summer. ~ 612 Route 143, Brian Head; 435-677-2013.

BRYCE AREA Nordic trails are groomed on the rim of Bryce Canyon. But within the park, skiers can break trail and wander through literally thousands of acres of wilderness, beyond the red-tipped fantasyland of rock spires and figures. Rentals and maps may be secured through **Best Western Ruby's Inn**. ~ Route 63, Bryce Canyon; 435-834-5341.

Sledding and tubing fans head toward Red Canyon, just west of Bryce Canyon on Route 12.

GOLF

Leave the masses behind and play the golf courses of southwestern Utah; scenic and uncrowded best describe the greens out here. Most golfing activity centers around St. George, but you can also find courses farther afield.

ST. GEORGE AREA Temperate weather, even in winter, means year-round play. In fact, many believe it's golf that has put St.

George on the map. There are eight public golf courses in the immediate city area, including the 18-hole **St. George Golf Club**, noted for its long fairways. ~ 2190 South 1400 East; 435-634-5854. **Entrada at Snow Canyon** is a pricey, rolling course designed by professional golfer Johnny Miller. ~ 2511 West Entrada Trail; 435-674-7500. Pine Valley Mountain provides a backdrop for **Green Spring Golf Course**. ~ 588 North Green Spring Drive; 435-673-7888. **Southgate Golf Course** borders the Santa Clara River. ~ 1975 South Tonaquint Drive; 435-628-0000. *Golf Digest* has ranked **Sunbrook Golf Course** as Utah's best. ~ 2240 West Sunbrook Drive; 435-634-5866.

One word of warning: Don't pick any pieces of petrified wood as souvenirs because legend has it that bad things come to those who do. Instead, buy a piece of wood at one of the rock shops located in Escalante.

The first golf course built in St. George, the nine-hole **Dixie Red Hills Golf Course** is surrounded by sandstone cliffs. ~ 645 West 1250 North; 435-634-5852. The nine-hole, par-three **Twin Lakes Golf Course** has been called Utah's "most picturesque." ~ 660 North Twin Lakes Drive; 435-673-4441.

ZION AREA   **Sky Mountain Golf Course** encompasses black lava outcroppings 15 miles east of St. George. ~ 1030 North 2600 West, Hurricane; 435-635-7888. **Thunderbird Golf Course** is a challenging nine-hole links where golfers must tee off over cliffs and ponds. ~ Route 89, Mount Carmel Junction; 435-648-2009. **Coral Cliff Golf Course** is another nine-hole course, wedged in the Red Canyon on the road toward Lake Powell. ~ 700 East Route 89, Kanab; 435-644-5005.

CEDAR CITY AREA   Cedar Ridge Golf Course is an 18-hole course open year-round, weather permitting. ~ 200 East 900 North; 435-586-2970.

RIDING STABLES

Riding through the sometimes-rugged Color Country on leisurely horseback trips is one of the best ways to explore steep canyons. The horses are likely to be as sure-footed as mules at the Bryce and Zion National Park concessions, the only horse rides allowed into these parks—the others are relegated to their peripheries.

ZION AND BRYCE AREAS   The main place to hitch up is with **Canyon Trail Rides**, the concessionaire in both of these national parks as well as the North Rim of the Grand Canyon. Inquire at the park lodges between April and October (Zion: 435-772-3967; Bryce: 435-834-5219), or reserve ahead. ~ P.O. Box 128, Tropic, UT 84776; 435-679-8665; www.canyonrides.com. Several Bryce trails are specifically set aside for riding.

Adjacent to Bryce Canyon, **Ruby's Red Canyon Horseback Rides** offers a variety of trips ranging in length from one hour to overnight. ~ Best Western Ruby's Inn, Route 12; 435-834-5341.

Day trips are also offered by **Red Canyon Trail Rides** from May through September, by reservation. ~ Bryce Canyon Pines Motel, Route 12, six miles northwest of the Bryce Canyon entrance; 435-834-5441, 800-892-7923. At Panguitch Lake, try **Black Mountain Outfitters**. ~ 435-676-2664.

ESCALANTE AREA Scenic Safaris will take you into the Kodachrome Basin area. ~ Cannonville; 435-679-8536. **Escalante Canyon Outfitters** reach some of the more forsaken corners of Grand Staircase–Escalante National Monument. ~ Boulder; 435-335-7311, 888-326-4453; www.ecohike.com. **Boulder Mountain Ranch** has trips that climb to the Aquarius Plateau. ~ Boulder; 435-335-7480; www.boulderutah.com/bmr. **Hondoo Rivers & Trails** offers guided horseback tours of the area. ~ 90 East Main Street, Torrey; 435-425-3519.

PACK TRIPS & LLAMA TREKS

Southwestern Utah's canyon country begs you to get out of your car and explore. While there's a lot you can do on your own, if you feel a bit timid about striking off cross-country, there are a few groups ready to help out.

ZION AREA For trips of several days, check with **Rick Marchal Pack Saddle Trips**. ~ P.O. Box 918, Hurricane, UT 84737; 435-635-4950.

BRYCE AREA Adjacent to the national park, you can take one-hour, two-hour, half-day, full-day, or overnight rides along the canyon rim with **Ruby's Scenic Rim-Trail Rides**. ~ Best Western Ruby's Inn, Route 12; 435-679-8761, 800-679-5859. Or you can hit the backcountry with **Red Rock Ride**. ~ P.O. Box 128, Tropic, UT 84776; 435-679-8665.

ESCALANTE AREA Red Rock 'n Llamas will get a beast of burden to carry your load into Escalante Canyon or Glen Canyon for a variety of adventures. ~ P.O. Box 1304, Boulder, UT 84716; 435-559-7325, 877-955-2627; www.redrocknllamas.com.

BIKING

Cyclists are starting to discover this region for its sights, interesting topography and varied terrain. While mountain bikers overrun Moab at certain times of the year, these trails are just being discovered.

ST. GEORGE AREA An intermediate loop ride is **Pine Valley Pinto**, a 35-mile trek across dirt road and pavement. Best ridden between April and October, the route is mostly gentle, although hills sneak in on occasion. Give yourself three to five hours. Take Route 18 north from St. George 25 miles to the town of Central. Turn right (east) toward Pine Valley recreation area. The loop begins on Forest Road 011, six miles from the Route 18 junction.

Snow Canyon Loop takes riders about 24 miles, passing through the towns of Santa Clara and Ivins before climbing through Snow Canyon State Park. (The part of the loop through the state park is on the highway and can be dangerous.) Start the loop at the northwest end of St. George along Bluff Street. Go west at the Bluff Street and Sunset Boulevard intersection. Route 91 takes you to Santa Clara, veer north to Ivins, then climb six miles to the park. After one climb, Route 18 is downhill all the way home.

ZION AREA An easy ride is Route 9 from **Springdale through Zion National Park** (11 miles), but there are steep switchbacks and a one-mile tunnel through which bicycles are not permitted to pass. You should arrange for a car to transport you and your bicycle through the tunnel. A bicycle is one of the best ways to tour Zion Canyon Scenic Drive from the south visitors center to the Temple of Sinawava, a massive rock canyon. Another good bike route in Zion is the two-mile **Pa'rus Trail**, which follows the Virgin River from the south entrance of the park to Scenic Drive.

> Snow Canyon has served as movie location for several films including *Butch Cassidy and the Sundance Kid*.

Mount Carmel Junction to Coral Pink Sand Dunes is also a favored road ride. Take Route 89 toward Kanab, and after three uphill miles you'll spot a turnoff sign to the park ten miles away.

CEDAR CITY AREA Both beginners and advanced riders will enjoy **New Harmony Trail** (3.6 miles), one of southern Utah's finest single-track rides. The trail offers a view point of Kolob Canyons, then a gradual uphill climb to Commanche Springs. Take Route 15 to Exit 42, then follow a westbound road four miles to the town of New Harmony and park your car at the far outskirts of town.

Fir and aspen forests enshroud Route 14, a scenic byway from **Cedar City to Cedar Breaks National Monument**. While the paved road is a delight, you'll need stamina and good lung capacity to make the more-than-4000-foot climb (25 miles).

When the snow melts, bike lovers hold forth on the trails around Brian Head. Mountain biking season at Brian Head usually begins in mid- to late June and runs into October, when cold weather and snow signals that ski season isn't too far off. Experts enjoy the single-track rides, while those less inclined to tight spaces go for the dirt roads and double-track trails. A moderate ten-mile loop in the Brian Head vicinity is the **Scout Camp Loop Trail**. Begin from the Brian Head Town Hall on Route 143 and ride to Bear Flat Road and Steam Engine Meadow. There's a cabin and, you guessed it, an engine on the trail. The trail continues toward Hendrickson Lake and the namesake scout camp.

Another popular ride that's relatively easy is **Pioneer Cabin**, about a six-mile journey on a wide, dirt road and single track that begins from Burt's Road. The 1800s-era cabin has aspen trees growing out of its roof!

BRYCE AREA   Dave's Hollow Trail (4 miles) near Bryce Canyon National Park is a pleasant ride through meadows and pine forests that's recommended for all abilities. At the boundary line to the park, about one mile south of Ruby's Inn, is a dirt road that heads west. Follow the road about one-half mile, then turn right about three-fourths mile along the trail. This begins a ride along a mellow, double-track trail that ends at the Forest Service station.

The **Red Canyon Trail** (5 miles) debuted in 2002 and was widely lauded, for obvious reasons. Not only does it run through beautiful landscape between Red Canyon and Bryce Canyon National Park, it does so on a paved bike path away from Route 12 traffic. It runs slightly uphill from the Red Canyon Visitor Center to the Coyote Hollow Parking Area.

From the Coyote Hollow Parking Area, experienced riders can pedal back to the visitors center via the more rugged **Thunder Mountain Trail**. This nearly 8-mile-long single-track trail winds through a ponderosa pine forest for part of the time before breaking out into a red-rock landscape.

ESCALANTE AREA   Atop the Aquarius Plateau, highest plateau in the United States, via the true-to-its name Hell's Backbone Road from Escalante, mountain bikers have a party on the spur roads near **Posy Lake** and the **Blue Spruce Campground**.

Bike Rentals   You can find guides, rent bikes and camping gear near Zion National Park from **Bike Zion**. ~ 1458 Zion Park Boulevard, Springdale; 435-772-3929; www.bikezion.com. Another outlet for bike rentals, repairs and guided trips near Zion National Park is **Springdale Cycle Tours**, next to the Mean Bean Coffee House. ~ 932 Zion Park Boulevard, Springdale; 435-772-0575; www.springdalecycles.com. For gear and equipment rentals in Cedar City call **Bike Route**. ~ 70 West Center Street; 435-586-4242.

HIKING   Some of the most spectacular hiking in the country can be found in this corner of Utah. Take your pick of national parks and monuments, fill your water bottle and head for the trails. All distances listed for hiking trails are one way unless otherwise noted.

ST. GEORGE AREA   Short on time and even shorter on endurance? We have just the place for you. Drive north on Main Street until it deadends, take a hard right and wind to the top of Red Hill. Park at the base of **Sugar Loaf**, the red sandstone slab with the white DIXIE letters, and start walking for a few yards. The view of St. George is nothing short of spectacular.

Snow Canyon offers several excellent hikes. One of the most popular is **Hidden Pinyon** (.75 mile), which takes you past a wide variety of plant life and geological formations. See if you can find the hidden piñon pine tree at the end of the trail.

Another popular Snow Canyon hike is to the **Lava Caves** (.75 mile) near the north end of the canyon. If you plan on exploring the rugged caves, take along a flashlight and good judgment. Watch for the sign along the road north of the campgrounds.

ZION AREA **Zion National Park** is considered one of the best hiking parks in the nation with a variety of well-known trails. A comprehensive list is included in the Zion National Park brochure. Regardless of which trail you choose, expect the unexpected—a swamp, waterfall, petrified forest or bouquets of wildflowers.

Also expect company, and lots of it, on **Riverside Walk** (1 mile), which traces the Virgin River upstream to Zion Canyon Narrows, just one of the tight stretches where 20-foot-wide canyons loom 2000 feet overhead. The concrete path winds among high cliffs and cool pools of water where many visitors stop to soak their tootsies. This easy trail begins at the Temple of Sinawava.

Angels Landing (2.4 miles) is a strenuous hike that begins at The Grotto Picnic Area and offers incredible views over the sheer drops of Zion Canyon. Believe it or not, the trail is built into solid rock, including 21 short switchbacks called "Walters Wiggles." The last half-mile follows a steep, narrow ridge with a 1500-foot dropoff. While a support-chain railing is of some help, the trail isn't recommended for the faint of heart or anyone with "high" anxiety.

Another heavily visited trail system is at **Emerald Pools**. The easy, paved trail (.6 mile) to Lower Emerald Pool is shaded by cottonwood, box elder and Gambel oak. Trail's end finds a waterfall with pool below. The more stout-of-heart can venture to the Upper Pool (1.3 miles), a rough and rocky trail. The trailhead is at Zion Lodge.

Views of the West Temple, Towers of the Virgin and the town of Springdale are the reward at the end of the **Watchman Trail**

THE ROAD LESS TRAVELED

Hole in the Rock Road from Escalante to Lake Powell is a drive/bike ride that's not to be missed. First forged by Mormon pioneers looking for a "shortcut" to southeast Utah to establish new settlements, the famous and now vastly improved dirt road (54 miles) skirts along the Straight Cliffs and sandstone markers to landmark Dance Hall Rock, a natural amphitheater where the pioneers were said to have held a party and dance. Just past this point are the Sooner Tanks, potholes that often fill with water. Beyond the holes is a set of natural bridges. But this is where the route really deteriorates; just imagine how tough the trail would have been 100 years ago when you were riding in a covered wagon! From the end of the road there is a steep foot trail down to the lake.

(1 mile). Considered moderately difficult, the trailhead is located at the visitors center.

Considered one of the most strenuous hikes within Zion, **West Rim Trail** (13.3 miles) takes two days, culminating at Lava Point. Hikers are blessed with scenic vistas including Horse Pasture Plateau, a "peninsula" extending south from Lava Point, surrounded by thousand-foot cliffs. Lightning strikes are frequent on the plateau, and uncontrolled wildfires have left some areas robbed of vegetation. Other views along the way include Wildcat Canyon, the Left and Right Forks of North Creek and Mt. Majestic. The trailhead starts at the Grotto Picnic Area.

Outfitters   Leave your hiking boots back home? Need a daypack or hiking staff? Then stop by **Zion Outdoor Gear and Clothing**, located a floor below the Zion Pizza & Noodle Co. ~ 868 Zion Park Boulevard, Springdale; 435-772-0630.

CEDAR CITY AREA   There are two developed trails within Kolob Canyons. **Taylor Creek Trail** (2.7 miles) follows a small creek in the shadow of Tucupit and Paria Points, two giant redrock cliffs. The creek forks in three directions, but the path straight down the middle goes past two of the three homesteading cabins that still exist in Kolob Canyons and ends at Double Arch Alcove, a large, colorful grotto with a high arch above. The trail starts from the Taylor Creek parking area two miles into Kolob Canyons Road.

The only way to see one of the world's largest freestanding arch involves a two-day trek along **Kolob Arch Trail** (7 miles), a strenuous descent following Timber and La Verkin creeks. After reaching the magnificent arch, which spans 310 feet from end to end, you might continue on to Beartrap Canyon, a narrow, lush side canyon with a small waterfall.

Two highcountry trails are within **Cedar Breaks National Monument**. Both explore the rim but don't descend into the breaks itself. **Alpine Pond Trail** (2 miles) is a loop that passes through a picturesque forest glade and alpine pond fed by melting snow and small springs. The trailhead begins at the Chessmen Meadow parking area.

Wasatch Ramparts Trail (2 miles) starts just outside the visitors center and ends at a 9952-foot overlook of the Cedar Breaks amphitheater. Along the way, pause at Spectra Point, a 10,285-foot viewpoint.

HIDDEN ►   The **Twisted Forest Trail** (1 mile) is a scattered grove of grey and gnarled bristlecone pine trees growing on the northern lip of Cedar Breaks National Monument. The trees, which somehow find nourishment in the barren reddish-pink soils, are found at the end of a nearly mile-long trail running just inside the Ashdown Gorge Wilderness Area. To reach the area, go to the Sugarloaf

Road, a dirt Forest Service road, just southwest of Brian Head. At the first junction you reach, bear left and continue to the parking area near the trailhead. Although the trail is less than a mile from the parking area to the trees, the 10,000-plus-foot elevation could tax hikers not accustomed to the elevation.

BRYCE AREA   Two hours worth of hiking time in **Red Canyon** can bring big rewards. The **Buckhorn Trail** (1 mile) begins at the campground and ascends high above the canyon past handsome rocks. **Pink Ledges Trail** (.5 mile) is a simple, short jaunt through brilliant-red formations. The trailhead starts near the visitors center. If you don't mind sharing your turf with a horse, try the **Cassidy Trail** (9 miles), named for that famous outlaw, that traverses ponderosa pine and more of those ragged rocks.

Bryce Canyon is hiking central because it's so darn beautiful. Uneasy around hordes of people? Either set out extra early or later in the day—the light shines deliciously on the rocks at both sunrise and sunset—or plan on spending a few days in the backcountry to wander into castles and cathedrals, temples, palaces and bridges. There are more than 60 miles worth of trails on which to wander.

The outstanding **Under-the-Rim Trail** (23 miles) connecting Bryce Point with Rainbow Point could be turned into a multiday trip if side canyons, springs and buttes are explored to their full potential.

Riggs Spring Loop Trail (8.8 miles) starts at Yovimpa Point and takes best advantage of the Pink Cliffs. More moderate is the **Bristlecone Loop Trail** (1 mile) that begins atop the plateau and leads to sweeping views of spruce forests, cliffs and bristlecone pines.

One of the most famous, and rightly so, trails within the Bryce boundaries is **Queen's Garden** (1.5 miles). Start from Sunrise Point and dive right into this amazing amphitheater. Taking a

CRACKS IN THE EARTH

Slot canyons are gorgeously fluted channels through the red-rock landscape. Cut by streaming flood waters that bore through sandstone, "slots" vary in size. Some might be 20 feet across and only 50 feet deep, others 100 to 200 feet high and only a few feet wide. Some might meander for a quarter mile, others for many miles. All can be deadly when thunderstorms spawn flash floods. Before heading out for a day of exploring these canyons, be sure to check the regional forecast, as storms ten miles away can create floods.

spur to the **Navajo Loop Trail** (an additional mile) brings you within view of the Silent City, a hauntingly peaceful yet ominous army of hoodoos. The trail ends at Sunset Point.

In the park's northern section is the **Fairyland Loop Trail** (8 miles). Moderately strenuous, the loop provides views of Boat Mesa and the fantasy features of the fairy area. Near the splitting point for the horse trail is the monolith known as Gulliver's Castle. An easier route is **Rim Trail** (up to 11 miles) along the edge of the Bryce Amphitheater that can be taken in small or large doses.

At **Kodachrome Basin State Park** the trails are short and sweet, offering plenty of satisfaction with little effort. From the **Panorama Trail** (3 miles) you get to see the Ballerina Slipper formation. At **Arch Trail** (.2 mile) there is—surprise, surprise—a natural arch. The most arduous of Kodachrome's trails is **Eagle View Overlook** (.5 mile), but the valley views make it all worthwhile.

Driving or hiking south of Kodachrome on the dirt road for about 15 miles brings you to **Cottonwood** and **Hackberry Canyons** which merit exploration for their fossils, springs, homesteaders' cabins and hidden wonders. Because the area is such virgin country, a good topographic map is imperative before setting out, and good route-finding skills are helpful in the backcountry.

ESCALANTE AREA   Because of high temperatures during the height of summer, the best hiking weather on the Grand Staircase–Escalante National Monument are April 1 to June 1 and September 1 to October 31. There are several access points to the awesome and somewhat mysterious **Escalante Canyons**. A main point of departure is east of town one mile on Route 12. Turn left on the dirt road near the cemetery and left again after the cattle guard. Follow to the fence line and begin at the hiker maze. The trail leads into the upper Escalante Canyon portion of Death Hollow, an outstanding recreation area. For an overnight or three-night trip continue on to where the trails come out 15 miles down the river.

Quite popular here is the **Lower Calf Creek Falls Trail** (2.8 miles), about a mile up the highway from the lower Escalante Canyon entrance. The sandy trail passes towering cliffs on a gradual incline. You are rewarded with a beautiful waterfall.

Outfitters   If you really want to get off the beaten path, hire **Escalante Outback Adventures** to guide you into the outback of south-central Utah. The company can lead you to slot canyons, dinosaur tracks and archaeological artifacts. They also offer stargazing trips. ~ 325 West Main Street, Escalante; 435-826-4967, 877-777-7988; www.escalante-utah.com.

Route 70 almost slices Utah in two as it runs east–west from the Colorado border. It ends at **Route 15**, Utah's main north–south artery that passes through Cedar City and St. George.

▼▼▼▼▼▼▼▼▼▼▼▼
Transportation

CAR

Route 14 branches east off Route 15 at Cedar City toward Cedar Breaks, while **Route 9** heads east from Route 15 to Springdale and the entrance of Zion National Park.

Route 89, a scenic byway, heads south from Route 70 through parts of Dixie National Forest before crossing Kanab, intersecting Routes 9, 12 and 14 en route. **Route 12** provides a pretty path to Bryce Canyon National Park and Grand Staircase–Escalante National Monument.

AIR

Skywest/Delta Connection serves both **St. George Municipal Airport** (435-634-3000) and **Cedar City Regional Airport** (435-586-3033). Airport shuttles are provided in St. George by **Quality Cab**. ~ 435-656-5222.

BUS

Greyhound Bus Lines (800-231-2222; www.greyhound.com) can bring you to southwestern Utah from around the country. The bus stops in St. George at a McDonald's restaurant. ~ 1235 South Bluff Street; 435-673-2933. There's also a depot in Cedar City. ~ 1355 South Main Street; 435-586-9465.

CAR RENTALS

Rental agencies at St. George Municipal Airport include **Avis Rent A Car** (800-331-1212) and **National Car Rental** (800-227-7368). Other agencies in town include **Budget Rent A Car** (435-673-6825), **Dollar Rent A Car** (800-800-4000), **Enterprise Rent A Car** (435-634-1556) and **Hertz Rent A Car** (435-652-9941, 435-674-4789).

At the Cedar City Municipal Airport, cars can be rented from **Avis Rent A Car** (800-331-1212) and **National Car Rental** (435-586-4004). **Speedy Rental** (435-586-7368) serves Cedar City as well.

TAXIS

In Cedar City, cab service is provided 24 hours by **Cedar City Cab**. ~ 435-586-9333.

SEVEN

Southeastern Utah

 How best to describe southeastern Utah? For starters, Teddy Roosevelt, America's quintessential outdoorsman, once traveled here. Then consider the fact that amusement-park thrills and manmade attractions have nothing on this place. Forget the Coney Island roller coaster. Plummet down a 30-degree incline at Moki Dugway or the Moab Slickrock Bike Trail. The rickety bridge on Tom Sawyer Island in Disneyland? You can sway and swing across a genuine suspension bridge over the San Juan River outside Bluff. And Gateway Arch in St. Louis becomes a mere modern toy after you see Mother Nature's natural design at Arches National Park.

This truly is a magic kingdom for the outdoors enthusiast, the naturalist, the archaeologist. Leave those luxury resorts, white-sand beaches and gleaming steel museums behind. In this region, the land reigns.

What's really ironic is that Mormon exiles thought they were entering America's wasteland when they fled to Utah in 1847—this land is anything but barren. Take all the earth's geologic wonders, toss them into a blender and you have southeastern Utah. An array of mesas abuts dense forests adjacent to broad deserts with red-rock canyons and slender spires thrusting out of semiarid valleys. In this portion of the Colorado Plateau lie the spectacular Arches and Canyonlands national parks, Glen Canyon National Recreation Area (Lake Powell), a national forest, two national monuments and a host of state parks.

Because southeastern Utah is so vast and diverse we have divided it into four geographic areas—Moab, Northern San Juan County, Southern San Juan County and Lake Powell. At the heart of the entire region sits Canyonlands National Park. Canyonlands divides into three sections, which though contiguous are not directly connected by roads. Therefore you will find The Maze section of the park described in the Lake Powell section, the Needles district in the Northern San Juan County listings and the park's Island in the Sky section within the Moab area listings.

Erosion is the architect of southeastern Utah. Over the millennia, land masses pushed through the earth's crust, rivers and streams carved deep canyons, wind and

350

water etched mountainsides. On some of the rock walls are pictures and stories left behind by early man that seem to transcend the ages.

The first known people in southeastern Utah were here long before the Europeans even knew about America. They were the ancestors of today's Pueblo Indians. Evidence of these early builders and farmers is abundant in the sites of their homes found among the cliffs, on the mesa tops and in the canyons.

When the tribes disappeared from southeastern Utah and the Four Corners region around the 13th century, they left dwellings, tools and plenty of personal possessions behind. Theories abound as to what prompted their hasty departure. Some look to about A.D. 1276 when a long drought ruined the harvest and depleted the food supply. There were dangers from marauding bands of fierce nomadic tribes. Others theorize that inexplicable fears caused by religious beliefs may have contributed. Still others—"The X-Files" generation—insist that they zapped back to their point of origin via flying saucers. Regardless of influences, the Pueblo peoples abandoned the region, and their living spaces and remnant continue to fascinate generations of archaeologists and amateur sleuths.

By the 14th century, the Navajo had become part of the landscape. Today, their reservation sprawls across 16 million acres of Utah, Arizona and New Mexico.

The first known contact by Europeans came in 1765 when Juan María de Rivera led a trading expedition north from New Mexico, hoping to establish a new supply route with California. That route, which became known as the Old Spanish Trail, opened portions of southeastern Utah near what is now Moab.

In July 1776, a small band led by Franciscan friars, Fathers Francisco Dominguez and Silvestre Vélez de Escalante, ventured from Santa Fe, New Mexico, intent on an overland journey to Monterey, California. They never made it, but their adventurous trek took them in a great loop through unexplored portions of the region including what is known today as Wahweap Marina at Lake Powell.

When traders finally realized that the crossing of the Colorado River near Moab bypassed more hazardous terrain in Colorado, the 1200-mile Old Spanish Trail opened great portions of Utah to commercial wagon trains. By 1830 the trail began to serve as a major trade route for European expansion into the West.

Nearly a century after the adventurous Spanish priests, a one-armed veteran of the Civil War, John Wesley Powell, led an expedition party on a thrilling and sometimes dangerous 1400-mile rowboat trip from Green River in Wyoming to the lower Grand Canyon, charting the Colorado River and a deep southern Utah canyon that almost a century later would be inundated with a manmade lake that would bear his name.

To extend its boundaries and promote its principles throughout Utah, the Mormon Church decided to settle the area. Brigham Young sent 42 men down the Old Spanish Trail to Moab. But after an attack by Ute Indians, the settlers departed. Twenty-two years later, however, another group of hearty souls tried again, this time establishing the town of Moab in 1877.

In April 1879, an exploration party scouted the San Juan country and reported that the area could be colonized. A group of 250 pioneers, 83 wagons and 1000 head of cattle left the relative safety of Cedar City in southwestern Utah for a 325-mile journey to what is now Bluff. Originally estimated as a trip of six weeks, their arduous journey took six months as they chiseled and chopped their way through sand and rock and at one point lowered wagons down the western wall of Glen Canyon through what is now the legendary Hole-in-the-Rock.

Settlers here discovered that Mother Nature rewarded southeastern Utah with more than scenic beauty. Rich with tremendous natural resources, the land bursts with coal, crude oil, oil shale, natural gas and more. In the 1950s uranium mining formed the heart of this area until the boom turned bust, but beds of potash and magnesium salts found deep within the soil continue to be mined.

Whether a pioneer Mormon or a modern-day adventurer, people have always found the weather to be a blessing. It gets hot here (summers average in the 90s), but during the other seasons the climate by and large is mild. Winter ranges in the 30s to low 40s, and precipitation is extremely low except in October, when there might be all of an inch of rainfall. Yet within the La Sal and Abajo mountains, skiers and snowshoers find abundant powder in wintertime.

To this day, southeastern Utah remains sparsely populated. Towns here are small (the largest, Moab, boasts just over 4000 residents) and exude a "pioneer" atmosphere. Tightly clustered buildings set up in traditional Mormon pattern along wide streets, these are sensible towns with a strong backbone. Youngsters still ride their bicycles at sunset or walk hand-in-hand to Sunday services. Going out for a drink is more likely to mean a soda pop than a beer.

Moab now supports a diverse and growing population based on tourism, mining, agriculture and retirement. It is considered one of the most cosmopolitan small communities in Utah and is one of its fastest growing.

Fifty-three miles northwest of Moab lies the town of Green River, which was founded as a waystation in the late 1870s for mail carriers and remains but a waystation. Truckers and other travelers along Route 70 stop for a bite to eat, some gas and perhaps a room for the night before moving on, east and west. Whitewater enthusiasts, meanwhile, both begin and end trips at the town, which practically straddles the river whose name it shares. While the rugged Book Cliffs and Tavaputs Plateau lie to the north of town, Canyonlands National Park sprawls to the south.

South of Moab, present-day San Juan County has a population of more than 12,000 scattered among farms, hamlets and communities like Monticello, Blanding and Bluff. Most growth can be attributed to natural resource–based industries. The Navajo and Ute Indian reservations comprise a large portion of the southern end of the county, with American Indians making up about 47 percent of the San Juan population.

In southeastern Utah, history and geology combine to draw the curious and the hearty. Though man has always explored the region by foot or automobile, the advent of mountain bikes opened up entirely new portals into the backcountry areas. John Wesley Powell's historic trip down the Green and Colorado rivers can now be easily run by whitewater enthusiasts. And onetime rugged cattle-drive routes are covered up with asphalt for the less-intrepid explorers.

Prized nooks and crannies are being "discovered" every day. This glorious land remains ever changing, continually revealing surprises long after any new wonders were thought to remain.

Movies made Moab famous, but the area has a lot more going for it. Used as a home base for many who explore southeastern Utah, the city has a well-preserved, colorful history. Add to this two wonderful national parks in the region, a neat loop drive, even a winery. What more could you want?

Moab serves as gateway to both Arches National Park and Canyonlands National Park—Island in the Sky. On your way to Island

Southeastern Utah

Price River

6
191

Green River

0   25 miles
0   25 kilometers

70

70

SAN RAFAEL REEF

24

128

Arches National Park

191

313

Moab

Island in the Sky 6000'

Green River

Manti-La Sal National Forest

Canyonlands National Park

Caineville   24   Hanksville

46

95

The Maze

The Needles

Glen Canyon National Recreation Area

Canyonlands National Park

Capitol Reef National Park

276

Colorado River

Manti-La Sal National Forest

Monticello

191

666

Burr Trail

95

Glen Canyon National Recreation Area

Natural Bridges National Monument

Blanding

276

261

95

191

Hovenweep National Monument

Glen Canyon National Recreation Area

Bluff

San Juan River

163

Lake Powell

Rainbow Bridge National Monument

Navajo Indian Reservation

Mexican Hat

191

Navajo Indian Reservation

Gouldings

A   R   I   Z   O   N   A

163

Monument Valley Navajo Tribal Park

160

Mexican Water

160

C O L O R A D O

N M

Text continued on page 356.

Rock of Ages

Day 1
- After a hearty breakfast at the **Sorrel River Ranch Resort** (page 362), your base camp for the next three days, return to Moab via River Road and then head north on Route 191 and then west on Route 313 to the **Island in the Sky** district (page 356) of Canyonlands National Park. Spend some time in the visitors center to gain an appreciation for this canyon-riddled landscape, then head into the district to get an up-close look at it. **Mesa Arch**, six miles south of the center, is an open window that tightly frames Buck Canyon.

- From Mesa Arch, drive five miles west to **Whale Rock**, a portly rock outcropping that invites scampering across. Jutting above the desert landscape, the rock provides great views in all directions. Nearby is a trail leading to **Upheaval Dome**, which is really a 1500-foot-deep hole in the ground, not a dome. Geologists are divided over what created the crater—a meteorite or the shifting of underground salt beds?

- From Whale Rock, backtrack towards Mesa Arch and then head south to **Grand View Point Overlook**, which provides spectacular views of the White Rim, the Colorado and Green rivers.

Day 2
- After loading your cooler with a picnic lunch and plenty of cold drinks, head into **Arches National Park** (page 358). A stop at the visitors center helps orient you and allows you to top off any water bottles. From there, head toward **Balanced Rock**, stopping at the **Park Avenue Viewpoint** and **Petrified Dunes Viewpoint**.

- From Balanced Rock, drive to the **Devils Garden Trailhead** and a hike towards Devils Garden, passing **Pine Tree Arch**, **Tunnel Arch** and **Landscape Arch** along the way. Hardy hikers will enjoy the **Primitive Trail** that gets little traffic.

- In late afternoon, backtrack to the **Delicate Arch** trailhead. The hike to the arch is not undertaken at mid-day, both because of the heat in summer and the high sun. By late afternoon things have started to cool a bit and the setting sun creates great light conditions for photography.

- After your hike to Delicate Arch, sate your hunger at **Center Café and Market** (page 369) or back at Sorrel River Ranch Resort.

Day 3 • The entire day could be spend exploring the **Slickrock Trail**, Moab's renowned mountain bike circuit that skitters across the desert's slickrock. Those not inclined for such an undertaking can tour **Castle Creek Winery** (page 361) or ride to the top of the **Moab Rim** via the **Moab Skyway** for a panoramic view of the area.

IF YOU ONLY HAVE ONE DAY

If you only have one day, spend it in **Arches National Park**.

HIDDEN ▶ in the Sky, be sure and stop at **Dead Horse Point State Park**. An isolated, 5250-acre island mesa, 5900 feet above sea level and surrounded by steep cliffs, Dead Horse Point State Park showcases 150 million years of canyon erosion, buttes, pinnacles, bluffs and towering spires plus the Colorado River 2000 feet below. Views from the park overlook 5000 square miles of the Colorado Plateau including the La Sal and Abajo mountain ranges. Admission. ~ Route 313; 435-259-2614, fax 435-259-2615.

CANYONLANDS NATIONAL PARK—ISLAND IN THE SKY   Route 191 connects with Route 313, a road leading into the northern portion of Canyonlands National Park. Natural boundaries of rock and water divide the park into three distinct districts— Island in the Sky, Needles and the Maze—and make travel between the sections almost impossible. Island could be considered the park's overlook, Needles leads visitors into the heart of rock country, while the remote Maze fulfills the promise of solitude and renewal that some seek. If ever you doubted Utah scenery could steal your breath away, this promontory will change your mind. Depending on weather and time of day, the Colorado River Gorge below is an artist's palate of ever-changing hues. For a spectacular view of the park, you can't beat the back deck of the **Visitors Center**. Nearby paths also offer an interpretive guide to regional flora. But don't make the center your only stop. From there drive another mile and a half to the park's majestic overlook. It won't disappoint. ~ 435-259-4712.

Wilder and less trodden than Arches National Park is Canyonlands National Park—Island in the Sky district. It's a broad, level mesa serving as observation deck for the park's 527 square miles of canyons, mesas, arches and cliffs. From this vantage point the visitor can enjoy views of the two powerful rivers (the Colorado and Green) that constitute the park's boundaries and the three mountain ranges (the La Sals, Abajos and Henrys).

Just past the Island in the Sky Visitors Center on the left side is the **Shafer Canyon Overlook** and the winding Shafer Trail Road, which swoops down the canyon to connect to the **White Rim Trail**, so named for the layer of white sandstone that forms its line of demarcation. The White Rim parallels the Colorado and later the Green River, forming a belt around Island in the Sky's circumference. Permits are required for campsites along the relatively level trail (reservations recommended; there is a $30 charge), which can be comfortably covered by bike or sturdy four-wheel-drive vehicle in two to four days.

Back on top of the mesa that is the Island, enjoy a bird's-eye view of **Lathrop Canyon** and the Colorado River via the **Mesa Arch** path. Short and sweet, this trail provides a vantage point for distant arches like Washer Woman, menacing Monster Tower and Airport Tower.

Just a quarter mile west, near the intersection of the park's only two roads, are the Willow Flat campground and the true-to-its-name **Green River Overlook**, a fine contrast to the muddy Colorado. On the road's north side is the short trail to **Aztec Butte**, where you'll find Indian archaeological sites.

At the end of this side road, see the bulbous **Whale Rock** jutting out of its parched home near the geologic paradox of **Upheaval Dome**, a 1500-foot-deep crater with a questionable origin. Theories are divided whether this was a natural occurrence or meteor-created. Weird, moonlike craters with peaks spring from its center.

At the most southerly end of the main road is the **Grand View Point Overlook**. From this vantage point at 6000 feet above sea level, Utah's geologic contrasts become crystal clear. There are totem pole-like spires and the rounded La Sal and Abajo mountains in the distance. The Colorado River cuts so deeply in the canyon below that it's invisible from the overview. Columns and fins

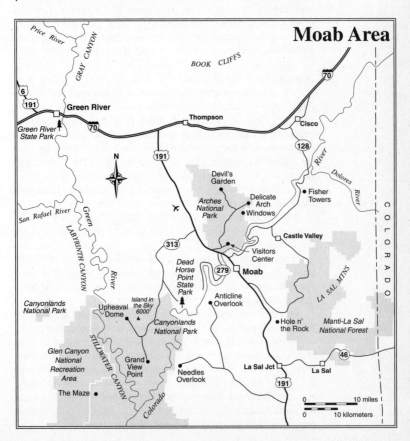

and other contorted rocks comprise a gang of soft sandstone structures called **Monument Basin**. By crossing the White Rim trail it's possible to get a closer look at these monuments.

ARCHES NATIONAL PARK Traversing the width and breadth of Arches National Park on the paved road that author Edward Abbey deplored in his book *Desert Solitaire* (a must-read for any visitor) is easy—maybe too easy. To truly experience the greatest number of natural arches in the country, get out of your car and wander. You won't want to miss the sensation of sandstone beneath shoe, the delicious scent of juniper and sage, even the hauntingly lonely sound of whistling desert wind on the short hiking trails. Admission. ~ Route 191, five miles north of Moab; 435-259-8161.

The world's largest concentration of natural stone arches, extraordinary products of erosion, makes this 76,519-acre park one of the most spectacular in red-rock country. Sandstone panoramas formed by weathering, movement of the earth's crust and erosion range in size from three to 306 feet. Natural monoliths in this semiarid land resemble everything from city skyscrapers to a whale's orb: The interpretation is all in the eye of the beholder.

Make your first stop the **Visitors Center** for a bevy of maps and other publications as well as a slide-show orientation, geology museum and history exhibit. Rangers can point out many of the best attractions. ~ Route 191 at the entrance to the park; 435-719-2299.

From the visitors center the main park road climbs into the heart of the arches region. **Moab Canyon,** a multi-hued example of geological slippage, opens to view about a mile from the center. About six million years ago activity along the Moab fault caused one section of the canyon to shift, resulting in rock formations on the bottom of one side that are identical in age with those on the far side of the canyon.

Farther along at the **South Park Avenue Overlook** you'll see giant sandstone rockfaces that rise sheer on either side of a dry creek bed.

Appearing to defy gravity is **Balanced Rock,** a formation that looks like it might fall from its pedestal at any moment. A short but strenuous trail (.3 mile) can be taken to examine all the boulder's vantage points.

One of the easiest areas to visit is **Windows**. Four large arches that provide natural picture frames for distant panoramas can be effortlessly viewed. The North and South Windows are a short walk in one direction from the parking lot. Take a jaunt the other way and see the Turret Arch. Splendid Double Arch is just across the road. Preludes to the panoramic windows via the Windows road are Garden of Eden viewpoint, providing sweeping views to the north, and Elephant Butte. ~ About 12 miles from the visitors center via the main park road and Windows turnoff.

Balanced Rock marks the start of a rough, four-wheel-drive road into the more secluded Willow Flats and **Herdina Park** sections. Herdina Park's claim to fame is that it's the home to five mini-canyons and the unusual **Eye of the Whale Arch**. With a little imagination, you can see the beast's orb.

Those with heavy-duty vehicles may want to venture another ten miles to the vast and scenic Klondike Bluffs, home to the **Tower Arch**, a hole in a wall of solid rock, and minarets that form the **Marching Men**. Check with the ranger for conditions before traveling this road.

The park's northern section, where the main park road ends, has the largest grouping of spires and openings-in-the-rock. No less than seven arches can be viewed in **Devil's Garden**, the park's longest maintained trail. The most distant of these arches is the Double O, which is about a two-mile trek from the trailhead that feels longer under the hot desert sun. If stamina allows, hike an extra quarter-mile on a more primitive trail to the ominous **Dark Angel** formation.

Some early explorers interpreted Delicate Arch as being a bow-legged cowboy!

Halfway to the trail end is **Landscape Arch**. At 306 feet long (and at one spot only six feet thick) it's one of the world's longest natural stone spans. **Navajo Arch**—did it protect Indians at some juncture?—is one and a half miles from the trailhead. Piñon plants, junipers—the most common tree in the park—the Mormon tea plant, the obnoxious prickly pear and evening primrose and Indian paintbrush flowers dot the area. Pick up an interpretive brochure at the visitors center before setting out to enhance your understanding of the desert garden.

From Devil's Garden it's about one mile south on the main road to the fins (yes, they do look like fish fins) of up to 100 feet high in **Fiery Furnace**, which does not live up to its threatening name on hot days. (Instead, the pinnacles provide a degree of relief when temperatures scorch.) The ranger-guided tour of the Furnace is recommended, since winter erosion and labyrinthine trails make this an easy place in which to get injured or lost.

Traveling back toward the park entrance, take the first turn-off to the left and drive two miles to the **Delicate Arch** trailhead. ◀ HIDDEN
Set aside several hours to really enjoy this graceful monument that stands 65 feet high with a 35-foot opening. Arguably Utah's most beautiful natural wonder, the sensuous bit of slickrock stands boldly against the desert and the distant La Sal Mountains. The one-and-a-half-mile trail skirts historic **Wolfe Ranch**, sole remains of a 19th-century cattle operation that somehow survived more than a generation in this harsh land. Those unable or uninterested in hiking to Delicate Arch can drive an additional mile from the trailhead to the **Delicate Arch Viewpoint** and gaze from there.

MOAB Moab truly is an oasis in the wilderness. Red-rock cliffs really do meet verdant valleys, all in the shadow of the towering La Sal Mountains. First settled in 1855 by missionaries, Moab is laid out in typical Mormon fashion with large, square blocks, wide streets and huge poplar trees. The city takes its name from a remote biblical kingdom east of the River Jordan. Present-day Moab is "sporting central" for the lean-and-mean Lycra-wearing crowd. Spring is high season in Moab, as thousands of ski bums and heat-seekers flock here for desert warmth.

For area information, stop at the **Moab Information Center**. Inside this multi-agency office you'll find information on recreation opportunities on state and federal public lands, as well as lodging, restaurant and outfitter brochures. You'll also find maps, guidebooks and a gift shop here. ~ Center and Main streets, Moab; 435-259-8825, 800-635-6622, fax 435-259-1376; www.discovermoab.com.

Moab's rich history is preserved in the **Dan O'Laurie Museum**. Though the collection is small, it is comprehensive, examining the geology and paleontology of Moab's beginnings. Dozens of photographs recount the development of mining, ranching, early transportation and the Old Spanish Trail. There's even the old switchboard that served all of Moab until 1951. Closed Sunday. ~ 118 East Center Street, Moab; 435-259-7985.

Star Hall, just northeast of the museum, is the start of the **Moab Historic Walking Tour** of 23 homes and commercial structures. Pick up a map at the visitors center.

It was young geologist Charles Steen who first discovered uranium deposits in the region, touching off the rush of miners. The "uranium king" built a **million-dollar home** overlooking the Moab Valley and rivers. The house is now the Sunset Grill (see "Dining"). ~ 900 North Route 191, Moab; 435-259-7146, fax 435-259-7626; e-mail emoab@hotmail.com.

When it gets so hot you think you're going to fry on the sidewalk, head to **Butch Cassidy's King World Waterpark**, where you and the kids can cool off on five waterslides, three pools or simply with a cool drink in the shade. There's even a pond for paddle

LOOK FROM AN OVERLOOK

Southwest of Moab off Route 191 is the **Anticline overlook**, a 2000-foot-high mesa overlooking archlike rocks, the mighty Colorado, Dead Horse Point and Arches National Park to the north. Here Canyonlands travelers can see where they've been and where they're going. ~ Keep an eye out for Anticline and Needles overlook signs when heading south of Moab on Route 191.

boats. What's Butch's connection? The 17-acre water park is built along a canyon the outlaw supposedly used to hide rustled cattle. Admission. ~ 1500 North Route 191, Moab; 801-259-2837.

Utah's first commercial winery, Arches Vineyard, was renamed **Castle Creek Winery** in 2002 and produces cabernet sauvignon, merlot, pinot noir, chardonnay, chenin blanc and gewürztraminer. Located along with the Red Cliffs Lodge (see "Lodging" below) on a working ranch along the Colorado River northeast of Moab, the winery has a tasting room that's open from mid-March through November. ~ Milepost 14, Route 128, Moab; 435-259-3332, 866-812-2002.

Spanish Valley Vineyards and Winery is Moab's other winery, a self-described "estate winery" that for years grew gewürztraminer and riesling grapes for other wineries. But in 1999 the company started bottling the fruits of its own labors, and today produces gewürztraminer, white riesling, and cabernet sauvignon wines. The tasting room is closed Sunday from February through November; appointments can be made in December and January. ~ 4710 South Zimmerman Lane, Moab; 435-259-8134.

Aching for a little respite from the frenetic tourist scene? The **Scott M. Matheson Wetlands Preserve**, jointly owned and managed by The Nature Conservancy and the Utah Division of Wildlife Resources, offers just such an escape. Encompassing nearly 900 acres where Mill Creek flows into the Colorado River west of Moab, the preserve is home to nearly 200 species of waterfowl, songbirds and raptors, as well as numerous amphibians and such riverine mammals as otters and beavers. Naturalists guide walks along the preserve's footpaths at 8 a.m. every Saturday from March through May and September through November. ~ Kane Creek Road, two miles west of Main Street, Moab; 435-259-4629.

Twelve miles south of Moab is **Hole n' the Rock**. You can't miss the gargantuan white letters painted onto the cliffside announcing the place. Attractions like this you either love or hate, and those intrigued by a 5000-square-foot home and gift shop inside solid sandstone will love it. Check out the sculpture of Franklin D. Roosevelt on the rock face above the entrance. Admission. ~ 11037 South Route 191; phone/fax 435-686-2250; www.moab-utah.com/holeintherock.

La Sal Mountains meet red rock along the **La Sal Mountain Loop Drive**. The roundtrip ride from Moab is about 60 miles from start to finish and can be driven in either direction. Plan on a minimum of three to four hours to fully enjoy the views and side trips in the evergreen-laden forests that rise 4000 feet above the red rock. ~ Look for the road marker about eight miles south of downtown Moab off Route 191. Turn left and head into the hills.

◄ HIDDEN

The land seems to change almost immediately as sandstone gives way to forests and foothills. A popular fishing hole and windsurfing spot, **Ken's Lake** is off to the left via a dirt road. Continuing on the La Sal Mountain Loop Drive brings you to a turnoff on the right called Geyser Pass. This road accesses a popular area for cross-country skiing.

Back on the loop road another few miles are turnoffs on the right to scenic lakes Oowah and Warner and a U.S. Forest Service campground. At this point the scenery may make it difficult to remain focused on driving.

Three miles farther on the left is the back entrance to Moab via Sand Flats Road. It's a 20-mile bumpy ride back into town. If you choose to continue on the loop road to the summit, you'll be rewarded with sweeping views of the Castle Valley below.

Nearby on the left side is a turnoff to the **Pinhook Battlefield Monument** and burial grounds. Here, eight members of a posse were laid to rest after battling Indians.

Across the loop on the right is the rough road to the site of an 1890s gold camp called **Miner's Basin**. This ghost town is reported to have produced gold ore valued in excess of $1000 per ton. Note: A four-wheel-drive vehicle is often needed to get to the 10,000-foot-elevation spot.

Beginning your descent into the Castle Valley brings you to Gateway Road on the right side—it's the rear entrance to Gateway, Colorado—and the abandoned mining town of **Castleton**, which boomed in the early 1900s with a hotel, two grocery stores, a school and two saloons.

The desert returns past Castleton as you ease into the truly stunning **Castle Valley**. At left is the volcanic remnant **Round Mountain**. There are the **Priest and Nuns** rock formations (yes, they do resemble a padre and his faithful sisters) jutting heavenward to your right, as well as the landmark **Castle Rock** that's been featured in more commercials than Michael Jordan.

In another four miles the loop road merges with Route 128 and the scenic river route back to Moab. A worthwhile stop before returning to the city is at the Big Bend picnic area for swimming, camping and picnicking.

LODGING

HIDDEN ►

One of the most picturesque, and nurturing, stays can be found 17 miles northeast of Moab at the **Sorrel River Ranch Resort**. Cupped by a bend in the Colorado River, the ranch is backed by towering red-rock buttes that inspired the name of the Castle Valley. Offering a variety of suites that front the river, and some that don't, some with fireplaces, some without, the ranch also contains a restaurant if you don't want to cook for yourself, as well as a swimming pool and spa. There is a barn for your horses, too. ~ Route 128, 17 miles northeast of Moab; 435-259-4642, 877-359-2715, fax 435-259-3016; www.sorrelriver.com, e-mail info@sorrelriver.com. ULTRA-DELUXE.

Edward Abbey

The most important modern writer on the deserts of the American West was undoubtedly Edward Abbey (1927-89). His nonfiction soliloquy *Desert Solitaire: A Season in the Wilderness* (1968) led him to be regarded as a Henry David Thoreau for the 20th century, and his tongue-in-cheek novel *The Monkey Wrench Gang* (1975) inspired a generation of environmental terrorist wannabes. In all, he published 21 books and a wide variety of essays and other writings.

Abbey was an enigma. Branded by conservatives as a liberal and by liberals as a right-wing conspirator, he never wavered from his contention that it was the duty of the true owners of the wilderness—the American people—to actively protect it from overdevelopment. A highly intelligent but irascible cynic, he was Mark Twain driving a battered pickup truck, toting a cooler of beer and a tome of Nietzsche.

Born in Pennsylvania, Abbey left the family farm at the age of 21 to see the American West. He graduated from the University of New Mexico (where his master's thesis was titled "Anarchism and the Morality of Violence") and spent many years as a part-time ranger and fire lookout for the National Park Service.

Two summers at Arches National Monument (now Arches National Park) provided the source material for *Desert Solitaire*. Always a rebel, Abbey spent much of his life rejecting societal expectations. He was more comfortable living in a rusty aluminum trailer, shading a colony of rattle-snakes, than in any city or town. His final home was a ranch near Tucson, Arizona, called "Fort Llatikcuf," a name intended to be read backwards.

After his death from complications of vascular surgery, his widow revealed his last request: to be buried in the desert, quickly and without ceremony. "If my decomposing carcass helps nourish the roots of a juniper tree or the wings of a vulture, that is enough immortality for me," Abbey had written. "And as much as anyone deserves."

Words of advice to an admiring public?

"Do not jump into your automobile next June and rush out to the Canyon country hoping to see some of that which I have attempted to evoke in these pages. In the first place, you can't see anything from a car; you've got to get out of the goddamned contraption and walk, better yet crawl, on hands and knees, over the sandstone and through the cactus. When traces of blood begin to mark your trail you'll see something, maybe."

Art and photography predominate at **Castle Valley Inn**, 16 miles northeast of Moab right off scenic Route 128. The bed and breakfast, located on five acres, is decorated with original Navajo art and signed prints by noted photographers such as Ansel Adams. The eight units all have private baths, and an outdoor hot tub offers spectacular views of both the red-rock monoliths and mountains. A hearty, healthy breakfast is served. ~ 424 Amber Lane, Castle Valley; 435-259-6012, 888-466-6012, fax 435-259-1501; www.castlevalleyinn.com, e-mail mail@castleval leyinn.com. MODERATE TO DELUXE.

Sandwiched between the Colorado River and the red rock of the Castle Valley is the sprawling **Red Cliffs Lodge**. The 40 rooms are set up as suites, with a bedroom, sitting area and kitchenette. This is cowboy country, and you can tell from the knotty pine trim and log furniture. All rooms face the river, and each has a private patio. There's also a swimming pool, a spa, two tennis courts and an exercise room, as well as a 50-horse stable (afternoon trail rides are available). Making this a destination resort is the lodge's restaurant, which has a wide deck with gorgeous views of Fisher Towers. ~ Milepost 14, Route 128, Moab; 435-259-2002, 866-812-2002; www.recliffslodge.com, e-mail info@redcliffslodge.com.

Don't be put off by the plastic and neon located along the Route 191 strip through Moab. While generic, two-story motels dominate, a few blocks off the main drag are some charming inns that welcome weary travelers with a personal touch.

Entering town from the north via Route 191, you can't miss the **Aarchway Inn**. This sprawling complex offers everything from simple rooms to executive suites and ultra-deluxe-priced two-room apartments. Set in the motel's courtyard is a pool and grassy common areas equipped with barbecue grills. There's also a hot tub and exercise room; the rooms are equipped with small

HOLLYWOOD'S BACKLOT

Director John Ford put the area on the map when he filmed the 1949 classic *Wagonmaster* here. Ford returned to film *Rio Grande* the following year, and Hollywood has favored it ever since. A detailed guide to area movie locations—including *The Greatest Story Ever Told*, *Cheyenne Autumn*, *Indiana Jones and the Last Crusade* and *Thelma and Louise*—is available at the visitors center. And you can pursue your own film career as an "extra" by filling out an application with the **Moab to Monument Valley Film Commission**, whose offices are lined with publicity stills and posters from movies shot in the area. ~ 40 North 100 East, Moab; 435-259-6388.

refrigerators, microwaves, TVs and phones. A continental breakfast is complimentary. ~ 1551 North Route 191, Moab; 435-259-2599, 800-341-9359, fax 435-259-2270; www.aarchwayinn.com, e-mail reservations@aarchwayinn.com. MODERATE TO DELUXE.

There are more than a dozen bed-and-breakfast establishments in the immediate Moab area, but none nicer than the **Sunflower Hill Bed & Breakfast Inn**. Though located just a few blocks from downtown, it is like a country estate with two separate homes sharing spacious central grounds. The Garden Cottage has six guest rooms with European-style antique furnishings and a Great Room with a fireplace and library, while the Farm House boasts five additional units with country-style decor. All rooms are air-conditioned and have private baths. Family suites are available. A full breakfast is served indoors or out, and there's a big hot tub in the garden. Laundry facilities are available. ~ 185 North 300 East, Moab; 435-259-2974, 800-662-2786, fax 435-259-3065l; www.sunflowerhill.com, e-mail innkeeper@sunflowerhill.com. DELUXE TO ULTRA-DELUXE.

The pink-adobe exterior with hanging dried chiles makes the **Kokopelli Lodge** easy to spot. Though small, the eight rooms are clean, and the service is friendly. Cyclists appreciate a secured area set aside for bikes, and breakfast is served on a garden patio each morning from March through October. There's also a hot tub in which you can soothe what aches. ~ 72 South 100 East, Moab; 435-259-7615, 888-530-3134, fax 435-259-8498; www.kokopellilodge.com, e-mail rick@kokopellilodge.com. BUDGET.

Best of the "strip" motels is the **Best Western Greenwell Inn**. Seventy-two rooms are conventionally furnished in pinks, mauves and blues with queen-sized beds and sitting areas. Bonuses include the on-site restaurant, an outdoor swimming pool, hot tub, laundry facilities, exercise room and bike storage. ~ 105 South Main Street, Moab; 435-259-6151, 800-528-1234, fax 435-259-4397; www.quinstar.com/greenwell, e-mail bwgreenwell@quinstar.com. BUDGET TO DELUXE.

The charming **Cali Cochitta Bed & Breakfast** is a lovingly restored adobe brick house that dates to the 1870s. There are three rooms and a suite; each offers its own bathroom and queen-sized bed. Out back you'll find a cottage that offers a little more privacy. ~ 110 South 200 East, Moab; 435-259-4961, 888-429-8112; www.moabdreaminn.com. MODERATE TO DELUXE.

A Colonial-style brick exterior houses the **Landmark Motel**. Thirty-five units feature tile baths, individual air conditioning and handpainted panoramic murals above the beds. Offering a pool, hot tub, guest laundry and continental breakfast, the motel is popular among families, especially large ones who appreciate the rooms with three queen beds and extra-thick walls. ~ 168 North

Text continued on page 368.

John Wesley Powell
and the Green River

Perhaps no individual had a greater impact on the opening of the canyonlands of the American Southwest than a one-armed college professor named John Wesley Powell (1834–1902). Powell enlisted in the military as the Civil War erupted in 1861. Commissioned a second lieutenant, he was wounded at the Battle of Shiloh in 1862 and lost his right arm below the elbow. Before the conflict ended he was made a brevet lieutenant colonel, but he preferred to be called "Major."

After the war, Powell became a geology professor at Illinois Wesleyan University. In 1867 and 1868, he led parties of students to the Rocky Mountains. Inspired by tales of the wild Colorado River and doomed attempts to navigate its rapids, Powell plotted his own expedition. With limited funding, he had four boats built in Chicago to his own design and specifications, and shipped them by rail to Green River, Wyoming. Seven mountain men joined Powell and his brother, Walter, as they launched an epic voyage on May 24, 1869. Fourteen weeks later and more than 1000 miles later, long since given up for lost, the Powell party reemerged at the mouth of the Virgin River in what is now Lake Mead, Nevada.

Powell was soon afloat once more, having this time obtained funds from Congress for exploration. In 1870, he cached supplies along the river and traveled extensively to establish friendly relations with the Indians. In 1871, with a party that included a surveyor and a photographer, he was back on the rivers. Between May and October, with Powell dramatically directing the voyage while lashed to a chair in the forward boat, the party undertook a detailed survey of the entire Grand Canyon region. From Lees Ferry to the mouth of the Kanab River, currents were exceedingly treacherous, but the party succeeded in its goals.

Powell's trip report, completed in 1878, is regarded today as one of the most important ever written about the American West. It discussed not only climate and physical geography, but also proposed a land classification system. He is buried in Arlington Cemetery along with other Civil War heroes.

When Powell first ran the Green River in 1869, the site of the town of Green River was a trail crossing. Ten years later a mail relay station was established at the site. Today the community of 850 people is a transportation hub on interstate Route 70, a center for river rafters and (surprise!) melon growers.

The story of Powell's expedition trials is detailed at the **John Wesley Powell River History Museum**. View a 20-minute multimedia show, then study full-size replicas of 19th-century river boats, such as the "bullboat" (buffalo hide over a willow frame) in which William Ashley traveled 200 miles in 1825. Working displays and models focus on more contemporary river guides and adventurers. Of special interest to whitewater enthusiasts is the River Runners' Hall of Fame. ~ 885 East Main Street; 435-564-3526.

Overnighters will find a few lodging options. The **Robbers Roost Motel**, a simple, pleasant hostelry, has 20 rooms with knotty-pine walls and charming country decor. Pets are welcome, except in the pool. ~ 225 West Main Street; 435-564-3452; www.robbersroostmotel.com. BUDGET. The **Book Cliff Lodge** offers family-friendly rates, clean, comfortable rooms, a pool and a restaurant. ~ 356 East Main Street; 435-564-3406, 800-493-4699. BUDGET.

It feels a bit sterile, but that might be because the **Deluxe Inn** is still fairly new. The rooms are comfortable if a bit on the small side. Amenities include an indoor pool and an adjoining hot tub, as well as a free continental breakfast. ~ 1117 East Main Street; 435-564-8441, fax 435-564-8445. MODERATE.

B&B enthusiasts will be pleased to find the 1897 **Bankurz Hatt Bed and Breakfast**. The four-square house features a trio of nonsmoking, antique-filled guest rooms. The large downstairs room has its own bath; two upstairs chambers share. An outdoor hot tub sits in tree-shaded grounds. Full breakfast is included. No pets or young children allowed. ~ 214 Farrer Street; 435-564-3382; www.bankurzhatt.com. MODERATE.

Ray's Tavern is the friendly "dive" where rafters congregate after river expeditions. Scores of their T-shirts and river photos line the walls, and they rate their burgers the best in Utah. The rest of the menu is basic grill: steaks, chops and the like. However, you will find a nice selection of microbrews, as well as some pool tables. The outside patio is popular when the heat isn't overwhelming. ~ 25 South Broadway; 435-564-3511. BUDGET.

If you don't have a lot of time, stop at **Cathy's**, which serves up burgers, pizza to sandwiches, fresh salads and shakes. ~ 185 West Main Street; 435-564-8122. BUDGET.

It seems most folks in Green River operate on a first-name basis. Why else would there be a third eatery that goes by a simple name: **Ben's Café**? The meals here have a Mexican influence, from fajitas and tostadas to enchiladas and burritos. You'll also find seafood, steaks, chops and chicken dishes, however. ~ 115 West Main Street; 435-564-3352. BUDGET.

For something a bit more upscale, consider the **Tamarisk Restaurant**. Classic American and Southwestern food, including Utah trout and local watermelon and cantaloupe, is served for three meals a day. ~ 870 East Main Street; 435-564-8109. MODERATE.

Main Street, Moab; 435-259-6147, 800-441-6147, fax 435-259-5556; e-mail landmark@aol.com. BUDGET TO DELUXE.

A complete make-your-own breakfast is the best reason to spend the night at **Cedar Breaks Condos**. The half dozen two-bedroom condominiums have full baths, kitchens and living rooms decorated with plants and black-and-white landscape photos. Upstairs units feature private balconies while downstairs units have patios; a complimentary full breakfast (March to mid-November only) is stocked daily for guests to prepare at their leisure. ~ Center Street and 400 East, Moab; 435-259-5125, 800-748-4386, fax 435-259-6079; www.moabutahlodging.com, e-mail info@ moabutahlodging.com. MODERATE.

Bright is one word for the paint used in the 43 rooms and suites at **The Gonzo Inn**. But if you play hard during the day in the surrounding national parks, you shouldn't have any trouble falling asleep at night. If money's not too much of a problem, splurge for the Gecko Suite with its gas fireplace, jetted tub, kitchenette, stereo and wet bar. ~ 100 West 200 South, Moab; 435-259-2515, 800-791-4044; www.gonzoinn.com, e-mail gonzoinn@ gonzoinn.com. DELUXE TO ULTRA-DELUXE.

The Redstone Inn is conveniently located on the north side of Moab just about five miles south of Arches National Park. These folks offer not only rooms but packages that cover white-water rafting, four-wheeling, and equestrian trips. ~ 535 South Main Street, Moab; 435-259-3500, 800-772-1972, fax 435-259-2717; www.moabredstone.com, e-mail office@moabredstone. com. BUDGET TO MODERATE.

HIDDEN ► Certainly off the beaten track, hidden behind a storage center, is the **Lazy Lizard International Hostel**. You can't go wrong at the cheapest sleep in Moab. Both the dormitory and the private rooms are clean, and bedding and towels are provided (there is a small extra charge for them if you're staying in the dorm). Log cabins are available for a few dollars more than the private rooms. There is also a common kitchen, a TV room, a hot tub and a laundry. It's popular with a European clientele. ~ 1213 South Route 191, Moab; 435-259-6057; www.gj.net/~lazylzrd, e-mail lazylzrd @lasal.net. BUDGET.

Hidden at the bottom of a red-rock notch known as Hurrah Pass, the **Camelot Adventure Lodge** offers a self-contained setting in southeastern Utah's canyonlands. Follow the backroads to this backcountry wilderness lodge and you'll reward yourself with a stunningly scenic retreat along the Colorado River. Take advantage of one of the lodge's five rooms and make your own fun during the day, or sign on for one of their camel treks or a jet boat ride up the Colorado. Rates include three meals a day. ~ Off Kane Creek Road, 18 miles south of Moab; 435-260-1783; www.cam elotlodge.com, e-mail camelot@camelotlodge.com. DELUXE.

Locals say Moab restaurants have improved greatly of late to meet **DINING**
demands of a more sophisticated, traveling public. As the town
is a center for so many outdoor activities, burning calories have
created a demand for decent fueling spots.

It's appropriate, perhaps, that the million-dollar 1952 home of
the world's richest uranium miner, Charles Steen, is now Moab's
most upscale restaurant. The spacious **Sunset Grill**, perched on a
bluff top at the north end of town, serves such classic American
and Continental dishes as escargot, *vol au vent*, Provimi veal rib
and Cajun shrimp fettuccine. The restaurant is reached via a steep,
winding third-of-a-mile drive above the highway. But don't feel
you have to dress up: Diners in T-shirts and shorts are welcomed,
and there's a separate children's menu. Dinner only. Closed Sunday. ~ 900 North Route 191, Moab; 435-259-7146, fax 435-259-
7626; e-mail emoab@hotmail.com. MODERATE TO DELUXE.

What looks like a log fort from the outside is actually a haven
for American cuisine. **Buck's Grill House** boasts grilled steaks,
fresh fish and game and luscious homemade desserts, served in
an understated Western atmosphere. House specialties include
buffalo meatloaf, duck tamales and, for vegetarians, a polenta-
zucchini pot pie. Dinner only. ~ 1393 North Route 191, Moab;
435-259-5201, fax 435-259-6092; e-mail grilling@lasal.net. MOD-
ERATE TO DELUXE.

Pizza reigns supreme at **Eddie McStiff's**, Moab's oldest legal
brewery. Pastas, salads, sandwiches and steaks are offered, but
the best bets are the special combination pizzas such as the Dosie
Doe topped with roasted garlic, sun-dried tomatoes, parsley,
scallions, and gorgonzola and parmesan cheeses. Beverages, including a selection of 12 house-microbrewed beers and homemade root beer, are served in mini-pitchers—a nice touch for
desert thirsts. Dinner only. ~ 57 South Main Street, Moab; 435-
259-2337, fax 435-259-3022. BUDGET TO MODERATE.

The **Slick Rock Cafe** has been a midtown favorite of the biking community since it opened in 1994. The ambience is as hip

AUTHOR FAVORITE

Going into the wilderness doesn't mean you need to deprive
yourself of some of the finer things in life. So after my wife and I return
from a day in Arches or Canyonlands, we clean up and head over to the
Center Café and Market for one of the best meals available in Utah.
The setting is intimate and elegant—white linen and fresh flowers adorn
the tables, Southwestern art and photography line the walls, and when
it's warm there's a charming adobe courtyard where you can take
your meal. See page 370 for more information.

as the staff itself. A half-lizard, half-coyote "critter" is the eatery's trademark, and the walls of the mezzanine level are decorated with six reproduced petroglyph panels. *Huevos rancheros* are a breakfast favorite; for lunch and dinner, choose between the likes of a uranium burger (mixed with fresh garlic and bleu cheese), a portobello mushroom sandwich, pork loin with a red-and-green-pepper sauce spiked with tequila, and Utah red trout baked with lime cilantro butter. ~ 5 North Main Street, Moab; 435-259-8004, fax 435-259-8003; e-mail slickrock@xmission.com. BUDGET TO MODERATE.

> More ice cream is consumed per capita in Utah than in any other state in the nation.

The **Center Café and Market** is year-in and year-out one of Utah's finest restaurants. The eclectic menu offers dishes ranging from seafood specials to beef, poultry and vegetarian entrées, such as roasted eggplant lasagna. The café's deli allows you to build a budget-friendly picnic lunch with a nice array of imported cheeses and meats. Closed December and January. ~ 60 North 100 West, Moab; 435-259-4295. DELUXE.

Breakfasts, and only breakfasts, are doled out at **The Jailhouse Café**. Housed in the town's historic jail, the restaurant churns out thick stacks of pancakes, french toast, a rich variety of omelets, as well as lower-calorie granolas. Get there early to avoid the long lines that often form in summer. Closed November to early March. ~ 101 North Main Street, Moab; 435-259-3900. BUDGET.

SHOPPING At first glance, Moab doesn't appear to be a mecca for shoppers. But take some time to look around town and you'll find not only the requisite souvenir and T-shirt shops but also a surprising number of noteworthy exceptions, ranging from art galleries to rock vendors.

The best rock shop in Moab also happens to be the best rock shop in southeastern Utah. The **Moab Rock Shop** not only has a large collection of fossils, crystals and minerals, but you also can find maps and guidebooks here. Closed January. ~ 600 North Main Street, Moab; 435-259-7312.

The **T-Shirt Shop** has a hefty inventory of locally designed prints it can affix to a shirt in less than 30 seconds. Interestingly, the shop also sells AKC-registered Italian greyhounds. ~ 38 North Main Street, Moab; 435-259-3347, 888-883-5271; www.moab tshirts.com.

Hogan Trading Co. carries an impressive variety of Indian art such as kachina dolls, pottery and alabaster sculptures. The store also carries Navajo rugs as well as Southwestern prints, baskets and sand paintings. ~ 100 South Main Street, Moab; 435-259-8118.

Inside the **Lema Indian Trading Company** are more Navajo rugs, alabaster carvings and pottery, as well as handmade gourd masks and pre-1900 Pima baskets. ~ 860 South Main Street, Moab; 435-259-5942; www.lematrading.com.

What must be one of the most comprehensive collections of books on the Southwest can be found at **Back of Beyond Bookstore**. Edward Abbey, Tony Hillerman and others with local ties take up the most shelf space, and there is a plethora of works on the outdoors, natural and Western history, American Indian studies and the environment. Popular novels are stocked, along with hiking, biking and river guides. ~ 83 North Main Street, Moab; 435-259-5154, 800-700-2859; www.moab.net/backofbeyond.

The desert Southwest offers some of America's most dramatic backdrops and landscapes for photos. If you left your camera at home or don't trust your skills, the **Tom Till Gallery** has some of the most striking landscape photos in the West, as well as posters, calendars and books. ~ 61 North Main Street, Moab; 435-259-9808, 888-479-9808; www.tomtill.com.

Utah's largest map store is virtually across Center Street from the Moab Visitors Center. **T. I. Maps, etc.** stocks any topographic map you might want for off-road biking or hiking, as well as road maps, atlases, river guides and geographic novelty items. ~ 29 East Center Street, Moab; 435-259-5529; www.moabmaps.com.

The hub for sports of all sorts, **Rim Cyclery** sells practical outdoor gear, footgear, regional guides and tools of the trade. Wise-cracking mechanics proffer knowing advice about destinations if you seem credible. "Cool central" for serious sporting athletes, or at least those who look the part. ~ 94 West 100 North, Moab; 435-259-5333, 888-304-8219; www.rimcyclery.com.

Not interested in sleeping out in a tent under the stars? How 'bout sleeping inside a tepee? You can find an impressive range at **Moab Outback**, which bills itself as Utah's largest tepee dealer. ~ 1080 Mill Creek Drive, Moab; 435-259-2667; www.moabout back.com.

NIGHTLIFE Utah's strict liquor laws mean an abbreviated bar scene. Moab fares better than most with a few nightspots.

One of the oldest nightly entertainments in the Moab area is **Canyonlands By Night**, a boat trip at sunset up the Colorado River. Complete with light and sound show, the voyage offers a unique perspective on river landmarks. Canyonlands also offers a nightly Dutch-oven dinner, cooked and eaten on the banks of the Colorado. April to October only. ~ 1861 North Route 191, Moab; 435-259-5261, 800-394-9978, fax 435-259-2788; www.canyonlandsbynight.com.

Live music and dancing on weekends keep **Rio Colorado Restaurant and Bar** hopping. This is a private club with cover on weekends. ~ Center Street and 100 West, Moab; 435-259-6666.

The **Sportsman's Lounge** has a huge dancefloor and live country music for two-steppin' every weekend. Occasional cover. ~ 1991 South Route 191, Moab; 435-259-9972.

Two brewpubs are popular haunts for telling tales of slickrock biking and four-wheel excursions. **Eddie McStiff's** is in the heart of downtown. ~ 57 South Main Street, Moab; 435-259-2337. One-half mile south is the **Moab Brewery.** ~ 686 South Main Street, Moab; 435-259-6333.

PARKS   **GREEN RIVER STATE PARK** This park, located about 40 miles northwest of Moab in the midst of melon fields on the west bank of the Green River, is a favorite embarkation point for river-rafting trips. The park has a small amphitheater for interpretive programs, restrooms and hot showers, a nine-hole golf course and boat ramps. Day-use fee, $5. ~ One-quarter mile south of Main Street, Green River; 435-564-8882.

▲ There are 42 sites; $14 per night. Reservations: 800-322-3770; parks.state.ut.us/parks/www1/gree.htm.

HIDDEN ►   **DEAD HORSE POINT STATE PARK** This 5250-acre mesa 2000 feet above the Colorado River has been preserved as a park that offers innumerable possibilities for hikers, campers and other outdoor enthusiasts. Park facilities include a wheelchair-accessible visitors center, picnic areas and restrooms. Day-use fee, $7. ~ From Moab go north on Route 191 nine miles, then south on Route 313 for 22 miles; 435-259-2614, fax 435-259-2615; parks.state.ut.us/parks/www1/dead.htm.

Dead Horse Point got its name, legend claims, when cowboys corraled wild horses here, selected the best of the herd, and left the rest to die.

▲ There are 21 sites with electric hookups (no water hookups for RVs); $14 per night. Reservations are recommended ($6 reservation fee): 800-322-3770.

CANYONLANDS NATIONAL PARK—ISLAND IN THE SKY This "island" mesa, 6000 feet in elevation, features rugged and beautiful terrain veined with hiking trails. The sparse vegetation and rain on the Island does not keep wildlife like foxes, coyotes and bighorn sheep from calling this land their home. The facilities at this park include picnic areas, a visitors center and vault toilets. The vehicle entrance fee is $10, good for seven days in all Canyonlands districts. ~ From Moab go north on Route 191 nine miles, then Route 313 for 26 miles; 435-719-2313, fax 435-719-2300; www.nps.gov/cany, e-mail canyinfo@nps.gov.

▲ There are 12 primitive sites at Willow Flat; $5 per night. No water available.

ARCHES NATIONAL PARK Popular with plenty of easily accessible geologic wonders, Arches National Park is a magnet for the recreational-vehicle crowd and backcountry enthusiasts alike. Guided walks are offered March through October and may be arranged through the visitors center. The park features picnic areas, a visitors center and restrooms. The vehicle entrance fee is $10, good for seven days. ~ Route 191, five miles north of Moab; 435-719-2299, fax 435-719-2305; www.nps.gov/arch, e-mail archinfo@nps.gov.

▲ There are 52 sites at Devil's Garden; $10 per night.

Northern San Juan County

Most people come to the northern portion of San Juan County to visit either Canyonlands National Park—Needles district or to drive the Trail of the Ancients. Time permitting, the two combined reveal more about the geology and history of southeastern Utah than almost any other tour. When you're ready to retreat from the red rock, you can head to Monticello or Blanding, two towns that got their start as agricultural outposts but are now warming to tourism.

SIGHTS

About 40 miles south of Moab, Route 211 (Squaw Flats Scenic Drive) heads west of Route 191. Blink and you might miss the turnoff that's opposite a cathedral-like geological upcropping called **Church Rock**. The road first sidles along Indian Creek, named for the area's first residents. As you approach the steep canyon curves leading to Newspaper Rock, sparse desert landscape turns lush and green: Is it any wonder numerous tribes settled here?

Newspaper Rock Recreation Site is a tiny park usually on the "hit and run" list of most visitors. Though somewhat tarnished by graffiti, the huge sandstone panel is etched with fascinating Indian petroglyphs. This "rock that tells a story" is a compendium of American Indian history over a 2000-year span. The petroglyphs span three distinct periods, making this giant mural an archaeological find. Some of the figures, such as the horseman with a bow and arrow, were not made by the Pueblo peoples but were done by later Indians (probably the Ute and Navajo), indicating that the sacred nature of the shrine was abandoned. A quarter-mile interpretive loop around the monument offers a chance to check out native flora and fauna, and some opt to set up camp here rather than amid the starker Canyonlands. ~ Route 211, 11 miles west of Route 191; 435-587-2141.

CANYONLANDS NATIONAL PARK—NEEDLES In the Needles section of Canyonlands National Park you tend to feel a part of the scenery rather than a casual and detached observer. With its myriad roads and trails, Needles is the most user-friendly of the Canyonlands sections. It also features the finest collection of petroglyphs and prehistoric sites in the park and is positively packed with natural stone sculptures in the form of arches and monoliths. Admission. ~ Route 211; 435-259-4711, fax 435-259-4266; www.nps.gov/cany, e-mail cany_info@nps.gov.

The adobe-style **Needles Visitors Center** can provide maps and advice to adventurers. From here a paved road leads six and a half miles into the park. Just past the visitors center a quarter-mile loop trail passes **Roadside Ruin,** an ancient Pueblo granary. Down the road, **Cave Spring Trail** loops three-fifths of a mile past a cave and former cowboy camp.

Needles Outpost Store is a necessary stop before heading into the backcountry. Ice, food, propane, firewood and guidebooks are sold at non-ripoff prices. Camping and four-wheel-drive rentals are also available. ~ Located .6 mile north of Route 211, outside the Needles district; 435-979-4007.

Farther along, **Squaw Flat Rest Area** is a fine place to get your bearings and absorb the magic of the orange-, rust- and white-striped stone fortresses ("the needles") ahead. Then follow the main road to **Pothole Point Nature Trail** (.6 mile), another short loop that passes a series of potholes formed in the eroding sand-stone. The vistas along the way of distant mesas are spectacular. At the end of the road you'll find **Big Spring Canyon Overlook,** gateway to a view of the Colorado and Green rivers' meeting place.

The Pueblo peoples left their mark throughout the Needles with Canyonlands sites dating from A.D. 900 to A.D. 1200. A four-wheel-drive vehicle or a well-equipped mountain bike and a good pair of legs are key to exploring the **jeep roads** leading to backcountry arches, canyons and the Pueblos' ancient drawings. A dirt road around the park's circumference is a fine way to view the Needles' unique topographic features. But beware: this route is not for the inexperienced driver.

For a grand view of the Needles section of Canyonlands, be sure to take in the **Needles Overlook** in the BLM-administered Canyon Rims Recreation Area. You'll be rewarded with a mesa-top vista that scans the Abajo and Henry mountains and the Colorado River and extends all the way to the park's Maze district. ~ Getting there means driving back on Route 211, heading north a few miles on Route 191, then turning west on a dead-end road.

MONTICELLO–BLANDING AREA   Fifteen miles south of the Nee-dles turnoff on Route 191, civilization reappears. Named for Thomas Jefferson's Virginia home, **Monticello** is the San Juan County seat. Complete information on the nearby national parks and monuments, state parks and local attractions can be obtained at the **Multi-Agency Visitors Center.** ~ Located in the County Courthouse, 117 South Main Street, Monticello; 435-587-3235, 800-574-4386, fax 435-587-2425; www.southeastutah.com, e-mail info@southeastutah.com.

Early area history is revealed at the **Monticello Museum** in the County Library. Besides Pueblo artifacts, the museum contains articles from pioneer life—an old stove, a wagon keg, a sewing machine, a vanity case, picture albums and flat irons. ~ 80 North Main Street, Monticello; phone/fax 435-587-2281.

For a break from desert sandstone, head west from Monticello into **Manti-La Sal National Forest**. A network of forest roads proceed west more than 30 miles through this largest unit of the 2187-square-mile national forest. Trails continue through the Dark Canyon Wilderness Area and BLM-administered Dark Canyon Primitive Area to Cataract Canyon in Canyonlands National Park and Glen Canyon National Recreation Area.

Spectacular views greet hikers who ascend 11,360-foot **Abajo Peak**. ~ From Monticello, take North Creek Road (an extension of Second South and Abajo Road) west six miles to the Dalton Springs campground, then turn south three miles on Forest Road 079 to reach the short but steep trail.

Another 20 miles south of Monticello on Route 191 is **Blanding**, once a trading center for nearby ranches. The log building a few miles farther along is home to **Huck's Artifact Hall of Fame**. Owner Huck Acton has assembled a stellar display of pottery and American Indian artifacts dating back to ancient times. The private collection of arrowheads, beads, pendants, effigy bowls, cooking pots and tools is sure to impress. Admission. ~ 387 South Main Street, Blanding; 435-678-2329.

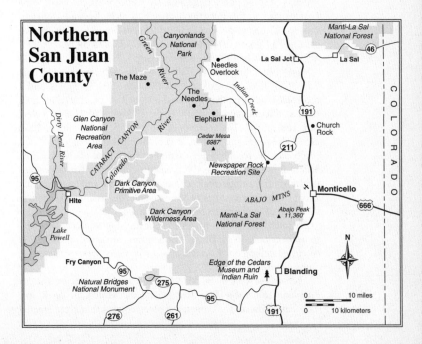

HIDDEN ►   A gem of the Utah state park system is **Edge of the Cedars Museum and Indian Ruin**. Site of an Anasazi Indian ruin, Edge of the Cedars allows visitors to explore the small village inhabited from A.D. 750 to A.D. 1200, even climbing down a wooden ladder into a large underground room. The modern museum details the many cultures—Anasazi, Navajo, Ute and Anglo—that have played a role in regional development. The exhibits include clothing, artifacts and tools as well as video presentations. The museum walls showcase reproductions of ancient Indian pictographs. Day-use fee, $5. ~ 660 West 400 North, Blanding; 435-678-2238, fax 435-678-3348; parks.state.ut.us/parks/www1/edge.htm.

Two other attractions are helping to make Blanding an important regional center for tourism. The **Nations of the Four Corners Cultural Center** resides on a low, sagebrush-covered hill at the edge of town. On the property you'll find several trails, including one half-mile-long path that winds past a central watchtower and replica dwellings of early Anglo, Spanish, Navajo and Ute cultures. It's a nice idea, and a free one, although most structures are kept under lock and key. ~ 707 West 500 South, Blanding; 435-678-4035.

Nearby, in a big, red warehouse, is the **Dinosaur Museum**. Well organized and nicely presented, this collection includes a wide variety of fossils, from skin and footprints to full skeletal replicas of some of the largest beasts ever to walk the earth. Film fans won't want to miss the history hall of Hollywood dinosaur movies! Closed mid-October to mid-April; closed Sunday. Admission. ~ 754 South 200 West, Blanding; 435-678-3454, fax 435-587-2054; www.dinosaur-museum.org.

Tying Blanding and Hanksville to the west together is Route 95, which takes a crooked path through stark badlands and a red-rock landscape that nurtured a flourishing civilization more than a millennia ago. Until 1976, the 133 miles of Route 95 were dirt and gravel. Then, in honor of the U.S. bicentennial, Utah paved the route and dubbed it the "Bicentennial Highway."

Today the road has been renamed the "Trail of the Ancients Scenic Byway," a nod to the prehistoric cultures that once lived in the Four Corners region. Travel this road and you can spy some of the last vestiges of the ancient Puebloan civilization in the form of well-preserved cliff dwellings.

A mile-long hike across slickrock and high desert takes you to an overlook of the **Butler Wash Ruins**, an amazing collection of cliff dwellings. ~ Located about five miles west of Blanding along Route 95.

Ten miles west of Butler Wash leads to two sets of ancient Puebloan ruins: the Cave Towers and the Mule Canyon Ruins. The **Cave Towers** site consists of seven towers that were erected on the canyon rim more than 900 years ago. ~ To reach the site, turn south off Route 95 onto a gravel road near Milepost 103. The road runs about a half-mile, and then you need to make a short hike to the towers. Don't enter or climb on the ruins—they are extremely fragile.

The **Mule Canyon Ruins** date to roughly 700 years ago. They consist of a kiva and a tower, as well as a block of rooms. ~ The ruins are on the north side of Route 95 near the Cave Tower turnoff. Watch for signs on the highway.

Travel farther west on the highway and you'll come upon **Natural Bridges National Monument**, which is home to three of the largest known natural bridges in the world: Sipachu, Kachina Bridge and Owachomo. The monument, the first in Utah, was established in 1908 by President Theodore Roosevelt. The monument maintains a visitors center, hiking trails, a campground and a paved, nine-mile loop road. Each mammoth stone bridge can be viewed by walking a short distance to an overlook. Archaeological sites can be seen from perches along the rim. Admission. ~ Route 95; 435-692-1234, fax 435-692-1111; www.nps.gov/nabr.

The monument area is mostly desert-like with a smattering of piñon-juniper trees, shrubs and grasses among the white sandstone. While ancient Indian tribes lived in the area, the canyons were apparently too small to sustain the farming activities of many families. Nonetheless, **Horsecollar Site**, the cliff dwelling remains of one community, can be viewed.

The three bridges, which resemble arches but are formed solely by flowing water, are known as Sipapu, Kachina and Owachomo. **Sipapu**, a flat-topped spur of rimrock, is the largest bridge in both height (220 feet) and span (268 feet). Its name means "the place of emergence." The "younger" **Kachina Bridge** was found to have prehistoric pictographs resembling kachinas (dancers). White Canyon floodwaters, frosts and thaws are still enlarging Kachina Bridge. **Owachomo**—"rock mounds" in the Hopi language—is so named for the large, rounded rock mass found nearby and is the oldest of the three bridges with only a narrow strip of nine-foot-thick rock remaining in the center of the bridge.

AUTHOR FAVORITE

Otherworldly is an apt description of **Canyonlands National Park—Needles**. This jumble of multicolored geology made me think the gods must have been playing with Play-Doh when they designed this corner of the park. See page 373 for more information.

LODGING As tourism generates most of this area's summer economy, hotels are numerous. Yet with few exceptions, most are of the motel variety, designed to provide a clean bed and bath but little else.

HIDDEN ► Without question the **Grist Mill Inn Bed and Breakfast** is an exquisite property. Originally an old flour mill, the meticulously restored inn maintains many original features like hand-hewn rough timber beams and loft ceilings. Seven rooms, each with private bath, are scattered among three stories for ultimate privacy. In addition, there are four similarly decorated guest rooms in the recently converted granary. Antiques, lace curtains, overhead fans and clawfoot tubs add to the luxury. Guests awake to a full country breakfast. Other amenities include a whirlpool, a television room, a library and an on-site country store featuring local handcrafted gifts. ~ 64 South 300 East, Monticello; 435-587-2597, 800-645-3762, fax 435-587-2579; www.thegristmillinn.com, e-mail reservations@thegristmill.com. BUDGET TO MODERATE.

Though nothing to write home about, the red-brick **Best Western Wayside Inn** is nevertheless a good place to hang your hat for a night or two. Rooms are large, with oak furniture and computer jacks. The on-site swimming pool and hot tub are pluses, as are the tastefully landscaped grounds. ~ 197 East Central Street, Monticello; 435-587-2261, 800-633-9700, fax 435-587-2920. BUDGET TO MODERATE.

Owachomo is tall enough to fit Washington's Capitol building underneath.

Clean, comfortable rooms, a heated pool and laundry facilities make the **Canyonlands Motor Inn** a reliable waystation. ~ 197 North Main Street, Monticello; 435-587-2266, 800-952-6212, fax 435-587-2883; e-mail canyonlandsinn@yahoo.com. BUDGET.

Budget-minded travelers will appreciate **Navajo Trail National 9 Inn**. Immaculate rooms have typical hotel decor but offer large, yellow-and-blue-tile showers. For a few extra dollars, a kitchen can be yours complete with stove, refrigerator and microwave. ~ 248 North Main Street, Monticello; 435-587-2251, 888-449-6463. BUDGET.

For those wanting a safe bet, **Days Inn Monticello** won't disappoint. The two-story complex is decorated in maroon and forest green. Rooms are large with ample drawer space. Adding to the hotel's popularity are complimentary continental breakfast and a huge indoor swimming pool with a whirlpool spa. ~ 549 North Main Street, Monticello; 435-587-2458, 800-329-7466, fax 435-587-2191. BUDGET TO MODERATE.

One of the better properties in the area, the **Best Western Gateway Inn** boasts nicely appointed rooms and a congenial staff. Contemporary appointments in blues and earth-tones are used in both the large lobby area and 60 spacious units. The swimming pool and free continental breakfast are nice extras. ~ 88 East

Center Street, Blanding; 435-678-2278, 800-528-1234, fax 435-678-2240. BUDGET TO MODERATE.

Walk through the leaded glass front door of the **Rogers House** and you'll enter a B&B housed in one of Blanding's original homes. Today the house, which was built in 1915, offers five guest rooms, each with its own bathroom and whirlpool tub. In the living room are a marble fireplace and a beautifully preserved antique mahogany piano. Outside, the front porch is still graced by the home's original porch swing. ~ 412 South Main Street, Blanding; 435-678-3932, 800-355-3932; www.rogershouse.com, e-mail hosts@rogershouse.com. BUDGET.

Designed by a student of architect Frank Lloyd Wright, the **Cliff Palace Motel** has many unusual features, including floor-to-ceiling windows, indirect lighting in bathrooms and dressing areas, tiled seats in showers and built-in luggage racks. Sixteen rooms are decorated in a Southwest style. Closed in winter. ~ 132 South Main Street, Blanding; 435-678-2264, 800-553-8093. BUDGET.

If you really want to leave it all behind when you head to southeastern Utah's canyon country, check into the **Fry Canyon Lodge**, which is on the way to nowhere. Founded in 1955 as a mining supply store, the lodge—which underwent an expansion in 1999—and its accompanying café, general store and gas station are 53 miles west of Blanding roughly halfway between Natural Bridges and Hite Crossing on Route 95. The ten rooms come in three flavors—deluxe, which feature queen beds or two double beds and have their own bathrooms; economy, which are smaller and might share a bathroom with another room, or be doubled up as suite; or standard, which are clean and simple and come with their own bathrooms. ~ Route 95, Fry Canyon; 435-259-5334; www.frycanyon.com, e-mail lodge@frycanyon.com. MODERATE.

◄ HIDDEN

Don't expect to watch your cholesterol in San Juan County. Basic country cooking is standard fare, with a real salad bar about as rare as a rosebush in the desert.

DINING

An adobe exterior replete with vigas houses **Los Tachos**. The menu offers burritos, chimichangas, enchiladas and burgers, and you can be certain it's authentic; in fact, you'll communicate much better in Spanish than in English. Closed Sunday. ~ 280 East Central Street, Monticello; 435-587-3094. BUDGET TO MODERATE.

A quick pizza fix may be had at **Wagon Wheel Pizza**. Fresh deli sandwiches, calzones and pizzas are prepared in a flash. Take out or hunker down in a blue-leather booth under mock Pepsi-Cola Tiffany lamps. ~ 154 South Main Street, Monticello; 435-587-2766. BUDGET.

Steaks are in ample supply at the **Homestead Steakhouse** in downtown Blanding. ~ 121 East Center Street, Blanding; 435-678-3456.

Another solid choice is the **Old Tymer Restaurant**, adjacent to the Comfort Inn at Blanding's south end. The exterior of this big gray building belies a rustic interior adorned with historic photographs. The three-meals-a-day menu is traditional American (steaks, prime rib, fish) with a sprinkling of Mexican items. ~ 722 South Main Street, Blanding; 435-678-2122. MODERATE.

HIDDEN ▶

You want remote? The **Fry Canyon Lodge and Cafe** is the only building for 122 miles on the highway from Blanding to Hanksville. It sits beside Route 95 about halfway between Natural Bridges and Hite Crossing. Founded in 1955 as a mining supply store, Fry Canyon initially served as a community center and tavern for 3000 isolated miners. The miners are long since gone, but the lodge, general store, gas station and vintage café remain. Solid home cooking with nightly specials is the hallmark of the café. ~ Route 95, Fry Canyon; 435-259-5334; www.frycanyon.com, e-mail lodge@frycanyon.com. BUDGET TO MODERATE.

At one point, the Fry Canyon Lodge and Cafe was a school for 67 miner children.

SHOPPING

After perusing the wares for sale at **Cedar Mesa Pottery** take a behind-the-scenes tour of the pottery factory. Here, you can watch American Indian artisans create and decorate their hand-painted pottery. Closed weekends in winter. ~ 333 South Main Street, Blanding; 435-678-2241, 800-235-7687.

Trading posts selling sandstone folk art, pottery, baskets, silver jewelry, pipes, papooses and rugs are **Thin Bear Indian Arts** (1944 South Route 191, Blanding; 435-678-2940), **Purple Sage Trading Post** (790 South Main Street, Blanding; 435-678-3620, 877-853-6149) and **Hunt's Trading Post** (146 East Center Street, Blanding; 435-678-2314).

PARKS

NEWSPAPER ROCK RECREATION SITE 🏃 Camping within this 50-acre park is encouraged, and the lush, evergreen area provides a sharp contrast to nearby Canyonlands. A short trail here leads to the base of the Newspaper Rock Petroglyph Panel. The only facilities available here are toilets. ~ From Monticello take Route 191 north for 15 miles, then Route 211 southwest for 11 miles; 435-587-2141, fax 435-587-1578; e-mail pgezon@ut.blm.gov.

▲ There are eight primitive sites; free.

CANYONLANDS NATIONAL PARK—NEEDLES 🏃 🚲 🐎 Sculptured rock spires, arches, canyons and potholes dominate the landscape. Grassy meadows like Chesler Park offer striking contrasts to the mostly bare rock. Traces of the Pueblo Indians can be found throughout the area in well-preserved pictographs and petroglyphs. The meeting place of the Colorado and Green rivers, before they join forces and rumble down to Lake Powell, can be seen from Confluence Overlook. If Island in the Sky is the observation deck for Canyonlands, then the Needles could be considered the main stage—you start out right at ground level and become immediately immersed in its unfolding tale. The park has a visitors center, picnic areas and restrooms. The $10 vehicle fee is good for seven days in all Canyonlands districts. ~ Proceed south from Moab on Route 191 for 40 miles (or north from Monticello 15 miles), then 35 miles southwest on Route 211; 435-259-4351, fax 435-259-4285, or National Park Office (Moab), 435-259-7164; www.nps.gov/cany, e-mail canyinfo@nps.gov.

▲ There are 26 sites in Squaw Flat Campground; $10 per night. Permits are required for backcountry camping. Nearby, there is also camping at Needles Outpost Store (435-979-4007) from March to October.

MANTI-LA SAL NATIONAL FOREST 🚶 🚴 🐎 🛶 ⛷ 🚤 Two southeastern Utah parcels are administered as part of this 1.4-million-acre national forest, the largest portion of which is south of Provo. Immediately west of Monticello, the national forest takes in the Abajo Mountains and stretches west to the Dark Canyon Wilderness; Anasazi relics can still be found in the canyon country on the west side. South and east of Moab, the national forest embraces the La Sal Range, capped by 12,721-foot Mount Peale. ~ Several roads access the national forest off Route 191; 435-587-2041 (Monticello), 435-259-7155 (Moab).

▲ There are six campgrounds (Devil Canyon, Dalton Springs and Buckboard in the Abajo sector, Warner, Oowah and Buckeye in the La Sal sector); $10 per night.

NATURAL BRIDGES NATIONAL MONUMENT 🚶 🚴 Three natural bridges, including the world's second and third largest, are within this 7500-acre, canyon-like park first discovered by white pioneers in 1883. You'll find a visitors center and restrooms, as well as picnic areas. Entrance fee, $5 per vehicle. ~ Off Route 95, about 40 miles west of Blanding; 435-692-1234, fax 435-692-1111.

▲ There are 13 primitive sites; $10 per night. Water is available at the visitors center.

DARK CANYON WILDERNESS AREA 🚶 🐎 🚤 Some 45,000 acres of plateau and canyon country are contained within this isolated region. Several long trails wind through the gorges, whose 1400-foot cliffs allow little sunlight to filter through. Adjoining Dark Canyon Primitive Area (in the Canyon Rims Recreation Area) provides a bridge to Cataract Canyon in Canyonlands National Park and Glen Canyon National Recreation Area. ~ Easiest access is off Woodenshoe Road, reached via Elk Ridge Road off Route 275 at Natural Bridges National Monument; 435-587-2041.

▲ Primitive camping only is permitted (pit toilets at some locations); free.

Southern San Juan County

Most of southern San Juan County lies within the Navajo Indian Reservation. Although towns are few and far between in this corner of Utah, attractions abound, from ancient ruins and incredible red-rock vistas to a national monument and state park.

SIGHTS   South of Blanding, at the intersection of Routes 163 and 191 is the tiny town of **Bluff**. While the Mormons first settled Bluff in 1880, some archaeologists believe Paleo Indian hunters may have stalked bison herds through the area 11,000 years ago. Kiva and cliff dwellings confirm the presence of ancient Pueblo tribes. Visitors to the town (the oldest community in San Juan County) may view sandstone Victorian-style homes left by early settlers, some of whom are buried in the historic **Pioneer Cemetery** overlooking the town. ~ The cemetery is easy to get to: Follow the Bluff Historic Loop past Rim Rock Drive to the end of the road.

On your way to Pioneer Cemetery you will pass the **Old County Jail**, a hand-hewn sandstone structure in the center of town. It was originally erected as an elementary school in 1896. ~ Bluff Historic Loop.

St. Christopher's Episcopal Mission, two miles east of Bluff, is a house of worship built of native sandstone. The Navajo Madonna and Child stand on the site of the original church, which was destroyed by fire. ~ Route 163.

About three miles east of Bluff, across a swinging footbridge that spans the San Juan River, is the **Fourteen Window Ruin** cliff dwelling (also known as the Apartment House Ruin). Take the dirt road on the south side of Route 163 to the bottom of the hill. After crossing the rickety bridge and coming to the clearing, the site can be spotted straight ahead in the rock. For closer inspection of these honeycombed dwellings, walk the additional mile on the dusty trail. Please be respectful—this site is on Navajo tribal land, and access can be denied at any time.

About 20 miles southwest of Bluff along Route 191/163, **Mexican Hat** is a tiny community separated from the Navajo Indian Reservation by the San Juan River. Its name comes from a stone formation resembling an upside-down sombrero just north of town. There are a few trading posts, motels, cafés, service stations and an RV park. ~ Two miles west of the Route 163 intersection with Route 261.

HIDDEN ▶   Located east of Mexican Hat by about seven miles (or fifteen miles west of Bluff) along Route 163 is one of the Southwest's hidden treasures: **Valley of the Gods**. Standing as sentinels within this patch of public lands at the base of Cedar Mesa are about a half-dozen or so rock monoliths that, collectively, offer a more intimate alternative to the better-known Monument Valley. Navajo lure claims the valley's towers and buttes are warriors turned into stone. Vivid imaginations have named some of the formations—Castle Butte, Rooster Butte, Battleship Rock, Setting Hen Butte, the Seven Sailors. A 17-mile dirt road loops through the valley. There are no marked hiking trails; you simply get out of your rig and start walking in whichever direction appeals to you. Numerous existing campsites (free) can be found along spur roads that break off from the main loop. Unlike Monument Valley, there's no need for tribal guides to tour the Valley of the Gods, and few tourists know of this attraction; as a result, solitude abounds.

MONUMENT VALLEY   It's about 25 miles from Mexican Hat via Route 163 to the Arizona border. A half-mile north of the state line is a crossroads: Go left two miles to Gouldings Trading Post and Lodge, or right two miles to **Monument Valley Navajo Tribal Park** headquarters and visitors center. Inside, you can see excellent views from a glass-walled observatory. This was the first Navajo Tribal Park, set aside in 1958. Within you'll see more than 40 named and dozen more unnamed red and orange monolithic sandstone buttes and rock skyscrapers jutting 400 to 1000 feet above the valley floor. Admission. ~ P.O. Box 360289, Monument Valley; 84536; 435-727-3287; www.navajonationparks.org.

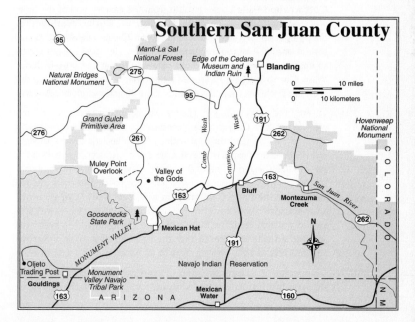

Southern San Juan County

Text continued on page 386.

Trail of the Ancients

A scenic, historical and archaeological tour of San Juan County begins at Edge of the Cedars, just northwest of Blanding, and follows a counterclockwise, 125-mile loop that includes more than a dozen sites of interest such as Natural Bridges National Monument and the towns of Mexican Hat and Bluff. The trail derives its name from Anasazi, "the ancient ones," and much of the tour passes ancient sites of this now-extinct people. Detailed maps are available at the Edge of the Cedars Museum and Indian Ruin.

WESTWATER CLIFF DWELLINGS   Just west of Blanding a paved access road from Route 191 leads across a swinging natural bridge to the Westwater cliff dwellings, which include five kivas (circular, underground structures used for gathering of kin groups) and open work areas. The dwelling was occupied from around 1150 A.D. to 1275 A.D. Unfortunately, much of the site has been destroyed by vandals searching for ancient relics.

COTTON, WASH, COMB   From Route 191, the trail turns west onto Route 95, passing Cottonwood Falls, Butler Wash and Comb Ridge. Only a large depression, almost 80 feet in diameter, marks the great kiva at **Cottonwood Falls**. Looking south from the eastern end of the hole, a prehistoric road may be spotted. Farther on, **Butler Wash** houses the highly developed stonework remains of a 20-room dwelling area plus several smaller Anasazi structures. The cliff houses can be viewed from an observation area at the end of a mile-long hiking trail. Beyond Butler Wash, **Comb Ridge** is an eroded monocline, or bending of the earth's crust in a single direction, and extends some 80 miles south into Arizona.

ARCH AND MULE CANYONS   The highway continues to cut through the red walls of Arch Canyon, where centuries of erosion have chiseled and sculpted massive sandstone formations. Seven ancient towers, thought to have been built more than 900 years ago, are clustered high atop the rim of Mule Canyon. Three of the seven are visible at the site and considered a rare find because only a few such tower-like ruins are still standing. At the **Mule Canyon Ruin and Rest Stop** is an excavated 12-room pueblo with a pair of kivas and a tower, all extremely well preserved and stabilized. The Bureau of Land Management has even constructed a sheltering ramada over the kiva, affording extra protection and interpretive signs offering clues to its history.

SALVATION KNOLL   Later explorers of the region included an 1879 scouting party that lost its way while looking for the Hole-in-the-Rock Trail.

The scouts climbed to the top of Salvation Knoll, from where they were able to regain their bearings and continue their search for a passable route to the east. What the scouting party didn't spot was **Natural Bridges National Monument** (page 377), which wasn't discovered by white men until 1883. You'll find the entrance to the park off Route 95 just past the junction with Route 261.

GRAND GULCH   From Natural Bridges, backtrack to the highway junction. and turn south on Route 261. This 34-mile segment of the trail first brings you to Grand Gulch, where Anasazi habitation was omnipresent. Found within the 50-mile-long canyon system (managed as an outdoor museum) are six representative sites from both Basketmaker and Pueblo periods. Extensive remains of Anasazi dwellings, tools and artwork may be seen. Travel is limited to horseback riders and hikers.

MULEY POINT OVERLOOK   Like stepping into a new world, Muley Point Overlook abruptly jolts travelers from cedar forests to austere desert scenes. In the distance, keen observers can spot the monolith-filled Monument Valley. Be warned: Route 261 leading to Muley Point travels over the **Moki Dugway**, a graveled, three-mile series of tight (and we mean tight!) switchbacks ascending to the lookout.

VALLEY OF THE GODS   Descending from the overlook, the road leads into the Valley of the Gods (page 382) which, with its unique rock formations jutting hundreds of feet into the air, is considered a mini-Monument Valley.

GOOSENECKS STATE PARK   From the canyon rim of Goosenecks State Park (page 389), you can view the San Juan River 1000 feet below forming a series of "gooseneck" switchbacks as it winds its way toward Lake Powell. ~ Route 261; 435-678-2238, fax 435-678-3348; e-mail nrdpr.edsp @state.ut.us.

ROUTE 163   Just north of the tiny Navajo border town of **Mexican Hat** (page 382), turn east on Route 163. This highway passes **Sand Island**, a primary boat launch for the San Juan River. Petroglyph panels here showcase five Kokopelli flute players—mythological Indian figures.

END OF THE TRAIL   Route 163 rejoins Route 191 at the little town of **Bluff** (page 382). Turn north and continue for 26 miles across the Ute Reservation to return to Blanding. Those with ample time may want to detour into **Hovenweep National Monument** (page 390), located in both Colorado and Utah.

Here you can arrange Navajo-owned jeep tours into the Valley Drive. For a fee, you can explore the **17-Mile Loop Drive** over a dirt road, badly rutted in places, to view a number of famous landmarks with names that describe their shapes, such as **Camel Butte**, **Gray Whiskers** and **Totem Pole**. At **John Ford's Point**, named for a famous Hollywood director, an Navajo on horseback often poses for photographs, then rides out to chat and collect a tip. A 15-minute roundtrip walk from **North Window** rewards you with panoramic views.

The Navajos and this land seem to belong together. A dozen Navajo families still live in the park, and several open their hogans to guided tours. For a small fee, they'll pose for your pictures. A number of today's residents are descendants of Navajos who arrived here in the mid-1860s with Headman Hoskinini, fleeing Kit Carson and his roundup of Navajos in the Canyon de Chelly area. Hoskinini lived here until his death in 1909.

The ultimate cowboy-Indian Western landscape, Monument Valley has been the setting for at least 16 movies—to name just a few: *Stagecoach*, *The Searchers*, *How the West Was Won*, *Billy the Kid*, *She Wore a Yellow Ribbon* and *The Trial of Billy Jack*.

A sleek, watermelon-colored complex on a hillside, the **Goulding's Trading Post, Lodge and Museum** blends in with enormous sandstone boulders stacked above it. The original Gouldings two-story stone home and trading post, which is now a museum, includes a room devoted to movies made here. Daily showings can be seen in a small adjacent theater. Admission. ~ Two miles west of Route 163, Monument Valley; 435-727-3231; www.gouldings.com.

From Goulding's it's nearly 11 miles northwest on paved Oljeto Road to the single-story stone **Oljeto Trading Post**, built in 1921 —its Depression-era gas pumps and scabby turquoise door are visible reminders of its age. Inside, ask to see a dusty museum filled with American Indian crafts hidden behind the turquoise bullpen-style mercantile. Often you can buy a fine used Navajo wedding basket for a good price. ~ Oljeto; 435-727-3210.

AUTHOR FAVORITE

An eeriness falls over me when I gaze at the **Butler Wash** cliff dwellings west of Blanding. The architects of these structures worked in union with their surrounding environment, yet what catastrophe struck that made them abandon their homes? See page 384 for more information.

Claustrophobes will find the **Kokopelli Inn** somewhat confining,   **LODGING**
but the 26 rooms are spotless. Surprisingly, baths are oversized
and there are walk-in closets. ~ Route 191 West, Bluff; 435-672-
2322, 800-541-8854, fax 435-672-2385; www.kokoinn.com, e-
mail office@kokoinn.com. BUDGET.

There's something very inviting about the **Recapture Lodge**.
An oasis of shade trees populates the site, shielding guests from
the hot Utah sun. There are 28 homey rooms, nothing fancy, but
quiet and comfortable. Lawn chairs, ideal for lounging, line the
upper deck. A nice-sized swimming pool provides another way
to beat the heat. Adventuresome souls can arrange geologist-
guided tours of the nearby canyons, cliff dwellings and American Indian sites—or even multiday llama treks—through the
lodge. ~ Route 191 West, Bluff; phone/fax 435-672-2281; e-mail
recapturelodge@hubwest.com. BUDGET.

Also in Bluff is the **Desert Rose Inn**. Backing up to the San
Juan River, the lodge looks north to rugged sandstone desert.
Along with the 30-room lodge, which is highlighted by massive
timbers, the Desert Rose offers a bit more privacy via six cabins,
each with two full beds, television, microwave, coffee maker and
small refrigerator. Each room in the lodge looks out over the red-
rock bluffs. ~ 6th East at Black Locust Avenue, Bluff; 435-672-
2303, 888-475-7673, fax 435-672-2217; www.desertroseinn.com,
e-mail reservations@desertroseinn.com. BUDGET TO MODERATE.

Tucked away in a corner of the desert at the foot of the Moki
Dugway is one of the unlikeliest outposts of civilization you'll
find in the Southwest. **The Valley of the Gods Bed & Breakfast**   ◄ *HIDDEN*
offers four charming guest rooms (all with private baths) in a
1933 stone ranch house and separate lodging in a two-story root
cellar. The B&B's architecture alone is worth a visit: two-foot-
thick walls of native rock, thick ceiling beams, and a wonderful
living room with comfy log furniture, a fireplace and great views
through the picture window. There is not another home within
miles . . . and this one is solar powered! From the rocking chairs
on the 75-foot-long covered front porch you have great views into
the Valley of the Gods. ~ One-half mile east of Route 261 on
Valley of the Gods Road, Mexican Hat; 970-749-1164 (cellular);
www.zippitydodah.com/vog. MODERATE.

Set into red cliffs on the north bank of San Juan River beside
the Route 163 bridge is the **San Juan Inn**, incorporating The
Olde Bridge Bar and Grille. The two-story motel has 40 rooms
including a pair of two-bedroom housekeeping units; it also features a coin laundry and an exercise room. Outside you'll find a
patio with wonderful views of the river. ~ San Juan Drive at
Main Avenue (Route 163), Mexican Hat; 435-683-2220, 800-

447-2022, fax 435-683-2210; www.sanjuaninn.net. BUDGET TO MODERATE.

If the views of the eroded Mitten Buttes aren't enough to stir your memories of actor John Wayne, **Goulding's Lodge** will rent you a movie starring "The Duke" to play on the VCR in your own room. The only lodging at Monument Valley since the 1920s, Goulding's blends into a sandstone hillside setting. Sliding glass doors in each of the 62 rooms open onto balconies, so guests can enjoy the panorama. The complex includes an indoor pool, a restaurant, a campground, a gift shop, a theater, a museum, a medical clinic, a laundromat, a gas station and a convenience store. ~ Two miles west of Route 163, Monument Valley; 435-727-3231, 800-874-0902, fax 435-727-3344; www.gouldings.com. DELUXE.

DINING

HIDDEN ►

Surprisingly, it's in the tiny town of Bluff where you'll discover some of the best dining. **Cow Canyon Restaurant** changes its entrées weekly and features traditional Navajo dishes as well as vegetarian—and sometimes even French—cuisine. One week the choices might be spinach lasagna, Greek salad or stuffed butternut squash. Desserts range from an apple dumpling to ice cream splashed with Kahlua and baked almonds. Housed in an old log-and-stone trading post, Cow Canyon's ambience more than matches the food. Dinner only. Closed Tuesday and Wednesday and from November through March. ~ Routes 191 and 163, Bluff; 435-672-2208; e-mail cowcanyn@sanjuan.net. BUDGET TO MODERATE.

There's also the **Cottonwood Steakhouse**. Many patrons enjoy dining outdoors, under a huge cottonwood tree and near a campfire; others enjoy the rustic decor inside. Barbecued ribs and chicken, as well as steak, are the house specials; they're served with salad, potatoes and baked beans. Dinner only. Closed November through February. ~ Route 191 West, Bluff; 435-672-2282; e-mail cwsteak@lasal.net. MODERATE TO DELUXE.

Sitting directly across the river from the Navajo Indian Reservation, it's no surprise that **The Olde Bridge Bar and Grille** does a wonderful job with American Indian dishes. Try the Navajo tacos or *haani gai*, a stew of lamb and hominy. A varied menu of Mexican and American dishes is served three meals a day daily at this eclectically decorated restaurant in the San Juan Inn. ~ San Juan Drive at Route 163, Mexican Hat; 435-683-2220. MODERATE.

The one place to eat in the Monument Valley Navajo Tribal Park is **Hashké Neeinii**. In this spectacular natural setting, you can eat traditional Indian food, such as Navajo tacos, fry bread and mutton stew. ~ Monument Valley; 435-727-3287. BUDGET.

The Stagecoach Restaurant at Goulding's Lodge may be best known for the dramatic view from its picture windows, but the regional American food is good, too. For breakfast, you can try

"The Duke" (corned beef hash and eggs); for lunch, the Navajo taco. Dinner runs the gamut from steaks to pastas. ~ Two miles west of Route 163, Monument Valley; 435-727-3231. MODERATE.

As gateway to Navajo tribal lands, San Juan County is blanketed with trading posts. Best of the lot is **Cow Canyon Trading Post**, a log-and-stone structure dating from the 1940s. Jewelry, pottery, rugs and ethnographic artifacts of the Navajo and Zuni are well displayed and honestly priced. New is a photo-graphic gallery. Closed October through March. ~ Routes 191 and 163, Bluff; 435-672-2208.

SHOPPING

Before man's ability to blast solid rock, Comb Ridge was a natural barrier to east–west travel.

Other trading posts to choose from, offering a variety of pottery, jewelry, pipes and rugs, are **Burches Trading Post** (Route 163, Mexican Hat; 435-683-2221, fax 435-683-2246), **San Juan Inn Trading Post** (Route 163, Mexican Hat; 435-683-2220, fax 435-683-2210) and **Twin Rocks Trading Post** (913 East Navajo Twins Drive, Bluff; 435-672-2341, fax 435-672-2370).

Margaret LaBounty's works at **Rock Speaks Studio** reflect both the Southwest landscape and cultures—pictograph reliefs, rock sculptures and a variety of totems. So impressed with her work was the Yuma County (Arizona) Airport Authority that it commissioned LaBounty to provide 13 sculpted clay totems for the Yuma International Airport. ~ 6th West and Rabbitbrush Avenue, Bluff; 435-672-2337; www.rockspeaks.com.

The Olde Bridge Bar and Grille is open Monday through Sunday for over-the-bar beer sales with occasional live music. ~ San Juan Inn, San Juan Drive at Route 163, Mexican Hat; 435-683-2220.

NIGHTLIFE

GOOSENECKS STATE PARK 🏃 An impressive example of "en-trenched meander," Goosenecks is a 1000-foot-deep chasm carved by the San Juan River as it winds and turns back on itself for more than six miles while advancing only one and a half miles west to-ward Lake Powell. A picnic area and restrooms are the park's only facilities. ~ Off Route 261, nine miles northwest of Mexican Hat; 435-678-2238, fax 435-678-3348; e-mail nrpdr.edsp@state.ut.us.

PARKS

▲ Primitive camping is allowed within the park; four sites; free. No water is available.

MONUMENT VALLEY NAVAJO TRIBAL PARK 🏃 🚲 🐎 Strad-dling the Utah–Arizona border is the jewel of tribally run Navajo Nation parks. With its 29,816 acres of monoliths, spires, buttes, mesas, canyons and sand dunes—all masterpieces of red-rock erosion—it is a stunning destination. Dozens of families still live here, making it also a sort of Williamsburg of Navajoland. There's a visitors center with shops, showers, restrooms and picnic tables. Day-use fee, $2.50 adults, $1 seniors, free under 7. ~ Route 163,

21 miles southwest of Mexican Hat. The visitors center is east another two miles; 435-727-3353.

▲ There are 100 sites at Mitten View campground; $5 per person per night.

HOVENWEEP NATIONAL MONUMENT 🧍 🚴 Within this 784-acre park, which straddles the Utah–Colorado border, are six major sites of American Indian ruins. The slickrock canyon and plateau country is characterized by sweeping unobstructed vistas of the pastel high desert. Monument facilities are limited to picnic sites and pit toilets; food, gas and supplies are available at Hatch Trading Post (16 miles west). The $6 vehicle fee is good for seven days. ~ From Blanding, head south on Route 191 for 15 miles, then turn left onto Route 262 and continue 16 miles to Hovenweep Road; 970-749-0510.

▲ There are 30 sites at Square Tower Ruin; $10 per night April through October (water available); free November through March (no water). Bring your own firewood; campfires are permitted in fire grates, but wood gathering is prohibited.

▼▼▼▼▼▼▼▼▼▼▼▼▼
Lake Powell Area

Like life, Lake Powell is grand, awesome and filled with contradictions. Conservationists considered it a disaster when Glen Canyon Dam was built in Page, Arizona, flooding beautiful Glen Canyon and creating a 186-mile-long reservoir that extended deep into the heart of Utah.

Today the environmental "tragedy" is Utah's second-most popular tourist destination. Part of the Glen Canyon National Recreation Area that covers one and a quarter *million* acres, the lake boasts nearly 2000 miles of meandering shoreline. Not only is that more shoreline than along the entire West Coast of the United States, much of it is in the form of spires, domes, minarets and multi-hued mesas.

SIGHTS

The depth of **Lake Powell's** turquoise waters varies from year to year depending on mountain runoff and releases from Glen Canyon Dam. An interesting cave discovered on one trip may well be under water the next season. The same holds true for favorite sandy beaches, coves and waterfalls. But part of the fun of exploring this multi-armed body of water is finding new hidden treasures and hideaways around the next curve.

Lake Powell's waters usually warm to a comfortable temperature for swimming by May or early June. During the summer months, when the majority of the three-million-plus annual visitors come, the surrounding temperatures can exceed a sizzling 100 degrees. Vacationers seek cool relief and a relaxing getaway in this stark desert ocean. Even at peak periods like July 4th and Labor Day weekends, when all the rental boats are checked out and hotel rooms booked, Lake Powell still manages to provide ample shoreline for docking and camping and, as always, clear, blue-green water for aquatic pursuits.

You can become acquainted with Powell from atop its sky-high buttes and adjacent byways, but those truly interested in getting to know its complex personality, curves and quirks must travel by vessel to the quiet box canyons and deep, gleaming pools for an experience akin to spiritual cleansing.

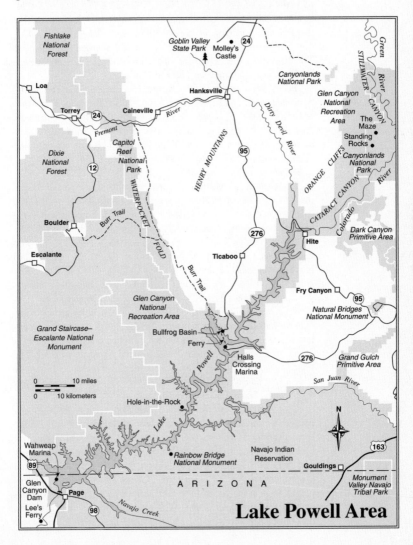

Lake Powell Area

Speedboats and houseboats are most popular for exploring, but a smaller water vehicle like a skiff or canoe will give access to outlying areas where you can just pitch a tent or throw down a sleeping bag on the shore.

The lake can be entered from four marinas accessible by car. From Natural Bridges National Monument, Route 95 leads to **Hite** (435-684-2278, 800-528-6154, fax 435-684-2358) the most northern facility. Also from the monument area, Route 276 runs to **Halls Crossing** (435-684-7000, 800-528-6154, fax 435-684-2319; e-mail fincher-carol@aramark.com), which is connected to neighboring **Bullfrog** (435-684-3000, 800-528-6154, fax 435-684-2355) marina by convenient car and passenger ferry service. The 20-minute ferry crossing, offered morning to evening at two-hour intervals, eliminates 130 road miles.

From Monument Valley, Route 163 crosses over the Utah–Arizona border and merges with Route 160 at Kayenta. Forty-two miles to the south, Route 98 heads 66 miles northwest to Page, Arizona. **Wahweap Marina** in Arizona offers the most services to boaters, sightseers and overnight visitors. ~ Route 89 near the Glen Canyon Dam; 928-645-2433, 800-528-6154, fax 602-331-5258; www.lakepowell.com.

Dangling Rope Marina, about seven miles southwest of the entrance to Rainbow Bridge Canyon, is a floating repair/refueling stop and supply store accessed only by boat. Enjoy a soft-serve ice cream cone while pumping gas. ~ Phone/fax 928-645-2969.

Before setting out, the logical place to become acquainted with the second-largest manmade lake in the country is the **Carl Hayden Visitors Center** at the Glen Canyon Dam in Page, Arizona. The visitors center has a relief map and changing exhibits. ~ Route 89, Page, AZ; 928-608-6404; www.nps.gov/glca.

Another way to explore Lake Powell is to take a **boat tour**, either a half-day tour to Rainbow Bridge, a full-day tour that enters many of the lake's high-walled canyons and includes a box lunch, or a sunset or dinner cruise aboard a paddle wheeler. The boat tours and paddle-wheel cruises depart Wahweap Lodge & Marina. ~ Lakeshore Drive; 928-645-2433, 800-528-6154, fax 602-331-5258; www.lakepowell.com.

The highlight of the Lake Powell boat tours is **Rainbow Bridge National Monument,** the world's largest natural bridge located about 50 miles from Wahweap. "Nonnezoshi"—or rainbow turned to stone, as it's called by the Navajos—spans 275 feet and rises 290 feet above the canyon floor. Declared a national monument in 1910, it wasn't until Glen Canyon Dam was completed 53 years later, and the lake started to fill, that the site became a favorite destination. Well touristed and commercialized on countless posters and cards, the stone arch with its awesome girth and prisms of color never ceases to amaze. Rainbow Bridge is reached only by boat, foot or horseback.

South of the awesome bridge, between Warm Creek and Wahweap bays, is **Antelope Island**, site of the first known expedition of whites to the area. Franciscan priests Francisco Dominguez and Silvestre Vélez de Escalante trekked across a low point in the river (before it became a lake) and established camp on the island. Nearby **Padre Bay** was also named for the priests. Within these waters is the rock fortress called **Cookie Jar Butte**.

Aficionados claim the best season to visit Lake Powell is early fall, when rates and temperatures drop to a comfortable level.

A landmark visible from the Wahweap section of the lake is the hump-backed, 10,388-foot **Navajo Mountain** and the striking **Tower Butte**, both located on the Navajo Indian Reservation. They are good landmarks to keep in mind when your directional sense gets churned in the water.

A primitive Indian "art gallery" is located approximately ten miles east of the Rainbow Bridge Canyon up the San Juan River arm in **Cha Canyon**. You must motor past what are termed the Bob Hope Rock (check out the profile) and Music Temple Canyon to reach Cha.

When the heat is on, you'll be spending a lot of time in the refreshing, crystal-clear water. Five miles upstream (while some landmarks and obstacles are marked with buoys, a map is still essential) from Dangling Rope Marina is a water cave in Cascade Canyon that invites exploring. If you're more interested in things that swim than swimming, throw in a line and wait for the bass, crappie, pike and trout to bite.

Highly recommended for fishing is the **Escalante River Arm**, located about 25 miles north and east of Dangling Rope. Bridges, arches and ravines also abound in the Escalante's coves. Keep an eye peeled for prehistoric dwellings and drawings on a ledge above the mouth to **Willow Creek**, nine and a half miles from the confluence with the main channel.

Continuing farther into the Escalante arm, at approximately the 20-mile mark, you'll come to **Coyote Gulch** and its natural bridge and pair of arches.

From the main channel, the steep sandstone ridges of the Straight Cliffs and the 100-mile-long rock uplift called the **Waterpocket Fold** loom to the north. Respect must be given to those who were unintimidated by these fortresses. Just imagine being among the 230 or so Mormons who reached the towering canyons above the river in 1880 en route to establishing a new settlement —and not turning back.

Men blasted in solid rock for more than a month to create the **Hole-in-the-Rock**, permitting passage through the earth's mantle.

The steep slope and landmark near the mouth of the Escalante River is still worth scaling, although erosion has partially closed the original notch.

North and east of the Hole-in-the-Rock is a little ol' swimming hole called **Annie's Canyon** about 12 miles from Bullfrog Marina. Boaters may notice more traffic and wake when nearing Halls Creek Bay, Bullfrog Bay and the busy marinas. Those on multiday excursions may want to stock up on ice and other necessary items at this point.

About five miles north of Halls Crossing is **Moki Canyon**. With its archaeological sites and petroglyphs, the area holds many secrets of the Pueblo peoples. Supposedly the canyon was a miniature city back in prehistoric times. From Moki Canyon upstream about five miles are the odd and eerie **Moki steps**, thought to be hand and foot holds of this same tribe of ancient climbers.

Turn right and follow the next water pocket to Forgotten Canyon. At the end is the **Defiance House Site**, believed to have been occupied during the Pueblo's peak years from A.D. 1050 to A.D. 1250. Defiance House represents the lake's finest restored sites and petroglyphs and includes unusual animal/man anthropomorphs.

You'll pass by Tapestry Wall on the left side of the channel before coming to the long stretch of water in handsome **Good Hope Bay**, below the mesa of the same name, that's usually a haven for flatwater—a waterskier's dream. The lake twists and turns past a handful of other canyons in the remaining 15 miles to Hite Marina, the start (or end, depending on how you look at it) of Lake Powell.

For more extensive history and sightseeing tips on Lake Powell, Stan Jones' *Boating and Exploring Map* is essential to your enjoyment and is available at any Lake Powell shop.

Northeast of Hite Marina via Route 95 and eventually Route 24 is **Goblin Valley State Park**, a testament to the artistic whims of nature. Fifteen miles of gravel road lead to the park, but even

TREAT WITH RESPECT

Rainbow Bridge is considered sacred by many American Indians, and the site has religious significance. To the Navajo, Rainbow represents guardians of the Universe. Boat tour passengers approach the bridge on a quarter-mile walkway that's part pontoon. The bridge may be photographed from a viewing area, but visitors are not permitted to walk under the bridge. Although signs that advise of the site's sacred status are clearly posted, many visitors tend to ignore the request to remain in the viewing area and must be called back by tour guides or boat crew members.

before you get there, you'll be stunned by the rock sculptures of Wild Horse Butte and Molley's Castle. Within the vast sandstone bowl of Goblin Valley is an enchanted land of countless standing rocks and troll-like figures that seem to change their shapes with the passage of the sun. Rock hoodoos and goblins (more often associated with Bryce Canyon National Park) crop up within these 3654 acres. While photographers try to capture the landscape, off-road enthusiasts flock to the hundreds of miles of dirt roads that wind through the area. Admission. ~ Temple Mountain Road west of Route 24, halfway between Hanksville and Green River; 435-564-3633.

CANYONLANDS NATIONAL PARK—THE MAZE   North of Lake Powell via Route 95/24, Henry David Thoreau would have liked the uncharted territory of Canyonlands' Maze District because it demands self-reliance. Services to this section, considered by some to be a "mini-Grand Canyon," are almost nonexistent save for the emergency water available at the **Hans Flat Ranger Station**. The ranger will probably check your vehicle for road-worthiness before allowing you to proceed. Extra gas, and of course plenty of water, must be on hand before proceeding because you may not see another car for days. The Maze remains some of the wildest land in the West and is accessible only by foot or high-clearance four-wheel-drive vehicle. ~ Ranger Station: 46 miles from the Route 24 turnoff via rough dirt road; 435-259-2652.

Puzzle-like chasms twist and turn through no-man's land where the junipers, piñon pine, sagebrush, yucca and spring wildflowers seem surprising given the desert dryness. From Hans Flat it's 34 miles to the Maze Overlook, a good starting point for hikes or for a bird's-eye view of the rock **Chocolate Drops**, which resembles candy bars left too long in the sun.

Hikers who drop into the steep canyon below the lookout are rewarded with eight-foot-tall pictographs at **Harvest Scene**. As with any remnants of ancient art, it is important not to touch these stunning works because human body oils can cause damage over time.

Traversing from one section to another in the Maze can be difficult and confusing because of the puzzle of canyons. Using Hans Flat as your starting point again, drive 45 miles past Bagpipe Butte Overlook and Orange Cliffs to the Land of Standing Rocks. There you'll have the option for further foot exploration of the **Doll House**'s red-rock spires and massive fins in Ernie's Country. You may actually see more people here than in other sections of the Maze because some backcountry outfitters and rafting companies access the canyons from the edge of the Colorado River. Still, it's far from a thoroughfare.

Horseshoe Canyon, on the northwestern edge of the Maze about 32 miles from the Route 24 turnoff, contains the prehistoric rock-art collection of the **Great Gallery**. Considered some of this country's best-preserved pictographs and painted art, the gallery is full of haunting, life-size drawings of people and animals. There is evidence that a prehistoric Indian culture, as well as the later Anasazi and Fremont tribes, dabbled on these walls.

LODGING

At the **Defiance House Lodge**, cool desert room colors mimic the canyon hues outside. Coffeemakers and mini-refrigerators are standard in all 48 rooms, many of which have lakeside views. ~ Bullfrog Marina; 435-684-3000; www.lakepowell.com/lodging/defiance.htm. MODERATE TO DELUXE.

Three-bedroom housekeeping cottages with linens, kitchens and utensils are a viable option for families. Cottages are available at **Bullfrog** (435-684-3000) and **Halls Crossing** (435-684-7000) marinas. **Hite** (435-684-2278) marina has mobile homes. ~ 800-528-6154; www.lakepowell.com. DELUXE.

Even those who don't enjoy roughing it in a tent and sleeping bag will take to the great outdoors experience on a **houseboat**. Under Lake Powell's silent, starry skies, waves gently rock the boat, providing the perfect tonic for deep sleep. During the day, is there a more relaxing pastime than reclining on the boat's flat-topped roof with book or drink in hand? The mobile floating homes come equipped with all-weather cabins, bunk beds, showers, toilets and kitchens. Four classes of boats sleep up to 12 people and are equipped for travelers with disabilities. **Lake Powell Resorts & Marinas** rents houseboats at the Wahweap, Bullfrog, Halls Crossing and Hite marinas. Prices vary depending on the season and the class of houseboat, but are not cheap by any stretch of the imagination. ~ Lake Powell Resorts & Marinas, 800-528-6154; www.lakepowell.com. ULTRA-DELUXE.

DINING

Restaurants are few around Lake Powell as most visitors opt to eat on their houseboats or at their campsites. But realizing that people need a break, Lake Powell Resorts & Marinas, which operates as the sole concessionaire for the National Park Service in Lake Powell, has a better-than-average restaurant at the Bullfrog end of the lake. The **Anasazi Restaurant** sits perched above the marina and serves Continental cuisine. Steaks, burgers, fish-and-chips and Southwestern specialties please most palates, especially those who've eaten houseboat food for a week. ~ Defiance House Lodge, Bullfrog Marina; 435-684-3000. MODERATE. The adjacent **Lily Pad Restaurant** specializes in pizza, burgers and shakes. Closed Labor Day to Memorial Day. ~ BUDGET.

PARKS

GLEN CANYON NATIONAL RECREATION AREA 🏃 🚣 ⛵ 🚤 🛥 🦆 Glen Canyon Dam confines the waters of the Colorado River forming Lake Powell, the second-largest manmade reservoir in the world. The 180-mile-long lake harbors countless inlets, caves and coves sheltering Pueblo Indian sites that are ever-changing because of the water level. Marinas are found at five separate locations on the lake: Hite, Bullfrog, Halls Crossing and Dangling Rope in Utah, and Wahweap in Arizona. All kinds of water sports, from skiing to windsurfing, kayaking to inner tubing, have their place at Powell. Largemouth and small-mouth bass, striped bass and catfish are common catches. You'll also find hotels, restaurants, boat rentals (except at Dangling Rope), groceries, visitors centers, picnic areas and restrooms. Entrance fee, $5 per vehicle, $10 per boat, for up to a week. ~ Routes 95, 276 and 89 lead to Lake Powell, where Routes 95 and 276 lead to Utah marinas; 520-608-6404, fax 520-608-6204; www.nps.gov/glca, e-mail glcachvc@nps.gov.

▲ There are sites at four campgrounds: Bullfrog, Halls Crossing, Lees Ferry and Wahweap; $10 to $18 per night. Primitive sites are available at Lees Ferry ($10), Bullfrog ($6) and Hite ($10). RV hookups are available ($28) through a private concessionaire (800-528-6154) at Wahweap, Bullfrog and Halls Crossing only. Backcountry camping is free. Camping is not allowed within one mile of marinas or at Rainbow Bridge National Monument.

RAINBOW BRIDGE NATIONAL MONUMENT 🏃 🚣 ⛵ Greatest of the world's known natural bridges, this symmetrical salmon-pink sandstone span rises 290 feet above the floor of Bridge Canyon. Rainbow Bridge sits on one square mile within the Navajo Indian Reservation in Glen Canyon. Tours of the monument leave regularly in the summer season from Wahweap and Bullfrog marinas; during the rest of the year there is sporadic service out of Wahweap. Facilities are limited to restrooms. ~ Accessible by boat, on foot or by your own horse. To go the land route means

LAKE POWELL HOUSEBOATING AND WATER SPORTS

The best way to see Lake Powell is from the stern of a boat with the breeze passing through your hair and water sprays cooling the temperature. **Lake Powell Resorts & Marinas** offers plenty for rent at the Wahweap, Bullfrog, Halls Crossing and Hite marinas, including flat-topped houseboats (they only average two miles a gallon, so many groups also rent a power-boat or jet skis for exploring the shoreline). Waterskis, tubes, bobsleds, kneeboards and water weenie-like "wavecutters" are also available. A word to the wise: Don't be in a hurry to check out boats. Lake employees seem to operate on a "desert clock" and the time-conscious visitor only adds stress to a vacation by trying to hurry the process. ~ 800-528-6154; www.lakepowell.com.

traversing mostly unmarked trails through Navajo Indian Reservation land and requires a permit (928-698-2801); the number for the monument is 928-608-6404; www.nps.gov/rabr.

HIDDEN ►

GOBLIN VALLEY STATE PARK 🏃 Curious rock formations created by erosion are the hallmark of this remote state park located off Route 24 and 26 miles south of Route 70. The effects of wind, rain and sand on rock play tricks on the imagination—goblin-like faces appear to stare from every corner of this small (just two miles by three miles) wonderland. Remote, yet not inaccessible, Goblin Valley would make a great setting for an episode of "The Twilight Zone." Gravel roads lead to beautiful Little Wild Horse Canyon, where there are two and a half miles of narrows to explore. A few short trails wind through rock hoodoos, goblins, mushrooms and other odd configurations. Day-use fee, $4. ~ Temple Mountain Road west of Route 24, halfway between Hanksville and Green River; 435-564-3633.

▲ There is one scantily shaded campground with 21 sites; $14 per night; 14-day maximum stay. Reservations: 800-322-3770.

CANYONLANDS NATIONAL PARK—THE MAZE 🏃 🚲 🐎 The Colorado and Green rivers naturally divide this 337,570-acre, unspoiled park into three distinct and separate districts: Island in the Sky, Needles and the Maze. Uncharted and untamed, wild formations of the Maze are enjoyed only after negotiating a labyrinth of canyons and jumbled rock. Another option for reaching the Maze is from the Colorado River's edge. The seemingly other-worldly formations and Indian artifacts in this 30-mile-wide jigsaw puzzle are found west of the Colorado and Green rivers. There are no facilities here. ~ Located via Route 24 south 46 miles to the dirt road turnoff to the east; 435-259-2652 or National Park Office (Moab), 435-259-7164.

▲ Primitive camping for backpackers and mountain bikers is allowed at Land of Standing Rocks and Maze Overlook with a permit ($15 to $30); no water available. Reservations are highly recommended: 435-259-4351. People planning to camp with a vehicle must provide their own portable toilet system, which can be rented or purchased in Moab.

▼ ▼ ▼ ▼ ▼ ▼ ▼ ▼ ▼ ▼ ▼ ▼ ▼ ▼ ▼

Outdoor Adventures

FISHING

Lake Powell is the most popular place in the region to go fishing; the expansive reservoir is rich in catfish, bass, crappie and rainbow trout. Elsewhere in the area, the Colorado, Green and San Juan rivers are hard to access because of the steep canyon walls that contain them. But several small lakes in the Manti–La Sal National Forest, west of Monticello and east of Moab, are stocked with trout.

For licenses, equipment and advice, visit **Canyonlands Outdoor Sports**. ~ 446 South Main Street, Moab; 435-259-5699.

The mighty Colorado River weaves its way through the desert rock of southeastern Utah en route to its final destination in the Gulf of Mexico. Burnt sienna–colored water rushes boldly in some sections, slowing to a near crawl in others. Kayaking, canoeing, whitewater rafting and jetboat tours are abundant throughout the region.

Running the rivers in Utah allows a pure view of the land from deep within the canyons. It's a different world, thousands of feet away from manmade distractions. Sometimes the only sounds are the whoop of a crane, the river's gurgle or a paddle dipping into the water. Novices shouldn't be deterred by the challenging Class V rapids of sections in Cataract Canyon; tours are offered in all degrees of difficulty. Because of the rivers' idiosyncracies, it's wise to verse yourself in their courses before taking the plunge.

> Those seeking rushing rapids must be willing to put up with frigid mountain runoff in early spring. By mid-summer, the rivers are warmer and mellower.

Along the Colorado River northeast of Moab via Route 70 is **Westwater**, which packs a real punch in a relatively short jaunt. Pre-Cambrian, black-granite walls line the deep canyons and stand in contrast to the red-sandstone spires above. Westwater, with 11 telling sections sporting names like Skull Rapid, is a favorite destination for whitewater junkies.

The most heavily used section of the Colorado River is below **Dewey Bridge** off Route 128. When runoff peaks, there are a few mild rapids between here and Moab. But for most of the year expect to kick back and enjoy a scenic float. **Fisher Towers, The Priest and Nuns** rock formations and **Castle Valley**—backdrop of many favorite Westerns—can be lazily viewed from a raft, kayak or canoe, or in low water on an air mattress or inner tube.

Floating along the sinuous Green River and in the rapidless **Labyrinth and Stillwater canyons** is a first choice for families and river neophytes more interested in drifting past prehistoric rocks than paddling through a wild ride.

When the Colorado meets the Green River in the heart of Canyonlands National Park, crazy things happen. Below the confluence is the infamous **Cataract Canyon**, where no fewer than 26 rapids await river runners. During the period of highwater (usually May and June), Cataract can serve up some of the country's toughest rapids, aptly named Little Niagara and Satan's Gut. When the river finally spills into Lake Powell at Hite Crossing, 112 miles downriver from Moab, boaters breathe a sigh of relief.

Unique to the **San Juan River**, another tributary of Lake Powell, are sand waves. These rollercoaster-like dips and drops are caused by shifting sands on the river bottom. Below the town of Mexican Hat, the San Juan meanders among deep goosenecks through the scenic Cedar Mesa Anticline and charges through reasonable rapids before spilling into Lake Powell.

Outfitters   **Holiday Expeditions,** which has an office in Green River, can arrange trips down the Colorado, Green, San Juan and Yampa rivers. Its Cataract Canyon trips through Canyonlands National Park begin in Green River. ~ 544 East 3900 South, Salt Lake City, UT 84107; 801-266-2087, 800-624-6323; www.bike raft.com.

To explore canyons such as Westwater (northeast of Moab via Route 70) by kayak or raft contact **Tag-A-Long River Expeditions.** ~ 452 North Main Street, Moab; 435-259-8946, 800-453-3292; www.tagalong.com. **Western River Expeditions** leads kayak and rafting tours as well. ~ 1371 North Main Street, Moab; 435-259-7019, 800-453-7450; www.westernriver.com.

Like ducks in a shooting gallery, you can't miss finding a professional river-running company along the Moab highway. All enjoy good reputations and can verse travelers in the water's idiosyncracies. Alphabetically first is **Adrift Adventures.** ~ 378 North Main Street; 435-259-8594, 800-874-4483; www.adrift. net. **Canyonlands by Night** is another reliable operator. ~ 1861 North Route 191; 435-259-5261, 800-394-9978; www.canyon landsbynight.com. **O.A.R.S.** runs the river regularly. ~ 543 North Main Street; 209-736-4677, 800-346-6277; www.oarsutah.com. Or take to the whitewater with **Sheri Griffith River Expeditions.** ~ 2231 South Route 191; 435-259-8229, 800-332-2439; www. griffithexp.com.

In the San Juan area, try **Wild Rivers Expeditions.** ~ 101 Main Street, Bluff; 435-672-2244, 800-422-7654; www.rivers andruins.com.

For more rafting companies, visit www.utah.com.

At Lake Powell, you can "see Rainbow Bridge and leave the driving to someone else." Guided full-day tours of the monument are available from **Bullfrog Marina,** which also leads an early-evening cruise past archaeological sites. ~ 800-528-6154. **Wahweap Marina** also leads tours of Rainbow Bridge and has shorter sight-seeing tours to Antelope and Navajo canyons. ~ 800-528-6154.

High Desert Adventures also offers Lake Powell trips, as well as raft trips down the San Juan River and through the Grand Canyon. ~ 435-673-1733, 800-673-1733; www.boathda.com.

AUTHOR FAVORITE

It took me a good 15 minutes to gather the gumption to push myself off a 100-foot-tall stone arch near Moab. But as I slowly twirled while rappeling off the arch, taking in the surrounding red rock, I knew that **canyoneering** was a sport I'd never grow weary of. See page 401 for a list of outfitters.

Desert summers heat up like a microwave oven. When tempera- **SWIMMING**
tures soar into the 90s and above, any body of water looks good.
Many people opt for a dip in the Colorado or Green rivers and,
of course, in Lake Powell.

For swimming, fishing, picnicking and nonmotorized boating
in the Monticello area try **Lloyd's Lake** on the road to Abajo Peak,
about three miles west of town. Another good swimming hole is
the multipurpose **Recapture Reservoir** about five miles north of
Blanding. Turn west off Route 191 and follow the signs.

Experienced climbers can test their mettle on the precipices near **CLIMBING**
Fisher Towers, Arches National Park and in the Potash region
near Moab and Indian Creek east of the Canyonlands Needles
entrance. Sunbaked walls make summer climbing a drag, but
temperatures are generally pleasant during the rest of the year.
Deep, sunless canyons are also prime ice-climbing spots in the
winter and perfect for canyoneering the rest of the year.

Gear, pointers and directions to climbs can be found at **Pagan
Mountaineering**. ~ 59 South Main Street #2, Moab; 435-259-
1117; www.paganmountaineering.com.

Rappeling often is the most enjoyable part of climbing, and
it's key to the canyoneering trips led by **Desert Highlights**. These
day-long adventures lead you off into the slickrock and red-rock
surrounding Moab for rappels down into canyons, which you
then hike out of. ~ P.O. Box 1342, Moab, UT 84532; 435-259-
4433, 800-747-1342; www.deserthighlights.com.

More canyoneering gurus can be found at **Moab Cliffs &
Canyons,** which also leads you into the red rock around Moab.
The company also has its eyes on adventures in the San Rafael
Swell and Cedar Mesa areas. ~ 63 East Center Street, Moab;
435-259-3317; www.cliffsandcanyons.com.

The only commercial ski area in the region, Blue Mountain in the **CROSS-**
Abajo range near Monticello is now defunct. But Nordic aficio- **COUNTRY**
nados still crisscross the slopes, ski the trees and camp out in **SKIING**
snow caves.

The La Sal Mountains are the second-highest range in the
state, so adequate white stuff is rarely a problem. There is continuing, but as yet unfulfilled, talk about developing an alpine resort here. Snow-filled meadows beckon cross-country skiers. **Rim
Cyclery** rents cross-country ski equipment in Moab. ~ 94 West
100 North; 435-259-5333, 888-304-8219; www.rimcyclery.com.

Much of Southeastern Utah's rugged, undeveloped wilderness re- **JEEP**
mains inaccessible to regular vehicles. For that reason, many vis- **TOURS**
itors opt for a jeep tour.

With **Adrift Adventures** discover the stunning beauty of the natural Gemini Bridges located northwest of Moab; from an overlook here, you'll see La Sal Mountain and the surrounding layers of red sculpted rock. ~ 378 North Main Street, Moab; 435-259-8594, 800-874-4483; www.adrift.net.

Dan Mick's Guided Tours will take you to the spectacular Onion Creek. You'll pass fluted red cliffs and drive through the creek with water splashing at your wheels. A one-man operation with a wealth of knowledge of the outback in this corner of Utah, Dan will take you out in your Jeep, a rented Jeep, or his own Jeep. ~ 600 Mill Creek Drive, Moab; 435-259-4567; www.danmick.com.

For a journey deep into the Needles, Maze or Island in the Sky districts of Canyonlands National Park, or if you have a specific itinerary in mind, contact **Tag-A-Long Expeditions**. Tag-A-Long offers packages ranging from half-day tours to week-long customized trips. ~ 452 North Main Street, Moab; 435-259-8946, 800-453-3292; www.tagalong.com.

GOLF

The desert heat seems to keep golf courses from springing up in southeastern Utah, but the few available ones are well-maintained, albeit not championship in caliber.

In Moab, there's the 18-hole **Moab Golf Course**. ~ 2705 South East Bench Road; 435-259-6488.

Monticello offers the nine-hole **Blue Mountain Meadows County Golf Course**. ~ 549 South Main Street; 435-587-2468, fax 435-587-5052.

RIDING STABLES

Clippity-clopping leisurely on horseback is one of the best ways to explore the red-rock landscape and river bottomlands around Moab.

Horseback rides can be arranged through **Sorrel River Ranch**. ~ Route 128, 17 miles northeast of Moab; 435-259-4642, 877-359-2715. A steed can also be found at **Red Cliffs Lodge**. ~ Milepost 14, Route 128, Moab; 435-259-2002, 866-812-2002.

BIKING

The Moab area has become mountain-biking central for gearheads throughout the West. Miles and miles of dirt, sandstone and paved trails within a 40-mile radius offer options for fat-tire enthusiasts of all abilities.

MOAB AREA One of Moab's claims is being the mountain bike capital of the free world. Any doubts you might have about this can be resolved by visiting the **Sand Flats Recreation Area** just a couple miles east of downtown Moab. Stop by this 7240-acre playground for those with wheels and you'll find the most challenging slickrock rides in the West. By far the most popular ride is the **Slickrock Bike Trail**, a technically demanding grunt.

Slickrock has become so well known that in spring cyclists line up wheel to wheel at the trailhead. Super steep to the point of being nearly vertical in some sections, Slickrock's 9.6-mile trail can take up to six hours to complete. But canyon, river and rock views, coupled with thrilling descents are dividends to those willing to work. Not for the faint of heart, leg or lung.

American Indians considered the humpbacked Kokopelli to be a magic being, and Kokopelli's Trail more than lives up to its namesake.

Wondering if you're up to the challenge of the Slickrock ride? Test your skills on the 2-mile-long practice loop if you have any doubts. Or, if you enjoyed the Slickrock trail and want another challenging ride, head to the far east end of the recreation area for the **Porcupine Rim Trail**. This nerve- and balance-testing ride runs 14.4 miles to Route 128. That translates into a roughly 30-mile roundtrip if you don't arrange a shuttle. Admission.

Kane Creek Road begins as a flat, paved, two-lane road that hugs the Colorado River. It's the gateway to numerous biking trails. Access Kane Creek from Route 191, just south of downtown Moab.

The **Moab Rim Trail**, about 2.5 miles from the intersection, is a short route for experienced cyclists that climbs steadily from the trailhead. Views of the La Sal Mountains and Arches vie for your attention; don't forget to look for ancient petroglyphs on rock walls.

Several miles down Kane Creek Road the pavement turns to dirt as it climbs through the canyon. You can head toward the **Hurrah Pass Trail** (17 miles) at this point. The nice thing about the Hurrah Pass ride is that it offers views of the Colorado River, takes you past petroglyphs, and threads you through gorgeous red-rock backcountry. The not-so-nice thing is that this is not a loop, so your total mileage pushes 34 miles. Another fun ride is **Behind the Rocks** (25 miles), which ends on Kane Creek Road. Pick up the trailhead 13 miles south of town via Route 191. The trailhead will be on the right side of the road marked Pritchett Arch. As its name suggests, ride behind the rocks and through Pritchett Canyon. Consult a detailed topographic or bike map before embarking on these journeys, as it is easy to get lost amid the sandstone.

There may be other traffic on the famous **Kokopelli's Trail**, but you're as likely to share space with animals as humans on this trail that links Moab with Grand Junction, Colorado. Single-track trails, four-wheel-drive roads, dirt-and-sand paths for traversing mesas, peaks and meadows—you'll find them all along the 128 miles. Detailed maps showing access points are available at bike shops and the Moab Visitors Center.

Follow your nose to **Onion Creek** four-wheel-drive trail. The colorful, easy-to-moderate, 19-mile trail, with views of rock, river and mountains, saves its toughest hill until the end. Take Route 128 north 20 miles from Moab; watch for the turnoff between mileposts 20 and 21, near the road to Fisher Towers.

Hidden Canyon Rim is also called "The Gymnasium." The eight-mile trip can be completed in three hours by almost anyone. About 25 minutes from Moab via Route 191 to Blue Hills Road, the trailhead is approximately three and a half miles from the road.

When the desert turns furnace hot, cyclists pedal for the hills. In the La Sal Mountains near Moab, try **Fisher Mesa Trail**. The 18-mile roundtrip passage appeals to less-experienced riders. Drive 15 miles north of Moab on Route 128 to the Castle Valley turnoff. Take the road about 13 miles to where the pavement ends. Look for Castleton/Gateway Road. The trail begins on the left side off this road about four miles from the turnoff.

NORTHERN SAN JUAN COUNTY **Gold Queen Basin** in the Abajo range near Monticello winds through nine miles of fragrant aspen and pine stands to the Blue Mountain skiing area. Mountain greens provide stark contrast to the red-rock country in the north. Take the ski area road due west of Monticello and follow the signs.

LAKE POWELL AREA Outfitters are an absolute necessity if you are planning to tour the remote **Canyonlands Maze District**. You can zigzag on the slickrock trails in Teapot Canyon en route to the rock fins of the Doll House. The inaccessibility of the Maze ensures that few others will traverse your cycling tracks.

Canyonlands is spectacular from any vantage point, but to really enjoy its splendor from the ground up, take the 100-mile roundtrip **White Rim Trail**. The trip typically takes about four days and meanders through rainbow-colored canyons and basins, skirting the Colorado and Green rivers. Since it's almost impossible to carry enough water and supplies in your panniers, a supported trip from an outfitter is recommended. The trail starts 40 miles from Moab via Routes 191 and 313 and Shafer Trail Road.

PERUSING THE SWELL

North of Green River is the long escarpment of the **Book Cliff Mountains**, whose colorful strata resemble the closed pages of a book. West is the wild country of the **San Rafael Swell**, 900 square miles of arid, jagged upland dominated by nearly two dozen steep-sided canyons and side draws. Trisected by the San Rafael and Price rivers, the region is a treasure trove of rockhounding and of American Indian and pioneer history. Except on Route 70, which crosses it from east to west, the Swell is mainly accessible only by four-wheel-drive vehicle, horseback or foot. See Chapter Five for more information.

Bike Rentals For friendly advice, bike rentals or to arrange private guides or fully supported tours try **Kaibab Adventure Outfitters and Moab Cyclery**. ~ 391 South Main Street, Moab; 435-259-7423, 800-451-1133; www.kaibabtours.com. **Western Spirit Cycling** also does the White Rim, as well as longer Telluride-to-Moab and Bryce-to-Zion trips. ~ 478 Mill Creek Drive, Moab; 435-259-8732, 800-845-2453; www.westernspirit.com. **Nichols Expeditions** offers a wide variety of excursions geared toward any level of experience. ~ 497 North Main Street, Moab; 435-259-3999, 800-648-8488; www.nicholsexpeditions.com. Also try **Rim Cyclery** for bikes and equipment. ~ 94 West 100 North, Moab; 435-259-5223, 888-304-8219; www.rimcyclery.com. Rim Cyclery's outfitter component is called **Rim Tours**. ~ 1233 South Route 191; 435-259-5223, 800-626-7335; www.rimtours.com. **Poison Spider Bicycles** also has bikes for rent. ~ 497 North Main Street, Moab; 435-259-7882, 800-635-1792; www.poisonspider bicycles.com. Don't forget **Top of the World Cyclery**, which rents and sells bikes and gear. ~ 415 North Main Street, Moab; 435-259-1134, 800-825-9791; www.topoftheworldcyclery.com.

Coyote Shuttle offers drop-offs for cyclists who want to do one-way rides. The firm also arranges trips through local bike shops. ~ 435-259-8656; e-mail campmoab@lasal.net. Shuttles for hikers, bikers and river runners also can be arranged through **Roadrunner Shuttle**. ~ 435-259-9402. Another option is **Moab Outback**. ~ 435-259-2667, 435-260-2171.

Expect the unexpected when hiking in the Utah desert. For around the next bend there could be Indian petroglyphs, a stunning rock bridge or, be prepared—a rattlesnake. All distances listed for hiking trails are one way unless otherwise noted.

HIKING

GREEN RIVER TO MOAB **Arches National Park** teems with miles of trails among the monoliths, arches, spires and sandstone walls.

◄ HIDDEN

Delicate Arch Trail (1.5 miles) sports a 480-foot elevation change over sand and sandstone to Delicate Arch. Along the way, you'll cross a swinging bridge and climb over slickrock. The most photographed of all the famous arches, Delicate Arch invites long, luxurious looks and several snaps of the Instamatic.

Another Arches favorite, **Windows** (.5 mile or less) culminates with an opportunity to peer through the rounded North and South Windows, truly one of nature's greater performances. This easy and accessible trail starts just past Balanced Rock at the Windows turnoff.

Canyonlands National Park—Island in the Sky, provides both short walks and long hikes for exploring some of its most outstanding features. **Upheaval Dome Crater View Trail** (.5 mile) is a short hike to the overlook of dramatic Upheaval Dome;

viewing its different stratified layers provides a glimpse into its millions of years of geologic history.

You can also traverse the entire dome via the **Syncline Loop Trail** (8 miles), an arduous route with a 1300-foot elevation change.

Neck Spring Trail (5 miles) also leads through the diverse landscape of the Canyonlands—Island in the Sky district. From the trail, hikers can view seasonal wildflowers and the sandstone cliffs of the Navajo Formation. The trail follows paths that were originally established by animals using the springs, so don't be surprised if a mule deer or chipmunk crosses your path.

MOAB AREA A stream will be at your side for the length of the **Negro Bill Canyon Trail** (2 miles), a favorite Moab stomping ground. Negro Bill ends up at Morning Glory Bridge, the sixth-longest rock span in the U.S. At canyon's end is a spring and small pool. From Moab, take Route 128 three miles east of the junction with Route 191.

Although short, the **Corona Arch Trail** (1.5 miles) involves climbing on large sandstone cliffs with the help of safety cables imbedded in the rock. At the top of the trail you'll be standing at the base of the 140-foot wide arch. The trailhead is located west of Moab on Route 279, 10 miles west of the Route 279/191 junction.

Fisher Towers (2.2 miles) is famous with climbers, but you can also hike to these stone pillars. Near the base of the towers you'll find yourself on a ridge that provides a striking view of Castle Valley and the Colorado River. From Moab, head 21 miles east on Route 128, then turn right to a parking lot at the trailhead.

The **Canyonlands Field Institute** sponsors seminars, workshops, field trips and naturalist hiking for groups of eight or more. Contact them for the schedule. ~ P.O. Box 68, Moab, UT 84532; 435-259-7750, 800-860-5262; www.canyonlandsfieldinst.org.

NORTHERN SAN JUAN COUNTY Like spires reaching for the sky, the striped rock formations of **Canyonlands National Park —Needles** beckon visitors to explore their secrets. A trail starting at Elephant Hill trailhead meanders through Elephant Canyon with optional side trips to Devil's Pocket, Cyclone Canyon and Druid Arch. Depending on your chosen route, the trip can be as long or as short as you choose.

Chesler Park (3 miles), one of the park's most popular routes, is a desert meadow amid the rock needles. Accessible from the Elephant Hill trailhead.

Lower Red Lake Canyon Trail (8.5 miles) leads to the gnarly Cataract Canyon section of the Colorado River. Start this steep and demanding multiday hike at Elephant Hill trailhead.

A spur of the Trail of the Ancients, the **Butler Wash** (.5 mile) interpretive trail is exceedingly well marked with cairns and trail symbols. After crossing slickrock, cacti, juniper and piñon, the hiker is rewarded with an Anasazi cliff-dwelling overlook. Take Route 95 west from Blanding. Turn right between mile markers 111 and 112.

Several scenic hikes are found within **Natural Bridges National Monument**. Paths to each bridge are moderate to strenuous in difficulty, and you may encounter some steep slickrock. But the National Park Service has installed handrails and stairs at the most difficult sections.

Owachomo Bridge Trail (.2 mile) is the shortest of three hikes at Natural Bridges National Monument; it provides an up-close and personal view of the oldest of the bridges.

LAKE POWELL AREA If you can tear yourself away from the water, Lake Powell has plenty of petroglyphs, arches and archaeological sites waiting to be explored.

Up the Escalante River arm, about 25 miles from Halls Crossing marina is **Davis Gulch Trail** (1.5 miles). Climb through the lovely "cathedral in the desert" and the Bement Natural Arch to what some consider one of the lake's prettiest sections.

John Wayne, Zane Grey and Teddy Roosevelt all visited the Rainbow Lodge. It's now the **Rainbow Lodge Ruins**. The trail (7 miles) begins about a mile past Rainbow Bridge National Monument and skirts painted rocks, cliffs and Horse Canyon en route to its destination in the shadow of Navajo Mountain.

Take the left-hand spur from the monument and head toward Elephant Rock and Owl Arch via the **North Rainbow Trail** (6 miles).

From the Glen Canyon Dam, there is a short hike to a lovely arch in a recently charted area called **Wiregrass Canyon** (1.5 miles). Drive about eight miles north of the dam on Route 89 to Big Water. Turn east on Route 277 to Route 12 and continue four and a half miles south on Warm Creek Road to the start of Wiregrass Canyon.

Transportation

CAR

From the Colorado border, **Route 70** heads due west forming the northern boundary of the region. **Route 191** travels north–south, passing through Moab, Monticello, Blanding and Bluff and intersecting the entrance roads to Arches and Canyonlands National Parks. Those traveling west from the Colorado border near Grand Junction should opt for **Route 128**, a scenic byway that connects Route 70 with Route 191 at Moab.

Route 95 branches off Route 191 west from Blanding toward Natural Bridges, while both Route 95 and **Route 276** lead to Glen Canyon National Recreation Area and Lake Powell.

AIR

Few visitors to southeastern Utah choose to come by commercial air. Perhaps one reason they don't is that commercial carriers are continually changing at Moab's **Canyonlands Field**. At last check, **Great Lakes Aviation** (800-554-5111; www.greatlakesav. com) was flying to Moab from Denver and Phoenix. Several flightseeing charters also operate from this airport. Shuttle service into Moab is provided by either **Coyote Shuttle** (435-259-8656) or **Roadrunner Shuttle** (435-259-9402).

Visitors to Lake Powell fly into Page, Arizona's **Lake Powell Airport**. Page is served daily by SkyWest Airlines. In Utah, airstrips help connect vast desert distances divided by mountains, canyons and rivers. There are public landing fields at Blanding and near the Bullfrog and Halls Crossing marinas.

TRAIN

The nearest **Amtrak** station servicing the Moab and San Juan County areas is in Green River, about 50 miles north of Moab. You will take one of three trains—the "Zephyr," "Desert Wind" or "Pioneer"—depending on your destination or point of departure. ~ 800-872-7245; www.amtrak.com.

FERRY

Lake Powell ferry service, on Route 276 between Halls Crossing and Bullfrog marinas, runs six times a day westbound (at two-hour intervals from 8 a.m. to 6 p.m.) and six times eastbound (9 a.m. to 7 p.m.) from mid-May through September. There are four crossings a day (8 a.m. to 3:30 p.m.) from November to mid-April, five transits daily during shoulder seasons. The 3.2-mile crossing aboard the 150-foot *John Atlantic Burr* saves 130 road miles. The charge is $12 per standard passenger vehicle. ~ Halls Crossing Marina; 435-684-3000.

CAR RENTALS

The main auto-rental firm in Moab is **Thrifty Car Rental** (435-259-7317, 800-847-4389). In addition to conventional vehicles, it offers four-wheel-drive vehicles, a must for exploring the backcountry roads and byways.

Other rental agencies strictly renting four-wheel-drive vehicles in Moab include **Farabee Adventures** (435-259-7494, 888-806-5337) and **Slickrock 4x4 Rentals** (435-259-5678).

TAXIS

Shuttle services take the place of taxis in Moab. For bike and raft shuttle service, or trips to or from the airport or Amtrak station, contact **Roadrunner Shuttle**. ~ 435-259-9402. Similar service is provided by **Moab Outback** (435-259-2667) and **Coyote Shuttle** (801-259-8656).

Index

Lodging Index

Dining Index

HIDDEN GUIDES

Adventure travel or a relaxing vacation?—"Hidden" guidebooks are the only travel books in the business to provide detailed information on both. Aimed at environmentally aware travelers, our motto is "Where Vacations Meet Adventures." These books combine details on unique hotels, restaurants and sightseeing with information on camping, sports and hiking for the outdoor enthusiast.

THE NEW KEY GUIDES

Based on the concept of ecotourism, The New Key Guides are dedicated to the preservation of Central America's rare and endangered species, architecture and archaeology. Filled with helpful tips, they give travelers everything they need to know about these exotic destinations.

Ulysses Press books are available at bookstores everywhere. If any of the following titles are unavailable at your local bookstore, ask the bookseller to order them.

You can also order books directly from Ulysses Press
P.O. Box 3440, Berkeley, CA 94703
800-377-2542 or 510-601-8301
fax: 510-601-8307
www.ulyssespress.com
e-mail: ulysses@ulyssespress.com

Order Form

HIDDEN GUIDEBOOKS

____ Hidden Arizona, $16.95
____ Hidden Bahamas, $14.95
____ Hidden Baja, $14.95
____ Hidden Belize, $15.95
____ Hidden Big Island of Hawaii, $13.95
____ Hidden Boston & Cape Cod, $14.95
____ Hidden British Columbia, $18.95
____ Hidden Cancún & the Yucatán, $16.95
____ Hidden Carolinas, $17.95
____ Hidden Coast of California, $18.95
____ Hidden Colorado, $15.95
____ Hidden Disneyland, $13.95
____ Hidden Florida, $18.95
____ Hidden Florida Keys & Everglades, $12.95
____ Hidden Georgia, $16.95
____ Hidden Guatemala, $16.95
____ Hidden Hawaii, $18.95
____ Hidden Idaho, $14.95

____ Hidden Kauai, $13.95
____ Hidden Maui, $13.95
____ Hidden Montana, $15.95
____ Hidden New England, $18.95
____ Hidden New Mexico, $15.95
____ Hidden Oahu, $13.95
____ Hidden Oregon, $15.95
____ Hidden Pacific Northwest, $18.95
____ Hidden Salt Lake City, $14.95
____ Hidden San Francisco & Northern California, $18.95
____ Hidden Southern California, $18.95
____ Hidden Southwest, $19.95
____ Hidden Tahiti, $17.95
____ Hidden Tennessee, $16.95
____ Hidden Utah, $16.95
____ Hidden Walt Disney World, $13.95
____ Hidden Washington, $15.95
____ Hidden Wine Country, $13.95
____ Hidden Wyoming, $15.95

THE NEW KEY GUIDEBOOKS

____ The New Key to Costa Rica, $18.95

____ The New Key to Ecuador and the Galápagos, $17.95

Mark the book(s) you're ordering and enter the total cost here ⇨ [   ]

California residents add 8.25% sales tax here ⇨ [   ]

Shipping, check box for your preferred method and enter cost here ⇨ [   ]

☐ Book Rate   FREE! FREE! FREE!

☐ Priority Mail/UPS Ground   cost of postage

☐ UPS Overnight or 2-Day Air   cost of postage   [   ]

Billing, enter total amount due here and check method of payment ⇨ [   ]

☐ Check   ☐ Money Order

☐ VISA/MasterCard _____ Exp. Date _____

Name _____ Phone _____

Address _____

_____

City _____ State _____ Zip _____

MONEY-BACK GUARANTEE ON DIRECT ORDERS PLACED THROUGH ULYSSES PRESS.

ABOUT THE AUTHOR

KURT REPANSHEK has been chasing stories around the Rocky Mountains since 1985, when he arrived in Wyoming as state correspondent for *The Associated Press*. A freelance editor and writer based in Park City, Utah, since 1993, he has scaled the Grand Teton, paddled portions of the Green, Colorado, Snake and Middle Fork of the Salmon rivers, wandered through the Grand Staircase–Escalante National Monument, and cross-country skied in the pre-dawn cold to catch sunrise on the North Rim of the Grand Canyon—all in the pursuit of stories. Kurt also is the author of *America's National Parks for Dummies* and *Hidden Salt Lake City & Beyond*. Among the publications that his work appears in are *National Geographic Adventure*, *National Geographic Traveler*, *Sunset* and *Hemispheres*.

ABOUT THE ILLUSTRATOR

DOUG MCCARTHY, a native New Yorker, lives in the San Francisco Bay area with his family. His illustrations appear in a number of Ulysses Press guides, including *Hidden Kauai*, *Hidden Tennessee*, *Hidden Bahamas* and *The New Key to Ecuador and the Galápagos*.